Portrait of Samuel Wesley by John Jackson, R.A. (1826)
(By permission of the trustees of Wesley's Chapel, City Road, London)

SAMUEL WESLEY (1766–1837):
A SOURCE BOOK

For Jamie and Hilary

SAMUEL WESLEY
(1766–1837)

A Source Book

Michael Kassler
Philip Olleson

Ashgate
Aldershot • Burlington USA • Singapore • Sydney

Published by
Ashgate Publishing Limited
Gower House
Croft Road
Aldershot
Hants GU11 3HR
England

Ashgate Publishing Company
131 Main Street
Burlington, VT 05401-5600 USA

Ashgate website: http://www.ashgate.com

British Library Cataloguing in Publication Data
Kassler, Michael
    Samuel Wesley (1766-1837) : a source book
    1.Wesley, Samuel, 1766-1837 2.Composers - England -
    Biography
    I.Title II.Olleson, Philip
    781.7'17' 0092

Library of Congress Control Number: 2001089789

ISBN 1 85928 357 8

This book is printed on acid free paper.

Typeset in Times New Roman by Computer Music Company, Sydney, Australia.

Printed and bound in Great Britain by MPG Books Ltd, Bodmin, Cornwall

CONTENTS

~ 5 ~ Literary Works

~ 6 ~ Portraits

~ 7 ~ Bibliography

ILLUSTRATIONS

PREFACE

This book celebrates the extraordinary life of the musician Samuel Wesley. Son of Charles Wesley and nephew of John Wesley, the founders of Methodism, he was acclaimed initially as a child prodigy and later as England's finest extempore organist. He is remembered now for numerous compositions that continue to be performed, recorded and appreciated, and for his fervent efforts to awaken interest in the music of J. S. Bach.

Because he was part of the Wesley family, Methodist collectors have been keen to preserve documents that bear his name. Their devotion, and the care of his daughter Eliza and his friend and colleague Vincent Novello to ensure that he be not forgotten, have resulted in a quantity of surviving source material which greatly exceeds that for most other English musicians of the Georgian era. The 1,100 letters summarised in this book, most of them for the first time, reveal much new information about London musical life and establish that Samuel Wesley's own affairs were considerably more complex than prior biographers have supposed.

This book could not have been prepared without the kind assistance of the archivists, collectors, dealers, librarians and scholars acknowledged below. We are especially grateful for the enthusiastic support of our publisher, Rachel Lynch, who persuaded us to expand our initially proposed calendar of Wesley's correspondence into a full source book and responded sympathetically to our several requests for additional time and space to make it more complete. We particularly thank Peter S. Forsaith for contributing the iconography section, Stanley C. Pelkey for his assistance in compiling the list of Wesley's musical works, and the Gibbs Family Charitable Trust for a grant that has enabled Wesley's portrait to be printed in colour. The Internet also deserves recognition for virtually eliminating the 17,000 km between Sydney and Nottingham, allowing us to exchange ideas with almost the same intensity as if we had lived in the same city.

Michael Kassler and Philip Olleson
Northbridge, NSW Australia and Nottingham, England
June 2001

ACKNOWLEDGEMENTS

Material for this source book has been gathered during the past 30 years. We lack space to thank everyone who helped us but would be remiss not to acknowledge gratefully the following people who gave us the benefit of their specialist knowledge, notwithstanding our persistence in asking them for further information.

We have had constant encouragement during the long period of this volume's gestation from the doyen of Methodist historians, the late Reverend Professor Frank Baker of Duke University, who shared with us not only his unsurpassed knowledge of Wesleyana but also information from manuscripts and notes in his personal collection, now in the Duke University Library. Our work in the Methodist Archives when they were at City Road, London has been greatly assisted by the Reverend Dr John C. Bowmer and Ms Sheila J. Himsworth; since their removal to Manchester, Dr Peter Nockles and Mr Gareth Lloyd of the John Rylands University Library have enabled us on numerous occasions to locate relevant materials.

Our access to other leading repositories of Methodist materials has been substantially aided by Dr Linda Matthews of Emory University, the Reverend Mr Page A. Thomas and Ms Wanda Smith of the Center for Methodist Studies in Southern Methodist University, Ms Louise Elliot of Queen's College, Melbourne, Ms Noorah Al-Gailani of Wesley's Chapel, London, Mrs Janet Henderson of Wesley College, Bristol, Dr Joe Hale and Ms Jeanette Robertson of the World Methodist Council and Museum in Lake Junaluska, North Carolina, Mr Sam Hammond of Duke University, Ms Kathryn Kimball of the Upper Room in Nashville, Tennessee, Dr Dale Patterson of the General Commission on Archives and History of The United Methodist Church, Madison, New Jersey, and Mrs Joyce Banks of Westminster College, Oxford.

The Reverend Dr Frederick E. Maser always encouraged our efforts and generously provided details of Samuel Wesley's letters in his private collection, recently donated to The United Methodist Church. Mr Bennett McGee, formerly of Painesville, Ohio, kindly provided information about the Wesley family letters that he owned. The Reverend Ms Lorna Khoo of the Methodist Church in Singapore and the Reverend Mr Scott Kisker, her successor at the Charles Wesley Heritage Centre, Bristol, facilitated our searches for relevant data.

Our work on the links between the Burney and Wesley families has been immeasurably assisted by the efforts of Burney family historians. Professor Joyce Hemlow of McGill University, Montréal, the founder of modern Burney studies, was always encouraging, and her colleagues and successors in Burney studies, particularly the late Professor Slava Klima, the Reverend Dr Alvaro Ribeiro, S.J., and Dr Lorna Clark have responded diligently to our numerous requests for information. Cynthia and the late John Comyn, who owned a significant collection of Burney family letters, have been unfailingly helpful. For access to the large collection of Burney materials in the Osborn Collection at Yale University we are indebted to Dr Stephen Parks and his assistants. For information about the Burney materials in the Berg collection of the New York Public Library we thank Dr Lola Szladits and Mr Rodney Phillips.

The late Ms Betty Matthews generously contributed her considerable knowledge about Samuel Wesley letters in England and, with Mrs Marjorie Gleed MBE, searched the archives of the Royal Society of Musicians for items relevant to him.

Dr Jamie C. Kassler shared her substantial information about English writers on music in the Georgian era. Professor Michael J. Crowe of the University of Notre Dame willingly disclosed connections between the Wesley and the Herschel families. Professors Simon McVeigh of the University of London and Nicholas Temperley of the University of Illinois replied promptly to our several queries. Dr Rachel Cowgill of the University of Leeds kindly made available portions of her transcript of Christian Ignatius Latrobe's journal. The staff of the Theatre Museum, London, responded quickly to numerous obscure inquiries, and Mrs Katrina Jowett of the United Grand Lodge of England diligently searched files for information about Samuel Wesley's fellow Freemasons.

We thank also Dr John Martin Robinson (librarian to the Duke of Norfolk), the Hon. Georgina Stonor (archivist to the Duke of Wellington), Messrs Peter Ward Jones and Michael Webb of the Bodleian Library, Mrs Chris Banks and Mr Robert Parker of the British Library, Ms Kate Alderson-Smith of the Brotherton Library,

University of Leeds, Dr Richard Andrewes and Mr Peter Meadows of the Cambridge University Library, Professor Richard Heitzenrater of Duke University, Mr Malcolm Lewis of the City of Nottingham Music Library, Ms Liz Fielden of the Fitzwilliam Museum, Ms Carol Lynn Ward-Bamford of the Library of Congress, Ms Katherine Hogg of the Royal Academy of Music, Dr Peter Horton of the Royal College of Music, Dr Yo Tomita of the Queen's University of Belfast, Mr Ray Currier, Dr Gabriella Dideriksen, Dr Andrew Drummond, Mr Lewis Foreman, Dr Roger Wesley Glenn, Dr H. Diack Johnstone, Dr Alyson McLamore, Mr Sander Meredeen, Mr Guy Oldham, Dr Edward Olleson, Dr Graham Pont, Mr Brian Robins, Mr Albi Rosenthal, Ms Ann van Allen-Russell, Dr John A. Vickers, Mr Ian Wells and Mr Peter Young for their valued help and support.

ABBREVIATIONS

The following three tables list abbreviations used in this book to identify persons, to designate repositories of manuscripts and to cite publications. The acronym 'SW', for example, stands for Samuel Wesley. Other abbreviations that relate specifically to SW's homes, to the calendar of correspondence, to the list of SW's musical compositions or to the iconography section of this book are defined in the introductions to these sections.

FREQUENTLY MENTIONED PERSONS

AD	Anne Deane (?–1806); schoolmistress; SW's 'dearest friend'
AFCK	Augustus Frederic Christopher Kollmann (1756–1829); music theorist; early publisher of JSB's music
Attwood	Thomas Attwood (1765–1838); composer and organist
BJ	Benjamin Jacobs [later Jacob] (1778–1829); organist; early performer of JSB's music
Bridgetower	George Polgreen Bridgetower (1778–1860); violinist
CB	Charles Burney (1726–1814); Mus. Doc.; historian of music
CFH	Charles Frederick Horn (1762–1830); teacher; early publisher of JSB's music
CLM	Charlotte Louisa Martin (1761–1845); married SW on 5/4/1793; after then CLW
CLW	Charlotte Louisa Wesley (1761–1845); married SW on 5/4/1793; before then CLM
Crotch	William Crotch (1775–1847); composer; professor of music at Oxford
CW	Charles Wesley (1707–1788); 'poet of Methodism'; father of SW
CW Jr	Charles Wesley (1757–1834); composer and organist; brother of SW
CW III	Charles Wesley (1793–1859); clergyman; son of SW and CLW
Dickinson	Peard Dickinson (1758–1802); Methodist minister
Emett	John George Emett (1787?–1847); organist

Emma	Emma Frances Wesley [later Newenham] (1806–1865); daughter of SW and CLW
EW	Eliza Wesley (1819–1895); daughter of SW and SS
Graeff	John George Graeff (1762?–?); composer and flautist
Handel	George Frideric Handel (1685–1759); composer
Hodges	Edward Hodges (1796–1867); organist and inventor
Jackson	Thomas Jackson (1783–1873); Methodist minister and editor
JSB	Johann [John] Sebastian Bach (1685–1750); composer
JW	John Wesley (1703–1791); founder of Methodism; uncle of SW
JWW	John William Wesley (1799–1860); son of SW and CLW
Kingston	William B. Kingston (?–?); friend of SW
Langshaw Jr	John Langshaw Jr (1763–1832); organist at Lancaster; pupil of CW Jr
Latrobe	Christian Ignatius Latrobe (1758–1836); Moravian minister and musician
MEW	Matthias Erasmus Suter Wesley (1821–1901); son of SW and SS
Pettet	Alfred Pettet (1788–1837); musician at Norwich
Picart	Samuel Picart (1775–1835); Canon of Hereford Cathedral; collector of JSB's music
RG	Robert Glenn (1776–1844); organist; married SW's daughter Rosalind
Rosalind	Rosalind Suter Wesley [later Glenn] (1814?–?); daughter of SW and SS; married RG
Salomon	Johann Peter Salomon (1745–1815); violinist and concert promoter
Sarah	Sarah Wesley (1759–1828); sister of SW
SGW	Sarah Gwynne Wesley (1726–1822); wife of CW; mother of SW
Shepherd	Mary Freeman [later Shepherd] (1731–1815); Roman Catholic literary woman
SS	Sarah Suter (1793?–1863); SW's 'partner' from 1810; mother of his second family
SSW	Samuel Sebastian Wesley (1810–1876); composer and organist; son of SW and SS
Stokes	Charles Stokes (1784–1839); organist and composer
Street	Joseph Payne Street (?–<1852); secretary of the Madrigal Society

SW	Samuel Wesley (1766–1837); musician; the subject of this book
Tooth	Eliza[beth] Tabitha Tooth (1793?–<1872); friend of SW, CW Jr and Sarah
VN	Vincent Novello (1781–1861); composer, organist and publisher
Wait	Daniel Guilford Wait (1789–1850); writer and scholar; rector of Blagdon
WH	William Horsley (1774–1858); composer and writer on music
WL	William Linley (1771–1835); author and composer

REPOSITORIES OF MANUSCRIPTS

Manuscripts of SW's correspondence and musical compositions are preserved in the following public and private collections in Australia, Canada, France, the United Kingdom and the United States of America:

1st United	1st United Methodist Church, Harrisburg, Illinois, USA
AdF	Archives de France, Paris, France
Albert	Private collection of Eugene Albert Jr, USA
Argory	The Argory, County Armagh, Northern Ireland
Arundel	Arundel Castle, Arundel, West Sussex
Baker	Frank Baker Collection, Special Collections Library, Duke University, Durham, North Carolina, USA
Bath	Bath Reference Library, Bath
Berg	Henry W. and Albert A. Berg Collection, New York Public Library, New York, New York, USA
BL	British Library, London
Bodl	Bodleian Library, Oxford
Bristol	The New Room, John Wesley's Chapel, Bristol
Burney-Cumming	Family collection in the possession of Michael Burney-Cumming, UK
Camb	Cambridge University Library, Manuscript Department, Cambridge
Cary	Mary Flagler Cary Music Collection, Pierpont Morgan Library, New York, New York, USA
ChCh	Christ Church College Library, Oxford
Cheshire	Cheshire Record Office, Chester

Comyn	Family collection of Cynthia Comyn, UK
Currier	Private collection of Ray Currier, USA
DLC	Library of Congress, Washington DC, USA
Dorset	Dorset Record Office, Dorchester
Drew	United Methodist Church Archives, General Commission on Archives and History, Drew University, Madison, New Jersey, USA
Duke	Special Collections Library, Duke University, Durham, North Carolina, USA (other than the Baker collection)
Euing	Euing Collection, Glasgow University Library, Glasgow
EUL	Edinburgh University Library, Edinburgh
Fitzwm	Samuel Wesley letters, Fitzwilliam Museum, Cambridge
GEU	John Wesley Collection, Special Collections Department, Robert W. Woodruff Library, Emory University, Atlanta, Georgia, USA
Gloucester	Local Studies Department, Gloucestershire Public Libraries
Hampshire	Hampshire Record Office, Winchester
Hyde	Private collection of Mary Hyde Viscountess Eccles, Somerville, New Jersey, USA
JRUL	John Rylands University Library of Manchester (other than the Methodist Archives), Manchester
K	Private collection of Jamie and Michael Kassler, Northbridge, New South Wales, Australia
LMA	London Metropolitan Archives, London
LRI	Royal Institution, London
LU	University of London Library, London
MA	Methodist Archives and Research Centre, John Rylands University Library of Manchester, Manchester
MB	Boston Public Library, Boston, Massachusetts, USA
McGee	Private collection formerly owned by Bennett H. McGee, Painesville, Ohio, USA
MH	Harvard University, Cambridge, Massachusetts, USA
NjP	Princeton University Library, Princeton, New Jersey, USA
NLS	National Library of Scotland, Edinburgh
NN	Music Division, New York Public Library, New York, USA
Norfolk	Norfolk Record Office, Norwich
Osborn	Osborn Collection, Yale University Library, New Haven, Connecticut, USA
PC–London	Private collection, London

PRO	Public Record Office, Kew
RAM	Royal Academy of Music, London
RCM	Royal College of Music, London
ROM	Royal Ontario Museum, Toronto, Ontario, Canada
RSCM	Royal School of Church Music, Dorking
SMU	Manuscript Collection, Center for Methodist Studies at Bridwell Library, Perkins School of Theology, Southern Methodist University, Dallas, Texas, USA
Texas	Harry Ransom Humanities Research Center, University of Texas, Austin, Texas, USA
UCSB	Department of Special Collections, Davidson Library, University of California, Santa Barbara, California, USA
Upper Rm	The Upper Room, Nashville, Tennessee, USA
VUQ	Queen's College Library, University of Melbourne, Melbourne, Victoria, Australia
WCL	Wesley's Chapel, London
Wcoll	Wesley College Library, Bristol
WDA	Westminster Diocesan Archives, London
WHS	Wesley Historical Society Library, Wesley and Methodist Studies Centre, Westminster Institute of Education, Oxford Brookes University, Oxford
WMM	World Methodist Museum, Lake Junaluska, North Carolina, USA

CITED PUBLICATIONS

The italic abbreviations below are used to cite the following publications:

Adam Clarke	*An Account of the Religious and Literary Life of Adam Clarke...by a Member of his Family [Mary Ann Clarke].* Volume II. New York, 1833.
AM	*Arminian Magazine*
Argent	Argent, Mark (ed.), *Recollections of R. J. S. Stevens, an Organist in Georgian London.* London, 1992.
Aspinall	Aspinall, George (ed.), *The Letters of King George IV, 1812–1830.* Cambridge, 1938.
Baker	Baker, Frank, *Charles Wesley as Revealed by his Letters.* London, 1948.
Barrington	Barrington, Daines, *Miscellanies.* London, 1781.

Bird	Bird, William, *Original Psalmody; 57 Psalm and Hymn Tunes in Score...revised by S. Wesley*. London, 1827.
Brown	Brown, Robert W., *Charles Wesley Hymnwriter: Notes on Research Carried out to Establish the Location of his Residence During the Period 1749–1771*. Bristol, 1993 [privately published; available from the Charles Wesley Heritage Centre, Bristol].
Bulmer	Bulmer, Agnes, *Memoirs of Mrs Elizabeth Mortimer with Selections from her Correspondence*. London, 1836.
Busby	[Busby, Thomas], 'Thomas Busby, Mus.D. LL.D. &c.', *Public Characters* v 5 (1803) p 371–394.
Chappell	Chappell, Paul, *Dr. S. S. Wesley, 1810–1876, Portrait of a Victorian Musician*. Great Wakering, Essex, 1977.
Cowden Clarke VN	Clarke, Mary Cowden, *The Life and Labours of Vincent Novello, by his Daughter*. London, [1863].
Cowden-Clarke Life	Cowden-Clarke, Mary, *My Long Life*. London, 1896.
Curnock	Curnock, Nehemiah (ed.), *The Journal of the Rev. John Wesley, A.M.* Standard Edition. 8 volumes. London, 1909–1916.
Dawe	Dawe, Donovan, *Organists of the City of London 1666–1850*. Padstow, Cornwall, 1983.
Doane	[Doane, J.], *A Musical Directory for the Year 1794*. London, [1794].
Dowden	Dowden, Wilfred S. (ed.), *The Journal of Thomas Moore* (6 volumes). Newark, Delaware, 1983–1991.
Elvin	Elvin, Laurence, *Bishop and Son, Organ Builders; The Story of J. C. Bishop and his Successors*. Swanpool, Lincoln, 1984.
EM	*The European Magazine*
Etheridge	Etheridge, John Wesley, *The Life of Adam Clarke*. Nashville, Tennessee, 1859.
GM	*The Gentleman's Magazine*
Gotch	Gotch, Rosamund Brunel (ed.), *Mendelssohn and his Friends in Kensington; Letters from Fanny and Sophy Horsley written 1833–36*. London, 1938.
H&S	Humphries, Charles and William C. Smith, *Music Publishing in the British Isles from the Earliest Times to the Middle of the 19th Century*. 2nd edition. Oxford, 1970.

Hemlow	Hemlow, Joyce, with Jeanne M. Burgess and Althea Douglas, *A Catalogue of the Burney Family Correspondence, 1749–1878*. New York and Montréal, [1971].
Hodges	Hodges, Faustina H., *Edward Hodges*. New York and London, 1896.
Jacobs	Wesley, Eliza (ed.), *Letters of Samuel Wesley to Mr Jacobs, Organist of Surrey Chapel, Relating to the Introduction into this Country of the Works of John Sebastian Bach. (Now First Published.)* London, 1875.
Kassler	Kassler, Jamie Croy, 'The Royal Institution Music Lectures, 1800–1831: A Preliminary Study', *Royal Musical Association Research Chronicle*, no. 19 (1983–1985) p 1–30.
Kassler Science	Kassler, Jamie Croy, *The Science of Music in Britain, 1714–1830; A Catalogue of Writings, Lectures and Inventions*. 2 volumes. New York and London, 1979.
Lightwood	Lightwood, James T., *Samuel Wesley, Musician; The Story of his Life*. London, 1937.
Liston	Liston, Henry, *An Essay on Perfect Intonation*. Edinburgh and London, 1812.
Logier	Logier, John Bernard, *An Explanation and Description of the Royal Patent Chiroplast or Hand-Director*. London, c1814.
Mackinlay	*A Catalogue of Original Letters and Manuscripts, in the Autograph of Distinguished Musicians, Composers, Performers, and Vocalists, with Portraits, collected by Thomas Mackinlay*. For private circulation, 1846. (A copy is in the British Library at S.C. 950(4).)
Marsh	Marsh, John (ed. Brian Robins), *The John Marsh Journals*. Stuyvesant, New York, 1998.
Matthews	Matthews, Betty, 'Charles Wesley on organs', *Musical Times* v 112 no. 1544 (1971) p 1007–1010, no. 1545 (1971) p 1111–1112.
MM	*The Monthly Magazine*
MW	*The Musical World*
NMMR	*New Musical Magazine, Review and Register*
O	Olleson, Philip (ed.), *The Letters of Samuel Wesley: Professional and Social Correspondence, 1797–1837*. Oxford, 2001.

Olleson	Olleson, Philip, 'Samuel Wesley and the *European Magazine*', *Notes* v 52 no 4 (1996) p 1097–1111.
Oxberry	*Oxberry's Dramatic Biography and Histrionic Anecdotes.* 7 volumes. London, 1825–1827.
Price	Price, Cecil (ed.), *The Letters of Richard Brinsley Sheridan.* Oxford, 1966.
QMMR	*The Quarterly Musical Magazine and Review*
Redford	Redford, Bruce (ed.), *The Letters of Samuel Johnson.* 5 volumes. Oxford, 1992–1994.
Rennert	Rennert, Jonathan, *William Crotch, 1775–1847; Composer, Artist, Teacher.* Lavenham, Suffolk, 1975.
Russell	Russell, William, *Job, a Sacred Oratorio...adapted from the Original Score...by Samuel Wesley.* London, 1826.
Schoelcher	Schoelcher, Victor, *The Life of Handel.* London, 1857.
Sidney	Sidney, Edwin, *The Life of the Rev. Rowland Hill, A.M.* London, Baldwin & Cradock, 3rd edition, 1835.
Smith	Smith, John Thomas, *Nollekens and his Times.* London, 1828.
Stevens	Stevens, W[illiam] S[eaman], *A Treatise on Piano-forte Expression...to which is added, An Exercise, Composed Expressly for this Work, by Mr Samuel Wesley.* London, 1811.
Stevenson	Stevenson, George J., *Memorials of the Wesley Family: Including Biographical and Historical Sketches of All the Members of the Family for Two Hundred and Fifty Years....* London, [1876].
Stevenson City Road	Stevenson, George J., *City Road Chapel and its Associations Historical, Biographical and Memorial.* London, [1872].
T	Telford, John (ed.), *The Letters of the Rev. John Wesley.* Standard Edition. 8 volumes. London, 1931.
Tyson	Tyson, John R. (ed.), *Charles Wesley: A Reader.* New York, 1989.
Wainwright	Wainwright, Arthur W. with Don E. Saliers, *Wesley/Langshaw Correspondence: Charles Wesley, his Sons, and the Lancaster Organists.* [Atlanta], 1993.
Ward Jones	Ward Jones, Peter (ed.), *The Mendelssohns on Honeymoon: The 1837 Diary of Felix and Cécile Mendelssohn Bartholdy Together with Letters to their Families.* Oxford, 1997.
WBRR	*The Wesley Banner and Revival Record.*

Willcocks/Jay   Willcocks, R. M. and B. Jay (eds.), *The British County Catalogue of Postal History. Volume 3—London*, by Barrie Jay. [London], 1983.

~ 1 ~

PRELUDE

WESLEY'S FAMILY

The relationship of the principal family members mentioned in Samuel Wesley's correspondence is shown in *Figures 1* and *2*.

SW's mother, Sarah Gwynne Wesley (SGW), was born in Garth, Wales on 12/10/1726[1] and died in London on 28/12/1822. She had three brothers and five sisters, of whom two—her sisters Rebecca Gwynne and Elizabeth Gwynne Waller—are frequently mentioned in SW's correspondence.

SW's father, Charles Wesley (CW), the 'poet of Methodism', was born in Epworth, Lincolnshire, on 18/12/1707. He graduated M.A. from Oxford in 1733, married SGW at Garth on 8/4/1749, and died in London on 29/3/1788. He was one of 19 children, of whom two—his brother John Wesley (JW, the founder of Methodism) and his sister Martha Wesley Hall—figure in SW's correspondence.[2]

Three of SGW's and CW's children survived infancy: SW's brother and fellow musician Charles Wesley (CW Jr, born in Bristol, 11/12/1757, died unmarried in London, 23/5/1834); SW's sister Sarah Wesley (Sarah, born in Bristol, 1/4/1759, died unmarried in Bristol, 19/9/1828); and Samuel Wesley (SW), the subject of this book, who was born in Bristol on 24/2/1766 and died in London on 11/10/1837.

SW's wife, Charlotte Louisa Martin (CLM), was born on 19/8/1761. They were married at St Paul's, Hammersmith on 5/4/1793, and she is referred to as CLW from this date. She died in London on 5/2/1845. Little is known about her family.[3] Her brother, 'Captain Martin', is mentioned in the correspondence.

After several periods of living apart, SW and CLW separated finally in early 1810 and executed a Deed of Separation on 25/3/1812.

---

[1] Dates are presented in this book in day/month/year format, i.e., the day precedes the month.

[2] CW's brother Samuel Wesley Jr (1690–1739) and their father Samuel Wesley Sr (1662–1735), with whom SW occasionally has been confused, died long before SW was born and appear in his correspondence only in relation to family history.

[3] CLM's father, George Martin, married her mother, Mary Nickelson, in London on 13/3/1754. George Martin was a surgeon at St Thomas's Hospital, London from 1768 until his death in 1784.

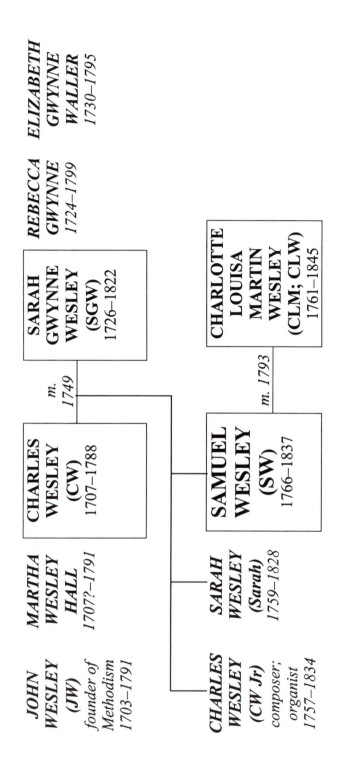

Figure 1. Members of Samuel Wesley's family to the time of his marriage who feature in the correspondence.

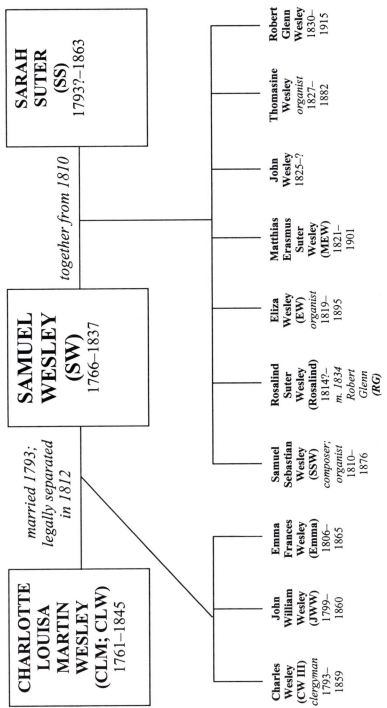

Figure 2. Samuel Wesley's children who survived infancy.

Three of their children reached adulthood: Charles Wesley (CW III, born at Ridge, Hertfordshire, on 25/9/1793, died in London on 14/9/1859); John William Wesley (JWW, born about June 1799, died in April 1860 before 17/4/1860); and Emma Frances Wesley (Emma, born in January or February 1806, died in November 1865).

A daughter, Susanna Wesley, who was born between 26/10/1794 and 12/11/1794, died before 22/12/1797.[4] Another stillborn or short-lived child appears to have been born about December 1795.

SW had a second family with Sarah Suter (SS, born about 1793, died 12/9/1863).[5] They had numerous children of whom seven reached adulthood: Samuel Sebastian Wesley (SSW, born in London on 14/8/1810, died at Gloucester on 19/4/1876); Rosalind Suter Wesley (Rosalind, born before 16/10/1814;[6]); Eliza Wesley (EW, born on 6/5/1819, died on 14/5/1895); Matthias Erasmus Suter Wesley (MEW, born on 19/4/1821 and died in 1901);[7] John Wesley (born about 1/7/1825); Thomasine Wesley (born about October or November 1827, died in 1882);[8] and Robert Glenn Wesley (born in London on 21/11/1830; died in November 1915).

There is uncertainty regarding the children of SW and SS who did not survive infancy, and their names are not known.[9]

---

[4] Her name is not found in the extant correspondence but appears on a copy of SW's song 'Beneath, a sleeping infant lies' that was offered for sale as item 153 in catalogue XVI of the Leamington Book Shop, Washington DC, *c*1958; its present location is not known.

[5] Very little is known about SS's family. An unnamed sister of SS is mentioned in SW's letters of 12/9/1810 and 10/10/1827, and someone called 'Suter', presumably a male relative, is mentioned in SW's letter of 1/10/1828.

[6] Rosalind's first mention in the extant correspondence is in a letter of that date from SW. She married SW's friend, the organist Robert Glenn (RG, 1776–1844), on 26/5/1834.

[7] MEW was christened Matthias Erasmus Suter.

[8] Thomasine's birth date is extrapolated from SW's remark in his 16/10/1827 letter to SS that he may find SS 'in the straw' when he returns to London on 21/10/1827.

[9] The correspondence indicates that a daughter born about 12/11/1812 died on 29/3/1813, and that an infant son died about 10/8/1816.

WESLEY'S HOMES AND ADDRESSES

The homes in which Samuel Wesley lived and their addresses are listed in *Figure 3*.[1] The first column gives the codes used in this book to specify each address. The second column has the street address by which a house was known while SW lived there. The third column provides the editors' estimate of the interval of time when he resided at each address.[2] The final columns list the dates of the first and last items of extant correspondence that are referable to each address.[3]

The following notes provide additional information about each of SW's homes. They explain the overlapping dates for several of his places of residence, the gap that follows SW's stay at Blacklands, and the uncertainties regarding SW living in Hornsey Lane and in Duke Street. We do not know where SW lived between early 1805 and early 1806.

CHARLES STREET, BRISTOL. Charles and Sarah Gwynne Wesley established their home in what is now Charles Street, Bristol on 1 September 1749,[4] a few months after their marriage on 8 April 1749.[5] About the time of Samuel Wesley's birth on 24 February 1776, they moved to another house in the same street. This house, now

---

[1] Places where SW stayed for only a short time—for instance, while visiting, lecturing, performing or copying music away from home—are not listed in *Figure 3*. However, all known dates of SW's travels outside the present Greater London area are given in the chronology section.

[2] When this information is used to date a letter, the symbol '🏠', which designates this interval, appears in the dating reason given in the calendar of correspondence for that letter. Our estimates of SW's periods of residence are based principally upon evidence in the correspondence and information in secondary sources. We have not examined rate books and other primary sources for evidence of transactions affecting these premises.

[3] Dr James Price, who died in 1783, bequeathed his house in Guildford to SW (*see* James Price will, 6/2/1783), who sold it about 1800 (*see* SW→Gentlemen, 5/1/1800). This house is not listed in *Figure 3* because SW does not appear to have lived in it.

[4] *Baker* p 71.

[5] The location of CW's Bristol homes is discussed in *Brown*.

Code	Address	Period of Residence	First Letter	Last Letter
Charles St, Bristol	Charles Street, Bristol	24/2/1766–9/1778	23/8/1766	late 1776
Chesterfield St	1 Chesterfield Street, Marylebone	5/1771–10/1792	9/10/1774	4/11/1804
Ridge	Ridge, Hertfordshire	10/1792–>15/2/1797	18/10/1792	15/2/1797
Finchley	Church End, Finchley	7/1797–1798	22/12/1797	23/5/1798
Hornsey Lane	Hornsey Lane, near Highgate	late 1798—5/1799	23/1/1799	23/1/1799
Highgate	5 Mile Stone, Highgate	6/1799–5/1803	18/10/1799	8/9/1802
Gt Chesterfield St	1 Great Chesterfield St, Marylebone	5/1803–early 1805	27/7/1797	16/11/1804
9 Arlington St	9 Arlington Street, Camden Town	}early 1806–1/1810	1/4/1806	30/5/1806
Camden Town	27 Arlington Street, Camden Town		14/1/1807	13/1/1810
Adam's Row	11 Adam's Row, Hampstead Road	7/1810–4/1812	17/7/1810	25/3/1812
Tottenham Ct	13 Tottenham Court, New Road	4/1812–9/1813	26/4/1812	31/3/1813
5 Gower Pl	5 Gower Place, Euston Square	}10/1813–3/5/1817	10/10/1813	25/11/1813
4 Gower Pl	4 Gower Place, Euston Square		22/7/1814	13/1/1817
Blacklands	Blacklands House, Chelsea	7–8/1817–>26/6/1818	24/8/1817	26/6/1818
Duke St	27 Duke Street, Grosvenor Square	early 1819	24/1/1819	15/2/1819
Euston St	16 Euston Street, Euston Square	6/1819–3/1830	5/6/1819	1/3/1830
Mornington Pl	1 Mornington Place, Hampstead Road	3/1830–>18/5/1831	23/4/1830	18/5/1831
Pentonville	8 King's Row, Pentonville	10/1832–11/10/1837	17/10/1832	17/4/1837

Figure 3. Samuel Wesley's homes and his times of residence there.

Dear Sir

Mr Aspurne has informed me that it is his Intention to discontinue the Musical Review in his Magazine: whether he mean that he rejects only my Services, but purposes to employ those of others, I cannot say, but the above Notice will account to you for not receiving any Matter for the Press from me in this Month as heretofore. — If he thinks that he can put it into abler Hands, of Course he is in the right to do so, but I cannot but consider the short Warning as far from handsome Treatment. — With sincere Thanks for your kind Assistance on all Occasions, believe me
    Dear Sir
        Yours very truly
Gower Place   S Wesley
13th Jan.y.
Monday.

Samuel Wesley's letter to Stephen Jones (13 January 1817)
(Collection of Jamie and Michael Kassler, Northbridge, NSW, Australia, by permission)

Samuel Wesley's *Twelve Short Pieces for the Organ*, No. 1 (10 July 1816)
(Royal College of Music, London, Ms 4025 f 57, by permission)

numbered 4 Charles Street, has been restored, and in 1997 it was reopened as the Charles Wesley Heritage Centre.[6]

After 1770, when CW was given the lease of a London house, he and his family spent increasing amounts of time there. CW and CW Jr arrived in London on 6 February 1771[7] and spent the following months there while SGW, Sarah and SW stayed in Bristol.[8] SW arrived in London, apparently for the first time, in the latter part of May 1771[9] but was back in Charles Street in September 1772.[10]

The Wesley family appear to have left Bristol finally about September 1778,[11] although some of their furniture apparently still remained in the Charles Street house as late as September 1780.[12]

CHESTERFIELD STREET/GREAT CHESTERFIELD STREET. CW was given the lease of this house by Martha Colvil Gumley (1702?–1787), a wealthy Methodist who wanted him to have it for his London

---

[6] According to *Brown* p 18, CW and his family lived from 1 September 1749 'to sometime in 1766 in a house close to 21 or 20 Charles Street (possibly no. 19)', and moved to what is now 'no. 4 Charles Street some time in 1766, but rates were paid for both houses for a period'. SW 'may have been born in the first house, although it is possible that the dual occupation of the house[s] was made so that the birth of Samuel could take place away from the rest of the family' (*ibid.*).

[7] CW→SGW, 10/2/1771, MA DDCW/7/96.

[8] In CW→SGW, 21/3/1771, CW asks why SGW cannot come with SW to London, pointing out that 'the additional travelling expenses will be saved by reduced housekeeping costs'.

[9] On 16/5/1771 CW wrote to SGW that he expected to see 'you all' [SGW, Sarah and SW] in London the following week and asked 'on what day and by what carriage' they planned to arrive.

[10] See the calendar of correspondence. The lack of correspondence in the calendar between 16/5/1771 and 22/9/1772 suggests, but does not prove, that the Wesley family were together for most of this interval. Calendar entries between 1772 and 1778 indicate times when SW was in Bristol, London or elsewhere.

[11] In CW→Sarah, 16/9/1778, CW says that Sarah should not regret the loss of the family house in Bristol. It was not earning them money, SW and CW Jr do not have time to visit Bristol, SW has no love for Bristol, and SGW will not leave London as long as her family are there.

[12] *Brown* pp 12, 21.

residence.[13] He paid ground rent on the property from 1770.[14] The area where this house was located was usually called 'Marybone' by the Wesleys rather than by its present name 'Marylebone'.

Some time in the 1790s Chesterfield Street was renamed 'Great Chesterfield Street',[15] but the Wesley family continued to use 'Chesterfield Street' interchangeably with the new name. Accordingly, when dating letters, we have utilised the distinction only to assert that letters containing the phrase 'Great Chesterfield Street' were written after 1790.

After SW moved away from his mother's home, first to Ridge, Hertfordshire, in October 1792 and later to Finchley and Highgate, he continued to stay in the (Great) Chesterfield Street house when business required him to spend nights in London, and he used (Great) Chesterfield Street as his postal address during this period in addition to Ridge, Finchley or Highgate.[16]

When he left Highgate, about May 1803, SW returned to live in Great Chesterfield Street, where he appears to have made his home until early 1805.[17] His place of residence until he settled in Camden Town the following year is not known.

---

[13] *Stevenson* p 404. Mrs Gumley, the widow of Colonel Samuel Gumley (1698–1763), an early Methodist, also was a godmother of CW Jr.

[14] A receipt by the representatives of Margaret Cavendish, Duchess of Portland, for the ground rent is at MA DDCW/6/61A.

[15] The first letter noted in the calendar to have a 'Great Chesterfield Street' address is dated 27 July 1797.

[16] It was economic for the Great Chesterfield Street address to be used in correspondence with Londoners. Ridge was beyond the area served by the London penny post, and Finchley and Highgate were in the country area rather than the town area of the penny post. Before April 1801, postage for a basic letter transported between town and country areas was 2d, twice the price of a basic letter carried within the town area. See *Willcocks/Jay* pp 50, 65.

[17] SGW & Sarah→SW, 16/11/1804, is addressed to SW at Great Chesterfield Street, where he was very ill and feared that he might die (*see* SGW & Sarah→ SW, 12/11/1804). SGW→Sarah, 1/5/1805, indicates that SW no longer lived at Great Chesterfield Street: he sleeps better elsewhere, although he still calls in most days. SGW appears to have moved from Great Chesterfield Street to Great Woodstock Street, Nottingham Place, some time before 15/10/1806.

The Wesleys' Great Chesterfield Street house was demolished about 1860.[18] In 1953 a commemorative blue plaque was erected at 1 Wheatley Street, Marylebone, to mark the site on which it had stood.

RIDGE. SW and Charlotte Louisa Martin began living here shortly before 18 October 1792, as Christian Ignatius Latrobe's journal entry for that day notes that SW has 'gone to live…in Hertfordshire…with a companion'. The Ridge house was described by SW as a 'wooden cottage',[19] and Sarah remarked several times on its comparative lack of amenity.[20] SW still lived at Ridge on 15 February 1797 but presumably left soon after then, as in a letter of that date Sarah says that the time is approaching for him and his family to leave Ridge. She hoped that their next home would be more comfortable.

FINCHLEY. SW and his family appear to have removed here about July 1797, as a letter from Sarah dated 27 July 1797, although addressed to SW at Great Chesterfield Street, presumes that he is in his new house. Only a few letters referable to the Finchley address have survived, of which the last is dated 23/5/1798.

HORNSEY LANE. The evidence that SW and his family lived here after Finchley and before moving to 5 Mile Stone, Highgate is sparse. He wrote the address 'Hornsey Lane, near Highgate' on a manuscript of a musical composition some time before 29/8/1798, and a 23/1/1799 letter from CLW to Sarah, posted from Highgate, mentions Sarah's departure from Highgate.[21]

---

[18] *Lightwood* p 43.

[19] SW→SGW, 7/11/1792.

[20] See, for example, her letters of 19/9/1794, 25/9/1794 and 30/9/1794.

[21] As SGW→Sarah, 12/6/1799, conveys that SW has taken a house near Highgate, i.e., the house at 5 Mile Stone, CLW and SW presumably were not yet living at 5 Mile Stone when CLW wrote to Sarah on 23/1/1799. We conjecture that SW and CLW made their home in Hornsey Lane about that time but lack sufficient evidence to establish this beyond doubt.

HIGHGATE. SW and his family presumably began to live at 5 Mile Stone, Highgate about June 1799, as a 12 June 1799 letter in which SGW tells Sarah that 'Sam is busy about a house which he has taken near Highgate'. This move may have been occasioned by the birth or expected birth of JWW. At the end of July 1801, SW and CLW separated.[22] CLW appears to have moved out of SW's house,[23] possibly to Pimlico,[24] while SW continued to live in his Highgate home.[25] On 30 April 1803, SGW wrote that the 'fatiguing time of giving up the house is nearer', suggesting that he left Highgate about May 1803 and returned to live in Great Chesterfield Street then.

9 AND 27 ARLINGTON STREET, CAMDEN TOWN. The earliest documentary evidence of SW's Camden Town residence is a letter from SW to SGW dated 1/4/1806, but this home presumably was established by SW and CLW before the birth of their daughter Emma about February 1806.[26] SW generally headed the letters he wrote from here 'Camden Town', adding the Arlington Street address only occasionally. This address appears to have been 9 Arlington Street until about June 1808[27] and 27 Arlington Street thereafter, as SW underscored the numerals '27' in a 23/6/1808 letter to Charles Burney. As SW and CB were in frequent correspondence at the time, the new address presumably took effect about that date. No indication has been found that SW moved house then, so this change of address may signify a house renumbering rather than a relocation.

---

[22] Sarah's memorandum of 28/7/1801 says that the separation is 'about to take place'.

[23] Sarah→SGW, 1/8/1801, states that CLW is now paying rent.

[24] In Sarah→SW, 2/9/1807, Sarah mentions her unsuccessful attempts to find lodgings for CLW and that CLW has found apartments in Pimlico without Sarah's help. However, it is not clear from this letter whether CLW moved to Pimlico in 1801 or after the Highgate house was sold.

[25] SW→Editor, *MM*, 13/9/1801, and some subsequent letters are written from Highgate.

[26] Shepherd→Sarah, 15/1/1806, says that CLW is ready to 'lay in'.

[27] SW→Street, 30/5/1806, is explicitly written from 9 Arlington Street, as is an undated letter from SW to Mr Freebairn.

SW's departure from 27 Arlington Street marked his final separation from CLW. His last letter explicitly written from Camden Town is assigned to 13/1/1810 but presumably he still lived there on 18/1/1810, as his letter of that date mentions Emma's whooping cough. Sarah Suter probably informed SW of her pregnancy about this time, as their first child, Samuel Sebastian Wesley, was born on 14 August 1810. Presumably SW had moved from Camden Town before he wrote to CW Jr on 16/2/1810 from James Ball's home in Duke Street, as in this letter SW declares that he has been CLW's 'dupe' and 'slave'.

ADAM'S ROW. The first report of SW's Adam's Row home is in his 17/7/1810 letter to CB. He was still residing here on 25/3/1812, when he executed the Deed of Separation from CLW, but he left within a month after that date.

TOTTENHAM COURT. The earliest indication of SW living here is his 26/4/1812 letter to Mr Freeling. He departed before 10/10/1813, when he invited Robert Glenn to his new home in Gower Place and described his former accommodation in Tottenham Court as a 'dark hole'.[28]

5 AND 4 GOWER PLACE. In that 10/10/1813 letter to RG, SW characterised his 'new home' at 5 Gower Place as 'more pleasant, neater and cheaper' than his last residence. His house number changed from 5 to 4 Gower Place, apparently about 22/7/1814, as in a letter to RG of that date SW underscored the numeral '4' in his address.[29] As with SW's Camden Town addresses, there is no evidence to suggest that he moved from one Gower Place home to another, so this change again may indicate merely a house renumbering.

---

[28] The last extant letter explicitly addressed to Tottenham Court is SW→SS, 9/7/1813.

[29] SW and RG were in regular correspondence at this time. The immediately previous extant letter from SW to RG was addressed from 'Gower Place' on 25/5/1814 without specification of a house number. No letter from RG to SW is known to have survived.

The code 'Gower Pl', without a preceding numeral, appears in calendar entries of letters that indicate that SW's home was in Gower Place but do not specify the house number.

SW remained at 4 Gower Place until 3 May 1817. On that night he came to his mother's home (in which CW Jr and Sarah also lived) at 2 York Buildings, New Road, in a state of mind so deranged that the family were 'obliged to have a keeper'.[30] Three days later, fearing the arrival of creditors, he 'flung up the window, and himself out of it'.[31] Although not expected to survive, he recovered and, after being accommodated briefly in Chapel Street, went in June 1817 to Southend for a month to recuperate. However, following medical advice, his family and friends determined that he should not return home to Sarah Suter and their children but should receive treatment for insanity.

SS presumably continued to stay at Gower Place for some time, but her movements from May 1817 until she rejoined SW at Euston Street, presumably in 1819, are not known.

BLACKLANDS. Although records of the private lunatic asylum at Blacklands House apparently have not survived, SW seems to have arrived there in July or August 1817.[32] His departure at the end of June 1818 is suggested by a letter from Sarah, assigned to 26/6/1818, stating that Dr Alexander Robert Sutherland, SW's physician at Blacklands, has pronounced him 'recovered' and has declared him free to change 'his place of abode whenever he likes'. The length of his stay at Blacklands is affirmed by another letter from Sarah, assigned to 4/3/1818, which remarks that doctors did not wish to risk their reputations by releasing patients from asylums before a whole year had elapsed.

SW consistently maintained that he was not insane, and that his confinement in Blacklands was a dreadful mistake. On a page of musical sketches written about 23/3/1818, he wrote: 'How the foolish

---

[30] Sarah→William Wilberforce, 12/5/1817?.

[31] *Ibid.*

[32] He was not yet there on 7/7/1817 (*see* Sarah→RG, 7/7/1817) but had arrived by 20/8/1817, when CW Jr recorded in his diary (MA DDWF/23/15) that Dr Sutherland had called to say that SW was better.

& the malicious confound pure Distress of Mind with Insanity, or Madness! As different things as sq[uare] □ & ○ round. Agitation proves no more than strong & irritable Feeling. What is he worth who never has these?'.[33]

Blacklands House, which earlier had served as a fashionable ladies' academy,[34] was located north of King's Road, Chelsea. In 1858 the licensees of the lunatic asylum there were 'Drs Sutherland' (Alexander Robert Sutherland and his son Alexander John Sutherland, who succeeded his father as physician to St Luke's Hospital), suggesting that at the time of SW's confinement there the elder Dr Sutherland may have been not only SW's physician but also the licensee of the establishment where he was kept.[35] The asylum removed to Tooting Common in 1890.[36]

SW's movements after his release from Blacklands are known only from the memoir published in *The Wesley Banner and Revival Record*. According to this account, after an excursion to the coast, SW returned to London 'nearly convalescent' and 'was kindly received under the roof of the skilful son of the Rev. John Gaulter [a Methodist minister], till his confirmed recovery enabled him to pursue his profession'.[37] By late 1818 SW was 'scoring' a symphony for the Philharmonic Society[38] and in January 1819 he resumed his post as organist of the Covent Garden oratorio concerts.

---

[33] Royal College of Music ms 4025 f 108ᵛ. f 108ʳ contains, amongst other items, two short vocal compositions 'Miserere miserorum' and 'Infelix homo' in SW's handwriting, between which he wrote the date 23 March 1818.

[34] Charles Burney had taught there. *See* CB→SW, 17/10/1808.

[35] If so, Dr Sutherland could have had a financial interest in keeping SW there.

[36] For information regarding the Blacklands asylum we are indebted to Patricia Allderidge, Archivist and Curator of the Bethlem Royal Hospital, and to the Chelsea Area Librarian, Royal Borough of Kensington and Chelsea.

[37] 'Memoir of Samuel Wesley, the musician', *WBRR* v 3 (December 1851) p 446; *Stevenson* p 521 reproduces this passage exactly. No corroboration of this reported excursion to the coast has been found, and it may be a mistake for SW's trip to Southend which took place in June 1817, before his confinement at Blacklands. The hospitality of Gaulter's son to SW, but not the dates when it occurred, is mentioned in Sarah→John Gaulter, 23/5/1825.

[38] *See* SW→VN, 17/11/1818, and Philharmonic Society Minutes of Directors' Meeting, 15/12/1818.

DUKE STREET. 27 Duke Street was the address of the home and piano manufactory of SW's friend James Ball. SW appears to have stayed here on at least two occasions. On 16 February 1810, after he had CLW and their Camden Town home, and before he had established his Hampstead Road home with SS, SW wrote from this address to CW Jr. Additional evidence links SW to Duke Street about this time.[39]

The 1819 *Literary Pocket-Book* lists SW as a teacher of organ and pianoforte at '23 Duke Street, Grosvenor Square'.[40] This appears to be a misprint for Ball's address, as SW wrote to Edward Hodges from 27 Duke Street in February 1819. Although there is insufficient evidence to prove that SW lived here in late 1818 and early 1819—an alternative hypothesis is that he used Ball's premises only as a teaching studio and as a place where he could meet people and receive mail—the limited available evidence suggests that he did live here at that time.[41]

EUSTON STREET. SW's period of residence here is known only from surviving correspondence. The first extant letter bearing this address is dated 5/6/1819, but SW may have moved to Euston Street some weeks or months earlier. He apparently moved directly from Euston Street to Mornington Place.

---

[39] The title-page of Charles Frederick Horn's and SW's 'adaptation' of six J. S. Bach organ trios, published serially at this time, was altered during publication of the series. The title-page of the first trio says that the trios were to be had only of Horn at 25 Queen Square and of Wesley at 27 Arlington Street, Camden Town. When the fourth trio was published CFH's address remained unchanged on the title-page, but in place of Wesley's Camden Town address those of 'Mr Birchall's' music shop and 'Mr Ball's piano forte manufactory, Duke St' were substituted.

[40] As Vincent Novello was in contact with SW at this time, and the *Literary Pocket-Book* was edited by VN's friend Leigh Hunt, its placement of SW in Duke Street seems credible.

[41] The additional evidence includes: a letter assigned to 17/11/1818 in which SW asks VN to meet him at Ball's; a letter dated 'Sunday 24th' from SW to VN (entered in the calendar of undated letters with a dating range of 1811–8/1820) in which SW writes Ball's address where he conventionally would write a return address and arguably is assignable to 24/1/1819 (although in this letter SW says that he will remain at Ball's home until 9 pm); and the absence of information that SW had any other home address at this time.

MORNINGTON PLACE. SW began living in Mornington Place about 22 March 1830, the date of a prayer that he wrote on removing to his new home.[42] He appears to have lived here beyond 18 May 1831, as he is placed at this address in CW Jr's will of that date.

PENTONVILLE. The earliest reference to Samuel Wesley living here is a letter from SSW to SS entered at 17/10/1832?. SW died here on 11 October 1837.[43] Following his death, SS continued to live in this house, as Mrs Wesley.

---

[42] This prayer is at BL Add 35012 f 108.

[43] An official copy of the 17 October 1837 entry in the register of burials in the Parish of St Marylebone, giving SW's abode at time of death as 'Kings Row Pentonville', is preserved at MA DDWes/6/61.

~ 2 ~

CHRONOLOGY

SIGNIFICANT EVENTS IN WESLEY'S LIFE

The following chronology lists significant datable events in Samuel Wesley's life.[1] Information about many other datable events is given in the calendar of correspondence and the iconography section.

Where not indicated explicitly, the source of information about an event is a letter of the same date in the calendar, a dated musical composition by SW, or—for concerts or lectures—an advertisement in *The Times*. Unless contrary news has come to our attention we have assumed that a public event advertised for a particular date did take place on that date.

The dates when SW's musical and literary works were completed, published or first performed, are stated (if known) in the lists of these works below. SW's periods of residence in particular houses are tabulated in *Figure 3* on page 8 above and are discussed in the section on his homes and addresses.

Where a date is followed by a question-mark the uncertainty is explained in the corresponding calendar entry. The symbols '<' and '>' preceding a date stand for 'before' and 'after', respectively.

1766–1778

24/2/1766	Born in Bristol. (*Barrington* p 291)
1–2/1769	Plays his first tune, 'when he was but two years and eleven months old'. (*Barrington* p 291)
1770	Teaches himself to read words from a copy of Handel's oratorio *Samson*, when 'between four and five years old'. (*Barrington* p 292)

---

[1] Events in which SW's participation is uncertain generally have been excluded from the chronology. For instance, John Marsh reports that he heard 'young Westley' play in a morning concert at the Thatched House Tavern on 14/5/1779 and at the Crown and Anchor Tavern on 21/11/1781 (*Marsh* p 197–198, 253). However, it is unclear whether Marsh heard CW Jr or SW play, and no list of performers at these concerts has been found. (For the spelling 'Westley' see the note to CB→Latrobe, 4/2/1799?, in the calendar of correspondence.)

1771	'When turned of five' knows all the recitatives and choruses of Handel's *Messiah* and *Samson*, 'both words and music, by heart', and can identify the composers of music played by CW Jr. Begins to compose extempore. 'Before he was six years old' composes his first oratorio *Ruth* 'in his memory', but is unable to write it down 'till he was eight'. (*Barrington* p 293)
5/1771	Lives at Chesterfield Street, London, apparently for the first time, but returns with family members to Bristol for extended periods until the Wesley family finally removes from Bristol to London in 1778. (Calendar of correspondence)
1772	'Between six and seven' learns to read music from David Williams, a Bristol organist, and studies with him for a year. (*Barrington* p 293–294)
3–4/1773	Plays the organ at St James's Church, Bristol. (CW→SW, 6/3/1773; SW→CW Jr, 20/4/1773)
1774	Learns to write music, and writes down score of *Ruth*. When 'full eight years old', family visited by William Boyce, who has heard from 'young Linley' [Thomas Linley Jr, composer and violinist, 1756–1778, WL's brother] that CW has 'an English Mozart' in his house.[2] Boyce inspects the score of *Ruth* and is much impressed.
	Teaches himself the violin, assisted for six weeks by 'a soldier', and subsequently by William Kingsbury, who gives him 20 lessons. Spends a month in Bath, plays several voluntaries on the organ at the Abbey, and plays the violin in several private concerts. Returns to London and learns music by Handel and Scarlatti. Taken by Martin Madan to visit Madan's friends. Heard by Sir Watkins Wynn, CB and others. Has smallpox 'between eight and nine'. (*Barrington* p 293–295)

---

[2] Thomas Linley Jr had been apprenticed to Boyce from 1761 to 1768. In April 1770 Linley met Mozart in Florence and the two became friends.

1775	Taken by Martin Madan to some of the 'first masters' of music, including Charles Frederick Abel [German performer and composer, 1723–1787, from 1759 resident in London]. Daines Barrington first hears SW 'at the latter end of 1775, when he was nearly ten'. (*Barrington* p 297–298)
6–7/1776	Extended stay with the Russell family at Guildford. Portrait painted about this time by John Russell, R.A. (exhibited at Royal Academy, 1777). Visits Martin Madan at Epsom. Returns to London, 27/7/1776.
20/5/1777	Plays at Hickford's Rooms in a concert organised by J. C. Bach. Other performers include Elizabeth Weichsel *later* Mrs Billington. (*Public Advertiser* 20/5/1777; *Lightwood* p 44)
1777	'Eight Sonatas for the Harpsichord or Pianoforte' [op. 1] published. (*Barrington* p 306)
8–9/1778	Revisits the Russell family at Guildford and visits his relatives, the Waller family, at Terriers near High Wycombe.
7/9/1778	Apparently expressing concern about SW's interest in Roman Catholicism, CW tells SGW that if she makes SW a 'living Christian' he 'will never wish to be a dead Papist'.

1779–1790

1779	Takes Crotch 'under his protection' and tests his abilities as a musical child prodigy. (CW→JW, 23/4/1779; *Barrington* p 313–316)
1779–1780	Gives music lessons to Miss Stretton [not identified]. (appointments and fees charged, MA DDCW/8/25(d))

14/1/1779; 28/1; 11/2; 25/2; 4/3; 11/3; 19/3; 25/3	First series of subscription concerts by CW Jr and SW at Chesterfield Street.[3]
8–10/1779	CW takes his family, including SW, on 'a long ramble' of 11 weeks on horseback, mostly through Wales, returning to London on 23/10/1779. (Rebecca Gwynne→SGW, 26/8/1779; CW→John Langshaw, 26/10/1779)
1780–1784	Begins teaching in Mrs Barnes's school, Oxford House, Marylebone. (In SW→George Smith, 23/4/1809, SW says he has taught there 'for 25 years'; in SW→George Smith, 9/5/1809, he says he has served there for 'nearly 30 years'.)
20/1/1780; 3/2; 17/2; 2/3; 16/3; 30/3; [13/4][4]	Second series of CW Jr/SW subscription concerts.
20/2/1780	Performs in concert at Lady Home's arranged by CW. (MA DDCW/8/21)
7/6/1780	CW Jr and SW 'sheltered' by SGW at SGW's aunt's home during the Gordon Riots; CW proposes to send SGW and SW to Bristol. (CW→Sarah, 8/6/1780)

[3] The CW Jr/SW concerts took place at Chesterfield Street from 1779 to 1787. Each of the nine annual series comprised seven concerts except the first series, which had eight. The primary source of data about these concerts is a set of CW's notebooks in which he wrote down the programmes, the names of performers, subscribers and attendees, expenses and other details. CW's register of the 1779–1781 concerts is at MA DDCW/8/21, of the 1782–1785 concerts (and also of subscribers to the 1779–1781 concerts) is at RAM Ms–L (Wesley), of the 1786 concerts is at MA DDCW/6/58 and of the 1787 concerts is at MA DDCW/9/15. Additional data by CW about the concerts are contained in MA DDCW/6/52A for 1779, MA DDCW/6/52B for 1780, MA DDCW/8/15(d) for 1782 and 1783, MA DDCW/6/57 for 1784, and MA DDCW/6/55 and MA DDCW/6/56 for 1786. In 1894, EW copied RAM Ms–L (Wesley), which then was in the possession of her brother MEW; her copy now is at BL Add 35017. *See* CW→William Russell, 21/12/1778, CW memorandum, about 14/1/1779 (which gives CW's reasons for having the concerts), CW→JW, 23/4/1779, and CW→John Langshaw, 22/12/1781. We are grateful to Dr Alyson McLamore for information concerning these concert registers.

[4] The 13/4/1780 date is not given explicitly in CW's register (MA DDCW/8/21).

9/11/1780	First dated Roman Catholic musical composition, 'Ecce Maria genuit nobis'.
25/1/1781; 8/2; 22/2; 8/3; 22/3; 5/4; 26/4	Third series of CW Jr/SW subscription concerts.[5]
25/1/1781	JW spends 'an agreeable hour' at CW Jr/SW concert but notes that he loves 'plain music' best.
31/1/1782; 14/2; 28/2; 14/3; 4/4; 18/4; 2/5	Fourth series of CW Jr/SW subscription concerts.
8/9/1782	Plays the organ at Queen's Square Chapel. (Elizabeth Waller→SGW, 12/9/1782)
10/1782	Relationship with CLM begins. (SW→SGW, 7/11/1792)
23/1/1783; 6/2; 20/2; 6/3; 20/3; 3/4; 24/4	Fifth series of CW Jr/SW subscription concerts.
7/2/1783	Plays, with CW Jr, Marsh's 'double pieces at sight' on the organ at Chesterfield Street. (*Marsh* p 278)
21/4/1783	Together with CW Jr meets John Marsh and plays on the organ newly built for him at the Wyche Street premises of the organ-builder Mr Hancock. (*Marsh* p 286)
3/8/1783	Suicide of James Price, who leaves SW £1,000 and a house at Guildford. (James Price will, 6/2/1783)
early 1784	Converts to Roman Catholicism. (>SW→ Shepherd, 26/12/1783; <Duchess of Norfolk visit to CW in 4/1784)
29/1/1784; 19/2; 4/3; 18/3; 1/4; 15/4; 29/4	Sixth series of CW Jr/SW subscription concerts.

---

[5] A copy of the printed proposals 'for a third subscription concert [series] by Messrs Charles and Samuel Wesley in Chesterfield Street, Marybone' beginning 25/1/1781 and continuing 'every other Thursday evening' is at MA DDWes/7/41.

12–30/4/1784	Duchess of Norfolk visits CW to inform him of SW's conversion to Roman Catholicism.[6] (Shepherd→SW→ Shepherd, 3/1794–1797).
2/5/1784	JW writes to CW Jr about CW Jr's and Sarah's concerns that SW has 'changed his religion', and asserts that SW has not done this but has merely changed his 'opinions and mode of worship'.
22/5/1784	*Missa de spiritu sancto* completed.
26/5/1784– 5/6/1784	Recalls, 29 years later, that he was 'seized' at the time of the Handel Commemoration festival (at Westminster Abbey) 'with a nervous horror against music', which caused him 'torment and pain'. (Thomas Green journal entry, 28/6/1813)
19/8/1784	JW writes to SW, apparently for the first time, to advise that there are 'weightier matters' than 'Protestant or Romish' opinions. JW declares that SW is on the wrong path; unless he is born again he 'cannot see the kingdom of God'.
9/1784	Presentation copy of *Missa de spiritu sancto* bound for dispatch to Pope Pius VI. (SW→Shepherd, 6/9/1784?)
3/2/1785; 17/2; 3/3; 17/3; 31/3; 14/4; 28/4	Seventh series of CW Jr/SW subscription concerts.[7]
6–7/1785	CW visits [Roman Catholic] Bishop James Talbot to ask him, as SW's pastor, to watch over SW's soul and to alert Talbot to SW's 'irregular conduct'. SW says that he would rather quit the Roman Catholic church than be the cause of a scandal in it. (SW→Shepherd, 7/1785?)

---

[6] Shepherd states in Shepherd→Sarah, 14/3/1794, that CW was informed of SW's conversion to Roman Catholicism by the Duchess of Norfolk 'between Easter and Whitsuntide 1785', but her statement of the year is clearly a mistake for 1784, as the duchess died on 26/11/1784, and SW did not profess to be a Catholic in 1783, *see* SW→Shepherd, 26/12/1783. In 1784 Easter occurred on 11/4 and Whit Sunday on 30/5. The duchess's visit presumably took place in April 1784, as SW's conversion is discussed in JW→CW Jr, 2/5/1784.

[7] A copy of the printed proposals for this concert series is at MA DDWes/7/42.

[9/2/1786; 23/2/; 9/3];[8] 23/3/1786; 6/4; 20/4; 4/5	Eighth series of CW Jr/SW subscription concerts.
12/5/1786	Performs with CW Jr at a free concert in Chesterfield Street to an audience of 54. (SGW→Sarah, 13/5/1786)
20/7/1786	Visits Brickendon, Hertfordshire.
1787	In his obituary (*Times*, 18/10/1837, published 50 years after the alleged event), SW said to have injured his head in a fall into a builder's excavation, to have 'obstinately refused' surgery which he 'ever after regretted', and to have been despondent for the next seven years, during which time he refused 'to cultivate his genius for music'.[9]
13/2/1787; 27/2; 13/3; 27/3; 10/4; 24/4; 8/5	Ninth and last series of CW Jr/SW subscription concerts. (MA DDCW/9/15).
21/3/1787	Plays an organ concerto and directs a performance of Felice Giardini's oratorio *Ruth* at the King's Theatre, Haymarket, for the benefit of Lock Hospital.[10] (W[illiam] T[homas] Parke, *Musical Memoirs*, London, 1830, v 1 p 92)
11/7/1787	Arrives in Hertford, where he plans to stay until 17/7/1787 in Mr Leach's house.
1788?	Spends a week at Cambridge. (SW→Latrobe, about 28/2/1799, says that this happened 'many years before'; Sarah→SW, 10/1789?, mentions a clergyman who knew SW at Cambridge; SW→CB, 7/7/1808, states that SW had not been to Cambridge for 20 years)
16/3/1788	JW agrees, while he lives, to be a 'father and friend' to CW Jr and SW when CW dies.

---

[8] The first three dates are not given explicitly in CW's register (MA DDCW/6/58).

[9] This story is uncorroborated by extant documentation from SW's lifetime.

[10] Parke ascribes these activities to 'Mr Wesley'. SW assumed to be the referent because CW Jr's 19/3/1794 performance of an organ concerto at Covent Garden was billed as his first appearance in public.

18/3/1788	CW near death. JW greatly concerned about SW. JW thinks that SW, under Shepherd's influence, is unlikely to heed JW, and advises SW to 'make a friend of' Peard Dickinson.
29/3/1788	Present at CW's death. (Sarah→JW, 4/4/1788)
17/12/1788	Admitted to Preston's [Masonic] Lodge of Antiquity. (United Grand Lodge records)
30/4/1789	CB includes 'the two Wesleys' [CW Jr and SW], as well as himself, in a list of the best players of keyed instruments in England. (CB, *A General History of Music*, v 4, London, 1789, p 682)[11]
1789	Elected a junior deacon of the Masons. (Cordell William Firebrace, *Records of the Lodge Original, No. 1, now the Lodge of Antiquity, No. 2, of the Free and Accepted Masons of England*, London, v 2, 1926, privately published)
7/1789	In Bromfield, Hertfordshire. (SW→SGW, 22/7/1789; Sarah→Penelope Maitland, 29/7/1789)
28/4/1790	JW desires Dickinson to invite SW without delay, as Dickinson has the opportunity to save SW's 'soul alive'.
29/4/1790	JW, sending what probably are his 'dying words' to SW, 'cares not' whether SW is called a Papist or a Protestant but is grieved that he is a 'heathen'. JW believes that SW is called to 'something better' than the 'refined heathenism' of the 'general religion both of Protestants and Catholics', and exhorts SW to 'give God his heart'.

1791–1800

1791	'Erased' from the Masonic Lodge of Antiquity for non-payment of arrears. (Cordell William Firebrace, *Records of the Lodge Original, No. 1, now the Lodge of Antiquity, No. 2, of the Free and Accepted Masons of England*, London, v 2, 1926, privately published)

---

[11] The publication date of this volume is given in Roger Lonsdale, *Dr Charles Burney: a Literary Biography* (Oxford, 1965) p 341.

2/3/1791	Knocks at the door of JW's house in City Road, London, at the moment of JW's death. (*Stevenson City Road* p 113; *Stevenson* p 509)
3–6/1791	Extended interchange of letters with Sarah about SW's conduct, his opinions of the Wesley family, and his views on marriage.
25/6/1791	Arrives in Taunton. (SW→SGW, 27/6/1791)
4/1792	Publishes *Vindex to Verax* 'to vindicate the motives' of JW from an attack in another pamphlet 'and to snatch his sacred ashes from the scourge of insolence'. (Shepherd→SW, 24/4/1792; *Vindex to Verax*, p 14)
4–5/1792	Indicates differences from Roman Catholics on points of doctrine. (SW→Shepherd, 26/4/1792; SW→'Reverend Sir', 5/1792?)
10/1792	Moves to Ridge, Hertfordshire, before 18/10/1792, and sets up house there with CLM. (Latrobe journal, 18/10/1792)
7/11/1792	Informs SGW that he has resolved to spend the rest of his life with CLM who, contrary to allegations, was a virgin before SW met her and who has become SW's 'wife by all the laws of God and nature'. No ceremony by 'divine jugglers' would make their union truer.
5/4/1793	Marries CLM at St Paul's, Hammersmith, apparently without informing his family.[12] (St Paul's marriage registers, Hammersmith and Fulham Archives)
about 9/6/1793	Robbed of his purse and watch by two men. (SGW & CW Jr→Sarah, about 10/6/1793)
8/1793	Maintains, in correspondence with Sarah who thinks that he has not married CLW, that the Bible nowhere requires that a marriage be celebrated in a public ceremony.
25/9/1793	CW III born at Ridge. (Ridge baptismal registers, Hertfordshire Record Office)

---

[12] A note in an unknown hand (MA DDWes/6/66) states that the marriage took place at Ridge and was witnessed by [SW's friend] James Kenton and William Hallett, clerk.

20/10/1793	CW III baptised at Ridge. (Ridge baptismal registers)
18/1/1794	Sarah meets CLW for the first time since SW's marriage and is relieved to know that they are married. Sarah records that 'all family enmities ceased'.
1/10/1794	Informs Sarah that he will have no further children with CLW after her current pregnancy, and that CLW would have been happier with 'a good and foolish husband'.
21/10/1794	Completes 'Begin the noble song', his ode to St Cecilia.
11/1794	Daughter Susanna born before 12/11/1794. (Sarah→SW, 12/11/1794)
9–11/1795	CLW, CW III and Susanna go to Bristol, apparently as a trial separation from SW. Sarah also is in Bristol.
3/3/1796	Tells Sarah that he esteems AD as 'his only female friend on earth'.
18/1/1797	Reveals particularly severe marital problems and the necessity of separation from CLW.
24/2/1797	Invites Bridgetower to a musical party at AD's mother's house. (SW→Bridgetower, 23/2/1797)
12/1797	Daughter Susanna dies before 22/12/1797. (SW→SGW, 22/12/1797)
5/1798	Applies unsuccessfully for post of organist at the Foundling Hospital. (SW→Thomas Merryweather, 6/3/1798; SW→William Seward, 16/6/1798; Foundling Hospital records, London Metropolitan Archives)
20/5/1798	Assaulted by CLW, who says that she wishes to separate from him. (SW→Sarah, 23/5/1798)
summer 1798	Visits William Seward twice in Richmond, Surrey. (Seward poem, *Whitehall Evening-Post*, 21–23/8/1798)

28/10/1798	New organ built by John Avery at St Nicholas, Sevenoaks, Kent, opened by 'Mr Wesley'. (handbill dated 17/10/1798, quoted in *Musical Times*, 1/12/1902, p 800)[13]
1/1799?	Meets CB at a dinner party, their first meeting since SW was a boy. (CB→Latrobe, 4/2/1799?)
22/2/1799	'Begin the noble song' first performed at Covent Garden oratorio concert, in which SW also plays a Handel organ concerto. (Hogan, Charles Beecher (ed.), *The London Stage 1660–1800, part 5 v* 3, Carbondale, Illinois, 1968, p 2148)
6/1799	JWW born before 1/7/1799. (SGW→Sarah, 14/5/1799; CLW→SGW, 1/7/1799)
14/8/1799	Completes *Confitebor*; subsequently sends it to CB for his comments. (SW→CB, 28/11/1799)
11/10/1799	Arranges to meet other musicians at James Ball's piano manufactory to play through *Confitebor*. (SW→Street, 6/10/1799)
16/10/1799	Has, with CLW, evening music party with SW's pupil Barry and Barry's brother. (SW→Street, 18/10/1799)
10/11/1799	Engagement at Watford. Advertised to play but did not play at charity sermon at Mr [Thomas?] Howard's church [location unknown]. (SW→Street, 9/11/1799)
11/1799	Corresponds with CB about details of CB's *General History of Music*. (SW→CB, 28/11/1799, 30/11/1799)
5/1/1800	Endeavours to sell house at Guildford left to him by James Price.

---

[13] The *Musical Times* misprints the year as '1788' but this is a mistake, as the opening was scheduled for 'Sunday, the 28th of October', which occurred in 1798 but not in 1788, and the quoted handbill [not located] refers to Admiral Horatio Nelson's victory over the French fleet, which took place on 1/8/1798. Although the handbill does not say whether the organist was SW or CW Jr, the event is listed here because other information in this *Musical Times* article is said by the writer, Frederick George Edwards, to have been supplied to him by EW.

21/3/1800	Discusses playing the organ in a proposed performance of Thomas Busby's oratorio *Britannia* and looks forward to meeting Busby's teacher Jonathan Battishill.
31/3/1800	Plays organ voluntary in François-Hippolyte Barthélemon's concert at Hatton House, Cross Street, Hatton Garden. (*Times*, 27/3/1800)
1/4/1800	Apologises to Sarah for hurtful words he uttered while inebriated, which had caused her to 'banish herself' from Chesterfield Street for a year.
21/4/1800	Plays the piano in Salomon's performance of Haydn's *Creation* at the King's Theatre and is soloist in his own organ concerto [probably his concerto in D]. (*Times*, 18/4/1800)
5/1800	Elected a governor of the Literary Fund. (SW→Thomas Busby, 3/6/1800)
20/7/1800	George III asks SGW about her children's 'genius for music' and whether CW liked this. (SGW→Sarah, 24/7/1800)
about 23/7/1800	Plays the organ with Johann Anton André at St Paul's Covent Garden and at the German Lutheran church in the Savoy. AFCK describes their performance as 'a great pleasure'. (AFCK→John Wall Callcott, 26/7/1800)
27/11/1800	Visits Concentores Society, where his 'While others, Delia, use their pen' and 'The Macedon youth' are performed. (Concentores Society minutes, Guildhall Library)

1801–1807

14/5/1801	Plays the organ in a performance of Thomas Busby's oratorio *The Prophecy* at the Theatre Royal, Haymarket. Richard John Samuel Stevens is astonished by SW's performance. (*Argent* p 122)
28/7/1801	Separation from CLW about to take place 'on account of AD'.

10/10/1801	Party with Miss Richardson, Graeff, François Cramer, George Frederick Pinto, and Johann Wilhelm Moralt, in which music by Haydn, Mozart and other composers is played. (SW→SGW, 16/10/1801)
4/2/1802; 25/2; 11/3; 25/3; 22/4; 6/5	Organises, with CW Jr, six subscription concerts at Hyde's Concert Rooms, Tottenham Street. They each lose £100 from this venture. (*Times*, 29/1/1802; SW→CB, 9/3/1802?; SW→SGW & Sarah, 8/9/1802; SW→CW Jr, 31/5/1811; SW→SGW, 4/7/1811)
27/4/1802	Symphony in B♭ completed.
8/1802	Assists Sarah in summarising parliamentary debates for Dr George Gregory, editor of the *New Annual Register*. (SW→Sarah, 12/8/1802)
8–9/1802	Extended period of mental depression. (SW→Sarah, 12/8/1802; SW→SGW, 27/8/1802; SW→SGW & Sarah, 8/9/1802)
23/10/1802?	Tells Sarah that his 'mind and body are failing most rapidly', and that he wishes before he dies to remove any false impression that she may have about AD.
6/3/1803	Becomes an Honorary Subscriber to the Royal Society of Musicians. (Royal Society of Musicians Governors' Minutes)
15/8/1803	Sarah affirms that SW's disease is of the mind, and regrets that SW cannot be influenced to follow advice.
12/6/1804	Visits Madrigal Society. (Madrigal Society Attendance & Transactions register 1785–1828, on loan to BL Music Library)[14]
12/11/1804	In constant misery, SW fears his 'speedy dissolution'.
1/5/1805	Apparently better, SW no longer lives in SGW's Great Chesterfield Street house but calls in there most days. Rapprochement with CLW presumably about this time.
>15/1/1806	Birth of Emma. (Shepherd→Sarah, 15/1/1806)

---

[14] The register names 'Mr Linley' and 'Mr Wesley'—presumably WL and SW, who both visited the Madrigal Society on several subsequent occasions—as professional visitors this day. No evidence has been found that CW Jr took part in this Society's events.

22/1/1806	AD buried. (St Mary Paddington Green burial records, London Metropolitan Archives)
1/4/1806	Visits Madrigal Society.[15] (Madrigal Society register)
4/1806	Financially distressed by bad debts and non-payment of fees, regrets that CW allowed him to have music for his profession and decides that CW III cannot remain at St Paul's school. (SW→SGW, 1/4/1806, 21/4/1806)
21/5/1806?	Completes manuscript transcription of '48' from copy lent to him 'some months ago' by Graeff.[16]
4/6/1806	Planned outing with CW III and Street to the Tower of London and Billingsgate. (SW→Street, 30/5/1806)
18/12/1806	Visits the Society of Harmonists, where he plays the piano and his glee, 'When Bacchus, Jove's immortal boy', is performed. (Richard J. S. Stevens 'Recollections', 18/12/1806; SW→CW Jr, 15/1/1807)
25/12/1806	Intended performance of his Responses to the Litany at St Paul's Cathedral postponed to Easter Day 1807. (SW→SGW, 12/1806; SW→CW Jr, 15/1/1807, 21/3/1807)
27/12/1806	Visits the Concentores Society, where his Dixit Dominus [III] is performed for the first time (autograph scores; SW→CW Jr, 15/1/1807; *Argent* p 150)
about 1807	Assists John Belfour [writer, 1768–1842] to prepare a translation of Tomas de Yriarte, *Music, A Didactic Poem, in Five Cantos* (London, 1807)[17]

---

[15] The register names the visitor as 'Mr Westley'. See note to the 12/6/1804 entry above.

[16] In his *Reminiscences* SW wrote that he 'first became acquainted with' the '48' 'through George Frederick Pinto', who died on 23/3/1806. The date of this first acquaintance has not been determined. Pinto had studied thorough bass with CFH in the 1790s and presumably could have become aware of the '48' then. Although in the extant correspondence Pinto is first mentioned in SW→SGW, 16/10/1801, he and SW presumably had met before the 10/10/1801 'musical party' described in that letter.

[17] In the 'advertisement' (p xii) to this translation, Belfour acknowledges SW's 'obliging alacrity and professional skill', particularly in regard to the poem's

11/1/1807	Goes to Dulwich with William Carnaby to visit Rev. Edward Barry. (SW→CW Jr, 15/1/1807)
14/1/1807	Attends lecture by Crotch at the Royal Institution. (SW→CW Jr, 15/1/1807)
29/3/1807	Responses to the Litany performed at St Paul's Cathedral.
19/6/1807	Organist in performance of Barthélemon's *The Nativity* at Hanover Square Rooms.
10/11/1807	Visits Madrigal Society. (Madrigal Society register)
24/11/1807	Visits Madrigal Society. (Madrigal Society register)

1808

23/1/1808	Admitted to Somerset House Masonic lodge. (United Grand Lodge records)
15/3/1808	Performs at Surrey Chapel. (*Argent* p 156)
22/3/1808	Renews contact with CB after a long period of non-communication, in order to introduce WL to CB. (SW→CB, 22/3/1808; CB→SW, 23/3/1808?)
12–14/4/1808	Seeks CB's opinion of the '48' and CB's advice about publishing the '48' by subscription. CB invites SW to propose a time when the two of them can 'compare notes' about JSB. (SW→CB, 12/4/1808; CB→SW, 13/4/1808?; SW→CB, 14/4/1808)
>15/4/1808	Visits CB, plays some of the '48' to him (the first time that CB hears any of the '48' played), and informs CB that CB's manuscript of the '48', given to him by Carl Philipp Emanuel Bach, contains only the first 24 of the '48'. (SW→BJ, 17/9/1808)[18]
17/4/1808	Responses to the Litany performed again at St Paul's Cathedral. (Latrobe→Joseph Foster Barham, 18/4/1808)

'third Canto, that treats of the Music peculiar to the church, in which he [SW] is himself so deservedly eminent'.

[18] The implication in SW→BJ?, 17/9/1808, that this visit occurred in 1807 is incorrect. See the entry of that letter in the calendar of correspondence.

5–6/1808	Mentions to CB Salomon's comment that SW could profitably arrange a 'morning party' in which he interspersed fugues from the '48' with his own voluntaries, and seeks CB's advice regarding SW giving a lecture course on JSB's music. CB advises SW not to risk the expense of printing an edition of the '48' until he has 'played them into favour' and recommends the Hanover Square Rooms as a suitable venue. CB and his daughter Sarah Harriet Burney approve SW's plans to lecture about the '48' but recommend that he defer lecturing until the next year. (SW→CB, 5/1808?; CB→SW, 5/1808?; SW→CB, 23/6/1808)
7/6/1808	Visits Madrigal Society. (Madrigal Society register)
11/6/1808	Benefit concert at Hanover Square Rooms. SW extemporises on the organ and plays 'preludes and fugues' by JSB on the piano. (*Morning Chronicle*, 7/6/1808; CB diary entry (Berg))
20/6/1808	Visits Madrigal Society. (Madrigal Society register)
27/6/1808	Raised to the rank of Master Mason at Somerset House Lodge. (SW→CB, 28/6/1808)
6–7/1808	Visits Cambridge for the award to his friend William Carnaby of a Doctor of Music degree; conducts choruses from Handel's *Messiah* and Haydn's *The Creation* in a concert on 1/7/1808; and plays music by JSB at private musical parties, returning to London on 6/7/1808. (SW→CB, 7/7/1808; *Cambridge Chronicle and Journal*, 25/6/1808, 2/7/1808, 9/7/1808)
7/7/1808	Seeks CB's advice about publishing, as a preface to a planned edition of the '48', a translated extract of Forkel's Life of JSB, including a portrait of JSB from a drawing lent to SW by AFCK.
8/1808	Plays music by JSB with BJ at Thomas Elliot's organ works. (*MM* 9/1808 p 151)
13/8/1808?	Proposes, in a letter presumably to BJ, the establishment of a society to promote and advance the cause of JSB's music.

27/8/1808	Plays music in the evening at a venue [not identified] outside London. (SW→BJ, 28/8/1808)
10/1808	Plans with CFH to publish a translation of Forkel's Life of JSB before publishing an edition of the '48'.[19] (CB→SW, 17/10/1808; SW→BJ, 17/10/1808; *The Librarian*, v 1 no. 5 (1/11/1808) p 238)
20/10/1808	Plans to play music at a party in Paddington where CFH's arrangement of JSB's fugues will be performed. (SW→BJ, 19/10/1808; SW→SGW, 20/10/1808)
28/10/1808	Plans to attend a 'musical meeting' at the Portuguese Embassy Chapel, and invites CW Jr to hear SW's new Te Deum and Jubilate performed at St Paul's Cathedral on 30/10/1808. (SW→CW Jr, 28/10/1808)
17/11/1808?	Agrees to sit for a portrait by John Bacon, at BJ's request.
25/11/1808	Advises Crotch to burn his 'London copy' of JSB's '48' (part 2 of the '48' published earlier in 1808 by Broderip & Wilkinson).
12/1808	Prepares lectures and seeks CB's advice on their topics and style. (SW→CB, 6/12/1808; CB→SW, 7/12/1808?; SW→CB, 20/12/1808; CB→SW, 20/12/1808)
20/12/1808	Visits Madrigal Society. (Madrigal Society register)
21/12/1808	Plans to meet John Bacon with BJ. (SW→BJ, 8/12/1808; BJ→John Bacon, 12/12/1808)
25/12/1808	Te Deum, Jubilate and Litany scheduled to be performed at St Paul's Cathedral. (SW→CW Jr, about 20/12/1808)
28/12/1808	Visits Richard Brinsley Sheridan at Randall Farm, near Leatherhead. (SW→John Bacon, 28/12/1808)

1809

3/1/1809	Planned sitting for his portrait by John Bacon. (SW→John Bacon, 1/1/1809)

---

[19] This plan to publish a translation of Forkel's biography did not succeed.

1–2/1809	Visits Bath: dines with SGW's cousin Thynne Gwynne, 22/1/1809; returns to London, 27/2/1809. (SW→SGW, 28/1/1809; SW→William Savage, 28/2/1809; *Bath Chronicle*, 19/1/1809)
about 21/3/1809	Dismissed from his teaching position at Mrs Barnes's school. (WH diary entry for 21/3/1809, Bodl Ms Eng. e.2134; SW→George Smith, 23/4/1809)
3/3/1809	About to send to the engraver the first of the set of six JSB organ trios lent to him by CFH.
10/3/1809	Begins course of lectures at Royal Institution. (CW Jr→ Sarah, 9/3/1809, 14/3/1809)
22/3/1809	Lectures at Royal Institution on improving the chromatic scale and demonstrates in the lecture an organ designed by William Hawkes and built by Thomas Elliot. This leads to 'J.P.'→Editor, *NMMR* , 4/1809, and subsequent controversy. (SW→William Savage, 16/3/1809, gives 22/3/1809 as the planned date of this lecture; SW→Charles John Smyth, 10/1/1810)
5/1809	Publication of 2nd edition of John Wall Callcott's *A Musical Grammar*, its fourth part revised by SW. (*MM*, 5/1809, states 2nd edition 'in the press')
<5/5/1809	First of the six JSB trios edited by CFH and SW published. (C. W. Pearce→Editor, *The Musical Times*, *Musical Times,* 1/6/1926, p 544)
3/6/1809	SW's 'musical morning party' at Hanover Square Rooms. 'Several' compositions by JSB performed including 'a grand sacred Motetto for five voices' ['Jesu, meine Freude']. (SW→BJ, about 15/5/1809, 25/9/1809?; *Musical Times*, 1/10/1896, p 654)
22/6/1809	Plays an extempore organ voluntary at Willoughby Lacy's benefit concert at the King's Theatre Concert Room. (*Times*; SW→Willoughby Lacy, 20/6/1809)
26/6/1809	Plays a 'piano fantasia' at Evans's Grand Vocal Concert at the Green Man, Blackheath.[20] (*Times*, 23–24/6/1809)

---

[20] Probably Charles Smart Evans, as SW is known to have assisted him by performing in at least one of his benefit concerts. *See* SW→Charles Smart Evans, 9/5/1825.

10/8/1809	Visits David Loeschman with BJ. (David Loeschman→ Editor, *NMMR*, 19/8/1809)
11/8/1809	Purchases JSB's 6 violin sonatas. Subsequently Salomon is informed of this purchase; he informs CB, who is anxious to hear them. SW plans to visit CB to play the violin part and seeks a pianist to accompany him. (CB→SW, 2/9/1809?; SW→CB, 4/9/1809; SW→BJ?, 30/9/1809?)
About 9/1809	Begins relationship with SS.[21] (SW→SGW, 2–3/1810, mentions SS's 'humane and tender attention' when SW was setting out for Tamworth)
19–23/9/1809	Visits Tamworth and Birmingham: leaves London by overnight coach, 18/9/1809; directs and plays in Tamworth Festival concerts, including new version of his organ concerto in D, 21–22/9/1809; travels to Birmingham and performs in a concert there, 23/9/1809; returns to London, 26–27/9/1809. (SW→SGW, 28/8/1809; SW→BJ, 4/9/1809, 25/9/1809; handbills and programme of Tamworth Festival, Tamworth Castle Museum)
11/1809	Portrait by John Bacon completed and delivered to BJ. (BJ→John Bacon, 18/11/1809)
7/11/1809; 14/11; 21/11; 28/11; 5/12; 12/12	Gives course of six lectures at the Surry Institution; one lecture (presumably given on 5/12/1809) attacks 'J. P.'. (Sarah→Adam Clarke, 25/9/1809?; SW→Editor, *NMMR*, 9/10/1809; SW→BJ, 5/11/1809, 6/11/1809?, 2/12/1809?; SW→Knight Spencer?, 9/12/1809)
29/11/1809	Performs with BJ, on the Surrey Chapel organ, 'fugues' by JSB and Handel alternately; also, plays violin part of JSB violin sonatas; about 3000 people attend. SW and BJ provide their services for free. (SW→BJ, 24/11/1809, 2/12/1809?; SW *Reminiscences*; BJ→Editor, Dictionary of Musicians, 15/1/1824)

---

[21] Apparently CLW had engaged SS as a servant. Sarah→John Gaulter, 23/5/1825, states that CLW flung 'temptation in the way' by admitting SS, 'whom she knew was not good', to wait upon SW.

1810

8/1/1810	Listens to the temperament of the Hawkes/Elliot organ at Elliot's home. (SW→Charles John Smyth, 10/1/1810)
13/1/1810	Notes that he has got AFCK to write out a list of JSB's works.
1–2/1810	Issues, with CFH, printed proposal to publish by subscription the first 12 preludes and fugues of JSB's '48'. (*MM*, 3/1810, p 170)
1–2/1810	Leaves CLW and the home he had shared with her in Camden Town. (presumably after SW→SGW, 18/1/1810; before SW→CW Jr, 16/2/1810)
21/1/1810	Planned performance of JSB's 'St Anne' fugue at St Paul's Cathedral. (SW→SGW, 18/1/1810)
30/1/1810	Performs his organ concerto in D at a performance of Handel's *Messiah* at Covent Garden. (*Morning Chronicle*, 23/1/1810; note on violino principale part, BL Add 35009; SW→CW Jr, 3/2/1810)
12/3/1810	Again performs his organ concerto in D at Covent Garden. (note on violino principale part, BL Add 35009)
1/4/1810	Plans to celebrate JSB's birthday at Edward Stephenson's house. (SW→Bridgetower, 29/3/1810)
24/4/1810	Visits Madrigal Society, where he is thanked for his present of a manuscript score of JSB's motet 'Jesus, decus meus'.[22] (Madrigal Society register)
15/5/1810	Visits Catch Club, introduced by WL. (Catch Club register, BL H2788yy; SW→'Dear Sir', 15/5/1810)

---

[22] CFH had lent this motet, 'Jesu, meine Freude', to SW, who adapted it to Latin words. *See* SW→BJ, about 15/5/1809.

19/5/1810	Plays organ and piano at morning benefit concert at Hanover Square Rooms. Programme includes first performance of SW's 'In exitu Israel' and 'Father of Light and Life', a JSB organ trio played as a duet (by SW and Joseph Major), a JSB solo violin sonata (Salomon), a JSB accompanied violin sonata (Salomon and SW) and parts of 'Jesu meine Freude'. Other performers include Street, Mrs Billington, Mr and Mrs Vaughan, Goss, Elliott (John Marsh journal;[23] *Musical Times* v 37 no. 644 (1/10/1896) p 655; *Lightwood* p 156, quoting *Morning Chronicle* advertisement)
26/5/1810	Plays an organ concerto in John Goss's benefit concert at Hanover Square Rooms, presumably the revised version of SW's organ concerto in D.[24] (*Times*; concert programme, Bodl 17405.d.8(26))
19/6/1810	Visits Madrigal Society. (Madrigal Society register)
20/7/1810	Plans to play, with VN, JSB's *Goldberg Variations* on two pianos at CB's apartments in Chelsea College. (CB→SW, 27/6/1810, 16/7/1810?; SW→CB, 17/7/1810; CB→SW & VN, 19/7/1810)
14/8/1810	SSW born. (SW→SGW, 12/9/1810)
17/9/1810	Book 1 of SW/CFH edition of the '48' published. (*Morning Chronicle*, 3/9/1810, 18/9/1810, quoted in *Musical Times* v 37 no. 644 (1/10/1896) p 656)
7/11/1810	Visits Birmingham, probably to discuss arrangements for the 1811 Birmingham festival with Joseph Moore. (SW→SGW, 3/11/1810; SW→SS, 7/11/1810)

---

[23] The citation 'John Marsh journal' refers to the journal of John Marsh [composer, 1752–1828] at the Huntington Library, San Marino, California, USA, ms 54457.

[24] The concert programme describes this performance as 'Concerto, organ, Mr S. Wesley...Bach' on the cover and as 'Concerto, organ, Mr Wesley...Wesley and Bach' inside. This description is presumed to refer to a performance by SW of the revised version of his organ concerto in D, the penultimate movement of which is an arrangement of JSB's D major fugue from part 1 of the '48'.

1811–1812

1/1811	Visits Rev. Christopher Jeaffreson in Tunstall, Suffolk: leaves London, 5/1/1811; returns about 23/1/1811. (SW→SS, 6/1/1811, 9/1/1811?, 15/1/1811, 20/1/1811)
1–5/1811	Book 2 of the SW/CFH edition of the '48' published after 15/1/1811 and before 22/5/1811. (SW→SS, 9/1/1811?, 15/1/1811; SW→VN, 22/5/1811)
2/1811	Begins course of lectures at Surry Institution after a postponement. The final lecture scheduled for 10/4/1811. (SW→Knight Spencer?, 3/1/1811, 7/4/1811; SW→Knight Spencer, 1/2/1811)
27/4/1811	Morning benefit concert at Hanover Square Rooms: programme includes first performance of SW's Trio for 3 Pianofortes played by SW, VN and Stokes, first performance of SW's glee to words by Peter Pindar (probably 'O Delia, ev'ry charm is thine'), SW's 'Dixit Dominus' and 'In exitu Israel', an organ improvisation by SW, a JSB solo violin sonata played by Salomon, and a JSB accompanied violin sonata played by Salomon and SW. (*Morning Chronicle*, 20/4/1811; *Times*, 24/4/1811; Richard J. S. Stevens 'Recollections', 27/4/1811)
22/5/1811	Confirms, in first preserved letter to VN, that he will deputise for VN by playing the organ at the Portuguese Embassy Chapel on 23/5/1811.
31/5/1811	Informs CW Jr that 'exorbitant demands' have been made upon SW in respect of CLW's debts. He needs money to avoid being sent to jail. (SW→CW Jr, 31/5/1811; CW Jr→Sarah, 5/6/1811; SW→SGW, 4/7/1811, 10/7/1811?; CW Jr & SGW→Sarah, 15/7/1811; SW→SGW, 1/8/1811)
3/6/1811	Writes recommendatory preface to Henry Liston's *Essay on Perfect Intonation*.

7/1811	Again visits Rev. Christopher Jeaffreson in Tunstall: leaves London and spends night in Ipswich, 11/7/1811; arrives Tunstall, 12/7/1811; returns to London by 1/8/1811. (SW→SGW, 10/7/1811?; SW→SS, 12/7/1811)
27/9/1811	VN asked to correct the proofs of Book 3 of SW/CFH edition of the '48', which SW received from Samuel Chappell. Book 3 published before 26/12/1811.[25]
2–4/10/1811	Visits Birmingham to direct festival: leaves London, 27/9/1811, for rehearsal on 30/9/1811; concerts 2–4/10/1811, including morning performances of Handel's *Messiah* and Haydn's *The Creation* and miscellaneous evening concerts. (*Aris's Birmingham Gazette* advertisements)
6/11/1811	Plays a JSB fugue with William Russell on the organ at St Stephen Coleman Street church.
11/1811–1812	Projects an edition of harmonised Gregorian chant.[26] (SW→VN, 11/11/1811, 27/6/1812; SW→Charles Butler, 7/10/1812)
25/2/1812	Visits Madrigal Society. (Madrigal Society register)
25/3/1812	Signs Deed of Separation, agreeing to pay George Oliver £130 *per annum* as maintenance for CLW.
about 18/4/1812	Plays at John Goss's benefit concert (venue and exact date not located), where he performs an extempore voluntary. (John Marsh journal)
10/5/1812	Plans to open the new organ at Christ Church, Blackfriars. (SW→VN, 6/5/1812)
13/5/1812	Invested as Grand Organist of the [Freemasons'] Grand Lodge. (United Grand Lodge records; Francis Rawdon-Hastings→Col. McMahon, 28/4/1812)

---

[25] In the *Quarterly Musical Register* no. 1 (1/1/1812, advertised in *The Times* on 26/12/1811), AFCK wrote (p 30) that 'Messrs S. Wesley and Horn, are now publishing those Preludes and Fugues [the '48'], with explanations, in four numbers, three of which are already printed'.

[26] This edition did not eventuate.

16/5/1812	Accompanies Salomon and Braham at Salomon's benefit concert at Hanover Square Rooms. (*Times*, 12/5/1812)
by 24/5/1812	Submits his madrigal 'O sing unto mie roundelaie' (autograph dated 27/2/1812) for the competition organised by the Madrigal Society (Madrigal Society register); he is unsuccessful. (SW→VN, 17/2/1813)
5/6/1812	Evening benefit concert at Hanover Square Rooms: programme includes first performance of SW's Grand Duet [I] for organ, played by SW and VN; SW's Trio for three Pianos, played by SW, VN and Stokes, and VN's arrangement for organ duet and orchestra of JSB's Prelude in E♭ major, BWV 552, played by SW and VN. (*Times* 6/4/1812, 3/6/1812; SW→VN, 6/5/1812; ms of VN arrangement, Gesellschaft der Musikfreunde, Vienna)
4/7/1812	Plans to play JSB's *Goldberg Variations* to VN and Bridgetower at Kirkman's piano manufactory. (SW→VN, 2/7/1812)
24/7/1812	Dines with Edward Harley, 5th Earl of Oxford.
5/9/1812	Arranges to play all the '48' on the organ to John Bernard Logier and others at the premises of the organ builder James Davis. (SW→Bridgetower, 4/9/1812)
9–10/1812	In Margate and Ramsgate with Samuel Webbe Jr: arrives in Ramsgate on 18/9/1812; gives concert with Webbe and Catherine Stephens on 3/10/1812; returns to London 5/10/1812. (SW→SS, 18/9/1812; SW→VN, 1/10/1812; SW→SGW, 6/10/1812; Gesualdo Lanza→Editor, *Theatrical Inquisitor*, 2/1814)
11/10/1812	Plays music by JSB for CB and Charles Butler. (Charles Butler→SW, 7/10/1812; SW→Charles Butler, 7/10/1812; SW→VN, 11/10/1812)
c12/11/1812	Birth of a child, presumably the daughter who died on 29/3/1813. (SW→SGW, 12/11/1812)
10–11/1812	Financial crisis and threat of imprisonment for debt. (SW→SGW, 21/10/1812, 4/11/1812, 12/11/1812, 19/11/1812; Sarah and SGW→RG, 18/11/1812; see also Sarah→SGW, 4/1/1813)

1813

1/1813	Appointed regular organist at Covent Garden oratorio concerts by Charles Jane Ashley. (SW→VN, 12/1/1813).
30/1/1813	Plays organ in Handel's *Messiah* at Covent Garden and is soloist in an organ concerto. (*Times*, 1/2/1813, 6/2/1813)
5/3/1813; 12/3; 17/3; 19/3; 24/3; 7/4; 9/4	Organist at Covent Garden oratorio concerts.
9/3/1813	Visits Catch Club.[27] (Catch Club register, BL H2788yy)
	Visits Madrigal Society and is thanked for five copies of his madrigal 'O sing unto mie roundelaie'. (Madrigal Society register)
17/3/1813	Gives first performance of his organ concerto in B♭ at Covent Garden oratorio concert.
29/3/1813	Death of infant daughter. Cancels projected visit to St Paul's Cathedral to play JSB fugues with VN. (SW→VN, 30/3/1813; SW→RG, 31/3/1813; SW's copies at RSCM)
14/4/1813	Plays at Anniversary Festival of the Freemasons' Charity for Female Children at Freemasons' Hall. (*Times*, 6/4/1813)
25/4/1813	Plays at charity sermon at Spitalfields Church. (John Marsh journal; *Times*, 24/4/1813)
26/4/1813	Plays piano at Salomon's benefit concert at Hanover Square Rooms. (*Times*, 24/4/1813)

---

[27] The register names the visitor as 'Mr Wesley' but there is no record that CW Jr ever visited the Catch Club.

4/5/1813	SW's benefit concert at Argyll Rooms. Marmaduke Charles Wilson plays SW's new piano concerto [not preserved]; the programme also includes SW's 'Father of Light and Life' and a 'Grand Symphony' by JSB, i.e., an arrangement by VN for organ four hands and orchestra of JSB's 'St Anne' prelude. The concert results in a financial loss. (*Morning Chronicle*, 12/4/1813, 1/5/1813; *Times*, 22/4/1813, 3/5/1813, 6/5/1813; SW→VN, 30/4/1813, about 1/5/1813; SW→SS, 9/7/1813)
20/5/1813	Plays, with VN, JSB fugues at St Paul's Cathedral after the service. (SW→RG, 18/5/1813; SW→VN, 26/5/1813)
6/6/1813	Performs 'the fourth organ concerto' by Handel with 'an additional movement' by JSB at the Ashleys' benefit concert at Covent Garden.
10/6/1813	Performs at Samuel Webbe Jr's benefit concert at Argyll Rooms.
21/6/1813	Attends a concert at Vauxhall, where one of his female pupils sings; meets James Hook there. (SW→VN, 21/6/1813, 23/6/1813)
6–7/1813	Visits Ipswich: leaves London 25/6/1813; dines with Thomas Green and Charles Hague on 28/6/1813; takes part in Ipswich Festival, 6–8/7/1813, playing his organ concerto in D and performing extempore on piano and organ; planned return to London, 11/7/1813. (SW→VN, 21/6/1813, 23/6/1813; SW→SS, 6/7/1813, 9/7/1813; Thomas Green journal entries 27/6/1813, 28/6/1813; *Suffolk Chronicle*, 10/7/1813; *Ipswich Journal*, 10/7/1813)
about 7/1813	Book 4 of SW/CFH edition of the '48' published. (SW→BJ, 10/5/1813, projects a 1/7/1813 publication date; SW→VN, 23/6/1813, indicates proofs not yet received)
9/1813	Planned trip with Samuel Webbe Jr, leaving London around 7/9/1813; returning around 17/9/1813. (SW→VN, 3/9/1813)

11/1813–1/1814	Applies unsuccessfully for the organist's position at the Foundling Hospital. His candidacy supported by William Kitchiner and the Duke of Sussex, whom SW sees at the Grand Lodge on 24/11/1813. (SW→Governors, Foundling Hospital, 8/11/1813; SW→RG, 9/11/1813; William Kitchiner→Christopher Idle, 10/11/1813; SW→Samuel Compton Cox, 24/11/1813; SW→RG, 25/11/1813; SW→VN, 23/12/1813; 4/1/1814; Foundling Hospital minute books (LMA))
<12/1813	Elected an Associate of the Philharmonic Society.[28]
28/12/1813	Plays the organ at the ceremonies marking the union of the two Grand Lodges of England, for which he writes a setting [not preserved] of 'Behold, how good a thing it is'. (SW→VN, 23/12/1813; *EM*, 1/1/1814, p 6–12, 49–51)

1814–1815

?1814	Daughter Rosalind born. (first mentioned in SW→SS, 16/10/1814)
27/1/1814	Attends musical party at Bridgetower's house; programme includes music by JSB, Purcell and Mozart. (SW→Bridgetower, 24/1/1814; SW→VN, 28/1/1814?)
2/1814	First regular column of music reviews in *EM*. (SW→VN, 17/3/1814)
25/2/1814; 4/3; 9/3; 11/3; 18/3; 23/3; 25/3; 30/3; 11/4	Organist at Covent Garden oratorio concerts. At 9/3/1814 concert gives first performance of his organ concerto in C. (SW→RG, 8/3/1814)

---

[28] SW was not a founding member of the Philharmonic Society at its establishment on 6/2/1813, but his name appears on a list of Associates of the Society that was printed before 31/12/1813 (BL Music Ms Loan 48.8). He presumably was elected an Associate before 1/12/1813, as his election is not mentioned in the Society's General Minute Book that contains entries of elections and other matters from 1/12/1813 (BL Music Ms Loan 48.3/1).

24/3/1814, 19/4/1814	Attends committee meetings to arrange a performance of William Russell's oratorio *Job* for the benefit of Russell's widow. (SW→VN, 17/3/1814, 23/3/1814, 20/4/1814)
25/4/1814	Visits Catch Club, introduced by WL. (Catch Club register, BL H2788yy)
	Directs concert of music by Thomas Linley at Hanover Square Rooms for the benefit of Queen's Lying-In Hospital, where he plays an organ concerto and voluntary. (*Morning Chronicle* 18/4/1814, 22/4/1814; SW→VN, 13/4/1814; SW→Bridgetower, 1/7/1814)
28/5/1814	Plays organ in C. Ashley's benefit concert [presumably General Christopher Ashley] at Covent Garden. (*Times*, 26/5/1814; *Morning Chronicle*, 28/5/1814; SW→RG, 25/5/1814; SW→VN, 26/5/1814)
6/6/1814	Accompanies Salomon in JSB violin sonata at Salomon's benefit concert at Hanover Square Rooms.
15/6/1814	Performs at Foundling Hospital Chapel concert for the benefit of William Russell's widow. The programme includes Russell's *Job* and the first performance of SW's Introduction to Bach's 'St Anne' fugue for organ duet, which SW plays with VN. (*Times*, 14/6/1814; VN annotation on BL Add 14344; SW→VN, 5/10/1814)
22/6/1814	Plays a piano concerto and an improvised piano piece at 'Messrs Elliott and Evans's' concert [presumably James Elliott and Charles Smart Evans] at the Green Man, Blackheath.
25/7/1814	Performance organised of SW's Trio for Three Pianofortes at Clementi's piano manufactory; SW invites leading pianists to attend. (SW→VN, 19/7/1814; SW→RG, 22/7/1814)
1/9/1814	Endorses the 'chiroplast' invented by John Bernard Logier.

10/1814	Visits Norwich: leaves London about 5/10/1814; stays in Norwich with WL and Ozias Linley; plays three services at the Cathedral; is given a special dinner at the Assembly Rooms, 15/10/1814; gives morning concert at St Peter, Mancroft, 20/10/1814; returns to London, 22/10/1814. (SW→VN, 5/10/1814; SW→SGW, 12/10/1814; SW→SS, 16/10/1814; Sarah→SGW, 23/10/1814)
30/1/1815	Organist at Covent Garden concert. (bill at Theatre Museum, London)
10/2/1815; 15/2; 17/2; 24/2; 28/2; 1/3; 3/3; 8/3; 10/3	Organist at Covent Garden oratorio concerts.
13/2/1815	Plans to attend first concert of the Philharmonic Society's season. (SW→RG, 13/2/1815?)
13/5/1815	SW's and Messrs Ashleys' annual benefit concert at Covent Garden. (programme at Bodl 17405.d.10(53))
1/6/1815	Elected to full membership of the Philharmonic Society. (BL Music Ms Loan 48.3/1)
2/7/1815	Plays a fugue with VN. (SW→VN, 5/7/1815)
7/1815	Visits Great Yarmouth with Charles Smith, stays with John Eager, and then visits Norwich: leaves London about 9/7/1815; gives concert at Great Yarmouth, 12/7/1815; performs Goldberg Variations there, 19/7/1815; travels to Norwich and performs in Anniversary Sermon, 27/7/1815; gives concert for his own benefit, 28/7/1815; returns to London by 30/7/1815. (SW→VN, 5/7/1815, 18/7/1815; SW→Pettet, 31/7/1815; *Norwich Mercury*, 15/9/1815, 22/9/1815)
9/1815	Plans to publish the Credo of JSB's *B Minor Mass* by subscription. (SW→William Shield, 13/9/1815; SW→Pettet, 22/9/1815, 29/9/1815; SW→Pettet?, 5/10/1815)
27/9/1815	Chairs committee meeting of the Philharmonic Society. (BL Music Ms Loan 48.3/1)

16/10/1815	Chairs committee meeting of the Philharmonic Society. (BL Music Ms Loan 48.3/1; SW→Bridgetower, 11/11/1815)
22/11/1815	Elected a director of the Philharmonic Society for the coming season. (BL Music Ms Loan 48.3/1)
8/12/1815	Attends committee meeting of the Philharmonic Society. (SW→VN, 9/12/1815)

1816–1818

8/1/1816	Informed that John Wall Callcott dislikes the changes that SW made to Callcott's *A Musical Grammar*.
30/1/1816; 8/3; 15/3; 22/3; 29/3; 5/4	Organist at Covent Garden oratorio concerts.
15/2/1816	Sends a psalm-tune and chant to BJ as his contribution to BJ's *National Psalmody*.
18/2/1816	Goes to Bavarian Chapel with Samuel Webbe Jr. (SW→VN, 22/2/1816)
24/2/1816	Attends Philharmonic Society rehearsal and directors meeting. Goes to Glee Club to 'preside over' a glee by WL. (SW→VN, 25/2/1816)
29/4/1816	'Father of Light and Life' performed at Philharmonic Society concert. (Myles Birket Foster, *History of the Philharmonic Society of London: 1813–1912*, London, 1912, p 25)[29]
18/5/1816	Trio for Three Pianofortes performed at Kirkman's piano manufactory. (SW→VN, 13/5/1816, 22/5/1816)

---

[29] On 8/4/1816 the directors of the Philharmonic Society requested SW 'to invite the singers required for his motet' (Philharmonic Society Minutes of Directors' Meetings 1816–1822, BL Music Ms Loan 48.2/1).

1/6/1816	SW's and Charles Jane Ashley's benefit concert at Covent Garden: programme includes SW's organ concerto in C with a new finale based on 'Rule Britannia'. (bill at Duke, Frank Baker collection; SW→VN, 22/5/1816, 1/6/1816)
c10/8/1816	Leaves for Norwich to play at the Anniversary Sermon on 15/8/1816 but, following the death of his little boy about the time of his departure, becomes severely ill on the journey, and returns to London without reaching Norwich. (SW→VN, 1/8/1816, 7/8/1816; SW→CW Jr and Sarah, 28/8/1816; Sarah→Kingston, 26/8/1817; *WBRR* v 3, 12/1851, p 444)
28/8/1816	Financial crisis resulting from his severe illness and his failure to fulfil engagements. Risk of imprisonment unless money can be raised.
25/9/1816	Performs the overture to Handel's *Messiah* and an organ concerto at All Saints, High Wycombe. (Downs, R. S., *The Parish Church, High Wycombe—A Descriptive Guide*, High Wycombe, 1904, p 21)
10/1816	Takes lodgings in Hampstead for a few days in order to recover his health. (SW→VN, 3/10/1816, 10/10/1816?)
1/1817	James Asperne discontinues the music review section of the *EM* which SW had conducted. (SW→Stephen Jones, 13/1/1817)
10/2/1817	'O sing unto mi roundelaie' sung at Madrigal Society Anniversary Dinner. (Madrigal Society register)
21/2/1817; 28/2; 7/3; 14/3; 21/3; 28/3	Organist at Covent Garden oratorio concerts.
24/4/1817	'As on fam'd Waterloo the lab'ring swain' sung at New Musical Fund concert. (New Musical Fund programmes, BL c.61.g.20.(5))
3/5/1817	Leaves SS and comes to SGW's house at night, his mind so deranged that a keeper is required. A lodging for SW is arranged in the neighbourhood, perhaps on 4/5/1817. (Sarah→William Wilberforce, 12/5/1817?)

6/5/1817	Jumps out of window, fearing arrest as writs had been issued against him by CLW. Sustains serious injury. Rev. Basil Woodd comes to pray with him. About this day Sarah removes SGW to the lodging she had arranged for SW and cares for him at her home. (Sarah memorandum, 6/5/1817; Sarah→William Wilberforce, 12/5/1817?)
8/5/1817	Doctors pronounce that SW has only a few hours to live. CLW and her children informed. Elizabeth Ritchie Mortimer comes to comfort SGW and talks to SW. (Sarah journal entry, 8/5/1817; WL→Sarah, 8/5/1817)
23/5/1817	Removed, by order of his physicians, to Chapel Street. (CW Jr diary, MA DDWF/23/15)
24/5/1817	SW's and Charles Jane Ashley's benefit concert, Covent Garden; SW not present. (*Times*, 20/5/1817, 22/5/1817; CW Jr diary entries for 5/1817)
about 28/5/1817	John Heaviside, SW's surgeon, says that if SW is kept quiet he should, through Providence, recover. (CW Jr diary)
3/6/1817	Apparently at WL's direction, goes to Southend to recover, where he stays for more than a month. (CW Jr diary)
7/7/1817	SGW requests WL to give up his charge of SW and entrusts SW to the care of Dr Alexander Robert Sutherland under the superintendence of RG and Kingston; Dr Sutherland is to arrange for Dr George Leman Tuthill to examine SW, presumably to sign a certificate of lunacy required for SW's admission to an asylum.
>7/7/1817 and <20/8/1817	Confined in Blacklands House, a private lunatic asylum in Chelsea.
23/8/1817	Kingston spends five hours with SW at Blacklands House. SW denies that he is insane and objects to a plan to send SSW to a school near Manchester. (Kingston→ Sarah, 24/8/1817; Sarah→Kingston, 26/8/1817)
28/11/1817	Thanks Hawes for accepting SSW as a Chapel Royal chorister.

1817–1818	Duties as organist of Kentish Town Chapel carried out by deputies. (CW Jr→RG, 27/12/1817; SGW→Mr Hornby, 5/1818)
3/1818	Remains at Blacklands because his doctors do not wish to risk their reputation by releasing him before a year has elapsed. RG and Kingston think that the longer SW is confined the more likely it is that SS will dispose of herself. (Sarah→CW III, 4/3/1818?)
17/6/1818	Benefit concert organised by Sir George Smart for SW and his family postponed. (*Times*, 16/6/1818; George Smart note, BL Add 41772 f 36v)
25/6/1818	Dr Sutherland tells SGW that SW has recovered and that he can safely leave Blacklands. (CW Jr diary entry, 25/6/1818; Sarah→'Dear Madam', 26/6/1818?)
during part of the second half of 1818	Stays in the home of a son of Rev. John Gaulter until well enough to pursue his profession. (Sarah→John Gaulter, 23/5/1825; *WBBR* v 3, 12/1851, p 446)
11–12/1818	'Scores' a symphony for the Philharmonic Society. (SW→VN, 17/11/1818; Philharmonic Society Minutes of Directors' Meeting, 15/12/1818)

1819–1823

1/1/1819	Publication by subscription of Credo from JSB's *B Minor Mass* announced to be 'in a state of forward preparation for the press'.[30] (*English Musical Gazette*, 1/1/1819, p 14; *Blackwood's Edinburgh Magazine*, v 5 (May 1819) p 237)
12/1/1819; 26/1; 5/2; 19/2; 26/3; 2/4	Organist at Covent Garden oratorio concerts.
6/5/1819	EW born.

---

[30] This publication did not eventuate.

1819–1822	At WH's suggestion asks Richard Mackenzie Bacon for work on a musical publication; becomes involved with WH in the preparation for Bacon of a dictionary of music. (SW→Richard Mackenzie Bacon, 5/6/1819; Thomas Moore journal entry, 2/11/1821)
17/6/1819	Dines with musical party at Gray's Inn where he presides at the piano in a performance of his 'O Lord God Most Holy'. (annotation by 'J. S' [Street?] on autograph ms of work, MB **M.408.2, item 6)
12/1819	Plans a benefit concert, to involve François Cramer, John Braham, Thomas Vaughan and possibly Catherine Stephens. (SW→VN, 3/12/1819, 9/12/1819, 23/12/1819)
22/1/1820	Dines with the same musical party at Gray's Inn as on 17/6/1819; his 'O Lord God Most Holy' performed again. (annotation by 'J. S.' [perhaps Street] on an autograph ms of work, MB **M.408.2, item 6)
20/11/1820	Begs VN for copying work. (SW→VN, 20/11/1820)
5/12/1820	Criticised by Sarah for declining work away from London. Sarah recommends that he leave SS.
19/4/1821	MEW born; baptised 14/12/1821. (St Marylebone baptismal records)
about 7/1821	Benefit concert for SW at New Argyll Rooms, at which SW plays extempore. (*London Magazine* v 4, August 1821, p 204)
4/8/1821	Canvases for organist's position at St Pancras New Church, but is unsuccessful. (St Pancras Church Estates Minutes, 21/2/1822)
21/9/1821	Receives £5 from Thomas Preston for the copyright of *24 Short Pieces or Interludes for the Organ.*
10/1821	Composes a 'short Magnificat' for VN. (SW→VN, 2/10/1821, 9/10/1821)
27/11/1821	Asks VN to recommend him for copying work.
5/3/1822	Writes 'While ev'ry short liv'd flower of sense' for Glee Club competition. (annotation on autograph ms)

9/1822	Appointed an honorary member of the Royal Academy of Music. (SW→John Fane, Lord Burghersh, 2/9/1822)
10–11/1822	Arranges music for the barrels of an organ being built for Walter McGeough in Northern Ireland. (SW→ Walter McGeough, 12/10/1822, 11/11/1822; *Elvin* p 97–100)
about 10/12/1822	Visits SGW on her deathbed and begs her forgiveness. She blesses all SW's children but calls SS 'an impudent baggage' and hopes that SW will be 'led in the right way'. (Sarah memorandum, about 10/12/1822)
22/12/1822	Death of SGW.
7–17/1/1823	Applies unsuccessfully for the post of organist at St Lawrence, Jewry. (St Lawrence, Jewry, vestry minute books, Guildhall Library)
1823–1825	Expresses wish to be buried near AD. (SW→VN, 4/7/1823, 14/6/1824; SW→CW Jr, 12/5/1825?)
12/1823	Resigns as 'perpetual visitor' to the Glee Club. (SW→Richard Clark, 4/12/1823?)
25/12/1823	Magnificat and Nunc Dimittis planned to be performed at St Paul's Cathedral. (SW→VN, 19/12/1823)

1824–1825

2/1824	Applies unsuccessfully for the post of organist at St George's, Hanover Square. (SW→VN, 17/2/1824)
2–3/1824	Solicits subscriptions for the publication of his Morning and Evening Service. (CW Jr→ John Trevor, 24/2/1824; CW Jr→Richard Edgcumbe, 24/2/1824; SW→Pettet, 8/3/1824; SW→VN, 8/3/1824)
3/1824	Apparently gives lectures; venue not known. (WL→CW Jr, 22/2/1824?)
3/4/1824	First complete performance of Morning and Evening Service, at St Paul's Cathedral. (SW→VN, 25/3/1824; SW→RG, 1/4/1824; SW→Pettet, 6/4/1824) A second performance planned for 25/4/1824. (SW→VN, 19/4/1824, 23/4/1824)

6/4/1824	Contributes 'Thou, O Lord, art praised in Sion' to Pettet's *Original Sacred Music.* (SW→Pettet, 8/3/1824, 18/3/1824, 6/4/1824)
20/5/1824	Appointed organist of Camden Chapel. (Minutes of St Pancras Church Trustees, 20/5/1824)
15/7/1824	Plays at the consecration of Camden Chapel by the Bishop of London. (Frances Burney d'Arblay→ Charlotte Francis Barrett, 17/8/1824 or 24/8/1824 or 31/8/1824)
8/1824	Visits Margate with SSW and Mr Tinney: arrives, 2/8/1824; planned return to London, 14/8/1824. (SW→SS, 3/8/1824)
9–11/1824	Arranges Handel's *Celebrated Italian Duets* for publication by the Royal Harmonic Institution. (SSW→SW, 10/9/1824; SW→VN, 13/9/1824; SW→CW Jr, 6/11/1824)
22/9/1824	Planned private performance with VN of music by JSB, to demonstrate the organ with pedals at the German Lutheran Church in the Savoy. (SW→VN, 18/9/1824, 20/9/1824)
29/9/1824	Planned meeting at St Sepulchre's to play music by JSB and others. (SW→VN, 25/9/1824, 28/9/1824; SW→John Harding, 27/9/1824)
10/1824	Biographical dictionary of musicians published by Sainsbury and Co. with article stating that SW had died about 1815. SW→Editor, *The Times*, 11/10/1824, points out that he is still alive; further correspondence ensues.
11/1824	Morning and Evening Service published. (SW→CW Jr, 6/11/1824; SW→VN, 12/11/1824)
12/1824	Plans to visit Sir Robert Peat at Brentford to perform, with SSW, VN and others, his Morning and Evening Service; visit postponed to 29/12/1824, by SW and SSW only. (SW→VN, 29/11/1824, 3/12/1824; Robert Peat→SW, 19/12/1824; SW→VN, 20/12/1824, 21/12/1824, 22/12/1824)

1–6/1825	Wounded by review of his Morning and Evening Service in the 1/1825 *Harmonicon,* prepares a reply that eventually is published in the 11/6/1825 *Literary Chronicle and Weekly Review.* SW suspects that WH wrote the anonymous review. (SW→VN, 8/1/1825, 17/1/1825, 20/1/1825, 27/1/1825, 31/1/1825, 25/3/1825, 29/3/1825, 12/4/1825, 27/4/1825, 15/6/1825)
18/2/1825; 23/2; 4/3; 9/3; 18/3; 23/3	Organist at Covent Garden oratorio concerts.
4–5/1825	Agrees to adapt William Russell's oratorio *Job* for publication.[31] (SW→Mary Ann Russell, 16/4/1825; SW→VN, 10/5/1825)
2–7/5/1825	Arrested for failure to pay £25 maintenance to CLW, 2/5/1825; confined in spunging house in Cursitor Street, 4/5/1825; released 7/5/1825. (SW→VN, 3/5/1825, 10/5/1825; SW→Sarah, 8/5/1825; SW→CW Jr, 10/5/1825?, 12/5/1825?; CW Jr→Emma, about 14/5/1825; CLW→CW Jr, about 21/5/1825; Sarah→John Gaulter, 23/5/1825; John Gaulter→Sarah, 26/5/1825; Sarah→SW, about 28/5/1825)
5/1825	Serves as 'umpire' for the appointment of an organist at St Matthew's, Brixton. (SW→VN, 19/4/1825; SW→Robert Williams?, 10/5/1825, 12/5/1825)
5/1825	Seeks to examine, and to edit for publication, music in the Fitzwilliam collection at Cambridge University that VN does not plan to edit. (Wait→SW, 11/5/1825; CW Jr→a sister of Wait, 14/6/1825)
18–25/6/1825	Visits Cambridge: leaves London 18/6/1825; returns, 25/6/1825. (SW→VN, 15/6/1825, 21/6/1825; SW→SS, 19/6/1825, 23/6/1825; SW→VN, 25/6/1825)
6–7/1825	Son John born, before 2/7/1825. (SW→VN, 2/7/1825)

---

[31] SW describes his adaptation of the instrumental parts for organ or pianoforte in SW→'The Musical Public', 8/5/1826, the preface to the publication of this adaptation.

7–8/1825	Visits Cambridge for about a fortnight; performs *Confitebor* with VN on the Trinity College Chapel organ, 1/8/1825; returns by 9/8/1825. (SW→SSW, 1/8/1825; SW→VN, 9/8/1825)
14/8/1825	Instigates the insertion of a paragraph in *The Examiner* that describes SW's and VN's performance of *Confitebor* on 1/8/1825 and announces that it will be performed next season. (SW→VN, 9/8/1825, 12/8/1825)
9/1825	Visits Sir George Gardiner at his house near Winchester; introduced to Lord Northesk; plays two services at Winchester Cathedral; returns about 10/9/1825. (SW→SS, 9/9/1825; SW→VN, 12/9/1825)
9–12/1825	Continues negotiations to obtain a grace from Cambridge University to transcribe and to publish music from the Fitzwilliam collection. (SW→VN, 19/9/1825, 22/9/1825, 3/10/1825, about 8/10/1825, 10/10/1825, 24/10/1825, 23/11/1825, 12/12/1825)
22/9/1825	Plans to visit Sir Robert Peat in Brentford.
10/1825	Visits Sir George Gardiner again: leaves London, about 11/10/1825; plans to leave Winchester and stay overnight in Bagshot, 21/10/1825; and to return to London, 22/10/1825. (SW→VN, 10/10/1825; SW→SS, 20/10/1825)

1826

5/1/1826	Chorus 'Magna opera Domini' from *Confitebor* planned to be performed at VN's Classical Harmonists' Society. (SW→VN, 12/12/1825, 29/12/1825)
6/2/1826	Plays an extempore organ piece in New Choral Fund annual concert at the Lyceum Theatre.[32] (SW→'Sir', 23/1/1826; SW→CW Jr, 2/2/1826; *Times*)
1/3/1826	Granted permission by University of Cambridge to transcribe and publish music in the Fitzwilliam collection. (Camb, Grace Book N, 1823–1836, p 117)

---

[32] The subject of this improvised fugue is preserved in BL Add 31239 f 1.

about 4/1826	Issues printed proposal to publish transcriptions of Byrd antiphons under the title 'The Fitzwilliam Music', which VN had already used. (>SW's 1/3/1826 'grace' from Cambridge University; <'Jubal'→Editor, *The Harmonicon*, 20/5/1826)
	Break in relationship with VN about this time, presumably a consequence of SW's 'Fitzwilliam Music' publication plans. (First volume of VN's *The Fitzwilliam Music*, preface dated 12/1825, reviewed *The Harmonicon* 2/1826 p 32; no extant correspondence between SW and VN from 29/12/1825 to 10/6/1830; SW→VN, 10/6/1830, suggests that the two had been 'violently at variance')
3–4/1826	Visits Cambridge to transcribe Byrd antiphons from the Fitzwilliam collection; leaves London about 27/3/1826; returns, 3/4/1826. (SSW→Emett, 25/3/1826; SW→Sarah, 27/3/1826; SW→RG, 4/4/1826)
14/4/1826; 21/4; 28/4; 5/5; 12/5; 19/5	Gives course of six lectures at the Royal Institution. (syllabus in *The Harmonicon* v 4 no. 41, 5/1826, p 94; SW→Sarah, 27/4/1826)
4/5/1826	Benefit concert at Argyll Street Rooms: programme includes extempore performance on the organ and first performance of *Confitebor*. (SW→RG, 4/4/1826; R. Carter→SW, 11/4/1826; SW→George Smart, 13/4/1826; SW→Sarah, 27/4/1826; SW→Domenico Dragonetti, 4/5/1826)
5/5/1826	Plays fugue by JSB on the organ at François Cramer's benefit concert. (*The Harmonicon* v 4 no. 42, 6/1826, p 131)
25/5/1826	Visits Madrigal Society. (Madrigal Society register)
26/5/1826	Unable to pay £80 debt for wine purchases. (SW→Sarah, 26/5/1826; Sarah→Thomas Marriott, 27/5/1826)
26/5/1826	Has ticket to attend Carl Maria von Weber's benefit concert in the Argyll Rooms. (ticket sold at Sotheby's 15/5/1979 in lot 202)
5–10/6/1826	Offers to play the organ at Weber's Requiem Mass; offer subsequently declined. (SW→Sarah, 10/6/1826)

6–8/1826	Attacked by 'Jubal' in *The Harmonicon* v 4 no. 42, 6/1826 p 113 over proposed Fitzwilliam publication; SW's reply deemed too immoderate to publish in *The Harmonicon*. ('Jubal'→ Editor, *The Harmonicon*, 20/5/1826; SW→Sarah, 8/7/1826?; *The Harmonicon*, v 4 no. 44, 8/1826, p 3)
29/7/1826	Postpones planned 31/7/1826 trip to Cambridge because of financial crisis.
9/1826	Visits Cambridge, where he discovers manuscript in Fitzwilliam collection of Handel's setting of hymns by CW: leaves London, about 11/9/1826; plans to return 23/9/1826. (SW→SS, 13/9/1826, 20/9/1826)
10/1826–1/1827	Proceeds to publish CW/Handel hymns, which he dedicates to 'the Wesleyan society', and seeks support from Methodists. (Sarah→John Gaulter, 25/10/1826; SW→Tooth, 31/10/1826; SW→Jackson, 8/11/1826; SW→Tooth, 8/11/1826; SW→Sarah, 13/11/1826; Sarah memorandum, about 15/11/1826; SW→John Jackson, 29/11/1826; SW→Thomas Roberts, 6/1/1827; CW Jr→Langshaw Jr, 11/1/1827; SW→ Sarah, 22/1/1827?)
9/11/1826	Applies for a British Museum reader's ticket. (admissions to the Reading Room, British Museum Central Archive)
12/1826–2/1827?	Lectures at Western Literary and Scientific Institution, Leicester Square; dates not known. (SW→Sarah, 14/11/1826; CW Jr→Langshaw Jr, 11/1/1827; CW Jr→ Marianne Francis, late February 1827)

1827–1828

2–3/1827	Arranges and publishes the CW/Handel hymns for use by choirs. (SW→Jackson, 12/2/1827; SW→Thomas Roberts, 8/3/1827)
1/3/1827	Directs 'Grand Selection of Sacred Music' at St Saviour, Southwark, and plays extempore voluntary. (bill in private collection)

5/3/1827	Plays with BJ at the trial of an organ at Flight and Robson's manufactory. SW plays an extempore piece; both play the JSB 'St Anne' fugue, and Mozart's 'Cum sancto spiritu' as duets. (*Times*, 8/3/1827)
22/3/1827; 29/3; 5/4; 12/4; 19/4; 26/4; 3/5; 10/5	Gives course of eight lectures at the Royal Institution.[33] (*Kassler* p 19; CW Jr→Marianne Francis, late February 1827; SW→Sarah, 29/4/1827; SW→CW Jr, 4/5/1827; CW Jr→Marianne Francis, 5/5/1827; CW Jr→Elizabeth Isabella Spence, 4/7/1827; SW→William Brande, 10/12/1827)
24/4/1827	Performs with SSW in concert at Christ Church, Newgate Street. (*The Atlas*, 27/4/1827, quoted *Lightwood* p 202)
3/5/1827	Attends breakfast for children of Methodist preachers. (SW→Sarah, 29/4/1827; SW→CW Jr, 4/5/1827)
11/6/1827	Gives organ recital at Beresford Chapel, Walworth. (*Times*, 8/6/1827)
24/6/1827	Gives recital to open the organ at Somers Town Chapel. (SW→RG, 15/6/1827)
10/1827	Visits Brighton, apparently to negotiate on behalf of Flight and Robson for a new organ for St Peter's church: leaves London about 9/11/1827; teaches pupils; asked to play the organ at the Sunday service, 14/10/1827; planned return on 20/11/1827. His profile sketched by John James Masquerier. (SW→SS, 10/10/1827, 14/10/1827, 16/10/1827)

---

[33] *The Harmonicon* v 5 (2/1827) p 38 reported that 'Dr Crotch will commence a course of lectures on music at the London Institution, on Wednesday the 7th of February; and Mr S. Wesley will begin, at the same place, a similar course, on the 22nd of March'. This announcement apparently misstates the venue of SW's lectures, as the minutes of the 16/11/1826 meeting of the Board of Management of the London Institution (Guildhall ms 3076 v 3 f 118) confirm that Crotch was to lecture on music in the ensuing season but do not mention SW. Moreover, Thursday 22/3/1827 is a plausible date for the commencement of SW's course of eight lectures at the Royal Institution, as such a course of weekly lectures would have ended on Thursday 10/5/1827, when SW is known, from SW→CW Jr, 4/5/1827, to have lectured there. The dates given here for SW's lectures are based upon this assumption.

10–11/1827	Birth of Thomasine presumably about this time. (SW→SS, 16/10/1827)
11/1827–2/1828	Board of Management of the London Institution approves proposal by William Pepys, a manager, that 'Westley' [SW] give 8 lectures on music in the next season. Pepys proceeds to negotiate with SW. (minutes of 8/11/1827 meeting, Guildhall ms 3076 v 3 p 131; SW→William Pepys, 23/11/1827, 19/12/1827, 1/1/1828, 12/1/1828?, 1/2/1828)
30/1/1828; 6/2; 13/2; 20/2; 27/2; 5/3	Gives course of six Wednesday lectures at the Russell Institution. (advertisement, *Literary Gazette* no. 574, 19/1/1828, p 46)
3–4/1828	Lectures at the London Institution. (Richard J. S. Stevens diary entry, 11/3/1828, states that the second lecture was on 11/3/1828)
3–5/1828	Gives course of six lectures at the Royal Institution. (*Kassler* p 19; SW→Joseph Fincher, 17/3/1828)
4–5/1828	Proposes that the Methodist Book-Room committee purchase, for £150, the copyright of his set of tunes to all the metres in the Methodist hymn book. (SW→Jackson, 21/4/1828, 17/5/1828)
5/1828	Visits Birmingham to open the organ at St Peter's, Dale End: leaves London, 21/5/1828; performs in concert, 23/5/1828; returns to London about 25/5/1828. (SW→CW Jr, 20/5/1828; SW→SS, 22/5/1828; St Peter's Vestry Minutes, Birmingham Archives, 27/5/2/1)
8/1828	*Original Hymn Tunes, adapted to every Metre in the collection by the Rev. John Wesley* published, using funds advanced by the Methodist Book-Room committee. (SW→William Upcott, 20/8/1828; SW→Jackson, 2/9/1828)

9/1828	In CW Jr's place and at his recommendation, goes to Leeds to open the organ at Brunswick Methodist Chapel on 12/9/1828.[34] Leaves London and breaks journey at Nottingham, 10/9/1828; arrives in Leeds, 11/9/1828; plans to leave Leeds, 16/9/1828. (SW→SS, 10/9/1828, 13/9/1828; *Leeds Intelligencer*, 11/9/1828, quoted in *Lightwood* p 207; CW Jr→SW, 18/9/1828)
19/9/1828	Sarah dies in Bristol, leaving nothing to SW in her will. SW consults Henry John Gauntlett for legal advice about his property rights in her estate. (Sarah will, 26/2/1826; Henry John Gauntlett→RG, 27/11/1828)
1828–1829	Offers to sell copyright and plates of *Original Hymn Tunes* to the Methodist Book-Room committee; offer declined. (SW→Jackson, 10/10/1828; Methodist Book-Room Committee minutes, 11/12/1828, 8/1/1829 (MA); CW Jr→Tooth, 1/8/1829; James Townley & Robert Newton→SW, 10/8/1829)

1829–1833

27/1/1829	Writes preface to revised edition of William Bird's *Original Psalmody*, in which SW has corrected musical 'inaccuracies'.
3/2/1829	Prepares to give a lecture, venue unknown. (SW→RG, 31/1/1829)
6/7/1829	Planned visit to Gravesend with SS to see Rosalind, leaving London 6/7/1829. (SW→Rosalind, 2/7/1829)

---

[34] The introduction of an organ into this Methodist chapel caused considerable controversy. The *Catalogue of Manuscripts and Relics...belonging to the Wesleyan Methodist Conference* (London, 1921) lists (p 179–181) some 35 pamphlets that were published about this 'Leeds organ dispute'.

9–11/1829	Visits Blagdon and Bristol: leaves London about 15/9/1829; stays with Wait at Blagdon and Hodges in Bristol. In Bristol tries St Mary Redcliffe organ 22/9/1829; plays at St Nicholas church, 28/10/1829; gives with SSW three recitals at St Mary Redcliffe to open the recently repaired organ, 1/10/1829, 5/10/1829, 7/10/1829; gives recitals at Moravian Chapel, 26/10/1829, St Nicholas, 28/10/1829; St James, 29/10/1829; plans to return to London about 3/11/1829. (SW→SS, 18/9/1829; Wait & SW→SS, 23/9/1829, 25/9/1829; Hodges journal entry, 1/10/1829, 4/10/1829; CW Jr→Tooth, 5/10/1829; Hodges journal entry, 5/10/1829; SW→SS, 7/10/1829; Hodges journal entry, 7/10/1829; SW→SS, 11/10/1829, 18/10/1829, 21/10/1829, 25/10/1829, 27/10/1829; Hodges journal entry, 28/10/1829; SW→SS, 29/10/1829, 30/10/1829; document in St Mary Redcliffe church quoted in *Lightwood* p 212; *Bristol Gazette*, 24/9/1829, 1/10/1829, 8/10/1829; *Bristol Mirror*, 3/10/1829)
17/11/1829	Avoids service of a tradesman's writ for £22 by 'harbouring in the house of a friend'; leaves for Watford where he plays in a concert organised by William Bird. (SW→Tooth, 17/11/1829; SW→SS, 17/11/1829)
1/1830	Visits Bristol: arrives with Joseph Collyer, 9/1/1830; dines with Hodges, 10/1/1830; gives course of eight lectures to the Philosophical and Literary Society of Bristol, 11/1/1830, 13/1, 15/1, 18/1, 20/1, 22/1, 25/1, 27/1; plans to return to London on 28/1/1830. (SW→SS, 10/1/1830, 14/1/1830, 17/1/1830, 22/1/1830, 26/1/1830; CW Jr→Tooth, 29/1/1830, 1/3/1830; SW lectures, BL Add 35014)
21/5/1830	Demonstrates new organ by Francis Day at the Royal Institution, as part of a lecture by Michael Faraday on Charles Wheatstone's new principle of musical instrument construction. (*Literary Gazette* no. 698, 5/6/1830, p 369; *Kassler* p 21)
25/5/1830	Asks Street whether the Madrigal Society might be interested to purchase SW's edition of Byrd antiphons, of which nine plates have been engraved.
6/1830	Reconciliation with VN. (SW→VN, 10/6/1830)

6–8/1830	Said to be seriously ill, 'drink is the cause' (CW Jr→ Tooth, 10/6/1830); 'deranged and strapped down' but better after being bled (CW→Tooth, 5/8/1830), and suffering from 'repeated fits of convulsion' (CW Jr→ Tooth, 27/8/1830).
21/11/1830	Birth of son Robert Glenn Wesley.
3/1831	Subscription to ease SW's financial problems organised by John Capel, WL and VN. Bailiffs said to be in possession of SW's property. (Richard J. S. Stevens memorandum, 3/1831; undated printed appeal at BL Add 56411 f 34, quoted in *Lightwood* p 219)
31/12/1832	SSW proposes that SW conduct a performance of his *Confitebor* in the 1834 Three Choirs Festival at Hereford.
26/7/1833	Felix Mendelssohn declines RG's invitation to play the organ at Christ's Hospital and expresses disappointment at missing this opportunity to meet SW.

1834–1837

1834	Writes hymn tunes for VN's *The Psalmist*.
6/3/1834	Writes to Lord Burghersh to suggest himself as organist for the forthcoming Handel Commemoration concerts, but is not appointed.
23/5/1834	Death of CW Jr; SW inherits £300 in his will. An annuity from the Methodist Book Room, formerly paid to CW Jr and Sarah, subsequently paid to SW in monthly instalments. (CW Jr will, 18/5/1831; Jackson, Thomas, *Recollections of my own Life and Times*, London, 1873, p 231)
26/5/1834	Attends marriage of Rosalind and RG at St Margaret Pattens church, of which RG was organist. (Copy of marriage certificate in the possession of Dr Roger Wesley Glenn.)

7/8/1834	Accompanies performance of 'All go unto one place', his funeral anthem for CW Jr, at a Sacred Harmonic Society concert. (article on SW in Grove, *A Dictionary of Music and Musicians,* 1st edition, London, 1879–1889)
9–11/9/1834	'In exitu Israel' performed at Three Choirs Festival at Hereford, directed by SSW.
2–3/1835	Attempts to sell the copyright of *Confitebor* for at least £150. (SW→Emett, 27/2/1835, 3/3/1835)
8/1835	SW and Crotch reaffirm their admiration of JSB's music. (Crotch→SW, 3/8/1835; SW→Crotch, 5/8/1835)
2–4/1836	Writes *Reminiscences.* Part one of his 'A sketch of the state of music in England from the year 1778 up to the present' published in the first number, 18/3/1836, of *The Musical World.* Possibly because of inaccuracies in this article, no further parts are published. (SW→Street?, about 2/1836; note on *Reminiscences,* BL Add 27593, dated 8/4/1836)
7/1836–5/1837	Composes a short song ('Orpheus could lead the savage race') for EW's album of musical autographs (BL Add 35026) and subsequently solicits further items for it. (SW→Attwood, 1/9/1836; Crotch→SW, 2/9/1836; SW→John Barnett, 15/3/1837; Ole Bull→SW, 5/5/1837; SW→Domenico Dragonetti, undated, >1/7/1836)
3/1837	Declines, because of ill health, Ignaz Moscheles's invitation to his 4/3/1837 concert. (Ignaz Moscheles→ SW, 1/3/1837; 11/3/1837)
5/1837	Invited by Ole Bull to attend his 'farewell concert' on 19/5/1837; expects Ole Bull's visit to try over some of SW's violin pieces. (Ole Bull→SW, 5/5/1837; SW→ Frederick Davison, 24/5/1837)
14/7/1837	Writes out from memory the score of his 'Begin the noble song'.
9/9/1837	Composes organ fugue on the theme that Felix Mendelssohn wrote in EW's album on 7/9/1837.

12/9/1837	Hears Felix Mendelssohn play the organ at Christ Church, Newgate Street, and plays the organ there at Mendelssohn's request. (Felix Mendelssohn→Cécile Mendelssohn, 14/9/1837)
10/1837	Composes eight further hymn tunes for VN's *The Psalmist*, including his last composition, 'Cesarea', on 7/10/1837.
11/10/1837	Dies after a short illness. (*Times*, 12/10/1837)
17/10/1837	Buried at St Marylebone Parish Church. (*Times*, 18/10/1837; copy of burial register, MA DDWes/6/61)

~ *3* ~

CALENDAR
OF
CORRESPONDENCE

INTRODUCTION

The calendar of correspondence marshals—in the editors' estimate of chronological order—more than 1,100 letters and related documents by, to or directly concerning Samuel Wesley that were written during his lifetime. Only a small proportion of these writings has previously been printed, often with unacknowledged excisions or inaccurate dating.

We have made considerable effort to locate the extant correspondence but cannot claim to have found it all. On 11 October 1790, for instance, SW informed his sister Sarah that he had ten or twelve letters to answer that day, of which only one—his letter to Sarah—has come to our attention. Dealers' and auctioneers' catalogues note letters that we have been unable to locate; some of these seem likely to survive in private hands. The considerable correspondence of members of the Wesley family has yet to be fully indexed and almost certainly contains references to SW that we have missed.

Some absences are striking: the calendar includes more than 170 letters from SW to his friend and colleague Vincent Novello but only one from Novello to SW, and we record more than 40 letters from Wesley to Sarah Suter but none in the other direction. We appeal to anyone who can fill gaps in our coverage to notify us through our publishers so that this information may be included in a supplement to, or a future edition of, this book.

The calendar has been compiled primarily from surviving autographs, with secondary sources used chiefly where the original manuscripts were unavailable for consultation or photographic reproduction. We have utilised a liberal criterion of what constitutes correspondence. Besides standard letters addressed to one person or to a few named recipients and delivered through the postal system or by hand, we include letters intended for larger audiences (such as letters to the editor of a periodical and epistolary prefaces that endorse a publication), notes left to advise the writer's attempt to visit a recipient who was away, notes written for the writer's private use (such as journal entries, drafts of wills and the memoranda written by Sarah Wesley that she called 'personal thoughts'), and a few legal documents such as family wills and Samuel and Charlotte Wesley's Deed of Separation.

All known letters written by or to Samuel Wesley, including drafts of letters, fragments of letters containing more than a signature, and letters signed pseudonymously, are recorded in the calendar; other letters are included only if their content about SW is deemed significant. (Letters, for example, whose sole reference to SW is a phrase such as 'Love to Sam' have been left out.) The calendar does not record writings that are principally not in prose, such as poems, household accounts, or musical quotations; it also excludes extracts and translations by SW of writings by others. Substantial entries about SW in contemporary journals are included, but brief references to him in church registers or pocket diaries are entered (if significant) in the chronology section of this book rather than in the calendar.

Structure of the Calendar. The calendar presents not only the first few words (following the salutation) of each letter—the standard practice of calendar compilers—but also includes a summary of its principal content.[1] For letters of which SW was neither an author nor a recipient the summary is limited to the portion of the letter that concerns him. The calendar accordingly may be read as a lightly interpreted biographical account of Samuel Wesley, from the appearance of his first tooth to his meeting, a month before his death, with Mendelssohn.

For each item in the calendar we provide a *dating reason* that indicates the logic we followed when assigning the item's composition to a particular day (or, when we could not do this with confidence, to a time interval larger than a day).[2] Where the writer asserts a date of composition in a letter we have generally accepted this assertion unless we had good reason to doubt it.

When, as frequently occurs, the writer has dated a letter incompletely (for instance, by stating the date only as 'Saturday

---

[1] We have respected the request of Wesley's Chapel, London, that the first lines of unpublished letters in their collection not be quoted as their contemplated publication of these letters has not yet appeared.

[2] Each dating reason is intended to present sufficient information to justify the editors' inference of an entry's assigned date or dating range. Additional information in support of this inference generally is not presented.

morning'), we have used other available forms of evidence to arrive at the assigned date. The types of evidence taken into account include the period of time when SW or some other named person lived at an address given in the letter, postmarks,[3] watermarks containing the year in which the paper used to write the letter was made, handwriting style[4] and, of course, the dates of people and events mentioned.

In most cases a combination of one or more of these varieties of evidence has led us to assign an entry confidently to a particular date. Where the evidence has been insufficient to allow this, we have endeavoured to assign the letter to a range of dates such as a particular month, or to a plausible date, indicating our uncertainty of the letter's actual date of composition by placing a question-mark after the assigned date.

In four circumstances[5] we have concluded that a letter was written on one of two non-consecutive dates but we have insufficient information to determine which one. In each of these cases the letter has been entered in the calendar under both dates, with a dotted line placed at the right of these entries to call attention to the ambiguity that is further explained in an accompanying footnote.

For a small number of letters we have been unable to narrow the range of conceivable dates of composition sufficiently to be confident of entering them correctly in the main chronological sequence. These 'undated letters' are presented, in approximate chronological order, in a second calendar that gives, for each letter, our estimate of the range of dates within which it appears to have been written.

In three instances we have been unable to decide whether a letter belongs in a calendar of Samuel Wesley's correspondence.

---

[3] For the interpretation of London postmarks we have relied principally upon *Willcocks/Jay*.

[4] In particular, we have assumed that documents written by SW in a childish style of handwriting in which every letter is printed antedate documents in which adjacent letters are connected. Also, the handwriting style of SW's last years is clearly distinguishable from that of earlier periods.

[5] Anne Gatehouse→Sarah, 9/7/1782? or 9/7/1783?; SW→SGW, 7/9/1808 or 7/9/1814; SW→VN, 1/3/1813? or 1/3/1819?; SW→VN, about 26/8/1825 or about 7/10/1825.

Information about these 'doubtful letters' is given in a third chronological calendar.

To present dating reasons succinctly in the calendar we use the symbols below with the following significations:

▣	The writer asserts in the letter that it was written on the (full or partial) date that follows this symbol
pmk	The letter was postmarked on the date or within the date range that follows this symbol[6]
wmk	The letter was written on paper bearing a watermark containing the year that follows this symbol (and therefore was written not before that year)
🏠	Samuel Wesley's home address, stated in the letter, limits its date to his period of residence there[7]
⬚i	The letter's assigned date

The symbols '<', '≤', '≥' and '>' stand for 'before', 'not after', 'not before' and 'after', respectively. The codes used to identify SW's homes are defined in *Figure 3* on page 8. Our abbreviations for frequently cited persons, manuscript repositories and publications are given in the tables on pages xv–xxiii above.

A dating reason such as '▣ Mon 18 Aug & 🏠→⬚i', for a letter written when SW lived at Highgate, accordingly should be interpreted as follows. The writer asserts in the letter that it was written on Monday, 18 August (but not the year in which it was

---

[6] Unlike today's practices, letters conveyed during SW's lifetime by the London penny post or twopenny post were marked with a date stamp not when they were received by the post office but shortly before they were sent out for delivery from the Chief Office or the Westminster Office. Accordingly, a letter bearing a postmark from either office of 8 am on a particular day can be presumed to have been written before that day, most likely on the preceding day.

[7] The editors' estimates of each period of residence are given in *Figure 3* on page 8 above.

written) and that Samuel Wesley's home address at the time was Highgate. From these data we have assigned the letter to 18/8/1800. Our inference is legitimised by the circumstance that although 18 August was a Monday in 1794, 1800, 1806 and in other years, only one of these years, 1800, coincides with the period of SW's residence at Highgate.

Where a dating reason cannot be presented succinctly in the main entry by means of such a formula or a short remark, our evidence for a particular assignment of date is given in a footnote to the entry. In each entry and any accompanying footnotes, the abbreviation 'ltr' is reserved specifically to designate the particular letter which is the subject of that entry.

The Form of Individual Entries. To show how entries in each calendar are structured we use, as an example, the entry for SW's 18/8/1800 letter from Highgate mentioned above.

SW→SGW   Highgate   **18/8/1800**
MA DDWF/15/11   I am prevented being in Town ToDay
▢ Mon 18 Aug & 📷→ⓘ

A 'very severe bilious attack' which seized SW on Saturday [16/8/1800] prevents him from being in London today. Mr Corpe [his doctor] insists that SW not go to business for two or three days to come, but he hopes to be sufficiently recovered on Thursday [21/8/1800] to be with SGW. He asks her to send the enclosed notes [not preserved, presumably cancelling his teaching engagements] immediately by Wilmot the shoe-blacker to High Street [Mrs Barnes's school] and to Paddington [AD's school]. SW hopes that SGW continues to recover from her 'late uncomfortable disorder' and that he will be able to give a better account of his health when he sees her on Thursday. CLW and Charles [CW III] 'desire their kind love'.

Each calendar entry comprises three lines of data followed by one or more paragraphs of text summarising the item's content.

The first line consists of three parts. The left part names the sender or senders and the addressee or addressees: the above entry therefore describes a letter from Samuel Wesley (SW) to his mother, Sarah Gwynne Wesley (SGW). The middle part of the first line, if not blank, specifies SW's address when the letter was written according to evidence given explicitly (e.g., by a stated address) or implicitly in the letter itself. The word 'Highgate' in the above entry therefore means that this letter contains an assertion that SW's address was 5 Mile Stone, Highgate, at the time when this letter was written. (We emphasise that the middle part of the first line presents SW's address when a particular letter was written, and not the whereabouts of other persons who may have sent or received this letter.) The right part of the first line gives the date or the dating range to which the editors have assigned the document. In our example the assigned date is 18 August 1800.

The second line of an entry consists of two parts. The left part shows, if known, the present location of the manuscript of the letter (or other document) and the catalogue number (if any) assigned to the manuscript by that repository. If the manuscript is not known to be extant, this part of the entry indicates the source of our information about the letter.

Thus, from the abbreviation 'MA', the above entry indicates that this letter is kept at the Methodist Archives and Research Centre in the John Rylands University Library of Manchester, and that it has been catalogued there as 'DDWF/15/11'.[8] If the full text of a letter is printed in a standard edition of letters, a reference to that edition also is given here.

The initial words of the letter following the salutation are entered in the right part of the second line.

The third line of an entry presents the dating reason that persuaded us to assign the letter (or other document) to a particular date or to a range of dates.

Each entry concludes with our summary of what we consider to be the item's principal content concerning SW. Where a summary includes direct quotations from a letter they are enclosed in inverted commas. Interpolations of information not contained in the original document, such as references to related correspondence or the identification of persons mentioned in the letter, are enclosed in square brackets.

---

[8] If a manuscript source has been foliated, an entry such as 'f 6' following the manuscript number indicates that the letter begins at folio 6 of that manuscript.

NEW INFORMATION ARISING FROM
THE CORRESPONDENCE

Samuel Wesley's life has been written by several authors, most extensively by the anonymous author of the 'Memoir of Samuel Wesley, the Musician' published in the September to December 1851 numbers of *The Wesley Banner and Revival Record,* by George J. Stevenson in a chapter of his 1876 *Memorials of the Wesley Family,*[1] and by James T. Lightwood in his 1937 biography *Samuel Wesley, Musician.* Accounts of SW also have appeared in numerous journal and encyclopaedia articles. A selective list of publications about SW is given in the bibliography section below.

The preparation of this book caused us to examine much correspondence not known to our predecessors and to reinterpret data that they did use. This effort has led to the discovery of considerable information that apparently was not taken into account by prior biographers and to the correction of some of their assertions, including the assignment of numerous letters to dates other than those proposed previously. The following new findings appear particularly noteworthy.

• Prior biographers fail to mention that Samuel Wesley was confined for nearly a year (from about July 1817 to June 1818) in a private lunatic asylum, Blacklands House in Chelsea.[2] It is remarkable that the extant letters that he wrote during his confinement there give no indication of mental disability.

• Lightwood entitled a chapter of his biography 'Visits Windsor'. This chapter purports to describe performances by SW before King George III in Windsor Castle on 22 and 23 July 1786, and clearly is based upon the first-person account of the visit in the

---

[1] As Stevenson's chapter follows the text of *The Wesley Banner and Revival Record* articles closely, although not exactly, he appears likely to have been the author of these anonymous articles.

[2] Stevenson clearly was aware of documents that refer to SW's confinement, as he cites them in other contexts. Perhaps he did not wish to detract from SW's reputation and that of the Wesley family by writing on this subject.

Methodist Archives.[3] However, this account is in the handwriting not of SW but of his brother, Charles Wesley Jr.[4]

• Although Wesley's perennial financial insecurity was noted by earlier commentators, they did not record his incarceration for debt in May 1825 in a 'spunging house' off Chancery Lane.[5]

• In 1875, Eliza Wesley issued a collection of 24 of her father's letters under the title *Letters of Samuel Wesley to Mr Jacobs, Organist of Surrey Chapel, Relating to the Introduction into this Country of the Works of John Sebastian Bach*. She must have realised that her title was not entirely accurate, as she noted that the 16th letter—which, incidentally, has no relation to Bach—was written not to Jacobs[6] but to Knight Spenser. From internal evidence we believe that another letter in her collection—letter 17—also was not written to Jacobs, and propose that the addressee was Charles Frederick Horn.[7] Although EW apparently arranged this collection in what she thought was the letters' chronological order, our calendar presents what we consider to be a more accurate ordering, so that (for instance) letter 11 of her collection appears in this book as the first extant letter from SW to Jacobs.

• By combining information in Wesley's correspondence with his family with information in his correspondence with friends and

---

[3] MA DDWes/6/60.

[4] Besides this handwriting evidence there is an account of CW Jr's Windsor concerts by Fanny Burney, who attended them. See her *Diary and Letters of Madame d'Arblay...edited by her niece* (London, v 3 (1842) p 26–27). The circumstance that SW, SGW, Sarah and (occasionally) SSW signed letters as 'S Wesley' has led to the incorrect cataloguing of some of their letters, but the handwriting of each of these persons is readily distinguishable.

[5] Lightwood was aware of this incident but says misleadingly (*Lightwood* p 87) that SW's 'failure to keep up the payments landed him in the King's Bench prison' 'some years' after 1812.

[6] Eliza Wesley correctly transcribed her father's spellings of Benjamin Jacobs's surname. Through 10/5/1813 Wesley and Jacob consistently used the spelling 'Jacobs'; from 15/2/1816 they consistently used the spelling 'Jacob'. We have not seen manuscripts or publications of Jacobs between these two dates and therefore cannot say precisely when BJ and his family changed the spelling of their surname.

[7] The autograph of this letter (RCM Ms 2130 letter 17) has no salutation and its address portion has not been preserved.

professional colleagues, we have revised and refined knowledge of his musical activities. By these means, for example, we have dated what we think is SW's first extant mention of J. S. Bach. This occurs in a letter bearing the date '21 May' that was written to the composer John George Graeff from SW's Camden Town home; the letter, therefore, was written after 1805 and before 1810. In this letter SW states that he has just finished transcribing Bach's 'preludes and fugues'—i.e., the '48'—from Graeff's copy, and mentions an overdue loan of £60 from 'a great man'. Coupling this latter remark with SW's statement in his 1 April 1806 letter to his mother that he has written off the £60 owed to him by Mr Casamajor,[8] we have assigned, with appropriate caution, this letter to 21 May 1806.

• Similarly holistic consideration of the correspondence also has yielded data about other musical activities in which Wesley was involved. The publishing history of the Wesley/Horn edition of the '48', for instance, is indicated not only in SW's letters to other musicians but also in his letters to Sarah Suter.

• Our work on this book has given us an opportunity to re-examine some problems that have puzzled previous researchers. For instance, according to Alfred Dürr, there has been 'much speculation' about the identity of the 'London copy' of the '48' that Wesley, in a letter dated 25 November 1808, advised William Crotch to burn.[9] Besides the Wesley/Horn edition of the '48', other editions were printed in London during the first two decades of the 19th century for Broderip and Wilkinson, for Lavenu and for Boosey. As both the Lavenu and Boosey editions apparently were first issued after 1808,[10]

---

[8] We take this man to be Justinian Casamajor, a former sheriff of Hertfordshire whose sugar plantations in the West Indies encountered financial difficulties. There are no other references to unpaid £60 loans in Wesley's extant correspondence between 1806 and 1809.

[9] Dürr, Alfred, 'On the earliest manuscripts and prints of Bach's Well-Tempered Clavier I in England', in Brainard, Paul and Ray Robinson (eds.), *A Bach Tribute: Essays in Honor of William H. Scheide*, Kassel, 1993, pp 121–134. Dürr's comments on this subject appear on p 134.

[10] [A. F. C. Kollmann], 'Of John Sebastian Bach, and his works', *Quarterly Musical Register* no. 1 (January 1812), pp 28–40, notes (p 30) that the Lavenu edition appeared 'but lately'. The Boosey edition was published from 28 Holles Street, where the Boosey firm operated from 1816 (*H&S*, p 80).

we have concluded that the edition which Crotch was advised to burn was the Broderip and Wilkinson edition of part 2 of the '48'. We interpret SW's statement in the same letter that 'Wilkinson in the Haymarket is trying to insult the public with a similar Grub Street performance' as a reference to a projected Wilkinson & Co. publication of part 1 that, as far as we know, never appeared.[11]

It is appropriate to mention here two stories about Samuel Wesley that are not corroborated by the extant correspondence.

• SW's obituary in *The Times* of 12 October 1837, and later biographical accounts, attribute many of his health problems to an accident which, it is said, occurred in 1787 when SW fell into a deep excavation near Snow Hill (a London street), spent the night there 'insensible', and then declined to have a surgical operation on his skull. No such event is mentioned in any surviving correspondence, although the earliest 1787 letter in the calendar dates from July.[12]

• SW wrote in his 1836 *Reminiscences*[13] that he was introduced to J. S. Bach's '48' by the musical prodigy George Frederick Pinto. This story is not implausible, as Pinto had studied thorough-bass with Charles Frederick Horn, from whom he could have become acquainted with JSB's music.[14] However, the story is unsupported by

---

[11] Like the earlier Bonn and Paris editions of the '48', Broderip and Wilkinson (whose edition of part 2 of the '48' has a title-page in French) called what is now considered part 2 of the '48' 'I. Partie', and thus could reasonably have published part 2 before considering whether to publish part 1. However, the partnership of Broderip and Wilkinson ended in 1808, after which the firm continued as Wilkinson & Co. (*H&S*, pp 86, 554). It is not known whether SW's criticism of the Broderip and Wilkinson edition influenced Wilkinson & Co. not to proceed with an edition of the 'II. Partie', i.e., of part 1 of the '48'. We are grateful to Dr Yo Tomita for help in resolving this puzzle, which is discussed further in Michael Kassler (ed.), *Aspects of the English Bach Awakening*, Aldershot, 2002, forthcoming.

[12] Sarah→SGW, 24/8/1782, says that SW's head is much better although it still bears a plaster, but there is no evidence to link Sarah's statement to the alleged Snow Hill accident five years later.

[13] BL Add 27593. An edition of SW's *Reminiscences* by Kenneth Hart has been announced but is not yet published.

[14] Pinto's studies are reported in Charles Edward Horn's unpublished memoirs of his father and himself (Nanki collection, Yomiuri Shimbun Symphony Orchestra, Tokyo). An edition of these memoirs by Michael Kassler is in preparation.

any of SW's extant correspondence, in which Pinto's name appears only once, in another context.[15] Indeed, SW's first extant mention of JSB, noted above, was written after Pinto's 23 March 1806 death.

In general, the correspondence presented in the calendar should be considered a more reliable guide to contemporary events than Wesley's *Reminiscences*.[16] SW wrote his *Reminiscences* near the end of his life and they are known to be inaccurate in several other respects.[17]

---

[15] SW→SGW, 16/10/1801, describes Pinto's presence as one of several people in a party that performed music mostly by Haydn and Mozart.

[16] For example, A. F. C. Kollmann, whose assistance to Wesley regarding Bach is well documented in the correspondence, is not mentioned at all in Wesley's *Reminiscences*, presumably because of a break in their friendship. This matter is treated further in Michael Kassler (ed.), *Aspects of the English Bach Awakening*, *op. cit.*

[17] For instance, about the same time as he wrote his *Reminiscences*, SW wrote 'A sketch of the state of music in England, from the year 1778 up to the present', which was published in *The Musical World*, v 1 no. 1 (18 March 1836), p 1–3. When a 'corrected' second edition of this number was issued ten weeks later, the publishers felt obliged to point out two errors in SW's account and included no more of his recollections in subsequent numbers, notwithstanding the promise of his title to bring his account, which ends as published with a discussion of Salomon's performance of Haydn's *The Creation*, 'up to the present'. SW→Street?, about 2/1836, also indicates that SW had planned to write more than *The Musical World* published.

HISTORY AND PRIOR PUBLICATION
OF THE CORRESPONDENCE

Manuscripts of the documents entered in the calendar are now preserved in more than 50 collections in five countries. Three collections each have more than 100 of these manuscripts: the British Library (more than 360), the Methodist Archives and Research Centre (more than 260) and Emory University (more than 140). Other repositories that hold more than ten of these manuscripts are the Fitzwilliam Museum, the Royal College of Music, the Osborn Collection in the Beinecke Library at Yale University, and the United Methodist Church Archives at Drew University.

A thorough study of the transmission of Samuel Wesley's correspondence from the original recipients to the present locations remains to be made. The following remarks may nevertheless be of interest.

Four people appear to have been chiefly responsible for the initial preservation of SW's correspondence: Sarah Wesley; Eliza T. Tooth (a friend, at least for a time, of each of CW Jr, Sarah and SW); Vincent Novello; and SW's daughter Eliza Wesley.

Sarah appreciated her family's importance and kept many documents concerning them.[1] At her death on 19 September 1828, her 'archive', together with many papers that had belonged to her parents, passed to her brother Charles Wesley Jr.[2]

We do not know when Eliza Tooth began her extensive efforts to preserve, to date and to annotate the Wesley family

---

[1] In the Introduction to his *Memoirs of the Wesley Family; Collected Principally from Original Documents* (2nd edition, New York, 1848), Adam Clarke noted (p 10) that he was 'chiefly indebted' to Sarah for lending original documents and providing him with other information about the family.

[2] CW's 28/5/1785 will bequeathed the contents of his Chesterfield Street house to SGW and then to CW Jr after SGW's death. During the last years of her life SGW lived with CW Jr and Sarah, who were the executors of SGW's 3/3/1818 will and received her household possessions. Sarah's 16/11/1827 will bequeathed all her property to CW Jr, with the injunction that he should deliver those of her manuscripts that he did not wish to retain to the Reverend Mr John Gaulter of the Methodist Connexion.

correspondence.[3] However, on 1 December 1828, CW Jr wrote to Mr Tilbury, a warehouse keeper, authorising Tooth to examine and to remove any of CW Jr's papers that were stored in Tilbury's warehouse.[4] Some of this examination apparently was done in conjunction with the Reverend Thomas Jackson, as CW Jr→Tilbury, 31/1/1829, gave permission for both of them to inspect furniture stored in the warehouse.[5] On 24/3/1829, CW Jr authorised Tooth to take away whatever she pleased from Tilbury's warehouse.[6]

By 1830, Jackson had become sufficiently convinced of the importance of CW's manuscripts and the necessity of preserving them for the Methodist Church that he borrowed money to buy them from CW Jr, as noted below. Presumably Tooth kept a residue of Wesley family papers,[7] as she later gave some of them away to friends.[8]

Tooth did not give all these papers away, and left a large quantity of remaining relics, including SW correspondence, to the

---

[3] An 1856 letter (WCL LDWMM 1997/6602) from Tooth to the Methodist minister Samuel Romilly Hall tells of her rescuing a 'burnt scrape' of a letter by CLW 'from the flames'. Letters annotated by Tooth, some still in the albums in which she pasted them, are preserved in many repositories including the Methodist Archives and Research Centre, Southern Methodist University, Queen's College, Melbourne, and Wesley's Chapel, London.

[4] MA DDWF/20/26. Following Sarah's death, CW Jr left the home he had shared with her (1 New Street, Dorset Square) and, after spending a short time with Mrs Elizabeth Mortimer in Kentish Town, moved about 20/11/1828 to the 20 Edgware Road home of his cousin Elizabeth Greene. Presumably the property stored with Tilbury was not required or could not be accommodated in CW Jr's new home. CW Jr→Tooth, 17/1/1829 (MA DDWF/20/28) states that Tilbury has sent '3 parcels of books' to Tooth's house, where CW Jr planned to spend 'a little time', presumably to examine them.

[5] MA DDWF/20/29.

[6] CW Jr→Tooth, MA DDWF/20/30.

[7] Jackson, Thomas, *The Life of the Rev. Charles Wesley* (London, 1841) v 1 p iv affirms that 'Miss Tooth was possessed of many papers relating to the family of Mr Charles Wesley, which she kindly placed in the hands of the author'.

[8] For instance, in 1841 she presented an album of Wesley family letters to the Rev. Henry Davies of Bristol. This album now is at Queen's College, Melbourne. Presumably her possession of a large quantity of manuscripts that had once belonged to Sarah led commentators to conclude erroneously that Tooth was Sarah's executrix (*see*, e.g., *Stevenson City Road* p 173, 399, 477).

mother of Mr J. A. P. Ingoldby. He subsequently consigned these relics to Sotheby's for sale on 10 July 1906.[9]

Vincent Novello kept many, although not all, of the letters that SW had written to him and presented them to the British Museum in 1840. 55 years later, Eliza Wesley bequeathed to the British Museum many letters by and to SW that she had retained.

The first substantial departure of Wesley family correspondence from England appears to have occurred in 1911, when items from the estate of the English collector Robert Thursfield Smith were acquired for Emory University in the U.S.A.

We now trace briefly how the seven principal current holders of SW correspondence acquired these manuscripts.

BRITISH LIBRARY. Samuel Wesley correspondence has come to the BL primarily from gifts by Vincent Novello and Eliza Wesley to the British Museum.[10] In memory of SW, VN gave to the British Museum in May 1840 what is now BL Add Ms 11729, a set of more than 170 letters that SW had written to him between May 1811 and December 1825.[11] EW, who died in 1895, bequeathed a considerable family archive to the British Museum, which subsequently has been catalogued as Add Ms 34996—35027. Her bequest included letters now in Add Ms 35012 from SW to Sarah Suter and other family members, letters now in Add Ms 35013 from SW to Robert Glenn and other friends, letters from Samuel Sebastian Wesley now in Add Ms 35019, manuscripts of SW's musical compositions described separately below, and much other material, including his lectures and

---

[9] 'Catalogue of autograph letters and historical documents, important letters & relics of the Wesley family', sale catalogue, Sotheby, Wilkinson & Hodge, London, 9–10/7/1806, p 28.

[10] The library departments of the British Museum were transferred to the British Library when the BL was established in 1973. BL letters summarised in the calendar are now primarily in the BL's music collections; a small remainder are in the BL's manuscript collections.

[11] VN also gave numerous musical manuscripts by SW to the British Museum, including compositions by SW and his copies of compositions by others. See the discussion below of SW's music manuscripts, and Chris Banks, 'From Purcell to Wardour Street: A brief account of music manuscripts from the library of Vincent Novello now in the British Library', *British Library Journal* v 21 no. 2 (Autumn 1991) p 240–258.

EW's scrapbook of newspaper cuttings about him. There were no letters by Sarah Suter in EW's bequest and none seem to have survived.

Two smaller collections of SW letters were acquired by the British Museum in 1970. Add Ms 56228, a set of 11 letters mainly to Joseph Payne Street, was presented by Street's great-great-granddaughter Hilda Whittaker. Add Ms 56411, a volume bound by Rivière of letters from SW to George Bridgetower, Domenico Dragonetti and others, was purchased in 1970 from the music antiquarian dealer H. Baron. The latter volume had been owned by the violin maker Arthur Frederick Hill (1860–1939) at least since 1908.[12] It was sold by his widow at Sotheby's on 17 June 1947, as lot 323 of his extensive music collection.[13]

DREW UNIVERSITY. The four letters by SW in this collection, and much other Wesley family correspondence, were donated to the United Methodist Church Archives by the Reverend Dr Frederick E. Maser. Three letters by SW now at Drew (which Dr Maser had purchased at auction through Bernard Quaritch Ltd and the Leamington Book Shop, then of Washington DC) have been printed and discussed by Frank Baker in *Methodist History*.[14]

EMORY UNIVERSITY. The John Wesley collection (collection no. 100 in the Special Collections Department of the Robert W. Woodruff Library) comprises letters, papers and memorabilia of John Wesley and his family. It includes: items from the estate of Robert Thursfield Smith that Warren Akin Candler (1857–1941, Methodist bishop, Chancellor of Emory University) bought in 1911 from Smith's son W. H. Smith; a 1929 gift by Candler's nephew Charles Howard Candler (1878–1957, president of the Coca-Cola Company

---

[12] According to 'Letters of a Bachist: Samuel Wesley', *Musical Times* v 49 (1/4/1908) p 236–237, where four letters now in BL Add Ms 56411 were first printed, Hill had acquired these letters 'recently'.

[13] It was purchased there by Cole, and we understand that it was subsequently owned by a director of the Hinrichsen firm before H. Baron acquired it.

[14] Maser, Frederick E., 'Discovery', *Methodist History* v 11 no. 1 (October 1972), p 52–56.

and a benefactor of Emory University); purchases in 1941 from the estate of William L. Clements (1861–1934, a Michigan industrialist and collector of rare books and manuscripts); and the 'Wesley/Langshaw' set of 32 letters bought in 1989 from the English autograph dealer John Wilson.[15]

FITZWILLIAM MUSEUM. The museum's set of 28 letters by SW, in a volume 'newly bound by Rivière', was offered for £21 in a December 1911 Maggs Brothers catalogue of autograph letters and manuscripts.[16] It presumably was purchased then by the autograph collector Alexander Meyrick Broadley (1847–1916), as the volume bears his bookplate dated 1911.[17] By December 1917 it had passed to the collector Ralph Griffin (1854–1941),[18] who presented it in September 1919 to the Fitzwilliam Museum.[19]

METHODIST ARCHIVES AND RESEARCH CENTRE. Charles Wesley's manuscripts that had passed to Charles Wesley Jr after the deaths of his mother in 1822 and sister in 1828 were acquired in 1830 by the Reverend Thomas Jackson for the Methodist Church.[20] These 'family papers' were acquired first by Jackson personally for an

---

[15] For information in this paragraph we are indebted to Laura Micham of Emory University. The entire Wesley/Langshaw acquisition is published in *Wainwright*.

[16] Catalogue no. 275, p 122, item 1259.

[17] In his book *Chats on Autographs* (London, 1910), Broadley wrote (p 261) that 30 years ago 'autographs of...Samuel Wesley averaged about 3' shillings, and that he 'lately gave £3/3/- for the signed ms. of [Charles] Wesley's "Ode on the Death of Boyce"'.

[18] With this volume now is a 31/12/1917 letter in which William Barclay Squire of the British Museum thanks Griffin for letting him see these SW letters and remarks that 'they are very interesting, but I do not think it would be advisable to publish them'.

[19] For information in this paragraph we are indebted to Liz Fielden of the Fitzwilliam Museum.

[20] J. Alfred Sharp, preface to *A Catalogue of Manuscripts and Relics, Engravings and Photographs...belonging to the Wesleyan Methodist Conference, and Preserved at the Office of the Conference, 25–35 City Road....* London, 1921, p. vi.

amount which Jackson borrowed and then, after the Methodist Conference approved the expenditure, were sold in 1831 to the Methodist Church for the same sum.[21] This acquisition, which possibly included some SW correspondence, has been supplemented subsequently by gifts and purchases from numerous sources. The Methodist Archives were transferred in 1977 from City Road, London, to the John Rylands University Library of Manchester.

OSBORN COLLECTION. The James Marshall and Marie–Louise Osborn Collection, named after its principal donors whose substantial collection of manuscripts included many relating to the Burney family, was 'installed' in the Beinecke Rare Book and Manuscript Library of Yale University in 1963.[22] Of the 20 letters in the Osborn collection that are entered in the calendar, 17 were written by or to the music historian Dr Charles Burney.

ROYAL COLLEGE OF MUSIC. Ms 2130, a bound volume that includes the 24 letters by SW to BJ and other persons published by Eliza Wesley in 1875,[23] appeared as lot 196 in the 26/4/1875 Puttick and Simpson auction of items from the library of the composer Sir William Sterndale Bennett (1816–1875),[24] where it was purchased by the Novello firm for £11.[25]

---

[21] Jackson, Thomas, *Recollections of my own Life and Times*, London, 1878, p 230; *Stevenson* p 469. The deed dated 4/8/1831 assigning CW's papers to the Methodist Book-Room, for which CW Jr received £105, is preserved in the Methodist Archives at MAW RA box 6. In addition, CW Jr was guaranteed continuation of the annuity which the Book-Room had previously paid to CW Jr and Sarah (Jackson, *op. cit.*, p 229–230).

[22] See Stephen Parks, 'The Osborn collection: a biennial progress report', *Yale University Library Gazette*, v 44 no. 3 (January 1970) p 1–30.

[23] In *Jacobs*. The volume also includes programmes of 1811, 1812 and 1814 performances of JSB's music by BJ and Crotch in the Surrey Chapel.

[24] Bennett was the principal founder of the Bach Society in London in October 1849, a purpose of which was to collect biographical works relating to J. S. Bach and his family. See J. R. Sterndale Bennett, *The Life of William Sterndale Bennett*, Cambridge, 1907, p 203.

[25] Coover, James, *Music at Auction: Puttick and Simpson (of London), 1794–1971* (Warren, Michigan, 1988) p 227–228.

The volume therefore was in the possession of Novello, Ewer and Co. when it published a number of letters by SW in its journal *Concordia*.[26] A few years later the company donated this volume to the Sacred Harmonic Society—the gift is recorded in the Society's 46th Annual Report dated 1877–78. The library of this Society, including this volume, subsequently was purchased by a group of benefactors and presented to the RCM library at its foundation in 1883.[27]

As the preface to EW's *Jacobs* book is dated 11/5/1875 she clearly was not in possession of the 24 SW autograph letters when her book was published. It is not known when or from whom Sterndale Bennett acquired these letters nor when EW had the opportunity to transcribe them, but her transcriptions appear to have been made not later than August 1870. A notebook in EW's handwriting, now British Library Add Ms 62928, includes in f 1–44 her copies of the letters printed in *Jacobs* and at f 47 her copy of SW→VN, 10/6/1830. As the latter copy bears her annotation 'copied August 10th 1870', she presumably had copied the 24 SW letters in *Jacobs* before then.

Prior Publication and Cataloguing of the Correspondence. Although this book presents for the first time a summary of Samuel Wesley's entire extant correspondence, substantial portions of this correspondence have been published in microform and catalogued by the repositories that possess them.

Much, but not all, of the large collection of Wesley family correspondence in the Methodist Archives and Research Centre, John Rylands University Library of Manchester, has been photographically

---

[26] The first letter in Ms 2130, SW→BJ?, 17/9/1808, was printed in *Concordia* v 1 no. 5 (29/5/1875), p 77. A prefatory note on p 76 states that the 'small and unpretending volume, labelled "Wesley's Letters to Jacobs"', occupied 'a most appropriate place' in Sterndale Bennett's library. The fourth letter in Ms 2130, SW→BJ, 17/11/1808?, printed in *Concordia* v 1 no. 34 (18/12/1875), p 541, with the omission of a paragraph said to be 'of no public interest', is described there as bearing 'no date in the handwriting of Wesley himself, but is pencil-marked "17 Nov., 1808"'. This description further establishes that *Concordia* transcribed these SW letters from the volume which is now Ms 2130, as EW's *Jacobs* book does not have this information.

[27] We are indebted to Dr Peter Horton of the RCM library for the information in this paragraph.

reproduced on microfiche by Inter Documentation Company bv (IDC), Leiden, Netherlands, as part of their series entitled *The People Called Methodists: A Documentary History of the Methodist Church in Great Britain and Ireland*. Reproductions of Samuel Wesley's 'out-letters and miscellaneous papers' in the Methodist Archives' DDWF/15 series are available from IDC as a set of six microfiches, order no. MP-661. SW's 'out-letters and miscellaneous papers' in the DDWes/6 series are available as a set of three microfiches, order no. MP-662. Reproductions of some letters to SW and other related correspondence in the Methodist Archives have been published by IDC in other microfiche sets of their collection.

Catalogues of portions of the Methodist Archives have been compiled and can be purchased from the John Rylands University Library. Of greatest relevance to SW are the two-volume catalogue of the Charles Wesley papers in the Methodist Archives' DDCW series and the three-volume catalogue of the Wesley Family papers in the DDWF and the DDWes series.[28] The information presented in these catalogues concerning SW's correspondence has been significantly revised in this book.

Almost all of the John Wesley Collection of manuscripts in the Robert W. Woodruff Library, Emory University is available for purchase as a three-reel set of microfilms. A printed guide to the collection is included on these reels and can be bought separately. The films follow an estimate of chronological order that, for SW's correspondence, has been substantially revised in this source book.

As mentioned, an edition of the 32 letters in the separate Wesley/Langshaw Collection at Emory University has been produced by Arthur W. Wainwright in collaboration with Don E. Saliers.[29] We have relied upon this edition in preparing our calendar.

Collections of SW's letters in the British Library and the Fitzwilliam Museum also have been microfilmed, and copies can be ordered from these repositories.

---

[28] These catalogues contain much information not in J. Alfred Sharp's 1921 *Catalogue of Manuscripts and Relics*, *op. cit.*

[29] Wainwright, Arthur W. with Don E. Saliers, *Wesley/Langshaw Correspondence: Charles Wesley, his Sons, and the Lancaster Organists.* [Atlanta], 1993. This edition includes a 33rd letter, which is at Drew University.

Finding aids for the John Wesley letters and for the Wesley Family letters now at Drew University have been published by the General Commission on Archives and History of The United Methodist Church.

An edition giving the full text of 439 letters by SW that have musical interest and were written after the year 1796 has been prepared by Philip Olleson.[30] Letters by SW whose full text is given in this Oxford University Press edition are identified in the calendar by the symbol *O*.

A new edition of the letters of John Wesley, begun by Frank Baker for Oxford University Press, is being continued by Richard Heitzenrater and others for Abingdon Press. This edition has not yet reached the years of John Wesley's letters to Samuel Wesley. For this Source Book, accordingly, we have relied upon the 'standard' eight-volume edition of JW's letters compiled by John Telford.[31] Letters by JW that are printed in Telford's edition are identified in the calendar by the symbol *T*.

An edition of Charles Wesley's letters has been proposed but has not yet begun publication.

An edition of the letters of Charles Burney, edited by Alvaro Ribeiro, is being published by Oxford University Press. It has not yet reached the years of Burney's letters to Samuel Wesley.

---

[30] Olleson, Philip (ed.), *The Letters of Samuel Wesley: Professional and Social Correspondence, 1797–1837.* Oxford, 2001.

[31] Telford, John (ed.), *The Letters of the Rev. John Wesley.* London, 1931.

CALENDAR OF DATED CORRESPONDENCE

CW→SGW   Charles St, Bristol   **14/7/1766**
MA DDCW/7/20   My dear Sally's letter is this moment delivered
☞ 'Monday night and Tuesday evening'; pmk 15 July[1]
  CW thinks that SW will escape the current bout [of illness].

CW→SGW   Charles St, Bristol   **27/7/1766**
MA DDCW/5/99   Yesterday I dined at Mrs Heritage's
☞ Sun 27 July={1766,1777,1783}[2]
  'Lady Robert' [Mary Manners, 1736?–1829, wife of Lord Robert Manners]
  entreats SGW 'to continue physicking Sally [Sarah] and Samme [SW] once a
  week for at least a month after' the doctors, apothecaries and nurses have
  finished their physicking.

CW→SGW   Charles St, Bristol   **9/8/1766**
MA DDCW/7/26   As Charles Jr is 'as fit to be trusted with care
☞ 9 Aug & ref. to SW's emerging teeth→ⓘ
  CW hopes that SW's teeth are appearing.

CW→SGW   Charles St, Bristol   **13/8/1766**
MA DDCW/7/23   My dear creature would commend my care
☞ Wed 13 Aug & ref. to SW's first tooth→ⓘ
  CW expects to hear by SGW's next letter that SW's first tooth has appeared.

---

[1] Assigned to 1766 because 15/7/1766 a Tuesday; ltr says CW's London host is
Mr Evans and CW→SGW, 12/7/1766 (MA DDCW/7/11), is written from Mr
Evans's house; the 12/7/1766 ltr says CW is to dine with Rebecca Gwynne on
14/7/1766 and this dinner is mentioned in 15/7/1766 portion of ltr; and ltr asks
SGW to get Mr Purnel's bill and CW→SGW, 25/8/1766, inquires whether
SGW has got Mr Purnel's bill.

[2] Not 1777 because on 27/7/1777 Sarah and SW were returning from Guildford
and SGW was not with them so could not be physicking them; not 1783 because
ref. to 'physicking' implies SW and Sarah young.

CW→SGW   Charles St, Bristol   **21/8/1766**
MA DDCW/7/12   What news of Sammy's invisible tormentors?
🖃 21/8/1776
   CW asks for news about SW's 'invisible tormentors' [his teeth]. When they break out he may recover his strength and looks and become once more the finest boy in Bristol.

SGW→CW   Charles St, Bristol   **23/8/1766**
MA DDWes/7/19   My dearest Partner's last is just come to hand
🖃 endorsed 'Sally' & 23/8/1766; pmk 25 Aug
   SW 'is gone out a-walking' [i.e., he has been taken out on a walk].

CW→SGW   Charles St, Bristol   **25/8/1766**
MA DDCW/7/27   Send for Mrs Bird, and tell her, her husband
🖃 25 Aug & ref. to SW's first tooth→ⅈ
   On his return [to Bristol] three weeks from tomorrow CW hopes to see SW's first tooth.

SGW→CW   Charles St, Bristol   **6/7/1768**
MA DDWes/1/50   This is to acquaint you that our Dr little babe
🖃 6/7/1768
   SGW informs CW of the death of their son John James Wesley [1768–1768] the previous night [5/7/1768]. The other children [including SW] are well but SGW does not know how long they may remain so. Smallpox is at the house next-door but one, and SGW fears for her 'little Sammy' [SW].

SGW→CW   Charles St, Bristol   **11/7/1768**
MA DDWes/7/20   I this day rec'd both my dearest Mr Wesley's
🖃 11/7/1768
   SGW describes her feelings on the death of her son Jacky [John James Wesley] who was buried on 'Saturday evening last' [9/7/1768]. SW's health gives cause for concern, as he 'eats but little animal food'. SGW intends to give him less food while smallpox is in the neighbourhood. All these means and 'physick' [medicine] were used for Jacky, but 'to no purpose'.

CW→SGW   Charles St, Bristol   **16/7/1768**
MA DDCW/7/15   Our preparation could not save the first Jacky
▣ 16/7/1768

CW's and SGW's actions could not save the life of 'the first Jacky' [John James Wesley] because God had a better place for him, but they should be thankful that SW still 'holds up'. If SW should have 'the distemper' [smallpox] soon, 'it will only lessen his beauty'. CW longs to see SW and SGW and asks SGW to write again, particularly about SW.

SGW→CW Jr   Charles St, Bristol   **2–5/1771**
Stevenson p 444   [not known]
Stevenson[3]

'Little Sammy' [SW] seems 'quite forlorn' because CW Jr [who is in London] is not in Bristol 'to play to him and with him'.

CW→SGW   Charles St, Bristol   **21/3/1771**
MA DDCW/7/59   Long before this reaches you I hope the Pain
▣ 21/3/1771

CW writes to SGW about their house in Chesterfield Street, London and asks why she cannot take SW with her [to London]. The additional travelling expenses will be saved by reduced housekeeping costs. CW sends love to SGW and SW.

SGW→CW Jr   Charles St, Bristol   **4/4/1771**
MA DDWes/7/23   By this time, I hope my dear Charles has recd
▣ Thurs 4 Apr={1771,1776,1782}[4]

SW was pleased that CW Jr has not forgotten him. SW's strength has been reduced by a cold, but he hopes that the approaching spring will rid him of it.

---

[3] *Stevenson* p 444 says ltr written when CW and CW Jr were in London, 'a short time before the family removed from Bristol to the metropolis'. CW and CW Jr arrived in London on 6/2/1771 (CW→SGW, 10/2/1771, MA DDCW/7/96) and were joined there by SGW, Sarah and SW in May 1771 (*see* CW→SGW, 16/5/1771).

[4] Assigned to 1771 because ltr addressed to CW Jr in care of CW at the Foundery rather than at Chesterfield Street, and CW Jr in London with CW while rest of the family still in Bristol; these circumstances preclude 1776 or 1782.

CW→SGW   Charles St, Bristol   **1/5/1771**
MA DDWes/4/7   The clouds drop fatness here.
☞ 1/5/1771
If SW would play [music] like CW Jr he must not reject CW Jr's first instructress [SGW]. Mr [William] Savage [organist, composer and bass singer, 1720–1789] offers to sing over with SW [Handel's] *Messiah* or any oratorios or operas. CW and CW Jr were sorry to disappoint Mr [John] Worgan [organist and composer, 1724–1790, CW Jr's teacher] yesterday, but the weather kept them at home.

CW Jr→SGW   Charles St, Bristol   **1/5/1771?**
MA DDWes/1/63   I hope you are very well. My Aunt's drank
☞ 1 May[5]
CW Jr supposes that 'Sammy' [SW] is 'quite a man now' and hopes that SW remembers 'all his songs'. When CW Jr comes [from London] to Bristol he hopes to hear SW sing them very well.

CW→SGW   Charles St, Bristol   **16/5/1771**
MA DDCW/7/30   My dear partner's last I expected, knowing
☞ Thursday 16/5/1771
CW hopes to see 'you all' [SGW, Sarah and SW] next week [in London] and asks on what day and by what carriage they plan to arrive. SW has not yet acknowledged CW's letter [not preserved].

Rebecca & Thomas Waller→SW   Charles St, Bristol   **22/9/1772**
MA DDWF/15/1A   *RW:*   I am very much oblige'd to my Dear
                          TW: as there is a half sheet of paper, spare, I
☞ 22/9/1772
RW: Rebecca Waller [daughter of SGW's sister Elizabeth Gwynne Waller, 1730–1795] thanks her 'dear cousin Sammy [SW] for his kind letter'. CW Jr was 'highly entertained at Gloucester'. Her uncle [CW] 'looked very well'. Her cousins 'long to see' SW. She sends respects and love to SW's family.
TW: Thomas Waller [*d*1781, son of Elizabeth Waller] loves SW but is 'not quite pleased' that SW wrote 'to his Cousin B' [Rebecca Waller] before he wrote to Thomas and supposes that this is 'because she was a young lady'. He entreats 'dear little Samson' [SW] to reply.

---

[5] 1771 presumed because CW and CW Jr then together in London while SGW and SW were in Bristol (*see* CW→SGW, 1/5/1771 and 16/5/1771). Also, ltr mentions being at the Foundery and not going to Marylebone, and CW Jr's handwriting is childish.

M. Foottit→SW   **22/11/1772**
MA DDWF/15/1B   It was no small Pleasure to me when I
☞ 22/11/1772

Mrs Foottit was pleased to hear of CW Jr's planned visit to London but is disappointed that SGW, Sarah and SW are unlikely to accompany him. Mrs Foottit thanks SW for his 'affectionate inquiry' concerning her arm and asks to be remembered to Prudence [Box, *d*1777, a servant of the Wesley family]. Mr Foottit sends love.

CW→SW   Charles St, Bristol[6]   **6/3/1773**
MA DDWes/4/70   Come now, my good friend Samuel, and let
☞ 6/3/1773

God made SW to be forever happy with Him; therefore SW should serve and love Him. 'Every morning and night', in SW's own words and in words he has been taught, SW should pray to God to make SW love Him. Formerly SW prayed 'in the sight of others'. Henceforth he should pray in a corner by himself.

SW 'should now begin to live by reason and religion'. There should be sense even in his 'play and diversions'. For this reason CW has furnished SW 'with maps and books and harpsichord'. Each day, SW should learn by heart whatever SGW recommends and should read one or more chapters in the Bible. CW supposes that SGW now will take SW to be her 'chaplain' in place of CW Jr, 'to read the psalms and lessons' when Sarah does not. Mr Fry [not identified] will assist SW to write better. SW will improve both in writing and in music. CW will die 'very soon', but God lives forever and SW may live forever with Him. CW hopes that this will happen when SW dies.

Music, for which SW 'has a natural inclination', in itself is 'neither good nor bad'. 'Foolish people' praise SW too readily; if they see any good in SW they should praise God for the gift rather than SW. CW Jr loves music 'much more than' SW but 'is not proud or vain' of this. SW is to send CW 'a long letter of answer' and should always look upon CW as both a loving father and a friend.

CW→Sarah   **8/4/1773**
MA DDCW/7/39   Go to bed at 9: & you may rise at six
☞ 8/4/1773

SW owes CW a letter. It is in SW's power to write 'very soon and very well'.

---

[6] Ltr addressed to SW humorously as 'Deputy Organist of St James's, Bristol'.

SW→CW Jr   Charles St, Bristol   **20/4/1773**
BL Add 35012 f 116[7]   Last Sunday I played a Psalm at St James's
▣ 20/4/1773
   Last Sunday [18/4/1773] SW played a psalm at St James's Church, Bristol.
Mrs [Anne] Vigor [*d*1774] hopes to see CW and CW Jr in Bristol. SW has
learned the 'Handel water piece' and today had 'some of the Highland Laddie'.
He saw Mr Rooke [CW Jr's music master in Bristol] last Sunday. Mr Allen
called yesterday [19/4/1773]. SW has not had a letter from Dr Ford and asks if
CW Jr has seen him. SW hopes that [John] Worgan and [Samuel] Arnold
[composer and organist, 1740–1802] are well.

John Worgan→CW   **20/12/1773**
MA DDWes/7/118   Be assured, not a jot of the Esteem I have for
▣ 20/12/1773
   John Worgan hopes that [his pupil] CW Jr is progressing, and trusts that his
'friend Samuel [SW], if he's in health, is as *pomposo* as ever, more especially in
the impulse he receives from great Handel's music'.

Anne Chapman→CW   **5/10/1774**
MA DDWes/2/79[8]   ...one before, but that Mrs Anne Stafford told
▣ 5/10/1774
   Mrs [Anne] Vigor, who is weak but not in immediate danger, was very pleased
with SW's letter [not preserved].

Hetty Rutter→   Chesterfield St   **9/10/1774?**
CW Jr, Sarah & SW
MA DDWF/25/4   *To CW Jr & Sarah:*   Why are you so ceremonious
                     To SW: I must write a few lines to my
▣ 9 Oct[9]
   To CW Jr and Sarah: not relevant to Source Book
   To SW: Hetty Rutter thanks SW for remembering her. He should write to her
often. He should not follow the example of CW Jr and Sarah, who are 'naughty
children'. Hetty Rutter showed SW's letter [not preserved] to Mrs [Anne] Vigor,
whose illness has caused concern. It pleased her.

---

[7] Ltr is written in SW's childish handwriting style: every letter is printed.

[8] Ltr is a fragment with considerable text missing.

[9] Assigned to 1774 on the assumption that the illness of Mrs Vigor's mentioned
is the one that led to her death later that year (*see* Anne Chapman→CW,
24/11/1774).

William Boyce→SW   **28/10/1774?**
Barrington p 294   Dr Boyce's compliments and thanks to
date calculated from date of SW's oratorio *Ruth*[10]
   William Boyce [composer and organist, *bap*1711–1779] sends 'compliments
and thanks to his very ingenious brother-composer' SW for the gift of SW's
oratorio *Ruth*. Boyce will preserve the manuscript carefully as the 'most curious'
item in his musical library.

Anne Chapman→CW   **24/11/1774**
MA DDWes/2/78   I join with you in thinking that there are few
☐ 24/11/1774
   Mrs [Anne] Vigor has left legacies to members of the Wesley family, including
£15 to SW.

JW→CW   **2/6/1775**
MA DDWes/3/43; *T* v 6 p 152   I thought it strange that poor S. F. should
T
   SW 'will not only be better but quite well' if CW does not 'kill him with
kindness'.

Philip Hayes→CW   Charles St, Bristol   **30/6/1775**
MA DDWes/2/80   I am not a little glad to find
☐ 30/6/1775
   Philip Hayes [*bap*1738–1797, from 1777 professor of music at Oxford
University] reveres Handel's genius and music and hopes that SW, when he
reflects upon what passed between them regarding Handel, will readily forgive
Hayes. SW and Hayes should be friends; Hayes hopes 'by gentle degrees' to
shake SW's bigotry. Hayes wishes SW success in his study of Latin and will be
happy to meet the Wesleys again in Oxford or London.

---

[10] The last date in the manuscript of *Ruth* (BL Add 34997) is 26/10/1774.
Barrington p 294 reports CW's statement that SW, as soon as he finished *Ruth*,
sent it to Boyce, who replied immediately with this letter.

Daines Barrington→CW   **6/1776**
MA DDWes/1/86   I think myself much obliged to you
☞ docketed by CW 'June 1776'; date within month not known
Daines Barrington [lawyer and antiquary, 1727–1800] thanks CW for allowing
him to peruse CW's memoranda regarding CW Jr. They cannot but be
interesting to any lover of music, and show that no church or cathedral can be
supplied with so able an organist as CW Jr, the favourite disciple of [Joseph]
Kelway [organist and composer, 1702?–1782]. Barrington hopes that CW will
collect a similar lot of anecdotes about SW.[11]

Daines Barrington→SW   Chesterfield St   **21/6/1776**
Lightwood p 32   Mr Barrington desires that Master Wesley
Lightwood p 32
Barrington sends SW a parcel of music. It is unworthy of SW's acceptance but
Barrington would be very happy if a few bars of the music should please him.

SW→SGW   Guildford   **26/6/1776**
BL Add 35012 f 2ʳ   I intended to write yesterday
☞ 26/6/1776
SW did not write yesterday because Sarah and Miss Russell [presumably a
daughter of SW's host John Russell, printer, 1711–1804, later mayor of
Guildford] wrote.[12] SW is pleased with Guildford, although not with Mr
Russell's organ, and intends to start a fugue tomorrow on the subject that CW
sent with SW. He is much diverted with things in the house. He sends his 'duty'
to CW, his love to CW Jr and both to SGW.

SW→CW Jr   Guildford   **26/6/1776**
BL Add 35012 f 2ᵛ   Excuse my not writing yesterday
ltr written on verso of SW→SGW, 26/6/1776
SW apologises for not having written yesterday. They [SW, Sarah and
Prudence Box] took Harley [a dog] to Mr [John] Russell's house. SW carried out
his promise of singing a solo, which he quotes, by [Samuel] Arnold. Dinner was
almost finished when they arrived; their arrival was a surprise as they were not
expected until the next day. Prudence and Sarah send their 'duty' to CW and
SGW and their love to CW Jr.

---

[11] CW's account of SW was published in 1781 in *Barrington* p 291–298.

[12] John Russell's son John Russell R.A., 1745–1806, painted a portrait of SW
aged 10, i.e., about this time.

Elizabeth Waller→SGW   Guildford   **29/6/1776**

MA DDWF/22/51   I hope this will find my Dearest Sis[r], Brother, and Charles
▣ Sat 29 Jun={1771,1776,1782}; ltr says SGW, CW & CW Jr in Bristol[13]

Elizabeth Waller [SGW's sister] hopes that SGW, CW and CW Jr are now safe in Bristol. 'Sister Beck' [Rebecca Gwynne, 1724–1799, SGW's and Elizabeth Waller's sister] wrote [not preserved] to SGW the night before last [i.e., on 27/6/1776], saying that Lady Anne [Gatehouse, d1793] had advised that 'Sally and Sammy' [Sarah and SW] were 'well at Guildford'.

Sarah→SGW   Guildford   **30/6/1776**

GEU in box 2   I was exceedingly surpris'd when I open'd my
▣ Sun 30 Jun & Prudence Box alive→{1771,1776}[14]

'Sammy [SW] does not seem to have a wish beyond his enjoyment'. Almost every day he 'lets off a cannon' before breakfast; in the evening he lets off [fire] crackers. Sarah thinks that he attends more to fireworks than to his music and suggests that SGW 'hint' this to him without disclosing Sarah as her source. SW has written to CW [not preserved], telling him that SW played [music] to Lady [Anne] Gatehouse. She was 'very lavish with her encomiums' and said that Mr [John] Russell 'had not spoke half enough of his [SW's] genius'. Whoever hears SW 'is astonished', but 'it is a great favour' if people can get SW to play, even though 'the company' comes to where he is. Sarah thinks that SW would not play 'if he was not to be rewarded by gunpowder'. He 'has contracted a great intimacy' with the man who makes gunpowder and is continually after him to let some off. SW 'strictly remembers his promise' of not doing this himself. His appetite has improved.

Tomorrow [1/7/1776] SW is going to Mr [Martin] Madan [author and clergyman, 1725–1790, SW's godfather] with 'less reluctance' because 'Mr William' [William Russell, musician, 1755–1839, John Russell's son] is going with him. Prudence [Box], who follows SW 'wherever he goes' (although Sarah is sure that this tires her), also will accompany SW. SW joins Sarah 'in duty and love' to CW, SGW and CW Jr.

---

[13] Of these years only in 1776 do SW and Sarah appear to have been in Guildford while SGW, CW and CW Jr were in Bristol.

[14] Of these years only in 1776 do SW and Sarah appear to have been in Guildford while SGW was elsewhere.

CW Jr→Sarah   Guildford   **7/7/1776**
GEU in box 2   You are very good my dear Sally to excuse
🖃 7/7/1776

Mr [Thomas] Lediard and others whom CW Jr has seen in Bristol send love to
SW. Samuel Hemings, 'a principal performer at Kingsburys Vauxhall' who
'plays concerts on his own', visited CW Jr. In his next letter [not preserved], CW
Jr will send SW a bill of Hemings's 'grand performances'.

SGW→Sarah   Guildford   **15/7/1776**
MA DDWes/1/51   My dearest Sally's Letter I have just rec'd
🖃 Mon 15 July={1771,1776,1782}; Sarah at Mr Russell's; SGW in Bristol[15]

As little SW 'continues well' and makes himself so agreeable to his good
godfather [Martin Madan], CW has given leave for SW to spend a night at
Epsom [Madan's home].

Elizabeth Waller→SGW   Guildford   **16/7/1776**
MA DDWF/22/53   I should long ere this have answered my Dearest S[rs] kind
🖃 16 July[16]

Elizabeth Waller's son [Thomas Waller] recently heard from Sarah and SW at
Guildford. Both are well and happy. If they return to London before CW and
SGW return the Wallers will look after them. Prudence [Box] has been 'pretty
well'.

Thomas Waller→Sarah   Guildford   **17/7/1776**
MA DDWF/22/54   If I am ask'd a question it is my place you know
🖃 Wed 17 July={1771,1776}; Sarah at Mr Russell's, Guildford[17]

SW's letter [not preserved] was received gladly. His 'lady from Angola' [a pet
rabbit] has given birth. It is expected that SW will 'go on with the songs, as
Charles [CW Jr] is only to write an overture'.

CW has written [not preserved] to James Waller [1723?–1802, husband of
Elizabeth Waller], begging that he insure his house 'when Sam [SW] came to
town', for there was 'great fear' that it would be 'blown up with his fireworks'.

---

[15] Of these years only in 1776 do SW and Sarah appear to have been in
Guildford while SGW, CW and CW Jr were in Bristol.

[16] Assigned to 1776 because ltr says SW and Sarah are at Guildford and SGW is
in Bristol, and ltr mentions SW's letter to Thomas Waller also mentioned in
Thomas Waller to Sarah, 17/7/1776.

[17] Not >1776 because Thomas Waller died <20/7/1781 (Elizabeth Waller→
Sarah, 20/7/1781, MA DDWF/22/55). Assigned to 1776 because Sarah known
to be at Mr Russell's, Guildford then and not known to be there in July 1771.

Sarah→SGW   Guildford   **18/7/1776**

GEU in box 2   I have the Pleasure to inform my Dr Mama

☐ Thu 18 July={1771,1776,1782}[18]

Yesterday [17/7/1776] the son and daughter of Sir Fletcher Norton [1716–1789, speaker of the House of Commons] came to hear SW [in Guildford]. They were 'very much delighted'. An acquaintance of Dr [John] Worgan [who became Mus.Doc. at Cambridge in 1775] also was at the performance. This man, 'who seemed to be a judge of music', gave SW a subject [upon which to improvise] and was amazed 'to hear how he pursued it'. This man's surprise was 'not lessened' when he saw SW 'the moment he rose from the harpsichord go and play cricket with some other boys'. SW has 'got acquainted with the whole town'. 'Crowds' come to hear him.

SW has written to CW Jr [not preserved] and has 'sent him a bill of his [SW's] fireworks which Mr [John] Russell printed'. The bill was 'scattered over the town', resulting in 'a good assembly' at the fireworks exhibition, which 'was very well conducted'.

SGW→Sarah   **23/7/1776**

MA DDWF/21/2   I rejoyced to find by my dearest Sally's letter

☐ Tue 23 July, 1776 because ltr replies to Sarah→SGW, 18/7/1776

SGW received Sarah's letter [Sarah→SGW, 18/7/1776] on Sunday [21/7/1776] and supposes that Sarah and SW will be back in London when this letter arrives. SGW is very glad that SW's visit was of service to John Russell's profession [of printing] and that SW has given 'such universal satisfaction'. SGW hopes that when SW is in London he will not become 'acquainted with any boys in our neighbourhood': Sarah or Prudence [Box] must always accompany him. Sarah should tell Prudence that the box and table that belonged to her late mother [in Bristol] are now in SGW's possession.

Sarah→SGW   **27/7/1776**

GEU in box 2   Tuesday morning we left Guildford

☐ 27/7/1776

After having spent an agreeable month in Guildford, Sarah left [with SW and Prudence Box] on Tuesday morning [23/7/1776] and arrived at Epsom, where they were received 'in a very friendly manner' by Mr [Martin] Madan and his daughter [Anne Judith Madan] and 'civilly' by [his wife] Mrs [Jane] Madan. SW again exhibited [played music] 'to the great wonder and delight of all' his several hearers. Madan and his son [Martin Madan Jr, 1756–1809] entertained

---

[18] Assigned to 1776 because SW and Sarah known to be at Guildford then and not known to be there in 1771. Ltr answered by SGW→Sarah, 23/7/[1776], when Prudence Box was alive. 1782 and later years can be ruled out for ltr because Prudence Box then was no longer alive.

SW with 'fireworks and trap ball'. [Martin] Madan insisted that they stay until Thursday [25/7/1776]. They left early that morning and arrived in London that evening.

Today SW received a letter from Madan who says he will call on SW next Thursday [1/8/1776] and take him to play 'to some gentlemen out of town'. Madan will bring SW back to Madan's house in Knightsbridge. Sarah asks whether SGW approves of Madan's plan. Everyone says that SW 'looks much better'.

Sarah→SGW   5/8/1776?

GEU in box 4　　　　　　　　　　　I am commission'd by Aunt Beck to inform you
ltr undated; pmk (London) 5 August; pmk 'Bristol'[19]

Yesterday SW went to Mr Ashlin's [not identified] with Prudence [Box]. On Wednesday [presumably 7/8/1776], Mrs Footit has invited 'us' [Sarah and SW] to dinner. Miss Russell has written to Sarah on behalf of the Russell family, desiring that SGW be thanked for allowing 'our company' [i.e., Sarah and SW] at Guildford. 'Sammy [SW] was not fatigued by his journey with Mr [Martin] Madan to Walthamstow'. Madan says that SW 'is a great favourite at Epsom, especially of Miss Maria's'. She took as much care as SGW could have taken to ensure that he did not get 'tired with playing'.

SW and Sarah send regards to Bristol friends and 'duty and love' to CW, SGW and CW Jr. 'Aunt Beck' [Rebecca Gwynne] asks Sarah to say that SW has been 'very orderly' and that great care has been taken to ensure that he does not 'overheat himself'.

---

[19] Ltr addressed by Sarah to SGW at the New Room, Bristol. This address subsequently was crossed out and ltr was re-addressed to SGW at the Foundery, London, with a note in an unidentified hand saying 'Returned from Bristol'. The London and Bristol postmarks are presumed to reflect ltr's journey to Bristol rather than its return trip to London. Ltr <9/1/1777, the date of CW's 'Poem on the Death of Prudence Box' (MA Charles Wesley mss, in box V). Assigned to 1776 because ltr follows a visit by Sarah to Guildford and by SW to Epsom, and the only such visits known before 1777 are the visits of 6–7/1776 documented in the preceding letters. This dating is consistent with Sarah→SGW, 27/7/1776, which reports Madan's desire to take SW out of town on 1/8/1776 to play music, and with CW, SGW and CW Jr being in Bristol while SW, Sarah and Prudence Box were in London.

Sarah→SW   8–12/1776

GEU in box 2   Thy Letter was not bad—but let me remonstrate to Thee
ltr undated[20]

SW's letter [not preserved] was 'not bad' but Sarah decries his conduct. Why
did he permit her to depart without offering his hand or his wishes? Did he
'sulkily and angrily turn the back' of his 'dirty scarlet coat' to her because his
'George and Dragon' [toys] were too large 'to be put in crammed pockets'? SW
also erred by commenting on CW Jr's repetition of Sarah's words.

SW knows 'the pleasures of Guildford': 'Jacky' Russell talks courageously of
fireworks but leaves it to Bennet [not identified] to 'let them off'. SW should
give Sarah's love to Mariane [not identified] if he sees her. He should present
Sarah's 'dues' to SGW, to Sarah's aunts and to Miss [Armine] Dyer, Prudence
[Box] and Nanny. 'Love and Innocence' [presumably two birds] are with SW;
he should be careful of them because they are Sarah's. He should 'teach them to
sing and answer them'. If SW is not angry he should write to Sarah again. He
knows that she is his sister; she is also his friend.

SW→Prudence Box   Charles St, Bristol   8–12/1776

Fitzwm ltr 2   I receiv'd your Letter a few days ago
>5/8/1776;[21] before Prudence Box's death about 9/1/1777

SW received Prudence Box's letter [not preserved] a few days ago. SGW did
not intend to change Prudence's room: she may sleep in the same [Chesterfield
Street] room as when they were in London [where they were in late July 1776
after visiting Guildford and Epsom, and where Prudence is now]. 'We' [SW,
SGW and Sarah] hope to come [from Bristol] to London soon. SW is 'quite sick'
of Bristol.

SGW will send [to London] the large box that belonged to Prudence Box's
mother [which passed after her death to SGW, *see* SGW→Sarah, 23/7/1776].
SW will bring [to London] books belonging to Prudence or to her [late] mother,
including [*The Life of*] *Nicholas Mooney* [an account of a highwayman executed
in Bristol in 1752], a 'physick book' and hymnbooks.

SW is about to fly a kite with a 'young gentleman'. He hopes that all his family
are well. He sends his love to Dr [Thomas Griffin] Tarpley and to Dr [Samuel]
Arnold, and asks how Mrs [Mary Ann] Arnold is.

---

[20] Ltr >25/7/1776 when SW and Sarah returned to London from Guildford and
Epsom (*see* Sarah→SGW, 27/7/1776) as no earlier travel of SW to Guildford is
known, and presumably >Sarah→SGW, 5/8/1776?, as SW and Sarah then were
still together in London. Ltr <Prudence Box's death on 9/1/1777.

[21] >23/7/1776 when SGW possessed Prudence Box's mother's box in Bristol
(*see* SGW→Sarah, 23/7/1776); >25/7/1776 when SW and Prudence Box
returned to London from Guildford and Epsom (*see* Sarah→SGW, 27/7/1776);
and >5/8/1776 when SW and Prudence Box were still in London (*see*
Sarah→SGW, 5/8/1776?).

Gustav Adam von Nolcken→CW   1/1777
MA DDWes/7/74   Baron Nolcken present his compliments
▣ Tuesday; docketed 'January 1777'; hence 7, 14, 21 or 28 Jan 1777
  Baron [Gustav Adam von] Nolcken [1733–1812, ambassador of Sweden] asks
if he may bring three ladies of his acquaintance with him tomorrow morning: the
Dowager Lady Essex [Elizabeth Capell, *d*1784, widow of William Capell, 1697–
1743, 3rd Earl of Essex] and the two Ladies Capell [presumably her daughters].
In consequence of von Nolcken's account of 'Master Wesley's [SW's] masterly
and surprising performance' they very much wish to hear him.

Mary Bertie→Daines Barrington   23/2/1777
MA DDWes/1/87   The Dutchess of Ancaster presents her compts
▣ Sunday[22]
  The Duchess of Ancaster [Mary Bertie, 1743–1804], is obliged to Barrington
for the amusement she has received on reading the account of 'the two young
gentlemen' [CW Jr and SW]. She thanks Barrington for arranging a musical
performance by them.

Daines Barrington→CW   24/2/1777
MA DDWes/1/87   Mr B presents his Compts to Mr Wesley
▣ Mon 24 Feb={1772,1777,1783}[23]
  Barrington apologises to CW for sending the 'two accounts' [of CW Jr and
SW] to the Duchess of Ancaster [Mary Bertie]. He received these accounts last
Saturday [22/2/1777] and will try to bring them with him on Friday next
[28/2/1777], when he will introduce Messrs Musgrave and Davies. Mr
Southwell [possibly Edward Southwell, 1738–1777, from 1763 to 1776 MP for
Gloucestershire] also will be there.
  The Bishop of Oxford [Robert Lowth, 1710–1787] has recommended SW to
the Bishop of London [Richard Terrick, 1710–1777] as 'a singing boy
extraordinary'. Barrington understands that this recommendation has the support
of the Bishop of Durham [John Egerton, 1721–1787]. It will leave SW's
education wholly in the hands of CW. However, Barrington can waive the
proposal on the grounds that he has not consulted sufficiently with CW. Lord
Kelly [Thomas Alexander Erskine, composer, 1732–1781, 6th Earl of Kelly] has
apparently mentioned CW Jr and SW by name at his concerts. The scheme of the
Queen's concert 'will never do' [for SW], as the 'grown musicians' will never
admit a child amongst them.

---

[22] Assigned to 23/2/1777 because ltr written on the same page as Daines
Barrington→CW, 24/2/1777 (a Monday), and Barrington says in that letter that
he received the accounts he sent to Lady Tryphena Bathurst on 22/2/1777.

[23] Assigned to 1777 because ltr >Barrington→CW, 15/6/1776, where Barrington
seeks CW's account of SW, and <1783, because the Earl of Kelly died in 1781.

CW→Sarah   11/10/1777
MA DDCW/7/40   I greatly miss you here, yet comfort myself
☞ 11/10/1777
Unless CW Jr makes more haste, SW 'will overtake him in Latin'.

Samuel Johnson→Hester Lynch Thrale   10/11/1777
Hyde; *Redford* v 3 p 94–96   And so supposing that I might come to town
Redford corrects ☞ 10/10/1777 to 10/11/1777 from ref. to Lord Mayor's Day
Samuel Johnson [lexicographer, 1709–1784] did not see the Lord Mayor's show today but saw 'Miss Wesley [Sarah] and her brothers [CW Jr and SW]'. Sarah 'sends her compliments' to Hester Lynch Thrale [author and hostess, 1741–1821, *later* Mrs Piozzi].

Thomas Waller→Sarah   21/11/1777
MA DDWF/22/62   Your unexpected billet came safe to hand
☞ Fri 21 Nov={1766,1777,1783}[24]
Dr [Samuel] Arnold and members of the Wesley and Waller families spent an evening with Dr Lloyd's family [not identified], when CW Jr and SW played [music] and the doctor sang with SGW.

Tryphena Bathurst→SW   26/1/1778?
MA DDWes/7/50   Lady Tryphena Bathurst's compts to
☞ 26 Jan; docketed 1777, presumably an incorrect year[25]
Lady Tryphena Bathurst [*b*1760, daughter of Henry 2nd Earl Bathurst, Lord Chancellor] thanks SW for his sonatas [presumably for a printed copy of SW's *Eight Sonatas for the Harpsichord or Pianoforte*, op. 1, published in late 1777]. She will take 'very great pleasure in learning them'.

---

[24] Not 1766 because of ref. to SW playing and singing. Not 1783 because Thomas Waller died in 1781.

[25] Assigned, with some diffidence, to 1778 for the following reason. Ltr presumed to refer to a printed copy rather than a manuscript copy of SW's sonatas, and to SW's op. 1 sonatas, the only SW sonatas published in the 1770s. The title-page of this publication states its availability at Welcker's music shop at 10 Haymarket, where John Welcker removed 'near the end of 1777' (*H&S* p 326). Ltr assigned to 26/1/1778 in accordance with Daines Barrington's report that these sonatas 'appeared in 1777, about the same time' as SW's 'portrait was engraved', i.e., William Dickinson's engraving dated 26/1/1778 of the 1776 portrait of SW by John Russell, R.A. (*Barrington* p 306–307). It seems plausible that Lady Tryphena Bathurst obtained SW's sonatas soon after they were published rather than a year or more later. However, evidence ruling out the possibility that ltr was written in a later year has not been found.

Philip Hayes→CW   **15/6/1778**

MA DDWes/7/65   I was favour'd with yours by our friend
☑ 15/6/1778

   Hayes regrets that too many of the musical profession 'judge and think very
narrowly', and sometimes uncharitably, of rising merit. His 'young friends' CW
Jr and SW need not be dismayed at 'some few idle remarks'. Hayes has always
mentioned their 'shining abilities' in 'the highest terms' and will continue to do
so. They have his best wishes not only for their publications but through life.
Hayes wishes that he had the power of patronage to convince CW of the
sincerity of his professions; CW should 'take the will for the deed' if Hayes is
unable to do as much as he would wish. Hayes will endeavour 'with much
pleasure' to dispose of their productions, which merit the notice of the public.
Mr Green [not identified] has left Hayes another book of SW's 'lessons' [i.e.,
another copy of SW's *Eight Sonatas*, op. 1]. 'Want of recollection' caused
Hayes not to ask for a few more copies when he was in London. These may now
be supplied whenever CW thinks proper.

CW→SGW   Guildford   **18/8/1778**

MA DDCW/7/34   I served West-Street Chappel yesterday afternoon
☑ 17/8/1778; the portion concerning SW written 'Tuesday' [18/8/1778]
   CW reminds SGW to ensure that SW goes riding every day [in Guildford].
CW's 'scholars' [CW Jr, Sarah and SW] also should keep at their Latin so that
they can make progress before CW returns [from Bristol, to where he is
travelling]. SGW or CW Jr or Sarah or SW may write to CW by every post. If
SGW can get franks, more than one of them may write at a time.

CW→Sarah & SGW   Guildford   **26–27/8/1778**

MA DDCW/1/68   *To Sarah:*   When Sam answers my last I shall write
                 To SGW: Guildford I perceive agrees with you all
☑ 26/8–27/8/1778
   To Sarah: When SW answers CW's last letter [not preserved], CW will write
to him again.
   To SGW: CW perceives that all his family find Guildford agreeable but is sorry
that SW has neglected his riding. CW has no objections to his family staying in
Guildford for a fourth week if the Russells agree. He asks if his 'three scholars'
[CW Jr, Sarah and SW] have read through the best part of the [Latin] grammar
and whether SW has written the solo [not identified] for his godfather [Martin
Madan]. If not, CW once more desires that SW does this.

Thomas Waller→Sarah 3/9/1778?

MA DDWF/22/63 This afternoon I had design'd for writing to you

⌨ 'Thursday 3[d],[26]

SW 'is entertaining himself at home God knows how' while SGW and CW Jr are in town getting food. While writing this letter, Thomas Waller was roused by the noise of horses and saw, through a window, SW 'on little gray', attended by his squire Jos[eph] on a cart horse.

CW→SGW & CW Jr Terriers[27] 7/9/1778

MA DDCW/7/36   *To SGW:*   I rode with my brother in his chaise
                To CW Jr: Send me a letter in the enclosed frank

⌨ 5–7/9/1778; passages concerning SW in 7/9/1778 portion of ltr

To SGW: SW 'will have many more escapes'. He will have great trials, 'but the Lord will deliver him out of all'; he 'wants more pains to be taken with him'. If CW does not live to help SW the duty will devolve entirely to SGW. If she makes SW 'a living Christian' he 'will never wish to be a dead Papist'.

To CW Jr: CW Jr should give CW's love to all 'our family' [the family of SGW's sister Elizabeth Waller] at Terriers and should look out for an opportunity of visiting 'his Lordship' [Garret Wesley, Mus. Doc., 1st Earl of Mornington and Viscount Wellesley (1735–1781), *see* CW→SGW, 10/9/1778].[28] CW Jr may 'get a scholar by it'. SW should go too, 'in gratitude as well as interest', and should oblige Garret Wesley 'to the best of his power'.

SGW tells CW that SW 'is very seriously inclined'. CW Jr and Sarah must make CW more satisfied in this respect [by becoming more seriously inclined themselves].

---

[26] Assigned, with considerable uncertainty, to Thursday 3/9/1778, chiefly on the grounds of SW's riding a little horse (CW→SGW, 26–27/8/1778, complained that SW has neglected his riding, and CW→SGW, 10/9/1778 says 'by all means' get SW his little horse); also, this is a time when SGW, CW Jr and SW could have been with the Wallers (as they were the following week at Terriers) while CW and Sarah were elsewhere. No reason has been found to suggest that ltr was written on other Thursdays on the 3rd of a month prior to Thomas Waller's death on 11/5/1781, but alternative dates for ltr have not been ruled out absolutely.

[27] Near High Wycombe.

[28] CW and Garret Wesley were distantly related. See *Stevenson MWF* p xi–xxiii and 387–388, and Stevenson's accompanying 'Pedigree of the Wesley Family'.

Sarah→SGW   Terriers   **7/9/1778**
GEU in box 5   Saturday Morning I sent John from the Foundry
⌨ Mon 7 Sep & pmk<1787→{1772,1778}[29]
  In her imagination, Sarah hears CW Jr in High Wycombe 'launching out in
praise of the woods, while sober Samuel [SW] regards them in silence, and
searches for a proper place for cricket'. She sends affection to CW Jr and to SW,
who should write to her at Wimbledon.

Garret Wesley→CW   **8/9/1778?**
WBRR v 3 (Oct 1851) p 363[30]   ...After saying so much about myself
Quoted in CW→SGW, 10/9/1778, apparently as recently received
  CW is right to have changed his plan to have Garret Wesley's 'two young
friends' [CW Jr and SW] introduced to 'a certain musical gentleman' [according
to *WBRR*, King George III]. 'Their merit will make its own way', and on a much
surer footing, if it is done independently [of royal patronage]. Garret Wesley
hopes that CW will live to see this, and assures CW of his great interest in and
desire to assist CW Jr's and SW's 'success in life'.

CW→SGW   **10/9/1778**
WBRR v 3 (Oct 1851) p 363–64[31]   Your welcome letter last night refreshed me
WBRR
  CW supposes that SW took a copy of Miss [Anne Judith] Madan's lessons 'to
make one of his new set'. [Martin] Madan fears that the solo that SW composed
for him [*see* CW→SGW, 26/8/1778] may be too hard for him. SW will consider
this. SW's ability to tune [musical instruments] is 'a valuable acquisition'. 'By
all means get Sammy [SW] his little horse'. SW prefers London to all other
places, perhaps because he is able to attend 'the rehearsal concerts'. The
Wesleys 'shall never more keep house in Bristol'. CW knows that SGW will be
pleased with the response from 'his Lordship' [Garret Wesley→ CW, 8/9/1778?]
and expects to hear from Sarah at Wimbledon.

---

[29] Assigned to 1778 because SW then at Terriers and Sarah about to go to
Wimbledon where she was in September 1778 (*see* CW→SGW, 10/9/1778).

[30] *WBRR* prints only an extract of this letter.

[31] *WBRR* prints only an extract of this letter.

CW→Sarah   **16/9/1778**
MA DDWes/4/26   Both my dear Sally's letters I have receiv'd
pmk 17/9 (so assumed to have been written from Bristol on 16/9)[32]
  Sarah should not regret the loss of the family house in Bristol. It was not
earning them money, SW and CW Jr do not have time to visit Bristol, SW has
no love for Bristol, and SGW will not leave London as long as her family are
there.

CW→SGW   **23/9/1778**
MA DDCW/7/35   Mr Cruger dined with us at Mr Lediard's.
◨ 22/9/1778 (a Tuesday); portion relevant to SW dated 'Wednesday'
  If CW and SGW live to 'see another summer' they should allow SW 'a whole
week at least' at Oxford. CW acquits Mr Chouquet [not identified, a friend of the
Waller family[33]] of 'any design' but is 'persuaded that his agreeable company
and conversation' gave SW 'his unhappy turn to P' [presumably, to Popery]. It is
time 'to shut the stable doors'. SW should be left free to write when he chooses.
'His music will recommend itself'.

CW→Sarah   **1/10/1778**
MA DDCW/7/41   Your friends and ours at the Common have
◨ 1/10/1778
  CW Jr has 'a turn to generosity', SW 'to parsimony'.

CW→SGW   **5/10/1778**
MA DDWes/4/59   My dear partner will be anxious to hear more
portion relevant to SW dated 'Monday' follows part of ltr dated Thu 1 Oct[34]
  SW 'by and by' may hear CW Jr and himself on St Catherine's organ 'for want
of Dr W' [perhaps a reference to Dr John Worgan, but a connection between him
and such an organ has not been identified].

---

[32] Assigned to 1778 because CW at Mr Lediard's near Bristol and Sarah at Rev.
Mr Bankes's at Wimbledon, where they appear to have been simultaneously
only in 1778 (as evidenced in CW→SGW, 23/9/1778 and CW→Sarah,
1/10/1778).

[33] Chouquet is mentioned in Thomas Waller→Sarah, 17/7/1776 and 14/9/1779?.

[34] Thurs & 1 Oct={1767,1772,1778}; assigned to 1778 because ltr mentions the
forthcoming marriage of Miss [Charlotte Sophia] Worgan (daughter of John
Worgan) to 'the singer Parsons' [later Dr Sir William Parsons], which took
place on 21/11/1778.

Edward Walpole→CW Chesterfield St **3/11/1778**
MA DDWes/7/83 I send you my small Performance
▣ 3/11/1778

Sir Edward Walpole [1706–1784, son of Prime Minister Sir Robert Walpole] encloses an anthem that he composed. He hopes that the Wesleys will receive it favourably and also that it will please the public if CW Jr and SW instruct 'the organist of their chapel' [to perform it]. CW Jr and SW are the 'the most extraordinary geniuses' that Walpole has met with, and their approbation of his music greatly honours him. If any of his compositions can be of use to them he will gladly send the music for them to copy. He wishes to see them again before long so that he may hear them play, preferably 'subjects of their own' rather than Walpole's 'dull heavy things'.

CW→Edward Walpole Chesterfield St **3/11/1778**
MA DDWes/7/83 You have the thanks of this House—of my Sons especially
▣ 3/11/1778

Replying to Edward Walpole→CW, 3/11/1778, CW expresses the thanks of his family—especially of CW Jr and SW—for Walpole's 'present to the Magdalen' [a charitable hospital and associated chapel for the relief and reformation of unfortunate women and penitent prostitutes]. CW Jr and SW have made a copy of Walpole's hymns and would appreciate a copy of his anthem. A 'proof of their natural turn to music' is that they have 'so readily' discovered Walpole's musicality. They, and CW, will be very happy to be 'farther acquainted' with him.

CW→William Russell **21/12/1778**
SMU We were quite tantalized by a glimpse of you
▣ 21/12/1778

CW and his family enjoyed glimpsing William Russell when he was in London and hope to see him when he comes 'for another [musical] instrument'. CW is sorry that Russell cannot avail himself of his 'two musical friends' [CW Jr and SW]. If Russell finds the time they 'will find instruction' which will make Russell master of his art. CW Jr wants Russell to send him an account of the 'gains' he receives 'by bespeaking [musical] instruments for others'. Russell buys instruments from [the firm of] Kirkman at a 'master's price'. CW asks Russell to send the prices 'of different instruments'. If Baker Harris [maker of musical instruments, *fl*1740–1780] 'will not make nearly the same allowance' as Kirkman, CW Jr may 'change his harpsichord-makers'.

Russell will be pleased to hear that CW Jr and SW propose 'to have every other Thursday at their own house' [in Chesterfield Street] 'an entertainment of their own music'. They desire 14 subscribers who will be charged £3/3/- for six nights [of music], which will start at 7 pm precisely.

The first concert will take place on 14/1/1779. The 'plan of the first night' includes, in the first act, music by CW Jr, Lord Mornington [Garret Wesley] and

SW's 'extempore on harpsichord'; the second act includes music by CW Jr and Handel, 'organ extempore' performances by SW and by CW Jr, a 'violin solo, composed and performed by' SW, and a performance by CW Jr and SW of a 'duet for two organs, composed by' CW Jr.

CW and his family 'join in love and respect' to Russell's father [John Russell] and to every branch of Russell's family.

CW memorandum   Chesterfield St   **about 14/1/1779**

MA DDWes/4/65   My reasons for letting my sons have a concert
Docketed by CW 'reasons for the concert Jan 14 1779'[35]

CW sets out four reasons for allowing CW Jr and SW to have 'a concert at home': (1) to keep them out of harm's way—i.e., of 'bad music and bad musicians' who might 'corrupt both their taste and their morals'; (2) that they might have a 'safe and honourable opportunity of availing themselves of their musical abilities', which have cost CW 'several hundred pounds': (3) that they may 'enjoy their full right of private judgement' and their 'independency', both of which must be given up 'if they swim with the stream and follow the multitude'; and (4) to improve their play and their skill in composing, the areas in which they may excel. CW Jr and SW do not presume 'to rival the present great masters who excel in the variety of their accompaniments' but aim, in their concert music, only at 'exactness'.

CW→JW   **23/4/1779**

AM v 12 (July 1789) p 386–388   By this time I presume you have read mine
AM

CW is 'clear without a doubt' that his sons' concert is 'after the will and order of Providence' [JW comments that he is 'clear of another mind'] and is confident that he has established them as musicians in 'a safe and honourable way'. The Bishop [Robert Lowth, who became Bishop of London in 1778] informed CW Jr and SW that he never heard any music he liked as well, and promises CW Jr five scholars next winter.

SW 'cherishes and recommends' a 'musical child from Norwich' [Crotch] and has sent him 'many customers', from whom Crotch's mother gets £10 a day.[36] Crotch has played before 'their Majesties' [King George III and Queen Charlotte]. CW and SGW neither envy Crotch's 'gains' or 'honours' nor regret that they 'did not make a show or advantage' of their 'two swans' [CW Jr and

---

[35] 14/1/1779 was the date of the first CW Jr/SW concert at Chesterfield Street. This memorandum presumably was written about then.

[36] Daines Barrington's 'Some account of little Crotch' (published in 1781 in *Barrington* p 311–325) is based partly on information provided by 'master Wesley' [SW], who tested Crotch's musical abilities and 'takes little Crotch much under his protection' (p 313–314).

SW]. If CW were to 'venture them into the world' they could make their fortunes, but he never wishes them to be rich. JW's and CW's father [Samuel Wesley Sr, clergyman and poet, 1662–1735, from 1695 rector of Epworth] neglected every opportunity to sell JW's and CW's souls 'to the devil'.

Edward Walpole→CW   7/1779
MA DDWes/1/90
▣ docketed by CW 'July 1779'; date within month not known
   Much as Walpole loves music and admires the abilities and performance of CW Jr and SW, he greatly prefers 'the acquaintance and conversation of a man of sense, virtue, and learning' to any other gratification. It was to CW and not to his sons (whom he nonetheless wishes to meet) that Walpole 'paid court' in his letter of last September [not preserved]. He found CW, on their first meeting, to be a 'plain dealing, sensible, good man', and he coveted CW's acquaintance. Walpole will be glad to see CW next Friday afternoon. Walpole also invites CW to visit with CW Jr and SW some morning when convenient. CW Jr and SW will see that Walpole has written 'several melodies to words with expression' but is 'very unfinished as to putting parts together'. He is 'by no means a master of composition'.

Rebecca Gwynne→SGW   Brecon   26/8/1779
MA DDWes/7/28   I rejoiced to hear of my Dearest Sister
▣ 26/8/1779
   Rebecca Gwynne rejoiced to hear that SGW and her family arrived safely at Brecon [Wales]. Their travel via the Hereford road must have been a pleasant surprise to [Joan Gwynne] Price [SGW's sister, 1728–1801]. Rebecca Gwynne hopes that SW 'is pleased with his situation, and receives benefit by change of air' [from London, where it appeared that he might become ill, *see* CW→John Langshaw, 26/10/1779].

Thomas Waller→Sarah & CW Jr   **14/9/1779?**
MA DDWF/22/64   I write now, tho you will not have it till this day week
☞ Tue 14th[37]
Thomas Waller is pleased to learn from SGW's letter that the Wesley family are well, 'not excepting' SW.

CW→John Langshaw   Chesterfield St   **26/10/1779**
GEU W/L; *Wainwright* p 40–41   Last Saturday we visited our house in peace
☞ 26/10/1779
After a 'long ramble of 11 weeks, mostly through Wales', CW and his family [including SW] returned [to London] last Saturday [23/10/1779]. CW tells Langshaw [organist, *c*1724–1798] that when SW left London he 'was threatened with a consumption', but 'constant riding has been the appointed means of his recovery'.

Anne Gatehouse→Sarah   **7/11/1779**
MA DDWF/26/50   here are 2 letters arrived for you
☞ 7 Nov; ltr says next Thursday is the 11th[38]
Lady [Anne] Gatehouse can receive Sarah 'any day after next Thursday' [11/11/1779]. If SW chooses to come with Sarah 'and would lay along with' [i.e., share the same bed as] CW Jr, Lady Gatehouse could accommodate all of them. She would be 'extremely glad' to have SW's company.

---

[37] Assigned to Tuesday 14/9/1779 for the following reasons: (1) Thomas Waller's respects are to be given to 'Mrs and Miss Pryce', presumably Joan (wife of the Rev. Hugh) Price and her daughter, whom the Wesleys visited en route to Wales (*see* Rebecca Gwynne→SGW of 26/8/1779) and presumably would visit on their return trip. (CW→Langshaw of 26/10/1779 says that CW and his family have just returned to Chesterfield Street after a ramble of 11 weeks, mostly in Wales.) (2) Ltr specifically mentions SW's health, and CW→Langshaw of 26/10/1779 states that SW was threatened with consumption when leaving London in August. (3) Ltr states that the Wallers continue to take evening walks despite the cold weather. This suggests a date following the warmest summer months; 14 September fits this description.

[38] Thurs & 11 Nov={1773,1779,1784}. Ltr presumably >1773 because Sarah then was only 14 and <Anne Gatehouse→ Sarah, 9/7/1783? (written no earlier than 9/7/1781), which says that SW does not approve of sleeping with CW Jr. Also, CW→Sarah of 17/11/1779 (MA DDWes/4/67) is addressed to Sarah at Lady Gatehouse's Guildford house. Therefore ltr assigned to 1779.

Brownlow Cecil→CW Jr & SW   Chesterfield St   **24/5/1780**
MA Letters Chiefly to Wesleys v 2 ltr 83   Ld Exeters compliments to Messrs
🖃 24/5/1780
  Brownlow Cecil [1724–1793, 9th Earl of Exeter] sends his compliments to
CW Jr and SW and desires to subscribe to their concerts next winter.

CW→Sarah   Chesterfield St   **8/6/1780**
MA DDCW/1/71   I have but a minute for writing. We are all well
🖃 8 Jun; assigned to 1780 because ltr presumed to refer to Gordon Riots
  CW has only a minute to write. SGW is 'not yet frightened out of her wits' [on
account of the Gordon Riots]. Last night she sheltered CW Jr and SW at Sarah's
aunt's, and sat up to guard them. SGW wishes to 'fly' to Wales. CW offers to
send SGW and SW to Bristol; CW Jr will stay with CW. Matters here [in
London] are 'in a dreadful situation'; Sarah is 'happily out of their reach'.

Garret Wesley→CW   **11/6/1780**
MA DDWes/1/91   I thought I should never find a quiet moment
🖃 11/6/1780
  Garret Wesley would love to 'transport' CW Jr and SW to his Irish home
[Dangan Castle] for an hour 'to get a few extempores' on his organ. He
considers it equal to any organ of its type that he has heard.

SGW→Sarah   **28/6/1780?**
MA DDWF/21/4   My dearest Sally's Packet came to hand
🖃 Wed 28 Jun={1775,1780,1786}; Sarah in Bristol[39]
  CW will write soon. SW also is 'employing his pen'.

SGW→Edward Walpole   **14/10/1780**
MA DDWes/7/22   Permit me, Honor'd Sir, to return my most grateful
🖃 14/10/1780
  CW and SGW are grateful for Edward Walpole's kindness, and especially for
his patronage of CW Jr and SW.

---

[39] Not 1775 because CW then in Bristol (*see* Philip Hayes→CW, 30/6/1775);
assigned to 1780 because Sarah known to have been in Bristol then, but 1786
has not been ruled out.

Robert Bremner→CW   18/11/1780
MA DDWes/7/110   I expect to have every note of the Concertos engraved
☞ docketed 18/11/1780
  Robert Bremner [music publisher, c1713–1789] expects that CW Jr's concertos
will be fully engraved by next week. CW should tell 'that ruffian Sam' [SW] that
Bremner will visit him soon, bearing a sword and 'determined to cut off any part
of his bow hand elbow that gets behind his back when he fiddles'.

JW journal entry   Chesterfield St   25/1/1781
Curnock v 6 p 303–304   I spent an agreeable hour at a concert
Curnock
  JW 'spent an agreeable hour' today at CW Jr's and SW's concert but was 'a
little' out of his element among 'lords and ladies'. JW 'loves plain music and
plain company best'.[40]

Edward Walpole→CW Jr?[41]   6/2/1781
Methodist Recorder 16/2/1899 p 13   You have made me a present
Methodist Recorder
  Walpole values the present [of a musical composition]. He expects that 'the
concerto' will make 'a great figure' in public, will do the composer much
honour, and will sound well in the composer's hands as he makes the most
difficult passages appear easy. In the composer's allegros 'the conduct of the two
hands' in many places requires such precision that 'the great players' have been
'tried'. The recipient has shown his strength 'as a writer [composer] and
performer'. Walpole likes the composer giving 'so large a part to the hautboy
with the organ in proper keys', as they will 'unite finely'. The musical world
probably will be indebted some day to CW Jr, and Walpole hopes equally to
SW, for many fine hymns.

---

[40] JW also attended two subsequent CW Jr/SW concerts, on 20/2/1783 and
29/1/1784 (attendance lists in the concert registers—*see* note to Chronology
entry for 14/1/1779; *Lightwood* p 53).

[41] CW Jr is proposed as the recipient, rather than SW as stated in the *Methodist
Recorder*, because CW Jr's *6 Concertos for the organ*, op. 2 (c1791), includes
an accompaniment for '2 hautboys', and no organ concertos by SW are known
to have been written before 1787, after Edward Walpole's death in 1784.

John Egerton→CW Jr & SW   Chesterfield St   **23/4/1781**
MA DDWes/1/93   The Bishop of Durham presents his Compliments
🖅 23 Apr; docketed 23/4/1781
'Want of health' precludes John Egerton, the Bishop of Durham, from attending CW Jr's and SW's next concert. However, he looks forward to subscribing to their concerts next winter.

CW→John Langshaw   **1/7/1781**
GEU W/L; *Wainwright* p 50   I had given my Letter to Jack
🖅 1 Jul & >1/7/1780[42] & <1/7/1782[43]→🖃
CW has not seen the [*Gentleman's*] *Magazine* [v 51 (April 1781), which on p 176–78 reviews Daines Barrington's *Miscellanies* and alludes to Barrington's account of CW Jr and SW as infant prodigies], but one effect of it will be to set 'the professors' upon CW Jr and SW 'to tear them in pieces'.

CW→John Langshaw   Chesterfield St   **22/12/1781**
GEU W/L; *Wainwright* p 56   Read Fabricius's most excellent Letters
🖅 22/12/1781
CW Jr and SW are 'busy, preparing for their concert' [the fourth series of Chesterfield St concerts, beginning 31/1/1782]. They do not expect to earn from the concerts 'much more than reputation and increase of skill'. CW need not tell Langshaw 'the hearts of the professors' towards CW Jr and SW, and does not want them 'to make more haste to be rich'. People should wish for no more 'than content with food and raiment'.

William Kingsbury→SW   **24/1/1782**
MA DDWes/7/115   I am greatly obliged to you for the Trouble
🖅 24 Jan; docketed 1782 by CW
William Kingsbury [an early violin teacher of SW, *d*1782] thanks SW for the care he has taken about the violin. Kingsbury has not 'a penny in the world' and would be grateful to receive the offered money and watch. He is cruelly treated where he is now [in a poorhouse]. He sends love to all his friends at the Wesley home.[44]

---

[42] Ltr mentions advertisements of CW Jr's concertos which were not published before November 1780 (*see* Robert Bremner→CW, 18/11/1780).

[43] George Langshaw, who was alive when ltr written, died on 23/5/1782 (*Wainwright*, p 51).

[44] Kingsbury died shortly after writing ltr. SW's song 'And is he then set free?', written 'on the death of Mr William Kingsbury', is dated 24/1/1782.

Elizabeth Waller→SGW   **24/3/1782**
MA DDWes/7/92   I have long wished to have thank'd my dearest Sisr
⊡ 24 Mar; 1782 from ref. in ltr to Elizabeth Waller's 'late heavy trial'[45]
Elizabeth Waller sends her love to SGW's children and hopes that SW 'has
found benefit of the blister'.

Anne Gatehouse→Sarah   Chesterfield St   **9/7/1782?**
MA DDWF/26/49   Mr Pollen return'd to his amiable Wife & family
pmk 9 Jul[46]
Mr and Mrs Pollen [presumably the Rev. George Pollen and his wife] will be
glad to have CW and SGW at their house [in Guildford]. Lady Anne Gatehouse
unfortunately cannot accommodate all the Wesleys; however, 'the day must
bring us all together constantly' and all the Wesleys are to dine with her. Sarah's
room will be in the same place, and a 'tent bed' or room can be found for CW Jr.
SW 'will not approve of sleeping with' CW Jr, 'so the Russells can furnish him'
with a room; alternatively, Mrs Pollen can accommodate Sarah, and CW Jr and
SW can stay with Lady Gatehouse. CW Jr and SW should not forget 'to bring
any music' they choose 'to perform here'. Mr [James] Price [alchemist, 1752–
1783] begins his lectures on Saturday evening.

CW→CW Jr   Guildford   **23/7/1782?**
MA DDWes/4/19   As soon as you receive this get T or J Russel to take 3 places
⊡ 'Tuesday night Marybone'; pmk (London) 24 July[47]
When CW Jr gets this letter he should have one of the Russells book three
places in Monday's coach [from Guildford to London]. CW Jr should give 2/6 to
Mr Pollen's manservant and should instruct SW to give 1/- to each of the maids.

---

[45] Her son Thomas Waller died in July 1781.

[46] Ltr < James Price's 3/8/1783 death, but not before 1781 when Price (who was
born James Higginbotham) assumed the name 'Price'. No visit or planned visit
by the Wesleys to Guildford in July 1781 is known. CW Jr and SW appear to
have been in Guildford in July 1782 (*see* CW→CW Jr, 23/7/1782?). A proposed
visit by the Wesleys to Guildford in 1783 involving Gatehouse and Pollen is
mentioned in Price→SW of 28/7/1783. No reason has been found to prefer 1782
to 1783 as the year of ltr, which accordingly has been entered ambiguously
under both dates.

[47] As ltr was written on Tuesday night it presumably was posted from London
on Wednesday 24 July, a date which occurred in 1771, 1776 and 1782. 1776 can
be ruled out because, although SW was in Guildford up to 23/7/1776, CW Jr
was not there with him (*see* Sarah→SGW, 27/7/1776 and preceding letters). Ltr
assigned to 1782 because CW refers in it to CW Jr as a 'man of fashion', a
designation that seems more appropriate to 1782 than to 1771, when CW Jr was
only 13 years old.

Sarah→SGW   Chesterfield St   **24/8/1782**

GEU in box 4   My dear Mothers few lines made us all happy

▣ 24 Aug[48]

SW's head is 'so much better' that he needs 'neither plaister nor todannil'
[perhaps tetanine, a former name for strychnine]. He has not yet removed his old
plaster but does not want to put on another 'and is in every respect well'. Sir
Joseph Andrews called yesterday [23/8/1782] and said he intends to subscribe to
next year's concerts. 'Miss Van' [Vancamp] combs SW's locks, but SW 'must
not know that this is known'. Both CW Jr and SW are out this evening. Sarah
has had no altercations with them and makes every effort to avoid altercations.

Elizabeth Waller→SGW   Chesterfield St   **12/9/1782**

MA DDWes/7/91   I just now received my dearest Sisr Wesley's kind letter

▣ Thur 12 Sep={1776,1782}[49]

[Martha] Hall [CW's sister, 1707?–1791] called this morning to say that she
dined yesterday [11/9/1782] with 'your young folks' [CW Jr, Sarah and SW] at
Mr Atwood's house [probably the home of Thomas Attwood, trumpeter, *c*1735–
>4/1817, Attwood's father, *see* SW→Sarah, 29/5/1826]. Last Sunday afternoon
[8/9/1782] Sarah listened to SW playing the organ at the Queen's Square
Chapel. He did not return with Sarah to the Wallers' home afterwards.

Since CW and SGW left for Bristol, CW Jr, Sarah and SW have each dined
once with Elizabeth Waller. She will let CW and SGW know if any of their
children should become seriously ill. She is sorry that SGW has not heard more
often from her children and suggests that the children's letters went astray.

Sarah→SGW   Chesterfield St   **13/9/1782**

GEU in box 3   I am very sorry, my dearest Mother should imagine

▣ 13/9/1782

SW and CW Jr 'continue very well'. Neither is fond of writing and both will
make excuses for not writing. In order 'to live together in harmony' Sarah
neither contradicts nor advises them, but she asks SGW not to tell them that
Sarah finds them 'unadvisable'. SW is going to have Mr Nicholas at Hampstead
'for a scholar on the violin'.

---

[48] Assigned to 1782 because ltr, written to SGW at Bristol, mentions that CW Jr
going to Deptford on 25/8; CW→CW Jr, 30/8/1782 (MA DDCW/7/37), advises
that CW and SGW are at Bristol and asks about CW Jr's visit to Deptford; and
no other trip by CW Jr to Deptford in this period has been discovered.

[49] Assigned to 1782 because ltr says CW not in London; 1776 excluded because
CW was in London on 12/9/1776 (*see* CW→John Fletcher, MA DDCW/1/66).

James Price will   Chesterfield St   **6/2/1783**
PRO PROB 11/1107[50]   James Price of Stoke near Guildford
will dated 6/2/1783

Amongst other provisions, James Price bequeaths to SW or his heirs or assigns Price's 'messuage or tenement' situated in Holy Trinity parish in the liberties of the town of Guildford and the appurtenances thereto, together with an adjoining tenement situated at Stoke-above-Bar in the parish of Stoke that is occupied now by Mary King, tenant for life. Price also gives SW £1,000 from Price's 3% consolidated annuities [at the Bank of England] and £50 in money. In addition, as a 'real mark' of his 'esteem and respect', Price leaves all his musical instruments, books of music and books 'upon musical subjects' to SW, and requests that if SW should desire to part with any of these [musical] instruments he give preference when disposing them to Price's executor, the Rev. Mr George Pollen of Stoke near Guildford.

CW→William Russell   **24/2/1783**
MA DDCW/1/67A   The Lord gave; but the Lord hath not taken away
✉ 24 Feb[51]

CW invites William Russell to come to the next [CW Jr/SW] concert on Thursday 6/3/1783 or to the following concert on 20/3/1783. SW hopes that Russell likes his fiddle. CW Jr's songs [presumably his *VIII Songs*, op. 3] have been 'retarded' by the concerts but are now ready and will soon appear. Both CW Jr and SW depend more upon their own industry than upon their 'great friends'.

Gasparo Pacchierotti→SW   Chesterfield St   **6/1783**
MA DDWes/7/116   Mr Pacchierotti presents his best compts & thanks
✉ docketed by CW 'June 1783'; date within month not known

Gasparo Pacchierotti [Italian castrato singer, 1740?–1821] thanks SW for the 'fine rondeau' [not identified]. Pacchierotti wishes that everyone would join him in praising its author.

---

[50] Document is the Prerogative Court of Canterbury copy of the original will, which was proved on 7/8/1783.

[51] Assigned to 1783 because the CW Jr/SW concerts on Thursdays 6 March and 20 March, which are mentioned in ltr, occurred only in that year.

Anne Gatehouse→Sarah   Chesterfield St   **9/7/1783?**
MA DDWF/26/49   Mr Pollen return'd to his amiable Wife & family
pmk 9 Jul[52]
 Mr and Mrs Pollen will be glad to have CW and SGW at their house [in Guildford]. Lady Anne Gatehouse unfortunately cannot accommodate all the Wesleys; however, 'the day must bring us all together constantly' and all the Wesleys are to dine with her. Sarah's room will be in the same place, and a 'tent bed' or room can be found for CW Jr. SW 'will not approve of sleeping with' CW Jr, 'so the Russells can furnish him' with a room; alternatively, Mrs Pollen can accommodate Sarah, and CW Jr and SW can stay with Lady Gatehouse. CW Jr and SW should not forget 'to bring any music' they choose 'to perform here'. Mr [James] Price [alchemist, 1752–1783] begins his lectures on Saturday evening.

CW→Sarah   Chesterfield St   **18/7/1783**
MA DDCW/7/43   I am just come with your particular friend and admirer
⊡ 17/7/1783; portion relevant to SW dated 18 July
 CW is not surprised at Sarah's affection for Bristol. He still hankers after it, but CW Jr and SW 'forbid' [living in Bristol] and SGW must remain [in London] to look after them.

James Price→SW   Chesterfield St   **28/7/1783**
photocopy of ltr in Baker   I acknowledge myself my Dear Sir
⊡ 28/7/1783
 Price has moved 'from the place where our intercourse subsisted' and apologises for not having corresponded with SW for a long time. For the last three months, Price has been very busy instructing two chemistry students and has spent many hours in his laboratory, where he made alloys in a wind furnace and observed that the human body can maintain 'a lower temperature than the surrounding atmosphere'. He has been very ill and still is 'far from well'. Since he last saw SW he has been in London and would have called except that the half-hour he had free coincided with SW's dinner time.
 Mr [Rev. George] Pollen is having a celestina stop put to Lady [Anne] Gatehouse's harpsichord during her absence. Price dislikes this stop because it has 'no bass', but believes that Lady Gatehouse will make it 'sing psalms'.

---

[52] Ltr < James Price's 3/8/1783 death, but not before 1781 when Price (who was born James Higginbotham) assumed the name 'Price'. No visit or planned visit by the Wesleys to Guildford in July 1781 is known. CW Jr and SW appear to have been in Guildford in July 1782 (*see* CW→CW Jr, 23/7/1782?). A proposed visit by the Wesleys to Guildford in 1783 involving Gatehouse and Pollen is mentioned in Price→SW of 28/7/1783. No reason has been found to prefer 1782 to 1783 as the year of ltr, which accordingly has been entered ambiguously under both dates.

Pollen, Lady Gatehouse and Price hope that SW will visit Guildford this summer. Price can offer a bed and 'such accommodation as a philosopher and bachelor's house affords'. He supposes that SW knows 'how confoundedly angry the Russells are' with Price about something which he did not do.

William Jackson→CW   16/12/1783
MA DDWes/7/114   I have just had your kind & friendly letter
🖃 16/12/1783
William Jackson ['of Exeter', composer and writer, 1730–1803] advises CW that CW Jr and SW will be more likely to flourish if 'planted out'. However, only CW Jr should be 'planted out' at present. Bath would be an ideal place for CW Jr and SW to flourish.

SW→Shepherd   26/12/1783
AdF S4619 dossier 5   You afford me a new opportunity
🖃 26 Dec={1777,1783,1788}[53]
SW thanks Shepherd for her letter [not preserved] and for her anxiety about his lost Cremona violin. In the past three weeks he has given up hope of recovering it. Few musicians in London are unaware of its loss. The violin is 'in the hands of a person who knows its value'; otherwise the £1/1/- reward would have secured its return. SW thinks Shepherd's plan of an advertisement is novel but is unlikely to work, as the thief would 'immediately suspect its being a contrivance'.
SW firmly intends to visit France within the next few years. Now is not the time, because CW is 'violently averse' to SW 'becoming a Catholic'. If SW consented to go abroad, CW would conclude that SW wished openly to profess himself a Papist: this would make CW extremely uneasy. SW will not distress CW by taking 'a step' that would rob CW 'of his comfort'.

SW→Shepherd   19/3/1784
AdF S4619 dossier 5   I do not judge exactly as you do
🖃 Fri 19 Mar={1779,1784} & ref. to recovery of lost violin→ⅈ
SW visited Dr [Alexander] Geddes [Roman Catholic translator and critic of the Bible, 1737–1802] this morning. SW had mentioned this visit to Sarah but thinks it prudent that his visits to Geddes not be mentioned to CW. SW is grateful for Shepherd's pains regarding his violin and invites her to call on Sunday evening [21/3/1784] to discuss 'her design for the recovery of it' with his family. Shepherd had disguised her handwriting in her last letter to SW [not preserved] but SW thinks that Sarah would identify any letter with 'Maribone' so spelt as

---

[53] Not 1777 because SW played the violin after 1777 but stopped after violin lost (*see* SW→CB, 4/9/1809). Not 1788 because CW alive when ltr written.

being by Shepherd. Lord and Lady Traquair [Charles Stewart, 1746–1827, 7th Earl of Traquair and his wife Mary], who had introduced SW to Geddes, stopped to see Geddes during SW's visit.

JW→CW Jr   **2/5/1784**
T v 7 p 216–17   I doubt not but both Sarah and you are in trouble
T

JW knows that Sarah and CW Jr are troubled because they think that SW has 'changed his religion'. However, he has not done this; he 'has changed his opinions and mode of worship' [to Roman Catholicism], which is 'quite another thing'. SW has sustained 'unspeakable loss by the change' because his new opinions and mode of worship 'are so unfavourable to religion' that they make religion 'extremely difficult'. Religion is 'happiness in God', or a 'heart and life devoted to God' or 'the mind which was in Christ Jesus'. If SW has this religion 'he will not finally perish, notwithstanding the absurd, unscriptural opinions he has embraced' and his 'superstitious and idolatrous modes of worship'. JW does not know if SW ever will have this religion, but if 'he has not given God his heart' his 'case is unspeakably worse', because his 'new friends will continually endeavour to hinder him by putting something else'—'forms, notions, or externals'—in its place.

JW has 'often lamented' that SW lacked the holiness necessary to 'see the Lord'. However, although he had not this holiness, 'in his hours of cool reflection' he did not hope 'to go to heaven without it'. Now SW will be taught [by the Roman Catholics] that he need only have certain notions and practise particular 'externals' to go to heaven, possibly after 'a few years in purging fire'. Therefore CW Jr and Sarah do 'have a great need to weep' over SW. But do not CW Jr and Sarah also need to weep for themselves? JW urges them 'earnestly and diligently' to give their hearts to God, otherwise he would not be surprised 'if God permits you also to be given up to a strong delusion'.

CW→SGW   **6/8/1784**
MA DDWes/4/16   My dear friend sees whereabouts we are
▣ Fri 6 Aug={1779,1784} & ref. to SW's house→ⓘ

Mr [Samuel] Tooth [timber merchant, builder of the (Methodist) City Road Chapel] must not sell SW's house [left to him in James Price will, 6/2/1783] for less than £650. CW thinks that SW would rather let than sell it. There are 'great lamentations' here [in Bristol] over SGW and her absent children. SW should bring SGW [to Bristol] as soon as possible.

JW→SW Chesterfield St **19/8/1784**

WCL LDWMM 1997/6598 As I have had a regard for you ever since you was
◼ 19/8/1784; pmk 25 Aug

JW often has thought of writing to SW and does so now with love. Many years ago JW saw that God gave SW 'a remarkable talent for music', 'a quick apprehension of other things', 'a capacity for making some progress in learning' and, most importantly, 'a desire to be a Christian'. However, JW often feared that SW 'did not set out the right way' with regard to 'weightier matters' than particular sets of opinions such as 'Protestant or Romish'. JW feared that SW was 'not born again'; unless SW is reborn he 'cannot see the kingdom of God'. SW 'might have thoroughly understood the scriptural doctrine of the new birth' had he used the many opportunities offered while he believed both CW and JW were 'teachers sent from God'. JW considers that SW has never been convinced of the necessity of rebirth and now there is 'greater danger than ever' that he never will. SW may be diverted from the thought of rebirth by new notions, practices and modes of worship which put together 'do not amount to one grain of true, vital, spiritual religion'.

SW is out of his way and is out of God's way. In his present state of mind, foolish zealots may puzzle him about this or that church. Instead, SW first should repent and realise he is a sinner; then he should know Jesus; then he should let the 'love of God be shed abroad' in his heart by the Holy Ghost. Only at that point, if SW has no 'better work' to do, will JW talk with him about transubstantiation or purgatory. SW should 'spread this letter before God, not before man'. JW expects to be in Bristol next week.

SGW→Sarah **25/8/1784**

GEU in box 4 I hope my Dearest Sally had a safe ride to Highgate
◼ Wed 25 Aug & CW alive→{1773,1779,1784}[54]

SW spent an evening at Mrs [Arabella] Mitz's home[55] with Mrs Hervey [not identified].

---

[54] Assigned to 1784 for the following reason. 1779 ruled out because SGW, CW and their family were in or *en route* to Wales on 25/8/1779 (see Rebecca Gwynne→SGW, 26/8/1779), whereas ltr refers to SGW just receiving a letter from CW. In 1773 SW was seven years old and therefore unlikely to be spending evenings away from home.

[55] Arabella Fountaine *bap*1741 married Abel Mitz on 30/12/1759. She was a skilled amateur violinist (*see* [Margaret Baron-Wilson], *The Life and Correspondence of M. G. Lewis*, London, 1839, v 1 p 17), a friend of several members of the Wesley family and a witness to the 9/8/1799 will of SGW's sister Rebecca Gwynne. Arabella Mitz attended many of the CW Jr/SW concerts in Chesterfield Street.

CW→SGW Chesterfield St **1/9/1784**
MA DDCW/7/32 My dear Sarah is, I suppose, by this time
▣ Wed 1 Sep={1773,1779,1784}[56]
SW should answer JW's kind letter [JW→SW, 19/8/1784].

SW→Shepherd **6/9/1784?**
AdF S4619 dossier 5 The Mass is bound up, and the following words
▣ Monday[57]
SW has bound [the presentation copy of] his *Missa de spiritu sancto* and cites
the Latin phrase he has used to dedicate his Mass to the pope [Gianangelo
Braschi, 1717–1799, from 1775 Pope Pius VI]. Dr [Alexander] Geddes has
supplied an address for Abbé [Peter] Grant [who assisted British travellers to
Rome, where he had died on 1/9/1784] via the merchants Marcharty and Son of
Livorno, Italy. SW seeks Shepherd's earliest advice regarding 'the most speedy
and safe method' of conveying his Mass. He tried to see her last Thursday
[2/9/1784]. Since then he has been 'perpetually employed'.

SW→Shepherd **16/1/1785?**
AdF S4619 dossier 5 I have not yet returned you my thanks
▣ 'Fest. Nomine Jesu'[58]
SW apologises for his delayed acknowledgement of Shepherd's 'very polite'
letter [not preserved] and thanks her for her gift of Cicero's *De Officiis*.
Shepherd has told SW 'that a circle never could be squared'; he believes,
however, that two propositions of Euclid prove that a circle is equal to a square.
Shepherd correctly regards SW as 'a young mathematician'. He is convinced of
the 'infinity' that mathematics 'and other deep sciences present to our short
sighted conceptions', and whimsically compares some geometrical figures to
human relationships such as friendship.

---

[56] Assigned to 1784 because ltr refers to JW preaching in Bath 'next Sunday'.
He preached there on 5/9/1784 (*Curnock* v 7 p 17) but not on 5/9/1773
(*Curnock* v 5 p 525) or 5/9/1779 (*Curnock* v 6 p 253).

[57] Assigned to 6/9/1784 because it is the first Monday after 1/9/1784, the date of
the bound presentation copy of SW's Mass (now Fitzwm ms 730).

[58] Addressed to 'Mrs Freeman Shepherd' so presumably after SW→Shepherd,
26/12/1783, which is addressed to 'Miss Freeman'. The youthful appearance of
SW's handwriting, and SW's reference to himself in ltr as a 'young
mathematician', indicate that ltr, addressed to Shepherd in London, was written
before her August 1785 departure from England; she did not return to England
until early 1792. Ltr assigned to 1785 rather than to 1784 because, in contrast to
SW's 1783/1784 letters to Shepherd, it does not concern Roman Catholicism,
but 1784 has not been ruled out. At this time the Feast of the Name of Jesus was
held on the second Sunday after Epiphany, which in 1785 was on 16 January.

Gianangelo Braschi→James Talbot 4/5/1785
WDA AAW/A v 42 no. 67[59] Venerabilis Frater Salutem
▣ 'IV non. Maias 1785'[60]
 Gianangelo Braschi [Pope Pius VI] sends greetings to Bishop James Talbot [1726–1790, from 1781 Vicar Apostolic of the London district]. The arrival of the beautifully and elegantly bound book [containing SW's *Missa de spiritu sancto*] presented by Talbot's fraternity in SW's name has given Braschi great pleasure, particularly as he understands from Talbot's letter [not located, presumably enclosed with SW's Mass] that the Mass was written to express SW's gratitude to God for his entrance into the Catholic Church, from which SW's ancestors were disbarred. Braschi by no means disapproves of sacred music—as pleasures experienced by the ears elevate weaker minds to a feeling of piety—but is most pleased by SW's skill in arguments of faith in which, according to Talbot, he excels, and by the high hopes that Talbot has of him. Talbot should transmit Braschi's gratitude to SW for his gift. If an opportunity presents itself, Braschi will demonstrate his gratitude by actions.

CW will 28/5/1785
PRO PROB 1/70 In the Name of God, Amen. I, Charles Wesley
will dated 28/5/1785[61]
 CW bequeaths [the leasehold of] his Chesterfield Street house and its appurtenances and contents to SGW for her life and to CW Jr or [if CW Jr has previously died married] to CW Jr's executors, administrators and assigns, after her death. CW also gives 'the yearly interest and produce' of all his 'moneys and personal estate' to SGW during her lifetime. He leaves to Sarah all 'moneys, personal estate and effects' which he shall have received or be entitled to at the death of his sister Martha Hall. As SW 'has in a great measure been provided for by a deceased friend' [*see* James Price will, 6/2/1783], CW therefore [makes no separate provision for SW but] wills that, after SGW's death, the principal of his money and his personal effects be given to his three children in equal shares. However, if any of CW's children should die unmarried while SGW is alive that child's share is to be divided equally amongst CW's remaining children, and if CW Jr dies unmarried while SGW is alive then the Chesterfield Street house and furniture are to be given in equal shares to Sarah and SW or to their executors, administrators and assigns.

---

[59] Ltr written in Latin. A draft of ltr is in the Vatican Library, Rome. A photocopy of this draft is in the Baker Collection, Duke University Library.

[60] The nones of May were on 7 May, hence 4th nones was 4 May.

[61] This will was proved in the Prerogative Court of Canterbury on 16/4/1788.

CW→Mary & John Fletcher   21/6/1785
MA DDCW/1/75   If you are weary of writing, I much more,
⊟ 21/6.1785

If Mary Fletcher saw SW 'in the cradle' she saw him 'in his best estate'. One
out of three [of CW's children] has 'some desire of salvation', but she [Sarah]
'seeks rather than strives'.

SW→Shepherd   7/1785?
MA DDWes/6/67[62]   I should have answered your Letter before
⊟ Thursday[63]

SW apologises for his delayed response to Shepherd's letter [not preserved]
which he received on Tuesday night. Replying to her question whether
'conscience' approves what SW endeavours to justify to his friends and
acquaintances, he notes that Shepherd is the only person to whom he has spoken
on the subject, which he regards as 'very trifling'. He is 'not conscious of having
appeared ashamed or confused', as Shepherd imputed. SW sighed because he
thought that CW's 'unfair and ungenerous conduct', accusing a party that 'had
not a power to defend', was 'so much below' [both] justice and CW himself.

Rashness is not a common fault of SW. Although he has been 'accused of
striking servants', he is aware of doing this only once, when 'the boy' [not
identified] 'positively' refused to obey SW's just orders. SW regards self-
examination as 'absolutely necessary on every occasion' and is not in danger of
taking 'any hasty step'.

Bishop [James] Talbot has told Shepherd that SW's behaviour, as recounted to
Talbot by CW, could cause a scandal. [In a note accompanying ltr, Shepherd
says that CW went to Talbot 'with great sorrow of heart' to complain about
SW's 'irregular conduct, in staying out to undue hours of night' and in 'tempers
of behaviour at home to the servants'. CW asked Talbot, 'to whose flock' SW
'now belonged', to watch over SW's soul 'as his pastor'. Talbot was uneasy that
news of a scandal 'would call in the Catholics' and insisted that Shepherd
'remonstrate' with SW, which she did in two letters [not preserved] and in
personal discussion, speaking to SW 'not harshly' but hoping that he would
accept her words in the 'spirit of good will and cordiality'.] SW informed
Shepherd that he would rather 'quit any communion than be a scandal' while he
remained in it. He will call on Talbot 'to hear the repetition' of what CW told
SW [about CW's conversation with Talbot]. SW thinks that 'when two persons
[SW and Shepherd] have friendship or esteem for one another, the discussion of
a topic whereupon they differ frequently produces disagreeable consequences'.

---

[62] Ltr is a copy in Shepherd's hand of SW's letter to her.

[63] Shepherd notes that she received ltr 'about six weeks before she left England
in August 1785'.

CW→SGW   **10/8/1785**
MA DDCW/7/71   My dearest partner has disappointed us of a letter
▣ 8/8/1785; relevant portion dated 'Wednesday morning' [i.e., 10/8/1785]
CW is glad that SW is well again and that CW Jr is fully employed. SW is
fonder than CW of 'physic' [medicine].

SGW→CW   **18/8/1785**
MA DDCW/6/42   The alteration[64] of the post Hour's by the new Act prevents
▣ Thurs 18 Aug & ref. to John Fletcher's 14/8/1785 death→ⅈ
CW Jr and SW are going to tea at Mr Wafer's house [presumably the home of
Richard Wafer, organist of Berwick Street Chapel, c1731–1795].

SW→CW   **22/8/1785**
MA DDWF/15/2   I should have written long before
▣ Mon 22/8/1784; pmk 22/8[65]
SW should have written 'long before' but waited until he could say that he has
finished a musical work which he has been advised to publish, and for which he
has issued proposals. It is the ode *Qualem ministrum* [to words by Horace],
which SW has set to music for six voices, and which has met the approbation of
judges both of Latin and of music. Dr Hopson [presumably Charles Rivington
Hopson, physician and translator, 1744–1796] has heard it and commends the
expression of the words, and CW Jr is 'much pleased' with the composition. SW
has done little else but write [music] since CW departed, and all his musical
acquaintances believe that 'considerable advantage' may crown his labours. The
ode will not be published unless he gains 'a good many' subscribers. He fixed
the number at 200 in the proposals but considers that it would be worth while to
publish if he receives only 150 subscribers as the subscription is to be 10/6.
SW seeks CW's judgement on two parts of the ode. One concerns a reading of
the Latin text; the other whether SW should include some verses which he thinks
'foolish'. SW has set them but could reject them 'without injury either to the
harmony or the effect'. Every day he reads some of Horace's finest odes and is
increasingly delighted with them; he concurs with CW that Horace improves on
further acquaintance. SW is glad that CW and Sarah find their 'present situation'
[at Bristol] agreeable and presumes that he will see CW at the beginning of next
month, when he will be glad to have CW's opinion of his 'late performance'.
CW remarked in the past that SW would like to be a scholar 'without taking the
pains which are necessary for it'. SW notes that one pursuit is a great effort for
one person; two are much more difficult. Music consumes a considerable

---

[64] SGW appears to have written 'alterelation'.

[65] 22/8/1784 was not a Monday. Assigned to Monday, 22/8/1785, as ltr says
Sarah with CW in Bristol where she was in August 1785 (*see* SGW→CW,
18/8/1785, MA DDCW/6/42).

amount of SW's time which he would gladly exchange for study, but as he was 'born with a trade not a fortune in [his] hands' it is necessary for him to make the most of it. There is little doubt that he will understand Latin perfectly within three years 'with moderate application'; whether he will have time to master Greek is another matter. If he does not, he will have no one but himself to blame, for nothing but music prevents his 'close application', and that must not be 'thrown aside' until his purse is 'fuller than at present'. He sees now 'no very promising symptoms' of this.

CW Jr→Langshaw Jr   20/9/1785?
GEU W/L; *Wainwright* p 68–69   I thank you my dear Friend for your Letters
☞ 20 Sep[66]
CW Jr is certain that SW's 'ode' [presumably SW's setting of Horace's *Qualem Ministrum*] will please people who like that style of composition. However, CW Jr tells [his pupil] Langshaw Jr that 'few real judges of music are to be found'.

JW→CW   6/4/1786
MA DDWes/3/61; *T* v 7 p 323–324   I am glad you are again able to officiate
T
JW is 'not sorry' that CW's 'concerts are come to an end' [presumably a reference to the CW Jr/SW concerts in Chesterfield St, although there were subsequent concerts in 1786 and 1787]. CW should remember his dream concerning 'Sammy' [possibly SW, although JW refers earlier in ltr to 'Sammy' Bradburn, Methodist minister, 1751–1816]. 'The damsel is not dead, but sleepeth!'

SGW→Sarah   13/5/1786
GEU in box 3   I hope this will find my Dearest Sally much better
☞ 13/5/1786
Yesterday [12/5/1786] the music room [at Chesterfield Street] was fuller than Sarah has seen 'since the alteration of it'. SGW counted 54 people, of whom very few did not have 'constant seats'. No one complained of inconvenience as the concert was 'free from expense', and the experience has shown how many people 'could be accommodated were they subscribers'. One 'musical lady' introduced by Mr Barnard [not identified] desired 'to have her name put down' [as a subscriber]. She said that, of 'all the music she attended', CW Jr and SW 'excelled'.

---

[66] Assigned to 1785 on the assumption that SW's ode mentioned in ltr is *Qualem ministrum*, completed about 22/8/1785 (*see* SW→CW, 22/8/1785).

SW→SGW   Mrs Phillips's, Brickendon   **20/7/1786**
typescript in Baker   The Trunk did not get hither till very late last night
▣ 20/7/1786
  SW's trunk arrived [in Brickendon, Hertfordshire] very late last night
[19/7/1786]. He was not much fatigued from his walk and he felt 'no kind of
lassitude' when he arose. He is enjoying the pure air and the pleasant scenery.
Mr Power [not identified] 'is in a snug situation and both of us make the most of
our time'. Mr [James] Kenton [poet, friend of CW and SW] has been attentive
and has run errands 1½ miles to the town; Kenton will see SGW tomorrow
[21/7/1786]. SW asks to be remembered to CW Jr and to Sarah, and promises to
reply to Sarah if she writes.

CW→SGW   **20/7/1786**
MA DDWes/4/37   I have been strengthened to go thro' the whole Service
▣ 16–20/7/1786; relevant portion dated 20/7/1786
  CW inquires when SW will return [from Brickendon] and whether he has
mentioned CW's letter [not preserved].

Henry Bergum→CW   **21/7/1786**
MA DDWes/7/112   O yez, O yez, O yez, Be it known
▣ docketed by CW 21/7/1786
  Henry Bergum announces his imminent release from prison. He is thankful for
the support he received during his confinement. He would like to hear CW Jr and
SW play again and invites them 'to tea and a little music' whenever convenient.

CW→SGW   **1/8/1786**
MA DDWes/4/50   My dearest Sally will rejoice to hear
▣ 1/8/1786
  If the paint annoys SGW, she should return to Mr Fountaine's house and let
SW live in the [fresh] air. It was kind of CW Jr to offer to teach SW's scholars.
CW is not 'sanguine' in expecting good from Windsor: it is a marvel if CW Jr
'has received no evil from it' [the 22–23/7/1786 performances by CW Jr in
Windsor before King George III].

CW→SGW   **7/8/1786**
MA DDWes/4/44   My dear partner, I hear, has not rec'd my long letter.
▣ 7/8/1786
  SW should not be too hasty in purchasing a house. Keeping a house in London
costs nearly £30 a year.

Sarah→SGW   7/8/1786
GEU in box 3   This is the third time I have absolutely sat down
▣ 7/8/1786
  CW has made Sarah and the family's Bristol friends happy by inviting SGW
[to Bristol]. Sarah wishes that CW Jr and SW would accompany SGW [to
Bristol]. CW Jr perhaps will do so, but [visiting Bristol] would give SW 'so little
pleasure' that it would be 'vain to assure him' that many people there would
rejoice to see him, particularly Miss Jones [not identified], who has charged
Sarah to convey 'everything affectionate' to SW.

CW→CW Jr & SGW   14/8/1786
MA DDCW/7/38   *To CW Jr:*   You are right in keeping up your interest
                 To SGW: My dearest Sally may write without putting
▣ 14 Aug, finished Tue 15 Aug={1775,1780,1786}[67]
  To CW Jr: not relevant to Source Book
  To SGW: CW sends his love to SW. SGW should tell SW that CW expects to
have first refusal when SW sells his organ. CW will pay at least as much as any
other bidder, so SW need not sell the organ for a song. SW should continue
riding every day. He still lacks 'one thing' to make him 'happy, or tolerably
easy'. He cannot believe what CW says, so 'must find it out as he can'.

SW→SGW   Hertford   11/7/1787
GEU Wesley Coll. ltr 48   I have arrived safely here about half an hour ago
▣ Wed 1787; pmk [London] 12/7/1787, a Thursday
  SW arrived safely in Hertford at 2 pm. He plans to stay until Tuesday
[17/7/1787] and expects to have a comfortable stay in Mr Leach's apartment
[possibly the musician Thomas Leach who, according to *Doane,* was living in
1794 at Cheshunt, Hertfordshire].

CW→Sarah   24/8/1787
MA DDWes/4/20   If God designs us to meet in Bristol
▣ 24/8/1787
  CW is increasingly frail. He soon must give up SGW to CW Jr's care, and CW
Jr—for his 'share'—must look after Sarah. SW must be entrusted to God's care:
'we know not for what he is reserved'.

---

[67] Assigned to 1786 because ltr says Sarah in Bristol where she was in August
1786 (*see* CW→SGW, 7/8/1786) and CW says in ltr that he thinks this is his
last visit to Bristol.

CW→SW **4/10/1787**
Stevenson p 508 My eyes will, I hope, suffice for a few lines.
Stevenson
   CW hopes that his eyes will allow him to write a few lines. Hitherto he has provided for CW Jr and SW 'with a willing mind'. This is no longer in his power; SW and CW Jr must now provide for themselves. CW leaves it up to them whether they 'board out' or continue to live with SGW. He cannot leave Bristol until he has a reply.

SW→CW **6/10/1787?**
Stevenson p 508 [not known]
A reply to CW→SW, 4/10/1787; CW at Bristol.
   Replying to CW→SW, 4/10/1787, SW resolves to remain a member of CW's household and of SGW's household when CW dies.

Rebecca Gwynne→SGW **10/10/1787**
MA DDWes/7/37 I am at a loss to know the meaning
▣ 10/10/1787
   SW spent a day with Rebecca Gwynne last week. He is looking 'quite hearty' and rather 'increased in size', which she thinks is a token of a 'sober and regular life'.

Latrobe journal entry Chesterfield St **21/1/1788**
JRUL English Ms 1244 f 3v went in rain to Sir Chas M house
journal entry dated 21/1/1788
   After breakfast, and following a visit elsewhere, Latrobe called at CW's house [Chesterfield Street]. SW 'played a new Mass of his composition' [not identified] for Latrobe, and then accompanied Latrobe to St James's Place.

Latrobe journal entry Chesterfield St **5/3/1788**
JRUL English Ms 1244 f 11v walked with Heithausen to the British Museum
journal entry dated 5/3/1788
   After a meeting elsewhere Latrobe proceeded with Mr Heithausen to CW's house and agreed to have tea there later. Then SW accompanied Latrobe and Heithausen to Bond Street. When Latrobe and Heithausen returned to CW's house SW entertained them 'most delightfully the whole afternoon with his enchanting fingers'. CW is 'but poorly' and seems to be 'going very fast'.

JW→CW Jr   **16/3/1788**
MA DDWes/5/17; *T* v 8 p 45   Before going down to preach I just snatch time
T

   Whenever God is pleased to call CW, JW—while he lives—will be 'a father
and friend' of CW Jr and SW.

JW→SW   **18/3/1788**
MA DDWes/5/18; *T* v 8 p 47   I have long had a great concern for you
T

   JW has long had 'great concern' for SW, but never more than now. SW is in 'a
critical situation'. CW appears to be 'just quivering over the grave' and ready to
leave SW under his own tuition, with all his 'first inexperience of youth'. There
was a time when SW might have taken JW's advice, but now 'Miss Freeman'
[Shepherd] has taught SW 'another lesson'. JW 'cares not' for 'one opinion or
another', nor who is head of the Church, provided that SW is a Christian.
However, it is a 'grievous loss' for SW to be cut off from 'that preaching which
is more calculated than any other in England' to make him a 'real scriptural
Christian'. If SW had neglected no opportunity to hear JW and CW preach he
would be a different man from the one he is now, but 'it seems the time is past'.
CW is 'on the wing'; SW is unlikely to see him for long, and may not see JW
much longer either. JW advises SW to make a friend of Dickinson, 'a sensible
and pious man' who has a tender regard for SW. JW commits SW to God, who
is able to carry SW 'through all temptations'.

Latrobe journal entry   **19/3/1788**
JRUL English Ms 1244 f 13v   Reading at 7. I read, but had no Organ.
journal entry dated 19/3/1788

   Latrobe hurried his dinner as he wished 'for once to hear the Roman Catholic
vespers'. SW had acquainted him with the times when the 2½ hour service,
which gave Latrobe 'very little satisfaction', took place. Then Latrobe called
with SW at CW's home. Latrobe could not see CW because it was so late.

SW→CLM   **27/3/1788**
MA DDWes/1/66   The Spirit of life just hovers over the Grave
▣ 27/3/1788

   CW is near death. The family expected that he would die today. It now appears
unlikely that this will happen until tomorrow [28/3/1788]. SW will consider it
miraculous if death does not occur then. If CW [who died on 29/3/1788] lives
through tomorrow everyone will be in the same anxious state. SW hopes that
CLM will excuse him from the 'performance of a promise' which nothing but
this circumstance could have forced him to forfeit.

Sarah→JW   **4/4/1788**
Tyson p 481–82   We were all present when my dear, respected father departed
pmk 4/4/1788 (according to *Tyson* p 481–82)
   The entire family were present when CW died [on 29/3/1788]. About
17/3/1788, CW took SW's hand when SW entered the room and blessed 'God to
all eternity' that SW was born. About 14/3/1788 CW prayed 'for all his enemies'
including 'Miss Freeman' [Shepherd]. He implored God 'that she may never feel
the pangs of eternal death'. When JW's 'kind letter' to CW Jr [JW→CW Jr,
16/3/1788] arrived, in which JW said that he would be a father to CW Jr and to
SW, Sarah read it to CW. CW responded that he was certain that JW would be
kind to all of CW's children after his death. SGW, CW Jr and SW join Sarah 'in
duty' and beg JW's prayers 'for the widow and the fatherless'.

JW→Dickinson   **15/4/1788**
T v 8 p 54   My brother never knew the value of Dr Coke
T
   JW has 'little fear' for Sarah, 'much hope' for CW Jr to whom he wrote lately,
and some hope for 'Sammy' [SW]. SW 'certainly fears God'.

JW→SGW   **21/4/1788**
MA DDWes/5/20; *T* v 8 p 55–56   You will excuse me, my dear sister
T
   JW wishes that CW Jr and 'Sammy' [SW] may follow SGW's example and
advice 'in keeping little company, and those of the best sort, men of sound
understanding and solid piety'. Only such people are 'fit for the acquaintance of
men of sense'.

JW→Dickinson   **27/4/1788**
Baker Box 6, Perronet family scrapbook   I really think it will be proper
⌧ 27/4/1788
   Dickinson 'should study every means of keeping up' his acquaintance with
SW. Both CW Jr and SW 'stand in much need of serious acquaintance' of men
or women.

Latrobe journal entry   Chesterfield St   **10/6/1788**
JRUL English Ms 1244 f 24v   went according to appointment to spend a day
journal entry dated 10/6/1788
   Latrobe spent today with SGW, looking over CW's papers; this gave Latrobe
'an opportunity of suppressing scandal'. The Wesley family were not yet up
when he arrived; when they came down they made him pray. In the afternoon he
had 'some music' with CW Jr and SW.

Sarah→SW   **1/9/1788**
GEU in box 3   I will thank you to endeavor to obtain Miss Deane's
🖃 1/9/1788
Sarah would like SW to obtain AD's 'decisive answer' concerning Mr Preston
of Beilby's Academy, Battersea. Sarah has nothing to relate that would interest
SW, as he 'detests descriptions of places' and she is not presently disposed to
point out 'varieties of character'. She is enjoying the air, the peace and the ocean
views in Ramsgate, but is too 'unentertaining a correspondent' and too
'unimportant a person' to trouble SW with further accounts of herself.

Latrobe journal entry   **6/9/1788**
JRUL English Ms 1244 f 41v   abt 7—calling at Huttons by the way
journal entry dated 6/9/1788
  Latrobe dined with SW. CW Jr and SGW came to tea.

Latrobe journal entry   **8/9/1788**
JRUL English Ms 1244 f 41v   breakf at Dr Lowders
journal entry dated 8/9/1788
  SW had supper with Latrobe.

SW→SGW   Bramfield[68]   **22/7/1789**
BL Add 35012 f 5   I should have written before, but as I knew Mr Kenton
🖃 22/7/1789
SW should have written sooner but knew that [James] Kenton would inform
SGW. SW has written [not preserved] to Biggs [not identified]. SW is
comfortable, has much attention paid to him and is very quiet. He has 'the sort of
situation' which no-one would enjoy except someone who loves 'retirement'. He
hates public life: 'it was a cruel mistake in my education, the forcing me into it'.
He needs to return next Wednesday [29/7/1789] because of the schools [where
he teaches]. He sends love to both CW Jr and Sarah and advises CW Jr to take
more exercise.

Sarah→Penelope Maitland   Bramfield   **29/7/1789**
Bodl Ms Eng. Misc. c.502 f 50   I have this moment received my dearest
🖃 29/7/1789
  SW, who is now in Hertfordshire, 'is not yet going abroad'. Sarah thinks this
would be imprudent 'in these commotions', although, 'as a Catholic', he 'might
be received safely where Protestants would be unwelcome'. She hopes and prays
that SW 'will not die' in the Catholic persuasion. She informs Penelope

---

[68] A small community in Hertfordshire.

Maitland [1730–1805] that he no longer holds its 'worst of doctrines', that 'no heretic can be saved'.

Latrobe journal entry 10/8/1789
JRUL English Ms 1244 f 112v   sat at home & worked
journal entry dated 10/8/1789
   Latrobe 'waited in vain' for SW to come to tea according to their appointment.

Latrobe journal entry Chesterfield St 21/8/1789
JRUL English Ms 1244 f 114v   went at 2 in a Coach
journal entry dated 21/8/1789
   On his way home Latrobe called at SW's home.

Rebecca Spilsbury→CW Jr 31/8/1789
MA DDWF/25/6   I have been disappointed at not having had
✉ 31/8/1789
   Rebecca Spilsbury and Mrs Tighe [with whom Spilsbury is staying in Ireland] would be grateful if CW Jr could send them two sets each of 'the scripture hymn' and one set of SW's 'prettiest lessons' for Miss Tighe.

JW→SW[69] Chesterfield St 16/9/1789
VUQ; *T* v 8 p 171   It gives me pleasure to hear that you have so much
ltr docketed 16/9/1789; pmk 'Froome'; pmk (London) 18/9/1789
   JW is pleased to hear that SW has sufficient resolution to go to bed at 10 pm and to rise at 4 am. He should not let the increasing cold 'affright' him from his purposes; he should bear his cross, and it will bear him. JW advises SW to read carefully the following publications [by JW of works by or about Roman Catholics] which are amongst CW's books: Thomas à Kempis [presumably JW's edition *The Christian's Pattern; or, a Treatise of the Imitation of Christ*, 1735], [JW's abridgement of] *The Life of Gregory Lopez*, and [JW's *An Extract of*] *the Life of Monsieur* [Gaston Jean Baptiste] *de Renty*, 1st ed., 1741]. JW remains SW's 'affectionate uncle and friend'.

---

[69] The address portion of ltr is written by JW to 'Miss Wesley', i.e., to Sarah, but the salutation to 'My Dear Sammy' and the close of ltr confirm that SW was the intended recipient.

Sarah→SW   **10/1789?**

VUQ   I send to You a Copy of an original letter from a worthy Nun
ltr undated[70]

Sarah sends a copy [not preserved] of a letter regarding 'the state of the clergy in France' that has lately arrived from a 'worthy nun' in Boulogne. Sarah received this letter from Mr Hunter, a Protestant clergyman who knew SW at Cambridge; Mrs Hunter, with whom Sarah is 'intimately acquainted here', is the aunt of Miss Smart, a [Roman] Catholic at Reading. Sarah plans to subscribe 5/- [to the cause identified by the nun] and hopes to collect £2/2/- or £3/3/-; she asks SW to use his 'interest in so good a cause'. She has translated 'the letter of St Francis' from the 'indifferent' French in which it was written. SW should write to her 'within the fortnight' if he has time. Sarah hopes 'to be in London about the end of the month'.

Sarah→SGW   Chesterfield St   **7/11/1789**

GEU in box 3   I write to thank you for your Letter
☞ 'Saturday 7 November'; pmk 1789

'Dear Sam' [SW] is to be thanked for his letter [not preserved]. Sarah proposes to return [to London from Reading] on Wednesday [11/11/1789].

JW journal entry   **28/12/1789**

Curnock v 8 p 35   I retired to Peckham
Curnock

The musical compositions of CW Jr and SW 'are not more excellent than the poetical ones of their father' [CW].

---

[70] Ltr placed here on the conjecture that Sarah wrote it from Reading, where she appears to have stayed for an extended time only in October–November 1789. Sarah→Martha Hall, 26/10/1789, (MA DDWes/6/12), written from Reading, states Sarah's intention to return to London in a fortnight; Sarah→SGW, 7/11/1789, also written from Reading, thanks SW for his letter [not preserved, but conjecturally a reply to ltr] and states her plan to return to London on Wednesday 11/11/1789. A 1789 dating also is consistent with concerns about the treatment of clergy in France following the Revolution and with SW's statement in SW→CB, 7/7/1808, that he has not been in Cambridge for the past 20 years.

JW→Sarah   **11/4/1790**
T v 8 p 213   Persons may judge I am not so well as I was once
T
    JW is glad that 'Sammy' [SW] is 'diligent in study'. This will 'save him many
temptations'. He will 'profit much' if he 'strictly follows the method of
Kingswood School' [which JW founded in 1748].

JW→Sarah   **28/4/1790**
MA DDWes/5/25; *T* v 8 p 216–217   Now if you was but sitting at my elbow
Telford
    They who fear the Lord 'can want no manner of thing that is good'. JW wishes
that CW Jr and 'Sammy' [SW] 'could find their way thither'.

JW→Henry Moore   **28/4/1790**
Duke in Adam Clarke papers   I have wrote freely to Sammy Wesley
☑ 28/4/1790
    JW has written freely to SW [presumably JW's draft of JW→SW, 29/4/1790]
and desires that Dickinson call on SW without delay. Dickinson should invite
SW to Dickinson's house. JW informs Henry Moore [Methodist minister, 1751–
1844] that if Dickinson 'strikes while the iron is hot he may save a soul alive'.

JW→SW   Chesterfield St   **29/4/1790**
Albert; *T* v 8 p 218–19[71]   For some days now you have been much upon
T
    For some days SW has been 'much upon' JW's mind. JW feared that he might
feel 'when it was too late' that he had been 'wanting in affection' to SW. If
SW's wants were 'clothes or books or money' then JW would soon supply him.
But JW fears that SW wants what he 'least of all' suspects: religion, 'the greatest
thing of all'. JW does not mean 'external religion' but 'the religion of the heart'
as enjoyed by [Thomas à] Kempis, [Blaise] Pascal and [François] Fénelon.
    When SW 'contracted a prejudice' in favour of Roman Catholicism, JW was
concerned, not by the opinions that SW embraced but by his 'being cut off from
those instructions' which he especially needed. If SW had read even a small part
of JW's writing, which 'Providence recommended' to SW's attention by his
being closely related to JW, or if SW had diligently attended JW's ministry as he
ought to have done, SW 'would have known more of that religion' than he does
now. JW laments SW's 'fatal step' of 'relinquishing those places of worship

---

[71] According to Telford, ltr is in the handwriting of Elizabeth Ritchie [1754–
1835, from 1801 the second wife of Harvey Walklate Mortimer, 1753–1819].
Elizabeth Ritchie Mortimer served JW and later also SGW (*see* SGW→SW,
29/8/1817) as an amanuensis.

where alone this religion is inculcated'. JW 'cares not' whether SW is called a Papist or a Protestant but is 'grieved' that he is a 'heathen'.

JW is certain 'that the general religion both of Protestants and Catholics is no better than refined heathenism'. However, SW is 'called to something better than this'. SW is called 'to know and love the God of glory' and should listen to the advice of JW who 'stands on the edge of eternity'. SW, 'in spite of prejudice', should 'go and hear that word' which can save his soul. He should give God his heart. 'Dear Sammy' [SW] should consider these 'as probably the dying words' of his affectionate uncle JW.

JW→Dickinson   12/6/1790

T v 8 p 221–222   I am exceedingly pleased that you have made a little tour
T

'Sammy Wesley' [SW] 'would probably be a real Christian' if the 'good impressions' which he 'frequently feels' could be changed. Dickinson has the possibility to 'save a soul alive' and 'should contrive' to see SW as often as possible.

JW→Dickinson   21/6/1790

Baker Box 6, Perronet   You send me good News concerning Sammy Wesley
family scrapbook
🖾 21/6/1790

Dickinson has sent JW good news concerning SW. The opportunity is not to be lost. Dickinson now should advise SW 'to give a serious reading to the three Appeals' [JW's *An Earnest Appeal to Men of Reason and Religion*, first published 1743, was followed in 1745 by his three-part *A Farther Appeal to Men of Reason and Religion*], although SW may have read them, cursorily or carefully, some years ago.[72] Dickinson should not let this week go before he sees SW again: 'delays are dangerous'. Dickinson perhaps 'might encourage Sally Wesley' [presumably Sarah rather than SGW, *see* JW→Sarah, 18/8/1790] to 'join' with him and 'speak a word in season' [to SW]. Dickinson also should provoke 'honest George Whitfield [Methodist minister, 1753–1832, from 1779 to 1804 steward of the Methodist Book-Room] to press on to the mark'.

---

[72] In his *Vindex to Verax*, published in 1792, SW would declare (p 32) that JW's *Appeals* contain arguments worthy of 'the most serious study of the most finished scholar'.

JW→Sarah 18/8/1790

MA DDWes/5/26; *T* v 8 p 233–34   I always mildly reprove the profane person
T

'Sammy' [SW] and Sarah 'should converse frequently and freely together'. Each might help the other. JW believes that SW has 'a mind capable of friendship'. JW hopes, if he lives, 'to be more acquainted with' SW.

SW→Sarah 11/10/1790?

MA DDWF/15/3   I answer your letter sooner than I do letters in general
pmk 11 Oct[73]

SW answers Sarah's letter [not preserved] sooner than he answers most letters; at present he has ten or twelve letters to answer. The introduction of Sarah's 'new friend' [not identified] to 'the old enemy of his profession' was a little unlucky, but SW respects [Edward] Perronet [minister and hymn-writer, 1721–1792, son of JW's and CW's friend Vincent Perronet] for not being overawed by the presence of his guest. SW thinks that any man who could say so much truth as one reads in *The Mitre* [a 'sacred poem' by Edward Perronet printed in 1757] would be a 'pitiful poltroon' to desert his cause or to hold his tongue except on the fullest conviction of having been wrong.

SW is the wrong person to ask for news. SGW dined at Paddington yesterday. SW was invited but preferred to come in the evening. This did not turn out well, for they had scarcely swallowed their coffee when 'Mr R' [not identified] did 'all but appear': he was heard walking upstairs, and was stopped by Miss Chouquet who ran out of the dining room to meet him. Their 'poor persecuted friend' was obliged to leave them for about 30 minutes, and then returned 'in agonies'. SW presumes that Miss Chouquet 'suffered additionally' because SW was in the house. Mr R is 'as jealous as spite can make him' and will kill her by his treatment if she does not kill herself with laudanum first.

SW has bought [John] Clarke's *Introduction* [*to the Making of Latin*; the 26th edition was published in 1790] and is certain that it will be 'serviceable' to Sarah. He means to go through it as regularly as he has gone through the French exercises, which he has almost finished. Verdion [not identified] believes that French can be thoroughly understood only by writing it as much as speaking it. SW thinks this is likely to be true for other languages too, in proportion to their difficulty.

SW writes, in Latin, that he sees no reason why Sarah should not acquire a meticulous knowledge of that language. He is at her service should she decide to employ him as her teacher. Sarah [presumably in an earlier letter] drew a

---

[73] Assigned to 1790 for the following reasons. Ltr not before 1790 as it bears a receiving-house stamp of the kind introduced that year (*Willcocks/Jay* p 18). Ltr does not appear to have the sorting-table mark introduced on 1/6/1791 (*ibid.* p 4–5). Addressed to Sarah at Mrs Whitcomb's, Margate where she was in October 1790 and also in October 1791, but the pmk, although not fully legible, does not appear to read '91'.

'mental portrait' of [Pascal] Paoli [Corsican general, 1725–1807, who lived in England for many years and who had subscribed to the CW Jr/SW concerts in 1785]. She must draw SW's 'mental portrait' also but, at that time, must forget her relationship with him, or she will 'extenuate some faults and exaggerate others'.

Sarah→SW   3–5/1791
GEU Wesley Coll. ltr 90   Your want of candour grieves me.
☑ 'Friday night'[74]

SW's 'want of candour' grieves Sarah. Wesleys other than SW 'dwelt with pleasure' on the virtues and talents of their ancestors. Differences of opinion did not lead them to 'depreciate their family'. JW 'attacked principles, not men'. CW 'exulted in intellectual eminence when joined with moral'; abilities [alone] did not 'tempt him to approve scepticism, or palliate vice'.

Sarah was not the only one to whom the [Wesley] family behaved well. JW's letters, visits and attention were to all of CW's children; he gave CW Jr £50 upon hearing of his 'intended match'. Sarah's aunt [Martha Hall, CW's and JW's sister] was kind to the entire family. Only hatred could cause SW to depreciate the Wesleys 'at every opportunity in the hearing of servants'. SW's constant pointing out of what he supposes are character faults in the Wesleys has the appearance of envy. Sarah thinks that, upon reflection, SW will 'condemn' his behaviour. If not, she asks that their 'altercations be private', as she loves her family much more than her 'unimportant self'.

SW→Sarah   3–5/1791
GEU Wesley Coll. ltr 75   Your letter has not at all convinced me that any word
☑ 'Saturday'[75]

Sarah's letter [Sarah→SW, 'Friday night', 3–5/1791] has not convinced SW that any word he uttered last night lacked 'candour or truth'. He does not defend

---

[74] Ltr placed here for the following reason. Ltr >JW's 2/3/1791 death and <Martha Wesley Hall's 12/7/1791 death because ltr answered the next day by SW→Sarah, 'Saturday', in which SW says that JW is dead and refers to Martha Hall in the present tense. Ltr written on a day when SW and Sarah were at the same place, as SW's 'Saturday' answer to ltr says that he uttered the words about which Sarah complains in ltr 'last night'. Hence ltr not written when Sarah was in Rochester (on 14/5/1791) nor while she was in Margate for some weeks immediately after. Sarah says in Sarah→SW, 16/6/1791, written from Margate, that she will not return to London until after SW has left London; he arrived in Taunton on 25/6/1791 (*see* SW→SGW, 27/6/1791) where he apparently planned to stay for a month (*see* Sarah→SW, 16/6/1791). Hence ltr presumably written before Sarah's departure for Rochester.

[75] Ltr written the day after the preceding letter, to which it is a reply.

or approve speaking 'in the hearing of servants', something for which Sarah herself has been blamed by Miss Darby [not identified].

Attacking 'principles and not men' is a 'cunning evangelical distinction'. JW had no rival; no one else proceeded upon his plan or assumed his authority. 'The only person who had anything like a chance with him' was CW, and between them 'a misunderstanding existed' up to their deaths.

SW was 'at variance' with CW not because their opinions differed but because CW was prejudiced and SW was stubborn. Although CW 'virulently opposed scepticism', he palliated what Sarah calls 'vice'. It was 'not excused' in Leach [possibly the musician Thomas Leach, *see* SW→SGW, 11/7/1787], Reinagle [probably Joseph Reinagle, 'cellist and composer, 1762–1825] or 'in other poor whoremasters', but 'it found protection in Lord Mornington [Garret Wesley] and Mrs Barry [Ann Spranger Barry Crawford, actress, 1734–1801, who was accused of adultery]'.

SW is not personally prejudiced against [his aunt] Mrs [Martha] Hall, but 'the Deist whom you detest' [SW] 'condemns with abhorrence' the treatment he has received 'from other parts of the [Wesley] family'. SW's veneration of JW and CW is due to their 'natural abilities alone', not to envy [as Sarah had suggested]. If SW had had 'similar advantages' to theirs he believes that he would have received 'similar honours'. He is not aware that he is their mental inferior.

SW is 'amazed' by Sarah's wish that their altercations be private. His preference is that they have no altercations. As their views always will be 'Alps' apart, silence is the only way to preserve peace.

SW→Sarah   3–5/1791

GEU Wesley Coll. ltr 73   I think tht [sic] our Controversy may be decided
📧 'Sunday'[76]

Sarah [presumably in a letter, not preserved, that replied to SW→Sarah, 'Saturday', entered immediately above] is inaccurate about the time of 'the misunderstanding between the brothers' [JW and CW]. This misunderstanding increased, but did not originate, with the ordination of laymen. 20 or 30 years ago [in fact, about 1758], JW published *Reasons against a Separation from the Church* [*of England*]. In the preface JW says 'that at present it is not expedient (whatever may be lawful) for us to separate'; in the same preface CW says that 'for me it is neither expedient nor lawful to separate'.

That JW and CW were not in agreement at CW's death 'is plain by the letter in the [*Arminian*] *Magazine*' in which the concept of 'consecrated ground', which CW respected, is ridiculed. SW knows that it has been not 'merely a religious

---

[76] Ltr follows the preceding letter, as SW provides in ltr further detail supporting his argument that CW palliated Lord Mornington's 'vice' and elaborates his view of the misunderstanding between JW and CW. As a letter [not preserved] from Sarah to SW presumably intervened between the immediately preceding letter and this ltr, ltr presumably was written eight days after the immediately preceding letter, and hence within the same dating range as that letter.

pretence' to attack principles and not men, but no one other than the contending parties [to an argument] has ever believed the distinction to exist.

Four or five of Lord Mornington's 'bawdy songs', written a few years before he died [in 1781], were in a drawer of CW's bureau. SW thinks that CW's dislike of 'Lady Ann' [probably Lady Anne Gatehouse, but perhaps a further reference to the actress Ann Spranger Barry Crawford, *see* SW→Sarah, 'Saturday', 3–5/1791, entered immediately above] came from his fear that she would 'seduce' Sarah 'to plays and other public amusements', and would thereby 'detach' Sarah from the principles that CW desired Sarah to adopt.

SW does not consider that he was 'ill treated (in the strict sense)' by JW. SW believes, however, that 'ridicule is less mercy than opposition'. He proposes to end this discussion. Sarah laments SW's 'want of faith'. He laments her 'excess of credulity' and regrets seeing her 'rich freight of talents wrecked on the sands of Methodism'.

Sarah→SW   Chesterfield St   **14/5/1791**
GEU in box 4   Hearing by Miss Deane of your Indisposition—I write
▣ 14/5/1791

AD has told Sarah of SW's indisposition. Sarah asks whether SW is lame 'from accident or gout'. She describes her activities, her travel plans and her attitude to servants.

Sarah→SW   Chesterfield St   **27/5/1791**
GEU in box 4   I thank you for giving me an opportunity
▣ 27/5/1791

Mrs Latrobe [Latrobe's wife Anna, *d*1824] often has told Sarah that SW seemed to retain a 'bad opinion' of CW's memory. CW was convinced that SW had made an unworthy 'connection' [with CLM] and had required SW to break it off, whereas SW was convinced that the aspersions against this connection were false and malicious and refused to end it. Sarah told Mrs Latrobe that the only part of SW's conduct which Sarah lamented was SW's continuance of the connection as an 'amour'.

SW had asked Sarah how a woman should be treated who was a man's constant companion, bore him children and showed 'every instance of disinterested affection'. Sarah's advice was that 'the man should marry her'. In addition to believing that marriage is a 'sacred institution', she considers that marriage is 'the mode best calculated for the education of children and the dignity of women'. She advises that SW will regret not marrying and asks why he will not marry [CLM].

Sarah reads daily and would be pleased to read together with SW [when she returns from Margate]. Margate 'brings many sad and sweet remembrances' of JW [who died on 2/3/1791]. People in Margate love Sarah on his account. Her health has benefited from this.

SW→Sarah   **5/6/1791**

Fitzwm ltr 3   I have but two objections to marrying.

☞ Sun 5 Jun={1791}, a reply to Sarah→SW, 27/5/1791

SW has two objections to marrying: he is not rich enough, and to 'tie' his person would be to lose his heart, to which 'she who valued it would hardly consent'. He agrees that 'legal order is a necessary thing', and that a man who truly loves must wish to make 'the object of his affection honourable as well as happy'. But 'would not a woman who loves rather sacrifice her honour than her happiness? Can she not better bear the sneers of a capricious world than one cold glance from him for whom alone she lives?' CLM 'has never once expressed a desire' to marry SW formally. Were she to do this, or to reproach SW 'for the injury done to her reputation', SW would 'marry her and hate her tomorrow'.

With respect to [CW's] 'management' of SW in 'that unfortunate business' [CW's requirement that SW break off his relationship with CLM, *see* Sarah→SW, 27/5/1791], SW was able to 'make allowances for parental anxiety, and the obstinate prejudices of old age'. However, CW should have been indulgent 'towards youth' and able to put himself in SW's situation. SW acknowledges that CW could not have meant 'otherwise than well'; had CW 'dealt candidly', SW would have been reasonable in his response. 'There seemed a fatal bar' to SW's loving CW, which SW could have done. SW's resentment towards CW was 'that of a heart damped or disappointed in the exercise of its best affections by one who best deserved them'.

SW will be glad 'to appoint an hour' [to read with] Sarah at any time that suits them both. He is glad that Sarah no longer uses the 'syrup' she has been taking [as a medicine] as Mr Anderson, a surgeon, told SW that it contains mercury. Before leaving London [for Taunton], probably about 24/6/1791, SW plans to call on Sir P[eter] B[urrell, 1754–1820, MP for Boston, Lincolnshire, 1782–1796, from 1796 1st Baron Gwydir]. SW is happy that his dog, Harley, died without his having to kill her.

Sarah→SW   Chesterfield St   **16/6/1791**

GEU in box 4   I thank you for your Candour

☞ 16/6/1791

Sarah thanks SW for his candour [in SW→Sarah, 5/6/1791] and is pleased that her candour has not offended him. She is consoled that SW is not acting against his principles, although her principles regarding marriage are very different. She trusts that their 'different modes of faith or action' will neither 'diminish' nor 'interrupt' their affection.

Sarah has felt affection for SW since he was 'a little child'. She regrets that he will leave London before she returns and hopes his stay away [in Taunton] 'will not be beyond a month'. She has received letters from family members and sends her love to AD.

SW→SGW   Taunton   **27/6/1791**
BL Add 35012 f 3   I got to Taunton safe about 5 o'clock on Saturday
🖃 Mon 27 Jun & pmk[77]→🖃

SW arrived safely in Taunton on Saturday [25/6/1791]. He is convinced that he
will never be able to live contentedly in London; for his health and peace of
mind he should not remain there. Were it not for the sake of 'a very few' people
in London he would live on his 'scanty pittance' in Taunton. Anyone wishing to
make his fortune by medicine should not come to Taunton as everyone here is so
healthy. He sends love and best wishes and asks SGW to tell Mrs [Arabella]
Mitz that he has not forgotten her.

Shepherd→SW   Chesterfield St   **7/12/1791**
BL Add 35013 f 28r   Although I dare scarce flatter myself
🖃 7/12/1791

Shepherd writes to SW in friendship. She hopes that his spirit is 'pure and
happy'. She understands from Abbey [Abigail Cox, SW's cousin] and from
other London friends that SW's family are well.

Although Shepherd doubts whether a recommendation from her 'will now be
of any great weight' with SW, she nevertheless proposes that SW consider being
'serviceable' to Mr Dumont, who presents this letter to SW. Dumont, a [Roman]
Catholic whose relations are in Paris, is a dancing master who went to Ireland
with his father, also a dancing master. There the father instructed the son and
also the children of the Countess of Moira [Elizabeth Hastings Rawdon, 1731–
1808], who has given the son a high recommendation. Dumont the son hopes to
work in London 'if he finds sufficient encouragement'. SW's profession gives
him the opportunity of assisting Dumont to teach 'in private families' and also
'in some genteel schools'. Dumont's 'interest' with Lady Moira's children, and
his prospects of introductions 'to other families of name', may enable him 'to be
grateful' to SW for his efforts.

Shepherd felt JW's death deeply. She 'will not look upon his like again' unless
SW, 'informed with a double portion' of JW's spirit, stands up in JW's place.
SW would not be 'hindered' in doing this by 'want of natural abilities'. He
possesses a 'strong sense of manly understanding' and 'powers of utterance and
address' to make his expressions eminently useful. [In an annotation, SW
comments that 'the plaister of Paris'—i.e., Shepherd, who is in Paris—'is too
coarse to produce the intended effect'.]

---

[77] Pmk type L6 or late L5 (*Willcocks/Jay* p 5) limits ltr's years to 1791–94.

Shepherd→SW   24/4/1792

MA Letters to Wesleys v 1 ltr 36[78]   It is now full five months since I wrote
🗎 24/4/1792

It is 'full five months' since Shepherd wrote [on 7/12/1791] to SW via Mr
Dumont. Although SW has 'taken no notice' either of her or of her letter, she has
observed 'with exquisite delight' every report about SW that sets him 'high in
the world's opinion' and gains him 'fresh additional honours from the wise and
the good'.

Yesterday [23/4/1792], Shepherd saw the pamphlet *Vindex to Verax* in a
bookshop window and could not resist looking at it. She asked who wrote it. The
bookseller said that the author was SW and, as proof, showed her a sample of
SW's handwriting, which she recognised. She bought the pamphlet and
subsequently produced it to several of JW's friends to whom she identified the
author, to their great delight. She showed it also to Mr Wathen [not identified]
and Miss Cope [not identified], and they 'carried home' the pamphlet.

It was 'noble' for SW to write this pamphlet, which 'must do him honour'.
Shepherd hopes that it may 'endear' SW to every branch of his family and
'increase all the comforts that stream from cordiality, sweet esteem, and the
union of affections'. She sends her warmest good wishes: may SW prosper and
'climb the utmost summit of genius and virtue'.

SW→Shepherd   26/4/1792

MA Letters to Wesleys v 1 ltr 36[79]   Let no apparent neglect be misconstrued
🗎 26/4/1792

SW assures Shepherd that his 'apparent neglect' [in answering Shepherd→SW,
7/12/1791] should not be 'misconstrued' as ingratitude. He has 'a lively
remembrance' of her 'past good offices' and has been 'of service' to Mr
Dumont.

SW's 'more distant' correspondence with Shepherd is caused by what he thinks
is their irreconcilable difference of opinion. He recently wrote [not preserved] to
a priest whom he has esteemed for a long time, setting out fully, explicitly and
freely his 'entire sentiments on two points', but has not yet received a reply.
SW's views on these points are 'very dissimilar' from Roman Catholic doctrine
and are likely to lead to his 'censure' or 'condemnation' by the Church. He cares
'not three straws' for excommunication and will not be 'drubbed' or 'flattered'
into orthodoxy. He refuses to be a hypocrite and will not cease to avow his
beliefs. The Vatican's [fire]crackers 'are no longer mistaken for the thunderbolts
of Heaven'. It is up to the Catholics whether they wish to 'retain' SW in their
society. His primary, principal ambition 'is to live and die quietly'.

---

[78] Ltr is a copy by Shepherd of the original letter [not preserved].

[79] Ltr is a copy by Shepherd of the original letter [not preserved].

Sarah→Penelope Maitland   **about 1/5/1792**

Bodl Ms Eng. Misc. c.502 f 43r–44v   It was with the greatest pleasure
ltr undated[80]

Sarah thanks Penelope Maitland for her 'flattering opinion of Vindex's performance' [SW's vindication of JW in SW's pamphlet *Vindex to Verax*]. Sarah now is 'at liberty' to tell her that SW is the author.

SW→'Reverend Sir'   **5/1792?**

MA DDWes/6/58[81]   I return you thanks for your Letter
ltr undated[82]

SW thanks the recipient [an unidentified Roman Catholic priest] for his reply [not preserved] to a letter [not preserved] that SW wrote to another [Catholic priest]. 'Young Mr D' [perhaps Derché, who is mentioned in SW→Sarah, 15/6/1792 and SGW→Sarah, 27/6/1792] considered that the opinions [on religious doctrines] which SW expressed [in his earlier letter] should be refuted by the recipient's 'masterly pen'.

SW quotes from, and responds at length to, the recipient's arguments concerning the necessity of baptism, the need to enter the Catholic Church in order to be saved, and the requirement for Catholics to submit to the authority of the Church's teaching. He takes issue with the argument that only marriages solemnised within the Catholic Church are valid, and points out the consequence that all those married within the Church of England would be 'living in fornication'.

SW's own definition of marriage is 'a mutual agreement of male and female to love and adhere to each other'. Such a contract deserves 'to be as inviolably kept, as that enforced by all the spiritual authority in Europe'. However, SW believes that having a 'public marriage ceremony' was deemed necessary for political reasons rather than for religious ones.

Although SW anticipates his recipient's response that SW is opposing his 'private judgement' to the authority of the Church, he argues for the right to exercise private judgement. He considers that private judgement is 'the true spring of all that implicit faith which is asserted by ecclesiastics to be so salutary and meritorious'.

---

[80] Ltr placed here because Shepherd→SW, 24/4/1792, reports seeing *Vindex to Verax* in a bookshop. Ltr <25/5/1792, when Sarah was *en route* to France.

[81] Ltr is a draft with several passages crossed out and the salutation altered from 'Reverend & Dear Sir' to 'Reverend Sir'.

[82] Ltr placed here for the following reason. In SW→Shepherd, 26/4/1792, SW mentions his recent letter to a Catholic priest on points of Catholic doctrine, to which SW has not yet had a reply. Presumably it is that letter which was referred for reply to the more 'masterly pen' of recipient of ltr, who presumably then wrote to SW about the end of April 1792. As ltr is SW's response to the latter, a May 1792 date for ltr appears plausible.

With regard to attending 'the public Catholic service', SW thinks that until 'authority *ex cathedra*' certifies whether or not his opinions are heretical it will be 'more modest and more candid' for him to remain in retirement than to pretend to be submissive [to the Catholic Church] when he is not. The latter position would be 'not humility but hypocrisy'. If his errors are 'not of a damning nature', he should be 'honourably recalled' [to the Catholic Church]. Otherwise, he should be 'honestly excluded' [from it].

Sarah→SW   Chesterfield St   **26/5/1792**
GEU in box 4   We came at seven o'clock last night to this place
▣ Sat 25; pmk 1792[83]
   Sarah arrived at Dover last night [25/5/1792] *en route* to Calais. She describes the town and people she has met. [SW annotates this letter, remarking that 'a ripened genius is the best of two legged things'.]

SW→Sarah   **15/6/1792**
GEU Wesley Coll. ltr 49   She whom I best love because She best loves me
▣ 15 June & addressed to Sarah at Calais→ⅰ
   Although the woman [CLM] whom SW loves best 'because she best loves me' wants to know some Latin, SW will be happy if she is a 'perfect mistress of English and French', which he anticipates that she will be. When Sarah returns [from Calais], SW probably will be in the country; he is planning to leave London on 21/6/1792 or 24/6/1792 and is likely to be away for not more than six weeks. Even if he finds 'a situation suitable for a continuance' he would have to return to London to get his effects [in Chesterfield Street] in order. SW doubts that he will be 'permanently fixed before next summer'. He knows his income and considers his prospects to be 'neither brilliant nor gloomy'. He does not wish to be idle. He considers his 'continued labours' to be 'the least recompense' he can make to the woman [CLM] 'who has sacrificed all to me' and has refused other offers in order to follow SW wherever he may go.
   AD intends to holiday in Flanders. She is a 'perturbed spirit' and a self-tormentor, who cannot be reasoned with or comforted. Mr Derché is 'a clever fellow', but SW doubts his honesty.

---

[83] Assigned to Saturday 26/5/1792 for the following reason. In Sarah→CW Jr, 25/5/1792 (GEU in box 4) Sarah says she leaves Rochester for Dover that day; this ltr says she arrived at Dover 'last night', i.e., on 25/5/1792.

SGW→Sarah   Chesterfield St   **27/6/1792**

GEU in box 4   My Dearest Daughters last Letter shou'd have been answered
🖃 27 June & Sarah in Calais→ⅈ

SGW conveys this letter by 'our kind friend' AD whom Sarah will rejoice to
meet [in France]. Yesterday [26/6/1792] SW and SGW dined with Mr Derché,
who is going with Mr Leviere [i.e., Rev. Peter Lièvre, *c*1754–1819, grandson of
SW's aunt Susanna Wesley Ellison] and his wife [Mary] to Leicestershire. SGW
does not know on what day SW is 'going into the country' [*see* SW→Sarah,
15/6/1792]. SGW will miss his company, particularly at meals, but it gives SW
pleasure 'to leave the dust of Marybone for fine fields', and SGW hopes that the
change of scene will be conducive to his health.

SW→SGW   **9/7/1792**

GEU Wesley Coll. ltr 50   I may now well say that I am at Heaven's Gate
🖃 9/7/1792

SW is now well but had been 'almost at death's door' since Friday [6/7/1792]
because of a fever and throat problem. His 'dear little friend' [CLM] 'had not a
moment's rest for two nights' because of her concern for him. She 'needs only to
be known' to be 'loved and believed'. He asks about Sarah and CW Jr. SW is 'at
no formidable distance from London' and hopes to visit Chesterfield Street
[SGW's house] in a week. SGW can write to him by the penny post in care of
[James] Kenton, 18 Charterhouse [where Kenton was a pensioner from 1790 to
1802].

Sarah→SGW   **16/7/1792**

GEU in box 4   I am with the Lediards, and probably may be in Town
🖃 16/7/1792

Sarah rejoices at SW's recovery. She wrote a letter to him [not preserved] from
Canterbury.

Latrobe journal entry   Ridge   **18/10/1792**

JRUL English Ms 1244 f 119r   Okely left London for Bedford
journal entry dated 18/10/1792

Latrobe went to see Mrs Wesley [SGW] this morning. SW 'is gone to live
somewhere in Hertfordshire' [Ridge]. He has 'taken a companion' [CLM]. It is a
pity that SW 'should be lost to the world and good society'.

SW→SGW   Ridge   **7/11/1792**
MA DDWF/15/5   I think I need not be told that every grand Step in Life
▣ 7/11/1792

SW does not need to be told that 'every grand step in life ought to be well weighed, and thoroughly considered before it be taken'. He has taken one such step within the past month [deciding to live with CLM away from home, *see* Latrobe journal entry, 18/10/1792], with much thought about its consequences. His 'acquaintance of ten years duration' [CLM] has confirmed SW's resolution to spend the rest of his life with her. Her actions have given the lie to her accusers; nonetheless, SW must comment on their charges. She has been painted as a 'fickle and unsteady character', yet CLM acknowledged that she loved him soon after he first 'became acquainted with her' in October 1782. Since then she has turned down several offers of marriage from men able to support her in the style in which she was originally educated, preferring SW in his 'wooden cottage' and his 'splendid fortune of £150 per year'.

CLM has been presented as having a 'careless, prodigal' disposition and as resembling her 'extravagant' father [George Martin, *d*1784, from 1768 a surgeon at St Thomas's Hospital, London] and 'vain' mother [Mary Nickelson, who married George Martin in London on 13/3/1754]. But CLM has managed for several years to live on £30, 'decently and out of debt'. SW has not helped her financially, although it was alleged 'by him who has gone to his own place' [CW] that SW would 'liquidate her debts and administer to her luxuries' as soon as he became of age.

CLM has been called 'a coquette, nay more, a wanton'. These allegations are false. They were 'engendered in the heart of envy and vomited from the mouth of malice'. SW has 'personal proofs' which 'it would not be delicate to adduce' that before she was his she was 'pure and untouched'. If CLM was seduced, SW was her seducer. It might be thought that SW would wish to make the woman he loves 'respected' by going through the ceremony of marriage with her. But she is 'truly and properly' SW's 'wife by all the laws of God and nature' and could not be made more so 'by the mercenary tricks of divine jugglers'. For CLM to be loved she needs only to be known. She is as guilty of the charges brought against her as SGW was of those brought by JW's 'wicked wife' [Mary Wesley, 1710?–1781, widow of Anthony Vazeille; she married JW in 1751 but subsequently parted from him].

SW→Sarah   **1st half of 1793**

MA DDWes/6/40   I thank you for your Letter which I had answered before now
ltr undated[84]

SW thanks Sarah for her letter [not preserved]. He would have replied sooner
but thought that his reply would not be worth four pence [in fact, postage for a
letter sent between London and Bristol was five pence]. He agrees with her that
'a long suspension of verbal or epistolary intercourse' often causes 'total
indifference' and finally ends in 'total oblivion'.

Bristol would probably be as 'melancholy' to him [as a place to live] as
London is 'hateful'. He could not enjoy the place [Bristol] where the 'first (and
most precious) opportunities of literary superiority were offered' [to him] but
were 'unfortunately refused'. While 'memory lives', he is bound to detest 'the
other place' [London], to which hunger drags him twice a week—it has been the
scene of most of his errors and of all his sorrows.

Mr Willis [not identified], whom Sarah has called [in her letter] the 'learned
doctor', is still a sociable acquaintance and a useful correspondent 'in all that
concerns Greek and Latin', but SW does not consider him a real friend.

SW has not 'parted' with Mrs Barnes's school: they have acceded to his terms.
If SW could earn the same elsewhere, he would leave this school: 'the profits are
inadequate to the slavery'. SW does not object to the walk, which is 'pleasant
and salutary', but to the 'unworthy employment of teaching sound without sense,
without honour, and without any real advantage'. Perhaps his profession is
intended as a penance for a few of his 'juvenile indiscretions'; he thinks that he
has already expiated them. The worst of these indiscretions might have been
'prevented, or at least reformed', by 'one encouraging word from the mouth of
reason and tenderness' [i.e., from CW].

SW doubts whether Sarah guesses what he considers to be his worst fault: it is
not 'the imprudency of intemperance' or 'the saying Latin instead of English
prayers' or the alliance [presumably with CLM] which has given him the
opportunity of respecting himself 'in an instance where most men secure to
themselves lasting and deserved contempt', but 'the neglect of those talents'
which SW would be hypocritical 'not to own uncommon'.

If SW had met justice from others and from himself, both his 'usefulness and
celebrity' would have 'run parallel' by this time. But he has almost given up
complaining and regretting. He is happy to know that he is sincere, and to feel
himself mortal: 'a Struldbrug's existence' [immortality] presents to him 'the
truest picture of Hell'. He has health and, in the country, peace. He would
willingly render happy all who love him.

SGW is 'very kind'. She appears to believe that the cause of his 'leaving father
and mother (though only half is now true)' [i.e., SW's moving from SGW's
home to live with CLM] is 'rational and defensible'. However, Sarah should

---

[84] Ltr addressed to Sarah at Mrs Ford's, at whose home in Clifton near Bristol
Sarah stayed apparently from at least 4/4/1793 and possibly earlier (*see*
Sarah→SGW, 4/4/1793, MA DDWF/14/8) to 22/6/1793 (according to
Sarah→SGW, 20/6/1793, GEU in box 4).

know that SGW considers that there was 'less absolute necessity' for Sarah's absence [from London].

AD is 'pretty well'. She is 'a delicious woman' whom SW loves, as he ought, 'second best [to CLM] in the world'.

SGW→Sarah 29/5/1793

GEU in box 4   We are all expecting to hear from my Dearest Sally

▣ 29/5/1793

CW Jr was 'miraculously saved from being murdered last Saturday night' [25/5/1793] when he was attacked by three villians at 10 pm. SW is here [at Chesterfield Street] today and unites with the rest of the family in sending love to Sarah [who is in Clifton near Bristol].

SGW & CW Jr→Sarah about 10/6/1793

WBRR v 3 (Nov 1851) p 406   *SGW:*   Your brother Charles is, thank God,

                                  CW Jr   What reasons have I, my ever dear

ltr undated in *WBRR*[85]

SGW: CW Jr is recovering [from his attack, *see* SGW→Sarah, 29/5/1793], although his bruises remain sore. But SW, returning home [to Chesterfield Street] through Savile Row about 11 pm last night, 'was stopped by two fellows; and, not choosing to be knocked down, delivered his purse with some money, and his watch', worth £9/9/-. CW Jr and SW thus 'have both by turns fallen among thieves'. SGW has been supported by her sense that 'we are yet the Lord's care' and is grateful that Sarah escaped SGW's 'frights and distress by not being here'.

CW Jr: CW Jr is thankful that God has miraculously spared him from death. He asks for Sarah's prayers.

---

[85] Ltr placed here because it is answered by Sarah→SGW, 14/6/1793?.

Sarah→SGW   **14/6/1793?**
GEU in box 8   Our Letters (I imagine) met on the road
ltr undated[86]

SGW's letter [SGW & CW Jr→Sarah, about 10/6/1793] was welcome, and the 'billet' [in that letter] from 'poor Charles' [CW Jr] was truly welcome. SW 'acted wisely in not contending with villains': losing a watch is a trifle compared with risking life or limb. Sarah feels that SW will miss his watch which, she recalls, was excellent and 'too valuable to be immediately replaced'. She desires that 'our hearts' be influenced by 'these deliverances' [of CW Jr and SW from danger].

SW→SGW   Ridge   **25/6/1793**
Fitzwm ltr 4   I send you a Goose together with the Giblets
◧ 25/6/1793

SW sends a goose which was killed today and should not be eaten immediately. His messenger expects to return [to Ridge] with the 'shower bath' and some music books which should be packed carefully to avoid damaging the bindings. SGW should forward any letters; SW expects one from Guildford. He expects to come to his 'well-beloved London' some time in the holidays, possibly when SGW is at Mrs Luther's home [in the country]. CLW sends her respects. SW asks to be remembered to CW Jr, whose name SW has seen in the newspapers as one of 20 or 30 people wounded by 'nocturnal assassins'.

SW→SGW   Ridge   **10/7/1793**
Fitzwm ltr 5   I hope that your Goose turned out as it ought
◧ 10/7/1793

SW hopes that SGW had an 'agreeable time' with Mrs Luther. He comments on the hot weather. He thanks SGW for the book of Oratorio songs, and thinks they must have been taken to Mrs [Arabella] Mitz's since their musical party there. He expects that SGW is waiting for the arrival of Sarah in London. He plans to be in London one day next week. There will be fireworks at Ridge on Saturday evening [13/7/1793]. CLW sends her respects: 'she is but indifferent at present: the heat and her own weight are almost too much for her'.

SW has written to [Samuel] Tooth about SW's house [in Guildford], but thinks that there is a curse on it.

---

[86] Ltr placed here because Sarah says she is planning to leave Mrs Ford's in Clifton in a week to go to Taunton, and Sarah→SGW, 20/6/1793 (GEU in box 4), fixes Sarah's departure from Clifton at 22/6/1793. Also, by the time of ltr, CW Jr has recovered sufficiently from his 25/5/1793 attack to have written to Sarah (in SGW & CW Jr→Sarah, about 10/6/1793). 14/6/1793 accordingly appears to be a plausible approximate date for this ltr.

SGW→Penelope Maitland   23/7/1793
Bodl Ms Eng. Misc. c. 502 f 95–96   I ought to have been much earlier
☑ 23/7/1793
SGW thinks that SW's 'appearance of low spirits' is caused by 'his great attention to books'. He has been studying Greek lately 'with scarce any help but that of knowing the letters' and appears to have learnt that language. Latin 'is quite easy to him'. Conceivably he 'may be called to preach' in 'our established Church' [of England]. SGW believes that SW will have Penelope Maitland's good wishes and prayers for whatever he undertakes.

Sarah→SW   10/8/1793
GEU Wesley Coll. ltr 89   You ask what could so suddenly turn a Monster
☑ 10/8/1793
SW [in a letter not preserved] asked 'what could so suddenly turn a monster [SW] into an angel of light' deserving Sarah's 'notice and society'. When Sarah was last at Margate she urged SW [in Sarah→SW, 27/5/1791] to 'do an act of justice' and marry the woman [CLM] 'of whose fidelity and good qualities' SW told Sarah he was 'well assured'. SW's reply [SW→Sarah, 5/6/1791] said that he 'abhorred the thought of marriage' and that marriage was not his friend's [CLM's] desire; 'if it had been', he 'would have complied and hated her'. Subsequently, SW has given out that he is married [SW married CLM at St Paul's, Hammersmith on 5/4/1793] and asks 'if a ceremony can change a character'. Sarah believes that marriage prevents 'the evils which would devolve on innocent children' and supports the respect of the community. She denies SW's assertion that she circulated reports that she heard [about him]; indeed, her warm defence of 'the absent [SW] and the dead [reference unclear]' led to some 'general altercations' with her family. She notes that SW declines her offer to visit [Ridge]; perhaps he 'will not easily forgive the offer'.

SW→Sarah   Ridge   14/8/1793
GEU Wesley Coll. ltr 51   I have read your Letter, I think without Prejudice
☑ 14/8/1793
SW has read Sarah's letter [not preserved] without prejudice or passion. He considers 'polemic divinity' to be amongst 'the worst of bad things' so will not cite Scripture which might be 'forced' into the support of either his or her positions. He has not lately consulted [Martin] Madan's book *Thelyphthora* which, though rational and apparently defensible by Scripture, has never furnished SW 'with any argument', nor has he established his 'system respecting marriage' on the basis of this book.
Sarah has mistaken SW's view of what forms marriage. It is not 'merely personal connection'; if it were, every prostitute would be a wife. Rather, in 'the eye of reason' and (SW believes) 'in the eye of God', a union of two persons who have 'faithfully united both body and soul' is 'as sacred and inviolable' as any union that 'human laws' can possibly sanction. The marriage ceremony is

not what distinguishes a concubine from a wife: a concubine 'cohabits with any man' without being tied to the relationship, whilst a wife loves and adheres to one man only.

Sarah's quotation from Deuteronomy [presumably xxii.28–29: 'If a man find a damsel that is a virgin, which is not betrothed, and lay hold on her, and lie with her, and they be found; Then the man that lay with her shall give unto the damsel's father 50 shekels of silver, and she shall be his wife'] is irrelevant because the quoted rule applied only to Jews, whereas Christians generally agree that 'the Ten Commandments are the only part of the Mosaic law' that applies to them, and that the Christian system superseded the earlier practices.

SW is not opposed to marriage; his argument with Sarah is about what forms marriage. He has always thought that 'the stigma of bastard' which the world applies to every child 'whose father has not paid a hackney parson his fare' is a 'tolerable excuse' for submitting to a marriage ceremony, particularly where 'great property is concerned'. However, he denies that a system [such as the one he advocates] is 'proved wrong' merely because some men have declared it to be wrong.

Sarah has suggested that SW might be injured by reports [that he has not had a formal marriage ceremony]. SW has few people whom he terms 'friends' and they know his sentiments. What his enemies think is of 'small importance'.

SW had no 'personal allusion' to any of Sarah's friends when he referred to 'the frail auditors in Chesterfield Street'. 'Severity on women' is not part of SW's conduct; those who know him know that he exhibits 'the contrary extreme'. Sarah's rigid principles should not prevent her continued attentions to a friend [SW] who has 'preferred the dictates of the God of nature' to 'the threats of the man of grace'.

SW→Sarah   about 18/8/1793

MA DDWes/6/54[87]   It is not easy to persuade an Antagonist that one had ltr undated but appears to follow soon after SW→Sarah, 14/8/1793[88]

SW continues discussing whether a marriage ceremony is required for marriage. He wants to present his arguments plainly and coolly but has no wish to prolong the discussion. Sarah said, in her letter [not preserved, presumably her reply to SW's statement in SW→Sarah, 14/8/1793, that the Ten Commandments are the only part of the Mosaic law that applies to Christians, and that the quotation from Deuteronomy was irrelevant], that 'Protestant divines assert that in the New Testament every part of the Jewish dispensation which is repealed is

---

[87] Ltr is incomplete. The four preserved pages of ltr contain no salutation or other explicit mention of the recipient. Sarah presumed as recipient because the content appears to be a continuation of matters discussed in SW→Sarah, 14/8/1793.

[88] Ltr presumably is a reply to Sarah's *c*16/8/1793 response [not preserved] to SW→Sarah, 14/8/1793. Sarah presumably replied *c*20/8/1793 [not preserved] to ltr, and SW then answered her reply with SW→Sarah, 22/8/1793?.

mentioned'. SW has no disagreement with this assertion. However, he has diligently searched the Bible chapters from Exodus to Deuteronomy, in which 'the whole Mosaic law is contained', and has failed to find any text 'which mentions any public ceremony relative to marriage'. He concludes that 'God never gave nor commanded any marriage ceremony to the Jews'; hence there was no such ceremony that could be repealed or for which some Christian ceremony might be substituted.

SW→Sarah   22/8/1793?
MA DDWF/15/6   I would not contend for a word.
🖃 Thursday night; presumably >10/8/1793 & <24/8/1793[89]

SW does not want to contend with Sarah about 'a word'. By 'lawfully' married, Sarah means 'according to those laws which priests have made, and lawyers daily unmake, if they are well paid'. All 'sensible people' know that a true marriage 'is the union of hearts and of persons'. The marriage ceremony, as JW said of transubstantiation, is 'a little harmless nonsense'; its form is a 'superfluity' other than as 'the means whereby property is secured, and confusion in genealogy prevented'. SW is ready at any time to prove that CLW belongs to him 'by leaping over a broomstick' in his kitchen or by 'worshipping her' in 'the presence of a drunken parson', but no ceremony would cause him to believe that she was thereby rendered 'a whit more honourable, or better either in body or soul than she has been for these eight years past' [presumably their time of intimacy].

SW is no 'stickler' for the morality of polygamy, although he is convinced that Martin Madan intended it as the lesser of two evils. Madan rightly maintained that 'fidelity is the true essence of marriage' and that the phrase 'he shall cleave unto his wife' is more accurately translated from its Greek original as 'he shall be cemented in his woman'. Christ never even hints that 'any outward form or ceremony' is essential to a true marriage. However, although SW despises the marriage ceremony, he does not condemn it, and he acknowledges that it can have practical value in some circumstances.

---

[89] The presumed sequence of correspondence is that Sarah initiated writing to SW <10/8/1793 (to congratulate him on reports of his marriage), SW then asked what could suddenly turn a monster [SW] into an angel of light, and Sarah replied to SW's letter [not preserved] with Sarah→SW, 10/8/1793. Other letters concerning the marriage ceremony, including the present ltr, are thus presumed to be >10/8/1793. Ltr presumably <SW→Sarah, 24/8/1793, in which SW remembers his 'definition of marriage' as 'the willing union of hearts and of persons'; as substantially that definition appears in the present ltr. Between 10/8/1793 and 24/8/1793 are only two Thursdays. Thursday 15/8/1793 discarded because SW wrote to Sarah on 14/8/1793 and the present ltr clearly is a response to a letter, not preserved, from Sarah. Therefore, ltr assigned to Thursday 22/8/1793.

SW→Sarah   Ridge   **24/8/1793**
WMM[90]   ...our Lord at an Ordinance of this kind was surely
☐ 24/8/1793
    SW remarks on Biblical references to weddings and discusses whether there
was a true wedding in Cana. All that SW can find in the Bible regarding 'any
matrimonial ceremony' is the statement 'God blessed them [male and female]
and God said unto them, Be fruitful, and multiply, and replenish the Earth'; this
is 'God's form of marriage'. If SW recalls correctly, his 'definition of marriage'
[in SW→Sarah, 22/8/1793?] is 'the willing union of hearts and of persons'—in
other words, a 'mental and corporal conjunction'. He is firmly convinced that
wherever such union is found 'a marriage is perfect, without any additional
ceremony invented or enforced by priests of any religion'. SW does not deny
that 'in the present state of human transactions (which is generally as
contradictory to reason and truth as can be)' a marriage ceremony may save a
woman from public disgrace, but believes that public opinion is an
unsatisfactory basis for determining right actions. People 'are bound in
conscience and honesty' to resist bad human laws which 'are as fallible as the
makers of them'. God says 'increase and multiply'; man says 'pay me before
you begin'; SW 'had rather take God's advice'.
    The cause of SW's debate with Sarah has not been polygamy (to which SW
refers, along with fornication and concubinage) but 'whether any outward
ceremony be any true, real, essential part of marriage or only a merely human
invention'. However erroneous Sarah may think SW's notions are, he is not to
be laughed or 'frighted' out of them although he is 'never averse to be reasoned
with upon them'. It is silly 'to be singular for singularity's sake' but it is wise to
be singular for the sake of truth.

Sarah memorandum   **18/1/1794**
GEU Wesley Coll. ltr 88   Had a great Anxiety taken from my mind
memo dated 18/1/1794[91]
    Obtaining confirmation of SW's marriage has taken 'a great anxiety' from
Sarah's mind. She saw CLW today and 'all family enmities ceased'.

SW→SGW   Ridge   **18/1/1794**
GEU Wesley Coll. ltr 52   We arrived here about half past 4
☐ 18/1/1794
    SW and his family arrived at Ridge about 4.30 pm. They were met by Mr
[Justinian] Casamajor [merchant with interests in West Indies sugar plantations,
1746–1820, who in 1792 inherited, and subsequently lived in, 'Potterells' in the

---

[90] Ltr is torn, with considerable text missing.

[91] This memorandum is part of a fragment of Sarah's notes entitled 'Mercies of
the Year 1794'.

nearby Hertfordshire parish of North Mymms]. Casamajor is willing to help find employment, possibly as a plantation overseer, for 'young Lloyd' [not identified], who is 30 years old, and has asked SW to call with Lloyd at Casamajor's 'counting house' in St Mary Axe in the City [of London] next Friday [24/1/1794].[92]

SW and CLW think it best to come to London on Wednesday [22/1/1794] and would like Hannah Williams [SW's cousin] to come to Ridge on Tuesday night [21/1/1794]. SW desires that his 'black hair dresser' [not identified] be with him on Thursday [23/1/1794] at 11 am. CLW can stay over in London until Sunday [26/1/1794], but SW cannot stay that long 'on account of the church'.

CW Jr told SW that [John] Ashley [bassoonist, 1734–1805, at this time a manager of the oratorio concerts at Covent Garden Theatre] advised CW Jr to advertise [presumably CW Jr's public debut, performing an organ concerto, which took place there on 19/3/1794], but SW thinks that unless £10 is spent on advertising it will be to no avail.

Shepherd→Sarah   **12/3/1794**
MA Letters Chiefly to Wesleys v 1 ltr 6   I this Instant receive your favor
⊡ 12/3/1794

Replying to Sarah's letter [not preserved], Shepherd says that she first was informed that SW was a [Roman] Catholic by Lord Traquair [Charles Stewart, *see* SW→Shepherd, 19/3/1784], who had heard this from the priest [Joseph Ferrers, Carmelite friar, 1725–1797] who was SW's confessor. Shepherd called on SW and told him what she had heard. SW seemed alarmed lest the news should reach CW. She urged some Catholics to 'stop their tongues, representing the consequences in the family'. Eventually, CW Jr was told. Shepherd thinks that when Mr Shepherd [not identified] said that SW 'had been seen at a Catholic chapel distributing the chalice at the altar' CW Jr came home 'brimful of anxiety'.

Shepherd then 'represented' to SW how much more proper it would be for him to break the news to CW than for CW to learn it from someone else. SW urged his lack of courage and his fear of the agitation that CW's anger would place him in, and asked Shepherd to tell CW herself. She said that if the news came from her CW would take it as an 'insulting triumph'.

SW and Shepherd then went together to consult with Bishop [James] Talbot, who proposed to send [Rev. Arthur] O'Leary [Irish priest, 1729–1802, whose 1781 publication *Miscellaneous Tracts* defended Catholics against criticisms made by JW in a letter 'containing the civil principles of Roman Catholics']. Shepherd said that sending O'Leary to CW would be like sending 'a Dymocke' [one of the family who held the hereditary office of King's Champion] with a challenge [at a coronation the Champion announces his readiness to defend the

---

[92] According to *Holden's Triennial Directory for 1805, 1806, 1807* (London, 1805), the business premises of Justinian Casamajor, merchant, were located at 18 St Mary Axe.

king's title to the crown]. CW, she added, was a gentleman and should be treated as such and with all tenderness due to a father. She wished the Duchess of Norfolk [Catherine Howard, 1718–21/11/1784, wife of Charles Howard, 1720–1786, 10th Duke of Norfolk] to go to CW and to tell him what SW had not 'the strength of heart' to say himself. In all her letters to and conversations with SW, Shepherd 'stimulated' him to act to all his family with a 'double portion' of charity and affection, thereby honouring the [Catholic] religion he had embraced.

After a quarrel, SW ceased corresponding with Shepherd. She has with her the last letter he wrote to her [SW→Shepherd, 7/1785?] before she left England [in 8/1785]. SW's letter came after Bishop Talbot had received a visit from CW with complaints of SW's conduct, when Talbot came to Shepherd and begged with her to 'expostulate' with SW. She wrote directly to SW [not preserved], and the letter in question was his reply. As a result of this a 'coolness' ensued, which 'ended in total silence'.

Shepherd→Sarah   14/3/1794

MA Letters Chiefly to Wesleys v 1 ltr 7   I think that you must have perceived
🖃 14/3/1794

In response to a letter [not preserved] from Sarah, Shepherd expands upon her previous letter [Shepherd→Sarah, 12/3/1794]. Shepherd loved SW as a 'fond mother' loves a 'darling child'. She formed such 'high hopes, expectations and ideas' of his understanding, his capacity and 'the strong powers and abilities of his mind and heart', that she wished and hoped he would help 'to build up in England a second temple, more glorious than the first' into which 'the Lord should come and reside'. She told SW that he should not suffer 'any of our people' [the Roman Catholics] to speak slightingly of CW, JW or any of CW's family. Shepherd saw CW's virtues. She counselled SW that CW's kindness 'deserves every return' and urged SW to offer to play the organ whenever CW preached 'a charity sermon in the afternoon'. Sarah should ask SW to confirm that this was Shepherd's advice to him.

Shepherd, who left England in August 1785, informs Sarah that SW's

---

[93] CW's deep affliction by SW's conversion to Roman Catholicism is indicated in a volume of poetry, now MA Charles Wesley mss, Samuel Wesley RC. The volume, which bears Sarah's annotation 'verses on his son Samuel on being made acquainted he had embraced the Roman Catholic religion', includes the following undated verses:

Farewell, my all of earthly hope,	But give I God a sacrifice
My nature's stay, my age's prop,	That costs me nought? My gushing eyes
Irrevocably gone!	The answer sad express,
Submissive to the will Divine,	My gushing eyes and troubled heart
I acquiesce, and make it mine;	Which bleeds with its belov'd to part,
I offer up my Son!	Which breaks thro' fond excess.

profession of Roman Catholicism was announced to CW 'sometime between Easter and Whitsuntide 1785' [the announcement, by the Duchess of Norfolk, can have occurred only in 1784, as the duchess died on 21/11/1784, and SW did not profess to be a Catholic in 1783, *see* SW→Shepherd, 26/12/1783].[93] On one occasion at Mrs [Elizabeth] Waller's home, Shepherd defended SW against some Methodists and apparently insulted them. Shepherd seeks a meeting [with Sarah] to try to heal old rifts.

SW→Sarah   **about 16/3/1794**
MA Letters Chiefly to Wesleys v 1 ltr 7   I think you must forgive
ltr undated but written on bottom of Shepherd→Sarah, 14/3/1794[94]
   Commenting on Shepherd→Sarah, 14/3/1794, SW notes that his 'quondam friend' [Shepherd] is sorry 'for all that her pride will suffer her to own'. The Wesleys have treated Shepherd harshly in some respects but justly in others. SW thinks that 'love and gratitude' are 'the strongest principles' in both Sarah and himself. If he were Sarah he would 'consent to an interview' [with Shepherd].

Shepherd→Sarah   **about 20/3/1794?**
MA Letters Chiefly to Wesleys v 1 ltr 26   I receive your favor and however
ltr undated[95]
   Shepherd refers to the altercation involving Mrs [Elizabeth] Waller [*see* Shepherd→Sarah, 14/3/1794] and to accusations that Shepherd alienated SW's affections from his family. Letters that SW wrote to her are now in France but she could possibly have them returned to her.

---

[94] Presumably Sarah sent Shepherd→Sarah, 14/3/1794, to SW for his advice about Shepherd's suggestion of a meeting with Sarah. Ltr, which gives SW's advice, presumably was written shortly after Shepherd's letter was sent to him.

[95] Ltr placed here because ref. to altercation involving Elizabeth Waller suggests that ltr shortly follows Shepherd→Sarah, 14/3/1794, in which Shepherd mentions this incident to Sarah, presumably for the first time.

Sarah→CW Jr   Ridge   **19/9/1794**
GEU in box 5   I must beg you to acquaint my Mother
▣ 19/9/1794

   Sarah will write to SW when she gets 'to the sea' [Ramsgate]. His illness 'afflicts' her: she fears 'he will be exhausted before he comes to the middle of life'. The distance [of Ridge] from London is unsuitable 'and may be fatal'. CW Jr should urge SGW to persuade CLW to take lodgings at Barnet. The 'present house [in Ridge] may be prejudicial to all their healths, especially in a lying-in'. Also, SGW 'would have more strength if she had a comfortable chamber' [when visiting CLW to assist her]. Sarah relies upon CW Jr to inform her if there are important developments concerning SGW or SW's illness.

Sarah→SW   Chesterfield St   **25/9/1794**
GEU in box 5   I designed to write to You at the end of my Journey
▣ 25/9/1794

   Sarah's thoughts and sympathies are with SW, whose health requires more attention than he gives it. By 'excess of labour and toil' he is jeopardising his future exertions and comfort. Why will he not hire a horse or enter a coach once a week? Sarah narrowly escaped an accident when travelling in a chaise.
   Sarah will be uneasy if SW and CLW stay at Ridge for the birth as one of them, probably SW, would have to sleep in a damp room and might become sick. She recommends instead that they try to find reasonable 'lodgings at Barnet'. She rejoices that SGW will attend CLW. Sarah would like to return [to London] before CLW lies in and hopes that CLW is 'tolerable'.

Sarah→SGW   Ridge   **30/9/1794**
MA DDWF/14/10   Yesterday, Mrs Keene & myself set out for this place
pmk (London) 1 October[96]

   Sarah wishes that SGW would stay with Mrs Bayles, who lives 'next door' to SW, rather than at SW's house in Ridge, where the only vacant bed is in a room that Sarah knows is cold. She would like SGW to mention this wish to SW, who would be very unhappy if SGW became ill as a result of her kind attention to CLW.

---

[96] Assigned to 1794 because ltr says Sarah has just arrived at Ramsgate, from where she wrote to SGW again on 9/10/1794, and both letters discuss SGW's planned visit to Ridge where CLW was expecting a baby.

SW→Sarah   Ridge   **1/10/1794**

GEU in box 5   I thank you for your Letter, wch I had probably answered

▣ 1/10/1794

SW hopes that he and Sarah can 'agree to differ without discording'. In the past SW may have 'opposed for the sake of imagined consequence and the love of singularity'. This happens 'no more'. He would be healthier if his mind were more tranquil, but his current exercise, particularly walking, does not seem injurious to his health or his life. He does not keep a horse because he can 'scarcely keep a family'. His future prospects are not good; he has few friends. He has 'many errors to lament, but only one crime, ingratitude'. Should he continue to live, he doubts not that his friendship with Sarah 'will be strengthened by age as it has existed by confidence'.

CLW is not 'tolerable' in any sense; within a fortnight SW expects her body 'must be lightened of the last load' he shall ever cause. SGW 'has not finally resolved' whether to attend CLW's delivery. The labour will be at Ridge; during CLW's confinement SW will be 'backwards and forwards' [to London] as usual. His presence at Ridge is necessary to avoid his property being wrecked by the servants and the nurse employed to attend CLW.

SW was shocked to hear of Sarah's accident. SW recently 'had an escape from robbery, perhaps murder'; he was travelling to London in Mr Wilkinson's carriage when they met a highwayman at night on Finchley Common. They were saved because of their 'lamps and pistols'.

SW likes the Quakers. He finds Erasmus 'admirable on all subjects'. He wishes that CW Jr was employed and out of SGW's way; he wishes that SGW were out of debt. CW thought and SW thinks that Sarah dips 'into too many books': if she read as deeply as she thinks, she 'would be too masculine'. SW has read 'too few books' because he was late in starting, but he is making up for this. He will know enough if he 'can make one human being happy'.

SW has been ill with colic but is now 'about'. He thinks that CLW would have been happier 'with a good and a foolish husband'.

Sarah→SGW   Ridge   **9/10/1794**

MA DDWF/14/11   By Charles's Letter I imagine this will arrive

▣ 9/10/1794

Sarah expects that SGW will be visiting Ridge shortly [where CLW is expecting a baby]. Sarah has been 'very anxious' on SW's and CLW's account, and hopes CLW 'will be happily brought through her hour of trial'. Sarah sends love to all and asks SGW to thank SW for his 'long letter' [SW→Sarah, 1/10/1794] to which Sarah will soon reply.

SGW→Sarah   Chesterfield St   **23/10/1794**
MA DDWF/21/10   I received My Dearest Sallys Letter at Ridge
▭ Thurs 23 Oct; pmk 23/10/1794

SGW stayed at Ridge until 'last Monday' [20/10/1794] and would have remained longer, but CLW's reckoning [of when her baby was due] was uncertain. CLW sends love to Sarah but 'is quite unfit for any exercise of mind'. CLW is 'very burthensome to herself' because of her size; she fears she may have twins, but SGW hopes otherwise. CLW 'begged' that Hannah Williams might come 'to stay with her and take charge of everything', particularly 'the dear sweet boy' [CW III] who is 'the best tempered child' that SGW ever saw. Hannah Williams sets off for Ridge tomorrow [24/10/1794]. SW is here [at Chesterfield Street] today but 'is not well in his bowels', a condition that has persisted 'for some days'.

SW→Sarah   Ridge   **26/10/1794**
GEU Wesley Coll. ltr 53   We are in daily or rather hourly expectation
▭ 26/10/1794

CLW's confinement is expected within hours. SW loves her and hopes that God will 'help her and make her happy whether she live or die'. However, 'the event has proved' that CLW was not designed to be SW's 'second self'. SW tries to dwell upon her virtues, but it is hard to esteem a person with 'an unbridled tongue'. SGW soon tired of her visit to Ridge and left on Monday [20/10/1794], thus defeating the aim of her visit which was to soothe and comfort CLW 'when she most needed it' [during her labour and childbirth].

SW believes that his and Sarah's thoughts on 'moral subjects' are generally similar, except those relating to marriage and polygamy. Other than with regard to CW, SW is guilty of 'no transgressions' besides those 'occasioned by a predominant and not a malignant passion'. SW's conduct towards CW was 'rather a sin of ignorance than malice'. Each was misrepresented to the other and taught 'to believe that each hated the other', whereas 'in truth neither hated either'.

SW remarks that the 'hypocrite [Thomas] Coke' [Methodist minister, 1747–1814, who in 1787 adopted the title 'bishop' in America, and in 1794 tried to establish bishops in the English Methodist church], is together with other 'bandits' making 'his episcopal church as similar in riches and power to the Court of Rome as he can'. 'Gain is now the godliness' of JW's successors. They should be allowed to 'dig their treasures' from CW's hymns; however, they should pay CW's 'lawful heir [SGW] a fair price for his property'. SGW has lent SW some 'curious letters' by CW and JW regarding ordination, which Sarah should see.

'Little Charles' [CW III] is well. Hannah Williams is here [in Ridge], spoiling him.

Sarah→SW   Chesterfield St   **12/11/1794**
GEU in box 5   I write to congratulate you on the Birth of a Daughter
☞ 12 Nov, ltr says Saturday is 15 Nov, & birth of child→ⅰ

Sarah congratulates SW on the birth of a daughter [Susanna Wesley, 1794–1797], whom she hopes 'may be happier than has been the fate of the females in our family to be'. She sends affectionate greetings to CLW. Sarah hopes to return from Rochester to London for Saturday dinner [15/11/1794] and 'longs' to see SW on Monday [17/11/1794]. She replies to SW's Biblical references to adultery and notes that CW III has not yet had whooping cough.

Sarah disapproves of the present form of infant baptism. She supposes that her 'aunt [Rebecca] Gwynne' will be the child's godmother, and asks whether, as previously discussed, SW intends to christen the child after their aunt [Emelia Wesley] Harper [1691?–1771?], whose name was 'Emily'.[97] Sarah notes, however, that 'the mother's name is commonly used for a first daughter'.

Sarah→SW   **29/11/1794**
GEU in box 8   The reason (if I recollect aright) of my observing at that time
☞ Sat 29 Nov={1783,1788,1794,1800,1806}[98]

Sarah had observed some time ago that the greater part of SW's life would be passed 'in controversy'. She always thought that he would leave the [Roman] Catholic Church, and she foresaw that when this happened his 'hand' would be against the Catholics and that they would oppose him. She recognises SW's 'talents and love for controversy' and attributes his 'aspersions on people and things' to 'a natural turn of opposition' rather than to delight of slander. However, his aspersions sometimes have the same effects as if he were malign, particularly in respect of his cousin, young 'Mrs L' [Mary Sturgis, who on 24/4/1783, at the age of 22, had married Rev. Peter Lièvre]. Her blameless life is undeserving of SW's accusations.

Sarah has proved some of SW's accusations false, including one that 'Mr L' [Peter Lièvre] sent 'Mr D' [presumably Derché and so identified by a later annotator, possibly Tooth] out of England. Mary, the Wesley family's 'vile servant', no doubt repeated to others the jests that she heard in the family parlour. Sarah hopes that her [male] cousin [Peter Lièvre] does not hear of SW's 'ill-founded conjectures', as they might embitter him forever.

---

[97] Susanna presumably was named after another aunt, Susanna Wesley Ellison [1695–1764], or after SW's grandmother Susanna Annesley Wesley [1670–1742].

[98] Ltr written after SW left the Roman Catholic Church. 1783 excluded because before SW's Catholic period. 1788 excluded because Sarah→Penelope Maitland, 29/7/1789, says SW was a Catholic then. Ltr calls Mrs Lièvre 'young'. 1800 (when she was 39) and later years excluded as she was unlikely to be so described then; also, Sarah is not known to have written letters to SW in 1800. Therefore ltr assigned to 1794.

SW→SGW   Ridge   **17/6/1795**
MA DDWes/6/47   Since I left London last I have been very ill
▣ 17/6/1795

SW has been very ill since last leaving London. He was taken ill on Finchley
Common and was nearly unable to proceed. He was able to reach Ridge and has
been very feverish and faint ever since. He is now somewhat better and would
have returned to London, except that his leg is still inflamed and painful, making
movement difficult. He hopes to come on Monday [22/6/1795], by some vehicle
if he is unable to walk. He asks SGW to send the enclosed [not preserved,
presumably notes cancelling his teaching engagements] to Paddington [AD's
school] and to High Street [Mrs Barnes's school] as soon as possible. He is
expected at the former between 12 and 1 pm and at the latter between 3 and 4
pm. SGW should tell [James] Kenton that SW regrets that he was unable to meet
him, and that Kenton will see him soon.

SW→Sarah   Ridge   **27/6/1795**
Fitzwm ltr 7   I was willing to answer your Letter at the first opportunity
▣ 27/6/1795

SW wanted to reply to Sarah's letter [not preserved] immediately, knowing that
she would be leaving Stoke, near Cobham [Kent], before the end of the month
[in fact, she had already done so]. SW's schools have now broken up so he has
more leisure to reflect on his state. He has never expected happiness in life, but
he 'aimed at comfort, and missed it'. He and CLW have spent the last two days
'without altercation', but considers this 'decent conduct' to be only a 'lucid
interval': whenever the 'fit of mania' returns, 'all its consequences will return
also'. SW still feels compassion for CLW, but 'esteem, delight and confidence
are no more'. CLW opened and read SW's mail while he was away. A planned
recent visit by SW to London was prevented by illness which confined him [in
Ridge] for three days.

CW Jr has sensibly given up the idea of organising a concert this year. It would
have been foolish for him to have done so in midsummer.

Few think alike on all subjects. SW considers different opinions to be the result
of differences in physiology—in particular, the structure of the brain. SW
believes 'true religion to have nothing (or little) to do with words; and nothing at
all with doctrines, at least such doctrines, the truth or falsity of which, nothing
but death can assure us'. He has clear evidence 'that height of good is height of
charity'. It is his greatest ambition to be 'all I can to the few who love me'.
Although he has been unfortunate, he has not been wicked.

SW→SGW Ridge **30/6/1795**

transcript in Baker[99] That I am one of the unfortunate I have too long known

◌ 30/6/1795

SW has known for too long that he is 'one of the unfortunate' and is mortified that he is causing 'uneasiness and disappointment to others'. Last night [29/6/1795] his leg suddenly became inflamed. He is now in much pain and is unable to stand on it. He had planned to be in London tomorrow [1/7/1795] and to meet Mrs [Arabella] Mitz at Cotton's [not identified] on Thursday [2/7/1795], and also to meet Mrs Mason [not identified] on Thursday, but cannot do so. Mr Corpe[100] [a doctor, see SW→SGW, 18/8/1800] is doing all he can for SW. SGW should send the enclosure [not preserved] by Mr Hull [not identified] or by another 'speedy messenger', as SW is expected to give Miss Mackenzie a lesson at Paddington [presumably at AD's school]. If SW cannot walk by Monday [6/7/1795] he will 'undoubtedly be conveyed' to SGW by some other means. He is impatient in his sufferings.

SW→Sarah Ridge **8/7/1795?**

Fitzwm ltr 8 Perhaps it may not be amiss to acquaint you

◌ Wed 9 July 1795, an incorrect date[101]

CLW probably has written to Sarah hoping that she will become CLW's friend and SW's enemy. Sarah can meddle or not in the dispute, as she wishes, but should know that 'no interference of any party or relation' will drive SW from the 'resolution' he has long made [to separate from CLW]. A 'favourable, or rather inevitable opportunity' appears to be present. He is well prepared for 'the worst that this woman [CLW] can say' of him or his loved ones. Her 'open violence' will have little effect other than to drive him 'more speedily into comfort' [presumably with AD] than he expected. Destroying SW's 'professional emolument' will concern him 'in a very trifling degree' as he can 'get bread' anywhere in Europe, and so can 'one who may be a similar sufferer with me' [presumably AD]. SW is 'fully prepared and determined to march boldly in the face of opposition, prejudice and ingratitude'. He will be in London on Monday [13/7/1795].

---

[99] The original ltr, from which SW's signature had been cut off, was sold at Sotheby's on 15/5/1979 to J. A. Gamble. Its present location is not known.

[100] The transcript reads 'Mr Caspe'.

[101] 9/7/1795 was a Thursday. Ltr assigned to Wednesday 8/7/1795 (rather than Wednesday 9/7/1794) as the discussion of SW's separation suggests 1795 rather than July 1794, when SW and CLW were expecting a child.

Shepherd→Sarah   5/8/1795
MA Letters Chiefly to Wesleys v 1 ltr 22   The honor of your letter, received
🖃 5/8/1795

Shepherd replies to Sarah→Shepherd, 4/8/1795 [not preserved, but identified by date in Shepherd→Sarah, about 10/8/1795, MA Letters Chiefly to Wesleys v 1 ltr 24, in which Shepherd asks for the return of her recent letters to Sarah and to CW Jr]. Commenting on CW Jr's and Sarah's accusation that SW's 'errors and misfortunes' were the consequence of his 'wrong choice of religion', Shepherd suggests that if SW has a reason to leave [the Roman Catholic Church], he should 'openly declare' this and should 'send his renunciation to Dr Douglas' [John Douglass, 1743–1812, who in 1792 succeeded James Talbot as Vicar Apostolic of the London district]. This action will be SW's 'full restitution in the eyes of all good Protestants'.

Shepherd declares that she will not bear a grudge or feel any shame or ill-will if this happens. She has love and tender affection for the [Catholic] Church, and wishes it 'cleansed' from every defilement. However, the Church cannot be guilty of all of SW's mistakes and misfortunes. The Church teaches obedience, mortification and self-denial, commands fasts and abstinence, and 'recommends corporal castigation' when necessary. The Church extols chastity, sobriety, temperance, poverty, humility and 'the life of angels'. Shepherd cannot conceive how the Church could have led 'a young man, a very boy [SW] to drunkenness, harlots and riotous living'. She adds that her phrase [in an earlier letter] 'the vermin of the bedstead' did not refer to SW's children.

Shepherd→CW Jr   6/8/1795
MA Letters Chiefly to Wesleys v 1 ltr 23   I have received rather an
🖃 6/8/1795

Sarah's letter [presumably Sarah→Shepherd, 4/8/1795, *see* Shepherd→Sarah, 5/8/1795] informed Shepherd that CW Jr had left open, on the breakfast table, a letter that she had written to him [possibly Shepherd→CW Jr, 26/7/1795, not preserved, but identified by date in Shepherd→Sarah, about 10/8/1795, MA Letters Chiefly to Wesleys v 1 ltr 24], and that SW saw this letter and copied a paragraph from it, which he showed to Sarah. This paragraph pointed out the advantages to a man like CW Jr of 'a connection with a virtuous wife' and the dangers of 'vicious connections'. Shepherd had not intended in this paragraph any specific allusion to SW's marriage.

Sarah→SW   Chesterfield St   30/9/1795
GEU in box 5   The reason I did not write sooner was, Mrs Wesley
🖃 30 Sep; pmk 1795

Sarah did not write sooner because 'Mrs Wesley' [CLW] intended to write every day. At Sarah's request, CLW has shifted to cheaper lodgings in Bristol costing 10/6 per week, where 'the Count' [not identified] also has taken a room.

Sarah sees her 'sister' [CLW] every day. On Sunday [27/9/1795] they went to the Moravian church.

CLW has not mentioned any 'disagreeable subjects' but is dejected and looks unhealthy. Her lodgings are more comfortable than at Ridge. CW III is fretful; he was 'a better child' when SW was with him than he is now. The daughter [Susanna Wesley] 'grows good humoured' and is much liked. CLW seems 'desirous of being economical' but has 'little skill in management'. Living at Ridge in a 'comfortless house' distant from a market did not provide the opportunity for her to learn 'habits of order', although she does not squander money on herself. The Count sets a good example. A number of Bristol friends have been seen and send regards. CLW's temper is mended but her spirits are not. Sarah believes that CLW will die soon and that SW will survive her.

Sarah reminds SW that in 1793 [the year of his marriage] the prayer of his soul was fully answered and he vowed obedience to God. SW should sin no more. SW's health was indifferent when Sarah left London. She is sorry that SGW is indisposed.

Sarah→CW Jr   6/10/1795
GEU in box 5   You will begin to think yourself forgotten
▣ 6 Oct[102]

CLW 'has very pleasant lodgings at Clifton' [near Bristol]. SW's letter to CLW [not preserved] indicates that SGW is 'not worse'. The bowel complaint is common in Bristol also: Sarah and the 'poor little girl' [Susanna Wesley] are both affected. Mrs Lewis [not identified] gave Sarah £1/1/- for SGW. Sarah gave this to CLW, 'whose cash dwindles', so SW should give SGW £1/1/-. Sarah's Bristol friends are very fond of CW III. They would like CLW also, if Sarah could persuade her to go out.

SGW→Sarah   Chesterfield St   21/10/1795
MA DDWF/21/11   As I find by your Letter (recd yesterday)
▣ 21/10/1795

CLW's health is more satisfactory than Sarah had apprehended from CLW's symptoms 'if she had not been breeding'. SW is in London and has gone to see [James] Kenton, who is ill. SGW let SW see Sarah's letter [Sarah→SGW, 6/10/1795], as it was about money. SGW is glad that CLW's 'dear offspring' are well. SW wrote [not preserved, presumably to CLW] 'the dear Babes,—kiss [them] for me'.

---

[102] Assigned to 1795 because Sarah at Kingsdown Parade, Bristol, to where SGW→Sarah, 21/10/1795 is addressed; also, CLW in Bristol at the same time.

CW Jr→Sarah   **31/10/1795**

MA DDWF/20/1   If I stood on ceremony you certainly would not be intruded

✉ 31/10/1795

Sarah [who is in Bristol] should be glad that she is not now at Chesterfield
Street. CW Jr hopes that CLW and her children 'are better, in health and spirits'.
SW 'went back [presumably to Ridge] this morning'. CW Jr mentions friends
and relatives he has seen including Shepherd, with whom he passed an
entertaining hour. SGW 'cannot accommodate you all here yet' and fears that
the [Chesterfield Street] house would 'give the dear children cold'. SW has a
bowel complaint.

SW→Sarah   Ridge   **12/1795?**

Fitzwm ltr 6   I cannot answer for what my Mother may have said

✉ Wednesday[103]

Discourse concerning SW's family is 'gloomy'. Both the females and the
males in the family have a 'happy talent' for 'betraying people into a dispute' by
'repeating every unguarded expression to their disadvantage'. SW does not
know exactly when he and SGW conversed about his children [CW III and
Susanna Wesley]. SW thinks that he said, when SGW was 'resenting' his cruel
punishment of 'the boy' [CW III], that 'one sound whipping' would be more
effective than 'very slight or even ridiculous punishments' for misbehaviour
such as standing in a corner, which CLW told him that Sarah applied to CW III
in Bristol 'without success'. SW also told SGW that CW III, 'young as he is',
acts best 'on reflexion'; he usually does as he is told when allowed a little time
to consider, except once when SW was forced to correct him 'with resolution'.

SW has not decided whether to bring CW III to London, where 'he is liable to
be foolishly indulged' and might get smallpox, or to leave him at Ridge, where
he is likely to be neglected and to disturb CLW 'in her bed' [presumably during
her impending confinement], for which CLW probably would reproach SW. He
is not concerned about CLW's conduct towards him. His heart is 'adamant to all
abuse and ill-usage' except from three or four quarters. He will have to decide
what to do about CW III in a week, judging by CLW's [presumably pregnant]
appearance.

---

[103] The dating of ltr is conjectural. Ltr > early November 1795 when CLW,
Sarah and CW III were still in Bristol (*see* CW Jr→Sarah, 31/10/1795). SGW to
Sarah, 21/10/1795 implies that CLW is 'breeding' and this ltr implies that
CLW's child is due shortly. There is no mention in the surviving 1796 letters of
CLW's pregnancy or of the birth of a presumably stillborn or short-lived child.

Sarah→SW   2/2/1796

GEU in box 5   I request the favor of You to relate faithfully to Mrs Wesley
⊟ 2/2/1796
SW should tell CLW all that Sarah wrote to SW from Bristol. CLW accuses
Sarah of writing unkindly to SW about CLW. However, if SW had shown CLW
the full letters, CLW would have perceived that Sarah was her sincere friend,
who went to Bristol to prevent SW and CLW parting, as Sarah maintained that
SW ought to bear with CLW's 'violent temper'. Sarah had imagined that she and
SW disagreed only on the 'fatal subject' of polygamy, yet SW told CLW,
falsely, that Sarah wrote [letter not preserved] that she was 'always quarrelling'
with SW and that CLW 'would never have a friend but on principle'. Sarah now
recognises that she was foolish to believe that 'any mediator between man and
wife' would be treated justly, kindly or gratefully by either.

Shepherd→Charles Howard   17/2/1796

Arundel
⊟ 17/2/1796
Shepherd asks Charles Howard [1746–1815, from 1786 11th Duke of Norfolk]
to use his influence to obtain the organist's post at the Charterhouse for CW Jr.
CW Jr is 'the Protestant, not the Catholic son [SW]' of CW. CW Jr has 'a
thousand prejudices to combat in those that would admire and encourage his
talents were it not that his name is Wesley'. The Methodists do not help him
because he is not a Methodist. [CW Jr did not obtain this post.]

SW→Sarah   3/3/1796

MA DDWes/6/34   It has been observed, & I believe truly, th.t people are
⊟ 3/3/1796
SW has never been treacherous to anyone. Although Sarah 'highly' resents SW
having quoted a passage [to CLW] from Sarah's letter [to SW], he never
considered the letter confidential, except from SGW. SW never imagined that
Sarah 'dreaded' CLW's knowing Sarah's opinion of 'any part' of CLW's
conduct. CLW and Sarah have exchanged letters in which CLW may have
detailed the 'dispute' [with SW]; he has no interest in the content of these letters.
His reason for quoting the passage was 'to check' CLW's 'insolence which
pretended that everyone' would defend her conduct against him. CLW also
maintained that Sarah agreed that CLW had cause for complaint against SW.
SW's quoting of the passage had 'the desired end': CLW was 'silenced' by
SW's statement that, however Sarah might condemn him, CLW's 'violence was
such as to leave her no firm friends but those who acted from principle'.
SW, far from being treacherous to Sarah, believes that Sarah may have been
treacherous to him. In consequence of Sarah's visit 'to her whom I now esteem
my only female friend on earth' [AD], SW had the 'utmost difficulty' in
convincing AD that SW 'had not endeavoured to render her an object of ridicule
and detestation' to both Sarah and CLW. AD wrote [not preserved] to SW that,

as a result of Sarah's conversation, AD was 'assured' that SW had 'fully disclosed' to Sarah 'every circumstance that could tend to disgrace and injure' AD. In consequence of what Sarah said, if SW had not been able to 'outweigh the impression' of Sarah's words, AD might well have been driven suddenly 'out of this world'. If SW had lost such a friend Sarah could never repair the loss.

Whatever Sarah's notions may be of SW's 'heart or conduct', SW 'shall always own' that Sarah intended him 'real service in the most distressful event of his life', for which he is very grateful. However, 'real candid friendship' can long subsist only 'between persons whose views, opinions and principles are the same'.

Sarah→SW   8/3/1796
GEU in box 5   That the utterance of mischievous, unkind, detrimental
📧 8/3/1796

Truths that are mischievous, unkind or detrimental should not be uttered, but truths that concern the good of society, the conviction of the guilty or the 'motions of conscience' should be disclosed. Sarah said nothing to SW that she did not also say in the same words 'to the person concerned' [AD]. SW's repeating these things without explaining their context must have injured Sarah in the eyes of the person to whom SW knows Sarah has been a friend. Sarah is astonished by SW's 'accusation'. SW gave Sarah 'the most arduous of commissions': to prepare his 'female friend' [AD] for 'the worst' by apprising her 'of a visit which must have destroyed' SW's interests and her 'establishment'. SW dreaded the truths that he had revealed to a person other than Sarah; nevertheless, Sarah, in carrying out her commission, 'concealed' these truths [to protect SW].

SW has been nearly overwhelmed by the fate resulting from his actions, not from Sarah's representations. In consequence of SW's 'system', a 'life would have been terminated wretchedly'. The 'danger is not yet averted' because, without restraint, SW's 'same inconstancy' may again tempt him 'to forsake one, as it has to slight another'. Given SW's opinions of Sarah's efforts to 'extricate' him, she is surprised that he has 'borne so long' the 'irksome appearance' of her friendship. She is deeply pained that 'the unhappy' CLW 'may at this time leave life' thinking that Sarah has been unkind to her and has 'held her up to detestation'. Nonetheless, whenever SW should need Sarah, she will be, on principle, his friend.

SW→Sarah Ridge **12/3/1796**

GEU in box 5[104] If I were less accustomed to bear false accusation than I am
⊡ 12/3/1796

As SW has 'now become dead to the good or ill opinions of all but a few', the 'misconstructions and unjust charges' in Sarah's last letter have not disturbed him. Sarah opposed SW's quoting some of her words to CLW; however, he did not consider this a breach of confidentiality, as Sarah had spoken 'the same words' to CLW and Sarah had asked him to conceal her letter only from SGW. SW's words promoted 'temporary peace and decency'; CLW's remonstrances were those 'of an unreasonable woman'.

SW and Sarah have different 'ideas of friendship'. SW would not shrink from serving a friend 'by making an enemy'. He 'never was more astonished at any human event' than Sarah's reconciliation with Shepherd, as Sarah had resolved never to enter into friendship with someone who had betrayed her. SW believes that the 'primary cause' of Sarah's breach with him is Shepherd's present great influence over Sarah. He has no doubt that Shepherd, a religionist, has been able to convince Sarah that he, a Deist, is incapable of having 'regard for justice, honour or truth'.

Before Sarah's 'coalition' with Shepherd, SW never perceived that Sarah was 'impatient, haughty or rancorous'. Now he finds that her temper has changed 'for the worse'. SW accordingly attributes Sarah's present 'acrimony and resentment' to 'the unfortunate power which a very unworthy person', Shepherd, has 'acquired' over her.

SW discusses problems of serving as a mediator in a dispute between two people. He acknowledges that Sarah has sacrificed time to him as well as conveniences and quiet from submitting 'to abide a night in this sad hovel' [Ridge], where Sarah witnessed and was disturbed by 'noisy altercations'. Sarah nevertheless should remember that her intervention was voluntary.

Sarah→SW **4/4/1796?**

Baker 'Wesley Family' folder in It is a painful task to me to enter into
unnumbered box of autographs discussions
⊡ 4 April[105]

It is painful for Sarah 'to enter into discussions' which recall 'the unkind treatment' of someone [presumably CLW] whom Sarah has loved 'tenderly' and supposed for the last two years to be her friend. Nonetheless, Sarah is induced to present a 'statement of facts'. From the moment that SW 'professed Popery' he 'calumniated' Sarah to many people, including Miss Vancamp, Mrs Harvey [not identified], Mrs [Arabella] Mitz and Mrs Spence [not identified]. Sarah 'never entered into any expostulations' with SW, but the 'littleness' of his 'mode of

---

[104] Ltr is incomplete; only the first four pages are preserved.

[105] Assigned, with some doubt, to 1796 from the context of the SW/Sarah quarrel evidenced in the preceding 1796 letters.

revenge' evidenced by his 'sullen reserve' silenced her. She considered then that SW 'was totally under the influence' of Shepherd and Miss Vancamp, both of whom were 'avowedly inimical to' CW and Sarah.

Sarah's 'own revenge was of a nobler kind'. She did SW 'all the good in her power' with CW. She spoke to CW of SW's good qualities and never mentioned his faults. When these faults became 'glaringly' apparent she reverted to SW's education which had 'naturally tended' to make him 'self-willed, tyrannic and uncandid'. SW was made his 'own object' from infancy and 'everything was to be subservient to this purpose'.

SW→Mr Livie   Chesterfield St   **2/9/1796**
Sotheby catalogue 11/3/1974 lot 116[106]   [not known]
Sotheby catalogue
  SW invites Mr Livie [not identified[107]] to meet a few musical friends next Tuesday [6/9/1796].

SGW→Sarah   **1/11/1796**
GEU Wesley Coll. ltr 41   My dearest Sally's Letter by post
◼ 1/11/1796
  SW is in London today. He is well.

Sarah→SGW   **14/12/1796?**
GEU in box 5   I am happy to hear your Cold is removed
pmk [London] 16 DE? 96; marked (by SGW?) 'ansd 17 Decr'[108]
  Sarah has 'not yet been able to serve the young man recommended by' SW and CLW. Provisions are so dear because of the war that people have been 'obliged to discharge some of their clerks'. Mr Holland, a blind man who teaches Miss Quincey [with whose mother Sarah is staying in Manchester] 'arithmetic and the use of globes', has undertaken to seek a situation for the recommended man and wants to know if this man can keep 'merchants accounts', has 'any acquaintance with business' or knows sufficient French to translate and to reply to letters. Until Sarah can communicate 'some satisfactory intelligence', which she hopes will be soon, she does not wish to put CLW to the expense of receiving a letter.

---

[106] Sold by Sotheby's to the bookseller Charavay in Paris, who sold it to M. Georgeot of Paris. The present location of ltr is not known.

[107] Conceivably 'Mr Livie' may be a misreading of 'Mr Lièvre', SW's relative, *see* SGW→Sarah, 27/6/1792 and Sarah→SW, 29/11/1794.

[108] Assigned to 14 December because Sarah(?) twice mistakenly dates this letter '14 March'.

SGW→Sarah   **17/12/1796?**
MA DDWF/21/13   My Dearest Sally will excuse my sending a short
ltr undated[109]
  SGW hopes to see SW on Monday [19/12/1796] and will let him know what
Sarah wrote [in Sarah→SGW, 14/12/1796] regarding CLW's request [to assist
in finding employment for a young man].

CW Jr→Sarah   Ridge   **27/12/1796**
GEU in box 5   *Multus et Felicis* used to be our Dear Father's health
☑ 27 Dec[110]
  SW did not come to London yesterday [26/12/1796] as the frost is severe and
the snow is deep. It is unfortunate that his home [Ridge] is not nearer. CW Jr
takes it kindly that SW is not 'visiting a certain lady [not identified] who seems
to have forgot the gentlewoman'; 'if she should reward him' he would be rich
indeed. CW Jr has learned a lesson from his youthful, inexperienced days: he
thinks that he was never before thought to be mercenary.

SW→Elizabeth Ritchie[111]   **1/1797**
Bulmer p 216   [not known]
Bulmer dates ltr 'January 1797' without specifying the day
  SW tells Elizabeth Ritchie [1754–1835, who had been JW's amanuensis, *see*
note to JW→SW, 29/4/1790] that 'we' [presumably CW Jr, Sarah and SW] were
kept 'closely at home, that we might escape the corruptions of the world'. Lord
Mornington [Garret Wesley], 'who was a passionate lover of music', had said
that 'we had no occasion to go into the world, for the world would come to us'.

Sarah→SGW   **4/1/1797**
GEU in box 5   I have just received your letter by the Post
☑ 4 Jan; pmk 1797
  Sarah has written to CLW 'about another place for the young man at St
Albans' [for whom SW and CLW sought Sarah's assistance to find employment,
see Sarah→SGW, 14/12/1796]. Sarah's letter [to CLW, not preserved] 'is
directed near Barnet so it may lay there for a week'.

---

[109] Assigned to 17/12/1796 by reference to Sarah→SGW, 14/12/1796? bearing
London pmk of 16/12?/1796, which asks if SGW knew that Mr Greenwood was
dead; in this ltr SGW says she 'never heard of young Mr Greenwood's death'.

[110] Assigned to 1796 because addressed to Sarah at Mrs Quincey's, Green Hay,
Manchester'; 1796 is the only year when she was there in December.

[111] Elizabeth Ritchie is presumed to be the recipient because *Bulmer* is a
biography of her. However, *Bulmer* does not name the recipient explicitly.

SW→James Kenton   Ridge   **18/1/1797**

typescript in Baker   If Mrs W. speak the Truth, which does not often happen
🖃 18/1/1797

If CLW is truthful, which is rare, she will have written to Kenton complaining of Kenton's 'cruel, unjust and treacherous conduct towards her'. Kenton has 'done many good works' for CLW and does not deserve ingratitude. CLW has no enemy but her 'diabolical, ungovernable, ferocious, ungrateful disposition'. SW and Kenton 'have long ago agreed' that she is 'incurable among lunaticks'. SW has tried reasoning with and being tender to her but has found that 'it is a useless prostitution to try' this any longer. He has decided to 'give it all up'.

Compared to her increasingly frequent and violent 'extravagant fits', CLW's 'lucid intervals are rare and short'. SW, 'about to leave this place' [Ridge], faces the 'sad prospect' of having his 'wretchedness' and her 'unworthiness' exposed 'among new people'. He wishes that he 'could find the friend who would insist on' SW parting from CLW. Although 'every evil cures itself in time', the afflicted parties 'often die before the cure takes place'.

The 'horrid effects' of CLW's 'enormous behaviour' have hurt SW's health more deeply than he would acknowledge other than to 'a chief friend'. SW is 'a dozen years older in constitution' than before he had CLW for his 'torment'. He cannot arrange ideas as he could in the past, his memory is 'exceedingly weakened' and his mind is very seldom calm. No alternative remains than for SW and CLW to 'drop' or to part. Waiting for the former is 'far worse than death' as it would make SW incapable of satisfying his children's wants. It will be impossible for him to attend properly to his business if he bears 'another such year as the last' when he was 'flagrantly neglected and rendered odious in the eyes of domestics and inferiors'.

Kenton often has told SW that his mind would change 'when these hurricanes were blown over'. SW has not contradicted him because up to now SW believed that 'a reformation' was possible. Now he is 'wholly convinced that no permanent change for the better will ever appear' while he and CLW are together. Therefore it is his duty, for the sake of his children, his friends and himself, to separate.

SW wrote to [Samuel] Tooth [not preserved] suggesting that SW go with him to Guildford tomorrow [19/1/1797]; Samuel Tooth has been asked to reply to 'Marybone' [Chesterfield Street] where SW is going today. SW does not return to his 'damned den' [Ridge] before Saturday [21/1/1797]. If he does not travel to Guildford he will call on Kenton tomorrow or Friday [20/1/1797] between 11 am and 2 pm.

SGW→Sarah   **23/1/1797**
GEU Wesley coll. ltr 40   My Dearest Sally is daily in my thoughts
✉ 23 Jan; pmk 1797
   SW 'begins [teaching at] the schools today'. CLW and the 'dear children' are
well. Charles Hill of Bristol called at Chesterfield Street *en route* to Paddington
to dine with SW. Instead, SGW and SW followed Hill [to Paddington] and
'drank tea with kind Mrs Deane' [AD's mother, proprietress of a school at which
SW taught].

Sarah→SGW   Ridge   **15/2/1797?**
GEU in box 5   My dearest Mothers Letter was, as hers always are
✉ Wed 15; pmk [London] 18/2?/1797[112]
   The knowledge that SGW has family near her, including CW Jr, SW and SW's
children, consoles Sarah. She often thinks about 'that poor little woman [CLW]
and the babes' and asks how CLW is. The time approaches 'when they will
leave Ridge'. Sarah hopes that 'the next house will better procure comfortable
necessaries to them'.

SW→Street   **21/2/1797**
BL Add 56228 ltr 2; *O*   I have received a letter from our Friend Vincent
✉ 21/2/1797
   SW has received a letter [not preserved] from 'our friend Vincent' [not
identified, perhaps J. Vincent or Zelophead Wyeth Vincent, both of whom are
listed as male alto singers in *Doane*], stating that he hopes to join the party on
Friday [24/2/1797] despite an attack of rheumatism. They expect to assemble by
7 pm at the latest. SW hears that 'young Danby' [probably Eustace Danby,
singer and organist, 1781–1824] will be present, so they will not be left 'quite
desolate' should Vincent not appear. SW wishes to sing over a *Miserere* for two
voices which he composed several years ago [his *Miserere mei, Deus*, of which
the autograph manuscript, BL Add 14342, is dated 7/4/1792]. He supposes that
Street would like to see the music in advance, and asks where it should be left
next Friday morning.

SGW→Sarah   **22/2/1797**
MA DDWF/21/16   I postpon'd writing to my Dearest Sally by post
✉ Wed 22 Feb & Sarah at Mrs Quincey's near Manchester→ ⅰ
   SW is well. He says that Sarah owes him a letter. SGW hopes that 'all his
family' are well, but she never sees them.

---

[112] Both 15/2/1797 and 15/3/1797 were Wednesdays when Sarah was in
Manchester. Assigned to February because the postmarked month appears more
likely to be a '2' than a '3', but some doubt remains about the month.

SW→Bridgetower   Chesterfield St   **23/2/1797**
BL Add 56411 f 7; *O*   Mr Samuel Wesley presents his best Compliments
▣ 23/2/1797
SW requests Bridgetower's company at the musical party tomorrow evening
[24/2/1797] at Mrs Deane's [AD's mother], Manor House, near Paddington
Church. SW apologises for presuming on his slight acquaintance with
Bridgetower, who can 'freely command' SW's services on a similar occasion in
the future. Should Bridgetower be willing to come, SW will arrange a 'proper
and careful porter' for Bridgetower's violin.

SGW→Sarah   **15/3/1797**
MA DDWes/6/41   I fear my dearest Sally will imagine
▣ 15 Mar & Sarah at Mrs Quincey's near Manchester→ ⓘ
SGW was with SW yesterday [14/3/1797]. He would have been glad to have
'some private conversation' with Sarah [who is near Manchester] if she had been
in London. SGW hopes that SW will return [to London] tomorrow [16/3/1797]
'as usual'.

Sarah→SW   Gt Chesterfield St   **27/7/1797**
GEU in box 5   I really do not recollect whether You or I wrote last
▣ 27/7/1797
At SW's request, Sarah wrote to SGW about 'pecuniary embarrassments'.
Sarah has been concerned about SGW's health and proposes to return to London
in a few weeks. SW has not been to a 'public watering place'. Sarah mentions
the 'various modes of life and manners of people' to be found there, and writes
about people she has visited. She presumes that SW is now in his 'new house'
[in Finchley] and asks to be remembered kindly to CLW.

Sarah→SW   **11/8/1797?**
GEU in box 5   The temptation of a private opportunity leads me to write
ltr docketed (possibly not by Sarah) 'Aug 1797'[113]
Sarah's letter to CW Jr [Sarah→CW Jr, 9/8/1797, GEU in box 5] mentioned
that she has not imposed upon Mrs Lee, so CW Jr's claims on Mrs Lee have not
been affected by Sarah's conduct, which has been unselfish. Sarah fears that her
uncle [James] Waller [*d*1802, husband of SGW's sister Elizabeth Waller] lends
money to SGW 'under the idea of' SW's and Sarah's 'justice'. SW should
'beware of this and tell him [Waller] so'. Sarah has given no hint to CW Jr about
what SW wrote [in a letter not preserved].

---

[113] >Sarah→CW Jr, 9/8/1797; <Sarah→SGW, 12/8/1797 (GEU in box 5) in
which Sarah says she has sent £4/4/- in her letter to London, i.e., in this ltr, to
pay Thompson.

Sarah and Mrs Lee never jarred during their time together. Mrs Lee has peculiar habits and some call her mad, but Sarah does not share SW's view of Mrs Lee's temper. Sarah expects to be in London in a few weeks time. She asks SW to deliver the enclosed £4/4/- to her aunt [Rebecca] Gwynne, who is to pay 'Thompson the Milliner in Oxford Street'.

SW→SGW   Finchley   **22/12/1797**
Fitzwm ltr 9   As my Aunt Gwynne seemed desirous of hearing
📧 22/12/1797

As SW's aunt [Rebecca] Gwynne wanted to hear news, SW tells SGW that CLW is 'as well as can be expected'. On the day that SW returned [to Finchley] she had a good deal of fever, but is now better and takes animal food. He is sure that she continues 'to feel the loss of that dear girl' [their infant daughter Susanna]. SW could not love another child as much as her. He expects to be at Marylebone next Tuesday [26/12/1797] but to dine out. Any letters received should wait for him to pick up.

SW was very ill today with his bile and his nerves, but has taken lemonade and onions and is now somewhat better. His remedies are 'simple and strange'. CLW sends her best love and duty to all, with Mrs Adams's respects.

SW→Thomas Merryweather   Gt Chesterfield St[114]   **6/3/1798**
LMA A/FH/A06/001/051/21/1; *O*   It being my Intention to offer myself
📧 6/3/1798

SW intends to apply for the organist's post at the Foundling Hospital Chapel and seeks information from Thomas Merryweather [*d*1799, from 1790 secretary of the Foundling Hospital] about 'the nature of the duty'. SW has to leave London early tomorrow [7/3/1798].

SW→Sarah   Finchley   **23/5/1798**
MA DDWF/15/7   Domestic Jars are never entertaining
📧 23/5/1798

Domestic quarrels are never entertaining but sometimes it is necessary to explain matters to concerned parties. SW does not like to make public the miseries of his own house and it is not flattering to talk of the evils he has brought upon himself; however, he feels a need to put the record straight. On Sunday evening [20/5/1798], without any new cause of provocation, CLW was 'villainously abusive' to him. When he insisted that she should not leave the room before hearing some words from him, she struck a 'sharp blow' in his face with her fist. Sarah will 'hardly conjecture that it was returned'.

---

[114] SW says in ltr that replies may also be sent to Church End, Finchley.

At that moment, SW felt that he had been a 'dupe' in remaining so long under the same roof with 'so brutal and shameless' a person. He decided long ago not to live with a woman who would strike him, and no penitence on CLW's part could change his mind. Nonetheless, he was prepared to see what might result from her reflection on her conduct, and left her to consider her 'prank' at her leisure, hoping that she might apologise. She has not done so; on the contrary, she says that she wishes to separate from SW and that she will have no chance of comfort until this happens.

SW now will 'coolly and quietly' pursue the issue of separate maintenance. He is 'somewhat ashamed' not to have done this earlier. He writes to inform Sarah of what she might otherwise learn only by hearsay and to show that he has not acted prematurely. This quarrel need not prevent 'the count' [not identified] coming to Finchley on Sunday [27/5/1798]. CLW always behaves well to her guests, and Sunday probably will be the last time when SW, CLW and the count will meet. Sarah therefore should not 'forbid' the count's visit.

SW→William Seward[115]   Gt Chesterfield St   16/6/1798
PC–London[116]
▣ 16/6/1798

SW is sorry if he disappointed William Seward [man of letters, 1747–1799] by not sending him the advertisement in which SW thanks his supporters in the recent Foundling Hospital election. SW asserts that he would have been elected if the election had been 'fairly conducted' and regrets that he expended 'so much time and trouble' in applying for the post. He guesses that the Hospital governor to whom Seward alluded is 'a certain great Commissioner of Customs' [Joah Bates, civil servant, conductor and organist, *bap*1740–1799], who consistently opposed SW in this election. SW sends verses ('Come all my brave boys who want organists' places…') satirising Bates [SW set these verses to music about this time]. SW looks forward to visiting Seward at Richmond[117] and will send him the 'Overture in [Handel's opera] *Ptolemy*' soon.

---

[115] SW names the recipient 'W. Sewart'.

[116] SW's satirical poem is printed in *Lightwood* p 92–93.

[117] A printed poem by 'S' [presumably William Seward] commemorating this isit, entitled 'To Mr Samuel Wesley, on his visiting Mr S— [Seward] at Richmond a second time in the summer of 1798' was published in the 21–23/8/1798 number of the *Whitehall Evening-Post* newspaper and again in *EM* v 34 (September 1798) p 161–162. In *EM* the poem is printed immediately after a paragraph, quoted in the Verbal Portraits section of this book, that calls SW a 'great musician' and likens his advancement from 'precocity' to Mozart's. A cutting of this poem from the *Whitehall Evening-Post*, with a few manuscript corrections, is at BL Add 35027 f 2.

CLW→Sarah Hornsey Lane?[118] **23/1/1799**
Drew Wesley Family Letters, CLW series I could not account for it, but I felt
▣ Wed 23rd; pmk 24/1/99
  CLW felt gloomy when Sarah left Highgate and wishes that Sarah had stayed longer, notwithstanding CLW's 'humble fare'. Sarah's brother [SW] had 'set out' [from Chesterfield Street] before Sarah arrived home [to Chesterfield Street], so CLW wants to hear whether Sarah arrived safely. CLW will be bringing CW III when she pays her 'respects in Chesterfield Street'. He 'does nothing but talk of his Aunt Sally' [Sarah].

CB→Latrobe[119] **4/2/1799?**
Osborn MSS 3, Box 4, folder 275 I have been a Scald-miserable ever since I
ltr undated[120]
  Since CB last saw Latrobe he has been able to accept only one invitation to a dinner or private concert. At this dinner CB was pleased to meet 'Sam Westley' [SW] of whom he 'had lost sight almost since his childhood, if ever he was a child'.[121] In music, SW now 'is somewhat more than man'; he pleased CB very much 'by his performance and compositions'. SW is 'a credit to our country, which certainly does not abound in native composers of the first class'.

---

[118] Ltr has no return address but was received by the post at Highgate and mentions CLW's gloom when Sarah left Highgate; this suggests that CLW and SW were living near Highgate at this time. They presumably were not yet living at 5 Mile Stone, Highgate, as their move to that address is first indicated in SGW→Sarah, 12/6/1799, which states that SW 'is busy about a house which he has taken near Highgate'. SW wrote the address 'Hornsey Lane, near Highgate' on an autograph copy of his musical composition 'Roses, their sharp spines being gone' (BL Add 14343 f 53), which bears an endorsement, not in SW's hand, that the copy was received on 29/8/1798. It therefore seems plausible that SW was living in Hornsey Lane when ltr was written.

[119] Ltr addressed to 'My dear friend'. Latrobe identified as recipient because ltr answered by Latrobe→CB, 7/2/1799.

[120] Assigned to 4/2/1799 because Latrobe says (in Latrobe→CB, 7/2/1799) that he received this ltr on 5/2/1799.

[121] The family name was spelt 'Westley' when SW's grandfather Samuel Wesley Sr was at Exeter College, Oxford in the 1680s; he later dropped the 't' (Adam Clarke, *Memoirs of the Wesley Family; Collected Principally from Original Documents*, 2nd edition, New York, 1848, p 15). The circumstance that CB and others occasionally misspelt SW's name as 'Westley' indicates that in SW's lifetime the name was pronounced with a voiceless 's' rather than a voiced 'z' sound.

Latrobe→CB   **7/2/1799**
Osborn MSS 3, Box 12, folder 867   Your kind note of __ I received the day
▤ 7/2/1799

Latrobe heartily subscribes to CB's view of SW [in CB→Latrobe, 4/2/1799?].
It is 'a shame to the nation' that SW and CW Jr 'pass unheeded' when 'a
Dibdin' [Charles Dibdin, composer and dramatist, 1745–1814, or possibly his
son Thomas John Dibdin, actor and composer, 1771–1841] 'rides triumphant
upon the asses ears of the town'.

SW→Latrobe   **about 28/2/1799**
MA [uncatalogued]; *O*   I have known enough of Printers to be little surprised
ltr undated[122]

SW is 'little surprised' at the delay in printing Latrobe's work [Latrobe's *Dies
Irae*, published in 1799 by Robert Birchall, c1760–1819]. The 40 subscribers to
this work that SW collected are 'fewer by some fifties' than he had hoped for.[123]
Unfortunately, one of them must be withdrawn: [Joseph] Bazley, for whose
character SW would have vouched, has been found to have committed a fraud
[upon his employer, the bankers Sir James Esdaile, Esdaile, Hammett, Esdaile
and Hammett].

SW thanks Latrobe for sending CB's 'very handsome note' [CB→Latrobe,
4/2/1799] and would be pleased if Latrobe could come to fetch it. SW is 'a very
accessible personage' on 'most Wednesdays and Saturdays'.

SW spent a week at Cambridge many years ago where he met Dr [Joseph]
Jowett [1752–1813, from 1782 professor of civil law at Cambridge]; he also met
Jowett's brother [Henry Jowett, *b* c1756], with whom SW 'sang glees and
catches'. SW has 'no present appetite for a doctorship' nor a desire to be a
'musical professor' at [the University of] Cambridge [succeeding John Randall
(*b*1717)]; he hates 'the thought of waiting for dead men's shoes' [Randall died
on 18/3/1799].

When Latrobe next is at Birchall's shop he should tell Birchall to hand over a
copy of SW's 'newly published sonatinas' [SW's *12 sonatinas for the piano
forte or harpsichord*, op. 4] as a gift. The sonatinas are 'trifles', so Latrobe
should consider the giver, not the gift.

---

[122] Ltr presumably written shortly after the announcement of Joseph Bazley's
conviction (reported in *The Times* on 23/2/1799) and <18/3/1799, when John
Randall died.

[123] SW himself subscribed to this work.

SW→Sarah   **26/3/1799**

BL Add 35012 f 113   As Rancour has never been any Characteristic of mine
▣ 26/3/1799

To show that he intends no ill-feeling, SW asks Sarah to deliver the enclosed note [not preserved] to Mrs [Rebecca] Gwynne. He leaves it open for Sarah to read first. He has given Rebecca Gwynne no provocation for her 'violent and vulgar' attack; even if he had, her behaviour would still have been shocking. Whatever errors SW may have committed are 'amply revenged' by the 'stinging vexations' he daily experiences. Neither of SW's two closest female friends contributes anything to his consolation: the 'continual violence' of one [CLW] and the 'frequent dejection and habitual melancholy' of the other [presumably AD] make his life bitter.

SW→Street[124]   **1/5/1799**

BL Add 56228 ltr 3; *O*   As I happened to pick up the most correct & perfect
▣ 1/5/1799

SW has picked up a copy of the 'most correct of perfect editions', a folio of the works of [William] Chillingworth [theologian, 1602–1644] and hopes that Street will accept it. Street can leave out, for the carrier, the other ugly old book which belongs to CW Jr. When CW Jr comes to study Chillingworth, SW will advise him to use a better edition.

SGW→Sarah   **14/5/1799**

MA DDWF/21/18   I wish my dear Sally has not written to any of us
pmk 14/5/1799 evening

'Poor Charlotte' [CLW] and 'her dear little boy' [CW III] visited SGW from Tuesday [7/5/1799] to Friday [10/5/1799]. SGW suspects that CLW is 'breeding' [she gave birth to JWW before 1/7/1799, *see* CLW→SGW, 1/7/1799] and hopes that the cause of her feeling poorly is pregnancy rather than consumption. Sarah will have read of the sudden death of 'Mr Sewart' [William Seward, *d*23/4/1799].

SGW→Sarah   **12/6/1799**

GEU in box 3   My dear Sally's former Letter to her Brother
▣ Wed 12 June; pmk 13/6/99

SW is 'busy about a house which he has taken near Highgate'.

---

[124] Ltr addressed to 'Dear Sir'. Street identified as addressee because ltr mentions Mark Lane (Street's address) as well as Chillingworth (*see* SW→Street, 6/10/1799).

CLW→SGW   **1/7/1799**
Wcoll D6/1/346   I was infinitely obliged to you for the loan of Betty Oliver
☞ 1/7/1799
  CLW is 'infinitely obliged' to SGW 'for the loan [presumably to assist CLW around the time of JWW's birth] of Betty Oliver' [*b c*1786, also referred to as Betsy Oliver]. CLW looks forward to visiting SGW, because 'constant solitude is fit for no one', but will not bring Anne [not identified, possibly a servant], as Betty Oliver 'will nurse the baby' [JWW] for CLW. CW III sends a letter to Sarah and greetings to SGW and CW Jr.

Rebecca Gwynne will   **9/8/1799**
PRO PROB 11/1332[125]   I Rebecca Gwynne of Chesterfield Street
will dated 9/8/1799
  After payment of debts and specified gifts, Rebecca Gwynne's capital comprising £1,000 in the 3% consolidated annuities in the Bank of England and £500 elsewhere is to be combined and invested in those annuities or in other public funds. She bequeaths the interest and dividends on the combined investment to SGW during her lifetime, subject to her paying £5/5/- annually to Rebecca Gwynne's niece Jane Weale. At SGW's death, legacies totalling £550 are to be paid out of Rebecca Gwynne's capital to various persons, including £100 to Sarah and £50 to each of SW and CW III. The entire remainder of Rebecca Gwynne's estate after SGW's death is bequeathed to CW Jr.

SW→Street   **6/10/1799**
BL Add 56228 ltr 4; *O*   I have appointed to be at Mr Ball's
☞ 6/10/1799
  SW has arranged to be at [James] Ball's piano manufactory at 1 pm next Friday [11/10/1799], when he will try over the *Confitebor* [SW's *Confitebor tibi, Domine*, completed on 14/8/1799] on the organ that Ball has there. SW knows that the middle of the day is an inconvenient time for Street to leave the City [of London] but, realising that Street wished [Thomas] Carter [alto singer and coal-merchant, 1769–1800] to get an early sight of the work, SW has taken his first opportunity and hopes that Street will be able to join them. If Carter can be with them, and 'will part with his coals for a song', he will be a great acquisition, particularly if he can persuade the 'busby-wigged parson' [not identified] whom they saw at his house to come too.[126]

---

[125] Document is the Prerogative Court of Canterbury copy of the original will, which was proved on 26/11/1799.

[126] As 'the Barrys' are mentioned in SW→Street, 18/10/1799, it is conceivable that the parson described in ltr is Edward Barry, whom SW visited on 11/1/1807, *see* SW→CW Jr, 15/1/1807.

SW asks Street to look into his copy of [the works of William] Chillingworth. SW believes that there is a misprint in his own edition which may be correct in Street's edition.

SW→Street   Highgate   **18/10/1799**
BL Add 56228 ltr 5; *O*   We were disappointed in not having the Pleasure
▣ 18/10/1799
SW and his friends were disappointed not to have Street's company last Wednesday [16/10/1799]. Mr Barry, his brother, SW and CLW were present. They had a convivial evening; the Barrys did not leave until 1 am. Barry, who is SW's 'scholar' and lives at 37 Queen Square, Bloomsbury, is a good musician and an agreeable companion. Barry wishes to make up a little glee concert, to which he means to invite Mr Wright who was at [James] Ball's [piano manufactory] on Friday 11/10/1799. Barry says that Wright is a good musician. The party will be on an evening when SW can remain in town, and Barry hopes that Street will be able to attend. SW suggests Friday 25/10/1799. He asks if this date will be suitable for Street and Mr Drummer [presumably either William Drummer or his brother], and desires a reply by return.

SW→CB?[127]   Highgate   **5/11/1799?**
Osborn MSS 3, Box 16, folder 1192; *O*   I address you at a Venture of speedy
▣ 5 Nov[128]
SW is not sure whether his correspondent has returned from the country but hopes to visit him some morning soon, for 'the instruction and comfort' of the correspondent's conversation.

SW→Editor, *MM*   Highgate   **9/11/1799**
MM v 8 no 5, 1/12/1799, p 875   I shall be thankful to any one of your learned
MM
SW asks if any reader of *MM* can inform him why the Latin word 'reclusus' signifies 'open' whilst the English word 'recluse' means 'shut up'.

---

[127] Ltr addressed to 'my dear Sir'. CB presumed as addressee because of ref. to the recipient's having been in the country (*see* SW→CB, 28/11/1799) and ltr's inclusion amongst the Burney papers in the Osborn collection.

[128] Not before 5/11/1799 as 1799 was SW's first year at Highgate. Assigned to 1799 because text appears to precede SW→CB, 28/11/1799.

SW→Street   Highgate   **9/11/1799**
BL Add 56228 ltr 6; *O*   Mr & Mrs Kingston hope for the Pleasure of your
⌧ Sat 9 Nov & 🖾→①

Mr and Mrs [possibly William B.] Kingston invite Street and Mr Drummer [*see* SW→Street, 18/10/1799] next Tuesday evening [12/11/1799]. SW will bring with him a new chorus for double choir [probably his *Deus majestatis intonuit*, the two autographs of which are dated 26/9/1799], the subject of which he played when they met last at Drummer's, and of which SW has not been able to make a fair copy until this week. SW will also bring his *Confitebor*.

SW was surprised to hear what Street had read in the newspapers. SW called today on [James] Ball, from whom he had had the invitation from Howard [probably Thomas Howard, organist], for an explanation. Howard had asked SW to oblige him [by playing at a charity sermon at his church] on Sunday [10/11/1799], which was impossible as SW had an engagement that day at Watford. He told Howard that if the charity sermon could be deferred to 17/11/1799 he would play then. However, it appears that the sermon will happen on 10/11/1799, so Howard must therefore 'thumb the musicks' alone. It would have been civil if Howard had informed SW of the changed circumstances before inserting his advertisement.

SW has been reading a 'very pretty account' of Mozart written by Dr [Thomas] Busby [writer and composer, 1755–1838] in the December 1799 [in fact, the December 1798] *MM* and recommends it to Street. He hopes that [Thomas] Carter will come on Tuesday.

SW→CB   Highgate   **28/11/1799**
MA DDWF/15/8; *O*   Your last obliging Letter having exprest the Probability
⌧ 28/11/1799[129]

In his last letter [not preserved], CB said that he expected to return to London about now. SW looks forward to visiting Chelsea [the Royal Hospital, known as Chelsea College, CB's home] one morning soon. He wants to ask CB about musical matters, and notes that CB kindly assisted him by condescending 'to revise' one of his compositions [*Confitebor*, according to SW's *Reminiscences*].

SW is very busy at present but has put aside an hour each day to study CB's 'excellent work' [CB's *General History of Music*]. SW asks a question relating to CB's discussion there of the Greek modes: he suspects a misprint in a musical example, and asks for CB's comments.

---

[129] The wrapper bearing the address portion of this ltr, postmarked 28/11/1799, is at Osborn MSS 3, Box 5, folder 319.

CB→SW **29/11/1799?**

Osborn MSS 3, Box 5, folder 319   I was on the point of reminding you
ltr undated[130]

CB was about to remind SW of SW's promise to breakfast with him in
November [1799] when he received SW's letter [SW→CB, 28/11/1799]
requesting a postponement, to which he agrees. Without 'looking into' his
History [CB's *General History of Music*], CB is certain that SW's suggestion is
right: 'the tetrachord to E♭ minor must be A♯'. Although on keyed instruments
the same key is used to produce both G♯ and A♭, 'with the voice and violin a
different sound' [for these notes] is produced. None of 'the sounds of the two
scales' [of G♯ and A♭] is 'the same'. By 'the triple progression' it takes a long
while to modulate from E♭ to G♯. CB cannot imagine how this 'blunder' escaped
him.

However, CB thinks SW also is 'in the wrong' regarding modulation. CB has
not thought about [ancient] Greek music since the first volume of his *History*
was published [in 1776] and has forgotten 'all about it'. The Dissertation [on the
Music of the Ancients, prefixed to CB's *History*] cost CB 'more trouble' than all
the remainder of the *History*, and CB is certain that it has been 'the least read'
part. However, he is 'glad that it is there', as it proves that he did not 'shirk
difficulties' in endeavouring to solve problems of this subject.

SW→CB **30/11/1799**

UCSB in Ms 33; *O*   This is really pestering You with my Letters
▣ 30/11/1799

SW apologises for pestering CB with letters. CB has 'clearly shown' that SW
misunderstood aspects of the Greek musical modes. SW has just finished reading
the 8th section of CB's Dissertation [on the Music of the Ancients] and is
obliged to CB for his illuminating researches. SW feels that CB [who concluded
that the ancients neither invented nor practised counterpoint] has
'demonstratively decided' this matter. SW concurs with CB against the idea of
[Pierre-Jean] Burette [French scholar, 1665–1747, who had suggested that the
ancients might have performed music not only in unison and in parallel octaves
but also in parallel thirds], and believes that CB's experiment of sounding just
the 15th and tierce stops of an organ provides 'invincible proof' of CB's
position.

---

[130] Assigned to 29/11/1799 because ltr is written on back of wrapper of
SW→CB, 28/11/1799, and is seemingly answered by SW→CB, 30/11/1799.

R. Perkins Jr→Editor, *MM*   **10/12/1799**
MM v 9 no 1, 1/2/1800, p 18–19   On the question proposed in your last
MM

   Replying to SW→Editor, *MM,* 9/11/1799, R. Perkins Jr proposes an
explanation of the different meanings of 'reclusus' and 'recluse'.

SW→Gentlemen   Highgate   **5/1/1800**
MA DDWF/15/10; *O*   Having been in Town almost all last Week
▣ 5/1/1800

   SW was in London for almost all last week and so did not receive his
correspondents' letter until yesterday evening [4/1/1800]. It is plain that Mr
[Thomas] Sibthorpe [of Guildford, attorney for the purchaser] is 'determined' to
be as litigious and troublesome as he can. SW has no vouchers for his legal
claim on the estate at Guildford other than what is given in Dr [James] Price's
will [*see* James Price will, 6/2/1783] and the title deeds. SW cannot understand
why these are considered insufficient, and cannot state facts which occurred long
before he knew Price. These delays have been 'contrived' by Sibthorpe in
revenge for SW not having entrusted the papers into Sibthorpe's possession. SW
has acted on the advice of Mr Foster [probably John Foster, London attorney],
who thought it 'highly imprudent' to entrust these papers to the purchaser's
attorney. It is 'vexatious' to find this business 'wantonly procrastinated'.
Sibthorpe might as well deny SW's right to the estate as to 'confound and
perplex matters' concerning SW's power of disposing of it. In that case Dr
Broxham [the intending purchaser] will be found to have made no legal purchase
and the property will belong to nobody. If the 'vouchers and instruments'
already produced do not enable SW to receive the purchase money, Broxham
must devise some other way of making his claim 'legal and indisputable'. If SW
had other 'explanatory papers', he would have produced them in order to
expedite an affair which has caused him trouble and which will bring him 'an
advantage by far inadequate to the real value of the premises'. The recipients
should address any response to SW at Chesterfield Street.

SW→Joseph Reid   Chesterfield St   **7/1/1800**
1st United; photocopy in Baker; *O*   I am really at a Loss how to apologize
▣ 7/1/1800

   SW apologises for his 'shameful delay' in not thanking Reid 'very long ago'
for the gift of a book, the *Life of [William] Chillingworth* [by Thomas Birch],
which SW obtained from their late mutual friend [William] Seward. SW will
always remain grateful for 'so valuable a present'.

SW→Thomas Busby   Charterhouse[131]   **21/3/1800**

ChCh 347/24; *O*   I received your Letter last Night, & presume

▣ 21/3/1800

SW received Thomas Busby's letter [not preserved] last night [20/3/1800] and presumes that Busby has got SW's earlier letter [not preserved]. SW is 'glad to find so promising an account of the business in hand'. [According to *Busby* p 388–390, in 1800 Busby proposed, to the Committee established to raise funds for the erection of a 'naval pillar' to honour admirals and seamen, that he compose a 'secular oratorio' named *Britannia*, whose performance 'at the opera-house, as a national concert, upon a scale adequate to the great occasion' would contribute to these funds.]

SW advises that Mr Gray [presumably William Gray, organ builder, *c*1757–1820] 'has been unable to explore any organ' likely to suit the planned occasion. SW asserts that the organ 'in the King's [Theatre] Concert Room' is best suited to Busby's purpose, not only 'on account of its intrinsic excellence' and power but also because of the 'loyal tendency' of the planned concert. Busby should write to SW next week at 'Marybone' [Chesterfield Street] to advise whether this organ is obtainable, as SW has resolved to perform only on 'a capital instrument'. If this organ cannot be had, SW will endeavour immediately to find 'some substitute'.

SW will be pleased to meet his 'friend' [Jonathan] Battishill [organist and composer, 1738–1801, Busby's teacher] at Busby's house, but SW's earliest available time for such a meeting is in the week after next [beginning 30/3/1800]. When there, SW would like to examine some of Busby's 'masterly productions' and to improve his 'acquaintance and intercourse' with Busby. SW comments that 'if musical Englishmen were laudably unanimous', a 'phalanx' might easily be formed 'against the invasion of continental locusts' [i.e., musicians]. He hopes to be able to attend two of Busby's rehearsals 'instead of one' and sends his compliments to Mrs [Priscilla] Busby.

---

[131] Possibly SW stayed occasionally with his friend James Kenton, who was a pensioner at the Charterhouse from 1790 to 1802 (*see* SW→SGW, 9/7/1792).

SW→Sarah   Chesterfield St   **1/4/1800**

typescript in Baker   I hereby recant or retract whatever I may
⊡ 1 April[132]

SW sincerely recants or retracts any utterance 'injurious or detracting' of Sarah
that he may have uttered 'at any moment of haste or inconsiderateness'.

Mercy Doddridge→Sarah   **26/4/1800**

MA DDWes/1/118   I had this Day the satisfaction of receiving
⊡ 26/4/1800

Mercy Doddridge refers 'with real concern' to the 'unpleasant circumstances'
that Sarah has mentioned [presumably in a letter not preserved] regarding SW
and CLW, whose conduct Mercy Doddridge 'cannot but reprobate' although she
is ignorant of the particulars. However, CW Jr's behaviour is 'a counterpoise
that greatly delights' her.

SW→Street   Highgate   **3/5/1800?**

BL Add 56228 ltr 7;[133] *O*   Mr Drummer has made a Promise of coming over
pmk 3?/5/1800—the '3' in the pmk is unclear

Mr Drummer has promised to visit SW in two or three weeks, and SW hopes
that Street will accompany Drummer. SW is thinking of inviting Drummer's
brother also. SW dined with Attwood last Friday [25/4/1800]; he promised to
visit SW at Highgate soon. SW would like to have a 'round sort of party' but the
size of his house prohibits it, particularly as he has only one spare bed. He can,
however, secure two beds in the neighbourhood, and it therefore will be possible
for Street to stay overnight.

SW asks Street to look at his copy of [the works of William] Chillingworth, as
he suspects a misprint in a particular section. SW has learnt that Salomon

---

[132] Assigned to 1800 for the following reason. Sarah→SW, 27/10/1802,
describing events of three years ago says that SW's inebriated words and
behaviour drove her from SGW's roof. Ltr presumably >1/4/1799 because
SW→Sarah, 26/3/1799, indicates no breach of communication between them
then; also, Sarah elsewhere indicates that some time elapsed between SW's
injury of her and his recantation. Sarah→SW, 2/9/1807, says that Dr George
Gregory received Sarah at time of her self-'banishment' and that she would not
return home while SW was there until he apologised. Sarah arrived at Dr
Gregory's home in Low Layton, Essex, about 12/4/1799 (Sarah→SGW,
12/4/1799, MA DDWF/14/16); Sarah→Mrs E. Delamain, 14/5/1800, written
from Low Layton, says that Sarah will return to Chesterfield Street on
17/5/1800. Hence SW's recantation presumably <17/5/1800. SW→Sarah,
23/10/1802, says SW that apologised 'long ago', which is consistent with an
1800 dating of this ltr.

[133] Ltr is torn, with some text missing at end.

intends to repeat Haydn's oratorio [*The Creation*] on Thursday 15/5/1800 and requires SW's participation [as organist and pianist].

[François-Hippolyte] Barthélemon [1741–1808, French composer resident in London from the 1770s] has requested (but in vain) a copy of SW's *Dixit Dominus* [probably *Dixit Dominus [II]*, of which the autograph manuscripts are dated 13/1/1800] and also has asked SW to play on Thursday 22/5/1800 at his 'Jerusalem Chamber' [presumably the Swedenborgian 'New Jerusalemelite' chapel in Friar Street, Blackfriars, where Barthélemon's children were baptised]. SW refused him. SW will oblige his friends but deals sharply with 'the trade', knowing that 'it is merely necessity, and never from good will' that they ask for his help.

SW→CB   Gt Chesterfield St   **12/5/1800**
UCSB in Ms 33; *O*   I trust, my dear Sir, that no bad Omen threatens me
☞ 12/5/1800

SW proposes to visit CB on 16/5/1800 at 10 am. The only obstacle might be Salomon's repetition of the oratorio [Haydn's *The Creation*], but a second performance this season now seems unlikely because of problems with singers [*see* SW→Thomas Busby, 3/6/1800] who gave Salomon an 'abundance of trouble' with the earlier performance [at the Concert Room in the King's Theatre on 21/4/1800, when SW 'presided at the organ and at the piano forte']. SW thinks that the present musical public can be divided into three classes: those who believe that only the so-called old masters such as Handel and Corelli are good; those who listen only to Mozart, Haydn and the few other modern masters; and those of inferior taste who admire simplicity and like only waltzes or strains produced by musicians such as [Michael] Kelly [Irish singer and composer, 1762–1826].

Sarah→Mrs E. Delamain   **14/5/1800**
GEU in box 5   I sensibly feel the kind part you have taken
☞ 14/5/1800

Sarah has 'much to bear from some part of her family' [presumably SW's part], but not from CW Jr, 'who is a kind hearted affectionate creature'. She has been 'extremely ill-treated' by CLW, whom Sarah 'had served in no common degree'. Sarah will go [from Low Layton, Essex] to Chesterfield Street on Saturday [17/5/1800].

SW→Thomas Busby[134]   Charterhouse   **3/6/1800**

ChCh 347/25; *O*   I this Morning received yours, the Contents of which require
▣ 'Tuesday 4 June 1800', an incorrect date[135]

   Busby's letter [not preserved], received this morning, requires further
consideration before SW can give his 'final answer' regarding Busby's 'intended
performance' on 16/6/1800 [when Busby's oratorio *Britannia* received its first
complete performance at Covent Garden]. SW believes that Busby
underestimates the difficulties of organising a performance so late in the season.
After the King's birthday tomorrow [4/6/1800], 'all the fine folk hurry out of
town' and the rest 'are likely to be deterred from attending' by the hot weather.
Although theatres are as full in summer as in winter, 'all manner of rabble will
go to a play in any weather', whereas the number of people curious to hear an
oratorio, or knowledgeable enough 'to relish it when they do hear it', is
comparatively small, even in winter, when the audience 'need not dread fevers
or fainting'. A 'thin audience would be another mortifying event added to those
which have already occurred'. [After Busby had completed *Britannia*, the
committee to raise funds for a naval pillar—*see* SW→Thomas Busby,
21/3/1800—decided not to proceed with the oratorio's complete performance
but to hold instead, on 28/4/1800, a 'miscellaneous' benefit concert comprising
selections from Handel's works and some music from *Britannia*, *see Busby* p
389.]

   SW thinks that Busby's 'most material' obstacle is the likely difficulty of
securing performers competent to do justice to his work; without such players
and singers the performance 'had better not be undertaken'. While not implying
that Busby would entrust his music to incompetent performers, SW notes that
people sometimes break their word, and reminds Busby that Salomon was thus
'misused' by [Henry] Denman [bass singer and actor, 1774–1816]. Denman 'had
engaged to sing a principal bass in [Haydn's] *The Creation* [in the 21/4/1800
performance directed by Salomon] and permitted his name to be repeatedly
advertised'. However, Denman 'attended not one of the rehearsals, and on the
evening of the performance, at 5 o'clock, sent to say that he could not sing at all'
without risking his engagement at the [Covent Garden] theatre. Busby may
consider SW a pessimist. However, SW has 'experienced so often how little
dependence a rational man ought to place' upon most professions and professors
that he is always 'agreeably disappointed' when a plan requiring the
'coincidence' of many people actually succeeds.

   'Ashley's organ' at Covent Garden [i.e., the organ used in the Covent Garden
oratorio concerts managed by John Ashley] is 'the most uncertain and intractable
of all the instruments' that SW has ever touched. It is unsuitable for the

---

[134] Ltr addressed to 'Dear Sir'. Busby identified as recipient from the context of
his recent election as a governor of the Literary Fund, the planned oratorio
performance on 16/6/1800, and SW's reference to Battishill as a mutual friend
(*see* SW→Thomas Busby, 21/3/1800).

[135] Ltr assigned to Tuesday, 3 June 1800, because the King's birthday, which
occurred on 4/6/1800, is said to be tomorrow.

performance of a concerto, and SW has 'sworn, by the diapason of Heaven', to have nothing more to do with it.

SW is 'fully sensible of the compliment' that the Literary Fund has bestowed upon Busby and himself [in May 1800 Busby was elected a governor of the Society for a Literary Fund, *see Busby* p 382, and SW, who subscribed to that Fund, presumably was elected to a similar post]. SW hopes to acknowledge such 'handsome attention' by participating 'at any performance for the benefit' of the Fund [on 2/5/1799 a glee that SW had composed for the anniversary meeting of this society was performed at that meeting].

SW is free to see Busby on Friday [6/6/1800] at Chesterfield Street for half an hour, either at 10 am or at 12.30 pm. If Busby writes immediately his letter will arrive on Thursday [5/6/1800], when SW expects to be in Marybone only for a few minutes before late at night.

SW's letter [not preserved] to [Alexander] Davison [naval agent, 1750–1829, treasurer of the 'naval pillar' committee] probably does not deserve [Jonathan] Battishill's 'hyperbolical commendation'. [According to *Busby* p 390, after CB, CW Jr, SW, Battishill and other musicians heard portions of *Britannia* performed in the 28/4/1800 concert, they wrote to the 'naval pillar' committee attesting to its merit.] Although Battishill's 'enthusiastic prepossession in favour of his friends' is 'highly satisfactory and delightful' to them, it is unlikely to influence people who hold contrary views.

SGW→Sarah 24/7/1800

MA DDWF/21/19 My Dearest Sally's wellcome Letter I received yesterday ☞ Thu 24 July={1800,1806}; pmk 18--[136]

SGW, CW Jr and Mrs Jeffreys have just returned from Windsor. George III 'immediately noticed' CW Jr and said that he should play on the king's own organ, which George III thought was better than the organ at St George's [Chapel]. On Sunday evening [20/7/1800] CW Jr met Dr [Theodore] Aylward [composer and organist, 1730?–1801, from 1788 organist of St George's Chapel] 'near the music room' [of Windsor Castle] and asked him 'if there was any impropriety' in 'our' [presumably SGW and Mrs Jeffreys] going 'to the adjacent room'. Aylward 'very civilly' placed SGW in the adjoining room where she could hear the music and see the Royal Family.

After some time, George III, being told who SGW was, came into the room to speak to her and asked her some questions about her childrens' 'genius for music' and CW's 'liking it'. George III said that he thought that music 'was intended for the noblest purposes'. SGW said that she believed music existed 'to raise our hearts above this world'.

George III's opinion of Handel's *Messiah* was 'higher than he chose to say'.

---

[136] The last two digits of pmk are illegible. Ltr assigned to 1800 because Aylward died in 1801; also, ltr is a reply to Sarah→SGW, 22/7/1800 (MA DDWF/14/19).

'Poor Charlotte' [CLW] was pleased to see SGW [at Highgate].[137] 'Dear little Charles' [CW III] rejoiced. CLW and CW III love Sarah. SW has asked after Sarah's health.

AFCK→John Wall Callcott   **26/7/1800**

BL Add 30022 f 22   I sincerely wish You joy to Your new Degree

▣ 26/7/1800

AFCK thinks that John Wall Callcott [composer and writer, 1766–1821] 'lost a great pleasure' by not hearing SW and Mr [Johann Anton] André [German composer, music publisher and pioneer of lithography, 1775–1842] 'when they tried the organs at St Paul's Covent Garden and at St Mary's Savoy Square [the German Lutheran church, one of the few in England that then had an organ with pedals], some days ago'.[138]

SW→SGW   Highgate   **18/8/1800**

MA DDWF/15/11   I am prevented being in Town ToDay

▣ Mon 18 Aug & 🖎→①

A 'very severe bilious attack' which seized SW on Saturday [16/8/1800] prevents him from being in London today. Mr Corpe [his doctor] insists that SW not go to business for two or three days to come, but he hopes to be sufficiently recovered on Thursday [21/8/1800] to be with SGW. He asks her to send the enclosed notes [not preserved, presumably cancelling his teaching engagements] immediately by Wilmot the shoe-blacker to High Street [Mrs Barnes's school] and to Paddington [AD's school]. SW hopes that SGW continues to recover from her 'late uncomfortable disorder' and that he will be able to give a better account of his health when he sees her on Thursday. CLW and Charles [CW III] 'desire their kind love'.

SW→SGW   Highgate   **26/9/1800**

MA DDWes/6/48   We are glad to hear that your Journey to Rochester

▣ 26/9/1800

SW is glad that SGW had a good journey to Rochester, although he thinks that she was ill-advised to travel while still suffering from her 'colicky complaint'.

---

[137] SGW's presence at Highgate at this time is stated in Sarah→SGW, 22/7/1800, MA DDWF/14/19.

[138] We are grateful to Professor Axel Beer for informing us that André's visit to London in the summer of 1800 is confirmed by his manuscript *Lebenslauf* (André archive, Offenbach, Germany). According to Alois Senefelder, *A Complete Course of Lithography*, London, 1819, p 36–37, André's brother Philipp André, who established the first lithographic press in England, did not go to England until after Johann Anton André had returned to Germany.

She is right not to contemplate going further into the country, and it will be well for her to return before the weather turns any colder.

Cold weather exacerbates SW's 'bilious disorder'. When he is free of this, he generally manages to go to [Martin] Madan [Jr]'s house, which is far colder than SW's Highgate house. SW is easier in his bowels than when SGW left and is so used to his complaint that he can prescribe for himself.

Miss [Hannah] Williams is 'pretty well' and sends best wishes. She says that she will attend to SGW's directions, but she and 'your girl' are 'continually jarring'. SGW's servant is very idle and unsatisfactory. Betsy Oliver [*see* CLW→SGW, 1/7/1799] would be a superior servant. Mary [a servant], who is at the infirmary, is said to be better. Oliver [not identified] continues much as before, but he is not expected to recover.

SW saw the coach master at Highgate yesterday [25/9/1800]. He promised to inquire about the mistake concerning two bottles of rum which have at last arrived at Chesterfield Street. SW will take care never again to send parcels by the Highgate stage. Mrs Foote, whom SW also saw yesterday, sends her best wishes.

SW asks to be remembered to the Lediards [with whom SGW is staying in Rochester].

Sarah memorandum   14/11/1800

GEU in box 8   Mrs Wesley came to Marybone and we were reconciled
memo dated 14 Nov[139]

Sarah and 'Mrs Wesley' [CLW] were reconciled when CLW came to Chesterfield Street today and 'repented her conduct'. CLW had 'espoused the cause' of Sarah's enemies and had 'so much injured and unjustly accused' Sarah that she thought not long ago of 'banishing' herself entirely from Chesterfield Street. 'Through this reunion' [with CLW] Sarah 'learnt the baseness' of SW; it took little to convince her of this. God disposed Sarah to forgive CLW. CLW's 'sudden revolution' also is God's work. Sarah implores God to help her to forgive SW and 'the instigator' AD.

CLW→Sarah   14/12/1800

Drew Wesley Family Letters, CLW series   I was happy to hear from you
📧 Sun 14 Dec; pmk 15/12/1800

CLW thinks kindly of Sarah and wishes that they were nearer. CLW is hurt that Sarah might suppose from CLW's 'absence' that CLW might again be giving 'credence to any cruel reports'. CLW now will not believe an 'informant' who

---

[139] Assigned to 1800 for the following reason: <Sarah's 28/7/1801 memorandum, in which Sarah says that her reconciliation with CLW occurred after Sarah committed her cause to God in 1799, when she was at Low Layton; hence not before 1799; but 14/11/1799 ruled out because Sarah then was at Low Layton, whereas this memorandum says that Sarah met CLW in Marylebone.

seeks 'mean revenge' by alleging what Sarah has said of her. If SW 'does dine out on Christmas Day', and if Sarah thinks SGW will not be inconvenienced if CLW, her children and the maid pass a day at SGW's house, then CLW will be 'particularly happy' to meet Sarah there.

Sarah has 'the best method with children' that CLW has ever seen and 'ought to be a mother'. CW III longs to see Sarah.

SGW→Sarah   **15/1/1801**
GEU in box 6   I expected my Dear Sally either Tuesday or Wednesday
☞ 'Thursday 15th'; pmk 15/1/1801 (a Thursday)

'Little Charles [CW III] sent to tell' SW that 'Aunt Sally' [Sarah] has been to see CW III. SGW finds that CW III 'has been in great danger'.

CLW→Sarah   **22/2/1801?**
Drew Wesley Family Letters, CLW series[140]   I should not have delayed
☞ 22 February; CLW at 5 Mile Stone, Highgate[141]

CLW apologises for her delay in replying to Sarah's letter [not preserved]. CLW has been 'in daily expectation of seeing' Sarah either at 5 Mile Stone, Highgate or at 'Miss Teulons' [a ladies' boarding school in Highgate kept by Misses Mary, Ann and Elizabeth Teulon]. CLW is unhappy not to see Sarah more often, as she is one of the 'very few' people whose society CLW wishes. CLW does not understand why Sarah and her brother [SW] 'should remain in cool regard of each other', as CLW knows that SW and Sarah 'respect and love each other'. CLW would enjoy Sarah's company at Highgate, where CLW's children 'would reap good' from Sarah's 'excellent mode of managing them'. Although CW III loves Sarah he fears her.

CLW hopes that 'dear Mrs Wesley' [SGW] is well. CLW will 'always love her' although CLW will 'not visit Chesterfield Street' [SGW's home] [rest of letter missing, but possibly saying that CLW will not visit while SW is there, *see* CLW→Sarah, 14/12/1800.].

---

[140] Ltr is incomplete.

[141] Ltr >6/1799 because of Highgate address and presumably <1/8/1801 when SW and CLW had separated (*see* Sarah memorandum 28/7/1801) and CLW was paying rent elsewhere (*see* Sarah→SGW, 1/8/1801). Of the two intervening years, 22/2/1801 seems more likely than 22/2/1800 because, in February 1800, Sarah was at Low Layton, Essex, having 'banished' herself from Great Chesterfield Street until SW apologised to her, and therefore CLW seems unlikely to have been in daily expectation of seeing Sarah at 5 Mile Stone, Highgate, which was SW's home. Although 22/2/1801 follows SW's apology to Sarah (SW→Sarah, 1/4/1800), her regard for him in February 1801 was 'cool' because she had learned, during her 14/11/1800 reunion with CLW, of his 'baseness' (*see* Sarah memorandum, 14/11/1800).

Sarah→CLW   5–7/1801?

GEU in box 8   After I left you it came into my mind that Charles might like
▣ 'Tuesday night'; addressed to CLW at 5 Mile Stone, Highgate[142]

Sarah recently visited CLW, bringing a proposal [from SW, not preserved] that
CLW receive [an allowance of] £100 per year [from SW] subject to conditions.
CLW should write out her objections as Sarah, having 'suffered too much from
all parties from friendly interference', will have 'nothing to do' with the dispute
between CLW and SW.

Sarah has not told SW of CLW's letter [not preserved]. Sarah does not know
with whom the proposal originated of 'taking the little one' [JWW] if CLW
'could not maintain him and have wine', which is necessary for both of them.
Sarah wanted CW III placed 'at the Moravians', who provide tender care of
children.

The Beardmores informed SW that [the singer] Miss Richardson, whom Sarah
never liked, has told people that SW's 'head is turned'. This has 'occasioned him
to lose some employment'. If such reports prevail, SW's scholars will decrease
and he will be unable to provide for his family, as his 'income depends on his
profession'. Sarah has done all she can to check such 'ill' reports.

Sarah suggests that CW III might like to go with her on Thursday to 'see the
Exhibition' [presumably the Summer Exhibition of the Royal Academy of Arts,
as the word 'Exhibition' at this time referred principally to this event]. On her
way back from visiting CLW, Sarah had called on CW III at his school and had
mentioned the possibility of his going with Sarah to the Exhibition, but the
earlier plans did not eventuate.

At CLW's request Sarah asked Mrs Delamain about 'Mrs Nicholson', to whom
CLW may be related [CLW's mother's maiden name was 'Mary Nickelson'].
However, Sarah is not 'curious' about family genealogies.

Sarah memorandum   28/7/1801

GEU in box 6   An important Event is about to take place in my Family
memo dated 28/7/1801

The separation of '— & —' [SW and CLW] is about to take place 'on account
of' Sarah's 'enemy' AD. Thanks to Providence, the 'very evil' which AD
intended to do Sarah has been returned upon AD's 'head with threefold
vengeance'. This outcome is due not to Sarah but to her Heavenly Father, to

---

[142] CLW lived at 5 Mile Stone, Highgate from 6/1799 to about 1/8/1801 when
she separated from SW (*see* Sarah memorandum, 28/7/1801) and began to pay
rent elsewhere (*see* Sarah→SGW, 1/8/1801). As ltr concerns SW's offer of
financial support to CLW after their separation it presumably follows Sarah's
'reunion' with CLW on 14/11/1800, and as ltr mentions the Exhibition it
presumably was written during the time of the 1801 Royal Academy Summer
Exhibition which took place in May–July 1801. Sarah→SW, 2/9/1807, notes
that Sarah went to Highgate to see if CLW concurred in the separation; ltr
presumably was written shortly after that visit.

whom, in 1799 at L[ow] Layton [Essex], she committed her cause in a special manner. God's wonderful ways are seen in the circumstances that (1) AD's 'baseness' towards Sarah convinced 'poor unhappy' CLW that Sarah had been CLW's 'faithful friend', and (2) SW's 'ill-conduct' towards Sarah effected CLW's confidence in Sarah's integrity. Sarah prays for grace that the 'approaching' separation may be 'set aright'.

Sarah has thought about her own fate and whether the 'same gracious Providence may appear in her favour' concerning 'X' [presumably SW]. She has besought her Saviour 'to bring the remembrance' of her 'cruel treatment' to the 'agonising soul' of her 'injurer'. However, Sarah's wrongs perhaps 'form the least part of the crimes of X'. She wonders at God's mysterious ways, which led a human being 'who was not barbarous herself' [AD] to fall 'into the power of a barbarous person' [presumably SW].

Sarah→SGW   1/8/1801
GEU in box 6   I waited for a private hand to convey a letter
☐ 1 Aug; '1801' on ltr possibly not autograph[143]

'Mrs Wesley' [CLW] sent Sarah 'a very civil letter' [not preserved] but waived 'all discussion' as she did not wish to make Sarah a 'concerned' party in a matter [CLW's separation, *see* Sarah memorandum, 28/7/1801] involving Sarah's brother [SW]. CLW 'has certainly acted very kindly' to Sarah so far. As SW 'effectively destroyed' any influence that Sarah might have had between CLW and SW, Sarah 'will have no concern in their disputes'. 'Mrs W' [CLW] pays 1½ guineas [£1/11/6] per week [in rent], which is 'not too much with wine included'.

CW Jr→SGW   12/8/1801
GEU in box 6   You may easily perceive my Dear Madam
☐ 12 Aug; pmk illegible[144]

SW promised that 'he would speak to his acquaintance Mr Christie' [possibly James Christie Sr, auctioneer, 1730–1803] regarding 'the Colonel's fine violin'. Mr Lord [not identified] could get it 'to a cheap shop', but CW Jr would prefer to have it appraised by [Ignatius] Raimondi [Italian violinist, 1735?–1813, from 1780 resident in London] or by Salomon, although SW 'is as good a judge [of violins] as they are'.

---

[143] Assigned to 1801 because ltr written from Rochester; Sarah was there in early August 1801 (her 28/7/1801 memorandum is written from there as is Sarah→SGW, 11/8/1801, GEU in box 6) but does not appear to have been in Rochester in other Augusts.

[144] Assigned to 1801 because ltr written from Dunstable, Bedfordshire where CW Jr was in August 1801 (MA DDWF/20/3) but does not appear to have been in other Augusts.

SW→Street Chesterfield St **18/8/1801**
BL Add 56228 ltr 8; *O* I believe that Saturday Week will be the first Day
▣ 18/8/1801

'Saturday week' [29/8/1801] will be the first day when SW can meet Mr Bell's party at Palmers Green. SW asks Street to convey his acceptance of the invitation. SW comments on the 'delirium' which Street experienced in consequence of their 'recreation' last Sunday [16/8/1801]. SW thinks that they did not have very much wine to drink and is surprised that it had the effect on Street that it did.

SW will be with Street on Saturday next [22/8/1801] by 2.30 pm, as he suspects 'the business' [the baptism of Street's son] is to be done before dinner. He has no objection to standing godfather, but feels that the duty of a godfather is 'one of the most solemn and obligatory in the whole theological system'. 'The ladies' are all 'sound, wind and limb'. 'Miss R' [possibly Miss Richardson, *see* SW→SGW, 16/10/1801] and SGW arrived at Marylebone half an hour before SW, and he 'went through his Monday's drudgery with great Christian forbearance and resignation'.

SW→Editor, *MM* Highgate **13/9/1801**
MM v 12, 1/11/1801, p 283 I shall be happy to receive the opinion
MM

SW seeks the opinion of 'learned' readers regarding a Greek passage by Lucian.

James Waller→SGW **21/9/1801**
MA DDWF/22/57 Your Daughter surpriz'd me yesterday by asking
▣ 21/9/1801

Sarah surprised James Waller yesterday [20/9/1801] by asking him, at SGW's desire, if more money could be raised for SGW from the £1000 in the 3% annuities [in Rebecca Gwynne's estate, *see* Rebecca Gwynne will, 9/8/1799]. This is impossible because the £1000 in stock 'would not fetch £600' now and, if its value should be still lower when SGW dies, would be insufficient to pay the £550 of legacies that Rebecca Gwynne willed, including £50 for SW when SGW dies. Therefore SGW must be content with the £30 annual interest on the £1000. However, if she wants £10 or £15 to go to Brighton, James Waller will advance this amount, to be reimbursed from her next half-yearly interest payment of £15, due after Christmas.

SW→SGW   Gt Chesterfield St   **16/10/1801**
MA DDWes/6/49   Your Letter, which I intended to have answered
🖃 16/10/1801

SGW's letter [not preserved] gave SW much pleasure as it proves that she has not regretted having gone to Brighton so late in the season. He feels that those who do not catch cold must be always in the same air, or perpetually changing it, like himself or JW. SW thought of SGW in the heavy thunderstorm on Saturday night [10/10/1801]. The same day 'we' had a delightful party consisting of Miss Richardson [singer], Graeff, François Cramer [violinist, 1772–1848], [George Frederick] Pinto [violinist, pianist and composer, 1785–1806] and [Johann Wilhelm] Moralt [viola player, 1774–>1842]; they played mostly Haydn and Mozart. Miss Jordan also came, and she and Miss Richardson were very much frightened by the storm.

SW's uncle [James] Waller does not intend to venture from London during the winter. Miss [Hannah?] Williams showed him SGW's letter. Miss Wise [not identified] has 'become quite raving' and has been moved to a madhouse, SW believes in Bethnal Green; he does not know if this is where she was sent before. Their friend Hannah is attentive and kind and both the Maries are ready and obliging. Miss Williams joins SW in sending best wishes. SW sends his love to all.

SW→CB   Highgate   **11/11/1801**
Comyn; *O*   I trust, my Dear Sir, to be with you on Tuesday next at 10
🖃 Wed 11 Nov & 🖎→🛈

SW intends to be with CB on 17/11/1801 at 10 am to seek his 'opinion and advice upon a business of more moment and magnitude than organ voluntaries', although the business [presumably the plans for CW Jr's and SW's 1802 concerts, *see* SW→CB, 9/3/1802?] is 'intimately concerned with them'.

A Translator of Lucian→Editor, *MM*   **15/12/1801**
MM v 12, 1/1/1802, p 484   I have this afternoon seen in your Magazine
M

'A translator of Lucian' has seen SW→Editor, *MM*, 13/9/1801, and notes how a Greek word that SW had queried is spelled in a 1619 edition of Lucian.

SW→CB[145]   **9/3/1802?**

Osborn MSS 3, Box 16, folder 1192; *O*   Your kind Note I would sooner have
ltr undated[146]

CB's 'kind note' [not preserved] would have been answered sooner if SW had
not been affected by the 'excessive pressure of harassing business'. [Elizabeth]
Billington [soprano, <1769–1818] 'would have laid us [CW Jr and SW] the
golden eggs' had she been engaged [to sing in their concerts], 'and would have
been a cheap bargain at any price' [in fact she was engaged to sing in a number
of presumably competing events, including a series of nine vocal concerts at
Willis's Rooms that commenced on 19/2/1802]. However, this is irrelevant now.

SW recently composed a 'duet for two organs' [not preserved] which he found
'after trial' to be 'too complicated' for 'general approbation'. Therefore 'we'
[CW Jr and SW] plan to play 'on Thursday next' a duet for two organs 'adapted
from the last chorus' of [Handel's oratorio] 'Esther'. This work will little
deserve CB's 'particular attention', as the music will be familiar to him. SW
writes out the programme of next Thursday's concert, which will begin with a
'symphony' by SW.

---

[145] Ltr addressed to 'My dear friend'. CB identified as the addressee because ltr
bears a symbol that his daughter Frances Burney d'Arblay used when sorting
through and evaluating family correspondence (*see* Hemlow, Joyce with Curtis
D. Cecil and Althea Douglas, *The Journals and Letters of Fanny Burney
(Madame d'Arblay)*, v 1, Oxford 1972, p xxxvi ff.).

[146] This undated ltr, which lacks an address portion, includes the programme of
one of the six CW Jr/SW subscription concerts that took place—according to an
advertisement on p 1 of *The Times*, 29/1/1802—in Hyde's Concert Rooms,
Tottenham Street, between 4/2/1802 and 6/5/1802. Ltr has been placed at
9/3/1802, with considerable uncertainty, because the address portion only of
SW→CB, 9/3/1802 (dated Tuesday 9 March and postmarked 10/3/1802)
survives in the Berg collection volume of 271 letters to the Burney family, and it
is conjectured that these two items may originally have constituted one letter. If
so, the concert on 'Thursday next' would refer to the concert announced for
11/3/1802. However, the alternative hypothesis—that the surviving address
portion originally belonged to another letter, not preserved, from SW to CB—
has not been ruled out. In particular, if the symphony by SW mentioned in ltr is
the symphony in B♭, of which the autograph score is dated 27/4/1802, then the
concert 'on Thursday next' could have been only the final concert of the 1802
series; in this case, ltr would have been written between Thursday 29/4/1802
and Tuesday 4/5/1802. However, no reason has been found to exclude the
possibility an earlier symphony by SW was intended to be performed 'on
Thursday next'.

SW→Sarah   Chesterfield St   **12/8/1802**
Fitzwm ltr 10   I was disappointed in not meeting you here
☞Thursday 13/8/1802, an incorrect date; pmk 13/8/1802, a Friday[147]

SW was sorry not to see Sarah at Chesterfield Street yesterday [11/8/1802]. He brought 'three debates' for her perusal: 'that of Cold Bath Fields [a prison], and of Martial Law in both Commons and Lords'. He has not had time to correct them and, according to Sarah, 'the Dr' [George Gregory, 1754–1808, editor of the *New Annual Register*, see SW→Sarah, 8/9/1802] needs them in a hurry. SW wishes to know exactly when Dr Gregory expects them [for publication in the *New Annual Register*]. The whole comes to 52 pages of SW's writing, which should come to the same amount of letterpress, and he calculates his present 'just demand' at £6/16/6. The Poor Relief Bill is now the only one remaining in the volume that Sarah gave him, and is comparatively short. SW thinks he can get through it in the course of the next week.

SW wishes to help William Westby, a young man 'in a starving state' whom he met 'in the Fields' last Tuesday [4/8/1802] while returning home. Westby had been employed as a bookseller but was 'wronged' of a considerable sum by a pretended friend, and has lost another friend who had employed him but who has now gone to Paris. Westby referred SW to several people for a recommendation, including a Mrs Connor of Duke Street, Portland Place. She confirmed that he had 'respectable connections' in Dublin and was capable of being useful either as a bookkeeper or a writer for an attorney. SW likes Westby's willingness to accept any situation, however menial. He seems to be well educated. SW accepts that the Irish are 'naturally eloquent' but feels that there is 'something above the common' in Westby's 'phraseology'. SW would have enclosed a sample of his writing, but this 'would have cost a double letter'. SW is 'a miserable patron' and is 'very shy of new protégés'. Mr Lloyd (*see* SW→SGW, 18/1/1794) has given him 'enough of venturing recommendation in weighty matters', but SW cannot see anyone in need of food without helping if possible.

The less said of SW the better. He remains 'heartless and hopeless, oppressed under an intolerable load of self-reproach for past irrevocable and irrecoverable follies', the consequences of which are daily tormenting him and sapping his health and strength. A 'certain friend' of SW's [not identified, conceivably CLW] told him yesterday that if it were not for Sarah's 'remonstrance' she would long ago have 'gone in person for the purpose of pulling down an establishment [presumably AD's school] by which she is fed'. Sarah did well to prevent this 'open violence', which would 'probably end in tragedy and massacre somewhere'. SW assures Sarah that his loathing of life is such that there are 'but two considerations' [presumably CW III and JWW] which still make him bear it. All who know SW have long been convinced that he has destroyed himself. If they have any regard for him they can only wish for his removal 'from this cruel scene of destruction and wretchedness'.

---

[147] So ltr presumably written on Thursday 12/8/1802 and incorrectly dated.

SW→SGW   **27/8/1802**
BL Add 35012 f 8   Your Letter was very welcome to me
📧 Fri 27 Aug={1790,1802,1813}[148]

SGW's letter [not preserved] was welcome and gave SW as much satisfaction
as anything he receives in his 'present miserable state'. His grievances are
'helpless and hopeless, unless God should please to work a miracle' for him. As
desired by SGW, SW will see Dr Benamore if he calls when SW is present, but
SW knows that Benamore's skill 'cannot remove maladies originating from the
mind'. SW is grateful for the invitation [from the Lediards] to Rochester [where
SGW is with Sarah], but a visit is not possible: his work 'must be minded' while
he can 'drag a foot, or speak a word of instruction'.

SW→SGW & Sarah   Highgate   **8/9/1802**
BL Add 35012 f 9   *To SGW:*   I received your letter on Monday
                        To Sarah: What Stevens may be able to 'do' is
📧 Wed 8 Sep & 📧→🖼

To SGW: SW has received SGW's letter [not preserved] and hopes that she
continues to benefit from the 'salubrious air' [at Rochester]. He feared that the
change of place and weather would be injurious to SGW, whose bowel
complaint persists, but presumes that she would hurry back to London if she felt
seriously ill.

Mrs B [not identified] is neither authorised nor qualified to judge SW's mind
and health. She has not seen him since SGW left; had Mrs B asked, Mrs Skinner
[not identified] would have given her a different account of him. SW knows that
his 'horrid state' is not exaggerated. The 'constant torment' of his mind is
'inexpressible and inconceivable' except to those who have known what a
'wounded spirit' is. His reflections on his own imprudence and the wrongs done
'against the kindest and most disinterested of friends' [AD] torment him. His
nights are 'comfortless' and his days are 'dreadful beyond the power of words to
express'. He is somewhat consoled by knowing that SGW is not in Marylebone
to be disturbed by his 'late paroxysms'. On some mornings he has been on the
brink of cancelling all his engagements. He may soon have to give up teaching:
often he is incapable of doing his pupils any good and is perplexed 'by the joint
distractions of mind and ear at the same time'. He has no one to blame for his
misfortunes but himself. His case is 'most lamentable and hopeless'.

'Honest' Mr Stevens [not identified] has sent another letter from his attorney.
There has also been a letter between Mr Burgess [presumably the attorney
representing the Wesleys] and Stevens. Burgess shares SW's opinion that

---

[148] Assigned to 1802 because ltr addressed to SGW in Rochester where she was
in August–September 1802 (SW→SGW & Sarah, 8/9/1802, also is addressed to
Rochester) and SGW does not appear to have been in Rochester in August 1790
or August 1813. Also, the content of ltr (SW turning down invitation from the
Lediards, attending to London pupils as long as he can, mental maladies) is
similar to SW→SGW, 8/9/1802).

Stevens embezzled part of the £46. Mrs [Sophia, née Corri] Dussek [singer and pianist, 1775–1847] has been paid £70 [for performing at the concerts in Hyde's Concert Rooms, Tottenham Street, earlier in 1802], leaving CW Jr's and SW's losses at £100 each. Another £20 each should settle the matter, unless the legal expenses are greater than SW expects.

SW has had no letter yet from Mr Thornton [whose family annually sent money to SGW] for SGW. SW is obliged by Mr [Thomas] Lediard's invitation [to visit the Lediards in Rochester] but must stay in London and work while he can, as he can find no 'safe or sufficiently skilful deputy' to do his business. He knows that a change of air 'is good for sick people', but he has 'no disease except that of the mind'. There is no better air in England than in Highgate; however, even 'the purest air can breathe no health into a wounded spirit'.

To Sarah: Mr Stevens 'will attempt his utmost against us'. SW's 'depression of spirits' cannot operate concerning a just or unjust claim; he would try the claim in a court of law rather than 'tamely submit' to the demands of such an 'infamous swindler'. He will be glad to see SGW next week, although he has done nothing to try and influence her decision to return. SW is 'worse rather than better' since Sarah left; however, 'the worst human miseries must end, in this life at least'. He has 'laboured' for Dr [George] Gregory [*see* SW→Sarah, 12/8/1802], but SW's brains are 'very different from what they were heretofore'. Some creditors have become rather importunate. This is a minor evil compared to 'those horrible and grim' evils with which SW has to contend.

SW→Sarah   **23/10/1802?**
GEU Wesley coll. ltr 64   After all the mighty & irreparable Mischief
▣ Saturday evening[149]

Throughout his life, SW has caused 'mighty and irreparable mischief, pain and injury' to innocent and good people. His conscience now motivates him to write to Sarah. She has 'frequently' given SW to understand that she has reason 'to complain of some unjust treatment' from his 'dearest friend' [AD]. AD has 'unjustly suffered' from SW's actions, and he wonders whether he may have been 'the original cause of any misconduct' to Sarah from AD. Sarah may remember SW's 'mortification' at her once attempting 'a degree of estrangement' between SW and AD, although Sarah thought this right. SW's 'pique' stimulated him to utter 'some hasty words' reflecting the natural resentment that one fears when faced with 'an utter deprivation of a beloved object'. SW pleaded 'the passionate impulse of the moment' in his apology to Sarah and thought she was satisfied that he regretted his 'unguarded expressions' and imputed no 'unworthy motive' to Sarah.

---

[149] Assigned to Saturday 23/10/1802 because SW's statement in ltr that Sarah has made him aware that she has a reason 'to complain of some unjust treatment' from his 'dearest friend' apparently is answered by Sarah saying 'you so urge me to state what ill treatment from Miss Deane I allude' in Sarah→SW, 27/10/1802.

'Not long ago' SW told AD that Sarah complained that AD had done her wrong. AD was much surprised and could not imagine the basis for the charge, as she said that Sarah had entrusted her only ever with one secret, which she has never divulged and will never reveal. SW asks Sarah to tell him 'what the real subject' of her resentment has been. He is confident that Sarah has a mistaken view of AD: he is as certain as he is of his 'misery' that AD is incapable of 'executing or meditating' injury to any creature. He will be pleased to assist in reconciling Sarah and AD, 'who were both once warmly attached friends'.

Sarah cannot suspect SW of any sinister motive in this matter. He is sad that his 'affection for the only object' [AD] he ever 'found upon experience to be worthy of it should have separated chief friends' [Sarah and AD]. He does not wish to die believing that a false impression of AD remains in Sarah's mind when he has the power to remove it. SW's 'mind and body are failing most rapidly'. He is therefore 'not for losing time'.

Sarah→SW   27/10/1802

GEU in box 5   I wished to have avoided everything relative to the past
☞ 27 Oct[150]

SW urged Sarah [in SW→Sarah, 23/10/1802] to specify the 'ill treatment' from AD to which Sarah alluded. SW's plea of ignorance is disingenuous because Sarah has repeatedly told SW that his conduct towards her 'three years ago' [in 1799] was instigated by 'avowed representations' of AD.

AD's remark to SW that she knew a 'secret' concerning Sarah led SW to believe that Sarah was a hypocrite. However, AD apparently did not discover this 'secret' until Sarah apprised her of news 'respecting her children' [pupils] and used this news to argue that AD's 'criminal intercourse' with SW should be broken off. Sarah gave the same news to SW who thanked her for it at the time. Subsequently, when SW was 'inebriated', he uttered 'words' and behaved so as to drive Sarah from SGW's 'roof'. Possibly SW never told AD that Sarah was 'banished' from home by his taunts on AD's 'representations'. AD did not 'calumniate' Sarah openly but 'whispered' something to SW, who then 'spread reports' that Sarah had been 'detected and found out by' AD, without mentioning any specific charge that Sarah might have refuted.

Although it was in her power, Sarah never 'revenged' by acquainting Mrs Boyer, Mrs Cozens or 'any of Mrs Deane's [AD's mother's?] friends' of the misery that AD occasioned in Sarah's family. SW is 'a striking instance' of this misery. If AD 'affects surprise again' at Sarah's claim that she has been 'basely, falsely and maliciously' injured by AD, Sarah will write down her reasons for so accusing AD, as Sarah does not fear the truth. SW would not have invented slanders to insult Sarah: they were infused into him by AD.

---

[150] Asigned to 1802 because ltr answered by SW→Sarah, 31/10/1802, which quotes several passages from ltr.

SW→Sarah   **31/10/1802**
GEU in box 5   My Letter has had one good effect, at least
⊟ Sun 31 Oct={1790,1802,1813}[151]

SW affirms [in reply to Sarah→SW, 27/10/1802] that, in the time he has been at AD's house, she never sought to lessen SW's opinion of Sarah or to prejudice him against her. When Sarah informed AD 'of reports about scaling ladders and holes bored in the wall to detect our [SW's and AD's] heinous crimes', AD pressed Sarah to name her informant. AD thought it 'unjust and ungenerous' that Sarah refused to do this, but has never defamed Sarah. Sarah has 'very unfairly accused' her of 'occasioning misery' in Sarah's family. SW has caused AD both misery and mischief, but God knows that she has been 'more sinned against than sinning'. AD never told SW that Sarah had entrusted her with a secret until within the last two months.

SW told Sarah long ago of the 'pain' he felt from Sarah 'endeavouring to detach, or at least partially to alienate' SW from 'the only woman likely to have rendered' SW 'blest and respectable' [AD]. SW's resentment of this endeavour 'betrayed' him 'into unadvised and indefensible expressions, most of them uttered when under the influence of wine'. SW 'long ago' made Sarah his '*amende honorable*' for 'using the harsh words of hypocrite', etc. [*see* SW→Sarah, 1/4/1800]. He has never 'spread any reports' of Sarah's 'detection' by AD, and 'never spoke of the subject but on that unlucky evening, when wine had inflamed' SW's 'transient resentment into a madness of unjust attack'. SW never told AD that Sarah was banished from SGW's house by taunts on AD's representations, and AD has never 'calumniated' Sarah either 'openly to the world' or secretly to SW. 'All real blame' in this 'sad business' is 'justly imputable' only to SW.

All the misery in 'our [Sarah's and SW's] family' has been 'by the misconduct and fatal mistakes in life' of CW Jr and SW, 'more especially' the mistakes of SW. AD's name 'might and would have been the comfort and honour of us all' if SW had not been 'infatuated' [with CLM] and 'suffered to split on the rock which has dashed me to pieces', perhaps for his 'original opposition' to CW's will [i.e., if SW and CLM had not got together and married, SW would have married AD]. It is cruel and untrue to say that AD has endeavoured to 'detach' SW from CLW and their children; AD has always 'sought the contrary by every human effort'. AD is as 'guiltless of injury' to Sarah as Sarah is to 'little Charles' [CW III].

Shepherd→SW   Chesterfield St   **17/11/1802**
MA Letters Chiefly to Wesleys v 1 ltr 36   Mr S Wesley's letter is received
⊟ 17/11/1802

Shepherd replies to SW's letter [not preserved] about his conduct, answering him point by point. Concerning his remarks that his 'immediate temporal

---

[151] Ltr >1792 as CW III alive and <1807 as AD alive; hence 1802 the only possible year.

destruction' was caused by an 'ignorant, irrational and low-minded woman' [presumably CLW], Shepherd asks whether SW's connection with that woman is lawful or unlawful. SW should remember that all unlawful relationships lead to 'destruction' and should immediately be broken off, and that a marriage cannot be dissolved except for adultery. He therefore should consider his position as a man and a Christian and should conscientiously discharge his duties as a husband and a father. Shepherd, in SW's place, would propose 'in a calm, kind, and dispassionate manner' 'some rational plan of future life and conduct' to CLW that would allow them to live comfortably together if possible. If both parties think this is not possible they should separate, at least for a time, and maintenance appropriate to CLW's needs and SW's means should be arranged. Decisions about the education of the children should be up to SW; the children should be 'put to board where their mother should, or should not, see them', whichever is best for them.

Concerning SW's allegation that he had broken off his connection at Shepherd's 'prudent instance', Shepherd replies that SW never confided to her that he had any connection, lawful or unlawful, with any lady whatever, and she never heard him mention her name, family or situation. She had heard from others that he 'secretly, and at undue hours' visited 'some young lady at a boarding place' and that 'young Worgan' [possibly a son of John Worgan] was his companion. When [Bishop] Talbot came to Shepherd to desire that she speak to SW about the complaints that CW had made about SW coming home 'at undue hours of the night', Shepherd 'delivered her message' to SW and expressed her fears about some 'improper connection' [possibly with CLM, *see* Shepherd→SW→Shepherd, undated, 3/1794–1797]. SW was angry and sent Shepherd a letter [not preserved], which she still possesses. After this, their correspondence 'declined and died'.

SW never told Shepherd that he had 'debauched a lady' and thought himself obliged to make reparation to her reputation by marriage. Shepherd therefore could not have advised him what to do on this occasion. In all her dealings with SW, Shepherd has 'exhorted' and 'earnestly entreated' him neither to injure the person or reputation of any woman. In fact, she wished him to abstain from any connection with women and to live 'if he could soar so high, the life of angels'. For this, Shepherd was rewarded with 'the sneer of contempt'. She had hoped that SW would be more than a mere musician. But the past cannot be recalled, and it remains for SW to be wise and good now, by making the best of the present.

Although SW may have reason to think his profession 'ill-chosen' it should not be irksome to follow it as a lawful way of earning his living. If any 'female wretch' having 'free-thinking notions', atheistic practices and 'bestial turpitude' should inflame SW's appetites in order to inflame her own appetites it would be vain for SW to think of any 'acceptance with God' or peace of mind. 'Scholars, were it a whole school, choice suppers, good wines, caresses and flattery' must all be given up. Sorrow for past sins is 'as the suppuration of an abscess'; the lancet that opens it gives ease.

Shepherd beseeches SW to make his peace with God and with his own soul, by removing every obstacle and weight of bondage.

Elizabeth Hamilton→Sarah   22/12/1802
MA DDWF/26/57 (typescript)   Where affection is founded upon something
MA typescript

Elizabeth Hamilton [author, 1758–1816] thanks Sarah for her two letters [not preserved]. The first letter presented 'a melancholy picture' of her brother's [SW's] sufferings.

Sarah→SGW   18/4/1803
GEU in box 6   I did not arrive in Dover till Saturday Night
▣ 18/4/1803

Sarah often has told SW that no one who expected good or who trusted 'the almighty Carer' has been disappointed. She has many hopes for SW and is anxious to hear about him. 'Chastening' seems grievous to him now but will bring forth righteousness, which Sarah trusts that SGW will live to see.

SGW→Sarah   30/4/1803
GEU in box 6   I know my Dearest Daughter will wish to hear of us
▣ Saturday; pmk 30/4/1803

SW's health is about the same as when Sarah [who is in Brighton] left: he is 'very ill'; 'his anxiety increases'. SW set off for Tottenham today doubting that he would have sufficient strength for the walk. Miss Cope gives him 'kind sympathy' for 'his present complaints'. As 'the fatiguing time of giving up the house [SW's house at Highgate] is nearer', SW often wishes that Sarah were here [in London]. CLW visited an acquaintance in London, who knew her father, for 'physical advice'. She does not want SW to go to her 'as she says it agitates her nerves' and she is advised to have quiet. SW kindly wants to do everything he can to make her happy and is planning, with Mrs Foote, to see CLW 'for a few hours' tomorrow [1/5/1803].

SW→Sarah   3/5/1803?
GEU in box 8   I believe that your Presence, & the utmost of your assistance
▣ Tue 3 May= {1791,1796,1803,1808,1814}[152]

SW never has needed Sarah's presence and assistance more than now. His brains are 'boiling over'. He needs her 'coolness' of mind, as actions must be taken 'without delay'.

---

[152] Ltr >1793 SW/CLM marriage and <1812 SW/CLW Deed of Separation after which SW no longer was concerned with CLW's wishes. Assigned to 1803 as ltr consistent with Sarah's being away and SW's desire to have her back, SW's being anxious and very ill, and CLW's illness (all of which are mentioned in SGW→Sarah, 30/4/1803). 1796 and 1808 have not been ruled out but appear less likely.

CLW has been ill lately. If 'the Yorkshire plan had been followed' SW could have been accused of sending her far off to injure her health, for sharp air hurts her lungs. Mr Burder's school at St Albans [where Samuel Burder, 1773–1837, was congregational minister] could be a possibility [perhaps for CW III's education].

As soon as Sarah can return, SW wants her to determine CLW's 'ultimate wish and resolution'. This might be 'one of the last essential services' that Sarah can confer upon SW. He is 'very ill', worse than when she left.

Mercy Doddridge→Sarah　　　　　　　　　　22/5/1803

MA Letters Chiefly to Wesleys v 1 ltr 129　　　I need not tell you how welcome
✉ 22/5/1803

Mercy Doddridge sympathises with [her friend] Sarah for the 'mortification' that she must have suffered from SW's and CLW's 'domestic jars, so disgraceful to both'.

CLW→SGW　　　　　　　　　　　　　　　　14/6/1803?

WCL LDWMM 1997/6601　　　　　　　　　　[not available]
✉ 14 June; pmk 180-[153]

CLW describes the sheets she requires, and proposes, with Mr Wesley's [SW's] leave, to send the table linen by Betty Oliver. They will not fetch much. SW and CLW never had a chafing dish or it would have been sent [presumably to Chesterfield Street]. CLW thanks SGW for her affectionate care of 'the dear children' [CW III and JWW].

Sarah→SGW　　　　　　　　　　　　　　　　15/8/1803

MA DDWF/14/17A　　　　　　　　　　　I wish to hear of You & Sam
✉ 15/8/1803

Sarah asks for news about SGW and SW, 'who we [Sarah and CW III] left in so melancholy a state'. Sarah and CW III are unable to leave Hillingdon [Middlesex] until the end of the week, as the coachman is ill. CW III's appetite is better. He 'desires his love and duty' to SGW and SW and seems 'mightily pleased' to be away from school. CW III 'forms a striking contrast to the little noisy boy' [JWW] who is 'the only child now at home' [at Chesterfield Street].

Dr [Robert] Willan [1757–1812, from 1783 to 1803 physician to the Public Dispensary, London], who has had 'great success' in the treatment of nervous

---

[153] The last digit of the postmark is illegible. >1801 because of the receiving-house stamp 'Highgate 2 Py P. Paid' (*Willcocks/Jay* L507, pp 71–72). Assigned to 1803 because ltr presumably refers to the distribution of possessions from the Highgate house (see SGW→Sarah, 30/4/1803, which says that the time of giving up this house is nearer), but 1802 not absolutely ruled out.

disorders, might do SW's health good, but 'it is in vain to advise poor Sam to follow advice'. SW's 'disease indeed is in the mind', for which God is the only physician; however, 'means [of treatment] ought not to be slighted'. But 'who has influence' [over SW]? 'We [Sarah and SGW] can only sympathise and pray and hope' that SW's 'afflictions are sent in mercy, and will end in happiness'.

SGW→Sarah   17/8/1803

GEU in box 6   My Dear Sally's Letter was very wellcome to me
▣ Wed 17 Aug={1796,1803,1808,1814}[154]

SGW was pleased by Sarah's letter [Sarah→SGW, 15/8/1803], containing an agreeable account of the situation in which Sarah and 'little Charles' [CW III] are staying with friends. Mrs Keysall called on SGW yesterday [16/8/1803]. SW was writing in the next room and joined them for tea. He and Mrs Keysall compared 'a few of their nervous sensations' and 'references to the only remedy in trouble'. SW is 'very much afflicted', but unites with SGW in sending love.

CW Jr & Sarah→SGW   20/9/1803

MA DDWF/14/21   *CW Jr:*   My ever dear and Hon'd Mother
                      Sarah: I have the pleasure to tell You
▣ Tue 20 Sep; pmk 1803
  CW Jr: not relevant to Source Book
  Sarah: 'Little Charles' [CW III] is highly pleased with where he is staying [in Milton, near Gravesend, Kent] with CW Jr and Sarah. She wishes that SGW and SW were with them. SW's mind 'could not receive benefit from change, but his health might'; he would then 'be better able to bear his afflictions' until God saw fit to lighten them. 'All we can urge' on this subject 'is vain'. If SGW and SW came next week [to Milton] Sarah would give them her room and the child's [CW III]; she would then 'keep house in town' [Great Chesterfield Street] until SGW and SW returned [to London]. Sarah sends love to SW.

SGW→CW Jr & Sarah   21/9/1803

GEU in box 6   I return my Dear Charles & Sally thanks
▣ Wed 21 Sep[155]

SW 'is much the same, (full of trouble)'. Betsy O[liver] saw SW 'very ill in a chair leaning as usual'. SW would not accept CW Jr's and Sarah's 'kind offer' at

---

[154] Not 1796 because CW III then only 3. Not 1814 because CW III then not little. Assigned to 1803 rather than 1808 because ltr appears to be SGW's reply to Sarah→SGW, 15/8/1803; also, Sarah and CW III are not known to have been away together in 1808, when SW seemingly was untroubled by 'nervous sensations'.

[155] Assigned to 1803 because ltr a reply to CW Jr & Sarah→SGW, 20/9/1803.

this time [to visit, *see* Sarah→SGW, 20/9/1803]. SGW wishes that SW were with them [CW Jr, Sarah and CW III], as SGW 'can administer no comfort but kindness'.

Sarah→SW   25/11/1803
GEU in box 6   To revert to Injury & Unkindness is always unpleasant
📧 25/11/1803

Sarah reverts reluctantly to the unpleasant subject of this letter only because SW said that a restatement of her feelings would afford him 'some comfort' in his 'agitated state of mind'.

Sarah considers that she has suffered 'injury and unkindness' from SW, who 'sacrificed' her because of his 'attachment' to AD. After Sarah wrote to AD and spoke to SW of a report that Sarah had heard, SW became continually quarrelsome. While Sarah was in the country, SW, apparently 'in liquor' and uttering curses, told Mrs [Arabella] Mitz and CW Jr in the presence of SGW that AD knew that Sarah was a 'hypocrite' and that Sarah had prevented Mrs Maud 'from placing her child' at [AD's] school. This was untrue. Sarah resolved then 'never to enter' SGW's house while SW was in it until SW 'made some apology'. Sarah kept her resolution and 'was banished many weeks' from her home, which grieved her friends, until SW 'made the slightest apology' [*see* SW→Sarah, 1/4/1800].

When Sarah saw 'Mrs SW' [CLW], she told Sarah what SW had said of Sarah when he was 'not inebriated'. Sarah also received an anonymous letter which she discovered was written by [Martin] Madan [Jr], to whom SW had represented Sarah 'in the same manner'. CLW has told Sarah 'many times' that Sarah 'was the sport of conversation' at SW's table before his guests. Sarah believes that AD is 'the cause of all this' and that SW took offence because of a sincere letter that Sarah wrote to her.

SW knows that Sarah lamented his conduct. She believes that his subsequent behaviour to her was 'revenge'. Sarah's conduct throughout has been sincere. She 'concealed the only secret' that SW entrusted to her respecting AD and, unlike CLW, never 'visited the person' [AD] who Sarah believes was responsible for SW's 'ill treatment' of herself.

CLW's behaviour 'during seven years could not but give pain to one who wished her well'. The ideas concerning Sarah that SW has impressed upon CLW's mind prevent Sarah 'ever being of service' to CLW, and 'will probably impede all future use' that Sarah might have to CLW's children. Children's impressions of people are formed by their parents, and SW may be right that CW III's 'apparent affection' to Sarah is 'only art'.

Sarah sympathises with SW's great affliction but it can be alleviated only by God.

SGW→Sarah   **24/5/1804**

MA DDWF/21/21   It was with pleasure I received my Dearest Sallys Letter
📧 Thurs 24 May; pmk 1804

CW Jr is much pleased with CW III's letter yesterday [23/5/1804] and 'will do
everything he can' to have CW III stay with 'us' [SGW and CW Jr] in the
vacation [from CW III's school at Wateringbury, near Maidstone]. However,
SW 'almost affronted' SGW by saying he would rather have CW III 'put
anywhere' but with SGW because she 'indulged' him and gave him butter,
contrary to SW's order. SGW reprimanded SW 'a little harshly', saying that his
feelings were far from those 'of a kind father'. She told SW that if 'he refuses
entirely' [to have CW III stay at SGW's home] she would not trouble about
SW's 'other child' [JWW] or go to see him. SW said he would pay Mrs Lediard
[with whom Sarah was staying at Maidstone] for CW III 'to be with her in the
holidays', as SGW emphasised to SW that it would be unkind to let CW III be
'the only scholar left at the school'. SGW 'won't despair' of Sarah's 'influence
and arguments' on this subject.

SGW told SW that if CW III were here [in Great Chesterfield Street] there
would be 'no expense' to SW [on account of CW III] and that Sarah should have
'the entire management' of CW III. SGW hopes that Sarah will be able to bring
CW III to them [at Great Chesterfield Street]. CW Jr and SGW send love to
Sarah and CW III. SW also sends love; his 'distress calls for all our prayers and
kind assistance'. SW said he was 'much obliged' by Sarah's 'ready attention and
kindness' to CW III.

CW Jr will write to [SGW's] cousin [Thynne] Gwynne [*d*1826] at Bath 'to
make inquiries'. SW is against CW Jr's going [to Bath].

CW III→SW   Gt Chesterfield St   **26/5/1804**

MA DDWF/16/1   I write these few lines to thank you & my Grandmother
📧 26/5/1804

CW III thanks SW and SGW for the presents he received and begs SW to allow
him to come home in the holidays, or at least not to stay at school. Sarah says
that she will bring him from Rochester to London if SW will let him come. Mr
and Mrs Lediard are both good to him. 'Master Henry' [Lediard] and CW III are
going [from Maidstone] to their school [at Wateringbury] tomorrow.

Sarah→SGW   **28/5/1804**

GEU in box 6   I did not reach my Journeys End till late last Night
📧 28 May; pmk (London) 31/5/1804

CW III has written to SGW. He loves Chesterfield Street [SGW's home] and
has not forgotten his family, as SGW imagined. Sarah is careful of SW's money
which pays for his schooling. Mr [John] Smith [of Dover, brother of Sarah's
friend Mrs Delamain] 'died as he lived—cursing and swearing just before'.
'Poor dear Sam' [SW] never was in such a state [as Smith]. Sarah wishes that
SW could see this as 'cause for gratitude and comfort'.

CLW→SGW   **30/5/1804**
Drew Wesley Family Letters, CLW series   I am hurt Mr Wesley shd think
▱ 30/5/1804; pmk 31/5/1804[156]
   CLW is hurt that 'Mr Wesley' [SW] should think that she 'ever tried to prejudice the children', or anyone else, against him. CW III 'is old enough to recollect the truth' of what she says. She must be 'a bad politician'.

CW Jr→Sarah   **9/6/1804**
Drew Wesley Family Letters, CW Jr series   I thank you for your epistle
▱ 9 June; pmk 1804
   CW III has written 'a kind letter' to SW [CW III→SW, 26/5/1804]. It appears that CW III's 'petition' [to return home or at least not to stay at school in the holidays] will be granted. Last Thursday [7/6/1804] 'young' Mr Marmaduke Coslett came to tea. SW has taken him three times on 'peregrinations'. CW Jr cannot walk with SW: 10 miles at one time 'is too much for a fat man'. It is remarkable that SW 'is never tired'. CW Jr would like SW to be happy. 'Only one thing is needful to make us contented', but SW 'hath not' that, 'poor fellow'.

SW→Sarah   **12/6/1804**
MA DDWes/6/35   I am sorry I cannot now answer your letter in Detail
pmk 12/6/1804
   SW apologises for not writing a detailed reply to Sarah's letter [not preserved] but his 'pen and brain have long failed' him. SW has permitted 'the boy' [CW III] to come [to London] on 20/6/1804 when his school [in Wateringbury] breaks up. CW III asked SW to inform Sarah of this. SW expects that what Sarah has reported about CW III is 'all true'. SW now expects from life only 'mortification, disappointment, disaster and disgrace'.
   A crisis is about to burst upon SW's 'guilty head'. 'Alas! that a family of such original merit, talents and virtues should be thus reduced to shame and sorrow!' SW will tell Sarah more when they meet. He has had 'fresh demonstration' of the damage which reports have done to his character: [Martin] Madan [Jr] and the Rev. S. White [not identified] 'are both become enemies.'

---

[156] The year '1804' appears to be written over an earlier date. The final digit of the postmark is unclear, but '4' appears to be the best guess.

Sarah will[157]   24/7/1804
Drew Wesley Family Letters, Sarah series   In the Year of our Lord 1804
will dated 24/7/1804

Sarah bequeaths to SGW the interest of £650 in the 3% consols[158] of the Bank
of England, to be paid annually to SGW during her lifetime. At SGW's death
this interest is to be paid annually to CW Jr during his lifetime. At his death this
interest is to be paid annually to SW during his lifetime. At SW's death the
principal of £650 is to be paid to 'his children now living, Charles [CW III] and
William Wesley [JWW] the day they become of age, and their heirs'. If Sarah is
bequeathed legacies she bequeaths them to SGW if SGW is alive and otherwise
to CW Jr and SW in equal proportions.

SW→Stokes   2/10/1804
BL Add 31764 f 18; *O*   I am unable to account for the reason of yr never
▣ 2/10/1804

SW does not know why Stokes has neither called nor written for so long. SW
supposes that if Stokes had wanted to be in SW's company, he would have
'contrived ways and means' of their meeting before now. SW is 'hurt at the
slight of a person for whom he has a regard'. He is conscious of having been
remiss with the Coopers [perhaps the family of George Cooper, organist, *c*1783–
1843], who sent him a kind invitation, but hopes that his illness and distraction
of mind will excuse him. SW proposes to meet Stokes at about 2 pm today.

SGW, Sarah & CW Jr→SW   Chesterfield St   4/11/1804
GEU in box 6   *SGW:*   My Dearest Sam. will be thankfull that we had
                  Sarah: It will be a great consolation & pleasure to myself
                  CW Jr: I have been much hurt my dear Saml for any thing
▣ 4/11/1804

SGW: SGW's safe journey to Bath 'would have been pleasant' if her reflecting
upon SW's troubles had not made her 'truly unhappy'. She would not have left
London on this short trip if her staying with SW would have made him better.
She asks SW to inform her if he has had 'any relief or comfort' from his
'anxious fears'.

Sarah: Sarah and SGW will be greatly consoled and pleased if SW is better
than when they left him. Sarah trusts that God will bring SW 'out of the deep
waters'. The 'blindness' has been removed from his eyes, which is a step
towards his salvation. Sarah hopes that SW 'will not cherish and seek out sad
thoughts'; instead, he should use his mind 'to hope better things'.

---

[157] Sarah made subsequent wills on 26/2/1826 and on 16/11/1827. Neither
explicitly revokes this will.

[158] I.e., the consolidated annuities, which were British Government debt
instruments with no maturity date.

CW Jr: SW's 'ill state of mind' must make all of his friends unhappy. CW Jr prays that SW will be better when CW Jr and his family return [to London]. Many people, including Sir Joseph Andrews, have inquired after SW.

SGW & Sarah→SW   Gt Chesterfield St   **12/11/1804**
GEU in box 6   *SGW:*   My Dear Sam.'s Letter I am thankful for
        Sarah: It will be a satisfaction to you to hear
◧ 12/11/1804

SGW: SGW is thankful for SW's letter [not preserved], but his account of his 'constant misery' is truly depressing, especially because he fears his 'speedy dissolution'. SGW hopes that this will not happen soon. Some old acquaintances have wished SW to come [to Bath] for a 'change of air'. SGW grieves that SW's present situation is 'so destitute of everything' he wishes; she hopes that this will change. Sarah will be glad to have CW III's letter—this can wait until she returns soon [to London]. SGW believes that Miss [Hannah] Williams would 'do everything she could' to oblige SW.
Sarah: Sarah wishes that SW could send a better account of himself. She strongly hopes that she will live to see SW 'in a happier state', which now appears impossible to him.

SGW & Sarah→SW   Gt Chesterfield St   **16/11/1804**
GEU in box 6   *SGW:*   My Dear Sam. is Extreamly on our Mind
        Sarah: If You can write it would comfort my Mother
◧ 16/11/1804

SGW: SGW has 'just received a letter from Miss [Hannah] Williams [not preserved] which distresses us all'. CW Jr has a scholar every day next week who should not be neglected. If SW has any regard for SGW, who 'prays to the Lord Jesus' to preserve SW 'from all the powers of darkness', he will remember that 'there is no repentance in the grave' and will be kept from doing 'any harsh action'. If SW asks SGW to come to him she will go 'as soon as possible'.
Sarah: SW probably will see SGW by the beginning of the [25/11/1804] week unless he requests her immediate departure. CW Jr has numerous engagements and fair prospects. Sarah does not doubt that God will 'preserve and bless' SW. If he can write, his letter would comfort SGW, who needs strength for her return journey [to London].

SGW→Sarah   **1/5/1805**
GEU in box 6   My dearest Sally's Letter I was glad to receive
pmk 1/5/1805

SW 'calls in for a few minutes most days'. Most people believe 'he looks better'. He sleeps better elsewhere [than at SGW's house]. He has 'many complaints', some of which he thinks came from 'those violent blows he often gave himself'. 'We all warned him' of the consequences of these blows.

CLW visited once, 'by the earnest desire of the dear little boy' [JWW] to 'see his grandmama' [SGW].

CW III→SGW   6/6/1805
MA DDWF/16/4   I receiv'd your kind Letter in which you wished me to write
✉ 6/6/1805
CW III received SGW's letter [not preserved], asking him to write to SW. CW III is going home [from his school in Wateringbury] on 19/6/1805 and asks SGW to inform SW of the progress he has made in his learning. He sends love to SW, CLW, CW Jr and JWW. Mrs Cooper sends her compliments.

Shepherd→Sarah   15/1/1806
MA Letters Chiefly to Wesleys v 1 ltr 40   I have often intruded my notions
✉ Wed 16/1/1806 but 16/1/1806 a Thursday; pmk 15/1/1806
CW III expressed 'much regret' to Shepherd concerning 'the intended arrangement of quitting' London [presumably the plan to remove him from St Paul's School, *see* SW→SGW, 1/4/1806]. She reprimanded him for expecting SGW, whose income has been 'spunged upon' both by CW and by her 'needy Welsh relations', to contract further debts, thereby hurting Sarah and CW Jr by depriving them of money to support their latter years. Shepherd told CW III that it was 'a shame' for a man [SW], who can earn his living and can strive with difficulties much better than a woman, to allow his sister [Sarah] to deprive herself of comforts that her old age will require, in order to pay for his son's [CW III's] schooling.

Shepherd urged CW III to practise 'temperance, soberness and even self-denial' and to have no 'false wants'. He did not seem to 'palate' these doctrines 'and no wonder: is he not the son of his father [SW]?'. SW is not like [Napoléon] Bonaparte [Emperor of France, 1769–1821], who conquered all the Low Countries, because 'great parts' of SW's revenue are affected by 'contributions' [payments] levied in respect of SW's 'low countries'.

Shepherd finds that CLW is 'ready to lay in' [for Emma's birth, in January or February 1806]. This will be another low-country contribution [that SW will have to pay]. 'By and by they [SW and CLW] will be quarrelling again like cats that fight when they cease caterwauling'.

SW→SGW   9 Arlington St[159]   **1/4/1806**
Fitzwm ltr 11   I fully intended to have written sooner
📧 1/4/1806

SW intended to write earlier but was interrupted on each occasion he sat down to write. He hopes that SGW concluded from his silence that nothing new was amiss. His whole situation is 'horrible' and his existence miserable: he hates to live, and fears to die. However, he bears his troubles as best he can, for the sake of his family. He is embarrassed at present for lack of money, not having been paid the half-year's account by 'the successor of my dear friend' [AD, who was buried on 22/1/1806]. He is assured that executors rarely pay the debts of a testator within a year of death, so he must expect to be 'seriously distressed'. He also has a bad debt of over £20 from the family of one of his pupils at Mrs Barnes's school. He has written off [Justinian] Casamajor's £60 and despairs of the £10 owed to him by Lingston [not identified]. There are no more hopes from 'honest and grateful' Miss Richardson, so SW is left with two alternatives: 'sinking [i.e., taking out] money in the funds', or borrowing on interest. He hesitates to call on [his relative] Dick Baldwyn as he has not seen him for a long time, and on the one occasion he called on Cotton he was denied. He imagines he will have to sink £100 [take £100 from his investments], which is preferable to his being arrested or dunned.

SW curses the day that his 'poor good father' CW suffered music to be SW's profession. Only 'impudent and ignorant wretches' make large amounts from music, except for singers, 'who often get a large sum over the devil's back, which they as soon expend under his belly'. The whole profession is a 'trivial and degrading business to any man of spirit or any abilities to employ himself more usefully'.

If SW had £300–400 at his disposal he would buy a large share in a gin shop, which would bring him substantial profits with no trouble. The investment could be made without the investor's name becoming known. With the exception of agriculture, SW thinks there is little to choose between the honour of one trade and another. If he could get CW III instructed in farming, SW would be sure that CW III had the best and most honest means of livelihood, and all CW III's knowledge of languages could go to the devil.

For financial and other reasons it is impossible for CW III to stay at St Paul's School. The doctor [Richard Roberts, 1729?–1823, from 1769 to 1814 High Master of St Paul's School] is almost disqualified from teaching but does not meddle with CW III's class; the usher who has succeeded Mr Braber is far from being a deep scholar. SW is anxious to try to find a job for CW III as soon as possible and is nearly indifferent as to how this should be done. A large fortune or patronage is needed for the 'three learned professions: law, physic [i.e., medicine] and divinity', so it would be cruel to encourage CW III in any of

---

[159] Ltr is headed 'Camden Town' with no street address stated. SW's address presumed to be 9 Arlington Street because his change of address from 9 Arlington Street to 27 Arlington Street, Camden Town, apparently occurred in 1808.

these. CW III is at an age when his destiny should be decided and 'not left to chance and caprice', which was the case with SW, and to which circumstance he attributes his 'utter ruin'.

SW has just seen Mrs [Arabella] Mitz. He is 'rather less uncomfortable' in health, which is fortunate, as he has 'little or no attention from the quarter' [CLW] where he has the greatest right to expect it. He has no hope of finding tranquillity, and 'a vessel so wrecked and shattered' as his mind cannot be repaired. He will consider himself fortunate if he can avoid jail. CLW is 'much as usual'. The children are well.

SW→SGW   21/4/1806
BL Add 35012 f 11   On Monday last before I left Mrs Barnes's, I was seized
◨ Monday 21 Apr; pmk 1806[160]

SW was taken ill last Monday [14/4/1806] on leaving Mrs Barnes's [school] and has been very unwell since. CLW has a severe cold and a swelled face, and is unable, even if she were willing, to help him. Because of his illness he has been unable to approach his friends about his financial difficulties, and he cannot get his half-year's dividend at the Bank [of England], as he has no Letter of Attorney. He is now down to his last £1/1/- and is pressed with daily visits from those to whom he owes money. He dictated a letter to Mrs Foote on Wednesday [16/4/1806], asking her to approach her brother on his behalf. He wrote yesterday [20/4/1806] to Cotton [not preserved], stating his inability to get to the Bank, and asking Cotton to advance the £30 due until he could get there. Cotton was unable or unprepared to help.

SW has now applied for a loan of £100 on interest. However, he considers that these 'temporary assistances' only postpone the 'inevitable mischief' which he feels is approaching. On his present income SW is unable to maintain himself and four other people [presumably CLW, CW III, JWW and a servant], not reckoning the infant [Emma], particularly as CLW is a 'determined spendthrift'. Even if another school were to offer SW employment this would not be a solution, as he cannot stand the drudgery of 'more dunces' assaulting his ears for six hours at a time. He is not averse to employment, but cannot increase this 'contemptible, frivolous work of hammering sounds into blockheads' without driving himself into madness or 'idiotism'. Graeff has told him that teaching so impaired his health that he had to give up half of it.

SW thus is without resource and is desperate. If he could find some 'quiet employment' that would pay him £200 per annum he would accept it. But he considers his health so bad that his 'wretched career' will not be much further extended. He will answer CW Jr's letter [not preserved] when he can. SW has sent to [Robert] Birchall for the music for Miss Wingrove.

---

[160] Although the day of this ltr can be read as either '21' or '27' ltr has been assigned to the 21st because that day was a Monday in 1806.

SW→Graeff   Camden Town[161]   **21/5/1806?**

BL Add 60753 f 122; *O*   At length I am enabled to announce to you

▣ 21 May[162]

SW has at last finished transcribing JSB's 'inimitable and immortal Preludes and Fugues' [the '48'] from Graeff's 'valuable book' [the edition of the '48' published by Nägeli in Zürich in 1801].[163] If SW had had no other obligations he would have returned this book 'some months ago', as he could easily have copied six to eight pages each day if he had been able to spend four hours on this task. However, necessity obliges SW to attend principally to the improvement of others [his pupils] rather than to his own improvement, for which he is left only snatches of time. As he wishes that his copy have 'not a single error', he requests permission to keep the book not later than next Saturday [31/5/1806], so that he may 'compare the copy with the original note by note'.[164]

SW apologises also for not yet repaying the 'pecuniary accommodation' that Graeff kindly provided. The money would have been returned to Graeff when due if a 'great man' [presumably Justinian Casamajor, who in 1800 had been sheriff of Hertfordshire; *see* SW→SGW, 1/4/1806], who had promised in February to pay the £60 he owes SW, had not 'chosen to delay' payment.[165]

---

[161] SW's Camden Town address appears to have been 9 Arlington Street until about June 1808 when it became 27 Arlington Street. In SW→CB, 23/6/1808, the numerals '27' are underscored, suggesting that the change of address was recent. It is not known whether this change signifies a new home for SW or was merely a renumbering of the houses on this street.

[162] SW lived at Camden Town in May during the years 1806–1809. Ltr presumably < SW→CB, 12/4/1808, in which SW says that he has laboriously transcribed all the '48'. Assigned to 1806 rather than 1807 because ltr says that a £60 loan has not been repaid, and SW→SGW, 1/4/1806, says that £60 owed by Mr Casamajor to SW appears to be lost forever; also, Graeff and SW's financial problems are mentioned in SW→SGW, 21/4/1806. No such references are found in the extant 1807 letters, but 1807 has not been absolutely ruled out.

[163] In his *Reminiscences*, written in 1836, SW said that he 'first became acquainted with the Preludes and Fugues' [the '48'] of JSB 'through George Frederick Pinto, one of the greatest musical geniuses that Europe ever produced, but who was cut off in the flower of his days' [he died on 23/3/1806] (*Musical Times* v 37 no. 642, 1/10/1896, p 653). No corroboration of this event or record of its date has been found.

[164] SW's copy of the '48' from the Nägeli edition now is at BL Add 14330 f 1.

[165] Justinian Casamajor experienced financial difficulties on several occasions. We are grateful to John Harris of the North Mymms Local History Society, Hertfordshire, for the information that Casamajor's will was marked 'insolvent', possibly because of the collapse of the sugar market about 1815. In 1816, because of personal disappointment, he was unable to continue to pay for his wife's and daughters' subscriptions to the Philharmonic Society (Justinian Casamajor→William Ayrton, 2/2/1816, BL Add 52342 f 74).

SW assures Graeff that his money is safe, and sends respects to Mrs [Mary] Graeff and to their young children.

SW→CW Jr   **28/5/1806?**
Dorset D/C00:G/C4   I purpose to reach the Bank on Friday next
☞ Wed 28 May={1800,1806,1817}[166]
SW proposes to meet CW Jr at the Bank [of England] about 11.45 am next Friday [30/5/1806], and will wait for him near the south door of the rotunda.

SW→Street   9 Arlington St   **30/5/1806**
BL Add 56228 ltr 9; *O*   I have a little Scheme to propose
☞ 30/5/1806
SW proposes a holiday plan for CW III, who has been 'diligent and assiduous' at his studies. CW III wishes to hear the Tower of London guns fired and has asked SW to take him there. SW can be free on Wednesday [4/6/1806, the birthday of George III] and suggests that he, CW III and Street should then pass the rest of the day together. SW proposes that they dine on fish at Billingsgate and then stroll towards Chalk Farm, where there is a pleasant tea-garden. Afterwards they can go to his Camden Town house, where they can have an 'unceremonious crust of bread and cheese'.

SW wishes that it were possible to change the date of George III's birthday as Wednesday is now one of the days he has 'the most oppressive work' [teaching], but he thinks that his 'assistant' will deputise for him for the afternoon. He seeks Street's opinion and decision on 'this momentous stratagem' and hopes that Street's son Joseph is better.

Sarah memorandum   **3/8/1806**
GEU in box 6   Falsely and cruelly accused Yesterday for not loving a Brother
memo dated 3/8/1806
Sarah was 'falsely and cruelly accused yesterday' [2/8/1806] for not loving SW. She has continually been treated unjustly by SW, who even has taken her enemies' side. Although Sarah once felt tenderly towards SW, he alienated himself from her, first by 'turning Papist' and afterwards by engaging with women in conduct that she 'openly reprobated'. As no one had ever contradicted SW before, 'he brooked it ill'. Yet he sought Sarah's counsel and 'extrication', which she gave as best as she could.

---

[166] Ltr presumably < SW→CW Jr, 31/5/1811, which says that SW no longer has property in the funds (which were administered by the Bank of England). Ltr assigned to 1806 because of other references in SW's letters to the Bank at this time (e.g., SW→SGW, 21/4/1806; SW→Marriott, 3/11/1807) but not in 1800.

When SW left CLW 'there was much difficulty in weaning the child [CW III] he resolved to take from her'. CW III was placed under Sarah's affectionate care. SW was 'tyrannical and cruel' towards CW III, who then 'had no resource' but Sarah. She nursed him when he had measles, 'accompanied him in winter 36 miles to school' [at Wateringbury], and placed him under Dr [Richard] Roberts at St Paul's School.[167] 'All this time' SW used Sarah 'like a brute'.

Sarah 'constantly remonstrated' with SW 'for keeping a mistress' [AD] after 'his marriage with one' [CLM]. His antipathy towards Sarah was evidenced by his traducing her character to his 'libertine friends', from one of whom [Martin Madan Jr] she received an anonymous letter.

SW then had 'an amour with one of our servants'. He came to Sarah 'in agony—to place her out', which Sarah accomplished with difficulty. Jealous of CW III's 'love towards' Sarah and 'wishing to counteract' all her plans, SW made CW III discontented with St Paul's School despite its obvious advantages, removed him [from the school] in May 1806, and did not permit him to see or to write to her. Last week Sarah received 'the younger child' [JWW] and allowed him to stay.

SW→SGW   Camden Town   **12/1806**

MA DDWes/6/50   I am very glad to find that you seem not to have suffered
ltr undated; pmk Dec[168]

SW is glad that SGW has not suffered damage from her journey [to Bath] but thinks that at her age it unwise to travel far. Jack [JWW] is recovered from the measles. The 'little child' [Emma] also has had them. 'Poor Ball' [conjecturally James Ball's father], who has a 'chronical' disease, is much better. There are hopes of his reinstatement, but from SW's awareness of this type of disease he is not confident of this.

SW is 'pretty certain' that CW III is 'superior to any sordid views of pecuniary advantage from the decease of any human being'. If SW believed that CW III were 'mean or interested', SW would consider disowning him.

SW is pleased that SGW's apartments [in Bath] are agreeable. Nothing gratifies him more than 'a rural prospect'; he often has hoped that if he ever has to go to jail it will be in the country. He asks SGW to give his love to Sarah and to CW Jr and his regards to Dr [Edward] Sheppard [1731–1813], Mr Millgrove and others [in Bath].

SW called today in Woodstock Street [SGW's new London home], but found [Mrs] Fletcher out. He was seeking the Sanctus that CW Jr wrote to be performed at St Paul's [Cathedral]; the performance might take place on

---

[167] CW III arrived at St Paul's School on 13/8/1805 (Mrs F. Roberts→Sarah, 16/8/1805, MA DDWes/9/107).

[168] Ltr assigned to 1806 because SGW said to be 80 years old; also, ltr says that SW will send an 'epitome' of his Responses to the Litany to CW Jr, and such an epitome was enclosed with SW→CW Jr, 15/1/1807. Ltr <25/12/1806 as a Christmas performance is said to be forthcoming.

Christmas Day if SW can get the music in time. SW has sent his Responses to the Litany to Attwood, who is keen for this composition to be performed well and wishes that it be 'well studied' beforehand. SW desires the same treatment for CW Jr's Sanctus. SW probably will send CW Jr an 'epitome' of the Responses so that he may try them over before Dr [Henry] Harington [physician, 1727–1816, founder of the Bath Harmonic Society]. Harington may scarcely remember SW.

SGW [in a letter to SW, not preserved] said that CW Jr's scholars are 'coming on'. SW has no doubt that they are making progress, but wishes that there were more of them. The other day, when SW was out, 'poor Mrs Weale' [presumably SGW's niece Jane Weale, *see* Rebecca Gwynne will, 9/8/1799] called here [Camden Town], and CLW pressed her to stay for dinner. He returned in time to see Mrs Weale, who seemed to be 'comfortable' while with them.

At Mrs Jeffreys's [school] SW has begun to instruct Miss Wyndham. She is slow, but SW will try to 'make her sure'. She takes an hour 'fumbling out' two pages of a sonata by [John Baptist] Cramer [composer, pianist and music publisher, 1771–1858], whereas Miss Margetts, a 'wonderful' girl at Mrs Barnes's school, played the whole movement at sight twice in ten minutes. The Jeffreys' friend Miss Paxton has been dangerously ill. SW will write to her. She and Jane Jeffreys are to go to Bath soon.

SW passes as 'a great liar' in showing SGW's letter and 'swearing that it was written by a woman of 80'.

Richard J. S. Stevens 'Recollections'   18/12/1806

Camb Add 9109 v 2 p 11   Thursday Decr 18th, was the first meeting
Entry for 18/12/1806[169]

On 18/12/1806, at the first meeting this season of the Harmonists' Society [which Richard John Samuel Stevens, composer and organist, 1757–1837, had founded with others in 1794], SW was 'one of our visitors'. After dinner, and 'not in the least flushed with liquor', his 'usual practice' at this time, SW played on the pianoforte 'some of the most ingenious and astonishing combinations of harmony' that Stevens had ever heard. SW concluded his extemporary performance by making a 'simple and pleasing movement' on the subject, 'O strike the harp'. This was a 'rare instance' of SW's 'wonderful abilities', and the audience 'were all delighted'.

---

[169] According to *Argent* p xv–xvi, v. 2 of Stevens's manuscript 'Recollections' was written in the 1820s on the basis of earlier diary entries. Extracts from both volumes of this manuscript are printed in *Argent*.

CW III→SGW   Camden Town   **14/1/1807**
MA DDWF/16/5   You will (I trust) pardon my seeming Neglect
☞ 14/1/1807

SW now is CW III's 'sole preceptor' and thinks that he does 'quite as much' reading of books as when he was at St Paul's School. He and JWW are well, but Emma is teething. SW 'finds himself better than he was, for the Camden Town air agrees with him very well'. The whole family, including CLW, send love to SGW, CW Jr and Sarah.

SW→CW Jr   Camden Town   **15/1/1807**
MA DDWF/15/12; *O*   I should certainly have sent you a Line long before now
☞ 15/1/1807

SW should have written long before now but waited to include a [printed] copy of his glee [*A New Glee for Three Voices*,[170] reviewed in the 1/2/1807 *MM*], which CW Jr desired. SW also encloses an 'epitome' of his Responses to the Litany [*see* SW→SGW, 12/1806] as well as his new Dixit Dominus [III] for three voices.

The latter was recently performed [on 27/12/1806] at the Concentores Society, which consists 'solely of 12 select musical professors', each of whom has to produce a new canon and glee on the day he is chosen to be president. SW was invited there as a visitor by [James] Elliott [bass singer and composer, 1783–1856], 'a very amiable sensible man' of whose skill and taste in singing SW need not tell CW Jr. At the performance were [Samuel] Harrison [tenor, 1760–1812], [Thomas] Greatorex [organist and composer, 1758–1831], [Richard John Samuel] Stevens, [John Wall] Callcott, 'little Master Tommy' [Attwood] and seven others. SW's Dixit Dominus made 'a great splash'. 'Old [James] Horsefall' was 'bawler maximus' and was 'so transported' that SW feared he would 'be seized with some mortal spasm or other'.

SW does not know the rules of CW Jr's 'Harmonic Club' [the Bath Harmonic Society, at which CW Jr directed a performance of glees on 19/12/1806] and so does not know whether they perform pieces on Latin scriptural texts among 'festive and Cytherean lays'. If they do, CW Jr is welcome to use Dixit Dominus [III] as he likes, but SW is anxious that no copies of it should 'get abroad' until it is published, as there is 'a danger (or rather the certainty)' that it would be 'mangled and mutilated in transcription'. CW Jr will remember the 'perfect scaramouch' that 'the learned Miss Abrams' [presumably Harriet Abrams, singer and composer, c1758–1822] made of [SW's glee] 'Goosy Gander'.

In reply to CW Jr's letter [not preserved], SW states that he has no objection to his music appearing in the 'first rate' [music] shops in Bath but would like it not to appear in 'an inferior window, as if soliciting purchase'. If the person CW Jr mentioned wishes to order copies of SW's Voluntaries [op. 6], his *New Glee* or whatever he should 'vomit out' next, this wish will be speedily complied with.

---

[170] This glee, 'When Bacchus, Jove's immortal boy', was first performed on 18/12/1806 at the Society of Harmonists.

'Master Jacky Owen, Archdeacon of York' [Rev. John Owen, 1773–1824, Archdeacon of Richmond, Yorkshire], brother-in-law to the crewel manufacturer John Beardmore [Owen appears to have been brother-in-law to the wholesale draper Joseph Beardmore, c1745–1829] has fallen in love with the violin solos by [Francesco] Geminiani. Beardmore's niece [Mary Beardmore, c1778–1838] has 'recommenced' music lessons with SW, and asked SW if these solos were 'practicable' in the form they appear for the violin. SW said they were not, but added that they were to be obtained in an arrangement by Geminiani for a keyboard instrument and offered to get them for her. He does not know where they may be found, as modern music shops 'disdain such trash', and those who love 'such obsolete stuff' are 'so bigoted to their fond prejudices' that they are loath to part with their own copies. He asks for CW Jr's assistance on this matter.

SW believes that CW Jr's 'selection' of [music by Venanzio] Rauzzini [Italian composer and male soprano, bap1746–1810, who lived in Bath from 1777] was a good one, as Rauzzini is 'thoroughly versed' in every type of good music. SW is glad to hear such a good account of the health of 'Dr H' [Henry Harington] and wishes that he could say the same of Harington's 'worthy and learned contemporary Dr B' [CB].

SW cannot understand how a 'real judge of music' could dislike Haydn or Mozart, and has been attempting to account for it. Their music must be heard often before it is thoroughly understood; but 'when the ear and mind become perfectly habituated to their rapid successions of harmony, the feast is rich indeed, and the surprise is still maintained, notwithstanding familiarity'. SW is uncertain 'how far taste in music is inherent' but is sure that taste, however acquired, 'may be wonderfully improved by cultivation'.

CW Jr mentions a movement in Handel's 'original MS'. SW recently saw a 'very curious original' of [Benedetto] Marcello's *Psalms*, which were 'the more valuable from their being almost impossible to read'. SW thinks 'very moderately' of Marcello: 'his writing is chaste; his style generally solemn, and his harmonies occasionally rich, but he wants the sweetness of [Agostino] Steffani [Italian composer, 1654–1728,], the strength of Purcell, and certainly the fire of Handel'. SW understands that Boyce thought that Marcello was overrated; whoever thinks so, SW is 'quite of his mind'.

SW turns to the 'business' of his Responses to the Litany. 'Little Master Tommy' [Attwood], despite having been organist of St Paul's Cathedral for 'a year or two (at least)' [in fact since 1796], seems ignorant of the rubric which states that the Litany is to be read or sung on all Sundays, Wednesdays and Fridays throughout the year. As Christmas Day [1806] fell on Thursday the Litany could not be performed then. Attwood is now anxious to have it performed on any Sunday that SW may appoint. SW shows his indifference 'by leaving it from time to time without fixing any day'. Attwood means very well, and one 'cannot be thoroughly angry with an honest blunderer'. SW regrets that some people who went to St Paul's purposely to hear SW's music [on Christmas Day] were disappointed. All that now remains is to perform it, together with CW Jr's Sanctus, at a time that is most convenient to SW.

SW hopes that Dr [Edward] Sheppard has recovered from gout and wonders where he picked it up. SW considered that 'a man of temperance had nothing to do with gout'. Sheppard is a very sensible, learned, energetic man, with interesting originality of thought. SW encloses 'a few lines' [not preserved] for CW Jr to forward to Mr Bowen. CW Jr should give SW's 'old love' to Mr Millgrove and ask if he remembers SW pestering him about a solo of Giardini [Sonata No 4 in A major, from *Sei Sonate,* op. 1], the incipit of which he quotes.

CW Jr is 'very sarcastic (tho' very just) about a certain English-German-Musician-Divine' [possibly Latrobe], whom he describes as being 'between Bath and Bristol'. SW does not wonder that professors stare at this man 'and know not what to make of his odd way of humour'.

SW called on the organ builder [William] Gray, who has been 'closely confined' for the last month as a result of an accident in which he hurt his leg. Consequently Mr Hoare's organ [probably the organ at Killerton House, Broadclyst near Exeter, ordered by Henry Hoare, banker, 1750–1828, for his daughter Lydia Elizabeth Hoare, 1786–1856, from 1808 Lady Acland] cannot be finished, and the remuneration due to CW Jr will be deferred.

John [Baptist] Cramer has sent SW some 'charming scraps' of his for the piano [Cramer's *A Collection of Rondos, Airs with Variations, and Toccata*], amongst which is a toccata [in G, no. 7 in this collection] which CW Jr will be delighted with if he can get it at Bath. The music is 'very difficult in various passages' but is 'a nut worth the cracking'.

If 'fame and flattery' could make a man fat, Sir John Falstaff would be a 'shrimp' to SW, as far as 'musical flummery' is concerned. SW's nerves, for some months past, have been in a less agitated state than he has known for years. In consequence, he can bear 'the bustle of society' with much less 'perturbation of spirits' than before. He has 'frequently mingled in those sort of public parties wherein alone a man is likely to be talked of to any purpose'.

SW attended [on 18/12/1806] the first meeting of the Harmonists' Society, to which he presented the glee mentioned above. [Richard John Samuel] Stevens proposed to the president [probably Augustus Frederick, Duke of Sussex, 1773–1843, 6th son of George III] that SW should perform on the piano. He did, and played much to his own satisfaction.

Last Sunday [11/1/1807], SW and [William] Carnaby [composer and organist, 1772–1839] went to visit Parson [Edward] Barry [1759–1822, curate of St Marylebone and grand chaplain to the Freemasons] at Dulwich. There were nine guests apart from themselves. Carnaby is a 'clever musician' and gave them some of his vocal compositions which were 'highly finished and extremely delightful'. One of them was 'Man can thy lot no brighter soul allow', which Carnaby says that CW Jr 'much approved', and he 'boasts everywhere' of CW Jr's good word. Carnaby 'carries himself pretty high among ordinary professors' and is gratified by the praise of only a few of them.

SW has promised to go next Sunday [18/1/1807] to Westminster Abbey, after which he is to dine with Robert Cooke [composer and organist, 1768–1814, from 1802 organist of Westminster Abbey] whose father, Dr [Benjamin] Cooke [organist and composer, 1734–1793], CW Jr knew. Robert Cooke is 'very knowing in music, and a pleasant man when you get at him, tho' he is rather shy and reserved at first'. Callcott has arranged for John [Baptist] Cramer to come too, so SW must mind his 'P's and 'Q's in such 'worshipful society'. The touch of the organ is 'remarkably good'; indeed it is rather too light for SW, in complete contrast to that at St Paul's, where CW Jr will remember that 'the keys are all as stubborn as Fox's martyrs, and bear as much buffeting'.

SW will convey news of 'domestic occurrences' in a letter that he will write to SGW [SW→SGW, 15/1/1807] after finishing this letter.

[John Wall] Callcott, 'who is indefatigable in searching out every information he can obtain concerning music', and who has erroneously conceived a high opinion of SW's Greek scholarship, has asked SW to look at Aristoxenus in order to discover if [Jean-Philippe] Rameau [1683–1764, musical theorist and composer] is not mistaken about how 'the ancients' conceived the fundamental bass of a particular four-note passage. SW doubts that he will be able to 'poke out any satisfactory intelligence' from Aristoxenus but has promised Callcott any help he can render. Callcott is 'so good a creature that no one but a morose and savage mind could bear to refuse him any request it could reasonably grant'.

SW went yesterday [14/1/1807] to Crotch's lecture [at the Royal Institution] on the merits of Pleyel, Kozeluch and Mozart [as composers]. SW feels that Crotch underrated Mozart and overrated Pleyel but rendered 'exact justice, and impartial praise' to Kozeluch. SW cannot understand how Crotch manages to play from score 'all the parts of a symphony of Mozart so that you do not miss the absence of any one instrument, whether stringed or wind'.

SW→SGW   Camden Town   **15/1/1807**
BL Add 35012 f 15   I should have written long before
⊟ 15/1/1807

SW should have written long before but deferred writing until he had finished transcribing the music he promised for CW Jr [*see* SW→CW Jr, 15/1/1807]. Mr Swan says that Hannah Williams is in 'a very indifferent situation' at present. Rather than supporting an increase in her salary, Swan proposes that four or five of her friends should contribute 1/- a week each to ease her situation. SW would be willing to pay his share, hard pressed though he is. He is also concerned at the financial situation of Mrs Coslett and Mrs [Jane] Weale, who called a few days ago. He thinks it would be no trouble for [SGW's] 'cousin [Thynne] Gwynne' to consider such cases: it would be a small amount for him, but a substantial benefit for them.

SW is much more recovered in health than he expected to be, for which he is thankful, as he is very busy. He wished his 'temporal circumstances' were in as good a state, but the situation of public affairs has increased taxes and prices, and all except the richest are feeling the effects. Miss [Mary] Beardmore and her younger sister [Frances Beardmore, c1789–1868] take lessons [from SW] once a week at Canonbury [i.e., at 5 Canonbury Place, Islington, where they lived]. Mrs Beardmore [their mother] has dropsy, which probably will confine her to her chamber for life.

SW hopes only to be able to provide 'bread and cheese' for his children. All relish and enjoyment has gone from his life following the loss of 'the dearest and most accomplished of characters' [AD]. He mentions Mrs [Arabella] Mitz, and asks to be remembered to Sarah if she is with SGW; he is sorry to hear that Mr Cowie has 'totally failed' and that Mr Maud's laboratory and premises were burnt down some time ago. Everyone sends their best wishes. Johnny [JWW] will write. SW asks when SGW intends to come to London, and hopes she is well. The frost has brought on SW's lumbago.

SW→CW Jr   21/3/1807

MA 9787; *O*   I am perfectly convinced that you would not grudge the Postage
☞ 21/3/1807

CW Jr 'knows too well' the 'miseries' and 'irreparable losses' that SW has suffered and therefore will understand that SW does not desire 'length of days'. While SW remains alive he must be 'employed wholly'; this is his 'only resource against insanity'. Although he often is 'almost faint with fatigue' from having to 'bustle about with a crazy carcase, as if nothing was the matter', he prefers these inconveniences to the 'horrors' of reflecting on the sacrifice of 'peace, liberty, honour and independence' to 'one of the most unworthy of mortals' [CLW].

SW is presently engaged with Mr [Rev. Robert] Nares [1753–1829, from 1793 editor of *The British Critic*, from 1795 assistant librarian at the British Museum, from 1801 archdeacon of Stafford] in a 'literary business' that cannot be disclosed for 'a few weeks' [SW's review of John Wall Callcott's *A Musical Grammar*, which appeared anonymously in the April and June 1806 numbers of *The British Critic*[171]]. CW Jr will remember Nares's father Dr [James] Nares [composer, 1715–1783] as a 'notable puppy' and a 'whoremaster'; now, however, he is highly regarded.

A performance of SW's Responses to the Litany is fixed for Easter Sunday [29/3/1807] at St Paul's [Cathedral]. SW will not be surprised if the organ blower chooses 'to observe the Sabbath' at the most interesting point in the music. SW is so hardened by vexations that his soul is 'become brawn': 'you may pull and tear at it with all your might, but it jerks back again to its old place, like a piece of India rubber'. SW includes a chant ['Venite, exultemus'] that he has 'cobbled up for the occasion'.

Attwood's brother [Francis Attwood, viola player, 1775–1807], who had just arrived from Ireland to see him, has died.

About a fortnight ago SW met 'our merry St Andrew' Latrobe at Beardmore's. 'Master Jacky [Rev. John] Owen' was with them. SW comments sardonically on the propensity of 'our sacerdotal Orpheus' [Latrobe] to speak German. Some music from Latrobe's 'collection' [his *Selection of Sacred Music from the Works of Some of the Most Eminent Composers of Germany and Italy*, the first volume

---

[171] AFCK identifies SW as the author of this review in *The Quarterly Musical Register* no. 1 (January 1812) p 5.

of which was published in 1806] was performed in the evening. Owen declared that the music was 'desperate dull', for Latrobe had selected 'all the most lachrymose, whining, caterwauling melodies he could stumble upon'. SW notes that there are plenty of such melodies by German and Italian composers when they set words relating to penitence or the Crucifixion.

SW agrees with [William] Boyce that 'chromatic subjects produce the worst fugues' and thinks that they also produce the worst vocal melodies. The best Italian melodies consist of diatonic intervals. SW does not concur with 'wire-drawing the chromatic scale, till your hair stands on end and then calling it melody', unless 'deep sorrow or acute pain are to be expressed'. He cites an example, 'O taste and see' from Handel's *Messiah* to show how 'the deepest sorrow may be completely expressed without one chromatic semitone'. He considers this composition to be 'the most finished specimen of the simple sublime in melody that ever was produced'.

[Rev.] Dr [Lucius] Coghlan [c1750–1833, later Chaplain of the Freemasons' Grand Lodge] is in London and wants SW's opinion of a piano which is to be sold. SW recommends the *Ariettes* by [Girolamo] Crescentini [Italian singer and composer, 1762–1846] for CW Jr's singing pupils.

SW→Bridgetower   **15/6/1807**
Upper Rm L-148; *O*   I am extremely sorry that I was under a Necessity
▣ Mon 15 June & pmk 16/6/180?→{1801,1807}[172]

SW apologises for having had to go out last Saturday evening [13/6/1807] but looks forward to seeing Bridgetower next Saturday [20/6/1807] and hopes that Bridgetower 'will come early that we may have a long gossip'. SW has been 'so occupied with correcting the copyist's blunders' in an oratorio [*The Nativity*] by [François-Hippolyte] Barthélemon [part 1 of this oratorio was performed in Barthélemon's benefit concert at the Hanover Square Rooms on 19/6/1807, at which SW played the organ] that SW has been unable 'to do justice' to Bridgetower's manuscript. SW will examine it as soon as he has a 'leisure moment'.

CW Jr→SW   **3/8/1807**
MA DDWF/20/5   I am truly shock'd to think you should use our good Sister
▣ 3/8/1807

CW Jr is 'truly shocked' that SW should use Sarah in 'such an ungentlemanly and low vulgar way' and is sorry that SW should lay blame upon her. CW Jr did not want to hear Sarah 'abused' and therefore chose not to come 'when she was hated'. CW Jr loves Sarah and respects her highly. He hopes that God will lead SW 'to see the evil of hatred and malice'.

---

[172] The last digit of the postmark is not clear. Ltr assigned to 1807 because of the performance of *The Nativity* on 19/6/1807 at Barthélemon's benefit concert in which SW took part.

Sarah→SW   2/9/1807
GEU Wesley Coll. ltr 82   Your First prejudice against me was taken
☒ 2/9/1807[173]

SW's first prejudice against Sarah arose from her disliking the Roman Catholics. Then SW took CLM 'as a mistress' and was enraged by Sarah's opposition to his system, which equated constancy with marriage. Sarah's home was 'rendered comfortless' by SW's open promulgation of his principles at CW's death and by SW's 'unworthy aspersions' upon CW after he died. In 1789 SW 'took up the subject of polygamy', which caused further dispute.

On 5/4/1793 SW married CLM and the whole family 'united in kindness' towards her. The family soon learned that SW was unhappy owing to CLW's 'ill-founded jealousy' of a talented, virtuous and esteemed woman [presumably AD]. To prevent SW and CLW separating—on which both seemed fixed—Sarah accompanied CLW to Bristol in 1795, as 'her health required care'. On CLW's return, SW showed CLW a part of a letter from Sarah to SW, in which Sarah said that CLW's temper was such that 'she could now have no friend but on principle' [*see* Sarah→SW, 2/2/1796]. This caused CLW to become exasperated with Sarah, but Sarah explained what she had meant, which seemed to satisfy CLW. When CLW later became ill, Sarah went to Ridge to be with her.

Sarah subsequently found that CLW had reason to be suspicious of SW. Sarah then became 'uniformly attached' to CLW's cause, which led to 'another great trial'. The person to whom SW was 'attached' was Sarah's 'particular friend' [AD]. In a 'moment of extreme anguish', SW confided in Sarah, who was ready to assist him and never betrayed his secret. CLW, however, 'furnished with proofs' of SW's conduct, betrayed the secret, an action that Sarah has 'always reprobated'. Sarah was in anguish whether to alert her friend [AD] to 'her danger' but could not do this without betraying SW.

Some time later, SW heard that Sarah had deprived her friend [AD] of a scholar. SW so abused Sarah that she resolved never to enter SGW's house while SW was there unless SW apologised. Dr [George] Gregory received Sarah at this time. One of SW's friends [Martin Madan Jr] sent Sarah an anonymous letter, accusing her of hypocrisy. In a place where her friend [AD] was not known, Sarah heard that some children at AD's school had discovered SW's 'connection' with AD. Sarah then told both SW and AD that their conduct was known and could lead to 'ill consequences'.

AD's illness 'did not contribute' to SW's 'happiness at home'. CLW 'tormented' SW with reproaches, 'blasted' his character and injured his fortune. SW was 'so much in debt' that he 'determined to part' from CLW. SW asked Sarah to 'interfere', which she declined to do; however, she went to Highgate to see if CLW concurred in the separation. CLW 'was fiercely determined to part' and said that 'all the world would know' that SW left her 'for a mistress'. Mrs Foote also called upon CLW and found her 'unalterable'.

The Highgate house was sold. CLW requested Sarah to bring a few things to her from the house and subsequently reproached Sarah for not saving more.

---

[173] At the head of ltr Sarah wrote 'A Letter to be deliver'd after my Death'.

CLW also 'commissioned' Sarah to find lodgings for her. Sarah 'wandered over Westminster' and found lodgings, but 'they were gone' before CLW decided to take them. Sarah had no role in finding CLW's apartments in Pimlico. She visited CLW there but, after CLW heard 'gossip from Highgate' [presumably gossip originating from SW] that perhaps Sarah was not CLW's friend, their 'intercourse' ceased.

SW's boy [CW III] was 'committed' to Sarah's charge. She nursed him through measles, 'attended' him to school at Maidstone in winter 1804 and visited him in summer. At this time SW's state of mind was 'little short of distraction'; his nights 'sleepless and raving'. SW surely will acknowledge in the future that Sarah treated him 'with kindness and compassion'. Then SW 'unfortunately connected' himself with 'a servant girl' under SGW's roof. SW supposed that the girl was 'with child', sent for Sarah, and Sarah sought 'habitation for the girl and future provision for her child'. Fortunately, no child 'was ever likely' to have been born. Sarah was 'resolute' in banishing this girl from the house, although SGW wanted the girl 'detained' to 'screen' SW from punishment.

In 1805 SW wished Sarah to place CW III at St Paul's [School]. Sarah 'gained him admission' and Dr [Richard] Roberts 'adopted' him 'as a child of his own'. However, SW and CLW 'became dissatisfied' and wished to take CW III back. In 1806 they 'took him away' from the school 'without apprising Dr Roberts', conduct which distressed Sarah. CW III now was 'never permitted' to come near Sarah, who had 'so affectionately fostered' him; by this action SW 'cruelly wounded' Sarah's heart. CLW falsely blamed Sarah for causing the marital separation, whereas the cause on CLW's side was 'well-founded jealousy' and on SW's side was CLW's extravagance. SW and CLW invited CW Jr to visit but he declined because SW had abused Sarah in CW Jr's presence. Sarah then withdrew funds from the bank to pay expenses at Dr Roberts's school.

SW lent SGW £100 'to defray expenses' in which his schemes had involved her, at which time Sarah and CW Jr gave their 'hands' so SW would suffer no loss. Without provocation other than 'Charles' [CW Jr] not visiting SW, SW sent Sarah a disgraceful 'scurrilous letter', insulting her 'without cause'. SW's children, from whom he has 'withheld all examples of good', may remind SW and CLW of 'the unmerited ill conduct and baseness exercised' towards Sarah, who once loved SW. This behaviour has embittered Sarah, who wished to direct SW to the 'path of peace'. SW has destroyed his children's 'root of gratitude'. She hopes that he will live to be 'an illustrious penitent'.

When CLW, who Sarah understands approved SW's sending the letter to Sarah, entered the apartment in which Sarah lives, she looked at Sarah without 'common civilities'. Sarah treated CLW 'as a stranger' and left the room, taking no notice of SW's 'infant child' [Emma].

SW→William Marriott Jr   Camden Town   **3/11/1807**
MA DDWF/15/13; *O*   I was rather surprized To=Day on applying at the Bank
📧 3/11/1807

SW applied at the Bank [of England] today for a half-yearly payment of interest on £1420 and was surprised when the clerk contradicted him. SW has not altered his stock since William Marriott Jr [1777–1834, at this time a stockbroker] 'last sold out' for him. SW's 'first money' [dividend] was £50; the second was £30. He accepted £25/7/8 from the bank today, knowing that it would be foolish then to dispute the amount that the clerk assured him was correct, but is 'far from satisfied'. SW desires Marriott's explanation of 'how this mistake could happen'.

SW→SGW   **6/11/1807**
BL Add 35012 f 13   My Absence from Woodstock Street has not been
📧 Fri 6 Nov & SGW at Woodstock St→{1807,1812}[174]

SW's absence from Woodstock Street [SGW's home] has not been occasioned by neglect or want of concern for SGW, but by the desire to avoid 'any personal altercation' [presumably with CW Jr or Sarah]. SW feels that any attempt to 'produce a union between persons of thoroughly opposite sentiments' would be a waste of time. The 'virtues and beneficence' of his 'dearest departed friend' [AD] are daily in his thoughts, and the 'cruel contempt and injustice' which she underwent excites his imagination.

SW considers CW Jr to be 'under the entire influence' of a person [presumably Sarah] whose mind is of a completely different cast to SW's, and he therefore bears CW Jr no ill will on account of their personal estrangement. SW regards CW Jr as 'a very good-hearted man' who is 'grossly misled', and wishes him well.

SW→Street   Camden Town   **9/11/1807**
BL Add 56228 ltr 10; *O*   My friend Madan used to maintain in Argument
📧 Monday & pmk 9 Nov & 📧→ⓘ

SW's friend Madan [presumably Martin Madan Jr] used to maintain that there was a 'physical perverseness' in things that upset the best laid plans. SW disagrees with this doctrine, but believes that 'we are apt to attribute the cause of our want of patience' to a deficiency in the world. He comments on the opinions of John Locke and Alexander Pope on this subject and wonders what has led him to indulge in metaphysical speculation. He supposes that it was the large size of his sheet of paper, which he was too lazy to divide (he is writing in bed),

---

[174] Assigned to 1807 because CW Jr estranged from SW in 1807 (*see* Sarah→SW, 2/9/1807, which says that CW Jr's not visiting SW provoked him) but not in 1812 (in SW→SGW, 12/11/1812, SW asks SGW to thank CW Jr and Sarah for their efforts on SW's behalf).

and which 'deserved something frightful and tedious to make it look grander'. On reconsideration, however, he thinks that his subject originated in the 'odd and vexatious see-saw engagements' that he and Street have been making.

SW has been unwell, to the extent of being 'precluded from officiating' at Covent Garden Church yesterday [presumably in place of the regular organist, John Wall Callcott, who was experiencing mental difficulties at this time] and was forced to cancel an engagement at Brompton, where he was to have passed the day with some friends who had appointed that day and place to meet him. SW is not sure that he will be well enough to meet Street tomorrow. If he is, he will be in Mark Lane [Street's home] as near to 4 pm as possible. If he has not arrived by 4.15 pm it should be assumed that he is incapable of attending.

He seeks the addresses of the Rev. Mr [George] Lock [c1780–1864] 'who has the living of Lee' [Kent], Lady [Gertrude Brand, Baroness] Dacre [1750–1819, whose country seat was at Lee], Sir Francis Baring [merchant and banker, 1740–1810], and Thompson Bonar [who in 1801 had been elected a governor of the Foundling Hospital]. These addresses are doubtless in [*Boyle's*] *Court Guide*, which SW does not possess but will buy next year.

SW was 'highly pleased' with the 'lines' *A Reckoning with Time* by [George] Colman [the younger, 1762–1836], which he read yesterday in [the 8/11/1807 number of] *Bell's Weekly Messenger*. He has not for a long time seen a collection of verses 'more uniformly witty and pointed'. He has been told that they appeared in the *Morning Post* of the previous Friday or Saturday [in fact, they did not] which he cannot believe, as he has not seen anything in that newspaper 'either rational or interesting' for the last six months.

SW→CB   Camden Town   **22/3/1808**
Osborn MSS 3, Box 16, folder 1192; *O*   Although your many and important
▣ 22/3/1808

Although SW and CB have not seen each other for a long time, SW's esteem for CB has not diminished. WL (brother of the late Mrs Sheridan) [Elizabeth Ann Linley, soprano, 1754–1792, first wife of Richard Brinsley Sheridan, playwright and politician, 1751–1816] desires to meet CB. SW asks if CB can spare a few moments some morning to see SW and WL.

CB→SW   **23/3/1808?**
Osborn MSS 3, Box 5, folder 319   Your remembrance after (I do believe)
ltr undated, a reply to SW→CB, 22/3/1808, thus assigned to 23/3/1808

CB is gratified that his 'old friend' SW has renewed contact after a long time when they 'unwillingly' lost sight of each other. CB did not know that 'the first dear Mrs [Elizabeth Ann Linley] Sheridan' had a living brother [WL]. CB listened to her singing 'with ecstatic rapture' and regarded her 'as an angel in voice, countenance and form'. WL does CB an honour by wishing to see him.

CB is now a 'worn out mortal whose eyes, ears and memory are so decayed that he is obliged to relinquish the great world'. He does not leave his apartments after sunset. He has 'weathered this severe winter' but 'the March lion' brought back his 'cough and complaints', and his medical advisers have told him to stay in bed until the weather improves. CB will be very happy to have SW and WL visit him after then.

SW→SGW   **5/4/1808**
WCL LDWMM 1997/6600   [not available]
◨ 5/4/1808

Because of the bad weather, Mrs Fletcher should send a boy to Paddington to collect SW's thick shoes if they have not already been collected. SW's bowels are much better. He thinks that this is due to SGW's peppermint drops.

SW→CB   **12/4/1808**
Osborn MSS 3, Box 16, folder 1192; *O*   Your kind Letter has reached me
◨ Tue 12 Apr={1803,1808,1814}[175]

CB's letter [not preserved] reached SW '5 minutes ago'. SW regrets that he cannot visit CB today but will immediately inform WL that CB is willing to see him. SW sent CB's 'former letter' [CB→SW, 23/3/1808] to WL, who read the part concerning [his late sister] 'Mrs Sheridan' to his mother [Mary Linley, *d*1820]. SW asks CB to name a time in the next week when it will be convenient for him to see SW and WL. SW trusts that CB's health will improve.

SW has 'long wished' for the opportunity to 'beg' CB's opinion and advice regarding a new edition of JSB's 'Preludes & Fugues' [the '48'], which have become 'exceedingly scarce in England' and are now 'almost unattainable'. For 'some months past' SW has 'paid much attention' to these works and considers them 'as the highest stretch of harmonic intellect and the noblest combination of musical sounds that ever immortalised genius'. SW has 'frequently played them among professors', of whom many had never heard them before and others 'had imbibed' a 'prejudice' that they were 'dry, harsh and unmelodious'. Therefore 'it was really a triumphant moment' for SW 'to witness their agreeable surprise'. Based upon this general satisfaction, SW thinks that publishing a new edition of these works by subscription might prove 'beneficial to the musical world as well as profitable to the editor' [SW]. SW has been told that the 'Zürich copy' [the edition of the '48' published by Nägeli in Zürich in 1801] is 'the best', but even this has 'several little omissions'. As SW was determined to have a true copy of this work he has not 'grudged the labour of transcribing the whole 48 preludes and their corresponding fugues' [*see* SW→Graeff, 21/5/1806?] and believes that he now has 'the most correct copy' of these works in England.

SW asks CB to communicate frankly his thoughts on this subject. SW recalls that CB said, some years ago, that 'subscriptions were troublesome things'. Yet, 'in the present instance', SW considers subscription to be the best mode of

---

[175] Ltr >CB→SW, 23/3/1808 and <12/4/1814, the day of CB's death, as CB did not exchange letters in his last days.

avoiding 'risk and dangerous expense'. He 'certainly would not think of publishing until the charges for printing were wholly defrayed'.

CB→SW   **13/4/1808?**

Berg f. 32 of coll. of 4 AL & 27 ALS, CB→CB Jr   The weather for some days
ltr undated but >SW→CB, 12/4/1808 & <SW→CB, 14/4/1808

Recent balmy weather has helped CB much. He appreciates SW's advice [in SW→CB, 12/4/1808] 'not to venture out too soon as the evenings are yet very sharp and wintry' and indeed has resolved 'never again to be in the open air after sunset'. CB offers SW and 'Mr L' [WL] any day for an appointment in the next week, either between 12 noon and 3 pm or between 5 pm and 8 pm, and recommends Tuesday [19/4/1808]. If SW 'individually' [i.e., without WL] wishes to 'compare notes' with CB about JSB, SW should propose a convenient day and hour.

SW→CB   **14/4/1808**

Osborn MSS 3, Box 16, folder 1192; *O*   I have sent your Letter to Linley
📧 Thurs 14 Apr & reference to WL→ⅰ [176]

SW has sent CB's letter [CB→SW, 13/4/1808] to WL. SW thanks CB for [offering to share] his thoughts concerning JSB. SW knows of no one who can give him better advice [regarding a new edition of the '48', *see* SW→CB, 12/4/1808].

Latrobe→Joseph Foster Barham   **18/4/1808**

Bodl Ms Clar. dep. c.378   I should before now have written to you
📧 18/4/1808

Tomorrow [19/4/1808], Latrobe will introduce SW to Mr Greville [possibly George Greville, 1773–1816] to play Greville's new organ. Latrobe wishes that Joseph Foster Barham [1759–1832, at this time MP for Stockbridge] could be there. For Latrobe, SW is 'the man': his organ-playing combines 'all the grandeur of old harmonies with the sprightliness and fancy of a most vivid and luxuriant musical imagination'. SW is 'unquestionably the most perfect extempore performer in this country' and 'as Salomon says, anywhere abroad'. On Easter Sunday [17/4/1808] Latrobe went to St Paul's [Cathedral] to hear SW's Responses to the Litany, which are 'very good and have much singularity about them showing his genius'. Latrobe visited the organ loft where he looked over the score of this composition.

---

[176] Ltr >CB→SW, 23/3/1808, in which CB says he had no prior knowledge of WL. CB no longer alive on 14/4/1814, when 14 April next occurred on a Thursday.

SW→CB[177]   **5/1808?**

MA DDWF/15/8A; O[178]   …However, having proceeded through half a Dozen
this fragment undated[179]

SW describes his performance of JSB's C major fugue from part 1 of the '48'
on a chapel organ [perhaps at the Surrey Chapel on 15/3/1808].[180] After initial
insecurity SW's fear subsided and, 'for two hours at least', he 'continued an
inquisitorial persecution' of his bellows blower. Salomon was there with 'two
beautiful women', whose 'deep attention' inspired SW. Salomon 'appeared to be
excessively pleased'. Although he had heard JSB's music played 'by some of the
best German organists' in Berlin and elsewhere, he told SW that they never
produced 'so smooth an effect' as SW had. This gratified SW, particularly as the
chapel organ has 'a very deep and a very obstinate touch'.

Salomon suggested that if SW were to arrange 'a morning party in some large
room capable of containing a large organ' to play fugues from the '48'
interspersed with SW's voluntaries, and made the tickets 7/- each, then SW
would make a profit. The Abbé [Georg Joseph] Vogler [1749–1814, German
musical theorist and organist] arranged a similar event at St Paul's Cathedral 'by
the private circulation of tickets' and cleared at least £200. Although SW has
previously experienced in Salomon 'more zeal in planning, than steadiness in the
execution of' his schemes, SW nonetheless thought this suggestion worth
consideration, and has paid it serious attention because of what CB has written
[letter not preserved] concerning 'performing the fugues in public'.

SW asks whether CB considers that there is sufficient time to prepare a lecture
course [on JSB's music] 'during the present advanced state of the season'. If SW
lives to 'another winter' he might be able to form 'at least an outline' of a
suitable course [of lectures].

CB→SW   **5/1808?**

Berg CB holograph draft   But this morning's business more complicated
ltr undated; a reply to the preceding letter (SW→CB, May 1808?)

If SW wants 'an immediate publication' [presumably of JSB's '48'] then his
'expedients for saving the expense of newspaper advertisements' seem prudent
to CB. In a 'long shop bill' [a large printed sheet displayed at music shops] SW
'may dilate on the excellence of the work at any length' he pleases. However,
CB recommends that SW not risk 'the expense of printing' [the '48'] until he

---

[177] CB identified as the recipient because ltr bears a symbol used by his daughter
Frances Burney d'Arblay; also, ltr is answered by CB→SW, 5/1808?

[178] Only the second sheet of ltr is extant.

[179] Ltr after SW and CB were reunited (presumably on 19/4/1808, *see* CB→SW,
13/4/1808) and before SW's morning concert at the Hanover Square Rooms on
11/6/1808.

[180] SW's performance at the Surrey Chapel on 15/3/1808, but not what he
played, is recorded in Richard John Samuel Stevens's diary (*Argent* p 156).

has 'played and lectured the work into favour', after which CB has 'little doubt' that 'all studious professors and dilettanti male and female' will make this music 'their future study', much as the duets of [Agostino] Steffani and the 'solfeggi' of [Leonardo] Leo [Italian composer, 1694–1744] 'were the morning studies of all the great Italian singers' during the early 18th century. CB rejoices that he and Salomon agree about SW's extemporary organ playing. There has been no communication between CB and Salomon about this, as CB has been 'ill in bed'.

Although SW fears 'attempting to comment' on and to explain 'the learning and beauties' of JSB's 'matchless work' [the '48'] 'without having a regular course of lectures to deliver', CB is sure that SW, if he 'were not subject to be nervous in public', has 'language, eloquence and science' at his 'finger ends ready for every bar, passage and period' [of the '48']. Given SW's fears, he should defer 'lecturing till next year but never cease thinking of it'. CB and his daughter [Sarah Harriet Burney, author, 1772–1844, who lived with and assisted CB at this time] 'see infinite credit and advantages that must necessarily flow' from SW's designs, by which SW will ensure himself to be 'not only a great musician' but also 'a scholar and a man of letters'.

CB and Sarah Harriet Burney have no doubt that SW 'will be called for [to lecture] at the Royal Institution' after Crotch [who lectured there on music in 1805, 1806 and 1807] and [John Wall] Callcott [who lectured there on music in January and February 1808] 'have expended all their ammunition'. CB thinks that 'great performing ladies' will attend SW's 'manual (and next year oral) exertions', and that their 'curiosity, respect and patronage' will make 'the whole audience more attentive'. SW should 'catch the country organists' in the manner that CB and Salomon suggested. SW's 'congress' should be 'assembled of a morning', CB recommends at the Hanover Square Rooms where 'there is always an excellent organ ready'. SW should 'secure the use' of the Rooms before he advertises. CB prays 'zealously' that God bless SW and 'speed the plough'.

SW→Editor, *MM*   Camden Town   **16/5/1808**
MM, 1/7/1808, p 503   The correspondent who subscribes himself Symphorus
MM

SW replies to the correspondent signing himself 'Symphorus', who in the May 1808 *MM*, pp 300–1, replied to an inquiry from CW III in the April 1808 *MM*, p 222, concerning the interpretation of a passage in Ovid's *Metamorphoses*.

SW→CB   27 Arlington St, Camden Town   **23/6/1808**
Osborn MSS 3, Box 16, folder 1192; *O*   I cannot advance a Step without your
⬚ 23 June[181]

SW 'cannot advance a step' without CB's advice and therefore continues to pester him. Yesterday [22/6/1808], the organist 'Mr Griffin junior' [George

---

[181] Assigned to 1808 because ltr refers to 'Nil desperandum' also mentioned in SW→CB, 14/4/1808 and to 'My Lady' also mentioned in SW→CB, 28/6/1808.

Eugene Griffin, organist and composer, 1781–1863] told SW that 'Lady Somebody or other' [in fact Lady Chambers, widow of Sir William Chambers, architect, 1726–1796, *see* SW→CB, 28/6/1808] had sent to Griffin to borrow his copy of JSB's fugues [the '48'] after searching in vain for them in 'every music shop in town'. Griffin told her that he had these fugues but 'they were so scarce' and precious that he could not part with them. This proves CB's prophecy that JSB's music 'might be played into fashion' [*see* CB→SW, 5/1808?]. SW has 'only risked one modest experiment' towards this end [his 11/6/1808 performance of JSB's music at the Hanover Square Rooms], but it 'electrified the town' in just the way that CB and SW desired. SW now wants CB to give him 'an order how to proceed'. Should SW 'immediately issue proposals about lecturing'? Or should he issue proposals 'about publishing' JSB's music 'with annotations and an explication'? Or is the season so far advanced that SW should wait until next season?

SW→CB[182]   28/6/1808
Upper Rm L-151; *O*   As your Words & Sebastian's Notes are to me equally
📧 Tue 28 June={1803,1808}[183]

SW requests the letter that CB promised to send him concerning 'my layady'. The lady that SW previously mentioned [in SW→CB, 23/6/1808] was Lady Chambers, wife [in fact, widow] of Sir William Chambers. SW undertakes to follow CB's advice fully. Yesterday [27/6/1808] SW became a Master Mason at Somerset House Lodge and took a solemn oath of sincerity.

SW→CB   Camden Town   7/7/1808
Osborn MSS 3, Box 16, folder 1192; *O*   I am just returned from the Cambridge
📧 7/7/1808

SW has just returned from the Cambridge commencement, to which he was invited by Professor [Charles] Hague [1769–1821] and [William] Carnaby. Carnaby wanted SW present when he [Carnaby] took his doctor's degree. Carnaby produced 'a very pretty and correct anthem' for the occasion, which was well performed. The principal singers were Mr [Thomas] Vaughan [1782–1843], Mrs [Elizabeth] Vaughan and Mr [Robert] Leete. On another morning [1/7/1808] SW conducted choruses from [Handel's] *Messiah* and [Haydn's] *The Creation*, to general satisfaction.

SW worked hard playing the organ in Cambridge. He enjoyed Cambridge immensely—he had not been there for 20 years—and regretted leaving. He made a point of playing JSB's music in Cambridge, even on the pianoforte at

---

[182] CB identified as the recipient because ltr bears a symbol used by his daughter Frances Burney d'Arblay.

[183] Assigned to 1808 because of ref. to 'my layady' which also is mentioned in SW→CB, 7/7/1808.

'glee parties', to considerable effect. Some musically talented listeners who tried playing a few bars of JSB's fugues or preludes commented that they previously thought Handel's were the best and hardest [to play] fugues in the world; now they realised they were 'mistaken in both suppositions'. This experience confirms CB's prophecy [*see* CB→SW, 5/1808?] that 'avidity for possessing' the '48' would be 'infallibly increased' by 'playing them into fashion'.

An artist friend of SW [not identified] has almost completed a painting of JSB from a small drawing lent to SW by AFCK. SW suggests that a translated extract [from the Leipzig 1802 publication] of the Life of JSB [by Johann Nicholas Forkel, German musicologist, 1749–1818] would make a good preface [to the planned edition of the '48']. A portrait [of JSB] could be prefixed to its title-page. SW seeks, and pledges to follow, CB's advice on this matter.

On his return to London on 6/7/1808, SW found CB's letter [not preserved] on 'my layady' [*see* SW→CB, 28/6/1808]. SW looks forward to telling CB all about the Cambridge journey, and plans to visit him at Chelsea [College] within a few days.

SW→Mary Beardmore[184]   Camden Town   **7/7/1808**
LU A.L. 293/1; *O*   The Reason of my long Silence & Absence
▣ Thurs 7 July; pmk 1808

SW apologises for his long silence. He has been at the Cambridge commencement to assist a friend [William Carnaby] to take his Doctor of Music degree, and stayed longer in Cambridge than originally planned. SW hopes to see Miss Beardmore [presumably Mary Beardmore, his pupil] next Saturday [9/7/1808] and will procure new music for her. He recalls recommending a 'beautiful song' by [John Christian] Bach from [Bach's additions to the 1770 London performance of Gluck's opera] *Orfeo* [published by Robert Bremner in *The favourite Songs in the Opera Orfeo* (London, 1770)].[185] This music is scarce, but SW will try to obtain it.

---

[184] Ltr addressed to 'Miss Beardmore'. The addressee presumably was Mary Beardmore, the elder of the two Beardmore sisters who were pupils of SW, as it was customary to address the oldest daughter without using her Christian name (e.g., as Miss Beardmore) and to address a subsequent daughter by using both a Christian name and and a surname (e.g., as Miss Frances Beardmore).

[185] SW later arranged, for organ, one of J. C. Bach's additional songs for *Orfeo*.

SW→BJ?[186]   Camden Town   **13/8/1808?**
RCM Ms 2130 ltr 11; *O*   I do not profess myself to be so great a Schemer
⊡ 13 August; 🖎→{1806–1809}[187]

SW does not profess to be 'so great a schemer as our late friend Dr [Samuel] Arnold', who 'speculated himself into mischief too often' [Arnold is believed to have lost £10,000 from an investment in Marylebone Gardens]. Nevertheless, SW seeks the recipient's written opinion of SW's plan to form a 'junto' of people 'who sincerely and conscientiously admit and adhere to the superior excellence of the great musical high priest' [JSB]. JSB's music manifestly produces the type of 'sensation' that causes 'musical pretenders' to divide into parties; for instance, 'those who know and like nobody but Handel'.

The proposed society will promote the cause of 'truth and perfection' [JSB] zealously. It should 'stigmatise such hypocrites as affect to be enchanted' with JSB one day and 'endeavour to depreciate and vilify him' the next. SW regards the state of music in England as 'very similar' to 'the state of the Roman [Catholic] Church when the flagrant abuses and enormities had arisen to such a height as to extort a Reformation'. The 'resolution and perseverance of a single friar', Martin Luther, quickly shook 'the whole fabric of ignorance and superstition' because he had 'truth for his firm foundation'. The proposed society 'in defence of the truth' [of JSB's music] should effect a comparable reformation in the 'republic of music'.

SW→George Smith   Camden Town   **14/8/1808**
BL Add 31764 f 24; *O*   On Thursday last I was informed by your excellent
⊡ 14/8/1808

Smith's 'excellent and very extraordinary' daughter informed SW last Thursday [11/8/1808] that George Smith had decided against organ lessons for

---

[186] Ltr addressed to 'My dear Sir'; the recipient's name is not preserved. The only known evidence that BJ was the addressee is EW's publication of ltr in her 1875 *Letters of Samuel Wesley to Mr Jacobs, Organist of Surrey Chapel, Relating to the Introduction into this Country of the Works of John Sebastian Bach*. But as EW explicitly notes in her *Jacobs* book that one included letter (no. 16) was not to BJ (and, incidentally, has nothing to do with JSB), it is unsafe to assume that all other letters in that volume necessarily were written to BJ. One such letter (no. 17), discussed below, appears much more likely to have been written to CFH than to BJ. Where there is no evidence other than the *Jacobs* book to support a claim that a letter in that book was written to BJ, this uncertainty is indicated by placing a question-mark after 'BJ'.

[187] Assigned to 1808 on presumption that (1) ltr follows the awakening of SW's enthusiasm for JSB evidenced by SW's correspondence with CB regarding JSB that commenced on 12/4/1808, and (2) references to forming a 'junto' to promote JSB's music and the 'sensation' it has caused indicate ltr comparatively early in SW's promotion of JSB rather than in August 1809. However, no year between 1806 and 1809 has been established to be impossible.

her. SW gathers from Mrs Barnes that Smith wishes his daughter to have
'private' piano lessons. SW recommends that she should give up the 'school'
lessons and have 'private' lessons only, and asks Smith to decide whether she
should have one or two hours of lessons per week. SW writes warmly of her
musical ability: she is 'possessed of the most illuminated musical intellect' that
SW has met for many years.

SW→BJ?[188]   **28/8/1808**
RCM Ms 2130 ltr 20; *O*   Many Thanks for your kind Attention
☛ Sun 28 Aug={1796,1803,1808,1814}[189]

SW returns a book, *The Centaur not Fabulous* by Dr [Edward] Young [1683–
1765], which he borrowed last Friday [26/8/1808] to read during his trip. The
book is 'among the bitterest of religious satires' and, like the majority of
Young's works, reflects 'an asperity of mind and a gloomy cast of disposition'.

SW was 'in very good humour for playing yesterday evening' [27/8/1808; the
venue has not been identified]. The introduction by his 'old rival' [not identified]
of 'two critical companions' put SW on his mettle. Mr Abbot [not identified]
seems knowledgeable about this matter. 'Mrs W' [CLW] sends 'her kind
respects'. SW will write again before next Sunday [3/9/1808].

SW→SGW   **7/9/1808**
MA [uncatalogued]   I mean to call upon You to-Day, but fear I cannot come
☛ Wed 7 Sep & >20/2/1805→{1808,1814}[190]

SW means to call on SGW today but cannot arrive before 7 pm. He will be
satisfied to eat 'a cold scrap of victuals'.

[188] Ltr addressed to 'My dear Sir'. Ltr included in *Jacobs* but BJ cannot be
confirmed as recipient from ltr's content.

[189] Assigned to 1808 because ref. to CLW sending regards indicates that she was
living with SW; they were not together in August 1803 or after 1810. 1796
excluded on the basis of SW's handwriting style.

[190] Ltr >20/2/1805 because sent to SGW 'by favour of Sir Vicary Gibbs', who
was knighted on that day. As no reason has been found to prefer 7/9/1808 to
7/9/1814, ltr has been entered ambiguously under both dates.

SW→BJ?[191]   **17/9/1808**

RCM Ms 2130 ltr 1; *O*   I am much obliged by your ingenious
☞ 17/9/1808

SW is delighted by his correspondent's letter [not preserved], received today, and rejoices at the recipient's 'success' with JSB, whom the recipient rightly calls 'Saint Sebastian'. Today, for the first time, SW read CB's critique of JSB, and is 'grieved' by its falsity and its erroneous comparison of JSB with Handel. SW is sure that CB now has a very different judgement of JSB.

In a letter to CB which SW thinks he wrote nearly 'a twelvemonth' ago, SW said that his study of the '48' had opened to him 'an entirely new musical world', which had surprised him no less than when he was 'thunderstruck' as a child by hearing about 100 people perform [Handel's] *Dettingen Te Deum* at Bristol Cathedral.[192] In reply [not preserved, but after SW→CB, 14/4/1808], CB referred to what he had written about JSB in his [*General*] *History* [*of Music*] and in other books, and added that he would be pleased to hear SW play JSB's 'elaborate and erudite compositions' [the '48'], as CB had never heard any of them [the '48'] performed. CB noted that he possessed a 'very curious and beautiful' copy of JSB's 'fugues' [the '48'], which had been given to him by [Carl Philipp] Emanuel Bach [German composer, 1714–1788, JSB's son].

When he visited CB, SW found this copy so full of notational faults that he had difficulty playing one of the fugues with which he was most familiar. CB, however, was 'extremely delighted' with the fugue and wondered 'how such abstruse harmony and such perfect and enchanting melody could have been so marvellously united'. CB's copy contains only the first 24 preludes and fugues of the '48', with the upper part written in the comparatively hard-to-understand soprano clef. CB, whom SW equally respects and loves, was astonished to learn that JSB had written an additional 24 preludes and fugues, of which SW has a copy.[193] Picart has told SW that JSB wrote 'innumerable' pieces of music, including some 'for three organs', that have not been sent to England owing to the 'contempt' that Germans feel towards the state of music in England.

SW is gratified that he has been accessory to the recipient's study of JSB and hopes that their friendship and enthusiasm for JSB 'may long continue'. SW trusts that he can rely upon the recipient as 'one of my right hand men against all the prejudiced Handelians'.

---

[191] Ltr addressed to 'Dear Sir'. The address portion of ltr has been torn out. Ltr included in *Jacobs* but BJ cannot be confirmed as recipient from ltr's content.

[192] SW presumably mistook the time that had elapsed since he first wrote to CB about the '48', and probably refers here to SW→CB, 12/4/1808. Both SW→CB, 22/3/1808 and CB→SW, 23/3/1808? indicate that SW and CB had lost sight of each other for a long time, and accordingly were not in correspondence in the latter part of 1807.

[193] CB's ms of JSB's 'Preludes and Fugues (24)' was sold in lot 626 of the 12/8/1814 posthumous auction by Mr White of part of CB's music library. The present location of this ms is not known.

CB→SW   **17/10/1808**

Osborn MSS 3, Box 5, folder 319   I am glad you like Mr Horn

▣ 17/10/1808

CB is glad that SW likes CFH. CB has never met him but believes him to be 'a worthy, ingenious and liberal-minded professor'. CFH's son [Charles Edward Horn, composer, tenor and actor, 1786–1849] is an amiable, well-liked gentleman who 'sings in a very good taste and accompanies admirably'. As CB wanted to employ a deputy organist at the Royal Hospital, Chelsea, he prevailed upon his neighbour, Lieutenant Colonel Wilson [probably John Wilson, *d*1812, deputy treasurer of the Royal Hospital], to ask Charles Edward Horn whether he would accept the position at £10 per annum. Horn replied that he would undertake the deputyship 'for nothing' in return for becoming acquainted with CB.

Col. Wilson then introduced Charles Edward Horn to CB, and the two got on as agreeably as SW has with CFH. CFH sometimes substitutes for his son as organist, as the son's health is delicate; the son has been 'advised to go to Cheltenham' [spa]. The organ is 'a bad one', but [Robert or William] Gray has 'put it in as good order as possible'. According to CB's daughter and amanuensis [Sarah Harriet Burney], who is SW's 'friend', Charles Edward Horn plays the organ 'in an elegant grave style' suited to sacred service.

CB will respond briefly to other subjects in SW's letter [not preserved]. From this letter, SW appears to be so busy 'during the first four days of the week' that he has no time even to read correspondence. CB knows 'the hurry of full teaching': while he was writing and printing his *General History of Music* he was employed at two of the largest boarding-schools in the London area—Mrs Shields in Queen Square, Bloomsbury, and in Blacklands, Chelsea—and in addition he gave 'from 40 to 50 private lessons' in different parts of town.

CB will be 'extremely glad to have a talk' with SW regarding SW's 'plan of publishing the life' of JSB 'jointly with' CFH. SW and his 'co-partner' CFH 'will confer honour' on themselves by 'blazoning the power' of JSB. CB 'formerly had some dealings' with [Johann Nicholas] Forkel [author of the biography of JSB]. CB does not know Mr [Edward] Stephenson [banker, 1759–1833]: if his translation of the biography 'is well done', it is a 'pity to undertake' a new translation. AFCK's criticisms always are exaggerated. Do SW or CFH have a copy of 'the original Life' [i.e., Forkel's biography, in German]?

When CB was in Leipzig in 1772, he procured all the information he could about JSB from [Johann Adam] Hiller [German composer, 1728–1804], who was 'music director there'. CB also obtained information about JSB from [Friedrich Wilhelm] Marpurg [German music theortst and composer, 1718–1795] in Berlin and from JSB's 'illustrious and most admirable son' Carl Philipp Emanuel Bach in Hamburg. Whenever CB met Carl Philipp Emanuel Bach, his father JSB, 'for whom he had a great veneration', was always 'part of our discourse'. CB has no idea how Forkel can subsequently 'have procured authentic materials' concerning JSB 'to furnish a book'. If SW can visit 'the old pensioner' [CB] at Chelsea College next Friday [21/10/1808] 'or on any other Friday', CB will be pleased to see him at any hour SW desires.

CB inserted, in his article on JSB in [Abraham Rees's] *Cyclopaedia*, 'all that was known' of JSB when CB was in Germany. CB 'can boast of being the first' to make his country 'acquainted' with JSB. When CB's *German Tour* was first published [in 1773], perhaps at most four professors 'in the Kingdom' had ever heard JSB's name: [CB], the Bristol organist [Edmund] Broderip [1727–1779], 'old [Thomas] Linley [1733–1795] of Bath', and perhaps CFH [who in fact arrived in England in 1782]. JSB was 'first mentioned as an author [i.e., as a composer] 20 years ago in Longman and Broderip's catalogue' [not located] and in [Nicolas Etienne] Framery's *Calendrier Musical* published in 1788.

SW→BJ[194]   **17/10/1808**
RCM Ms 2130 ltr 2; *O*   We are going on swimmingly.
☞ 17/10/1808

CFH, who had arranged 12 of JSB's fugues for four instruments before SW met him,[195] is 'furthering the cause of our grand hero' [JSB] mightily. Prior to editing JSB's 'fugues' [the '48'], CFH and SW propose to publish by subscription an 'authentic and accurate' *Life* of JSB, including a list of all the works of 'our Apollo' [JSB], which the banker [Edward] Stephenson, 'a most zealous and scientific member of our fraternity' [of JSB enthusiasts], has translated 'from the German of [Johann Nicholas] Forkel'. This will cause a 'considerable sensation' in the musical and literary worlds. CFH possesses many unpublished JSB works, including organ trios of which AFCK published one in his 1799 *Essay on Practical Musical Composition*. CFH wants to publish a complete edition of JSB's compositions. He has transcribed all the '48' and is as 'indefatigable' as BJ.

SW has promised Attwood to be at St Paul's [Cathedral] on Sunday morning [23/10/1808]. BJ is asked to send the enclosure [not preserved] to [Charles] Neate [composer and pianist, 1784–1877], whose address SW does not know. SW sends 'kind regards' to his 'friend Mrs [Mary] Jacobs' [BJ's wife].

SW→BJ[196]   Camden Town   **19/10/1808**
RCM Ms 2130 ltr 3; *O*   I thought you would be gratified in gaining
☞ Wed 19 Oct & 🖎→🖺

SW thought that BJ would be gratified by 'gaining early intelligence' of 'our [CFH's and SW's] intention' to publish 'memoirs of our matchless man'

---

[194] Ltr addressed to 'My dear Sir'. BJ confirmed as addressee by SW conveying his regards to 'Mrs Jacobs'.

[195] *A Sett of Twelve Fugues, Composed for the Organ by Sebastian Bach, Arranged as Quartettos, for Two Violins Tenor and Bass…by C. F. Horn* was published by CFH in 1807. The preface is dated 1/5/1807.

[196] Ltr addressed to 'My dear Sir'. BJ confirmed as addressee by SW and CLW sending best wishes to 'Mrs J'.

[Edward Stephenson's translation of Forkel's Life of JSB]. The book will defy JSB's 'would-be critics' in the British Empire. Salomon has rightly said that the English know very little of the works of German masters other than Handel; however, Handel has little claim to be regarded as an original genius because he pilfered his subjects from many other composers and utilised his own subjects over and over. A great majority of teachers such as 'Gaffer' [Richard John Samuel] Stevens, whom BJ saw recently, are incompetent. The appreciation of JSB in England, like the progress of truth, will come to pass, however slowly. BJ's brother organists are envious of his industry on behalf of JSB, however much they may criticise BJ.

   SW has been confined to his chamber all day because of a bilious complaint but is engaged tomorrow [20/10/1808] to be at a party [in Paddington, *see* SW→SGW, 20/10/1808], where CFH's arrangement for 'two violins, tenor and bass' of music by JSB will be played [*see* SW→BJ, 17/10/1808]. SW intends to be with BJ by 1 pm on Sunday [23/10/1808] when he will identify 'a man of real musical judgement, some science and admirable talent on his own instrument', who incredibly compared a fugue from JSB's '48', arranged by CFH, to 'a hog floundering the mud'. CLW joins in sending best wishes to BJ and his family.

SW→SGW   Camden Town   **20/10/1808**
WCL LDWMM 1997/6599   [not available]
☞ Thurs 20 Oct & 🏛→ⅰ
   Although SW has had a 'bilious complaint' he wishes to keep his engagement to play at a party in Paddington. He would like a bed for the night in case bad weather should prevent his return to Camden Town. His bowels are in a tender state.

SW→CW Jr   **28/10/1808**
WMM   If you & my Mother will come over & dine with me
☞ Fri 28 Oct={1808}[197]
   SW proposes that CW Jr and SGW should dine with him next Thursday [3/11/1808] at any time after 2 pm. SW will not ask anyone else 'so that we may have the organ all to ourselves' and 'play the right sort of music on it'. On Sunday [30/10/1808] SW's new Te Deum and Jubilate will be performed at St Paul's Cathedral. SW would like CW Jr to hear it. SW has just been rehearsing it and 'playing the choir service throughout', which is difficult because the singers are '1000 miles distant from the organ'. At 8 pm this evening [28/10/1808] there is a 'musical meeting' at the Portuguese Embassy Chapel. SW wishes that CW Jr would come, as 'the organ is a most sublime one' and '£400 has lately been expended on its repair' [by George Pike England, organ builder, c1768–1815].

---

[197] Assigned to 1808 because the autograph of SW's Te Deum and Jubilate (BL Add Ms 14342) is dated 1808.

SW→BJ[198]   **17/11/1808?**

RCM Ms 2130 ltr 4; *O*   I always suspect the Sincerity of sudden Conversions.
17/11/1808 written on ltr in pencil; this date is used in *Jacobs* p 13

SW is suspicious of CW Jr's apparent sudden conversion to JSB's music on
Monday night [14/11/1808].[199] Regrettably, CW Jr's 'transcendent musical
knowledge and skill' has been 'betrayed by bad company'. SW is glad that BJ
performed the 'hymn tune' that SW set to music [possibly SW's 1807 'Might I
in thy sight appear', set to words by CW, which SW quotes in SW→BJ,
21/11/1808?], as its style particularly pleases CW Jr, whose 'best compositions
are pathetic'. If CW Jr tells Sarah about it 'she will be extraordinarily chagrined
in finding that' SW, whom she characterised [perhaps in a letter not preserved]
as 'destitute of every sentiment of justice, honour or integrity', has set religious
words to music. CW Jr's harpsichord master [Joseph] Kelway, who was 'one of
the most accurate critics of [musical] performance', said that CW Jr played
Handel better than Handel himself.

SW agrees to BJ's request that SW sit for a portrait by [John] Bacon [1777–
1859, the younger of two sculptors so named] and asks BJ's assistance in
arranging a suitable time. This should not be on a day that SW goes to Cossens's
[presumably a school], when SW is occupied with work 'from morning to
night'. BJ should inform [George] Gwilt [architect, 1775–1856] that SW will be
pleased to 'attend him' on Wednesday [23/11/1808] at 'your organ' [at Surrey
Chapel, where BJ was organist] about 4.30 pm., after SW finishes teaching in
Paddington. BJ can tell [Thomas] Elliot [organ builder, 1759?–1832, who built
the Surrey Chapel organ] that SW will dine with Elliot sometime between
20/11/1808 and 27/11/1808, 'as desired'. SW asks to be remembered to BJ's
wife [Mary] and to 'all my young Bachists' [presumably BJ's children].

---

[198] Ltr addressed to 'My dear Sir'. BJ explicitly identified as addressee in *Jacobs*
p 13 (conceivably on the basis of a subsequently discarded address portion of ltr
that also included a date or postmark); this identification is supported by ltr's
assertion that the request that a portrait of SW be made by John Bacon
originated with the recipient who is asked to arrange an initial meeting of SW
and Bacon (*see* BJ→John Bacon, 12/12/1808, in which BJ makes arrangements
for SW to sit for this portrait and BJ→John Bacon, 18/11/1809, in which BJ
praises the resulting portrait).

[199] However, a manuscript 'Ode to Sebastian Bach' by CW Jr appeared as lot
138 in the 13/7/1835 posthumous auction of his property by Phillips. (An
unpriced copy of the sale catalogue is at BL Add Ms 35019 f 214.) The present
location of CW Jr's ode is not known.

SW→BJ[200]   **21/11/1808?**
RCM Ms 2130 ltr 5; *O*   Although I fully hope & expect to enjoy
22/11 written on ltr in pencil[201]

Replying to BJ's letter [not preserved], SW agrees that CW Jr would be 'an acquisition to any musical cause' he espouses. However, SW thinks that CW Jr's conversion to the cause of JSB unfortunately is likely to be intermittent: when CW Jr is with Handelians he will 'readily relapse' into the 'blasphemy' of defending the pre-eminence of Handel.

SW looks forward to being with BJ next Wednesday [23/11/1808] at Charlotte Street [BJ's home], where he proposes to spend the night if convenient. A day for [SW to see John] Bacon can be appointed then. SW will 'endeavour to manage a meeting' at [Thomas] Elliot's on Saturday [26/11/1808], even though he teaches from 1 to 5 pm on Saturdays in Paddington. The governess [of the Paddington school] is a difficult woman who often puts on airs.

'Charles' [CW III] anticipates using [the Rev. Richard] Lyne's Latin grammar; this embodies a 'beautifully simple' method by which BJ could acquire, in a few months, all the Latin that he will ever need. SW asks to be remembered to BJ's wife [Mary], and quotes in this connection the opening of 'Might I in thy sight appear' [a sacred song by SW that BJ and his wife presumably knew].

SW→Crotch   Camden Town   **25/11/1808**
Norfolk in Ms 11244; *O*   I hope that I shall always feel ready to render
☞ Fri 25 Nov; pmk 1808

SW is always happy to help 'the cause of real good music' and acknowledges Crotch as an 'eminently conspicuous' promoter of it. SW at this moment cannot state the dates of JSB's birth and death but advises that CFH and SW 'are preparing for the press the whole Life' of JSB 'together with an accurate list of all his works'. The Life of JSB, written in German by Forkel, 'has been translated by Mr [Edward] Stephenson of Queen Square', who is 'a great enthusiast in the cause [of JSB] and a most excellent judge of music'. If Crotch's query regarding JSB's dates is urgent, SW will apply to CFH, who can instantly supply the answers by referring to the biography.

Although JSB and Handel both wrote large amounts of music, JSB's compositions are 'totally unknown' in England, 'even by their titles'. This does

---

[200] Ltr addressed to 'My dear Sir'. BJ is designated as the recipient because ltr mentions SW spending the night in Charlotte Street, where BJ lived.

[201] 22/11/1808 was a Tuesday. Ltr assigned to Monday, 21/11/1808 on the assumptions: (1) that ltr's 'Wednesday next' when SW plans to see BJ is the same Wednesday as that mentioned in SW→BJ, 17/11/1808, i.e., Wednesday 23/11/1808, because of the references in both letters to appointing times for SW to see John Bacon and to meet Thomas Elliot; and (2) the pencilled annotation records a postmark on the address portion of ltr that has not been preserved. (If SW had referred to 23/11/1808 in a letter written on 22/11/1808 he presumably would have written 'tomorrow' rather than 'Wednesday next'.)

little for England's honour. Although Handel outlived JSB the two were contemporaries. JSB had 'a high respect for' Handel and sought several times to meet him, but without success.

Crotch's 'pains' to analyse 'every note in the fugue' to which he is 'justly so partial' [presumably JSB's E major fugue in part 2 of the '48', which Crotch published c1809 in v 3 of his *Specimens of Various Styles of Music Referred to in a Course of Lectures*] have convinced SW that Crotch is 'fully determined to appreciate' JSB's true worth. SW's own esteem of JSB's music, in which SW continually finds 'new beauties', exceeds 'all power of language'.

Crotch should burn his 'London copy' immediately [presumably the edition of part 2 of the '48' published by Broderip and Wilkinson under the title *Preludes et Fugues pour le Forte-Piano...I. Partie* not later than 1808, when the firm became Wilkinson & Co.], as its errors 'libel' JSB. Anyone forming an opinion of JSB's music from such a 'nefarious specimen' [based upon, but not identical to, the edition published by Simrock in Bonn in 1801] would be fully justified in asserting JSB's ignorance of the rules of harmony and counterpoint. SW understands that [the music publisher, C.] 'Wilkinson in the Haymarket is trying to insult the public with a similar Grub Street performance' [presumably a proposed edition of part 1 of the '48' that Wilkinson would have called *II. Partie*]. SW will 'write him [Wilkinson] down publicly with a pen dipped in gall'.

SW made his manuscript copy of the '48' [now BL Add 14330] from the 'Zürich edition' [*see* SW→CB, 12/4/1808], the only edition 'on which any tolerable dependence can be safely placed', yet he has found at least 30 errors in it. He comments on its notational practices. Presumably in response to a query [not preserved] from Crotch, SW discusses a textual problem in the 24th bar of the E major fugue in part 2. JSB composed the '48' to make performers proficient 'on the Clavier' in all 24 [major and minor] keys. SW thinks that the German phrase is 'the compleatly well tempered Clavier'. The term 'Clavier' is 'alike applicable to clavichord, harpsichord, piano forte or organ', but SW believes that the 'sublime and beautiful' effects of the '48' can be 'truly' heard 'only on the organ'. If SW's 'life and health are spared', he will endeavour to produce editions of JSB's music besides an edition of the '48'.

SW→CB   **6/12/1808**

Burney-Cumming[202]; *O*   'The Time cries Haste & Speed must answer it'.

⊡ 6/12/1808

SW wishes to prepare his lectures carefully and soon, and asks whether CB approves that two lectures should be 'On the power of musical prejudice' and 'On the power of music upon morals'. SW inquires what CB thinks would be the most 'taking' style for the introductory lecture. SW aims to dispel some of the 'partiality and prejudice' that have for too long 'overshadowed Apollo' [JSB] in England.

---

[202] The address portion of ltr seemingly is in Osborn MSS 3, Box 5, folder 319.

CB→SW   **7/12/1808?**

Osborn MSS 3, Box 5, folder 319   The Morality of Music has been mentioned

ltr undated[203]

CB [presumably commenting upon SW's plan to lecture on music and morals, *see* SW→CB, 6/12/1808], notes that Pythagoras, Plato and Aristotle mentioned the morality of music; however, these 'venerable ancients', who wrote 'previous to [preserved notations of] solo instrumental music', called poetry 'music'. CB said much about the moral effects of music in his Dissertation on the Music of the Ancients. Perhaps it must not be said that German music has been improved by the 'grace and facility' of Italian music. However, Italian drama—written, set [to music], sung and performed by Italians—was present in all the courts of former times. Recent German composers of instrumental music, such as Haydn, Mozart and Beethoven, availed themselves of this; 'in their slow movements', [these German composers] 'surpass the Italians themselves'.

SW→BJ[204]   Camden Town   **8/12/1808**

RCM Ms 2130, ltr 6; *O*   Previously to the Receipt of your last kind Letter

▣ 8/12/1808

SW received BJ's letter [not preserved] today. SW had decided earlier to have nothing to do with 'that infamous libeller, the Satyrist' [*The Satirist, or Monthly Messenger* had attacked the Surry Institution in September 1808, pp 136–139 and published 'Hints to Lecturers' in December 1808 pp 508–513]. SW arranges to meet [John] Bacon with BJ on 21/12/1808 about 6 pm; on that day SW teaches at the Manor House [the school in Paddington run by AD's successor] until 5.30 pm.

SW is glad that 'Sebastian' [JSB's music] is to be heard 'even out of the mouths of babes and sucklings'. SW and BJ's venerable friend and fellow JSB-enthusiast 'agonidzomenos' [a sinner who so signed himself in a letter to the Rev. Rowland Hill, minister of the Surrey Chapel, 1744–1833, *see Sidney* p 217] have good opinions of each other. SW regrets that this man is not likely to come to live in London. SW heard an excellent sermon by Hill on Sunday [4/12/1808] and is grateful that he considers SW worthy to be BJ's successor [as organist of Surrey Chapel]. However, SW would rather be BJ's joint organist than his successor. 'Mrs W' [CLW] and the rest of SW's family unite in sending 'kindest regards'.

---

[203] Assigned to 7/12/1808 because ltr apparently written on address portion of SW→CB, 6/12/1808. Ltr is an incomplete draft; there is some uncertainty where it begins.

[204] Ltr addressed to 'My dear Sir'. BJ confirmed as addressee by ref. to Rowland Hill's suggestion that SW could be BJ's successor as organist of Surrey Chapel.

SW→CW Jr   **10/12/1808**
Bristol Watkinson album p 68, ltr 834   I cannot send you a Hare
☞ 10/12/1808

SW regrets that he cannot send CW Jr a hare or a brace of partridges for the celebration of his [51st] birthday tomorrow [11/12/1808], but encloses 24 'bars of descant' [not preserved] which he thinks that CW Jr will like to analyse. SW will withhold the name of the author [perhaps JSB] until he knows CW Jr's opinion of 'the air and the bass'. SW asks to be remembered to SGW and to all friends who inquire for him.

BJ→John Bacon   **12/12/1808**
GEU in box 6   Mr Wesley has named Wedy 21st as a day
pmk 12/12/1808

SW appoints 6 pm on Wednesday 21/12/1808 to dine with [John] Bacon, Bacon's wife and BJ. BJ is delighted that Bacon's children are 'Bachists', as this proves the naturalness and beauty of JSB's subjects. 'Infants' in several families within BJ's 'circle' are singing JSB's 'strains', and BJ agrees with SW [and quotes from SW→BJ, 8/12/1808] that an 'assiduous cultivation' of JSB's 'divine strains' is necessary to render them 'the chief delight and solace of all truly harmonised souls'. BJ has cleverly deciphered Bacon's 'hieroglyphics' [not preserved] as the subjects, which he writes out, of the F major and A♭ major fugues in part 2 of JSB's '48' [which may have come to Bacon's and BJ's attention through the recent publication of the Broderip and Wilkinson edition of part 2, *see* SW→Crotch, 25/11/1808].

SW→CB   Camden Town   **20/12/1808**
Osborn MSS 3, Box 16, folder 1192; *O*   I am eternally pestering you
☞ 20 Dec[205]

CB has endured SW's continual 'pestering' so patiently that SW now asks him two further questions. He promises 'to be quiet' after this until he comes to Chelsea College to rehearse his first lecture in front of CB. Although SW has played in public since childhood and is not embarrassed to do this if his 'tools are good', 'to speak in public is another affair', about which SW is diffident. He asks whether he should make 'a little prefatory apology' before the lecture, to avoid 'censure which might be excited' by deficiencies in SW's 'manner of delivery'. His second query is whether it is necessary to 'adduce' practical [musical] examples in his first lecture, which will be 'on music considered as an art and as a science'.

---

[205] Ltr assigned to 1808 because CB's reply of the same date (CB→SW, 20/12/1808) mentions the death of Richard Thomas Burney which occurred in 1808.

CB→SW   **20/12/1808**

Osborn MSS 3, Box 16, folder 1192   I am over head & ears in bed

▣ 20 Dec[206]

CB is in bed with his former complaint. He fears that his eldest daughter [Esther Burney, 1749–1832] is 'dangerously ill', and he is full of sorrow because of the death of his youngest son [Richard Thomas Burney, 1768–1808]. Even if CB were well, these calamities would 'prevent, for a time' his 'going out, or letting friends in'. In reply to SW's two questions [in SW→CB, 20/12/1808], CB approves SW making a 'prefatory apology' regarding his inexperience as a public lecturer, and advises that SW 'should keep back' his [musical] performances [during a lecture] until they are necessary 'to illustrate some remarkably pleasing style of composition'.

SW→CW Jr   **about 20/12/1808**

BL Add 35012 f 119; *O*   Perhaps you or some of your friends will like to hear

ltr undated[207]

SW suggests that CW Jr or some of his friends might like to hear his Te Deum, Jubilate and Litany at [Matins at] St Paul's [Cathedral] next Sunday, Christmas Day [25/12/1808]. They always keep this service for 'high days and holidays', so there is hardly any other opportunity to hear it but at the four great festivals. The service begins at 9.45 am. SW is sorry that CW Jr cannot come to Mr Smith's [not identified] on Saturday next [24/12/1808], particularly as SW will have no other day free this month.

The people at Bath are begging SW to come there without delay: Dr [Henry] Harington, [Venanzio] Rauzzini and other [Bath] musicians are already making great preparations.

SW→John Bacon   Randalls, near Leatherhead   **28/12/1808**

GEU in box 6; *O*   You must forgive my Non-attendance To-morrow

▣ 28 Dec; pmk 29/12/1808

SW cannot be present [presumably to sit for his portrait] on 29/12/1808 because Richard Brinsley Sheridan is detaining him [at Randall Farm, which Sheridan had rented in 1808, *see Price* v 3 p 39]. As soon as SW gets to London he will advise Bacon.

---

[206] The numerals '20' are not clear, but ltr is a reply to SW→CB, 20/12/1808. Assigned to 1808 because of the death of Richard Thomas Burney that year.

[207] Assigned to 1808 for the following reason. Ref. to performance of SW's Te Deum composed in 1808 (*see* SW→CW Jr, 28/10/1808) implies ltr >1807; ltr says Christmas Day is a Sunday, which it was in 1808 and 1814, but 1814 impossible because Rauzzini, who was alive when ltr written, died in 1810. Ref. to 'next Sunday, Christmas Day' implies ltr >17/12/1808; ref. to 'Saturday next' [24/12/1808] suggests ltr <23/12/1808.

Sarah→Marianne Francis   28/12/1808?

Berg vol. of 271 letters to the Burney family   But yesterday dearest Marianne
📧 28 Dec[208]

Sarah is not surprised that Marianne Francis [1790–1832, CB's granddaughter] was delighted with the talents of Sarah's 'unhappy brother' [SW, possibly a reference to the 25/12/1808 performance of his Te Deum, Jubilate and Litany at St Paul's Cathedral]. He possess talents 'in no common degree', but genius can cause its possessor misery, 'especially if united with convivial powers, which woefully mislead'. Sarah prays that SW's 'mind may be turned before he leaves this world'.

Sarah was much surprised when CW III called today. He was under her care as a child and she loved him 'so much', but afterwards he 'never came near' her. Sarah 'spoke to him of his want of gratitude'. He confessed that he may have given an impression of this, but always wished 'to please the persons with whom he lived'. He was bred up in 'extremely difficult' circumstances because SW and CLW 'were always on different sides, and their discords terrified him to any submission', as he loved 'his ease'.

CW III 'is a very acute boy'. He seems aware that Sarah's interest [in him] 'may serve him'. She is inclined to help him, especially as his parents are too 'intent on jangling to promote the welfare of their children'. CW III hopes to be a surgeon.

SW→John Bacon   Camden Town   1/1/1809

GEU in box 6; *O*   Mr S. Wesley presents his Respects to Mr Bacon
📧 1/1/1809

SW proposes to attend [John] Bacon [presumably to sit for Bacon's portrait of SW] on Tuesday 3/1/1809 at about 1 pm.

SW→SGW   Bath   28/1/1809

Wcoll D6/1/444(a)   I take this Opportunity of sending by Mr Major
📧 28 Jan; pmk (London) 30/1/1809[209]

SW sends this letter by [Joseph] Major [organist and composer, 1771–1828], who is returning from Bath to London. SW continues 'in very good health and condition'. 'The Bath people are most extremely and universally kind and polite'; he has received many invitations and does not know when he shall be 'suffered' to leave. Last Sunday [22/1/1809] he dined with [SGW's cousin]

---

[208] Dated 1808? by Berg collection and in *Hemlow* and assigned to that year for this reason, as text is consistent with such a dating. Ltr written from Woodstock Street, where SGW lived in Decembers from 1806 to 1812.

[209] The year stamped by the pmk is hard to read, but assignment of ltr to 1809 follows also from SW's presence in Bath, where he was in January 1809 but not in other Januaries.

Thynne Gwynne. SGW should tell CW Jr that SW is obliged to him for his letter [not preserved].

SW→William Savage   Camden Town   **28/2/1809**
LRI; *O*   Mr Samuel Wesley begs leave to inform Mr Savage that he arrived
▣ 28 Feb; 🖎→{1807–1809} & SW's return from Bath→ⓘ
SW returned to London last night [27/2/1809] from Bath where he was 'detained some weeks longer' than he had planned. He now has a bad cold 'with swelled glands of the throat'; because of his very hoarse voice he cannot speak 'without much inconvenience'. Accordingly, he asks to delay the first lecture to 'Wednesday next' [8/3/1809], by which time he hopes to have recovered. He informs William Savage [printer, 1770–1843, at this time Assistant Secretary of and printer to the Royal Institution] that 'nothing short of illness' would have 'occasioned this procrastination'.

CW Jr→Sarah   **28/2/1809**
GEU in box 6   I this momt recd your welcome Letter
▣ 28/2/1809
SW is 'in great request not only at Bath, but all the musical world are mad for his instruction'. He is 'coming to town' [London]. CW Jr has been told that SW 'begins his public lecture at the [Royal] Institution next Friday' [3/3/1809].

SW→BJ[210]   Camden Town   **2/3/1809**
RCM Ms 2130, ltr 7; *O*   Here I am once more, and shall rejoice
▣ 2/3/1809
SW has returned [to London from Bath]. He looks forward to seeing BJ at the first opportunity 'after so a long an interval of separation', and apologises for not writing to him [while away]. SW was very busy during the holidays, amongst other tasks preparing his course of six lectures [to be read at the Royal Institution]. The first lecture 'has been in readiness for some days'; the next two have been outlined. The 'miracles' of JSB should furnish material for the final lecture.

SW has borrowed JSB's many 'exercises' for the harpsichord [presumably some or all of JSB's four-part *Clavierübung*, which was published in Leipzig under the title *Exercices pour le Clavecin*], which are 'every whit as stupendous as the preludes and fugues' [the '48']. Amongst these exercises is 'a beautiful air which is published along with a set' of C.P.E. Bach's 'Lessons' which SW saw in Bath. SW thinks that C.P.E. Bach 'made little scruple of robbing his father' [JSB].

---

[210] Ltr addressed to 'My dear Sir'. BJ confirmed as addressee by ref. to his son Rowland Jacobs.

SW's first lecture is 'not to be read before next Friday week' [10/3/1809]. He hopes to see BJ and his wife [Mary] before then, and asks to be remembered to 'Rowley' [their son Rowland George Benjamin Jacobs *later* Jacob, composer, 1800–1817] and 'all the young Powlies' [presumably their daughters Mary Lucretia Jacobs and Elizabeth Ann Jacobs, both *bap*1804].

SW→BJ[211]   Camden Town   **3/3/1809**
RCM Ms 2130, ltr 8; *O*   I have just received your very prompt Answer to mine
⬛ 3/3/1809
SW has just received BJ's very prompt answer [not preserved] to his letter [SW→BJ, 2/3/1809]. He regrets that he cannot be with BJ tomorrow or Sunday [5/3/1809], but proposes to meet him next Wednesday [8/3/1809] about 5 pm.

JSB's works would 'furnish materials for 600 as easily as for six lectures'; however, SW and BJ should not promote JSB too hastily. BJ's information that [Richard John Samuel] Stevens is 'beginning to revoke his blasphemies' [his negative views of JSB's music] proves that slow promotion of JSB will achieve good results. SW is glad that BJ likes WL. WL is 'a great favourite' of SW.

SW left BJ's book of 'Bach's Lutheran Hymns' at John [Baptist] Cramer's house and will reclaim it shortly. SW is about to send to the engraver 'the first trio of the six' [JSB organ trios] lent to him by CFH. It is best that the trios be printed singly. SW asks to be remembered to BJ's wife and children.

CW Jr→Sarah   **9/3/1809**
GEU in box 8   I thank you for your last favour wch I received yesterday
⬛ 9 Mar[212]
SW begins [a course of lectures] tomorrow [10/3/1809] at the Royal Institution.

CW Jr→Sarah   **14/3/1809**
MA DDWes/6/73   It gave us much satisfaction, hearing from you on Monday
⬛ 14/3/1809
Mrs Roberts went to the Royal Institution to hear SW [lecture]. She and CW Jr 'made a few observations', in which CW Jr thinks that Sarah would have joined.

---

[211] Ltr addressed to 'My dear Sir'. BJ confirmed as addressee by ref. to 'Mrs J.'.

[212] Assigned to 1809 because ltr addressed to Sarah at Miss Swinburne's, Arundel, Sussex, where she was in March 1809 (amongst other letters, CW Jr→Sarah, 14/3/1809 is addressed to her there) and is not known to have been in March of other years.

SW→William Savage   **16/3/1809**
LRI; *O*   Having heard nothing from you to the contrary, I conclude
▣ Thurs 16 Mar={1809}[213]
Having heard nothing to the contrary from William Savage [Assistant
Secretary of the Royal Institution], SW assumes that next Wednesday
[22/3/1809], the day he proposed to read [his next lecture], is agreed. The
principal subject of the lecture will be the 'improvement of the chromatic scale'
as shown in the construction and effects of the patent organ designed by William
Hawkes and built by [Thomas] Elliot.

SW→Bridgetower   Camden Town   **25/3/1809**
GEU Wesley Coll. ltr 61; *O*   I need not multiply Words (I trust) to assure you
▣ 25 Mar; pmk 27/3/1809
As SW must dine at Somerset House Lodge on 27/3/1809 to vote for a
deserving new member, he regretfully must defer Bridgetower's planned visit
that day. SW proposes instead that Bridgetower visit him at 4 pm on Good
Friday, 31/3/1809, when, as is customary in England during Lent, salt fish rather
than fresh fish will be served.

SW→Bridgetower   Camden Town   **14/4/1809**
MA DDWF/15/14; *O*   S Wesley is compelled to inform Mr Bridgetower
▣ 14 Apr; pmk 15/4/1809
VN has 'put off the party' at the Portuguese Embassy Chapel [where he was
organist], as all the priests are 'engaged in absolving their penitents from the
crime of slandering the Duke of York's reputation'.

'J.P.'→Editor, *NMMR*   **4/1809**
NMMR, v 1 no. 3, May 1809, pp 43–44   Through the medium of your
ltr undated[214]
SW chose to make the organ and piano patented [on 25/7/1808] by [William]
Hawkes 'a part of his lecture at the Royal Institution' [on 22/3/1809, *see*
SW→William Savage, 16/3/1809], but did not point out the imperfections of the
system of tuning of these instruments. If SW had not discovered these
imperfections at the time of his lecture, his failure to mention them may be
regarded as 'an oversight'. If he knew of these imperfections, then his failure to
mention them 'bears a strong resemblance to deception'.

---

[213] Assigned to 1809 because ltr mentions SW's Royal Institution lecture on
Hawkes (*see* 'J.P.'→Editor, *NMMR*, 4/1809).

[214] Ltr >22/3/1809 as it discusses SW's lecture of that date. Dated letters
published in the *NMMR* generally were written not later than the middle of the
month preceding publication.

As part of his lecture, SW played 'Surely He hath borne our griefs' from Handel's *Messiah* and 'Return, O God of hosts' from Handel's *Samson*. 'J.P.' cites particular passages that he asserts cannot be played correctly on Hawkes's organ or piano, and asks SW to reply publicly whether he played these compositions 'correctly'. 'J.P.' finds it 'almost incredible' that 'both the ear and understanding of so eminent a professor as' SW could have been deceived to consider Hawkes's system worthy of introduction 'under the sanction of a royal institution'.

SW→George Smith   Camden Town   **23/4/1809**
BL Add 31764 f 20; *O*   I feel it my Duty to apprize you
▣ 23 Apr[215]

SW advises that he has been dismissed by the 'Mesdames Barnes' after 25 years of service, under the 'pretence' of his having allowed his pupils too little time for each lesson. Another master [in fact, WH] has been engaged.[216] No similar complaint has ever been made at four other schools in which SW has taught, and at two of which he still teaches. SW gave up one of the schools because the number of pupils did not make his attendance worthwhile. The governess of the other school retired.

SW received an 'exceedingly flippant and ungenteel' letter [not preserved] from Mrs B[arnes], stating that George Smith would be 'extremely angry' when he knew how much his daughter had been neglected by SW. This 'neglect' was merely SW's continued stay at Bath for a fortnight longer than he had originally intended. Mrs Barnes had no cause to complain, as SW had appointed Cooke [probably Matthew Cooke, organist and composer, 1761?–1829] to deputise for him.[217] However, SW had not thought it proper to appoint Cooke to teach Smith's daughter without having first consulted Smith. SW has subsequently made up the missed lessons and on several occasions has given her an hour's lesson. He has always been 'warmly interested' in her improvement.

SW asks whether Smith wants him to go on teaching her, or whether she is to be 'turned over' to whomever the governesses appoint in SW's place. SW assures Smith that his daughter is making good progress, especially in playing at sight, and that her facility in this area gives him much pleasure.

---

[215] Assigned to 1809 because SW was in Bath earlier that year and subsequent 1809 letters from SW to George Smith are on the same subject.

[216] WH's engagement is stated in his 21/3/1809 diary entry (Bodl Ms Eng. e.2134).

[217] Robert Cooke (*see* SW→CW Jr, 15/1/1807) was organist of Westminster Abbey at this time, so it seems unlikely that SW would have engaged him to carry out comparatively menial teaching duties at this school.

SW→George Smith[218]   Camden Town   **26/4/1809**
GEU Wesley Coll. ltr 60; *O*   Frankness on one Side demands it on the other
▣ Wed 26 Apr & 🖎→ⓘ

As Smith believes that his daughter 'is more likely to improve with Mr [John Baptist] Cramer' than with SW, SW recommends that Cramer be immediately engaged. SW will inform Cramer of Smith's intention.

SW→BJ?[219]   **26/4/1809?**
RCM Ms 2130, ltr 9; *O*   I am a great Fool—I forgot whether I desired You
ltr undated[220]

SW forgot whether he asked BJ to bring SW's 'two books' of JSB's music tomorrow [27/4/1809]. They will be busy performing tomorrow so will have little time to talk. BJ's copy of JSB's *Choral Vorspiele* [*für die Orgel*, published by Breitkopf in Leipzig in four volumes] should be with [John Baptist] Cramer now. SW will bring his copy tomorrow [of volumes 1 and 2, given to him in 1809 by Joseph Gwilt, architect and musician, 1784–1863, George Gwilt's brother; this copy now is at RCM], if only to 'electrify' CW Jr by performing JSB's prelude [BWV 680, of which the beginning is quoted]. SW will then lend his copy to BJ.

'Sermonising' [i.e., lecturing] now is part of SW's 'profession', but he makes no apology for the possibility of being accused of 'canting' [insincerely advocating JSB's music], as he and BJ know 'better things' [the true value of JSB's music]. SW and BJ will give 'a death wound' to the 'prejudice and impotence' of 'all the stiff Handelians and Wolfians' [preachers of cold, lifeless sermons who followed the system of Christian Wolf, German philosopher, 1679–1754]. The 'Portuguese fun' [presumably an event at the Portuguese Embassy Chapel, *see* SW→Bridgetower, 14/4/1809] is not yet 'settled'.

SW→George Smith   Camden Town   **9/5/1809**
BL Add 31764 f 22; *O*   As I am not conscious of having 'acted any Part'
▣ Tue 9 May & 🖎→ⓘ

SW does not consider that he acted incorrectly either to Smith or to Mrs Barnes, and is therefore keen to enter into 'the most unequivocal explanation' of his conduct 'relative to the misunderstanding at Oxford House' [Mrs Barnes's school]. During SW's stay 'in the West' [at Bath] he engaged 'a professional

---

[218] Ltr addressed to 'Dear Sir'. Smith identified as recipient because ltr's discussion of the suitability of having his daughter study with John Baptist Cramer is continued in SW→George Smith, 9/5/1809.

[219] Ltr addressed to 'My Dear Sir'. Ltr included in *Jacobs*. BJ presumed to be the recipient although this is not explicitly indicated in ltr.

[220] Assigned to 26/4/1809 because ltr is so annotated in pencil (not by SW), possibly on the basis of a subsequently discarded address portion.

man of real worth and talents' [probably Matthew Cooke, *see* SW→George Smith, 23/4/1809] to teach his school pupils until his return. SW regrets that he did not ask Smith whether he would have wished his daughter to have her 'separate lessons' from Cooke; if he had done so, Smith would probably have agreed to SW's proposal, and 'all these unpleasant consequences' would have been avoided. SW is at a loss to understand why Mrs Barnes, who when SW returned to London had expressed 'the highest approbation' of Cooke's attention and punctuality, should suddenly have informed SW that she intended to engage another master after the midsummer holidays. SW leaves it to 'all dispassionate and unprejudiced persons' to judge whether this was 'a becoming behaviour' to someone who had served them for 'nearly 30 years'.

SW cannot guess why Smith should have wanted to remove his daughter to another master, as he has appeared to have been satisfied with her rapid progress with SW. It is Smith's 'unquestionable right' to engage as many masters and to change them as often as he likes, but SW regards Smith's behaviour as inconsistent with the 'complete approbation' that he has previously expressed regarding SW's teaching. SW has always felt 'considerable zeal' to make Smith's daughter a good player, and he had always supposed it was Smith's intention that SW should have 'the full credit' for his exertions, and that she should be considered exclusively his pupil.

The friendship subsisting between SW and [John Baptist] Cramer will always prevent the possibility of Cramer suspecting SW of 'an atom of jealousy' about the 'eminence of his abilities'. SW does not retract his opinion given to Smith that Cramer is 'the prince of pianoforte players', or rather 'the emperor, for the word prince has deservedly fallen into some disrepute'. At the same time, Cramer knows that, after 30 years of teaching experience, SW understands the principles of piano playing as well as Cramer. If Smith should decide that he wishes his daughter to continue with SW, SW would have no objection to attending her, whoever Mrs Barnes may employ to teach the other pupils.

BJ→Editor, *NMMR*   about 12/5/1809

NMMR, v 1 no. 5, July 1809, pp 76–77   Having read in your Publication
ltr undated in *NMMR*[221]

BJ 'cannot overlook ''J.P.'s' 'impudent attack' on SW ['J.P.'→Editor, *NMMR*, 4/1809]. SW's 'integrity and independence of spirit' are well known, and his unrivalled 'genius and skill in the art and science of music' are acknowledged by everyone 'who knows what music is'. 'J.P.'s accusation that SW, in his lecture at the Royal Institution, concealed or was ignorant of the imperfections in [William] Hawkes's 'improvement of the chromatic scale', is envious, malicious and hypercritical. In that lecture SW 'candidly' confessed that Hawkes's 'organ was not perfect beyond five sharps and flats' and illustrated this by musical examples. BJ indicates passages in compositions that SW played at the Royal

---

[221] Ltr placed here because it apparently precedes SW→BJ, about 15/5/1809, in which SW characterises 'J.P'. as BJ's correspondent.

Institution 'that can be made little or nothing of on an organ or piano-forte according to the old system' but 'had a most beautiful effect' on the new system [of Hawkes]. BJ believes that his arguments prove that it is not SW but 'J.P.' 'who is guilty of deception' by attempting 'to obscure the merit' of Hawkes's 'valuable improvement'.

SW→Crotch   15/5/1809

RCM Ms 3073; *O*   I am much obliged to your Attention concerning Bach.
⬛ Mon 15 May={1799,1809,1815}[222]

SW thanks Crotch for his 'attention' concerning JSB. SW obtained JSB's *Choral Vorspiele* some months ago [from Joseph Gwilt, *see* SW→BJ?, 26/4/1809?]. He is glad that Crotch now has a copy and is sure that it will give him much delight. SW particularly recommends certain pieces. He points out that the German titles are the first words of Lutheran hymns, to which JSB added 'all that florid counterpoint in fugue and canon' which 'produces on the organ the most magnificent effect'. SW will try to attend Crotch's lecture tomorrow [16/5/1809, at the Hanover Square Rooms] but unfortunately is not likely to have returned from Turnham Green in time for it.

SW→BJ[223]   about 15/5/1809

EUL Dk 7.38 3[224]; *O*   I am told (how truly I cannot answer) that my
no date on extant portions of ltr[225]

SW has been told (how accurately, he does not know) that his 'antagonist' and BJ's correspondent ['J.P.', *see* 'J.P.'→Editor, *NMMR*, 4/1809] is the blind organist John Purkis [1781–1849]. When told recently that SW defended the 'new temperament' [of Hawkes], Purkis replied 'does he?' [remainder of page missing].

SW's 'lecture' [at the Royal Institution] has been held back. The managers pretend that the reason is that they did not receive SW's 'heads' [the subjects of the lecture] in time to have cards printed, but 'all the fools of fashion', who are a large majority of SW's audience, are 'running helter-skelter, pell-mell to the Epsom races' [held 18–20/5/1809], leaving the lecture room 'as empty as their own heads'.

---

[222] Assigned to 1809 because ltr addressed to Crotch at Duchess Street where he lived from 1808 to 1813 (*Rennert*, pp 50, 64).

[223] Ltr addressed to 'Dear Sir'. The recipient is identifiable as BJ because he was 'J.P.''s correspondent (*see* BJ→Editor, *NMMR*, 13/3/1809?).

[224] Ltr is torn, with considerable text missing.

[225] Ltr assigned to 1809 from ref. to 'J.P.' (*see* 'J.P.'→Editor, *NMMR*, 4/1809). 15/5/1809 appears to be a plausible approximate date because ltr suggests that the Epsom Races will take place in the coming week, and in 1809 they were held from 18 to 20 May.

Only two lectures have been scheduled [at the Royal Institution] this week: one by [Sir Humphry] Davy [1778–1829] [end of page missing].

SW begs BJ's pardon for disappointing him of [copies of the first of] the [CFH/SW edition of JSB's organ] trios: SW's carrier does not deliver as far as BJ's address.[226] SW will send some copies to [Muzio] Clementi's [music shop in Tottenham Court Road] with a note saying that they are for BJ. SW has fixed to have his 'morning party' [concert] on Saturday 3/6/1809 [at the Hanover Square Rooms]. CFH has lent SW a 'divine motet' by JSB ['Jesu, meine Freude'] for five voices, which SW is adapting to Latin words ['Jesus, decus meus']. The original German words are 'always harsh, and mostly unintelligible to an English audience'. SW hates the German language as much as he respects the German people. The reason why the cards announcing the trio [probably the first JSB organ trio arranged by CFH and SW] were not delivered [end of page missing].

SW is informed 'that it will be advisable for us to print' [as had been announced in the 1/12/1808 *MM*] the anthems by [William] Croft [1677?–1727] and [Maurice] Greene [1696?–1755] on 'less expensive paper'; otherwise 'the concern is by no means likely to answer'.[227] SW desires a meeting on this subject and will summon [John] Page [1760?–1812, vicar choral of St Paul's Cathedral and editor of music, who participated with SW in this publication]. SW would appreciate BJ's presence [at the meeting] and hopes that there will be 'an improvement in arrangements'. Today SW received five subscribers' names from a Dean and Chapter and is promised five more from [end of page missing].

SW→Tebaldo Monzani   Camden Town   26/5/1809

K; *O*   Mr S. Wesley desires Mr Monzani's Acceptance of the enclosed
▣ Fri 26 May & 🖅→ⓘ

SW wishes [Tebaldo] Monzani [1762–1839, of the firm Monzani & Hill, music publishers] to accept the 24 enclosed tickets [probably for SW's 'musical morning party' in the Hanover Square Rooms on 3/6/1809] for sale, and to notify SW if more tickets are required.

---

[226] As noted below in the Editions and Arrangements section of the list of SW's musical works, the first trio was published not later than 5/5/1809.

[227] Publication of the first number of SW's edition of Croft's and Greene's anthems was noticed in the *MM*, v 27 (1/2/1809) p 66, whose commentator particularly praised the 'fine execution' done by the music engraver, [James] Balls. No evidence that subsequent numbers of this edition were published has come to our attention.

SW→BJ?[228]   **29/5/1809?**
RCM Ms 2130, ltr 21; *O*   You must play the Trio, will ye nill ye
▣ Monday morning[229]
   The recipient must play 'the trio' [presumably the first of the six JSB trios
'adapted' by CFH and SW]. SW cannot fix Thursday [for a meeting] until the
day of 'our grand vocal rehearsal' is settled. This depends upon Mrs [Elizabeth]
Vaughan and the other singers being gathered to prove that JSB was 'no mere
organist' [by performing JSB's motet *Jesu meine Freude* in SW's 3/6/1809
concert]. 'Cerberus' [not identified] has been known to say that JSB wrote good
organ music, but his vocal music must have been 'strange stuff'.

SW→Willoughby Lacy   Camden Town   **20/6/1809**
K; *O*   Mr Samuel Wesley will have the Pleasure of calling on Mr Lacey
▣ 20/6/1809
   SW will be pleased to call on 'Mr Lacey' [Willoughby Lacy, actor and theatre
manager, 1749–1831] between 11 am and noon tomorrow [21/6/1809] to
examine 'the state of the organ at the room in the Haymarket' [the Opera
Concert Room in the King's Theatre, where Lacy was licensed to hold a musical
performance for his benefit on 22/6/1809, at which SW played an extempore
organ voluntary].

'J.P.'→Editor, *NMMR*   **about 10/7/1809**
NMMR v 1no 6, August 1809, p 93–94   I address you with deference
ltr undated in *NMMR* but printed following a letter dated 8/7/1809
   If SW will not himself venture to say that 'J.P.' is incorrect regarding SW's
lecture [at the Royal Institution concerning William Hawkes's organ], nothing
that BJ can say on the subject [*see* BJ→Editor, *NMMR*, about 12/5/1809] is
worthy of 'J.P.'s notice.

---

[228] Ltr addressed to 'My dear Sir'. Ltr included in *Jacobs* but BJ cannot be
confirmed as recipient from ltr's content.

[229] Ltr assigned to 29/5/1809 because ref. to forthcoming rehearsal of JSB vocal
music presumed to be rehearsal for SW's 'musical morning party' in Hanover
Square New Rooms on 3/6/1809, when JSB's motet *Jesu meine Freude* was first
performed in England. Ltr >SW→BJ, about 15/5/1809, when SW informs BJ
that the date of this concert has been set. Monday 22/5/1809 not ruled out, but
29/5/1809 preferred on presumption that there was only one 'grand vocal'
rehearsal of this concert and that this occurred close to the concert date.

Picart→SW   Camden Town   **22/7/1809?**
ltr quoted in SW→BJ, 24/7/1809[230]   ...I am sorry my confused expressions
ltr undated in quotation[231]
    Picart explains the type of music manuscript paper he has in mind and is sorry
that his 'confused expressions' have troubled SW.

SW→BJ[232]   Camden Town   **24/7/1809**
RCM Ms 2130, ltr 10; *O*   The Reverend Canon Picart hath a most unhappy
▣ 24/7/1809
    When SW returned [home] today he received news of several 'vexations and
impudent things' which put him 'out of humour'. He was glad to be diverted by
a letter from Picart, 'our sacerdotal Bachist', concerning music manuscript
paper, from which SW quotes [Picart→SW, 22/7/1809?]. SW also describes
humorously the 'cheap' greasy writing paper that he is using to write this letter.

SW→Graeff   **28/7/1809?**
Add 60753 f 120; *O*   You will excuse my asking you upon a Sheet of Coarse
▣ Fri 28 July & wmk 180- →{1809,1815,1820}[233]
    SW asks if Graeff can visit this evening. SW knows that Graeff has 'no taste
for the sublime or beautiful in music', otherwise SW might offer some operatic
music by [Vincenzo] Pucitta [Italian composer, 1778–1861, from 1809 to 1814
composer and music director of the King's Theatre, London] or 'divertimentos
with triangular accompaniments' by [Louis] von Esch [*d*1825]. As it is, they will
have to 'drudge through some of old Bach's [JSB's] humbug dismal ditties, all
so devoid of air, taste, sentiment, science or contrivance' that SW is astonished
how a sensible man like Graeff could ever have admired such an 'impostor'.
This demonstrates what 'ignorant pretenders to musical knowledge' Germans
such as Graeff are. SW apologises for writing on a sheet of 'coarse copy paper'.

---

[230] The quotation may be not the first line of ltr. The original ltr has not been
located.

[231] Ltr assigned to Saturday 22/7/1809 on the assumption that SW→BJ,
24/7/1809 was written immediately after ltr's receipt.

[232] BJ named as recipient in ltr , which is addressed to 'My dear Sir'.

[233] Ltr assigned to 1809 because of the watermark year (the last digit of wmk is
unclear) and because Pucitta was in London then: three of his operas were
performed in London in 1809 before 28 July. Also, SW's mention of his use of
poor-quality writing paper accords with his similar comments in SW→BJ,
24/7/1809. In July 1820 SW was in a very low state, contrary to the exuberance
of this letter. However, 1815 has not been ruled out.

SW→'J.P.'   Camden Town   **10/8/1809**
NMMR v 1 no 7 (Sept. 1809) p 113   I am perfectly ready and willing to defend
🖻 10 Aug; 1809 because ltr replies to J.P.→Editor, *NMMR*, about 10/7/1809
   SW is 'ready and willing' to defend every position he advanced in his course of
lectures at the Royal Institution. He is 'totally unconcerned' by 'J.P.'s
'unprovoked attack'. However, BJ [in BJ→Editor, *NMMR*, about 12/5/1809] has
already ably and fully refuted 'J.P.''s alleged arguments. SW has 'long
determined' against 'controversy with anonymous adversaries'. 'J.P.' must
disclose his name if he desires SW's future notice.

David Loeschman→Editor, *NMMR*   **19/8/1809**
NMMR v 1 no 7 (Sept. 1809) p 113   I conceive that the letter I addressed
🖻 19/8/1809
   The 8/7/1809 letter by David Loeschman [inventor of the Grand Harmonic
Piano-Forte] to the editor of the *NMMR* [published in v 1 no. 6 (August 1809)
p 113] 'brought' BJ and SW to Loeschman's house on 10/8/1809. BJ then
'confessed himself in error with regard to what he had sent to your magazine'
[BJ→Editor, *NMMR*, about 12/5/1809] to Loeschman's detriment. Several
eminent musicians have approved Loeschman's invention. Loeschman wants the
publicity of the present letter to counteract BJ's 'unjust aspersions'.

SW→SGW   **28/8/1809**
UCSB in Ms 33   It is very probable that some of your communicative
🖻 Mon 28 Aug & ref. to Tamworth music meeting held 21–22/9/1809→ 🛈
   SW is travelling to Tamworth, Staffordshire next month to conduct 'at a grand
music meeting'. There will be two concerts and two oratorios in the church. SW
would like to spend a quiet day with SGW before he leaves and asks what day
next week would be convenient. He hopes that her Brighton trip was agreeable.
'Mrs W' [CLW] and the children send best regards.

SW→Mary Beardmore[234]   Camden Town   **31/8/1809**
LU A.L. 293/1; *O*   I delayed answering your last obliging Letter
🖻 31 Aug; pmk 1/9/1809
   SW delayed answering Mary Beardmore's letter [not preserved] as he had
hoped he would be able to rearrange his engagements and attend her and her
sister [Frances Beardmore] at Canonbury [their home at 5 Canonbury Place,
Islington], according to their wish. He is afraid he cannot do so at all regularly,
as he is too busy to be able to clear three hours in a morning. He suggests that a
place should be found within half an hour's journey from Camden Town and

---

[234] Ltr addressed to 'Miss Beardmore'. Recipient presumably Mary Beardmore
for the reason given in the footnote to SW→Mary Beardmore, 7/7/1808.

that he should teach them there. If this would be convenient, he will arrange to secure a piano at some musical friend's house, and will teach them there. He will look out some music and will send it to Milk Street [their father's business premises].

Sarah & CW Jr→Henrietta Fordyce   2/9/1809

Baker 'Wesley Family' folder in	*Sarah:*	The pleasure I received from the
unnumbered box of autographs	*CW Jr:*	How I should rejoice My Dear

✉ 2 Sept; pmk 2/9/1809

Sarah: not relevant to Source Book

CW Jr: As Sarah has 'met ingratitude of no common kind from a near quarter' [presumably SW], CW Jr could not introduce to Mrs Fordyce 'a near relation' [presumably SW] when at Bath. CW Jr wishes this relative 'good' and wants him 'to see things in a better light' regarding his real friends. It is charming 'when genius and morals unite'; when 'they do not, good advice raises enmity'.

CB→SW   Camden Town   2/9/1809?

ltr quoted in SW→BJ, 4/9/1809[235]   ...I believe Mr Salomon is now out of Town
SW→CB, 4/9/1809, says ltr received '5 minutes ago'[236]

Salomon told CB at their last meeting that SW possesses some sonatas by JSB with a fine violin part.[237] Salomon wants CB to hear these sonatas. When CB returns to London [from Buckinghamshire] he would like Salomon and SW to play the sonatas to him. As CB has 'no violin in order', SW should prevail upon Salomon to supply one of his own violins. CB anticipates 'rapturously applauding the composition and performance'.

'X.Y.Z.'→Editor, *NMMR*   3/9/1809

NMMR, v 1 no. 8, Oct 1809, p 134   Having perused in your last number
NMMR

An anonymous correspondent signing himself 'X.Y.Z.' writes that 'eminent professors', including SW, were invited by David Loeschman to see his 'first attempt' to build a musical instrument that could produce 17 sounds in each 'septave' [the 'space' of seven consecutive notes of a diatonic scale]. SW 'played on the instrument, but did not see the mechanism' that moves the

---

[235] Only a portion of ltr is quoted. The original ltr has not been located.

[236] Assigned to Saturday 2/9/1809 because ltr written in Buckinghamshire.

[237] On 11/8/1809 SW purchased, at Henry Escher's bookshop for 18/-, JSB's *Clavier Sonaten mit obligater Violine*, BWV 1014–1019, published in Zürich *c*1801 by Nägeli. SW's copy is now at the RCM, shelf-mark H414 (score) and H515 (violin part).

hammers, for which Loeschman later received a patent [British patent 3250, granted 26/7/1809]. After trying out the instrument SW 'most ungenerously' and untruly wrote a letter [not preserved] to [William] Hawkes at Newport, Shropshire, asserting that Loeschman had infringed upon Hawkes's patent [British patent 3154, granted 25/7/1808]. SW did this 'unhandsome act' without informing Loeschman, 'who would readily have undeceived him'. Subsequently, in March 1809, Hawkes wrote to Loeschman rudely 'demanding satisfaction' for the alleged infringement.

SW→CB[238]   Camden Town   **4/9/1809**
Osborn MSS 3, Box 16, folder 1193; *O*   I am glad to find that your welcome
⊟ 4/9/1809
SW received CB's letter [CB→SW, 2/9/1809?] five minutes ago. CB should let SW know when he is returning from Bulstrode [the Buckinghamshire country house of William Henry Cavendish Bentinck, 3rd Duke of Portland, 1738–1809, at this time Prime Minister] so that SW can arrange to perform the 'lovely sonatas' [JSB's violin sonatas] that Salomon mentioned. CB's comment that JSB's preludes [in the '48'] are 'as modern, as if composed only yesterday' applies equally to the sonatas. The Allegro of the first sonata [BWV 1014] has a 'very original and plaintive' motif, which SW quotes.

SW played the violin 'very well some 30 years ago' but stopped playing after losing a favourite violin in a hackney coach [*see* SW→Shepherd, 26/12/1783]. JSB's sonatas have 'regenerated' SW's 'liking of the instrument' and he can now play the sonatas 'without much difficulty or blundering'. If Salomon is unavailable, SW could bring a good pianist to Chelsea College with whom he could perform these sonatas for CB.

The words of SW's oratorio *Ruth* were written by [Thomas] Haweis [1734–1820], 'an excellent judge of music' and a clergyman in Lady Huntingdon's Connexion [Selina Hastings, Countess of Huntingdon, 1707–1791, a friend of JW and CW, notwithstanding religious differences].

SW agrees with CB that [Christopher] Smart [poet, 1722–1771] was 'a very superior man'. If SW mistakes not [apparently he did mistake], Smart wrote the words for [Samuel] Arnold's oratorio *The Cure of Saul*.

SW hopes to receive another letter from CB before he leaves Bulstrode.

---

[238] CB identified as addressee because ltr bears a symbol used by his daughter Frances Burney d'Arblay.

SW→BJ[239] **4/9/1809**

RCM Ms 2130, ltr 12[240]; *O*   I omitted to observe to You either on Saturday
▣ Mon 4 Sep={1809} & SW's forthcoming visit to Tamworth→⊡

SW forgot on Saturday [2/9/1809] and on Sunday [3/9/1809] to ask BJ to get
him some good, cheap music manuscript paper so that he can complete the parts
of his [organ] concerto [in D] before going to Tamworth. CB's letter [CB→SW,
2/9/1809?], which SW has just received and from which he quotes, shows CB's
conversion to the cause of JSB and establishes that 'one is never too old to
learn'. CB's past criticisms of JSB's music should now be 'cordially' forgiven; it
would be unreasonable to expect CB 'when tottering over the grave' to revoke
them publicly.

SW plans soon to set down his views 'on the various and inimitable
excellencies of THE MAN' [JSB]. He refers to 'our challenge to Jack Pudding'
['J.P.']. Before leaving for Tamworth SW desires one more meeting [with BJ] at
Surrey.

SW→BJ   Birmingham   **25/9/1809**

RCM Ms 2130, ltr 13; *O*   I have the Comfort of acquainting You
▣ 25/9/1809

SW travelled to Tamworth by overnight coach in bad weather last Monday
night [18/9/1809]. His Tamworth visit was successful and his health improved.
The location of the church organ 'obliged' him to use a mirror to see Frank [i.e.,
François] Cramer [who led the Tamworth Festival orchestra in a gallery at the
west end of the church]. SW's [organ] concerto [in D major] was 'excessively
praised' and the 'fugue of our Sebastian' [SW's arrangement of the D major
fugue from part 1 of JSB's '48' (BWV 850), forming the concerto's penultimate
movement] 'produced a glorious effect' [on 22/9/1809].

In Birmingham SW played on the piano, to great acclaim, a fantasia
[improvised piece] which he concluded with 'Roly Poly Gammon and Spinach',
at a concert [at the Theatre Royal on 23/9/1809] arranged by [Samuel] Buggins
[Birmingham musician, *bap*1766]. SW plans to leave Birmingham tomorrow
morning [26/9/1809] via 'the Oxford two day coach', to avoid excessive fatigue.
He longs 'to see all our Sebastian squad' [the admirers of JSB's music] when he
returns to London.

---

[239] Ltr addressed to 'My dear Sir'. BJ identified as recipient because ltr refers to
Surrey and. to 'our challenge' to 'J.P.'.

[240] A four-line poem in SW's autograph, entitled 'J.P.', is preserved at RCM Ms
2130 f 45r and may (as asserted in *Jacobs* p 33) have been sent to BJ with this
ltr.

Sarah→Adam Clarke   **25/9/1809?**

MA DDWF/14/25   I hope to be with you Tomorrow at Two

☞ Monday morning; pmk 1809[241]

Sarah hopes to see Adam Clarke [scholar and Methodist minister, 1762–1832] tomorrow [26/9/1809] regarding the Surry Institution [of which he was Secretary at this time]. She thinks that SW 'would not come'. She understands that SW is 'in Leicestershire'. SW's terms [for lecturing] 'are not only high, but he wants [musical] instruments'. Instruments were procured for him 'last year' [presumably last season, i.e., earlier in 1809, at the Royal Institution].

Sarah wishes that Clarke 'could prevail' on CW Jr 'to accept the lectureship' [at the Surry Institution]. He has 'yet more science' than SW but 'is more diffident of his abilities than those who possess them in such a degree commonly are'. Sarah has told CW Jr that 'he could obtain the situation if he would take it'. She is sure that Clarke 'would wish to engage any modest man of merit', especially one named 'Wesley'. All of SW's musical knowledge 'is derived from' CW Jr. Because SW has 'a more brilliant imagination and confidence in his powers, he carries off much of the glory'. CW Jr does not envy this. Sarah must introduce CW Jr to Clarke, whom CW Jr is 'very desirous' of meeting.[242] CW Jr is 'a worthy man' inclined 'to everything good', is not spoiled 'by the favour of the great' and is 'fond of the Methodists'.

SW→BJ   **28/9/1809?**

EUL Dk 7.38 3;[243] *O*   ...the Mind, increases the Indisposition of the Body.

☞ 'Thursday 28th 1809'={28/9/1809,28/12/1809}[244]

SW encloses 7/-, which he is ashamed not to have sent earlier for the cards that BJ has had printed. SW likes the way BJ's printer has done them and will use him again. SW hopes that BJ will approve of 'the proposals annexed' [not identified] which SW longs 'to see floating about in the world without further loss'. SW was informed yesterday 'in the most confident manner' that 'our 'J. P.'' [their *NMMR* correspondent] is the Honorable Mr [George] Pomeroy

---

[241] Ltr <SW→Editor, *NMMR*, 9/10/1809, as SW then was engaged to lecture at the Surry Institution. Ltr assigned to 25/9/1809 because (1) Sarah says in ltr that she believes SW is in Leicestershire; (2) the only known 1809 trip by SW to places near Leicestershire is his September trip to Tamworth and Birmingham; SW did not leave London for Tamworth until Monday night 18/9/1809 (*see* SW→BJ, 25/9/1809) and so was away from London on a Monday only on 25/9/1809, when he was in Birmingham.

[242] CW Jr recorded in his diary (MA DDWF/23/12) that he and Sarah called to see Adam Clarke about 8/11/1809 and saw his library.

[243] The manuscript of this ltr is badly torn with considerable text, including the beginning of ltr, missing.

[244] Assigned to 28/9/1809 because of the currency of the ref. to 'J.P.'. However, 28/12/1809 has not been ruled out.

[*b*1764, son of Arthur Pomeroy, 1723–1798, 1st Viscount Harberton], whom SW has 'always extremely disliked' as 'a most conceited pretender to musical criticism'. SW regrets that he cannot see BJ next Sunday but will let him know when a visit is possible. SW sends best wishes to BJ's wife and children.

SW→BJ?[245]   **30/9/1809?**

RCM Ms 2130, ltr 18; *O*   I am in the utmost Distress, and there is no one
ltr undated[246]

SW is 'in the utmost distress'. Only the recipient can help. CB is 'stark staring mad' to hear JSB's [violin] sonatas [*see* CB→SW, 2/9/1809?]. After hearing from SW about the recipient's 'adroit management' of JSB's music, CB has resolved to hear these sonatas performed by the recipient on the keyboard and SW on the violin [*see* SW→CB, 4/9/1809].

CB has appointed next Monday [2/10/1809] at noon for the performance 'as this is the only time he has left before a second excursion to the country' [presumably to stay again at Bulstrode]. SW will 'put off to Tuesday' [3/10/1809] the 'three private pupils' he had planned to see on Monday and hopes that the recipient can do likewise, as 'the triumph' of CB 'over his own ignorance and prejudice [regarding JSB] is such a glorious event' that some sacrifice is appropriate to enjoy it.

SW told CB that 'young Kollmann' [George Augustus Kollmann, pianist and organist, 1789–1845, AFCK's son] was 'quite capable' of playing [the keyboard part of] these sonatas but, in the enclosed letter [to SW, not preserved], CB says that he prefers to hear the recipient play. Unless the recipient 'comes forward' tomorrow [1/10/1809, presumably to rehearse the sonatas] 'we are utterly ruined'. SW cannot dine with the recipient tomorrow but proposes to breakfast with him at 9.30 am. SW will bring the sonatas then so that the recipient can 'peep' at them before Monday's performance.

SW anticipates the effect of announcing to the public that CB, 'who has heard almost all the music of other folks', listened 'with delight at almost 90 years old' [in fact, he was 83] to the music of JSB, 'whom he so unknowingly and rashly

---

[245] Ltr addressed to 'Dear Friend'. Ltr included in *Jacobs* but BJ cannot be confirmed as recipient from ltr's content. In extant letters that are unquestionably to BJ SW consistently used the salutation 'Dear Sir' or 'My dear Sir' and not 'Dear Friend'.

[246] Ltr presumably after the Duke of Portland's 28/9/1809 letter to CB (Osborn) inviting him to visit Bulstrode for a second time that year. Ltr assigned to 30/9/1809 on the assumptions (1) that CB received the Duke's letter on 29/9/1809 and decided to return to Bulstrode the following week, and (2) that CB then wrote to SW on 29/9/1809 requesting to hear JSB's violin sonatas on the following Monday, 2/10/1809. A later date for ltr appears unlikely because, shortly after writing to CB, the Duke became seriously ill: he resigned from government not later than 4/10/1809 (when the new prime minister, Spencer Perceval, assumed office) and died on 30/10/1809.

had condemned'. This announcement will confound and silence such 'pygmy puerile puppies' as [George Ebenezer] Williams [1783–1819, deputy organist of Westminster Abbey] and [John Stafford] Smith [1750–1836, Master of the Children at the Chapel Royal].

SW→CFH?[247]   **1/10/1809?**

RCM Ms 2130, ltr 17; *O*   Huzza!—Old Wig for ever, and confusion of Face
ltr undated[248]

[Samuel] Chappell [c1782–1834] of [Robert] Birchall's [music publishing firm] stopped SW in New Bond Street [where Birchall's shop was located] and said that people are demanding to know when SW intends 'to bring forward the fugues in all the 24 keys' [the planned SW/CFH edition of JSB's '48']. Chappell advised that 'twelve of the first set' should be published as soon as possible. SW perceives that Chappell and Birchall would be glad 'to get the concern' [the copyright] into their hands but tells CFH that 'we shall be too cunning to suffer that'. SW suggests that CFH make without delay a 'strict revision' for the press of the first 12 preludes and fugues from SW's own copy, which CFH now has.

Chappell has sold six copies of the second [JSB trio in the CFH/SW edition] and wants six more copies directly.[249] Chappell also wants all copies SW can find of his organ voluntaries [opus 6] printed by [William] Hodsoll [music seller and publisher]. SW urges CFH to make known everywhere the demand for JSB's music at Birchall's, 'the most brilliant music shop in London'.

SW cannot express sufficiently his thanks that God made his organ performances a 'humble engine' in bringing JSB's music 'into due notice'. SW and CFH should lose no time 'in forwarding such harmony on earth', which tends to bring mankind 'to the celestial'. It is remarkable and providential that JSB was 'an exemplary instance of unaffected piety, and of the mildest Christian virtues'. Men such as [George Ebenezer] Williams and [John Stafford] Smith 'may be considered as Satan's implements to thwart the designs of Providence'.

---

[247] Ltr has no salutation or address portion. CFH presumed as addressee because SW says in ltr that 'we' shall be too cunning to let the copyright of the SW/CFH edition of the '48' fall into Birchall's hands.

[248] Ltr presumed to date from about the same time as CW→BJ, 30/9/1809?, because both letters refer to the vanquishing of Williams and Smith. Also, the first of the CFH/SW editions of JSB trios was published in early May 1809; and presumably several months elapsed before the second trio was published and multiple copies of it were sold.

[249] As the trios were published by CFH and SW jointly, they presumably were responsible for supplying music shops with copies.

SW→Tebaldo Monzani   4/10/1809
WCL LDWMM 1997/6603   [not available]
▣ Wed 4 Oct={1797,1809,1815}[250]
   SW asks if Monzani wishes to purchase for £10 the copyright of SW's 'little burlesca' ['I walked to Camden Town'], which SW thinks has 'every chance of becoming popular'.

SW→Editor, *NMMR*   Camden Town   9/10/1809
NMMR, v 1 no. 9 (Nov 1809) p 154   Having engaged to deliver a course
NMMR
   SW has engaged to deliver a course of lectures at the Surry Institution, commencing in 'the next month' [11/1809]. He invites his adversaries 'J.P.' and 'X.Y.Z.', who have criticised him anonymously in the *NMMR*, to attend and to hear 'their gross ignorance and defamatory falsehoods duly exposed'.

SW→BJ[251]   5/11/1809
RCM Ms 2130, ltr 14; *O*   Enclosed is the Card I promised.
▣ Sunday night 5 Nov; pmk 1809
   SW encloses the promised card [not preserved, probably an admission ticket to his 7/11/1809 lecture] and hopes that BJ will attend SW's first Surry Institution lecture on Tuesday [7/11/1809]. Although BJ has 'both heard [presumably at the Royal Institution] and read' this lecture before, SW has improved it in a few places and seeks BJ's opinion of the changes. SW looks forward to conversing with BJ afterwards at 'the lock-up house' [a house of detention, presumably a humorous reference to BJ's home, where SW sometimes spent the night], especially about BJ's 'party at the [Surrey] Chapel' and 'the immediate promulgation of THE MAN' [JSB].
   SW's services today 'to the Scarlet W. of Babylon' [the Roman Catholic Church, probably at the Portuguese Embassy Chapel] were gratefully received. If 'Roman [Catholic] doctrines were like the Roman [Catholic] music we should have Heaven upon earth'.

---

[250] Assigned to 1809 because of ref. in ltr to SW's 'burlesca'. As far as is known, SW composed only one 'burlesca', entitled 'I walked to Camden Town'. Of all the years when 4 October was a Wednesday, SW lived in Camden Town only in 1809.

[251] Ltr addressed to 'My dear Sir'. BJ presumed to be the recipient because of SW's ref. to promulgating 'THE MAN', a name of JSB previously used in SW→BJ, 4/9/1809 and not known to have been used by SW in letters to others.

SW→BJ[252]   Camden Town   **6/11/1809?**
RCM Ms 2130, ltr 22; *O*   You will think me sufficiently stupid
▣ Monday evening[253]
  In his letter to BJ last night [presumably SW→BJ?, 5/11/1809], SW forgot to say that he intends to visit BJ tomorrow before lecturing nearby [at the Surry Institution]. BJ had previously invited SW to Charlotte Street [BJ's home] after the lecture.

BJ→John Bacon   **18/11/1809**
GEU in box 6   A thousand praises are due to you for so excellent a portrait
▣ 18/11/1809
  Extensive praise is due to Bacon for his 'excellent' and 'correct' portrait of BJ's friend SW, which BJ had requested. BJ often has been astonished and delighted by SW's performances, and Bacon's written description [not preserved] of one makes BJ 'glow with rapture'. BJ is amused by Bacon's idea of SW 'being the dragon', as SW 'is supposed to be a Roman Catholic'.

SW→BJ   **24/11/1809**
RCM Ms 2130, ltr 15; *O*   I wish your Opinion of delivering to each Person
▣ Friday; pmk 24/11/1809 (a Friday)
  SW seeks BJ's opinion about delivering a card announcing [the CFH/SW publication of] the JSB Trios to each person who presents a ticket [to the concert at the Surrey Chapel] on Wednesday [29/11/1809]. SW thinks that [the Rev. Rowland] Hill could hardly object to this. SW will bring a supply of cards tomorrow [25/11/1809], but will leave the decision [about distributing them on Wednesday] to BJ. SW has sent notices of Wednesday's event to Hoare, [Thomas] Wright, Hammersley 'and some other bankers of consequence', and

---

[252] Ltr addressed to 'My dear Sir'. BJ identified as addressee from ref. to Charlotte Street [BJ's home].

[253] The statement in ltr that BJ's Charlotte Street home is 'at so near a distance' from the place where SW lectures on Tuesday is taken to imply that the lecture was at the Surry Institution. SW engaged to read six lectures there in 1809 (*see* SW→Knight Spencer?, 9/12/1809), and also lectured there in 1810 and 1811. The 1810 lectures were on Monday and Thursday evenings; the 1811 lectures appear to have been on Wednesdays (*see* SW→Knight Spencer?, 7/4/1811). SW appears therefore to have lectured at the Surry Institution on Tuesdays only in 1809. His first 1809 lecture there was on 7/11/1809 (*see* SW→BJ?, 5/11/1809) so 6/11/1809 is the earliest possible date for ltr. Ltr assigned to 6/11/1809 because it says SW wrote to BJ the previous night and SW→BJ?, 5/11/1809 is plausibly that letter; no later letters from SW to BJ written on Sunday nights in 1809 are known, but the possibility that ltr was written on a later Monday in 1809 has not been ruled out.

asks if BJ can borrow a *Court Guide* for the names of other appropriate recipients. All these bankers are musical and will 'prate' about the event, so there is a good chance that SW and BJ will be paid for their work 'at a future opportunity'. SW has not notified M[atthew] P[eter] King [composer, 1773?–1823] about Wednesday's event and leaves this to BJ.

SW 'longs to know' what BJ has written to CW Jr [not preserved], who probably will regard BJ's 'setting J.C.B. [John Christian Bach, or possibly a mistake for JSB[254]] before G.F.H. [Handel]' as 'an unpardonable sin'. SW fears that 'no lecture on prejudice will ever eradicate' CW Jr's [prejudice].

For tomorrow's rehearsals SW proposes that BJ borrow Joseph Gwilt's copy of the 'Zürich fugues' [the Nägeli edition of JSB's '48'] and a Stradivarius violin from 'Professor Perkins' [perhaps James Marshall Perkins, violinist], although SW doubts that this will prove as suitable as his 'own tender Stainer' [a violin made by Jacob Stainer, 1617?–1683]. SW, who now (2 pm) is at Turnham Green, plans to see BJ about 6 pm today.

SW→BJ[255]   **2/12/1809?**
RCM Ms 2130, ltr 19; *O*   Many Thanks for your early and kind Attention.
▣ Saturday[256]
SW thanks BJ for promptly sending the 'numbers' [of the *NMMR*] including the number containing 'the commencement of the attack' [on SW]. They will

---

[254] EW supposed that SW had made this mistake, as she silently altered SW's 'J.C.B.' to 'J.S.B.' on p 38 of *Jacobs*.

[255] Ltr addressed to 'My dear Sir'. BJ presumed as recipient because of ref. to SW and recipient having fun next Tuesday in connection with 'J.P.' and 'X.Y.Z.'.

[256] Ltr refers to SW's lecture next Tuesday in which he will attack two anonymous writers who he thinks are one person. SW→Knight Spencer?, 9/12/1809, is SW's response to a complaint about this lecture, which therefore presumably took place on Tuesday 5/12/1809. Ltr accordingly has been assigned to 2/12/1809, the immediately previous Saturday. This assigned date is consistent with Mrs Billington thanking SW for the 'feast on Wednesday', which plausibly refers to the performances by SW and BJ of JSB's music at Surrey Chapel on Wednesday 29/11/1809. The possibility that SW's lecture took place on Tuesday 28/11/1809 and that ltr was written on 25/11/1809 seems unlikely, as SW→BJ, 24/11/1809, states SW's plan to be with BJ on 25/11/1809, making it improbable that SW would that day write to thank BJ for his early and kind attention in sending numbers of the *NMMR*. Although earlier November Saturdays have not been positively eliminated the assignment of ltr to 2/12/1809 plausibly presumes that Spencer? responded quickly rather than protractedly to the complaint. The occasion for complaint cannot have been SW's first Surry Institution lecture on 7/11/1809, as SW→BJ, 5/11/1809, makes clear that this lecture was substantially a repeat of a lecture that SW had earlier read elsewhere.

have 'fun alive' next Tuesday [5/12/1809, at SW's Surry Institution lecture]. SW is convinced that 'J.P.' and 'X.Y.Z.' are one person; if this person comes [to the lecture], SW may have 'some murder to answer for'. Mrs [Elizabeth] Billington has sent SW a letter [not preserved], thanking him for the feast on Wednesday [presumably the Surrey Chapel concert on 29/11/1809] and inviting him to a feast 'of the alderman sort' at her house. In a letter [not preserved] to SW, WL has asked for the return of his two books. SW would like BJ to arrange to have this done before Tuesday, if possible.

SW→SGW   **9/12/1809**
MA DDWF/15/15   A reverend Friend of mine in the Country, a Mr Jeaffreson
☞ Sat 9 Dec & SGW at Woodstock Street→ ⓘ
   The Rev. Mr [Christopher] Jeaffreson [1770–c1847, at this time curate of Tunstall, Suffolk], whose wife SW taught when she was recently in London, has sent SW two brace of birds. SW presents one brace to SGW. If she arranges to get both brace from his house [at Camden Town] this evening he will arrange to get the remaining brace tomorrow [10/12/1809] from Woodstock Street [her house]. He asks to be remembered to CW Jr and to 'all inquiring friends'. SW also received a hare which he probably will 'reserve for home'.

SW→Knight Spencer?[257]   **9/12/1809**
RCM Ms 2130, ltr 16; *O*   I have received the Favour of your Letter
☞ 9/12/1809
   Replying to a letter [from an officer of the Surry Institution, not preserved], SW defends his actions in raising, in his recent lecture there on the subject of 'Musical Deception', the controversy between himself and 'two anonymous antagonists' ['J.P.' and 'X.Y.Z.'], whom he suspects are one person. SW was not discussing a private squabble but was responding to an attack on 'the whole body of musical professors'. He is disinclined to 'make amends' for an act which he cannot 'consider in the light of an offence'. Because of 'pressure of engagement', he declines his correspondent's suggestion that he read an additional lecture beyond the six he had engaged to read.

---

[257] Ltr addressed to 'Sir'. A non-autograph pencil note on ltr names the recipient as 'Knight Spenser Esqre/Surry Institution', possibly copied from an address portion of ltr that subsequently was discarded. Knight Spencer succeeded Adam Clarke as Secretary of the Surry Institution in 1809, but the date of his succession has not been determined.

SW→Langshaw Jr Camden Town **26/12/1809**
GEU W/L; *Wainwright* p 71–72; *O* Although you may not have entirely
📧 26/12/1809

For a long time, SW and Langshaw Jr have neither seen each other nor corresponded. SW understands that an organ is to be constructed in Langshaw Jr's 'quarter of the world' [Lancaster], for which estimates have been or are being supplied by 'various makers'. SW states that 'there is no organ builder in England' better suited to the task than [Thomas] Elliot, who built SW's 'own organ'. SW agreed to have this organ limited 'to three stops' to obtain 'the advantage of an octave of double base pedals'. 'All the judges who have heard' the organ have been delighted with its tone. SW sends best wishes to Langshaw Jr's family.

SW→SGW **8/1/1810**
BL Add 35012 f 18 When I saw your Superscription yesterday, I supposed
📧 Mon 8 Jan={1798,1810,1816}[258]

When SW yesterday [7/1/1810] saw a letter [not preserved] addressed to him in SGW's hand, he thought that the text of the letter would be written by her. However, the letter was from CW Jr, inviting SW to visit next Thursday [11/1/1810]. SGW should tell CW Jr that SW will be glad to accept. He is very busy and hopes that 4 pm is not too late for them to dine as he cannot arrive earlier. He may bring one of the boys with him, probably John [JWW].

SW→Charles John Smyth Camden Town **10/1/1810**
BL Eg. 2159 f 68; *O* I am sorry that I have not sooner had an Opportunity
📧 10 Jan; pmk 11/1/1810

In a letter [not preserved] to 'our friend Linley' [WL or his brother, the Rev. Ozias Linley, 1765–1831], the Rev. Charles John Smyth [writer on music, 1760–1827, at this time rector of Great Fakenham, Suffolk] asked about [Thomas] Elliot's organ 'constructed upon Mr [William] Hawkes's plan of temperament', which SW 'exhibited at the Royal Institution' [during his 1809 lectures]. SW apologises for his delay in replying; a satisfactory answer required him to consult Elliot.

This organ had only three stops: two diapasons and a principal. Smyth correctly noted that the beatings of an imperfect consonance 'would be multiplied by the compounds' [mixture stops] and that 'the thirds ought to be good, or compounds excluded'. In 'the false old temperament', in which E♭ and D♯ (like other enharmonic equivalents) 'passed for the same tone', the former sounded 'highly delightful' and the latter 'quite intolerable'. SW quotes comments by Elliot on

---

[258] Ltr >8/1/1798 because JWW then not yet born. 1816 ruled out because CW III then was aged 22 so not a boy and SSW was not welcome at CW Jr's house. Therefore ltr assigned to 1810.

temperament: that certain beats (for instance) 'are so faint that the most critical ear cannot distinguish them from perfect'. SW can certify the truth of these comments as a result of 'various experiments' that he made 'at Elliot's house two days ago' [8/1/1810]. Theory may always be refined 'beyond what can ever be reducible to practice'. If 'harmony on an organ can be sufficiently improved by temperament to entirely remove objectionable sounds', and to bring every chord to something approaching perfection, one ought to be content. SW believes that Hawkes's scheme has done this 'in the extraneous keys' and that 'Elliot's temperament has sufficiently improved the others'.

SW→SGW   Camden Town   **13/1/1810**
GEU Wesley Coll. ltr 54   You were perfectly right in your Conjecture
📧 'Saturday 12 January', an incorrect date[259]
SGW correctly conjectured that 'Charles' took away the list of JSB's works [presumably CW Jr, as CW III is not known to have been interested in JSB's music]. SW apologises for causing trouble but, as he had mislaid a former list and had got AFCK to write out a new one, he was 'the more ashamed' of his carelessness. Jack [JWW] will mend as many of SGW's pens as she likes; she has been a kind friend to him. SW looks forward to spending a day with SGW when she is 'quite at leisure'. He asks on what morning he made an appointment 'to breakfast with Miss Cope'.

SW→SGW   **18/1/1810**
MA DDWes/6/55; *O*   I hope that you did not wait Dinner for any of my People
📧 18/1/1810
SW hopes that SGW did not delay dinner or provide extraordinarily for any of his 'people'. It was impossible for SW to come yesterday [17/1/1810] and he had no way of letting SGW know in time. Emma has the whooping cough but is much better. SGW's intelligence came too late for him to breakfast with 'Miss Coope' [Miss Cope]. He thinks that her address is 14 New North Street, Bloomsbury, although he is unsure of the house number. SGW should give SW three or four days notice when she next wishes him to dine with her as he is 'widely distributed' and letters frequently arrive too late for him to give a 'commodious' answer.
SW asks to be remembered to CW Jr. If CW Jr should go to St Paul's Cathedral on Sunday [21/1/1810] he will hear the fugue in three movements (with three flats) [JSB's 'St Anne' fugue, BWV 552] that he played with SW the other night, and which he was so delighted with, on that 'noble organ with the double base'. The service begins at 3.15 pm.

---

[259] 12 January was not a Saturday during the years that SW lived at Camden Town. Ltr assigned to Saturday, 13/1/1810, as SW's planned breakfast with Miss Cope mentioned in ltr also is mentioned in SW→SGW, 18/1/1810.

SW→CW Jr   **3/2/1810**

GEU Wesley Coll. ltr 68; *O*   You have often heard & read in the Gospel
🖃 3/2/1810

In a letter to SW [not preserved], CW Jr said that he was prevented by another engagement from going on 30/1/1810 to a theatre [to Covent Garden Theatre, where SW was performing his organ concerto in D major]. However, CW Jr was observed in a lower box of that theatre on that date, enjoying a concerto. SW inquires whether the observation was of CW Jr or of his ghost.

SW→CW Jr   c/o Ball's, Duke St, Grosvenor Sq   **16/2/1810**

Fitzwm ltr 14; *O*   I send you a divine Scrap of 'the old Wig'
🖃 Fri 16 Feb & CW Jr at Great Woodstock Street→ ⓘ

SW encloses 'a divine scrap of the old wig' [JSB's organ chorale prelude 'Schmücke dich, O liebe Seele', BWV 654]. It is on an old Lutheran tune which SW remembers having heard many years ago at the Savoy [German] chapel. SW and Hugh Reinagle ['cellist and composer, 1759–1785] went into the chapel around 10 am and then to some other places of worship, returning about two hours later, where they found the congregation and the organist [Charles Frederick] Baumgarten [*c*1738–1824] hard at work on the same tune. It is sung while people are receiving the sacrament.

SW is devising a plan [presumably an agreement to support CLW and their children] which must deliver him from many vexations and which, if delayed, would eventually cause him to 'look through a grate' for life. He has been a 'dupe' and a 'slave' to the most unworthy of women [CLW].

SW→SGW   **2–3/1810**

MA DDWes/6/53   I am much concerned to find that you are being pestered
ltr undated; written not long after SW's departure from Camden Town[260]

SW is 'much concerned' that SGW is being 'pestered continually' on his account by 'bad people'. He has had a violent cold and toothache but is much better, and is well cared for [presumably by SS]. This 'was never the case at Camden Town', where he was 'shamefully neglected' [by CLW] and 'might have perished' just at the time he was setting out for Tamworth [in September

---

[260] SW's last letter explicitly written from Camden Town is assigned to 13/1/1810, but SW apparently still lived there when he wrote SW→SGW, 18/1/1810, which mentions Emma's whooping cough and SW's 'people' coming to dine at SGW's house. SW presumably had left Camden Town (and CLW) before he wrote, from James Ball's house, SW→CW Jr, 16/2/1810, which calls CLW the most unworthy of women and states that SW is devising a plan, presumably to support her and their children. Ltr placed here because SW declares in it that he will never return to Camden Town, that a settlement [with CLW] 'must shortly take place', and that he wishes to see his children at SGW's house without CLW.

1809] were it not for the 'humane and tender attention' of a person [SS] falsely represented to SGW as a 'worthless abandoned strumpet'.

SW will 'no longer remain with an abominable creature in female shape' [CLW] whose extravagance was hurrying him to ruin and whose 'insolence and vulgarity' can no longer be borne. CLW's claim to be SW's wife (other than having a claim on part of his property) is 'a joke' or a lie. She has not been SW's wife (in the scriptural sense) since the birth [in February 1806] of the last child [Emma], and therefore, according to 'one of the highest legal authorities', SW can enforce a plea of divorce in the ecclesiastical court whenever he chooses. He will not desert 'an object [SS] who has been scandalously abused' unless she should reverse her behaviour towards him.

No other man would have had 'half the forbearance' that SW has shown towards CLW's 'unworthy conduct'. He is now 'acting under the most calm and prudent advice' and will do nothing unjust. He does not intend to leave CLW 'distressed, or even straitened' as far as his circumstances permit, and will do his best for his children, whom he loves. Time will prove that he is not deserting his family. But he will not again enter his [Camden Town] house to meet the 'disgusting and violent behaviour' that he experienced when he last went there on business. A settlement [with CLW] 'must shortly take place'. He wishes to meet his children at SGW's house on any day when she is 'quite alone'.

SW→Bridgetower   29/3/1810
BL Add 56411; *O*   I much regret having been unable to fix a moment hitherto
▣ Thu 29 Mar; pmk 1810
SW regrets his delay in fixing a date for a meeting with Bridgetower and proposes next Sunday [1/4/1810], when a few of the 'orthodox harmonists' will meet at [Edward] Stephenson's home, 29 Queen Square, to celebrate JSB's birthday.[261]

Sarah→?   20/4/1810
GEU in box 6   I was in the Country when your Friend brought your Letter
▣ 20/4/1810
CW Jr has 'arrived at much honour'. He proves that 'happiness attends a virtuous life'. Sarah wishes that she could say the same of the rest of her family. One [SW's] branch 'has caused us much trouble'; 'without morals, we cannot expect tender affections or social duties'.

---

[261] JSB was born on 21 March 1685 OS, which converts to 1 April 1685 NS.

SW→SGW   25/4/1810

MA DDWF/15/16   I can manage to dine with You To=morrow at half past 4.

▭ Wed 25 Apr & SGW at Great Woodstock Street→ⓘ

SW can dine with SGW tomorrow [26/4/1810] at 4.30 pm but must leave early, as he is engaged to play in a concert in the evening. They will talk over the subject she mentions, on which she need not be uneasy, as Mr [James] Ball 'is doing everything for the best'. SW will come at the first opportunity but will not be able to bring 'Johnny' [JWW].

SW→'Dear Sir'   15/5/1810

McGee[262]   ...Please to favor me with the Name of any one of them

▭ 'Tuesday 15 May'={1810} & SW at Catch Club→ⓘ [263]

SW asks who his correspondent thinks is 'best qualified to take a part' in the enclosed Glee by Salomon and seeks a reply at the Catch Club this evening, where SW will remain until 10 pm.

Shepherd→Sarah   4/6/1810

MA Letters Chiefly to Wesleys v 1 ltr 46   I am going to answer you by

▭ 4/6/1810

Shepherd thinks that 'it can do no harm' for Sarah to see 'the poor little infant' [Emma] when Emma comes to SGW's house, but if Sarah went to see Emma at CLW's home this 'might give cause for lies and misapprehensions' [regarding Sarah's loyalty to SW]. Shepherd advises that Emma be removed from CLW; otherwise, CLW might perhaps 'rear up a little viper to sling you all to madness'.

CB→SW[264]   27/6/1810

BL Add 11730 f 33   Since we last met, I have been but 3 days see-able

▭ 27/6/1810

Since CB and SW last met, CB has been 'seeable' on only three days because of various ailments, but the recent warm weather has enabled him to leave his

---

[262] Ltr is a torn sheet, in which the initial portion including the salutation is missing. SW's enclosure has not been preserved with ltr.

[263] Assigned to 1810 because the Catch Club register (BL H2788yy) states that SW visited that club on 15/5/1810 at the invitation of WL (who had been elected a member in 1809), and no record has been found that SW visited the Catch Club on any other Tuesday 15 May.

[264] SW not named in ltr but identified as recipient in annotation on ltr probably by VN, who presented Add. Ms 11730 to the British Museum in 1840. This identification is confirmed by subject of ltr (*see* CB→SW, 16/7/1810?).

bedroom and to 'breathe the more pure air' of his library. CB will be happy to receive SW and his 'illustrious Portuguese friend' [VN], but cannot do this until the following week. SW's 'comprehensive encomia' on the talents and intellect of VN make CB impatient to meet him. CB asks SW to name his choice of day.

CB→SW   **16/7/1810?**
DLC Music Div. Moldenhauer Archives   Now my French Packet is off my
ltr undated[265]
CB has thought further about SW's plan for 'rehearsing' JSB's [*Goldberg*] *Variations* in his presence. Although CB's initial reaction 'must have seemed very cold'—he had thought his 'little parlour' had insufficient room to accommodate 'two large instruments of equal force and magnitude'—he now realises 'that there would be sufficient space' if this room were 'unbe-littered'. Moreover, CB's earlier suggestion that SW and VN perform the *Variations* in a pianoforte shop on two instruments 'nicely tuned together' was made without recalling his intention never to go 'into the open air again'. CB has 'caught a fresh cold' and has two painful teeth, but begs that the planned performance take place 'during the warm weather'. CB then will be able to tell the larvae that he meets after he dies 'how the wonderful wonders' of JSB were played 'by the zealous and indefatigable' SW and VN. SW accordingly should send his instrument and name his day or days and hours for the promised performance 'before the end of the present month'. CB suggests that the 30 variations be 'decimated' into three sets of ten, performing each set once or twice each day, as this 'will allow us time to breathe, digest and judge'.

SW→CB   Adam's Row   **17/7/1810**
Osborn MSS 3, Box 16, folder 1193; *O*   I am right glad to find that upon
⌨ 17/7/1810
SW is glad that CB no longer fears that placing 'one additional instrument' in CB's apartment might cause its collapse. All is now set for performing the 'comical pieces' [JSB's *Goldberg Variations*] there. SW expects to see VN today or tomorrow when a time will be fixed that least interferes with CB's 'more important concerns'. SW thinks that CB's proposal [in CB→SW, 16/7/1810?] to 'decimate' the *Variations* [to perform ten variations on each of three days] would be 'cruel'. The 'whole series' of variations can be played in not 'much more than one hour', and as they 'are all upon one theme' they should be heard together. Nevertheless, SW will defer to CB's wishes on this matter.

---

[265] Assigned to 16/7/1810 because ltr is answered by SW→CB, 17/7/1810.

CB→SW & VN   Adam's Row   **19/7/1810**
BL Add 11730 f 35r   With best Comp. a. Virtuosissmo Sigr Vincenzo
⬛ Thu 19 July & 🖎→🛈
   CB asks SW and VN to send their 'lumber-dy instrument' before 10 am
tomorrow [20/7/1810], so that it can be tuned in unison with CB's own piano.
CB would rather meet them at 11 am than at noon or 1 pm. He is now 'entirely
for' the performance of [JSB's *Goldberg*] *Variations* 'de suite' [consecutively].
If there is time after a complete performance, they can discuss the *Variations* or
can play them again.

SW→SGW   **12/9/1810**
MA DDWes/6/51   You have been grossly misinformed concerning the State
⬛ 12 Sep; pmk 1810
   SGW has been 'grossly misinformed' about the state of SW's household. The
only people who have been 'inmates' in his lodgings are the nurse and SS's
sister, who has saved the expense of washerwomen. A lying-in month [for the
birth of SSW on 14/8/1810] was never gone through with less expense: a great
contrast to the 'reign' of CLW, 'when the house was full of gossips and hangers-
on from morning till night'. SGW should not to listen to the tattle of CLW's
servant, whom CLW uses to 'propagate all manner of villainy'.
   SW was never so little embarrassed financially as at present.

SGW & CW Jr→Sarah   **28/9/1810**
MA DDWF/21/24   *SGW:*   I thank you for your letter &
                         CW Jr: I thank you for your letter, which I
⬛ 28/9/1810
SGW: SGW expects SW and his children [CW III, JWW and Emma] to dine
with her next Thursday [4/10/1810].
   CW Jr: SW is 'pretty well'.

SW→Street?[266]   Adam's Row   **11/10/1810**
BL Add 56228 ltr 1; *O*   I have this Day experienced a little Disappointment
⬛ 11 Oct[267]
   SW today 'experienced a little disappointment'. About a year ago, an
acquaintance 'obligingly' lent him £20. When he repaid it, the acquaintance said
that he would be happy to lend him more money on a similar occasion. On the

---

[266] Ltr addressed to 'My dear Sir'. Street, to whom most other letters in this
manuscript are addressed, is a plausible recipient (*see* SW→Street, 25/5/1830),
but no specific evidence that he was the recipient of ltr has been found.

[267] Assigned to 1810 because ltr mentions SW's removal from Camden Town to
Hampstead Road, which occurred in 1810.

strength of this offer, SW applied to him yesterday [10/10/1810] for the loan of £50, on whatever terms he might consider 'not only safe but even advantageous'. The acquaintance refused, saying that he had recently advanced a large sum 'on account of a brother' [presumably a fellow Freemason] and was therefore unable to help.

SW knows that if the recipient can lend SW £20 he will. SW wishes the recipient to advise the date when he requires repayment. SW asks that if the recipient is not able to lend SW the money himself he might negotiate the loan among his 'numerous and respectable City monde'. SW wishes to have a 'tête-à-tête talk' with the recipient about a number of matters which have 'conduced' to his 'migration from Camden Town' to his 'present place of abode'.

SW→SGW   3/11/1810

MA DDWF/15/47   I am sorry that it is not in my power to dine with You
☞ Sat 3 Nov={1804,1810,1821}[268]

SW is unable to dine with SGW today. He is engaged to his friend [Joseph] Major, who has a party of 'ladies' with music. SW will sleep at Major's house. SW has no apprehensions about his journey. The nights have now become moonlit, and the Mail [coach] in which he has booked a place [to Birmingham] is known to be the safest coach available. He asks to be remembered to CW Jr. SW probably will call in to see SGW tomorrow about 2.30 pm.

SW→SS[269]   Birmingham   7/11/1810

BL Add 35012 f 29   You see I pick your Pocket sadly by sending you Letter
☞ Wed 7 Nov; pmk 1810

SW writes again to SS [earlier letters to SS not preserved] about the book that [Thomas] Vaughan sent him to take to Birmingham. SW left this book— Haydn's *La Tempesta*, with Italian words—behind. If SS and Mrs Rowley cannot find it, SS is to send for [Robert Thomas] Skarratt [music engraver and composer]. Someone must call on Vaughan in Dean Street, Soho, for the English words, on account of [Joseph] Moore [Birmingham benefactor and promoter of music festivals there, 1766–1851]. If SS can accomplish this by 4 pm tomorrow [8/11/1810], she should direct the parcel to Moore, and send it to the Green Man and Still [an inn] in Oxford Street, to go by the Mail coach [to Birmingham].

SS must not expect 'Mr Pug' [a nickname at this time for SW] until Sunday [11/11/1810]. He will leave Birmingham on Saturday evening [10/11/1810] at 8

---

[268] Assigned to 1810 for the following reason: 1804 excluded because on 3/11/1804 SW was in London and SGW was in Bath; 1821 excluded because SGW then was no longer reading or writing letters. Also, ltr mentions SW's planned coach journey; SW→SS, 7/11/1810, establishes that he arrived in Birmingham before that date.

[269] SW always addressed his letters to SS as 'Mrs Wesley'.

pm and arrive at the Green Man and Still about 1 pm Sunday [11/11/1810]. SS may come there and wait for 'Mr Faw' [another nickname for SW].

CW Jr→Sarah   15/12/1810
MA DDWF/20/44   I fear much my Dear Sarah, I shall intrude
⊟ Sat 15 Dec & CW Jr at Woodstock Street, Nottingham Place→ ⓘ
  CW Jr hears that SW will be 'here' [Woodstock Street, Nottingham Place] on Wednesday [19/12/1810], to take leave of SGW 'before he goes to Suffolk to a clergyman for the Christmas holidays' [in fact, SW arrived at Rev. Christopher Jeaffreson's home in Tunstall, Suffolk, on 7/1/1811, *see* SW→SS, 6/1/1811].

SW→Knight Spencer?[270]   Adam's Row   3/1/1811
Currier; O   I have received the Favour of your Letter
⊟ Thu 3 Jan & 🖎→ⓘ
  The recipient's letter [not preserved] has been received. SW is concerned that his first lecture [of his course of lectures at the Surry Institution] cannot be postponed, because the text he planned to read has 'fallen among thieves' and he will be pressed for time to prepare a new one.
  For his course of lectures SW will require only one piano (not two) and the same organ [built by Thomas Elliot] that was used last season. As the first lecture will be on temperament, it will be necessary to make 'an alteration in the management of the pipes of the organ', which Elliot informs SW will cost £5. This expense is necessary if SW is to make clear 'a doctrine in the distribution of the musical scale which is of the utmost importance in the improvement of harmony on keyed instruments'. He hopes that there will be no objection to the expense. Elliot, whose address is Tottenham Court, New Road, requires an answer as soon as possible if he is to complete the work before 14/1/1811 [the scheduled date of the first lecture].

SW→SS   Woodbridge   6/1/1811
BL Add 35012 f 30[271]   Mr Pug has not got to Mr Jeaffreson's yet
⊟ Sun 6 Jan; pmk 1811
  'Mr Pug' [SW] has not yet arrived at [the Rev. Christopher] Jeaffreson's in Tunstall, but will go there tomorrow [7/1/1811] in a post-chaise. They [SW and an unidentified companion] got to Colchester yesterday afternoon but could not go further, on account of snow drifts, and had to stay overnight. Early this morning they decided to walk 18 miles to Ipswich, leaving their luggage to be

---

[270] Ltr addressed to 'Dear Sir'. Text of ltr indicates that the recipient was associated with the Surry Institution. As SW wrote to Knight Spencer on a similar subject on 1/2/1811, he presumably also was the recipient of this ltr.

[271] Ltr is incomplete.

sent on after them. They arrived at Ipswich at 2 pm and set off in the Woodbridge coach about 4 pm. SW asks Pexy [SS] to send him more money.

SW→SS   Tunstall, Suffolk   **9/1/1811?**
BL Add 35012 f 32   I could not get a Letter sent to the Post Office
ltr undated, pmk Melton [near Tunstall]²⁷²
SW was unable to send a letter earlier. He has received SS's letter [not preserved] and the £1 note. He is not yet sure whether [Rev. Christopher] Jeaffreson will consider SW's loss in the way that SS desires; if Jeaffreson does, SW will have money to spare, but SW does not intend at present to hint to Jeaffreson that he wants the loss made good. SW is sorry that 'little Boy Blue' [SSW] is poorly. SS should ask VN about the proofs of the 'fugues' [of book 2 of the SW/CFH edition of the '48'] sent to VN by Lomax, the engraver.

SW→SS   Tunstall   **15/1/1811**
BL Add 35012 f 36   I received your Letter last night.
☞ 15/1/1811
SW is sorry to hear from SS's letter [not preserved] that she is short of money. He has not spent any money while at Tunstall but will need to give the servants a present on his departure. He thinks he will leave next Monday [21/1/1811] at the latest and will let SS know where and when she is to meet him in London. He longs to talk to her. The Jeaffresons are very kind and obliging. He has been riding, and went to the seaside yesterday [14/1/1811]. The sea in a storm is 'the very grandest effect in the world'; it is 'quite as astonishing as' JSB. SW is anxious about CW III, JWW and Emma, and wishes he could learn some news of them. He hopes that SSW is better.

SS should keep her spirits up. If she is distressed for money, she should apply to [James] Ball: an additional £1 would be a trifling addition to what SW already owes him. Despite the lavishness of life at Tunstall, SW wishes to be back home: he wants not luxury but comfort. SS should write. She should remember him to Mr [Richard] Twiss [writer, 1747–1821, who 'perambulated' Camden Town with SW, *see Smith* p 149] and to other friends. SW asks her to 'get the proof forward' of the 'fugues' [of book 2 of the SW/CFH edition of JSB's '48', *see* SW→SS, 9/1/1811?]; otherwise he will be in disgrace.

---

²⁷² Assigned to 9/1/1811 on presumption that SS received on 7/11/1811, and immediately replied to, SW→SS, 6/1/1811, in which SW says that he is going to Tunstall on 7/11/1811 and wants SS to send money. On this presumption SW would have received £1 from SS on 8/11/1811. which is consistent with SW saying in a 9/1/1811 ltr to SS that he could not write to her sooner and has received her £1. However, a later date for ltr cannot be ruled out.

SW→SS   Tunstall   **20/1/1811**
BL Add 35012 f 38   I have taken my Place for next Tuesday
▣ 20/1/1811

SW has reserved a seat for next Tuesday [22/1/1811] but does not know when
the coach will arrive in London. He supposes that it will stop at the Four Swans
[inn in Bishopsgate Street] or at the Spread Eagle [inn] in Fenchurch [in fact,
Gracechurch] Street. SS should inquire, as he wishes her to meet him on his
arrival.

[Rev. Christopher] Jeaffreson has not said anything about giving SW a present.
Jeaffreson paid 18/- for SW's travel and SW will repay him. SW then will have
only 11/- left. He cannot give the servants more than 5/- between them, and then
will have only 3/- to bring him to London. However, Mr [Zebedee] Tydemann [a
music teacher who lived in Framlingham, near Tunstall] asked Jeaffreson to pay
SW for two books of the 'fugues' [the SW/CFH edition of the '48', to which
Jeaffreson had subscribed]. This payment will give SW an additional 18/- for
emergencies.

SW→Knight Spencer   Adam's Row   **1/2/1811**
NjP John Wild Autograph Coll., vol. 13, leaf 103; *O*   When I called on
▣ 1/2/1811

SW called at the Surry Institution last Wednesday [30/1/1811] but Spencer was
out of town. SW wishes to know how many free tickets he may have to admit
friends to his lectures. His first lecture will be 'On the most eligible method of
acquiring an easy command of keyed instruments'.

Sarah→Sarah Tooth   **6/2/1811**
MA DDWes/6/23[273]   Many thanks for your kind Epistle, but the report
▣ Wed 6 Feb={1811}; pmk (on address portion) 6/2/1811

SGW was seized with 'a numbness in one hand' but now is much better.
Sarah's illness this winter stemmed from her damp bedroom, from which she
twice had to 'seek shelter' with friends. Sarah informs Sarah Tooth [*d*1830,
widow of Samuel Tooth] that the owners of the [Great Woodstock Street]
lodgings were 'far from civil' about the dampness. As they had 'gained peculiar
favour' with SGW 'by canting', and by receiving Sarah's 'unhappy brother'
[SW], SGW did not take up the matter as she might otherwise have done, but
was willing to wait until spring.

---

[273] The address portion of ltr is at MA DDWes/6/24.

SW→Knight Spencer?[274]   7/4/1811

BL Add 56411 f 25; *O*   I have written to Mr Spagnoletti

📧 Sun 7 Apr={1811}, docketed 7/4/1811

SW has written to [the violinist Paolo] Spagnoletti [1768–1834] desiring an immediate answer to the request of the subscribers concerning SW's final lecture next Wednesday [10/4/1811, at the Surry Institution]. Its subject, which SW announced at the end of his last lecture, will be 'the necessity of establishing a standard pitch for all keyed instruments, and the propriety of teaching beginners on good instruments'.

Richard J. S. Stevens 'Recollections'   27/4/1811

Camb Add 9109, v 2 p 127   Saturday April the 27th, we went to Mr Samuel
Entry for 27/4/1811

Stevens and his wife [Anna Maria] went to SW's morning benefit concert at the Hanover Square Rooms on 27/4/1811. A trio by SW was performed by SW, Stokes and VN 'on three grand piano fortes, the first attempt in England'. The composition was 'noisy' and not what Stevens expected to hear.

CW Jr→Sarah   30/4/1811

GEU in box 6   I thank you for yr kind favour but am not able

📧 30 April; pmk 1811

SGW is angry that CW Jr did not go to [SW's 27/4/1811] concert. CW Jr thought that Sarah 'would approve' his action. CW Jr hears that SW called on SGW when CW Jr was not at home, and that SW also is not pleased that CW Jr did not go. CW Jr asks Sarah 'not to mention the hints' he has given regarding this concert. 'All the world were there, applauding.' Therefore CW Jr thinks that he could not have been 'wanted or missed' at the concert.

SW→Sir   Adam's Row   21/5/1811

MA DDWF/15/24A; *O*   Upon consulting the State of my Engagements

📧 Tue 21 May & 📧→ⅈ

SW has consulted his diary for the time mentioned as the most likely for the writer's 'musical meeting' [not identified]. The lowest terms that SW can offer without detriment to his business in London is £42. SW has fixed this rate on the understanding that the concern is 'a matter of experiment' rather than of profitable certainty.

---

[274] Ltr, addressed to 'Dear Sir', refers to the recipient's 'institution'. Knight Spencer is presumed to be the recipient as ltr concerns Surry Institution lectures.

SW→VN 22/5/1811
BL Add 11729 f 1; *O* You may have been probably informed by a Lady
☞ Wed 22 May & SW/CFH edition of '48' partly complete→ⅰ

VN may have heard from a lady with whom SW dined on Sunday [19/5/1811]
that he stopped yesterday [21/5/1811] at VN's house to ask if VN wished him to
deputise [for VN as organist of the Portuguese Embassy Chapel] tomorrow
[23/5/1811, Ascension Day, requiring a sung Mass with organ]. The answer was
affirmative. SW will be at the Chapel tomorrow from 11 am to 1 pm. He asks
what music is to be performed.

VN is asked to leave out for SW 'Mr F's 2nd volume of the Zürich' [the copy
of the Nägeli edition of JSB's '48' owned by the Rev. William Victor Fryer,
1768–1844, Principal Chaplain of the Portuguese Embassy Chapel]. Fryer shall
have SW's '2 first numbers' [i.e., the first two books of the SW/CFH edition of
the '48'] 'with all expedition'. He also shall have the '2 latter' [the last two
books of this edition], if SW lives to edit them.

SW→SGW Adam's Row[275] 30/5/1811?
GEU Wesley Coll. ltr 69[276] In Consequence of a Demand rather suddenly
ltr undated by SW but annotated in pencil (by SGW?) 30/5/1811[277]

SW has to pay 'a demand rather suddenly made' upon CLW's account. This
has drained the cash which otherwise would have lasted him 'very well' until
Midsummer [24/6/1811], when he receives his half-yearly payments from the
two schools [at Paddington and Turnham Green] in which he teaches. If SGW
can lend SW 'a few pounds' now he will 'return them' as soon as he receives his
money. SW would not have troubled SGW 'had not the case been very urgent'.

SW→SGW Adam's Row 30/5/1811
Wcoll D6/1/444(b) I will call in after I have been at Paddington
☞ 30/5/1811

SW will visit SGW after he has been at Paddington.

SW→CW Jr 31/5/1811
BL Add 35012 f 117 I believe that you are not likely to suspect me
☞ 31/5/1811

SW is sure that CW Jr will not misunderstand his motives and will give him
credit for representing facts 'fairly, justly, and openly'. SW is always unwilling

---

[275] Ltr annotated in pencil (by SGW?) 'Hampstead Road'.

[276] The manuscript of ltr is incomplete.

[277] This assigned date is consistent with SW's statement in SW→CW Jr,
30/5/1811, that he regrets having had to trouble SGW on money matters.

to give SGW trouble of any kind, particularly on money matters. Nonetheless, CW Jr will be aware that the 'exorbitant demands' that have been made on SW for the payment of CLW's debts have made it very difficult for him to keep his head above water, or 'to avoid being dragged to jail'. Although SW little values 'money for its own sake' he must make every effort to save his children from 'absolute distress and want'.

CW Jr will remember that, after 'those concerts which failed at the Tottenham Street Rooms' [in 1802], he and SW were 'mutually hampered' how to clear their obligations to the performers, many of whom could 'scarcely be persuaded to relax in any part of their demands'. CW Jr also will remember that—in addition to sharing the expenses with him—SW, at the 'very pressing solicitation' of Sarah, consented to procure £100, at a time when he had property in 'the funds', 'which time is now past'. For this sum SW received a 'note of hand' [a promissory note] signed by both CW Jr and Sarah. SW is sure that CW Jr remembers this transaction and relies on CW Jr's sense of justice and honour to repay the debt.

SW is now hard pressed financially. He requests CW Jr and Sarah to advance whatever sum they can manage.

SW→Henry Liston	Adam's Row	**3/6/1811**
Liston p xv–xvi	Mr Samuel Wesley presents his respects to Mr Liston	
Liston		

SW has been falsely accused of inconsistency because he has praised both [William] Hawkes and [David] Loeschman for their different inventions designed to improve the production of harmony on the organ. SW likes the 'facility and simplicity' of Hawkes's invention. He also admires Loeschman's invention because it produces greater perfection of harmony, although at the cost of greater mechanical complexity. The improvements of [the Rev.] Mr [Henry] Liston [inventor of the 'euharmonic organ', 1771–1836] are different from the others' and also are meritorious: they enable 'minute intervals of sound' to be 'truly obtained', although considerable study and practice is required for a performer to master the system. SW assures Liston that he regards his invention as ingenious, practicable and a 'delightful acquisition to a nice musical ear'.

CW Jr→Sarah	**5/6/1811**
GEU in box 8	I hope you continue well, and that Miss d'Anvers is better.
☞ 5 June[278]	

SW 'is much distressed'. He has desired SGW to raise £100 from the money that Rebecca Gwynne left to him and to CW III [*see* Rebecca Gwynne will, 9/8/1799]. Mrs Roberts thinks that this is a good idea provided that SW gives a receipt and 'security in writing to pay the interest' to SGW. It would be hard for

---

[278] Assigned to 1811 because ltr discusses SW's plan to raise £100 from Rebecca Gwynne's legacy (*see* SW→SGW, 4/7/1811).

SGW, in her situation, to lose these interest payments. CW Jr pities SW and hopes that the Lord will turn SW's heart 'to the right channels'.

SW→Stokes   **6/6/1811**

MB **M408.2; *O*   I am neither 'a Liar', nor 'the Son of Darkness'

▣ Thu 6 June={1811,1816}[279]

   SW has called repeatedly, wanting to see Stokes. SW thinks Stokes, VN and he could 'make a few guineas' by performing 'the trio' [SW's Trio for three pianofortes, first performed by Stokes, VN and SW at SW's musical morning party in the Hanover Square Rooms on 27/4/1811] in the approaching holidays. Next Monday [10/6/1811] SW will 'take the pianoforte for Salomon' [i.e., will play the piano in the benefit concert for Salomon at the Hanover Square Rooms]. SW asks Stokes if he can turn [pages] for SW and come to the rehearsal on Saturday [8/6/1811] at 11 am.

SW→VN   Adam's Row   **3/7/1811**

BL Add 11729 f 3; *O*   Read (if you can, for 'tis a funny Hand) the Piece

▣ Wed 3 July; pmk 1811

   SW comments on the enclosed 'piece of paper' [not preserved]. SW and VN had a 'horrible disagreeable evening' at [Joseph] Gwilt's home on Sunday [30/6/1811]. WL, who lives at 11 Southampton Street, Strand, is 'impatient' to know the worst: SW asks VN to write to him.

   SW means to be with VN at Vespers on Sunday [7/7/1811] and will bring with him an organ pupil, a young man [not identified] from Birmingham. SW hopes that VN will come to hear WL's 'antim' [an unidentified anthem], which is to be tried over and criticised at SW's house on Sunday. SW sends his 'duty to honoured Madam' [Mary Sabilla Novello, VN's wife, *c*1789–1854].

SW→SGW   **4/7/1811**

MA 9788   I believe you know me utterly averse from giving you

▣ 4/7/1811

   SW is 'utterly averse' to giving SGW any uneasiness, especially on money matters. Nonetheless, he approaches her for financial assistance. When SW wrote to CW Jr [SW→CW Jr, 31/5/1811] about the £100 he advanced 'in addition to the equal share of the expenses' of the concerts 'which succeeded so ill' [at Hyde's Concert Rooms, Tottenham Street, in 1802], SGW gave SW 'some expectation' of raising about £25 in a short time and said it would be difficult to raise more in the short term. She sent him £5, which is all he has received since raising this matter.

---

[279] Assigned to 1811 because ltr mentions SW's *Trio for 3 Pianofortes* of which the manuscript is dated 20/4/1811; also, 1816 is after Salomon's death.

SW now wishes to discuss another way in which SGW can help him without any inconvenience to herself. SGW will remember that [her sister] Mrs [Rebecca] Gwynne bequeathed £50 to CW III, and that Mr [James] Waller was able to persuade her, 'much against her inclination', to leave SW the same amount, on condition that SGW received the interest on the whole £100 during SGW's life [*see* Rebecca Gwynne will, 9/8/1799]. SW asks if SGW has the inclination and power to give him his £50 soon. This would be a 'considerable help', for until he receives his half-yearly payment from both schools [at Paddington and Turnham Green], he cannot pay various bills that he is expecting. Even if SGW can let him have the £50 he must adopt a 'less expensive scheme' for the provision of his children. He has yet to pay £50 for CW III to 'his master' Mr Rivers [an apothecary]; this bill falls due in August, and SW will be hard pressed to meet it.

SW presumes that Mr [James] Pettit [from 1798 to 1821 an employee of the Bank of England] can give SGW a 'sound opinion' of the legality of her making over the legacy to SW while she lives.[280] SW is willing to pay SGW the interest she currently receives [from the legacy], so she would not be worse off by the change he proposes. He stresses the urgency of the situation and begs her to approach Pettit without delay.

SW→SGW   **10/7/1811?**
MA DDWF/15/25   The News you send is indeed as bad as can be
ltr undated[281]

The news that SGW sends [presumably James Pettit's advice that SGW cannot alter the terms of Rebecca Gwynne's will, according to which SW inherits £50 after SGW's death, *see* SW→SGW, 4/7/1811] is 'as bad as can be'. SW is 'not persuaded' that Mr P[ettit] has told the strict truth; however, 'that is of no consequence at present'. Time is 'too short' for SW to apply to his friends [for money], and 'it is not a little mortifying' that 'in two quarters' where SW is asking only for a part of what is really his own [the legacy, and money advanced in respect of the 1802 concerts], 'no one will come forward 'with spirit and propriety'.

SW's landlords are demanding their quarter's rent, which he promised them some days ago on the assumption that he could obtain some money from the family. CLW also expects her monthly allowance, which SW is unable to pay at present.

---

[280] Pettit's duties from 1805 concerned the 3% consolidated annuities in which the capital bequeathed by Rebecca Gwynne was invested. We are grateful to Sarah Millard, Deputy Archivist of the Bank of England, for information about Pettit's work at the Bank.

[281] Assigned to 10/7/1811 because ltr apparently written soon after SW→SGW, 4/7/1811, and SW's taking his 'place for tomorrow' is presumed to refer to a place in a stagecoach to Ipswich, where he arrived on 11/7/1811 (*see* SW→SS, 12/7/1811).

SW has taken his 'place for tomorrow' [booked a place in the 11/7/1811 stagecoach for his journey to Ipswich, *en route* to Tunstall], but matters will be 'in much perplexity' unless some money can be raised immediately 'to stop the present demands'.

SW→SS Tunstall **12/7/1811**
BL Add 35012 f 34 I am but just arrived here
▣ Friday 12; pmk 13/7/1811
SW has just arrived in Tunstall. He is safe and sound but could not get a conveyance from Ipswich last night, and had to stay there until today. He will write again tomorrow. If Evans [not identified] does not send the money, SS should 'serve him with a Marshalsea Writ and be damned to him'.

CW Jr & SGW→Sarah **15/7/1811**
MA DDWes/6/70 *CW Jr:* By what I heard from worthy Mrs Gregory
 SGW: My dear Sally will perceive I have no room
▣ Mon 15 July={1799,1805,1811,1816}[282]
CW Jr: Mr [James] Pettit has brought SGW a little money from the legacy left by CW Jr's aunt [Rebecca Gwynne] but 'cannot raise the sum at present' for SW [that under Rebecca Gwynne's will would come to SW after SGW's death]. SW has gone from town [to Tunstall].
SGW: Poor Sam' [SW] would be thankful to have £25 of his £100 [*see* SW→SGW, 4/7/1811, in which he had asked for £50, not £100] but SGW 'cannot get it' [*see* SW→SGW, 10/7/1811?].

SW→SGW Adam's Row **1/8/1811**
GEU Wesley Coll. ltr 70[283] Your Assistance was very Welcome & opportune
▣ 1 August; pmk 1811
SW thanks SGW for her 'very welcome and opportune' assistance. He trusts that in the not too distant future he will have 'some prospect of comfort' through the remainder of his life, without inconveniencing his friends. SGW knows that, 'had it not been for the vilest of women' [CLW], he would have been able to look after his needs. He has heard of 'an excellent school within 12 miles of London', to which he is contemplating sending JWW.

---

[282] Assigned to 1811 because ltr discusses SW's proposed transfer of Rebecca Gwynne's legacy, which is mentioned in other July 1811 letters but not in July letters of the other listed years; also, SW out of London on 15/7/1811.

[283] Only a portion of ltr is preserved.

SW→SGW   **5/8/1811?**

Dorset D/C00:G/C2   I am sorry it is out of my Power to see you To-Day

📧 Mon 5 Aug={1799,1805,1811,1816}[284]

SW is sorry that he cannot see SGW today. He is 'obliged to dine and sleep' at
his friend [Joseph] Gwilt's [home], from where he has just come. Tomorrow
[6/8/1811] SW must be at Turnham Green. He expects to return home by 6 pm.
SGW should write to him at home if there is anything urgent to communicate.
He can manage to see her on Wednesday [7/8/1811] if she is free.

SW→VN   **12/8/1811**

BL Add 11729 f 5; *O*   I have been groping in my Scapula's Lexicon

📧 Mon 12 Aug; pmk 1811

SW has been looking in his lexicon for a translation of a Greek inscription [on
a house] in Welbeck Street. He asks if VN requires him at 11 am or at 3 pm on
Thursday [15/8/1811, the Assumption of the Blessed Virgin Mary], and requests
that VN come to see him tomorrow [13/8/1811].

SW→VN   **3/9/1811?**

BL Add 11729 f 7; *O*   I saw J Elliott at Paddington Yesterday

📧 Tue 3 Sep={1805,1811,1816,1822}[285]

SW saw J. Elliott [probably the singer James Elliott, *see* SW→CW Jr,
15/1/1807] yesterday at Paddington. Elliott said that he intends to visit VN this
evening. SW will call in on VN on his return from the school, probably between
7 and 8 pm.

---

[284] Assigned to 1811 because SW's friendship with Joseph Gwilt appears to
have begun after 1805 and to have ended before 1816.

[285] Assigned to 1811 because if ref. to Paddington and school implies ref. to SW
teaching at Paddington no references to his teaching there have been found after
1813. 1805 unlikely because no <1808 references to VN associating with SW
have been found. However, the other listed years have not been specifically
ruled out.

SW→VN   **12/9/1811**
BL Add 11729 f 8; *O*   S. Webbe called on me Yesterday Evening
☞ Thu 12 Sep; pmk 1811

Yesterday evening [11/9/1811], SW discussed, with Samuel Webbe Jr [organist and composer, 1768–1843], VN's plans to visit Samuel Webbe Sr [composer, 1740–1816, VN's predecessor as organist of the Portuguese Embassy Chapel]. SW proposes next Sunday [15/9/1811] for the visit.

SW intends to be with VN at Vespers. Gwilt [probably Joseph Gwilt], with whom SW spent yesterday morning, wants to acquire a 'handsome' breviary. SW told him that he is negotiating with Victor Fryer, who wishes to dispose of one, and asks VN to convey Gwilt's interest to Fryer.

SW→VN   **27/9/1811**
BL Add 11729 f 31; *O*   Chappel has very conveniently sent me all
☞ Fri 27 Sep={1811} & ref. to proofs of the '48'→ⅈ

[Samuel] Chappell [who had left Robert Birchall earlier in 1811 to form the music publishing firm Chappell & Co., which with Robert Birchall printed books 3 and 4 of the SW/CFH edition of the '48'] has sent SW the [proofs of the] preludes and fugues of book 3 for correction. SW is 'going off' at 3 pm [to Birmingham, to direct the music festival there] and asks VN to assist him by correcting the engraver's proofs [in SW's absence].

SW→SGW   Adam's Row   **24/10/1811**
Fitzwm ltr 15   We find that there remains no other possible Method
☞ 24/10/1811

The only way to manage SW's affairs with his 'beloved wife' [CLW] is by 'proceeding to last extremities'. Her landlord 'some days ago' demanded another quarter's rent from SW, despite having been warned 'in the presence of witnesses not to trust her a shilling' on SW's account. SW is unwilling to advance any more money than at the rate of £100 he has agreed to allow her. He would go to prison rather than change his mind. CLW's landlord subsequently served a writ on SW which he 'bailed' until 6/11/1811. SW is confident that he will win the legal action as he had informed CLW's landlord that he would not be responsible for her debts, and Mr Swan [who was acting on behalf of SW, *see* CW III→Sarah, 5/6/1817] also knows this.[286]

SW has to pay £7/10/- by 6 pm today to settle the last bill he has out, and asks SGW for £5 towards this bill. If he dishonours it, his credit will be destroyed. He

---

[286] Perhaps this is the legal action mentioned by *Stevenson* p 443, who records that in 1812, in her 87th year, SGW was required to give testimony in a lawsuit 'commenced by a lawyer in an unjust claim upon her son'. That suit was settled out of court by arbitration, but the lawyer 'subsequently was struck off the rolls' for misconduct.

will call on SGW between 5 and 6 pm after he comes from [his teaching at] Paddington. He encloses a letter [not preserved] just received from John [JWW] and his [school] master.

Richard J. S. Stevens 'Recollections'   6/11/1811
Camb Add 9109 v 2 p 146   Wednesday November the 6th I went to St Stephens
Entry for 6/11/1811
  Stevens went to St Stephen Coleman Street on 6/11/1811 to hear SW, William Russell [organist, 1777–1813, from 1801 organist of the Foundling Hospital chapel, not the William Russell (musician) of earlier correspondence] and VN perform on the organ built by [John] Avery [organ builder, 1738–1808]. While SW was playing a fugue by JSB Russell doubled the bass notes an octave lower. This had 'a most grand effect'.

SW→VN   11/11/1811
BL Add 11729 f 10; *O*   I conclude by your not looking in last Night
☞ Mon 11 Nov={1805,1811,1816}[287]
  SW thinks that VN doubted SW's resolution of accompanying him to the Foundling Hospital chapel, as he did not call on SW last night [10/11/1811]. If VN can lend his Gradual to SW tomorrow he can make extracts before Saturday [16/11/1811], when he will return it. SW is considering where to begin the task of providing harmonisations for all the Gregorian chants and fears that it will prove impractical, in terms of the time it will take and the size and expense of the completed volume. He wishes to discuss the matter with VN and asks him to call in this evening. SW inquires if VN has heard anything '*touchant l'Etablissement de l'Ambassadeur*' [of Portugal], and would like to know whether there is 'a prospect of success'.[288] SW has been reading Rousseau.

SW→VN[289]   9/12/1811
EUL Dk 7.38 3; *O*   To Catholick Choirs & Organists. An erroneous Manner
☞ 9/12/1811
  SW informs 'Catholic choirs and organists' that, of the eight ecclesiastical modes, the first four 'ought always to be accompanied with a minor third upon their final note' and the latter four with a major third. SW will be pleased if his explanation, which includes musical examples, proves 'useful towards

---

[287] Assigned to 1811 because ltr discusses SW's harmonising Gregorian chants, an activity that occupied SW in 1811 and 1812 (*see*, for instance, SW→VN, 29/10/1812).

[288] The purpose of this inquiry has not been identified.

[289] The address portion names VN as the addressee. This item may have been enclosed with another letter that is now missing.

producing correctness and uniformity in this point of the Evening Church office', which has 'long needed' amendment owing to a failure to distinguish rightly the first from the sixth psalm tone.

SW→VN **24/12/1811**
BL Add 11729 f 111; *O*   I hope you remembered to remind Mr G.
🖃 'Tuesday 24'[290]

SW hopes that VN remembered to remind 'Mr G' [probably Joseph Gwilt] that SW and VN had forgotten their 'Xtmas Carol', and that Mr G had undertaken to return it to them in time for High Mass tomorrow [25/12/1811]. Salomon was in good form on Sunday [22/12/1811].

Timothy Essex→SW **14/1/1812**
ltr recorded in Madrigal Society Attendance & Transactions   [not known]
register 1785–1828 (BL Music Ms Loan)
Madrigal Society Attendance & Transactions register, entry for 14/1/1812

On behalf of the Madrigal Society, Timothy Essex [composer and organist, 1764–1847] invites SW to compose a madrigal for the Society's competition.[291]

SW→VN **8/2/1812**
BL Add 11729 f 12; *O*   Gwilt is engaged out To-morrow, but wishes us
🖃 8/2/1812

Gwilt [probably Joseph Gwilt] is engaged tomorrow but would like SW and VN to dine with him on the following Sunday [16/2/1812]. SW cannot be with VN at High Mass, having promised to meet 'Master Beale' [not identified] at Beale's church, St James, Clerkenwell. SW is not certain of being at Vespers, and so encloses a piece of music which could be rehearsed for one of VN's 'compline evenings': it is 'one of the sweetest descants on the 6th tone' that SW knows. SW hopes to be able to be at Vespers tomorrow [9/2/1812]; if he is there, he hopes that VN will return home with him afterwards, for a chat.

---

[290] Assigned to 24/12/1811 because the reference to a Christmas carol tomorrow suggests ltr written on Tuesday 24 December={1805,1811,1816}: 1816 excluded because Salomon then no longer alive; 1805 considered unlikely because no <1808 references to VN associating with SW have been found.

[291] According to the Madrigal Society register, similar invitations were sent at this time by Essex and others to Attwood, Crotch, WH, BJ, Salomon, Samuel Webbe Sr and Jr, and others. The prize was a silver cup valued at £10/10/-.

SW, CLW & George Oliver deed   Adam's Row   **25/3/1812**

MA DDCW/6/88   Whereas great and unhappy disputes and differences have
Deed of separation dated 25/3/1812

Because 'great and unhappy disputes and differences have arisen and do still
subsist' between SW and CLW they have agreed to live apart. SW agrees to pay
£130 a year 'for the maintenance and support' of CLW and her infant child
Emma.[292] This amount will be paid in 12 equal instalments, on the 25th day of
each month starting 25/4/1812, to George Oliver, linen draper of Skinner Street
in the City of London, as trustee for CLW. Oliver agrees to pay these sums in
full to CLW or to her appointees.

Under the will of her deceased maternal grandmother Nickelson of South
Carolina, USA, CLW is entitled to a share of this grandmother's residual
property. SW, who became entitled to this share 'by the rights of marriage',
agrees to pay half of the portion of that share to CLW, or to Oliver in trust for
CLW, that becomes due and payable during SW's and CLW's lifetime.

SW covenants that he will henceforth permit CLW, 'notwithstanding her
coverture', to live wherever she likes without molestation, challenge or demand,
'as if she were a *feme-sole*'. Oliver agrees that CLW shall not 'institute any
proceeding in any ecclesiastical or other court' against SW and, moreover,
indemnifies SW against his losses and costs if she does institute such
proceedings, unless SW's payment of any instalment of the agreed annuity is in
arrears by 14 days. This indenture also binds the heirs, the executors and the
administrators of the signatories.

SW→VN   **27/3/1812**

BL Add 11729 f 13; *O*   I could not meet you this Morning
⬛ Fri 27 Mar[293]

SW was unable to meet VN this morning or to be at the rehearsal yesterday
[26/3/1812], but wishes to know if VN will be at the [Portuguese Embassy]
Chapel this evening. If so, SW will meet VN in South Street [the location of the
Chapel] beforehand. SW will bring with him the '1st Nocturn of the Officium
Defunctorum'. He wishes to know why VN had mentioned being 'below stairs'
[at the Chapel] on Wednesday [25/3/1812].

---

[292] By 1825 SW's annual payment had been reduced to £25. *See* SW→VN,
3/5/1825.

[293] SW describes ltr's date as 'technically, *Feria sexta in Parasceve*', i.e., Good
Friday. Good Friday occurred on 27 March in 1807 and 1812. Assigned to 1812
because no references <1808 to VN associating with SW have been found.

SW→VN 31/3/1812
BL Add 11729 f 14; *O*   Your Organ at South Street is certainly 'strong
☐ 'Vigil of April Fools Day 1812'; pmk 31/3/1812
SW comments humorously on the recent mechanical failings of the Portuguese
Embassy Chapel organ and regrets that [George Pike] England does not pay
more attention to its maintenance [*see* SW→CW Jr, 28/10/1808]. SW discusses
arrangements for his concert on 5/6/1812: [Angelica] Catalani [Italian soprano,
1780–1849] has authorised SW [in a letter not preserved] to announce her
willingness to sing 'in aid of a forlorn (nearly blind) organist' [presumably a
humorous reference to SW himself, *see* SW→VN, 6/5/1812, which discusses
Catalani's cancellation]. SW has been recommended to speak to her 'on the
[Teresa] Bertinotti [Italian soprano, 1776–1854] question after her half pint of
Madeira'.

SW→Mr Freeling   Tottenham Ct   **26/4/1812**
Osborn file folder 15908; *O*   Mr Samuel Wesley presents his best Respects
☐ Sun 26 Apr & 📧→ⅈ
SW will be happy to attend Mr Freeling [not identified] tomorrow [27/4/1812],
as arranged by WL.

Francis Rawdon-Hastings→Col. McMahon   **28/4/1812**
Aspinall v 1 p 71   Among the other cares of Empire which assail the Prince
Aspinall
At the last Grand Lodge [Masonic meeting], it was voted to create the office of
Grand Organist. SW offered to play the organ without fee at all ceremonies in
the hall. The Lodge wished to designate SW Grand Organist, but Francis
Rawdon-Hastings [1754–1826, created 2nd Earl of Moira in 1793, Acting Grand
Master of the Society of Freemasons, 1790–1813] thinks that this decision
should be up to the Grand Master [the Prince Regent]. He asks Col. McMahon
[private secretary to the Prince Regent] to solicit the Prince's pleasure regarding
the appointment of SW. The Grand Feast will be on 13/5/1812, when officers for
the following year will be appointed.

SW→VN 6/5/1812
BL Add 11729 f 16; *O*   I am in great Tribulation & Discomfort until we meet
☐ Wed 6 May; pmk 1812
SW is distressed. [Angelica] Catalani has announced that, in consequence of
her new contract with [William] Taylor [co-manager of the King's Theatre,
1753–1825], she is prohibited from singing except at the Opera House [the
King's Theatre], and thus cannot sing at SW's concert [on 5/6/1812]. SW doubts
her veracity, as her appearance at Ashley's benefit [the benefit concert on
16/5/1812 for General Christopher Ashley, violinist, 1767–1818, and his brother

Charles Jane Ashley, 'cellist, *c*1773–1843, who following the death in 1805 of their father John Ashley became joint organisers of the Covent Garden oratorio concerts] has already been announced [in *The Times*, 6/5/1812]. Also, she continues to sing at [Samuel] Harrison's concert every Friday. If she reneges on her agreement with SW [to sing at his concert] he will 'expose the whole transaction' in the newspapers. SW asks VN's opinion of the advisability of a meeting with 'Vallabreguez' [Paul Valabrègue, Catalani's husband and manager], whose letters to SW [not preserved] would 'excite universal reprobation' if published.

Several weeks ago VN told SW that he thought he could secure [Teresa] Bertinotti (*see* SW→VN, 31/3/1812). SW thinks that she is a better singer than everyone in England except [Elizabeth] Billington, and 'a dish worth a whole course of Catalanis'. He asks VN for an immediate line on his news, and on the progress of 'the symphony' [VN's arrangement for organ duet and orchestra of JSB's Prelude in E♭ major, BWV 552, the manuscript of which, in the Gesellschaft der Musikfreunde, Vienna, is dated 28/5/1812 and bears VN's annotation that the arrangement was first performed by VN and SW on 5/6/1812].

SW is 'up to the a—e with all manner of *omnium gatherum*': 'honouring bills for such as have done me the honour to ruin me', 'laying a musical siege to Badajos for Mr [Thomas] Preston' [the printer of SW's piano sonata *The Siege of Badajoz*], teaching 'those never meant to learn', 'signing tickets' and making other arrangements for his 5/6/1812 concert [where the 'symphony' was first performed], and endeavouring to find time to complete his duet for the same occasion [his *Grand Duet* in C, for organ].

After opening the organ at Christ Church, Blackfriars, on Sunday [10/5/1812], SW is to dine with [Joseph] Gwilt. SW invites VN to call in on them both in the evening. Gwilt's wife [Luisa] is in labour.

SW→SGW   **22/5/1812?**
BL Add 35012 f 19   I fully intended calling before now
✉ Friday 23 May 1812[294]

SW has meant to visit SGW but has always been prevented by some 'cross accident or other'. He will look in today if he can. He was out in the storm on Tuesday night [19/5/1812], coming from Turnham Green. If he had waited until the lightning ceased, he would have been away from home all night; as it was, he had to shelter at a house during the worst of the storm, when a man and his horse were both struck dead near Kensington. He is sorry that SGW heard reports of him being dead. This was a mistake, which arose because of a confusion between SW and [Joseph] Wölfl [Austrian composer and pianist, 1773–1812], who died on 'Tuesday last' [19/5/1812]. SW is 'at present rather in a hobble'

---

[294] In 1812 23 May was a Saturday. Ltr assigned to Friday 22/5/1812 on the assumption that SW wrote an incorrect date rather than an incorrect day of week.

financially. He needs to honour a bill of £35 next Monday [25/5/1812], but has only £10 available. He is himself owed money from two sources, but cannot get hold of the money at present. He therefore wishes to borrow £25 for a month, and asks SGW if she knows anyone who might oblige.

Sarah memorandum 20/6/1812

GEU in box 6   On looking into papers which casually presented themselves memo dated 20/6/1812

Sarah found, in a drawer, a letter that her 'unfortunate brother' [SW] wrote to her many years ago 'detailing his wretchedness in affecting terms'. Yesterday [19/6/1812], she had been moved 'at hearing the vile opprobrium' that the 'infamous' AD, when 'living in sin and brazen audacity' [with SW], had cast upon all in Sarah's family except SGW. AD's letter, which had been given with other letters by 'Mrs Wesley' [CLW] to Mrs Charles Dyer, revived Sarah's 'anger and abhorrence' and tempted her to vent 'violent deprecations on the head' of AD and her 'lover' [SW].

However, when Sarah read SW's letter, she felt commiseration, and wondered whether SW 'would terminate his life as he already has wasted it, in sensuality, malice and oppression'. She prayed for his conversion. Although her prayers 'have not extended to the temporal prosperity' of any of his progeny, she wishes 'their salvation'. If Sarah was not still suffering from his injustice she would feel 'much more kindness' towards them. She 'shudders' at the thought of 'association' with SW's family other than SW himself. She would like him to show 'signs of sorrow' for the 'base and accumulated injuries' he has 'heaped upon' her without cause. SW is a 'poor, deluded man' who 'never can be happy, however penitent'. Unlike Sarah, he has 'lost the enjoyments of existence'.

Sarah has 'denounced the wicked' before God and prayed 'more like a Jew than a Christian' that her 'enemies might be punished in this world', yet reconciliation with them would be possible if they became penitent. She prays that she 'may bless instead of curse them'.

SW→VN 22/6/1812

BL Add 11729 f 20; *O*   I have written the annexed for Wednesday
☞ Mon 22 June={1807,1812,1818,1829}[295]

SW has written the enclosed piece [probably his 'Ut queant laxis', for the feast of St John the Baptist] for performance by VN's choir on Wednesday [24/6/1812], the feast of John the Baptist. SW asks if VN will call on him Wednesday at 3 or 3.30 pm.

---

[295] Assigned to 1812 because 1818 impossible as SW was at Blacklands and 1807 and 1829 outside the period when SW was assisting VN's choir at the Portuguese Embassy Chapel.

SW→VN?[296]   **24/6/1812?**
BL Add 11729 f 18; *O*   SW feels the UTmost Satisfaction in REturning his
📧 24 June[297]
   In a humorous note based upon the Guidonian musical syllables (*ut, re, mi,*
etc.), SW thanks the recipient for his favourable comments on SW's 'tune'
[presumably the music enclosed in SW→VN, 22/6/1812]. SW thinks, however,
that the recipient's comments may have been biased by their friendship.

SW→VN   Tottenham Ct   **25/6/1812**
BL Add 11729 f 21; *O*   You are a very fine Spark upon my Say So
📧 Thu 25 Jun & 📧→1
   SW remonstrates with VN, who first wrote [not preserved] to SW and then sent
Mr Boyle [not identified] to tell him that VN was 'engaged to the little Jack of
Trumps' [not identified] to conduct his concert. On arrival at Jack Straw's Castle
[an inn on Hampstead Heath], SW discovered that the remainder of the party had
almost finished their meal. Afterwards he was 'set down to accompany Te
Deums' with 'a gallon of bucellas' [a Portuguese white wine] in his 'sconce'
[head].

Sarah→Mr Bingham   **26/6/1812**
MA DDWF/14/29   I am harrassed about a little nephew of mine
pmk 26/6/1812
   Sarah tells Mr Bingham [a surgeon in Uxbridge] that she is 'harassed' about
the future prospects of her nephew [JWW], whom SW is about to take away
from school at the 'early age' of twelve. JWW has sense and the capacity to
learn 'if assisted'. Sarah had placed another of SW's children [CW III] at St
Paul's School. He showed great talent and would have been sure to have gone to
Oxford [University] 'with £100 per annum'. He is now apprenticed to Mr
Rivers, an apothecary. This occupation requires time 'to procure independence'.

---

[296] Although not named as recipient VN is the likely recipient because ltr is
surrounded by other letters from SW to VN in manuscript given by VN to the
British Museum in 1840.

[297] Assigned to 1812 on presumption that content (particularly the use of
solmisation syllables) appears to relate to SW's composition discussed in
SW→VN, 22/6/1812; however, other years have not been ruled out.

SW→VN **27/6/1812**

BL Add 11729 f 94; *O*   I am concerned to state that there is very discouraging
▣ Sat 27 June={1807,1812,1818,1829}[298]

SW has discouraging news about his efforts to harmonise the Gregorian chants.
He had initially proposed to [Rev. William Victor] Fryer to provide
accompaniments to all psalms, anthems, responsoria etc. of the Office. Fryer
objected that there might be variations between the 'large choir book' and
Fryer's own 'small' book copied by [John Francis] Wade, [1710?–1786], from
which SW had made arrangements so far. This might cause confusion; also, it
would be prudent not to introduce this method of performing the Office all at
once as some people might condemn it as a novelty. SW saw the force of the
latter objection and agreed that the organ should be silent until the beginning of
the Mass. On comparing the two books, SW became aware of great
discrepancies, some of which he outlines. He considers these to be a 'ten-barred
gate' to his proceeding with his planned publication. To decide whether to
continue he needs to examine and compare the books of Gregorian chant in use
in all the chapels and must determine whether this effort will be worth his while.
Even though [Joseph] Gwilt has liberally offered an 'entire indemnity' for the
cost of printing and paper, SW thinks that this would not adequately recompense
him for so tedious a job. He seeks VN's advice on the matter.

SW→VN **2/7/1812**

BL Add 11728 f 26; *O*   An unexpected Obstacle (which however is likely
▣ Thursday morning[299]

SW cannot meet VN at Kirkman's [piano manufactory] tomorrow [3/7/1812].
If VN can instead fix Saturday [4/7/1812] at 7 pm, SW will be there. VN should
not let the opera [presumably Mozart's *The Marriage of Figaro*, performed at
the King's Theatre on 4/7/1812] 'prove the veto': he can hear that more often
than the 30 variations [JSB's *Goldberg Variations*]. Bridgetower, who called at
VN's house last week to ask whether 'the Mass of Mozart' [not identified] was
to be performed [presumably at the Portuguese Embassy Chapel] last Sunday
[28/6/1812], will be with them [at Kirkman's].
SW asks the name of the reviewer in 'Akerman's Magazine' [the *Repository of
Arts*, published by Rudolph Ackermann, 1764–1834; the music reviewer was
Gottlieb Lewis Engelbach], who [in the July 1812 number] praised SW's piano
composition *The Deserter's Meditations* 'to the size of Sadler's balloon' [a
reference to James Sadler, balloonist, *d*1828]. SW comments on newspaper
reports of 'throats cut lately on the continent' [*The Times*, 2/7/1812, describes

---

[298] Assigned to 1812 because 1818 impossible as SW was at Blacklands and
1807 and 1829 outside the period when SW was assisting VN's choir at the
Portuguese Embassy Chapel.

[299] Assigned to 2/7/1812 because of the battle report in *The Times* that day and
ref. to the review of SW's *The Deserter's Meditations* in the *Repository of Arts*.

the 1/6/1812 battle of Bornos, in which there were 1,000 enemy casualties] and supposes that he and VN will perform a Te Deum [at the Portuguese Embassy Chapel] shortly in thanksgiving.

SW→VN   **7/7/1812**

BL Add 11729 f 23; *O*   I send you a Twopenny Tune
⊟ Tue 7 July={1807,1812,1818,1829}[300]

   SW encloses a 'twopenny tune' [his 'Ave verum corpus' [II], the manuscript of which is dated 6/7/1812], which VN may like to rehearse with his choir after Vespers on Sunday [12/7/1812]. SW has written the upper [boy treble] part for Lanza [possibly a son of Gesualdo Lanza, singer, 1779–1859]. The 'motivo' is at least 32 years old, but SW 'put in a few furbelos' for 'this gimcrack age'.

   SW wants to show VN some Gregorian chant and wishes that VN would visit him this evening, instead of going to 'that devilish Opera House' [the King's Theatre].

Thomas Green journal entry   **9/7/1812**

GM n.s. v 8 (Nov 1837) p 455   Went to a large musical party in the evening
GM

   Thomas Green [author, 1769–1825, of Ipswich] attended a 'large musical party' [in London] in the evening. He was 'enchanted' by SW 'seizing whatever [musical] subject presented itself and working upon it' with 'stupendous' mastery of modulation. Green was 'delighted with the harmony' but did not understand how 'a perfect scale of temperament' could permit 'the passing of the gap' [i.e., how equal temperament, which employs the same pitch to play notes such as F♯ and G♭, allows all major and minor keys to be satisfactorily played without retuning the instrument]. Green found SW 'very intelligent, and pleasant and complying'.

---

[300] Assigned to 1812 because of discussion of Gregorian chant in ltr.

SW→RG   Tottenham Ct   **24/7/1812**
BL Add 35013 f 52; *O*   I think that we had a little Conversation
✉ 24 July; pmk 1812

SW and RG conversed the other night about the appointment of an organist for Huddersfield. RG observed that there was an objection to a blind organist. SW was not certain whether the objection was insurmountable, and had made application on behalf of [Thomas] Grenville [1744?–1827], the blind former organist of the Foundling Hospital, who had called on him in the meantime. SW has a high opinion of Grenville's abilities: he holds him to have 'no inconsiderable pretension to the situation of an organist either in the country or in London'. SW asks RG to call and discuss the matter. SW then will communicate with Grenville.

SW→VN   **24/7/1812**
BL Add 11729 f 24; *O*   I can meet you at 4 & stay till 5 at Davis's
✉ Fri 24 Jul; pmk 1812

SW can meet VN at [the manufactory of James] Davis [organ builder, 1726–1827] at 4 pm today and can stay until 5 pm, but supposes that this will not suit [Muzio] Clementi [composer, piano manufacturer and music publisher, 1752–1832]. SW could not be with VN today as he was unexpectedly invited to dine with Lord Oxford [Edward Harley, 1773–1849, 5th Earl of Oxford, whose wife Jane Elizabeth Harley, 1777–1824, and daughter Jane Elizabeth Harley, 1796–1872, had both subscribed to the SW/CFH edition of the '48'] on a matter of potential importance to SW.

SW→VN   **11/8/1812**
BL Add 11729 f 28; *O*   I have lately heard that there are two different
✉ Tue 11 Aug & ref. to Prince Regent→{1812,1818}[301]

SW comments sardonically on the Prince Regent's order for the execution of two criminals tomorrow [the Prince's birthday, 12/8/1812]. SW wishes to know by Thursday [13/8/1812] whether VN wants SW to deputise for him next Saturday [15/8/1812, the feast of the Assumption of the Blessed Virgin Mary] at 11 am and 3 pm. SW is not unwilling to do this, but would need to 'cut and contrive'.

---

[301] Assigned to 1812 because of the execution of two criminals on 12/12/1812 (reported in *The Times*, 13/12/1812). In August 1818 SW does not appear to have been deputising for VN.

SW→VN   **13/8/1812?**

BL Add 11729 f 43; *O*   My dear Doctor of the Sorbonne—(Sorebone I fear is
ltr undated[302]

SW comments on VN's criticism of SW's phrase 'of increased universal
popularity' [used by SW in SW→VN, 11/8/1812]. Although VN does not need
SW on the 'approaching day of obligation' [15/8/1812, the feast of the
Assumption of the Blessed Virgin Mary], SW nonetheless would like to take
down the Introit and Alleluia. If the Gradual could be left at Blackett's [not
identified] on Saturday morning [15/8/1812], SW could call and 'scratch it out'
in [Rev. William Victor] Fryer's apartment. SW has not been able to see [Rev.
James] Archer [priest, 1751–1834, from 1780 to 1826 Principal Chaplain of the
Bavarian Embassy] but hopes to call on him. Charles Butler [Roman Catholic
lawyer and historian, 1750–1832] has invited SW to a 'smoking haunch' next
Monday [17/8/1812] at 6 pm. SW must be on his best behaviour in such
'worshipful company'.

SW→VN   **16/8/1812**

BL Add 11729 f 30; *O*   I am sorry that I cannot have the Gratification
☞ Sun 16 Aug={1807,1812,1818,1829}[303]

SW regrets that he will not see VN at [Joseph] Major's home this evening. SW
and Major are dining at the house of a friend of Major's. Consequently, SW
cannot be at South Street [the Portuguese Embassy Chapel] 'this evening' [for
Vespers] but will be there [for High Mass] on Wednesday morning [18/8/1812].
SW relates an anecdote concerning a 'Te Dum' [sic] 'psalm'.

---

[302] Assigned to 13/8/1812 for the following reason. In SW→VN, 11/8/1812, SW
said that the Prince Regent is 'increasing his universal popularity'. VN
presumably criticised this phrase in a letter to SW of 12/8/1812 [not preserved]
to which ltr replies. SW in ltr proposes an event on 'Saturday morning'
[15/8/1812]; had ltr been written on 14/8/1812 he probably would have said
'tomorrow'.

[303] Assigned to 1812 because 1807 and 1829 outside the period when SW was
involved with the Portuguese Embassy Chapel, and 1818 considered unlikely
because SW had then just left Blacklands.

SW→Bridgetower Tottenham Ct **4/9/1812**
BL Add 56411 f 11; *O* I have appointed a few Friends to meet me
4/9/1812

SW has arranged to meet with a few friends tomorrow morning [5/9/1812] at the premises of the organ builder [James] Davis in Francis Street, Tottenham Court Road. [John Bernard] Logier [German music educator, 1777–1846, for many years resident in Dublin] wants to hear the whole of the Preludes and Fugues [JSB's '48'], and SW has promised to play them all through. SW will be glad to have Bridgetower's presence.

SW→SS Ramsgate **18/9/1812**
BL Add 35012 f 40 Here we are, all safe & sound
'Thursday 18 September', pmk (London) 19/9/1812[304]

SW has arrived in Ramsgate after a journey by boat. Many passengers were sick, but he was not. He writes in haste to catch the post. SS is to take care of herself, SSW and [James] Ball, and is to send Picart his music books. SW will write again in a day or two. [Robert Thomas] Skarratt is to address any mail for SW to the Post Office at Ramsgate.

SW→SS Ramsgate **29/9/1812**
BL Add 35012 f 42 In the first Place, the Concert is doing as well as we can
29 September & SW in Ramsgate→ⅰ

SW is planning to give a concert with Samuel Webbe Jr in Ramsgate. It has been delayed until Saturday night [3/10/1812] for reasons that SW has not time to explain now. Preparations are going as well as they can expect: their many good friends in Ramsgate are doing all they can to find them a good room, and SW considers that they are not likely to be losers now. SW is embarrassed by an awkwardness with Webbe Jr about money: SW has little money at present and Webbe Jr is presently obliged to pay all their daily expenses. SW will apply [by letter] to [Joseph] Major, whom he desires to call on SS. SS says nothing about Gray [possibly the organ builder William Gray], who if he is in town surely would lend £5; otherwise, 'Mr Glenn' [RG], who lives at Stewart Street, Spitalfields, might lend £5 until SW's return. SW asks SS to apply to RG.

SW likes Ramsgate because of the sea but finds it less pleasant than Margate. He hopes that SS has let [Joseph] Gwilt know that SW is out of town, and that Gwilt does not suspect SW of neglecting him. Nothing can be done about 'Mrs Wesley's [CLW's] money' until SW's return. CLW should know that SW has come to Ramsgate in the hope of getting money. SW will write tomorrow to Corbett [not identified]. Kingston is never pleased about anything except what he does himself. He says that whatever SW does is wrong, although SW has acted on his advice throughout.

---

[304] Assigned to 18/9/1812, a Friday, because of the postmark the following day.

SW and Webbe Jr will not get away from Ramsgate until next week. SW wishes very much to be back home, even if it is 'only to be plunged into hot water', and longs to see all who are dear to him. He wishes he could hear better news of 'poor Mrs Rowley' but supposes that Mrs Perry is attentive to SS. He supposes that SS gave her the trouble of writing the letter.

SW asks SS not to delay if there is good news, and hopes that there is no bad news that could make it 'dangerous' for him to remain in Ramsgate. He must write to VN and [Marmaduke Charles] Wilson [composer and pianist, *b*1796] to 'secure their services for a day or two extraordinary' at the schools [where SW teaches].

SW and Webbe Jr could have had their concert a week ago if it were not for 'two damned parsons' [*see* SW→VN, 1/10/1812]. He asks SS to kiss 'Boy Blue' [SSW] for him. 'Mrs S' [not identified] has a fine lot of pretty shells and seaweed for SSW. SW's letter to Major [not preserved] will reach him at the same time as this letter reaches SS.

SW→VN   Ramsgate   **1/10/1812**

BL Add 11729 f 33; *O*

▣ Thu 1 Oct & SW in Ramsgate→⚊

SW and his 'coadjutor' Samuel Webbe Jr have had mixed fortunes in Ramsgate and Margate. Their offer to the vicars in both places to give free recitals at their churches was rebuffed. Much time was wasted waiting for their decision. After much deliberation, SW and Webbe Jr have fixed 3/10/1812 as the date for their concert. SW is not over-optimistic about their making a profit, but will be happy if they can avoid burning their fingers. They have engaged [Catherine] Stephens [soprano, 1794–1882] as their singer. She has a very sweet voice and sings in a pretty style. She is to sing two songs, SW and Webbe Jr will join her in two glees, and SW will play a sonata by Pleyel, of which the opening is quoted. Also in the programme will be 'one of Dussek's most stately pieces', played by Webbe Jr as a solo, the 'Duet of the Sisters' at VN's suggestion, 'another of Clementi', and a Fantasia 'with some St Giles Ditty or other for the edification of the learned critics now resident in the Isle of Thanet'.

SW thanks VN for taking over his teaching commitments. SW doubts that he and Webbe Jr will be able to set out on their return journey before Monday [5/10/1812] and asks VN to stand in for him then; he will inform VN immediately on his return to London, which he expects will be on Tuesday [6/10/1812]. SW comments on his love of the 'main ocean'; if he were able, he would always live close to the sea. He and Webbe Jr swim naked in the sea every day. Yesterday they met WH, his fiancée [Elizabeth] Callcott [1793–1875] and her mother [Elizabeth Callcott, 1775–1825, wife of John Wall Callcott]. SW comments on the poor quality of the 'pianoforte artists' that he and Webbe Jr have met.

SW has seen VN's name as a subscriber to the concerto by [Francesco] Panormo [Italian composer, 1764–1844]. From knowledge of Panormo's other compositions, SW thinks that VN has a lot to learn.

SW→SGW   Tottenham Ct   **6/10/1812**
BL Add 35012 f 21   Mr Webbe & I arrived in Town last night
▣ 6/10/1812

SW and Samuel Webbe Jr returned to London last night after a pleasant journey [from Ramsgate]. Their 'music party' at the Assembly Room on Saturday night [3/10/1812] was attended by all the 'fashionable folk' left in Ramsgate, but there were not as many as had been hoped because of the 'devilish election' which had obliged many of them to come to London. Their friends in Ramsgate feel that if they were to organise 'an oratorio' and further concerts at the Assembly Rooms next year they would have a great success. SW expects that they will have just broken even on this concert, but that they have laid the foundations for a greater success on a future occasion.

SW gathers that Mr [James] Ball called on Sunday last [4/10/1812] and said that SGW would be willing to help SW with his financial problems. SW hopes that these problems will be temporary and that better times lie ahead. He is anxious about John [JWW] and must try to place him in some 'safe and useful state of employment'. SW feels that JWW would be a credit to anyone who employs him, and hopes that SGW will make known SW's wishes to friends of the family.

He comments on SGW's forthcoming 'jaunt' to Brighton. Although he is sure that sea air will be beneficial, he is doubtful about the effects of the journey at SGW's time of life. He does not know how long SGW intends to stay there, and cannot comment on the business that Ball has consulted her about.

SW needs to come forward with £40 by the middle of next week. He has already had difficulty putting off payment until then and will be in severe trouble if he cannot pay the bill at the due time. He is obliged to go into the City [of London] and cannot call on SGW but asks her to reply by post. He wishes that CW Jr may get something out of the Prince [Regent, at Brighton], but fears that he is 'only purchasing honour' at a dear rate.

Charles Butler→SW   **7/10/1812**
BL Add 11729 f 36   I have a note from Dr Burney expressing the wish
▣ 7/10/1812

CB has written to Charles Butler, asking him and SW to visit next Sunday [11/10/1812] about noon so that SW can play music by JSB to CB. Butler requests SW's reply by return of post. Butler is serious about 'the Gregorian note' [Gregorian chant] and has sent to Paris for a book about it.

SW→Charles Butler   Tottenham Ct   **7/10/1812**
MA DDWes/9/20; *O*   I have just now received your Letter
▣ Wednesday evening; pmk 8/10/1812 (a Thursday)

SW has just received Butler's letter [Charles Butler→SW, 7/10/1812] and accepts CB's 'summons'. CB had shown SW his manuscript copy of the first part of JSB's '48' given to him by C.P.E. Bach, imagining it to be the whole work. SW then brought forward the second part of the '48' and played some of the compositions to CB, to his great delight. SW considers this proof that CB on occasion has been 'precipitate in his decision' on musical matters; his present 'slight knowledge of the Gregorian note' seems to be another example. SW has mentioned to Butler the 'general wish' for Gregorian melodies to be harmonised, for the use of organists. SW is convinced that such a work would be universally valuable and is willing to undertake it, particularly if Butler would contribute a prefatory essay.

SW→VN   **11/10/1812**
BL Add 11729 f 35; *O*   The enclosed will account for my not being with you
◨ Sun 11 Oct={1812} & SW's enclosure of 7/10/1812 letter→ ⒤

SW encloses a letter [presumably Charles Butler→SW, 7/10/1812] which explains his 'summons from a man of 90 years' [CB, who in fact was born in 1726] and indicates why SW cannot be with VN this morning. SW cannot be with VN this afternoon either, as he must see WL then. If the Gregorian books can be left for SW on Wednesday [14/10/1812], he thinks he can manage to make a rough copy of the Mass that he and VN revised in the course of the week. SW believes that there is no feast requiring High Mass before next Sunday [18/10/1812].

SW→SGW   Tottenham Ct   **21/10/1812**
MA DDWes/6/52   As you left me no Direction where you could be found
◨ 21/10/1812

SGW left SW no direction where she could be found in Brighton. By chance he was given her address by Miss Harington, who called a few days ago. He hopes that SGW's return to London will be speedy. The weather begins to grow worse, and SW supposes it is the same in Brighton.

SW is in no doubt that 'some immediate arrangement' must be made to render him 'a little present aid'. If not, dire consequences will follow which SGW would not want to witness, especially if 'timely assistance' on her part could avert them. SW expects 'unpleasant and rough applications' from a number of directions which could be avoided if he could receive part of his claim in 'the common stock' [i.e., receive some of his inheritance during SGW's lifetime]. He assures SGW that he has 'ever disdained the contemptible idea' of relying on legacies. If SGW is about to write to Miss Harington, she can give SW a line in her letter, stating when will be the earliest convenient time for SGW to return home. SW stresses that the matter is urgent.

SW knows little or nothing of the present situation at Brighton. He will be glad to hear that CW Jr 'may have made his excursion answer' (*see* SW→SGW, 6/10/1812). SW has informed John [JWW] that SGW is expected home shortly. As soon as SW's financial worries are sorted out he will attempt to find employment for JWW.

SW→VN   **24/10/1812**

BL Add 11729 f 37; *O*   There seems to be some Prevalence of Incantation
☞ 24/10/1812

SW was unable to call at the [Portuguese Embassy] Chapel until 1 pm today.
When he arrived he was unable to make anyone hear him and was obliged to go
away. He had hoped to write out the antiphon for the Vespers tomorrow as well
as the Gregorian Mass. This may yet be done: if VN can get the two books sent
to Blackett's [not identified] by 9 am tomorrow, SW will do the job there and
will then return the books in time for High Mass. Samuel Webbe Jr and
[presumably Joseph] Gwilt expect to come to Vespers. Gwilt would be pleased
to hear the antiphons sung with a bass on the organ.

SW→VN   **29/10/1812**

BL Add 11729 f 39; *O*   Mr No Well O, I spell it so on Purpose
☞ 29/10/1812

SW remonstrates humorously with VN for breaking his promise to visit SW at
his house last Tuesday [27/10/1812]. He has spent three hours trying to 'claw
hold of supple Jack's [not identified] woundy exercises'. SW desires VN's
repentance and his 'satisfaction', the nature of which will not be disclosed before
the Feast Day of All Saints [1/11/1812] between the hours of 11 and 12. They
are to be merry after their 'sad solemnity and black' next Monday [2/11/1812].
SW hopes that Gastang [a boy treble] will be there, as he is curious to see him
eat plum pudding and wishes to hear him sing 'Sweet bird' [by Handel] and
'The soldier tired' [by Arne]. SW is busy with Gregorian harmonisations.

SW→SGW   Tottenham Ct   **4/11/1812**

BL Add 35012 f 24   I was much surprized to hear from Miss Harington
☞ 4 Nov; pmk 1812

SW was 'much surprised' to hear that SGW, who is in Brighton, intends to stay
on the coast until Christmas. He feels that as winter approaches 'nothing but
absolute necessity' could induce those who value comfort to stay by the sea.

SW is in another financial crisis. Unless £100 can be found he will be
imprisoned. He has done all he can in SGW's absence, but had she returned a
fortnight ago when expected he would have been saved much trouble. He
apologises for taking SGW to task, but the pressure on him is extreme. £200
would see him 'compleatly free of embarrassment', and as he is in 'good health
and tolerable spirits' he knows that his exertions in the music profession must be
ultimately successful. Given this, he feels it hard that the advance of £100
(which in any case is his own) should have been so long delayed.

SW→Salomon?[305]   Tottenham Ct   **5/11/1812**

MB **M.408.2; *O*   I beg you to accept my Apology for not having sooner

▣ Thu 5 Nov & ✉→ⓘ

SW apologises for not having earlier sent thanks for the letter, book and invitation. He intends to call at 'No. 70' [presumably the recipient's home] between now and Sunday [8/11/1812] to make arrangements. SW intends to be at Vespers and to proceed from there with the recipient to the 'Feast of Philosophy'. The service will last for at least an additional 15 minutes or so until nearly 4.30 pm on account of 'scraps of pribbles and prabbles for one lousy saint or another'. SW hopes that 'our sage Deroise Stewart' [not identified] will be patient if they are delayed.

SW→SGW   **9/11/1812**

Fitzwm ltr 16   Matters are now come to an Extremity with me.

▣ 9/11/1812

SW is in hourly expectation of a summons to a prison. His crisis arises from the failure of his £100 to be advanced, which would have stopped all demands on him. The term has now begun, and Mrs Mace has arrested SW and is proceeding against him at law 'on account of [failure to pay for] John's [JWW's] schooling'. SW feels that, unless immediate aid is forthcoming, 'slinking off to Brighton' [where SGW is staying] will be his best recourse and the only way he will avoid jail 'before the end of next week'.

---

[305] Ltr addressed to 'Dear Sir'. Salomon suggested as recipient because he lived at No. 70 Newman Street and was a friend of SW.

SW→SGW   Tottenham Ct   **12/11/1812**
Fitzwm ltr 17   Mr Mason refuses to pay me a Farthing
⬛ Thu 12 Nov & 📬→🔲

Mr [Thomas] Mason [an attorney] refuses to pay SW anything and wonders at Sarah's lack of sense in writing to him in the terms she did. For the lack of £100, SW is in hourly expectation of an 'execution [of a warrant] in the house' and the 'arrest' of his 'person', at the moment when his 'poor companion' [SS] is in absolute labour'. SW called on Mr [James] Pettit [of the Bank of England] for an explanation. Pettit thinks that Mason's designs were 'none of the honestest', and that 'only legal compulsion' will now wrest SGW's property from Mason.

SW asks SGW to approach an attorney [in Brighton] to draw up a Power of Attorney empowering Pettit to raise £100 from SGW's stock. She should send this immediately to SW, together with an order to Pettit to pay the sum to SW. SW doubts that this will avert the 'evil' he dreads, but hopes that she will do it nonetheless. He asks SGW to thank CW Jr and Sarah for their 'exertions', although CW Jr's were 'much too late', as SW's arrest was made 'long ago'. SW is preparing to pay legal costs as well as 'the debt' [for JWW's schooling].

SW→James Asperne   **14/11/1812?**
MA DDWF/15/42; *O*   Mr S. Wesley called on Mr Asperne to solicit his
⬛ Sat 14 Nov={1807,1812,1818}[306]

SW agrees to the proposal received several days ago [not preserved] from [James] Asperne [bookseller and publisher, *d*1821] about the portrait. SW possesses a portrait [of himself] which was considered a good likeness when taken 15 years ago [presumably (Thomas?) Robinson's portrait of SW, made when SW was about 30], but 'the furrows of age have been so much increasing in indenture that a facsimile might appear somewhat ridiculous at the present period'. SW is willing to sit for the artist [not identified] whom Asperne mentioned, but is 'averse' to and 'incapable' of becoming 'his own biographer'.

Sarah & SGW→RG   **18/11/1812**
WHS   *Sarah:*   I cannot but assure you that I admire and respect
                 SGW: Your kind Letter with the Intelligence it brought
pmk 18/11/1812 (Brighton)
Sarah: Sarah admires and respects RG's 'kindness and humanity'. He has taken 'much trouble and interest in the perplexities of others'. Sarah has long

---

[306] Ltr written from 32 Cornhill where Asperne worked between 1802 and 1821. Assigned to 1812 because 1807 seems less likely from SW's reference to 'the furrows of age', and 1818 seems unlikely as Asperne had decided in 1817 to discontinue SW's music reviews in the *European Magazine*, which Asperne published (*see* SW→Stephen Jones, 18/1/1817). No evidence has been found to link Asperne's publication of that magazine with his interest in SW's portrait.

known of the generosity of her 'friend' Mr [James] Pettit, of which this is a fresh and unforgettable instance. As soon as Sarah returns [from Brighton] she, SGW and CW Jr will see that Pettit is repaid.

SGW: RG's kind letter [not preserved] to CW Jr, conveying that SW had been supplied by Mr Pettit and was 'secure from the cruel power of the law and its consequences', gave considerable satisfaction. SGW hopes before long 'to prove Mr [Thomas] Mason has money' to pay her 'through Mr Gregory's demands', although Mason refused to provide money to SW. SGW's eyesight is failing. She sends best wishes for RG's mother's health, and love to SW.

SW→SGW   **19/11/1812**

BL Add 35012 f 25   The Supply I obtained in Consequence of your very
☞ Thu 19 Nov ={1812}[307]

Because of SGW's prompt actions, SW received a supply of money in time to avert the crisis. He is puzzled that [James] Pettit should suddenly be able to advance £50 and is 'mortified' to think that SGW's money is entrusted to such 'unsafe hands' as [Thomas] Mason's. The weather has become raw and cold, and SW imagines that SGW must long for her fireside at home. He has been suffering from toothache, which is not surprising considering his 'continual exposure in all weathers'. He is glad to hear that SGW will be in London on Saturday [21/11/1812] and wishes her a safe journey. He asks her to thank CW Jr and Sarah for their exertions on his behalf.

SW→VN   **5/12/1812**

BL Add 11729 f 41; *O*   I leave with you the prior Piece of the Sanctus
☞ Sat 5 Dec={1807,1812,1818}[308]

SW leaves with VN 'the prior piece of the Sanctus' [probably from SW's *Missa pro angelis*]. SW has nearly finished [harmonising] the Mass of the 5th Tone [his incomplete *Missa de sanctissima trinitate*], after which he will not bother with Gregorian [harmonisations], as there is little prospect of profit. He will attempt to sell his Mass [probably his *Missa pro angelis*], but would rather it mouldered in a chest than to sell it for a song.

The Gregorian [chant] is beginning to be proscribed by the clergy themselves, so this is not a good time to be promoting it, even when it is 'presented with florid advantages'. Had SW been aware of the 'silly revolution' in VN's choir, he would not have spent so much time on this. He asks VN to gather up all the 'scraps of square notes' [the notation of Gregorian chant] that SW has written down and to return them to him. He parodies the text of the Magnificat antiphon

---

[307] Assigned to 1812 because of SW's being supplied with money by Pettit (*see* Sarah & SGW→RG, 18/11/1812).

[308] Assigned to 1812 because SW's harmonisations of Gregorian chant were made that year.

for the 5th Sunday after Epiphany: gather together all the Gregorian Masses and burn them, but preserve all church music by [Samuel] Webbe [Sr] and David Perez [1711–1778, from 1752 chapel master to the king of Portugal], together with other pieces by Portuguese composers.

SW→VN   14/12/1812
BL Add 11729 f 42; *O*   Mr Picart has again been assailing me
⌨ 14/12/1812
   Picart has asked SW for the 'symphony' by JSB that VN arranged [*see* SW→VN, 6/5/1812] and also for SW's organ duet [presumably SW's *Grand Duet* in C, mentioned in the same letter]. Picart has been 'so very liberal' in accommodating SW's requests for music that SW 'cannot consistently or decently refuse' him, although SW does not like to send manuscks 'abroad' for various reasons, including 'the probability of their being erroneously transcribed'. SW asks VN to lend him VN's own manuscript copy of the duet, which is more legible than SW's original. SW asks for all his 'sanctified shreds and patches' [presumably his harmonisations of Gregorian chant] to be returned. He wishes to make 'an orderly arrangement' of them, whether or not they will be printed. He will be glad when VN has copied out SW's Sanctus in B as SW wishes to 'scratch it out' in a bound book.

Sarah→SGW   4/1/1813
GEU in box 6   May this Year bring more Comforts & Blessings
⌨ 4/1/1813
   Sarah has delayed answering the letter [not preserved] from 'poor Sam' [SW] because she has been 'devising all possible means to help him'. Miss Harris has no friend to whom she could now apply for £100. John Jeffreys, who lives in Cliffords Inn, might help SW to obtain money or would 'lend him sufficient for the journey' to the country, where he has some promise of success.

SW→Muzio Clementi?[309]   Tottenham Ct   6/1/1813
BL Add 31764 f 26; *O*   Since I saw you last I have received full Authority
⌨ 6/1/1813
   SW has been authorised to make decisions regarding the piano ordered by W. Williams, a barrister from Weymouth. The piano required is the one at 42 guineas [£44/2/-], together with a set of strings, a tuning hammer and whatever

---

[309] Ltr addressed to 'Dear Sir'. Muzio Clementi presumed as the recipient because his company was both a piano manufacturer and a music publisher, and SW's *Variations on 'The Bay of Biscay'* mentioned in ltr was dedicated to Clementi and was published by his company. However, the possibility that the recipient was an employee of the Clementi firm other than Clementi himself has not been ruled out.

is usual for an order for the East Indies. Williams (whom SW does not know) approached WL to procure an instrument for his daughter, and WL has made the commission over to SW. SW understands that the order is to be completed without delay. He asks the recipient to find out if a ship sails for the East Indies soon. WL wishes to see the instrument before it is dispatched.

SW has not obtained any copies of his 'Tune with Variations' [his *Variations on 'The Bay of Biscay'*, published about this time by Clementi (it is reviewed in the 1/2/1813 *MM*) and dedicated to him], which he expected this morning at the latest.

SW→'Dear Sir'[310]   Tottenham Ct   **12/1/1813**
MA DDWF/15/17A; *O*   I have just received a letter from our good Friend
▭ Tue 12 Jan & 🖾→🗓

SW advised their 'good friend' [the Rev. Christopher] Jeaffreson that his correspondent would have liked to have 'given [SW] the meeting' [to have appointed a time and place to meet SW] during SW's stay in Tunstall. Jeaffreson, in a letter SW just received [not preserved], asked SW to invite his correspondent to travel with SW to Tunstall and to stay with Jeaffreson for a few days. SW has been confined by a knee injury but hopes to be fit to travel by stagecoach in two or three days. He asks his correspondent to call or to write if he desires to take up Jeaffreson's invitation.

SW→VN   **12/1/1813**
BL Add 11729 f 47; *O*   In Consonance with your Wish I give you the earliest
▭ Tue Jan 12={1813,1819}[311]

SW and Charles [Jane] Ashley have struck a bargain about the [Covent Garden] oratorio concerts. Ashley has agreed to SW's terms [of appointment as organist]. SW told him about the plan of [Sir George] Smart [conductor and organist, 1776–1867] to introduce sacred music of more modern composers [at the Drury Lane oratorio concerts] and suggested that Ashley might like to do the same [at Covent Garden], but he objected on grounds of trouble and expense.

---

[310] Ltr conceivably written to Zebedee Tydemann, who had purchased parts of the SW/CFH edition of the '48' and who lived in the same area as Jeaffreson (*see* SW→SS, 20/1/1811), and who therefore could plausibly have asked Jeaffreson to arrange a meeting with SW when SW was in Tunstall. However, no evidence to confirm this conjecture has been found.

[311] Assigned to 1813 because SW's role as regular organist of the Covent Garden oratorio concerts began in that year.

SW→VN **13/2/1813**

BL Add 11729 f 49; *O* I suppose you mean to eat Victuals somewhere
▣ 'Saturday evening', pmk 15/2/1813 (Monday)

SW invites VN to dine with him on Monday [15/2/1813] at 4 pm. RG, 'a sensible modest man', will be with SW then. After dinner, VN will have the opportunity to play [on an organ in SW's house] the 104th Psalm and the 'Black Joke [probably Clementi's *The Black Joke with 21 Variations* (1777)] upon the Horgins' [i.e., on the organ].

SW→VN **17/2/1813**

BL Add 11729 f 51; *O* I cannot exactly determine whether your Reason
▣ Wed 17 Feb={1813}[312]

SW cannot decide whether VN's reason for not appearing at SW's house on Monday [15/2/1813, *see* SW→VN, 13/2/1813] is satisfactory until they meet tomorrow [18/2/1813]. The point will be argued then in a 'true parliamentary manner' by their friend Samuel Webbe [Jr] who, in the time of Thomas Paine [writer of radical tracts, 1737–1809], was 'a celebrated man in matters of political discussion', in consequence of which he narrowly escaped prison. SW expects Webbe tomorrow at 6 pm. They will have all the 'dull and dolorous ditties' ready for VN's solace, including 'the madrigal that lost the prize' [SW's 'O sing unto mie roundelaie', submitted unsuccessfully to the 1812 Madrigal Society competition]. [Joseph] Gwilt is having SW's madrigal printed, and [Robert Thomas] Skarratt is now engraving it.

SW comments on a hostile review [of performances of Handel's *Messiah* at Drury Lane and Covent Garden on 30/1/1813] which appeared in *The Times* on 1/2/1813. He has copied this out and has lent it to Webbe [probably Webbe Jr]. SW is determined to write a rejoinder for publication in 'next month's magazine' [not identified]. He suggests sardonically [possibly because Timothy Essex had invited SW to write for the madrigal competition, *see* Timothy Essex→SW, 14/1/1812] that he can arrange for VN to have lessons concerning the chord of the 7th with Essex 'in his doctorial capacity' [Essex became doctor of music at Oxford in 1812], on the 'moderate terms' of £1/1/- per lesson.

---

[312] Assigned to 1813 from ref. in ltr to Leigh Hunt and his brother being in jail.

SW→VN   **1/3/1813?**

BL Add 11729 f 52; *O*   If you can manage at such short notice
☞ Mon 1 Mar={1813,1819,1824}[313]

SW asks VN to visit him this evening. 'Honest James Ball of Duke Street' is expected and no one else. SW asks VN to bring with him a book into which he copied some of SW's 'pot-hooks and hangers' [musical compositions], as the originals are 'a little astray' in various corners of SW's 'palace'.

SW→VN   **30/3/1813**

BL Add 11729 f 57; *O*   You will readily give me Credit for the Regret
☞ 'Monday 30/3/1813', an incorrect date[314]

SW's infant daughter [with whom SS was in 'absolute labour' on 12/11/1812, *see* SW→SGW, 12/11/1812] died last night [29/3/1813] between 9 and 10 pm. SW had to give up engagements yesterday with VN and with George Gwilt, at whose house SW was to have dined. He had firmly intended to be at St Paul's [Cathedral] yesterday with VN, and had written out the fugues in D♯ minor, G♯ minor, and B♭ minor [from part 2 of JSB's '48'] into 'the more commodious keys'. [SW's manuscript of these transposed fugues is preserved at the Royal School of Church Music.]

SW→RG   Tottenham Ct   **31/3/1813**

Baker 'Samuel Wesley, musician' folder; *O*   I am deeply concerned to inform
☞ Wed 31 Mar; pmk 1813

Because of the death of his little child, who lately was inoculated with smallpox (SW would have preferred a cowpox inoculation but SS had her way), SW is 'unavoidably precluded' from joining 'the agreeable society' at the home of RG's friend Mr Savage [not identified] tomorrow [1/4/1813]. As SW must be at his 'post' [as organist of the Covent Garden Oratorio concert] on Friday evening [2/4/1813], he hopes that RG will call at SW's home at 5 pm that day. 'Sarah' [SS] is 'very ill' now and SW wants to remain with her 'as much as possible'. He will write directly to Mr Savage and suggests that RG might 'negotiate' with Savage another day in the following week for SW to 'wait upon him'.

---

[313] Ltr presumably <1824 because SW→VN, 29/8/1820, says that Ball insulted SW and he does not like to go there, and Sarah→Mr Probyn, 19/8/1822 says that Ball is less in SW's favour than previously, suggesting that SW and Ball had little or no contact after 1820. However, no reason has been found to prefer 1813 to 1819 as the year of ltr, which accordingly has been entered ambiguously under both dates.

[314] Assigned to Tuesday 30/3/1813 because SW→RG, 31/3/1813, says that SW's child died Monday night [29/3/1813].

SW→VN **31/3/1813**

BL Add 11729 f 59; *O*   Herewith is a Tune, put together in Sorrow of Heart
☞ 31/3/1813

SW encloses a 'tune' ['Ecce panis angelorum', dated 31/3/1813] 'put together
in sorrow of heart' [because of the death of his daughter], which he thinks VN
will like. SW suggests meeting VN at [Joseph] Major's home on Sunday
[4/4/1813] at 6 pm, when they can chat and play Major's piano. Because of SS's
illness, SW is unable to have music in his own house at the moment.

SW→VN **2/4/1813**

BL Add 11729 f 60; *O*   I guessed that my Ditty would suit your Complaint
☞ 'Friday'; pmk 3/4/1813 (Saturday)

SW is 'obliged to [his] low spirits' [following the death of his daughter] for the
melody of his 'ditty' ['Ecce panis angelorum'] that he guessed would suit VN
during Lent. SW is uncertain whether he can see Picart between now and
Sunday [4/4/1813]. Tomorrow [3/4/1813] is impossible because SW has to go to
Turnham Green, and on Sunday morning Picart is likely to be 'engaged in his
trade' [as a clergyman].

For the concluding Oratorio [concert at Covent Garden] next Friday [9/4/1813],
SW has engaged VN to assist him in performing VN's arrangement of
'Sebastian's [JSB's] Symphony' [*see* SW→VN, 6/5/1812]. SW hopes that VN
will be able to attend the rehearsal, which probably will take place that morning.

SW→VN **14/4/1813**

BL Add 11729 f 87; *O*   I says as how that I owes you three Pints of Beer
☞ 'Wednesday 14' & 'Holy Week'[315]

SW owes VN three pints of beer, £3, and a 'Lamentation of Jeremias'. VN will
be given his beer tomorrow [15/4/1813], but the £3 must wait until after SW's
benefit [concert at the Argyll Rooms, 4/5/1813]. SW comments on the 'pretty
diaboliad' made of *Don Juan* 't'other night' [perhaps a rehearsal or private
performance of part of Mozart's *Don Giovanni*], and adds 'but Griffins may do
any thing, being non-descript honey-mills' [meaning unclear].[316]

---

[315] Assigned to 1813 for the following reason. The 14th day of a month occurs
in Holy Week only when Easter Sunday is on 18 April, which happened in 1813
and 1824. 1824 is excluded because ltr is addressed to VN at 240 Oxford Street,
where he lived in 1813 but not after 1820.

[316] Perhaps a reference to George Eugene Griffin, who had helped to arrange
concert performances of *Don Giovanni* in London in 1809 and earlier. See Alec
Hyatt King, 'The quest for Sterland – 3: *Don Giovanni* in London before 1817',
in his *Musical Pursuits* (London, 1987) p 137.

SW→VN   **30/4/1813**

BL Add 11729 f 61; *O*   Mr Glenn & myself were disappointed at your

☞ Fri 30 Apr={1813,1819,1824}[317]

RG and SW were disappointed by VN's non-appearance last Sunday [25/4/1813] and attributed this to the bad weather. SW's Trio for three pianofortes cannot be performed [at SW's benefit concert on 4/5/1813] because the orchestra at the Argyll Rooms cannot easily accommodate three pianos, and the organ will take up much space. 'Silly' [James] Bartleman [bass singer, 1769–1821] prevents his boy King [possibly C. M. King, son of the composer Matthew Peter King] from singing. This does not upset SW, but WL had wanted the boy to sing one of WL's songs. SW is concerned about recruiting his orchestra as Tuesday is an opera night, but some people say that 'opera on Tuesday there will be none'.

SW→VN   **about 1/5/1813**

BL Add 11729 f 62; *O*   I should have liked to perform the Organ Duet

ltr undated[318]

SW would have liked to perform [with VN at SW's benefit concert on 4/5/1813] the organ duet [SW's *Grand Duet* in C], but the organ [at the Argyll Rooms] has only one manual; consequently it would be impossible for them to perform the Andante, which has some 'criss-cross work'. SW is still worried about recruiting his orchestra: he was led to believe that he would have no difficulties in finding sufficient people independently of the opera, but this turns out not to be the case. 'The brute' [James] Bartleman prevents his boy [King] from singing [at SW's concert, *see* SW→VN, 30/4/1813]. This hurts WL, as the boy was to have sung one of WL's canzonets, which now has had to be withdrawn.

SW assumes that VN will 'take a hand' with SW in the 'symphony' of JSB [arranged by VN]. SW desires that VN look in at Flight and Robson's [the organ builders supplying the organ for the concert]. VN will like the pedals, his special concern in the JSB symphony.

---

[317] Assigned to 1813 for the following reason. 1819 excluded as Argyll Rooms unavailable that year (the old Rooms were destroyed in 1818 and the New Argyll Rooms opened in 1820). 1824 excluded as Bartleman then no longer alive.

[318] Ltr >30/4/1813, as SW then was uncertain (*see* SW→VN, 30/4/1813) whether there would be an opera on 4/5/1813; and not later than a few days before 4/5/1813, as SW discusses in ltr the not yet settled arrangements for his benefit concert that day.

SW→BJ[319]   **10/5/1813**
RCM Ms 2130, ltr 23; *O*   I have the Pleasure to inform You that I have
▤ 10/5/1813
SW has arranged a plan with [Robert] Birchall to bring out the '4th number of
the Preludes and Fugues' [book 4 of the SW/CFH edition of the '48'] by
1/7/1813 and intends to advertise this within a few days. The subscribers have
been remiss in their applications for the '3rd number' [book 3 of this edition],
which is the main reason why the remaining volume has been delayed. SW
sends best wishes to BJ's wife and family.

SW→RG   **18/5/1813**
BL Add 35013 f 58; *O*   Mr Novello & myself have appointed to meet
▤ Tue 18 May=(1802,1813,1819}[320]
VN and SW have agreed to meet on Thursday [20/5/1813] at St Paul's
[Cathedral], at the beginning of the service. They intend afterwards to 'rattle
some of the old boy's [JSB's] fugues' on the organ. They hope that RG will
come and will bring a friend or two.

SW→VN   **26/5/1813**
BL Add 11729 f 63; *O*   I find all the Papers we took to St Paul's right
▤ 26/5/1813
SW has found all the music that he and VN took to St Paul's [Cathedral] except
for the manuscript organ duet; if VN has this he should let SW know. [Samuel]
Webbe [Jr] was indignant at not being told of their meeting [at St Paul's] last
Thursday [20/5/1813]. He has invited SW to visit him on Saturday [29/5/1813]
to learn [Samuel] Webbe Jr's duet. SW wishes VN to meet him there.

SW→VN   **21/6/1813**
Osborn file folder 15900; *O*   I am concerned to report unto You a twofold
▤ Mon 21 June={1813}; pmk 1813
SW regrets that he cannot meet VN at the Philharmonic Society concert this
evening. It conflicts with a performance of a song at Vauxhall Gardens [sung by
SW's 'girl', presumably his pupil, *see* SW→VN, 23/6/1813] that SW wishes to
hear. He is 'truly vexed' that the meeting on Wednesday [23/6/1813] cannot take

---

[319] Ltr addressed to 'Dear Sir'. BJ identified as recipient because ltr conveys
SW's greetings to 'Mrs Jacobs and family'.

[320] Assigned to 1813 for the following reason. 1819 excluded because ltr
addressed to RG at Stewart Street where he lived in 1813; from 1815 RG lived
in Kirby Street, Hatton Garden. 1802 excluded because SW's interest in JSB's
fugues began after then. Also, SW's 20/5/1813 meeting with VN at St Paul's
Cathedral is confirmed in SW→VN, 26/5/1813.

place because of the many other things he must do before leaving London [for Ipswich] this week. He will inform VN of his movements. Except for copying, these are unlikely to be musical movements until he gets to the country. He advises VN to 'take things quietly as they are' and not to fret because things 'are not as we could wish them'. He promises to get VN's two tunes done before leaving London.

Today SW heard the unpleasant news that SGW has had 'the touch of a complaint' that could be paralytic. This diagnosis is plausible as she is 'nearly 86 years old' [in fact, she was nearly 87].

SW→VN   **23/6/1813**
BL Add 11729 f 64; *O*   Herein are the Tunes required
◻ 23/6/1813

SW encloses the 'tunes required, written at a mail coach pace'. His 'girl' [*see* SW→VN, 21/6/1813] was well received at Vauxhall, and 'the manager' [George Rogers Barrett] seemed pleased. SW introduced himself to [James] Hook [composer, 1746–1827], who surprised SW by his courtesy and by saying that he had just published a voluntary 'at Bland and Weller's' dedicated to SW. SW ordered three copies and has given one to 'little Joey' [Major]. SW is impressed with it: the fugue is better than anything he has heard Crotch perform on the organ. Hook played a 'praeludium' at the opening of each part [at Vauxhall], which was 'in thorough organ style, and with knowing modulation'.

SW intends to leave London [for Ipswich] on Friday [25/6/1813]. He suggests that VN call in tomorrow evening [24/6/1813]. SW will show VN Hook's voluntary and will appreciate VN's opinion of it. 'Birchall's people' have promised to send the JSB proofs [of book 4 of the SW/CFH edition of the '48'] to VN, but he should 'jog some of their heavy-arsed memories'.

Thomas Green journal entry   Ipswich   **27/6/1813**
GM n.s. v 9 (May 1838) p 468   Went to the Tower church
GM

Thomas Green went to [St Mary le] Tower Church [in Ipswich]. After the service, he took SW and [Professor Charles] Hague [a promoter of the Ipswich Festival on 6–8/7/1813, in which SW performed, *see* SW→SS, 9/7/1813] to the organ loft, where SW 'romanced [on the organ] in a most stupendous style' for more than an hour. SW said that he 'never thought beforehand' about his improvisations nor remembered them afterwards, but 'could always play when he sat doggedly about it'. A voluntary that SW played 'took away the breath'.

Thomas Green journal entry   Ipswich   **28/6/1813**

GM n.s. v 9 (May 1838) p 468   Wesley, Dr Hague, and others, dined with me
GM

SW, [Charles] Hague and other persons dined with Green. At the dinner SW was 'full of life and spirit and anecdote'. He recounted a visit by Dr [Samuel] Johnson to CW's house: Johnson said then that as CW's 'boys' [CW Jr and SW] were 'skilled in music' he would like to hear them but, as soon as they started to play, Johnson read a book. Although Johnson once described singing as 'howling', he told CB that he envied CB's 'sixth sense' [for music]. SW said that CB 'possessed rather more taste than science' and was 'too much attached to the Italian school' [of composers]. The Germans, SW said, were 'far their superiors in harmony', and in Mozart 'both excellencies' were united.

SW said that, at the time of the Commemoration of Handel [at Westminster Abbey from 26/5/1784 to 5/6/1784], he had been 'seized, from particular circumstances, with a nervous horror against music', which had caused him 'torment and pain'.

During the evening SW got 'prodigiously elated'. He 'joined in the singing, with good effect' and 'extemporised most stupendously'. He declared that he was 'perfectly versed in all the minutiae of the Roman Catholic religion' and 'could perform Masses as a priest'. He was 'wonderfully quick and brilliant'. He 'drained all the bottles' and Green had difficulty 'getting rid of him' at midnight.

SW→SS   Ipswich   **6/7/1813**

BL Add 35012 f 45   I am extremely concerned to hear such a bad Account
▣ 6/7/1813

SW is about to go to the first rehearsal at the [St Mary le] Tower Church and cannot write as much as he would like. He cannot be sure when he will return, but will let SS know by letter. He intends to write to WL about 'the bill', and will not be offended even if WL cannot help. If possible, SW must prevent [George] Oliver [CLW's trustee] from doing SW mischief. SW will require Oliver to apply to SGW, which will save SS some trouble.

SW is extremely concerned about SSW's poor health and wishes that SS could have 'Boy Blue' [SSW] 'at some near place' where SW and SS could see him almost every day. SW hopes that SSW does not fret after him. SS should kiss SSW for SW and should tell him that SW will come home soon. She should fatten SSW with arrowroot and let him have as much good air as possible.

SW→SS   Ipswich   **9/7/1813**

BL Add 35012 f 46   I mean to come in the morning Coach on Monday next
▣ 9/7/1813

SW plans to return in the morning coach on Monday [11/7/1813]. It will stop at the Four Swans [inn in Bishopsgate Street, London] around 5 pm. When SS learns that Dr [Professor Charles] Hague has lost £150 in promoting the Ipswich Festival, she may consider that SW's loss at his benefit concert [at the Argyll

Rooms on 4/5/1813] was a good thing. SW told Hague that he wished he could afford to donate his services, but that this was out of the question.

SW has written to WL [not preserved, presumably concerning the bill mentioned in SW→SS, 6/7/1813], who has agreed to SW's request. SS is likely to receive a letter addressed to SW before she sees him on Monday [11/7/1813]. She is to open it and to 'proceed accordingly'. He hopes to find SSW recovered. Mrs J [not identified] is in a bad way. SW thinks that she will die or will destroy herself before long.

SW→VN   **18/8/1813**
BL Add 11729 f 68; *O*   I shall expect You, selon votre Promesse
▣ 18/8/1813
SW expects VN 'next Saturday' [21/8/1813] about 7 pm and will try to persuade Bridgetower to come and 'scrape out one of the old humbug's country dances'. Samuel Webbe Sr has asked SW to intercede with VN to procure a deputy for Webbe Sr's 'Sardinian [Embassy Chapel] organ'. The salary is inconsiderable, only £10 or £10/10/- per annum. SW intends to ask Samuel Webbe Jr to come on Saturday, when VN will have an opportunity of discussing the matter with him.

CB→SW   **29/8/1813**
BL Add 35027 f 12v   Though the weather grows daily more cold
▣ 29/8/1813
CB takes SW to task for failing to appear at a meeting with CB that SW had himself arranged. CB reminds SW that this has happened before, and is unwilling at the moment to arrange another meeting. CB has been 'so long detached from the active world and weaned from musical delights' that he does not wish to renew them unless coaxed by 'the civilities of such a performer as' SW.

Commenting on SW's statement that 'the little Paton' [Mary Anne Paton, soprano, 1802–1864] is to be of SW's party 'in the country', CB notes that it was he who was the first to hear her in England, having been requested by Lord Buchan [David Steuart Erskine, 1742–1829, 11th Earl of Buchan] to hear her and to recommend her to the patronage of CB's friends.

SW→VN   **3/9/1813**
BL Add 11729 f 70; *O*   On Tuesday next friend Webbe & I mean to commit
▣ 3/9/1813
Next Tuesday [7/9/1813] SW and [Samuel] Webbe [Jr] plan to 'commit [their] carcases to the mercy of the winds and waves' [possibly to Margate or Ramsgate, but the location of their journey has not been determined]. SW wonders if VN would like to accompany them, as he had hinted he might. SW also reminds VN of his promise to teach SW's 'eight young yahoos' at

Paddington on one Monday and one or two Thursdays during his 'days of banishment', which should be for not more than ten days at the most. SW may appear in VN's 'cock loft' [at the Portuguese Embassy Chapel] on Sunday morning [5/9/1813] if the organ there is working again.

John Farey→'Mr Urban'[321]   1/10/1813

GM v 84 part 1 (Feb 1814) p 135–137   Observing that the Rev. Henry Liston's *GM*

John Farey [geologist and writer on musical temperament, 1766–1826] has listened several times 'with peculiar delight to the fine and novel effects of the perfect harmony' produced on the Rev. Henry Liston's euharmonic organ at the rooms of Messrs Flight and Robson. Farey witnessed there the facility with which, after 'slight practice', SW and other performers could manage the pedals of this organ to produce such effects.

SW→RG   5 Gower Pl   10/10/1813

GEU in box 6; *O*   I have been very much longing for a Call from You

'Sunday evening'; pmk 11/10/1813 (Monday)

SW is concerned because he has not heard from RG. SW would like RG to hear SW's plans for the coming season and to see his new home at 5 Gower Place, which is more pleasant, neater and cheaper than his previous 'dark hole' in Tottenham Court.

SW→Governors, Foundling Hospital   5 Gower Pl   8/11/1813

LMA A/FH/A06/001/071/19/1; *O*   Having this day been informed that

8/11/1813

SW heard today that the post of organist at the Foundling Hospital Chapel has become vacant by the death [which in fact did not occur until 21/11/1813] of William Russell. SW offers his services.

---

[321] 'Sylvanus Urban' was the pseudonym of the editor of the *GM*.

SW→RG?[322]   **9/11/1813**
MA DDWF/15/17A; *O*   Will you take a Beef Steak with me To=morrow at 2
▣ Tue 9 Nov={1813}[323]
  SW asks his 'dear friend' [presumably RG] to 'take a beef steak' with him
tomorrow afternoon [10/11/1813] and then, if possible, to accompany him to
Deptford [presumably to meet or to hear John Charles Nightingale, organist,
1790–1833, former deputy of the organist William Russell, *see* SW→RG,
25/11/1813]. SW has 'started for the Foundling' [i.e., has started applying for
the post of organist at the Foundling Hospital]. He understands that he has 'no
bad chance', but 'nothing now disappoints' him.

William Kitchiner→Christopher Idle   5 Gower Pl   **10/11/1813**
MA DDWF/15/17B[324]   Allow me to recommend to your patronage my old
▣ 10/11/1813
  William Kitchiner [writer on music, cookery and other subjects, self-styled
medical doctor, 1775–1827] recommends his 'old friend' SW to the patronage of
Christopher Idle [in his capacity as a governor of the Foundling Hospital]. SW is
'a worthy man and an incomparable organist'.

SW→Samuel Compton Cox   5 Gower Pl   **24/11/1813**
LMA A/FH/MO1/001.004; *O*   Mr Samuel Wesley presents his Respects to Mr
▣ 27/11/1813
  SW informs Samuel Compton Cox [Treasurer of the Foundling Hospital] of his
willingness to play the organ there on Tuesday [30/11/1813], in the morning or
the evening or at both times. If necessary, SW also will attend a rehearsal with
the vocal performers on Saturday [27/11/1813].

SW→RG   5 Gower Pl   **25/11/1813**
BL Add 35013 f 59; *O*   You are long ere now informed of poor Russell's
▣ Thu 25 Nov & 🖎→🛈
  RG will have heard that [William] Russell died [on 21/11/1813]. SW now can
openly express his interest [in the organist's position at the Foundling Hospital],

---

[322] Ltr addressed to 'My dear Friend'. RG presumed as addressee because SW
apparently used this salutation at this time only in letters to him (for instance, in
SW→RG, 25/11/1813).

[323] Assigned to 1813 because ltr says SW starting his application for the
Foundling Hospital post (*see* SW→Governors, Foundling Hospital, 8/11/1813).

[324] Ltr written on the bottom of a printed sheet prepared by SW to canvas
support for his application for the 'place of organist to the Foundling Hospital'.
Presumably SW had sent this sheet to Kitchiner.

and has spoken to 'Mr Treasurer [Samuel Compton] Cox'. SW thinks that Cox supports another candidate. SW's offer to play for services next Sunday [28/11/1813] was declined on the grounds that [John Charles] Nightingale, Russell's former deputy, already had been engaged, but the Drummers tell SW that Nightingale will be at his Deptford church on that day. At the Grand Lodge yesterday [24/11/1813], SW saw the Duke of Sussex [Augustus Frederick, who on 12/5/1813 had succeeded the Prince Regent as Grand Master], who promised to support SW's candidacy. SW asks RG to call, and will be sure to be at home on Saturday evening [27/11/1813].

SW→VN Gower Pl[325] **23/12/1813**

BL Add 11729 f 75; *O* I know your readiness to adopt the Gospel Advice

✉ 'Thursday evening'; pmk 24/12/1813 (Friday)

SW is in distress for want of time to complete a composition which must be performed next Monday [28/12/1813]. At the command of [Augustus Frederick,] the Duke of Sussex, SW has 'half composed' an anthem ['Behold, how good a thing it is'] to be sung next Monday [28/12/1813] at the meeting of reconciliation of the ancient and modern Freemasons [the union of the two Grand Lodges of England, forming the United Grand Lodge]. He asks VN to help him copy out the chorus parts.

SW will come to High Mass [at the Portuguese Embassy Chapel] on Saturday [Christmas Day] but requests a reply immediately. He notes that the Foundling Hospital appointment 'goes on rather in favour of the long-nosed man' [perhaps a reference to SW himself, *see* the portrait of SW in the frontispiece].

SW→VN **26/12/1813**

BL Add 11729 f 76; *O* The Bearer will convey the MS. safely.

✉ 'Sunday' & '*Festum Sancti Stephani*' [26 Dec]→{1802,1813,1819,1824}[326]

SW sends the manuscript [presumably of his anthem 'Behold, how good a thing it is']. He has omitted to write out the second tenor part and will do that as soon as he gets hold of the score. He is about to go to [James] Perry [a Masonic official] to arrange for a rehearsal. SW has already tried, on VN's account, to have the rehearsal take place between 1 pm and 3 pm or alternatively after 5 pm, and will let VN know what is agreed.

---

[325] Ltr does not specify the house number.

[326] Assigned to 1813 for the following reason. 1824 excluded because ltr addressed to VN at 240 Oxford Street from where he moved in 1820. 1802 excluded because outside the period of known correspondence between SW and VN. 1813 preferred to 1819 because SW is not known to have been involved in rehearsals with VN in December 1819 and a Masonic official named James Perry was involved in the 28/12/1813 meeting of reconciliation (*see* SW→VN, 23/12/1813).

SW→VN   **4/1/1814**

BL Add 11729 f 79; *O*   I am sorry we did not better understand each other
🖃 4/1/1814

SW regrets the misunderstanding about the meeting at [Joseph] Major's house.
SW was prevented from calling on Major before dinner by a conversation with a
new 'scholar'. SW dined with 'Pokey' [not identified], but set off as soon as he
could. He brought his manuscript book and JSB's motets with him as he was
sure that he would find VN in Carmarthen Street [presumably where Major
lived]. SW will be at home this evening and invites VN to take 'a quartern of
gin' with him. VN perhaps is not aware that SW has 'missed the certainty of
being kicked and cuffed about by the worthy governors of the Sunday bawdy
house' [the Foundling Hospital Chapel]. SW today met [John] Immyns
[organist, 1764–>1818, from 1798 to 1801 organist of the Foundling Hospital
Chapel], who congratulated SW on his escape [from being appointed organist]
and said that SW 'should not have been a fortnight in the situation without
spitting in Mr Treasurer [Samuel Compton] Cox's face'.

SW→Bridgetower   Gower Pl[327]   **24/1/1814**

BL Add 56411 f 12; *O*   I saw my Friend Linley on Monday last
🖃 Mon 24 Jan & 🖼→🛈

WL, whom SW last Monday [17/1/1814], will be happy to join the party on
Thursday [27/1/1814] if possible, but it is his birthday and a dinner for him has
been arranged. VN, whom SW saw yesterday [23/1/1814], will 'make a point of
attending' Bridgetower's party. VN is the most completely music-loving of
SW's 'professional friends', although SW considers Bridgetower to be VN's
equal in this respect.

SW→VN   **28/1/1814?**

BL Add 11729 f 69; *O*   I fear that something serious has been the Cause of
ltr undated[328]

SW fears that 'something serious' prevented VN appearing between 7 and 10
pm last night [27/1/1814] at 20 Chapel Street, Grosvenor Place [Bridgetower's
house], and asks what it was. The participants experienced a 'luxurious treat of
harmony'. The music played included a trio by Mozart, two trios by Purcell, one
trio by JSB, another by JSB arranged from Prelude and Fugue 1 in book 3 of
SW's edition [with CFH of the '48'], and the Chaconne [from JSB's *Partita* II,
BWV 1004] and the Fugue in C from the 'solos' [JSB's *Sonata* III, BWV 1005;

---

[327] Ltr does not specify the house number.

[328] Assigned to 28/1/1814 on the presumption that the party at Bridgetower's
house described in ltr is the 27/1/1814 party anticipated in SW→Bridgetower,
24/1/1814. No other party arranged by Bridgetower involving SW has been
identified.

the incipit of the fugue is quoted]. The performances were 'admirably given' by Bridgetower, and the whole was 'the most classical affair in the crotchet and quaver line' that SW has witnessed for a long time. If anything further could have been desired it was either Beethoven's 'Pastoral' Symphony or Webbe [Sr]'s 'Cantantibus Organis'.

SW→VN   **31/1/1814**
BL Add 11729 f 80; *O*   You were so good as to say (some Weeks ago)
▱ Mon 31 Jan={1814,1820,1825}[329]
   VN told SW some weeks ago that he still had the privilege of nominating a subscriber for the Philharmonic Society [of which SW had become an Associate Member in 1813]. A lady known to SW [Mrs Tyndale, *see* SW→VN, 4/2/1814] is anxious to acquire a subscription for her daughter, and SW promised to use his influence with VN. Today is the last day for applications, and SW hopes that she is not too late. He had told her that he hoped to see VN last Thursday [27/1/1814]; she was 'sadly vexed' when SW told her on Saturday [29/1/1814] that he did not see VN on Thursday.

SW→VN   **4/2/1814**
BL Add 11729 f 81; *O*   From the Threat in your last I fully expected
▱ 'Friday night'; pmk 5/2/1814 (Saturday)
   From VN's last letter [not preserved], SW expected to see him this evening and invites him to visit on Sunday [6/2/1814]. The Drummers and Street will be with SW on Sunday and hope to 'besiege' VN's 'holy citadel' at 11 am [for High Mass at the Portuguese Embassy Chapel]. They would very much like to hear Haydn's '1st Mass'. SW has 'done a good piece' of VN's *Missa Defunctorum*. Mrs Tyndale, 'a sort of a blue stocking worthy', thanks VN for acquiring a ticket [for the Philharmonic Society's concerts] for her daughter [*see* SW→VN, 31/1/1814]. SW asks if VN has seen January's *European Magazine* [which reported the union of the two Freemason lodges, *see* SW→VN, 23/12/1813, and SW's part in the proceedings]. SW has finished the slow movement of his sonata [not identified].

---

[329] Ltr assigned to 1814 because ref. to mother and daughter consistent with SW's description, in SW→VN, 4/2/1814, of Mrs Tyndale and her daughter; also, ltr's statement that SW expected to see VN last Thursday but did not is consistent with VN's non–appearance at Bridgetower's party on Thursday 27/1/1824 mentioned in SW→VN, 28/1/1814?. Philharmonic Society ref. makes 1814 the earliest possible year for this ltr.

Gesualdo Lanza→Editor, *Theatrical Inquisitor* 　　　　**2/1814**
Oxberry v 2, 18/6/1825, p 124–128 　　　　To what or to whose malevolence I
Oxberry[330]
　Gesualdo Lanza affirms that Catherine Stephens was his pupil when she sang at 'concerts given' by SW and Samuel Webbe Jr in Ramsgate on 3/10/1812. SW said that 'she received the greatest and most deserved applause' for her performances there.

SW→RG 　　　　**8/3/1814**
BL Add 35013 f 61; *O* 　　　　I am in a Dilemma concerning Mr Savage.
☞ Tue 8 Mar; pmk 1814
　VN helped to copy SW's [organ] concerto [in C, the autograph score is dated 5/3/1814] until 1 am last Sunday [6/3/1814] and wishes to be near SW when SW performs it [for the first time] tomorrow [9/3/1814, at the Oratorio concert, Covent Garden]. SW also expects RG [to be near SW at the organ]. The Ashleys [General Christopher Ashley and Charles Jane Ashley] allow no more than two people to be near the organ at concerts. This presents a problem with Mr Savage [RG's friend, *see* SW→RG, 31/3/1813], who perhaps will agree to attend on some other evening when a concerto is performed. SW asks RG to negotiate the matter with Savage as best he can, and hopes that this can be done without offending him.

SW→RG 　　　　**16/3/1814**
MA DDWF/15/18; *O* 　　　I trust that you are not displeased at my not having come
☞ Wed 16 Mar; pmk 1816
　SW apologises for not having come to RG at the Chapel [presumably the Portuguese Embassy Chapel] last Sunday [13/3/1814]. SW could not easily leave the party, as Mrs Foote [presumably his hostess] did not want him to 'slip' away, even for half an hour. He intends to be in Houndsditch tomorrow by 5 pm and will meet RG there.

SW→VN 　　　　**17/3/1814**
BL Add 11729 f 83; *O* 　　　The Cramers & Horsley have appointed to meet me
☞ 'Thursday morning'; pmk 17/3[331]
　[John Baptist and François] Cramer and WH have arranged to meet SW at Chappell's [either the home of Samuel Chappell or the premises of his music publishing firm] on Saturday [19/3/1814] at 8 pm. SW hopes that VN will join them. SW has nominated Samuel Webbe [Jr] as a member of the 'committee on

---

[330] The day on which ltr was written is not given in *Oxberry*.

[331] Assigned to 1814 because of ref. to error printed in the February 1814 *EM*; also, 17 March was a Thursday in 1814.

Russell's business' [to arrange a performance of the oratorio *Job* by William Russell, organist, 1777–1813] and will advise Webbe [Jr] of the meeting. VN should inform SW if he intends to be at the [Covent Garden] theatre with SW tomorrow [18/3/1814, at an oratorio concert where SW played the organ] so that SW can make the necessary arrangements. VN would hardly believe how SW is 'bothered by applications from overturners' [page turners].

SW has asked the editor of the *EM* to correct, 'in the next number', a mistake in a review [presumably by SW] in last month's number [the February 1814 *EM*]. Instead of 'a side drum', the *EM* printed [on p 138] 'a sick dream'.

SW told Ashley [General Christopher Ashley or Charles Jane Ashley] that SW would like to perform VN's arrangement of JSB's 'prelude' [for organ duet and orchestra, *see* SW→VN, 6/5/1812]. Ashley consented to this, but the piece must be rehearsed.

SW→VN   **23/3/1814**

BL Add 11729 f 85; *O*   J. Cramer informs me that Horsley had undertaken
☛ Wed 23 Mar={1814}[332]

John Baptist Cramer has told SW that WH failed to inform members of the committee [set up to discuss the performance of William Russell's *Job*; *see* SW→VN, 17/3/1814] that their meeting could not take place last Saturday [19/3/1814]. Another meeting is proposed for Thursday [24/3/1814] at Chappell's at 7 pm.; SW will be there. SW regrets he was unable to be with VN last Sunday [20/3/1814]. SW will have more time 'when the oratorio shop is shut'.

---

[332] Assigned to 1814 because of ref. to meeting at Chappell's (*see* SW→VN, 17/3/1814).

SW→VN   **13/4/1814**

BL Add 11729 f 89; *O*   Your Note to the Committee convinced us
▣ Wed 13; pmk 14/4/181-;[333] Wed 14 Apr={1808,1814,1825}& pmk →▣

VN's note to the [Philharmonic Society] committee convinced them that he has 'no notes beside to attend unto' [i.e., that VN has no copying work remaining to be done]. SW asks when the Te Deum will be performed [presumably at the Portuguese Embassy Chapel] and whether he can help with copying.

'Harry Smart' [Henry Smart, violinist, 1778–1823, from 1812 leader of the Drury Lane Theatre orchestra] will let SW and VN appear in the [Drury Lane] orchestra 'at all godly opportunities'. 'Kean's *Richard* is a Monday go' [i.e., Edmund Kean [actor, 1787–1833] performs the title role in Shakespeare's *Richard III* at Drury Lane Theatre on Mondays]. However, Smart previously promised [a right of admission in the orchestra] next Monday [18/4/1814] to WH. Monday week [25/4/1814] is Linley's 'do' [a concert of music mainly by Thomas Linley, composer, 1733–1795, WL's father; the concert was directed by SW, who also played the organ]. Therefore VN and SW must postpone [the opportunity of seeing Kean's performance] and be patient.

SW→VN   **20/4/1814**

BL Add 11729 f 90; *O*   If the Report from the Paper be true, Louis XVIII is
▣ Wed 20 Apr={1814} & departure of Louis XVIII →▣

SW read in a newspaper that Louis XVIII is to leave England on Sunday next [24/4/1814, to take the throne as king of France]. SW assumes that the Te Deum is postponed, but wishes for more certain news. Ill-health prevented him from hearing what he understands was a very bad [Philharmonic Society] concert on Monday [18/4/1814].

SW supposes that [Samuel] Chappell failed to inform VN of the committee meeting last night [19/4/1814], which was attended by F[rançois] Cramer, [Samuel] Webbe [Jr], WH, Attwood, [James] Elliott and SW. They went through two Acts of [William] Russell's 'poor' oratorio [*Job*] and agreed that it could be performed only once in public, and that it was lucky that the place fixed is a chapel, as in a room or theatre there would certainly be 'serpentine symptoms'. If VN's 'grand do' is not fixed for Friday [22/4/1814], SW will depend on him to assist SW at the rehearsal. SW will dine with the Jeaffreson family tomorrow [21/4/1814] at 6 pm at 41 Duke Street, Manchester Square; he asks VN to call on him there. The committee meets on Friday [22/4/1814] to go over the third act of Russell's oratorio; SW hopes that VN will be present.

VN will find [James W.] Windsor [composer and pianist, 1776–1853] to be a 'sensible' and 'modest' man who knows almost as much about harmony as [James] Bartleman. [Thomas] Greatorex believes that 'chorus singers never can be harmonists'.

---

[333] The last digit of the postmarked year is illegible.

SW→RG 14/5/1814
BL Add 35013 f 64; *O*   Pray are you alive or dead? If the latter, I am sure
pmk 14/5/1814
   SW inquires humorously whether RG is alive or dead. If the latter, RG will feel
it his duty to come to see SW without delay.

SW→RG Gower Pl[334] 25/5/1814
BL Add 35013 f 66; *O*   I shall most willingly attend You on Sunday
☑ Wed 25 May; pmk 1814
   SW will be pleased to be with RG on Sunday [29/5/1814] to meet Mr James
[not identified], and will be happy to see RG if he calls on SW on his return from
[Christ's] Hospital [of which RG was music master]. SW asks RG to turn pages
for him [at a concert at Covent Garden] on Saturday evening [28/5/1814]. He
thinks VN will come too, so cannot invite anyone else without cross looks from
'the rascally Ashleys' [*see* SW→RG, 8/3/1814].

SW→VN Gower Pl[335] 26/5/1814
BL Add 11729 f 92; *O*   I have but just now received your Letter
☑ Thu 26 May={1814}; pmk 27/5/1814
   SW has just now received VN's letter [not preserved], which arrived too late
for SW to think of dining with 'the gentlemen at Hampstead'. He had not
expected to be invited there. He has asked RG to be with him on Saturday
evening [to turn pages at a Covent Garden concert on 28/5/1814 in which SW
played organ, *see* SW→RG, 25/5/1814] and would like to have VN also by his
side [at the organ during the concert]. SW invites VN to take coffee with him at
5.30 pm on Saturday.

SW→Bridgetower Gower Pl[336] 1/7/1814
BL Add 56411 f 14; *O*   Being now comparatively a disengaged Animal
☑ Fri 1 Jul; pmk 1814
   SW now is less busy than when 'the performance of Linley's and Russell's
music was in preparation' [for the concert of Thomas Linley's music on
25/4/1814 and the performance of Russell's *Job* on 15/6/1814]. SW has
promised CW Jr that Bridgetower would play for him JSB's 'exquisite [violin]
solos' and asks when Bridgetower can do this. If he names a convenient evening
in the next week, SW will inform CW Jr immediately. SW will attend and hopes
that Bridgetower will allow VN to come also.

---

[334] Ltr does not specify the house number.

[335] Ltr does not specify the house number.

[336] Ltr does not specify the house number.

SW→VN   1/7/1814

BL Add 11729 f 96; *O*   I have not been yet successful in discovering
▣ Fri 1 Jul; pmk 2/7/1814 (Saturday)

SW has not found the original score of his Trio [for three pianofortes] but
hopes to locate it by Sunday [3/7/1814]. Meanwhile, VN should ask [Samuel]
Webbe [Jr] if he has it. If it cannot be found, a third copy can be made from
VN's copy or from [Charles] Stokes's copy. However, this cannot be done by
Sunday.

SW→VN   9/7/1814?

BL Add 11729 f 66; *O*   I mounted Guard, selon ma Promesse for you
▣ Fri 9 Jul[337]

SW deputised [at the Portuguese Embassy Chapel] for VN yesterday [8/7/1814,
the feast of St Elizabeth of Portugal, marked by a sung Mass at the Chapel].
They could not perform anything complex, as VN had forgotten to leave the key
of his 'bum-fiddle box' [presumably a music bench with a lockable
compartment], and therefore decided to perform the Mass in G Major by
[Samuel] Webbe [Sr]. 'Little [John Francis] Prina' [organist, 1798–1841?, at this
time a chorister at the Portuguese Embassy Chapel] ran to VN's house for the
key, but VN's brother [Francis Novello, b1779, bass singer in the Chapel choir]
said that it was better to be not too ambitious with a small choir.

[James] Asperne, editor [in fact, publisher] of the *EM*, 'scruples' to pay SW
for his review until he discovers what other reviewers get. SW asks what VN
was paid when he 'once reviewed in a magazine'. SW would rather receive an
annual sum than be paid by the sheet and supposes that 25 guineas [£26/5/-] is
'not out of the way'. He expects to see VN on Sunday [10/7/1814] and hopes
that VN's 'aquatic affair' [not identified] turned out well. SW was 'glad to be all
day out of the reach of the Royal Blackguard' [the Prince Regent], who he hears
was 'hissed all the way [during a procession to celebrate the ending of the
Peninsular War: *see The Examiner*, 10/7/1814] in a jolly style'. SW requests
VN's reply, as the 'rascally bookseller' [Asperne] awaits SW's 'requisition'.

SW→VN   19/7/1814

BL Add 11729 f 98; *O*   I have compleated the Transcript of the Trio
pmk 8 am 20/7/1814, hence ltr presumably written the previous day

SW has transcribed his Trio [for three pianofortes] and suggests Monday
[25/7/1814] as the most suitable day to perform it, when he will be free from 1
pm. Salomon is 'agog' to come and Clementi has promised to attend. SW will

---

[337] Assigned to 1814 because SW's reviewing for the *EM* presumably began in
this year. In 1814, 9 July was a Saturday, contrary to what SW wrote. (9 July
was a Friday in 1813 but SW was in Ipswich then and on the immediately
preceding days, *see* SW→SS, 6/7/1813 and 9/7/1813).

invite [John Baptist] and [François] Cramer but has no hope of the former coming, especially as he may have heard how well [Marmaduke Charles] Wilson can play his music. The performance of the 'selected' [Mass in VN's *A Collection of Sacred Music* (1811)] went well on Sunday [17/7/1814], despite Lanza's absence [presumably the boy singer, *see* SW→VN, 7/7/1812].

SW→RG   4 Gower Pl   **22/7/1814**
BL Add 35013 f 68; *O*   You remember that when Moses went
📧 Fri 22 Jul & 📧→ⓘ
SW wonders what has become of RG. On Monday [25/7/1814], at 5 pm in Clementi's [piano] manufactory in Tottenham Court Road, [Marmaduke Charles] Wilson will play [John Baptist] Cramer's [piano] Concerto in D minor. SW's Trio for three pianofortes also will be performed. SW has 'summoned some of the great guns', including [John Baptist and François] Cramer, Kollmann [presumably George Augustus Kollmann] and [Jean T.] Latour [French pianist and composer, 1766–1840]. SW invites RG to come too.

SW→VN   **29/7/1814**
BL Add 11729 f 100; *O*   I am not certain whether you will esteem Two Pence
📧 Fri 29 Jul; pmk 1814
SW encloses a 'bagatelle' [not identified]. If VN considers the music worth two pence he will perhaps let it be sung [at the Portuguese Embassy Chapel] next Sunday [31/7/1814]. SW suggests ironically that the choir should not need 'more than a dozen rehearsals'. He will be with VN at High Mass to learn the fate of this 'abstruse piece of counterpoint'.

SW→VN   **11/8/1814**
BL Add 11729 f 101; *O*   I was not at Vickery's on Tuesday evening
📧 Thu 11 Aug; pmk 1814
SW was prevented by a 'plaguey bilious colic' from being at Vickery's [presumably the home of Rev. Francis William Johnson Vickery, *c*1787–1866, a member of the Madrigal Society] on Tuesday evening [9/8/1814]. SW now is considerably recovered and hopes to see VN at 3 pm next Sunday [14/8/1814]. Vickery called on SW today and said that VN had not joined the party on Tuesday [9/8/1814]. SW explained that VN probably was still out of town then. Vickery wants to hear the South Street [Portuguese Embassy Chapel] organ and means to meet SW and VN after Vespers. He wants also to buy VN's two volumes of church music [VN's *Collection of Sacred Music*, published in 1811]. SW told him that he would ask VN the best way of obtaining them.
The Mass on Sunday [7/8/1814] went very well. [Rev. William Victor] Fryer requested Mozart, to which SW had no objection. SW has not found his 'harmonised Gregorian *De Angelis*' [his *Missa pro angelis*] and asks if he lent it to VN. It was 'a favourite foster child', which SW would be sorry to lose.

SW→John Bernard Logier   4 Gower Pl   **1/9/1814**

Logier p 24[338]   I feel much satisfaction in expressing my hearty and entire
Logier

SW expresses his 'hearty and entire approval' of Logier's 'very ingenious and
useful machine', the Chiroplast. He considers it 'a most valuable invention'
which cannot fail to produce correct fingering and a 'secure and graceful
position of both hands' in performing on a keyed instrument.

SW→SGW   **7/9/1814**

MA [uncatalogued]   I mean to call upon You to-Day, but fear I cannot come
▣ Wed 7 Sep & >20/2/1805→{1808,1814}[339]

SW means to call on SGW today but cannot arrive before 7 pm. He will be
satisfied to eat 'a cold scrap of victuals'.

SW→VN   Gower Pl[340]   **14/9/1814**

BL Add 11729 f 102; *O*   It was ridiculous in me to conjecture
▣ Wed 14 Sep={1814}[341]

SW was foolish to suppose that the music had not been returned from [George
or Joseph] Gwilt's home. SW now realises that he and VN subsequently took the
music to Islington Chapel on the Saturday when they 'displeased' Mr [John]
Purkis by 'pleasing everybody else'. SW is anxious about the 'Green Book'
which was taken to the Chapel with the rest of the music, and which [George
Pike] England's 'young man' was engaged to bring back to SW's house.

SW has found the book containing the *Choral Vorspiele* [by JSB] and the
'triple Mass', [BWV Anhang III 167, for three choirs, published by Breitkopf &
Härtel under JSB's name but now not attributed to JSB], but has not found the
other book.[342] England's 'young man' declares that he brought back two bound
books, one of which ought to have been SW's manuscript of the [JSB] *Exercises*
and organ pieces. If it is not found SW will have to undergo the drudgery of

---

[338] Logier reprinted this letter with slight alterations in a number of his later
publications.

[339] Ltr >20/2/1805 because sent to SGW 'by favour of Sir Vicary Gibbs', who
was knighted on that day. As no reason has been found to prefer 7/9/1808 to
7/9/1814, ltr has been entered ambiguously under both dates.

[340] Ltr does not specify the house number.

[341] Assigned to 1814 because of ref. to *The Examiner* article published on
11/9/1814.

[342] This volume, a contemporary binding of books 1 and 2 of the *Choral
Vorspiele* and the 'triple Mass' in G, is now at RCM. On the latter SW noted
that 'this admirable and stupendous *Messa* was the gift of the Revd Christian La
Trobe to his very sincere friend S. Wesley' in 1809.

copying the music again from Picart's book. SW refers teasingly to an article in *The Examiner* [the 11/9/1814 number], which refers to VN as 'a young man of great promise'.

SW asks VN to write and not to forget to come on Friday [16/9/1814], and inquires how 'Pokey' [not identified] got on on Sunday afternoon [11/9/1814].

Kingston→SW 27/9/1814
BL Add 11729 f 104   Independent of my being unable to feel otherwise
☞ 'Tuesday night'[343]

Kingston wishes to know VN better. He asks SW to invite VN to accompany SW on Thursday [29/9/1814] for a 'brew-house beef-steak', not later than 4 pm, and assures VN of a warm welcome.

SW→VN 28/9/1814
BL Add 11729 f 103; *O*   Fully expecting you To=Night, according to your
☞ Wed 28 Sep; pmk 1814

SW expected VN tonight and would have given him the enclosed letter [Kingston→SW, 27/9/1814]. It is an invitation to an 'unceremonious dinner' tomorrow [29/9/1814] at 3.30 pm at the Weston Street Brewery, 16 Weston Street, The Borough, where the meal consists of steaks cooked in the brewery stoke-hole. SW can promise good conversation and good wine. He knows that VN had a prior engagement at Cristall's [not identified] tomorrow evening but hopes that VN will be able to attend for 3 or 4 hours. The 'master of the concern' is Mr Probyn, who has been a friend of Kingston's for 10 or 12 years.

SW→VN 5/10/1814
BL Add 11729 f 105; *O*   You will probably be surprised at my besetting you
☞ 5/10/1814

VN, who is 'in the thick of Handel's best Psalm Tunes' [at the Birmingham Festival], probably will be surprised to hear from SW. SW leaves on the Norwich Mail [coach] tomorrow [6/10/1814]. He had hoped to take with him his organ duet [*Grand Duet*] in C, and also the JSB organ duet [VN's arrangement of JSB's 'St Anne' fugue, BWV 552] that he and VN played at the Foundling [Hospital, on 15/6/1814 in the benefit concert for the family of William Russell, the Foundling Hospital organist]. SW's concert at the Norwich church [St Peter Mancroft] has been postponed on account of the Assize Week and a bereavement in the family of one of the principal singers, [Edward] Taylor [bass singer and writer on music, 1784–1863]. On VN's return to London he should write to SW in care of the Rev. Ozias Linley, Norwich, and enclose the duets.

---

[343] Assigned to 27/9/1814 because ltr enclosed with SW→VN, 28/9/1814 (a Wednesday).

The service [at the Portuguese Embassy Chapel] went well on Sunday [2/10/1814]. They performed Mozart's 'Kyrie and Gloria', the Credo of the 'selected' [Mass in VN's *A Collection of Sacred Music* (1811)], the Agnus [Dei] of Mozart, and VN's 'Tantum [ergo]' and '[O] sacrum [convivium]'. [John Francis] Prina searched the organ music that VN had removed from 'the box' [the organ music bench at the Portuguese Embassy Chapel] to his home, but has written to SW [not preserved] that 'neither of the duets is findable'.

SW→SGW   Norwich   **12/10/1814**
GEU Wesley Coll. ltr 55   Thinking that you would like to know how I am
✉ 12/10/1814
SW is 'in the most comfortable situation' [in Norwich], staying with 'Messieurs Linley' [WL and Rev. Ozias Linley]. He has already been introduced to 'all the principal people of the city', including the clergy at the cathedral. He will be performing at the church [St Peter Mancroft] on 20/10/1814 and has 'a fair prospect' of doing well financially: the admission fees of only 50 people will cover all his expenses. He has already played 'the Choir Service' three times at the cathedral. The Norwich people are hospitable, the air and the sights are good, and the journey which was safe and pleasant has benefited SW's health. SW and WL plan to return to London on Friday week [21/10/1814] on the Mail [coach], arriving in London early Saturday [22/10/1814]. SW asks to be remembered to Sarah and CW Jr, and is much obliged to Sarah for a loan of £1 until he returns. Any letter to SW should be addressed care of the Rev. Ozias Linley, Dean's Square, Norwich.

SW→SS   Norwich   **16/10/1814**
BL Add 35012 f 48   Your Letter and the pound Note in it arrived safely
✉ Sun 16 Oct={1814}[344]
SS's letter containing £1 arrived safely yesterday. SW could not reply immediately because he was busy with rehearsals for his concert [at St Peter Mancroft church] on Thursday [20/10/1814]. He has been entertained at a dinner at the Assembly Rooms organised by several of the gentlemen of the town, including Miss Forth's father [not identified]. SW is very popular in Norwich, and it has been difficult to persuade them that he must return to London on Friday [21/10/1814]. [Marmaduke Charles] Wilson should go to Mrs Magrath's [not identified] for SW on that day. The Mail [coach] gets to London about 7 or 8 am on Saturday morning [22/10/1814]. WL has invited SW to breakfast with him then, as Southampton Street [where WL lives] is on SW's way home.

SW asks SS to send someone, possibly Robert Batt [not identified], to the General Post Office in Lombard Street to pick up his trunk. SS's lodger is 'a rum concern', and SW will not put up with any 'gammon' from her on his return.

---

[344] Assigned to 1814 because of ref. to SW's Norwich concert on 20/10/1814, *see* SW→SGW, 12/10/1814.

SS has requested SW to bring some food back with him. SW hopes that some of his admirers will give him a brace of partridges or pheasants, but he cannot ask for them, and they cannot be bought. He does not think it worthwhile to bring back a goose as it would not be any cheaper [than in London]. SW hopes that SS will think of him on his 'grand day of exhibition' on Thursday [20/10/1814], and will pray that he has a 'church full of people'.

SW has had two letters [not preserved] from 'Mrs J' [not identified] since he has been in Norwich. They show that her state is worse than ever. He is afraid that she will 'make away with herself'. It is 'an unfortunate affair' that he and she ever met. SW fears that 'Sammy Sixpence' [SSW] is not well; SS can now tell him that he will see SW soon. SW is annoyed that SS packed only one pair of drawers. He is comfortable in Norwich but will be glad to be back home. He asks SS to kiss Sam [SSW] and Raz [Rosalind] for him. [The Rev. Charles John] Smyth says that everyone in Norwich is so taken with SW that SW may make excellent connections for a concert at any time in the future.

Sarah→SGW   **23/10/1814**
GEU in box 6   We have just received your kind Letter
☞ 'Sunday 23 October 1813' (an incorrect date); pmk 1814[345]
Sarah is glad that SW has returned [from Norwich] to dine with SGW on her birthday [23/10/1814] and is pleased that SGW 'will dress the ham'. Sarah has reflected painfully about 'poor Sam' [SW] and CW's 'dying hope of him'. A 'sunny ray would be diffused' over SGW's 'evening' if SW should be 'called to repentance' during SGW's lifetime. Sarah trusts that SW will repent 'at last' and prays that 'we all may live to see it'.

SW→RG   **27/1/1815**
BL Add 35013 f 54; *O*   If not pre-engaged, I shall be glad of your Company
☞ 'Friday evening'; pmk presumably 30/1/1815[346]
SW invites RG to 'take a chop' with SW on Monday [30/1/1815] before the [Covent Garden] Oratorio concert [at which SW played the organ in a performance of Handel's *Messiah*], and asks RG to assist at SW's right hand [to turn pages and draw organ stops]. SW does not know what Ashley's arrangements are about [free] admission into the orchestra so thinks it would be safest for SW to take no one else with him on this occasion.

---

[345] Assigned to 23/10/1814 because that date was a Sunday; also, ref. to SW's return consistent with his planned return from Norwich on 22/10/1814 (*see* SW→SS, 16/10/1814).

[346] The final digit of the postmarked year appears to be either a '3' or a '5'. Ltr assigned to 1815 because addressed to RG at Hatton Garden and therefore >1814 (in 7/1814 RG was still at Bishopsgate); also, SW known, independently of ltr, to have played at the Oratorio concert on 30/1/1815.

SW→RG   Gower Pl[347]   **13/2/1815?**
BL Add 35013 f 56; *O*   I had quite forgotten that Tonight is the first Meeting
☞ '13 February'[348]
SW apologises for not being able to see RG tonight. SW had forgotten that
'tonight is the first meeting of the Philharmonic Society', which he is obliged to
attend. He also has had to refuse an invitation to the Somerset House Lodge
dinner today for the same reason. He invites RG to take a chop with him next
Wednesday [15/2/1815] at 4 pm, before 'our Oratorio business' [an Oratorio
concert at Covent Garden, at which SW played].

SW→RG   **4/3/1815**
BL Add 35013 f 70; *O*   I have been reflecting upon the Circumstance
☞ Sat 4 Mar; pmk 1815
SW is wondering whether to apply for the organist's position at Lambeth
Church, which he is told is worth £70 p.a. He asks RG to make inquiries. Several
friends have told SW that if he were to 'volunteer' his services to the church
wardens this would 'terminate the idea of any competition'. SW is not convinced
of this and would welcome RG's opinion.

SW→Editor, *EM*   Gower Pl[349]   **3/5/1815**
EM v 67 (May 1815) p 388   In reply to the request of your Correspondent
EM
In reply to a correspondent's query in a prior number of the *EM*, SW reports
that he experiences 'great ease and convenience' by washing his face with warm
water and strong soap before shaving.

---

[347] Ltr does not specify the house number.

[348] Assigned to 1815 on the presumption that 'first meeting of the Philharmonic
Society' refers to the first Philharmonic Society concert of the year. Of the years
that SW lived in Gower Place the first concert took place on 13 February only in
1815. An 1815 date for ltr also is consistent with SW's playing at the Covent
Garden oratorio concert on 15/2/1815.

[349] Ltr does not specify the house number.

SW→VN **5/7/1815**

BL Add 11729 f 113; *O* There certainly is a Devil, which I prove thus:
⬛ Wed 5 Jul={1809,1815}[350]

SW sent to 'old Horn' [CFH] for the '30 Variations' [JSB's *Goldberg Variations*], and received the enclosed disappointing reply [not preserved]. SW expects VN tomorrow [6/7/1815] at 6 pm and thinks that they will have 'some fun'. Samuel Webbe [Jr] will be with them. Salomon will try to come if he can 'get off his engagement' to go to the opera with 'Parson [Frederick William] Blomberg' [1761–1847, from 1808 to 1822 Prebendary of Westminster Abbey].

SW is summoned to Yarmouth [in Norfolk, now called 'Great Yarmouth']. He must leave on Sunday [9/7/1815] at 2 pm and thus cannot repeat the pleasure that he and VN 'experienced in the fugue' last Sunday [2/7/1815]. VN should remind SW tomorrow to give him the French essay that SW transcribed. VN should bring 'a trio or two' by JSB so that they can be played 'in their right way'. SW has all of JSB's trios bound in one volume.

SW→VN [Great] Yarmouth **18/7/1815**

BL Add 11729 f 115; *O* I was informed that you expected me to write
⬛ 18/7/1815

SW and his 'coadjutor' Charles Smith [bass singer and composer, 1786–1856] have had mixed fortunes in [Great] Yarmouth. Their receipts amounted to £22, which they will share. The attendance at their concert [at St Nicholas Church, Great Yarmouth] was poor, as Smith had not sufficiently considered the best time for it to take place, which would have been during the time of the races. Those who attended, however, were delighted. The organ is the 'most magnificent' that SW has yet heard. VN's manuscript music book has been of great service: the triple fugue in E♭ [JSB's 'St Anne' fugue] was received with the same wonder as people express when they see a balloon ascend for the first time. SW and Smith intend to try the '30 Variations' [JSB's *Goldberg Variations*] on the organ tomorrow. This will be a treat for [John] Eager [1782–1853] the organist [of St Nicholas, Great Yarmouth], at whose house SW is staying and whose musical attainments SW describes. Eager is an extraordinary man who plays many instruments, is a dancing master, is well read and knows German and Italian. He expects to come to London in the Christmas holidays, when he wishes to be introduced to VN.

SW expects to return to London at 9 am on Friday [21/7/1815]. He probably will be with VN on Sunday [23/7/1815] at the morning or the evening service [at the Portuguese Embassy Chapel] when they can further discuss SW's doings in [Great] Yarmouth.

---

[350] Assigned to 1815 because ltr refers to SW's forthcoming trip to Yarmouth, where he was on 18/7/1815 (*see* SW→VN, 18/7/1815). No earlier trip by SW to Yarmouth is known. Ltr <1816 as Salomon alive when ltr written.

SW→Pettet   Gower Pl   **31/7/1815**

MA DDWF/15/19; *O*   You will perhaps be a little surprized at this unexpected
▣ 31/7/1815

SW regrets that he and Pettet did not have more time to talk before SW's
departure [from Norwich, where he went from Great Yarmouth]. He was
extremely busy and hopes that Pettet did not feel neglected. SW is sorry not to
have had time to transcribe the 'disquisition' which he lent to Pettet. It is SW's
only copy, so he asks him to return it. SW also asks Pettet to remind Mr Sharp
[not identified], who SW presumes is now at Great Yarmouth, of his promise to
send SW the words of 'that excellent funny song of the Noachic Procession into
the Ark'.

SW seeks Pettet's advice about possible overcharging on SW's journeys from
London to [Great] Yarmouth and from Norwich to London.

SW returned [to London] to find '12 or 14' letters awaiting his answer. VN has
asked him 'to do his Popish drudgery' [to deputise for VN] at the Portuguese
Embassy Chapel for 'two Sundays to come' [6/8/1815 and 13/8/1815]. SW
sends best wishes to Mrs [Harriot] Pettet and to 'all inquiring friends' [in
Norwich].

SW→VN   **1/9/1815**

BL 11729 f 117; *O*   Since we parted on Wednesday Night I have been
▣ Fri 1 Sep={1809,1815,1820} & pmk 181-[351] →ⅈ

Since leaving VN on Wednesday night [30/8/1815], SW has been 'seriously ill'
with a 'damned violent cholic'—the 'learned physickers' call it *'cholera
morbus'*. He was unable to go out yesterday and used the time to catch up with
his correspondence [of which only SW→Editor, *EM*, 1/9/1815 is preserved]. He
is going to Turnham Green today in a coach. He has given up the idea of going
to see the jugglers tomorrow but hopes to be with VN on Sunday [3/9/1815].

---

[351] The last digit of the postmarked year is illegible.

SW[352]→Editor, *EM*   1/9/1815

EM v 68 (Sept 1815) p 218–19   The late ingenious Mr William Jackson
EM

Using the pseudonym 'Philomusicus', SW notes in this epistolary article that William Jackson ['of Exeter'] published in 1798 a book entitled *The Four Ages, together with Essays on Various Subjects*. These essays showed 'uncommon acumen and solidity of thought' and exhibited 'much novelty and originality'. In view of the current 'extraordinary rage among mere amateurs' to attain the rank 'not only of performers but composers', SW quotes at length from one of the essays, 'On Gentlemen-Artists', which attacks the pretensions of such people.

SW→Editor, *EM*   Gower Pl   8/9/1815

EM v 68 (Sept 1815) p 219   To the question of your Correspondent
EM

Responding to a correspondent's query why a hump-backed man is called 'my Lord', SW cites an entry in a lexicon by Cornelius Schrevelius that links the Greek word 'lordos' with the Latin word 'curvus'.

SW→William Shield   Gower Pl   13/9/1815

BL Eg. 2159 f 70; *O*   I have repeatedly besieged your Mansion
☞ Wednesday 12/9/1815, an incorrect date[353]

SW has repeatedly called on William Shield [composer, 1748–1829] since Shield's departure for the country. SW was told on his penultimate visit that Shield had returned to London. SW accordingly left word that he would call this morning, when he was assured that Shield would be at home. Finding him once more out, SW left his card.

SW has been informed by [the organ makers] Flight and Robson that Mr [John] Fuller came one day to hear the music that SW had prepared for Fuller's organ, and had approved the results. SW asks whether Fuller is now in town, as he wishes to visit him at his Devonshire Place home. Fuller had been expected to hear the organ on the day it was exhibited to several professional gentlemen. SW supposes that Shield saw the report of this meeting in the newspapers.

SW asks if he left the Credo [from JSB's *B Minor Mass*] with Shield. SW remembers taking it with him to Berners Street [Shield's house], but thinks he did not take it away when he took the book of motets from which the movements

---

[352] The identification of SW with 'Philomusicus' (made in *Olleson* p 1103–1104) derives from SW's statement in SW→VN, 7/12/1815, that he wishes to reply to 'the gentleman who does not like me and Mr [William] Jackson'. This gentleman was 'H.W.', who replied to ltr in 'H.W.'→Editor, *EM*, about 1/11/1815.

[353] Assigned to Wednesday 13/9/1815 on the presumption that SW mistook the date rather than the day of the week.

he prepared for Fuller's organ were selected. SW is planning to publish the Credo if he can secure 70 subscribers. He wishes only to clear his expenses, which would amount to about £60–£70.

SW→Bridgetower   Gower Pl   **22/9/1815**

GEU Wesley Coll. ltr 56; *O*   Will you favour me with a Line, just to inform
☐ 22/9/1815
SW asks whether he lent Bridgetower a manuscript copy of 'Bach's violin solos' some time ago. SW has been searching for this in vain. If it really is lost or stolen, SW will copy the music again. As the missing item was a gift from Salomon, SW cannot 'decorously' tell him about the loss. Salomon has a printed copy of these compositions which SW thinks is from the edition that Bridgetower owns.

SW→Pettet   **22/9/1815**

MH Shaw Theatre Collection; *O*   Our Friend W. Linley franks this to You
☐ 22/9/1815
SW encloses with this letter a composition for [Edward] Taylor, and asks Pettet to thank Taylor for actively promoting 'the Cause of the Credo' [SW's plan to publish the Credo from JSB's *B Minor Mass* by subscription]. SW now thinks that this may receive sufficient support 'to come forth into the world'. SW told WL 'last Wednesday' [20/9/1815] that, in view of the 'very cordial reception' SW had on his two previous visits to Norwich, he would be pleased to return there to assist without fee 'at the Charity Meeting about to take place for the benefit of the blind', providing that his travelling expenses were reimbursed. He asks Pettet for 'early intelligence' regarding this proposal.

SW asks Pettet to thank Mr Sharp for the funny song ['The Noachic Procession', *see* SW→Pettet, 31/7/1815], about which 'friend Ozee' [Ozias Linley] has made 'wry faces'. Although SW thinks the song 'perfectly innocent', it ought not to be sung 'in the presence of Bob Elwyn' [Robert Fountain Elwin, 1783–1853, at this time Rector of Wilby, Norfolk], to whom SW sends best regards. SW plans to spend this evening with VN. Pettet may rely upon receiving the parts he requires in time.

SW is waiting to receive his manuscript book containing 'The Chimney Sweepers' [presumably the glee composed *c*1795 by John Beckwith, 1750–1809, with whose son John Charles Beckwith, Norwich organist, 1788–1819, SW was in correspondence, *see* SW→Pettet, 5/10/1815] from the binder, who is unacceptably slow.

SW→Pettet   Gower Pl   **29/9/1815**
BL Eg. 2159 f 74; *O*   I should have not thus instantaneously pestered you
☑ 29 September[354]

SW thanks Pettet for his present of game and for his efforts in the cause of the Credo [from JSB's *B Minor Mass*]. SW has received an additional four subscribers' names from the [Norwich] Hall Concert, for which he understands he has [Edward] Taylor to thank. He regrets not having earlier offered his services to the approaching [Charity] Meeting [in Norwich, *see* SW→Pettet, 22/9/1815] and will hold himself in readiness in future. Pettet should inform WL that SW went to Preston's [music shop] in search of the music book required, and has obtained it; he will now go to work according to the instructions in WL's last letter. SW desires Pettet to thank 'Mr Pymer of Beccles' [Thomas Pymar, *c*1764–1854, organist of St Michael's, Beccles, Suffolk] for the gift of birds. SW has no important musical news to impart, except that the gentlemen of the Professional Concerts have made a proposal for union with the Philharmonic Society. In consequence, a committee [of the Philharmonic Society] has been set up to consider the matter. SW feels that no solid agreement will be reached and that the end result will be the 'annihilation' of both societies.

SW→Pettet?[355]   Gower Pl   **5/10/1815**
SMU; *O*   With this will arrive (I trust) a spiritual & a convivial Dish
☑ 5/10/1815

The hymn *Adeste Fideles* and 'the Chimney Sweepers' May Day Adventure' [*see* SW→Pettet, 22/9/1815] should arrive with this letter. VN wants 'the score' returned as soon as the desired transcripts have been made. SW asks the recipient to thank [John Charles] Beckwith for his last letter [not preserved] concerning 'the [JSB] Credo', and to tell 'Mr Linley' [presumably WL] that SW's 'score of the songs etc. is in great forwardness'. SW is pressed for time.

'H.W.'→Editor, *EM*   **10/11/1815**
EM v 68 (Nov 1815) p 399–400   A correspondent under the assumed title
☑ 10/11/1815

'H.W.' considers SW's reasoning [given under the pseudonym 'Philomusicus' in SW→Editor, *EM*, 1/9/1815] 'loose and desultory'. In contrast to SW and William Jackson, whom SW had quoted, 'H.W.' considers that the 'pinnacle of excellence is almost (not quite) as attainable to the [musical] amateur gifted with genius, as to the professional votary'.

---

[354] Assigned to 1815 from ref. to the collection of subscribers for SW's proposed edition of the Credo from JSB's *B Minor Mass*.

[355] Ltr addressed to 'Dear Sir'. Pettet presumed to be the recipient because SW→Pettet, 22/9/1815, says that the manuscript containing the 'Chimney Sweepers' song', presumably sent with ltr, was then still at a bindery.

SW→Bridgetower   Gower Pl   **11/11/1815**
BL Add 56411 f 16; *O*   Mr Ball, of Duke Street, informed me that you have
☑ Sat 11 Nov & 🖼→ⓘ

SW has been informed by [James] Ball that Bridgetower wishes to introduce to
SW 'a new great gun in the musical way'. SW supposes that this is the person
whom [Muzio] Clementi lately proposed, and SW seconded, for election as an
associate of the Philharmonic Society [on 16/10/1815 SW chaired a meeting of
that society at which Clementi's pupil August Alexander Klengel, German
pianist, 1783–1852, was proposed as an associate].

SW inquired 'some months ago' [in SW→Bridgetower, 22/9/1815] whether he
had lent his still missing manuscript copy of 'Bach's violin solos' to
Bridgetower. This earlier letter must have gone astray.

SW & others→Philharmonic Society   **4/12/1815**
BL Music Ms Loan 48.7/1 f 2   We recommend Wm Lacy Esqr of Manchester St
☑ 4/12/1815

SW and others recommend William Lacy [bass singer, 1788–1871], an
associate of the Philharmonic Society, for full membership of the Society.

SW & others→Philharmonic Society   **4/12/1815**
BL Music Ms Loan 48.7/1 f 3   We recommend Mr John Loder of Bath
☑ 4/12/1815

SW and others recommend John [David] Loder [violinist, 1788–1846] of Bath,
an associate of the Philharmonic Society, for full membership of the Society.

SW→VN   **7/12/1815**
BL Add 11729 f 122; *O*   I regret that I shall not be able to see you
☑ 7/12/1815

SW has a 'vile cold'. He regrets that he cannot be at the [Portuguese Embassy]
Chapel on Sunday [10/12/1815] but surmises that he will meet VN soon at a
Philharmonic [Society] committee meeting. SW voted for VN [at the committee
meeting] on Monday [4/12/1815], but [Giuseppe] Naldi [Italian bass singer,
1770–1820] was elected. VN should let SW have 'the [*European*] *Magazine* in a
day or two'; otherwise SW will be too late with his answer to 'the gentleman
['H.W.', *see* 'H.W.'→Editor, *EM*, 10/11/1815] who does not like me and Mr
[William] Jackson' [a reference to SW→Editor, *EM*, 1/9/1815]. SW has nearly
finished VN's Masses and has 'taken one or two liberties' with his own Masses.

SW→VN   Gower Pl   **9/12/1815**
BL Add 11729 f 123; *O*   Among other prudential Arrangements, it was
☞ Sat 9 Dec; pmk 1815

At last night's meeting [of the Philharmonic Society] it was decided that some members should be deputed to correct and superintend the copying of parts from manuscript scores. VN's name was put forward and SW expects that VN will be appointed 'President in the said department'. It was wished that VN would be present at the general meeting next Monday [11/12/1815]. SW feels that VN's involvement in this way would be very valuable. Because of an engagement at Islington made 10 days ago SW cannot take up VN's invitation to meet him at Robertson's [presumably the home of Henry Robertson, treasurer of Covent Garden Theatre] this evening. SW wants the [*European*] *Magazine* as soon as VN can let him have it [*see* SW→VN, 7/12/1815].

SW→Editor, *EM*   **about 15/12/1815**
EM v 68 (Dec 1815) p 486–88   In your number for last Month (at page 399)
ltr undated[356]

Again using the pseudonym 'Philomusicus', SW replies to 'H.W.'→Editor, *EM*, 10/11/1815. As 'H.W.' has much misunderstood SW's 'design' [in SW→Editor, *EM*, 1/9/1815], SW feels it necessary to explain, at length, what 'H.W.' misapprehended. SW states that 90% of amateurs who play or sing are 'sadly deficient in the two primary requisites for correct performance'—the ability to sing or play 'exactly in time and tune'. He asserts that musical amateurs will perform well only 'by chance' unless they join theory with practice, and that study of theory ought to precede practice. Musicians should begin their study with 'thorough base' and should gradually 'become acquainted with true harmonic progressions, and consequently qualified to reason upon them'. Only then, and after studying 'from the models of the best acknowledged masters', will an interested student have had the preparation 'to extend the consequences of his researches to attempt original composition himself'.

---

[356] Ltr >SW→VN, 7/12/1815, when SW requests the November 1815 *European Magazine* so that he can reply to 'HW', and >SW→VN, 9/12/1815, in which SW reiterates his request. Ltr <25/12/1815 as it is printed in the December 1815 *European Magazine*.

SW→VN 18/12/1815

BL Add 11729 f 124; *O*   You vanished some how at the Chapel Door
☞ Mon 18 Dec={1809,1815,1820}[357]
SW failed to make contact with VN at the [Portuguese Embassy] Chapel
yesterday [17/12/1815]. He wanted to tell VN about a blind man [not identified]
who desires to establish himself as a piano tuner. This man has asked to tune the
pianos of some professional musicians, in order to obtain recommendations. He
has tuned John [Baptist] Cramer's piano several times, and tuned SW's piano
'very well' some weeks ago. The man, whose name SW has forgotten, proposes
to call on VN tomorrow or Wednesday to ask if he may tune VN's piano.

SW→VN 30/12/1815

BL Add 11729 f 125; *O*   The Somerset House Lodge does not meet
☞ Sat 30 Dec={1809,1815,1820} & pmk 181-[358]→ⅰ
Somerset House Lodge does not meet next Monday [1/1/1816] but SW is
otherwise engaged then. He suggests Tuesday [2/1/1816] for 'being with' the
Rev. Cleaver Banks [John Banks Cleaver *later* John Cleaver Banks, clergyman,
1765?–1845, a subscriber to the SW/CFH edition of JSB's '48']. If VN writes to
Banks at Knightsbridge, near the Barracks, Banks is likely to appear at the
[Portuguese Embassy] Chapel on Sunday morning [31/12/1815]. SW said
yesterday [29/12/1815] that he thought that the origin of the phrase 'pot pourri'
was 'Popery'.

SW & others→Philharmonic Society 8/1/1816

BL Music Ms Loan 48.7/1 f 73   We recommend Mr Hullmandel, of 51 Great
☞ 8/1/1816
SW and others recommend Mr Hullmandel [Nicolas-Joseph Hüllmandel,
Alsatian pianist and composer, 1788–1846], as a person suitable for election as
an associate of the Philharmonic Society.

WH→SW 8/1/1816

BL Add 11730 f 77   You have, without doubt, heard of the deplorable relapse
☞ 8/1/1816
SW has undoubtedly heard that Dr [John Wall] Callcott [WH's father-in-law]
has had a 'deplorable relapse' and is again under the care of Dr [Joseph Mason]
Cox [medical doctor and writer on insanity, 1763–1818] at his 'melancholy

---

[357] Assigned to 1815 for the following reason. 1820 excluded because ltr
addressed to VN at 240 Oxford Street, an address he had left before December
1820. 1809 presumed unlikely because no correspondence between SW and VN
is known to have been written before 1811.

[358] The last digit of the postmarked year is illegible.

abode' [Cox's private lunatic asylum at Fishponds near Bristol] in Gloucestershire.

Before Callcott's 'departure' he had been 'superintending the printing of a third edition' of his *Musical Grammar* which 'is now advanced almost to the 4th part, on rhythm'. Callcott intended to see SW regarding the alterations which SW made 'in that part, in the second edition' but was prevented from this by 'repeated attacks' of 'mental irritation'. A few days before Callcott's 'departure', he conversed at length on this subject with WH and asked him to inform SW 'that the three first pages of the 4th part should be restored' to the way 'they stood in the first edition'. Callcott acknowledged his obligations to SW [for his work on the second edition] and regretted that he lacked the opportunity to tell SW personally 'the reasons which induced him to differ' from SW. WH's role in this matter is that of 'an honest agent, whose sole business is to obey the will of his supervisor' [Callcott].

SW→VN Gower Pl **15/1/1816**
BL Add 11729 f 127; *O* We cooked the Hash Yesterday as well as we could
☞ Monday; pmk 15/1/1816 (Monday)

SW and the [Portuguese Embassy Chapel] choir managed as well as they could in VN's absence yesterday [14/1/1816]. SW thinks that the Mass 'went very well'. [Francesco Pasquale] Ricci's Kyrie, Gloria, Sanctus, and Agnus, the 'selected' Credo, and the Roman Domine were performed. Miss Stamp, an 'intimate' of Miss Harington, was introduced into the choir. The feast was 'Of the name of Jesus' and [James] Turle [1802–1882] and [John Francis] Prina sang 'O Jesu pastor bone', a 'treacly lollypop of old [Samuel] Webbe' [Sr], which had 'a ravishing effect'. They are to sing a Te Deum next Thursday [18/1/1816]. VN's choir wish to have a rehearsal and suggest Wednesday evening [17/1/1816]. SW encloses the hymn of yesterday's feast, which VN is to harmonise with the rest. SW supposes that VN had a 'roaring day' yesterday with [Leigh] Hunt [editor, essayist and poet, 1784–1859].

SW→Stephen Jones Gower Pl **15/2/1816**
MA DDWF/15/20; *O* As the Examination of 'a Sonata by Wm Beale' did
☞ 15/2/1816

As the review [by SW] of a sonata by William Beale [composer, 1784–1854] did not appear in the January number [of the *EM*, which Stephen Jones, 1763–1827, edited], SW presumes that it will be printed in the February number, together with the reviews he encloses [not preserved; presumably those printed in the February *EM*]. SW would be grateful for a proof sheet. He asks Jones 'to calculate the account of the pages of the musical review' [SW's reviews in the *EM*] from Midsummer to Christmas 1815, and inquires how Jones is getting on with [Martin Madan's book] *Thelyphthora*.

SW→BJ[359]   4 Gower Pl   **15/2/1816**
RCM Ms 2130, ltr 24; *O*   You are perfectly welcome to the Psalm & Chant
📧 15/2/1816

BJ is welcome to the Psalm and Chant annexed [presumably SW's setting of 'He's blest, whose sins have pardon gain'd' and the Te Deum double chant] if they are suitable [for inclusion in BJ's *National Psalmody*, published in 1817, where these two SW compositions are printed].

SW also sends some proposals for the publication of the Credo [from JSB's *B Minor Mass*] which SW feels that BJ will 'find no inclination to decry'. SW's purpose is not financial gain, which is 'seldom to be expected' in London 'from any masterly musical productions', but to correct the view that JSB could not compose 'truly vocal music'. The Credo also should 'be regarded as a study for masters in orchestral composition'. SW needs 70 subscriptions at £1/1/- each to cover the costs of publication. At present he has only 40. BJ will be 'surprised at some of the gigantic features of the admirable Credo'.

SW sends his 'best respects' to BJ's wife [Mary].

SW→VN   **22/2/1816**
BL Add 11729 f 129; *O*   I think you will not conclude, that from neither
📧 Thu 22 Feb; pmk 1816

SW accepts that VN had good reason for not being at the musical evening in SW's 'nutshell of a house'. 'Pokey' [not identified] substituted for VN [at the piano] in the JSB sonatas; SW played the violin. SW hopes to have another similar evening before the end of Lent.

SW assumes that VN is aware of the [Philharmonic Society] rehearsal tomorrow evening [23/2/1816] at 6 pm at the Argyll Rooms, when he hopes that they will meet. He expects 'some entertainment with a mixture of disgust' if the 'sextuple citharian humbug' [Ferdinand Ries's *Bardic Overture* with six harps, first performed by the Philharmonic Society on 26/2/1816] is to be practised. SW was told that Attwood suggested it; however, SW suspects that he was merely 'the puppet' and that the 'real fundamental' was the 'mountebank knight' [Sir George Smart].

A pupil [not identified], who subscribes both to the Philharmonic Society and the Professional Concerts, informed SW that attendance was poor at both recent concerts of the latter. The performance of [Robert] Lindley ['cellist, 1776–1855] was the chief attraction; [Francesco] Vaccari [Italian violinist, *b*1773] appeared to be playing on a 'very inferior' violin. SW was obliged to go with Samuel Webbe [Jr] to the Bavarian Chapel; otherwise he would have been with VN. He relates a comment that [Edward] Du Bois [barrister and author, 1774–1850] told him a few days ago regarding the 'late prank' [an affair] of [John] Braham [tenor, 1777–1856] with Mr Wright's wife.

---

[359] Ltr addressed to 'Dear Sir'. BJ confirmed as addressee by SW conveying in ltr his regards to 'Mrs Jacob'.

SW→VN   **25/2/1816**

BL Add 11729 f 132; *O*   I communicated the Contents of your Letter
☞ Sun 25 Feb={1810,1816,1821,1827}[360]

During the [Philharmonic Society] rehearsal yesterday [24/2/1816], SW communicated the contents of VN's letter [to SW, not preserved] to [William] Ayrton [writer and composer, 1777–1858, a director of the Philharmonic Society at this time] and required him to read it. Ayrton accepted the 'remonstrance' but pointed out that setting up the Correcting Committee was intended to lighten the expense to those members of the [Philharmonic] Society who refused to play in the orchestra without fee. He said that most of the orchestra were now paid, so few had the privilege of a [complimentary] ticket in the way instanced by VN. Ayrton recommended that SW come forward with 'the proposition', which he did. However, he was unable to carry the motion upon the principle that VN wished to establish. It was nevertheless agreed to arrange complimentary tickets so that each committee member may admit a friend to two concerts in the season. SW found yesterday's meeting of the [Philharmonic Society] directors unsatisfactory but he is only one of twelve; although he is the most recently elected director aside from Clementi, he is the eldest.

SW had to leave the directors' meeting at 4 pm to go to the Glee Club. His right eye is inflamed, and he would not have gone to the Glee Club at all had he not promised WL to preside over the performance of one of WL's glees. Because of his eye infection, SW cannot be at VN's 'sanctum' [the Portuguese Embassy Chapel] this morning, nor will he go to the [Somerset House] Lodge or be with 'Pokey' [not identified] this evening. SW suggests that VN call on him tonight. Notice of the change of the [Philharmonic Society] rehearsal from Friday [23/2/1816] to yesterday came too late for SW to inform VN.

SW→VN   **26/2/1816**

BL Add 11729 f 131; *O*   The enclosed was designed to have been given
☞ Mon 26 Feb; pmk 1816

SW intended the enclosure [presumably SW→VN, 25/2/1816] to have been given to VN yesterday [25/2/1816] after Vespers but was unwilling to send his female messenger out in the rain at 3 pm. SW assumes that he will meet VN this evening.

SW→VN   **4/3/1816**

BL Add 11729 f 133; *O*   There seems Fatality against my ever hearing
☞ 'Monday evening'; pmk 5/3/1816 (Tuesday)

SW seems fated never to hear [Beethoven's] 'Grand Battle Symphony' [*Wellingtons Sieg*, op. 91] nor to learn how to conduct choruses from 'the noble

---

[360] Assigned to 1816 because ltr refers to SW being a Philharmonic Society director, which occurred only in 1815–16.

knight-man' [Sir George Smart]. This morning SW received a summons from the [Freemasons'] Grand Lodge to attend the 'quarterly communication' on Wednesday [6/3/97] and to be at the organ there for the rest of that evening. He asks VN to come tomorrow evening [5/3/1816], when SW will be at home from 6 pm.

WL→SW   10/4/1816?
ltr quoted in SW→William Ayrton, 10/4/1816[361]   [not known]
dated on the basis of SW→William Ayrton, 10/4/1816[362]
WL asks SW to attend 'the practice' of WL's musical composition at the Philharmonic Society on Saturday [13/4/1816] and 'to speak and act' for WL there, as he must be at the Beef-Steak Club at that time. He does not know which of his two pieces (his dirge 'Pardon Goddess' or his little ode 'Tell me where is Fancy Bred') will be played but is certain that 'they will try one'. He gives instructions regarding their performance.

SW→William Ayrton[363]   Gower Pl   10/4/1816
NLS Ms 2207 f. 188; *O*   I have just now received a Letter from our Friend
▣ Wed 10 Apr & 🖎→ⓘ
SW has just received a letter from WL [WL→SW, 10/4/1816?] regretting that he is unable to be at the Argyll Rooms on Saturday evening [13/4/1816] to hear the trial of his music at the Philharmonic Society rehearsal; he has asked SW to be his *locum tenens* in the trial. The Beef-Steak Club meets that evening, and the Duke of Sussex [Augustus Frederick] has particularly requested that every member be present. SW sends WL's instructions to Ayrton in case SW should mislay WL's letter 'or omit to bring it on Saturday'.

SW memorandum   26/4/1816
MA DDWF/15/21   Mr Samuel Wesley is entitled to the third Part of £700
memo dated 26/4/1816
SW is entitled to 'the third part' of three investments: £700 in the 4% [securities]; £300 in the 'consols' [government stock paying 3% annually]; and a 'trifling' annual interest of about £8 in the 'long annuities'. This property was owned by CW; at the decease of his widow SGW, who is now 89, each of

---

[361] Only a portion of ltr is quoted. The original ltr has not been located.

[362] SW→William Ayrton, 10/4/1816, which was written on Wednesday evening, 10/4/1816, states that ltr has been 'just now received'.

[363] Ltr addressed by SW to 'T. Ayrton Esq[re]/James Street/Buckingham Street'. From ltr's content and this address it seems clear that William Ayrton was the intended recipient.

CW Jr, Sarah and SW will inherit it in equal shares. Under CW's will, this property 'is subjected to the benefit of survivorship', so neither CW Jr, SW nor Sarah can 'will away more than their own life interest'. If any one of these three dies 'the remaining property devolves to the two survivors'.

SW→VN **13/5/1816?**

BL Add 11729 f 135; *O*   As you did not call according with your Intention ltr bears non-autograph date (possibly in VN's handwriting) of 13/5/1816[364]

SW informs VN that they will perform [SW's] Trio [for three pianofortes] in Kirkman's [piano manufactory] room on Saturday [18/5/1816]. Stokes cannot participate [as one of the pianists], but Joseph Major is studying Stokes's part and SW is confident that he can do it justice. SW has 'got rid of' half his 'scholars' on Friday [17/5/1816] so that a rehearsal can take place that evening at Kirkman's. SW asks VN to find him this evening during the interval [of the Philharmonic Society concert].

Clementi intends to come to the [Trio] performance. SW also has invited [Frédéric] Kalkbrenner [pianist and composer, 1785–1849]. [John Baptist] Cramer is too grand to attend: SW and VN must be content with the attention of 'Clementi, his master'. SW hears that Cramer's performance on Thursday [9/5/1816, at the Great Room, King's Theatre] was 'extraordinarily great'.

The 'Quebec business' [not identified, possibly concerning the Quebec Chapel, Portman Square, London] yesterday [12/5/1816] went on very agreeably. SW never knew an affair concerning singers which was more smoothly negotiated.

SW→VN Gower Pl **22/5/1816**

BL Add 11729 f 136; *O*   When we parted on Saturday, we did not notice ☞ 'Wednesday 23 May'; pmk 23/5/1816 (a Thursday)[365]

When they parted on Saturday [18/5/1816], SW and VN forgot their intention of going to Mrs Elliston's ball [Elizabeth Elliston, c1774–1821, wife of Robert William Elliston, actor and theatre manager]. VN may have attended, but SW was too tired to go.

SW reminds VN to approach Leigh Hunt about a 'word of annunciation concerning the Oratorio on Saturday week' [i.e., publicity for SW's and Charles Jane Ashley's benefit concert at Covent Garden on 1/6/1816]. No time should be lost if a notice is to be inserted.

---

[364] The plausibility of this date is enhanced by a presumed reference to a Philharmonic Society concert on this date and a reference to John Baptist Cramer's performance on the preceding Thursday. However, the date of this letter has not been confirmed by additional evidence.

[365] Assigned to Wednesday 22/5/1816 rather than Thursday 23/5/1816 on the assumption that SW was more likely to have mistaken the date than the day of the week.

SW met Picart in St James's Street today. Picart was hoping to run off with 'some of the old boy's [JSB's] tunes' from the [second day of the] sale [of John Baptist Cramer's library at White's auction rooms]. Picart feared VN most [as a rival bidder; both were at the sale]. SW asks if VN 'pounced upon a stave of Sebastian [JSB] extra' [at the sale].

SW spent a charming hour with [August Alexander] Klengel today at [the music seller C.] Guichard's shop, where Klengel played the piano. He performed a toccata of his own composition, which was 'quite in the great man's best style'.[366] From the firmness and equality of Klengel's touch, SW thinks that he must be a good organist.

Klengel will come to the [Portuguese Embassy] Chapel on Sunday [26/5/1816]. He commended VN's arrangement of the fugue they are to play, which Charles Smith had showed him.

In consequence of VN's disapproving the idea, SW has given up any thoughts of advertising the performance of his Trio [for three pianofortes] in the newspapers. He now thinks that this would not bring much advantage, as the piece will not be played at his benefit concert [on 1/6/1816]. He asks VN to write.

SW→VN   Gower Pl   **1/6/1816**
BL Add 11729 f 138; *O*   Pray come & take your Coffee with me at 5 exactly
☞ Sat 1 Jun; pmk 1816
SW would like VN to take coffee with him this afternoon at 5 pm to discuss 'the distribution of stops in the last movement' of SW's 'old new tune' [SW's Organ Concerto in C, which he performed, with a new last movement based on 'Rule Britannia', at that evening's concert at Covent Garden].

SW→Sarah   **3/6/1816**
WBRR v 3 (Dec 1851) p 447   I have been consulting the 'Cyclopaedia' upon
WBRR
To assist Sarah, who has been quibbling with a 'Popish antagonist', SW consulted the article 'Inquisition' in [Abraham Rees's] *Cyclopaedia*, from which he quotes. SW believes that the 'horrible account' in this article is true and demonstrates that the Inquisition was established by the [Roman Catholic] Church. He cites a remark about Popery in a book by his godfather [Martin] Madan, which 'the [Roman Catholic] bishops bought up wherever they could find it' [to lessen its circulation]. SW plans to be in Percy Street [Sarah's home] on Wednesday [5/6/1816] before 4 pm and is 'pretty sure' that he, assisted by [writings by William] Chillingworth, can help Sarah to dumbfound her 'hoary hypocrite'.

---

[366] This 'great man' may have been JSB or possibly Klengel's teacher Muzio Clementi.

SW→VN **25/6/1816**

BL Add 11729 f 140; *O*   As you are concerned in the enclosed, I must trouble
☞ Tue 25 Jun={1811,1816,1822}[367]

As VN is involved in the enclosed [matter discussed in a letter from Picart to
SW, not preserved, *see* SW→VN, 28/6/1816], SW cannot answer Picart without
VN's authority. The Vespers [at the Portuguese Embassy Chapel] went smoothly
on Sunday [23/6/1816]: SW 'bespoke' the litanies instead of David's humdrum
ditty 'God bless us' [perhaps a composition by David Perez, *see* SW→VN,
5/12/1812]. SW will be at [Joseph] Major's home from 8.30 to 10.30 pm this
evening. Perhaps VN will call in there.

SW→VN **28/6/1816**

BL Add 11729 f 141; *O*   I am rather desirous to send an Answer to Picart
☞ Fri 28 Jun={1811,1816,1822}[368]

SW cannot reply to Picart until he hears whether VN can lend to Picart the
Stabat Mater by [Emanuele] Astorga [Italian composer, 1680–1757?] that Picart
mentioned in the letter which SW enclosed to VN [with SW→VN, 25/6/1816].
SW proposes to be at VN's 'transubstantiation manufactory' [the Portuguese
Embassy Chapel] on Sunday morning [30/6/1816] and will expect VN's answer
then. A music master from Norwich [not identified] also intends to come.
[Joseph] Major has left town, taking SW's 'brace of pages', which VN will have
as soon as possible. SW has finished his 'cut throat *Waterloo [Battle] Song*'; he
is also writing 'little tiney nimminy pippiny volunataries' [his *Twelve Short
Pieces* for the organ, of which the autograph, RCM Ms 4025, is dated
10/7/1816]. He will bring two or three voluntaries with him on Sunday.

SW→VN **15/7/1816**

BL Add 11729 f 142; *O*   I could not send the accompanying Parcel till now
☞ Mon 15 Jul={1811,1816,1822}[369]

SW could not send the accompanying parcel earlier or would have done so. He
is summoned to Norwich [to play a voluntary at the Anniversary Sermon in
Norwich Cathedral on 15/8/1816, according to Norwich newspaper
announcements] and hears that much may be done at [Great] Yarmouth in the
week following the week [starting 15/8/1816] of the [Norwich] Assizes. He asks

---

[367] Assigned to 1816 because ltr mentions an enclosed letter from Picart that
presumably is the letter from Picart mentioned in SW→VN, 28/6/1816.

[368] Assigned to 1816 for the following reason. Ref. to *Waterloo Battle Song*
implies ltr >18/6/1815, the date of the Battle of Waterloo. Ref. to SW's having
finished this song implies that ltr <24/4/1817 when this song was performed at a
New Musical Fund concert.

[369] Assigned to 1816 from ref. to Clementi's publication of SW's *12 Short
Pieces for the Organ*, which he called 'voluntaries' (*see* SW→VN, 28/6/1816).

VN to call. All the voluntaries [SW's *Twelve Short Pieces*] are done. SW must send them to Clementi [the firm that published them] in a hurry.

SW→'Dear Sir'   Gower Pl   **23/7/1816**

GEU Wesley Coll. ltr 57; *O*   As I have a sincere Confidence in the Reality of
▣ 23/7/1816

About six weeks ago, the Rev. Mr [John] Davies of Brompton Row, whom SW had not met previously, approached SW regarding the possibility of his setting to music 'some stanzas' which Davies had written on the victory at Waterloo. The two agreed on terms, and Davies asked SW who would be 'the most eligible tenor' to perform the song 'on the stage'. As [John] Braham was unavailable, SW recommended [Charles Edward] Horn, who agreed and who 'handsomely' volunteered his services.

After indicating that he wished to perform the song tonight [23/7/1816], Horn visited SW on Friday morning [19/7/1816] and then said that he was delighted with the song but desired that the latter movement be shortened to make it suitable 'for an English theatrical audience'. SW complied 'instantly' with Horn's request and Horn left with SW's score, promising to engage a copyist immediately. Davies accordingly told many people that the performance would take place tonight and mustered 'a grand party' to attend the [Lyceum] theatre. However, SW yesterday [22/7/1816] received a letter [not preserved] from Horn declining to sing this song, offering excuses which, if valid, ought to have been put forward earlier.

SW values his correspondent's cool judgement and seeks his opinion whether this circumstance, which has disadvantaged both Davies and [Samuel James] Arnold [dramatist, 1774–1852, Samuel Arnold's son, at this time manager of the Lyceum Theatre], does not indicate that Horn is 'an unstable character' or, alternatively, that he has been unfairly influenced to break his promise to perform SW's song.

SW→VN[370]   **27/7/1816?**

BL Add 11729 f 143; *O*   A Dialogue which happened on Saturday, July 27th
manuscript undated[371]

[Edward] Jones [Welsh historian and composer, *bap*1752–1824], William
Ayrton and SW met at Chappell's music shop on 27/7/1816. Jones asked why
SW had not attended White's auction [on 21–22/5/1816] of musical items [from
John Baptist Cramer's library], at which several compositions by JSB were sold.
SW replied that he had seen the catalogue before the sale and had found no JSB
compositions there with which he was not previously acquainted. He added that
he has been lent 'six curious and grand preludes and fugues with an additional
bass line entirely for the pedals' [by JSB, possibly his *Sechs Praeludien und
Sechs Fugen für Orgel oder Pianoforte*, BWV 543–548, published in Vienna
and Pest in 1812]. Ayrton believed that these were sold at Salomon's auction.
SW doubted this and said that he thinks he has the only copy in England.
Ayrton then said that Salomon's library included several JSB works that
Ayrton thought not worth bringing forward [at auction] and that the work lent to
SW probably was one of them. SW wondered at Ayrton's omission [of a JSB
composition from the auction], asserting that 'every note of this author [JSB] is
valuable'. Ayrton sneered that very few people shared SW's opinion of JSB. SW
retorted that his opinion of JSB is shared by 'all those who deserve the name' of
musician or judge of music. He added that JSB's works 'are the finest study
possible' for all musical doctors in England; if JSB were alive he 'would stare
not a little at how they had ever acquired their title'.
SW reminds VN that Ayrton's father [Edmund Ayrton, organist and composer,
*bap*1734–1808] was a doctor of music [from Cambridge in 1784] and was 'one
of the most egregious blockheads under the sun'. SW left this meeting 'in high
good humour'. VN will appreciate SW's vanquishing of 'these vermin' [Jones
and Ayrton].

SW→Pettet   **29/7/1816**

BL Eg. 2159 f 72; *O*   Your obliging Letter reached me Yesterday
29/7/1816

SW thanks Pettet for his letter [not preserved] which arrived yesterday and for
his strenuous exertions on 'turkey-ish topics'. SW is looking forward to his visit
to Norwich and is thinking of setting off in the middle of next week. He asks

---

[370] VN not identified as recipient but presumed as addressee because ltr is in
collection given by VN to the British Museum and the style of ltr (including an
assumption that SW and the recipient have a similar exalted opinion of JSB's
music, SW's use of French and his frank comments about other musicians) is
consistent with that of other letters from SW to VN written about this time.

[371] Assigned to 27/7/1816 on the presumption that it was written on the date
when the events described took place. However, the possibility that it was
written shortly thereafter has not been ruled out.

Pettet to arrange where he is to stay. SW has had invitations from [John Charles] Beckwith as well as from Pettet, and proposes to stay for part of the time with each. SW must contact [John] Eager [of Great Yarmouth], who has not answered his letter, and will inform VN of Pettet's 'honest principle' concerning *Adeste Fideles*. VN is as much a faithful Roman Catholic as Pettet or SW, as he believes not a word of the Church's doctrines.

Beckwith has told SW that he is avid in SW's cause. On SW's former visit [to Great Yarmouth, *see* SW→VN, 18/7/1815], Charles Smith's wrong-headedness prevented some good. Eager was helpful despite Smith's failure to consult him. SW is grateful to Eager for this and for his hospitality during SW's stay in [Great] Yarmouth.

SW has paid [John] Braham a 'visit of condolence'. The 'little Gergashite' seems not to relish 'the slight contribution levied upon him' [damages of £1,000 awarded against Braham to Mr Wright, with whose wife Braham had run off to France; *see* SW→VN, 22/2/1816].

SW→VN   1/8/1816
BL Add 11729 f 144; *O*   I purpose leaving Town on Saturday Week
☞ 1/8/1816

SW is planning to leave London [for Norwich] on Saturday week [10/8/1816] at the latest, and is making arrangements to find deputies to cover his London commitments. He does not want to put VN to any inconvenience or financial loss, and asks VN to inform him candidly about VN's morning engagements. SW also will write to [Marmaduke Charles] Wilson, but VN will be more welcome at Turnham Green [in the school where SW taught]. SW has only two 'private scholars in town' [London]; he will ask them to defer their lessons until he returns. VN should write if he is not able to call tomorrow evening [2/8/1816]; SW then will try to see him on Sunday [4/8/1816], before evening.

SW→VN   7/8/1816
BL Add 11729 f 146; *O*   Our little Boy is in so precarious a State
☞ Wed 7 Aug={1811,1816,1822}[372]

SW's 'little boy' [who died *c*10/8/1816, about the time that SW left for Norwich, *see* Sarah→Kingston, 26/8/1817] is so ill that SW expects that he cannot be with VN at the Surrey Chapel tomorrow [8/8/1886] at 1 pm. SW must attend two pupils in the Cheapside area tomorrow, but would feel 'totally disqualified for any musical exertion of energy' if the child dies. He hopes that VN will meet BJ [at the Surrey Chapel] and asks VN to call tomorrow.

---

[372] Assigned to 1816 for the following reason. 1811 excluded because SW calls BJ 'Jacob' rather than 'Jacobs' (BJ and SW consistently used the spelling 'Jacobs' until at least SW→BJ, 10/5/1813 and consistently used the spelling 'Jacob' from at least SW→BJ, 15/2/1816). 1822 excluded because ltr addressed to VN at 240 Oxford Street which he left before 1822.

SW→CW Jr & Sarah   **28/8/1816**
MA DDWes/6/44   It is very painful for me to be troublesome to you
📧 Wed 28 Aug={1805,1811,1816,1822}[373]

It is very painful for SW to trouble CW Jr and Sarah about money or about
anything else, but 'pressing circumstances' make this unavoidable. SW has been
unable to raise £100 in the manner that they had proposed to [James] Ball,
which was that they would give security for this sum at SGW's death, should
SW predecease her. One 'unreasonable person' would have given SW £50 on
the [promise to pay] £100, which would have been useless and an 'absurd
sacrifice'.

SW's 'severe illness, and the loss of nearly £100' which he 'would have
certainly cleared had not Providence thought fit to prevent' his journey [to
Norwich and Great Yarmouth], have placed him in 'the present distressful
situation'.[374] Without 'immediate assistance', he must 'surrender' himself into
the hands of 'officers', whose visit he 'hourly' apprehends. If he cannot
discharge certain debts on Saturday [31/8/1816], he will be 'hurried away' in his
'weak and nearly delirious state', which 'certainly' would soon terminate his
'sad existence'. If CW Jr and Sarah can let him have £90, the remaining £10
would be two years' interest to SGW in advance. SW has not exaggerated his
case: nothing but extreme need would have forced him to make this request. He
will send tomorrow morning [29/8/1816] for an answer.

SW→VN   **3/10/1816**
BL Add 11729 f 147; *O*   I called Yesterday at Frith Street to apologize
📧 3/10/1816

SW called [at the Kirkman piano manufactory] in Frith Street yesterday
[2/10/1816] to apologise for not meeting VN on Sunday evening [29/9/1816].
'Mr K' [Joseph Kirkman Jr, piano manufacturer, 1790–1877] was out, but SW
left a card. SW was not in the mood for music [on Sunday] and would have been
useless as a participant; in addition, [Handel's oratorio] *Samson* 'especially
revives unpleasant recollections' [i.e., the name 'Samson' = 'son of Sam'
presumably reminds SW of his recently deceased son].

---

[373] Assigned to 1816 because statement in ltr that SW would have cleared nearly
£100 if 'Providence' had not prevented his journey is consistent with his plans
to perform in Norwich and Great Yarmouth in August 1816 that were not
realised. No journeys have been identified that SW planned to take but did not
take in August 1805, 1811 or 1822.

[374] Sarah→Kingston, 26/8/1817, states that the death of SW's child (*see*
SW→VN, 7/8/1816) drove SW 'frantic on the road to Norwich'. According to
WBRR v 3 (12/1851) p 444, SW 'was on the road to Norwich to take parts in the
splendid ceremonial of a musical festival, and actually travelling thither in the
mail coach, when the excitement of the journey, acting upon his tremulously
nervous system, threw him into a paroxysm of phrenitis, so violent that he was
obliged to be left at an inn, and when partially recovered he returned to town'.

SW asks VN to deputise for him tomorrow [4/10/1816], when VN should bring the 'annexed roll' [not preserved] with him. SW has taken lodgings at Hampstead for a few days; he means to go there this afternoon and plans to stay there at least until Saturday [5/10/1816]. Miss Cresswell [one of SW's pupils] is to begin studying a piece by Handel from the selection published by [John] Clarke [organist and composer, 1770–1836, from 1814 John Clarke-Whitfeld]. The governesses [of the school at which SW teaches] require that 'each brat' be allocated 15 minutes [of instruction].

SW→VN   10/10/1816?

BL Add 11728 f 148; *O*   I fear that I shall not be able to reach Hammersmith
▣ Thu 11 Oct[375]

SW cannot reach Hammersmith before noon tomorrow [11/10/1816] at the earliest; he asks VN to assist him. Should VN be able to reach Turnham Green by about 11, they could travel together from there.

VN should know confidentially that SW has been 'sadly nervous' since Tuesday [8/10/1816], despite the Hampstead air. He is 'thoroughly ashamed' by the 'tiresome test' he is imposing upon VN's friendship.

SW→VN   Gower Pl   11/12/1816

BL Add 11729 f 150; *O*   I am informed that you mean to call here To-morrow
▣ Wed 11 Dec; pmk 1816

SW will be 'ready to receive' VN tomorrow [12/12/1816] between 1 and 2 pm. VN should advise if he cannot come at that time. SW needs VN's help in [writing] the 'review for the approaching month' [for the *EM*] and will explain what help is required when they meet. The printer's deadline is 20/12/1816 so there is no time to lose. SW will do the little he can in conjunction [with VN].

SW asks if VN knows the whereabouts of SW's 'green fat' music book which SW cannot find. He is sure that VN was with him when it was last used. VN's memory is better than SW's, although SW still is reminded of 'all the useless, mischievous, disastrous and distressing events' in his life.

---

[375] Assigned to 10/10/1816 for the following reason. Ltr <1821 because addressed to VN at 240 Oxford Street. Ltr docketed '1816' by an unknown hand; the ref. to Hampstead makes this a plausible year as SW had planned to take lodgings in Hampstead for a few days from 3/10/1816 (*see* SW→VN, 3/10/1816). 11 October was a Friday in 1816. Ltr assigned to 10/10/1816, a Thursday, on the presumption that SW mistook the date rather than the day of the week.

SW→'Dear Sir'[376] Gower Pl **26/12/1816**

MA DDWF/15/22; *O* You will much oblige me by an Estimate of the Pages
📧 26/12/1816

SW requests an estimate of the [number of] pages of [his] musical review in
the *EM* from 'midsummer to the present Christmas' [presumably so that he may
request payment of money due to him].

SW→Stephen Jones Gower Pl **13/1/1817**

K; *O*[377] Mr Asperne has informed me that it is his Intention
📧 Mon 13 Jan; pmk 1817

SW has been informed by [James] Asperne that he intends 'to discontinue the
Musical Review in his Magazine' [the *EM*]. SW does not know whether Asperne
intends to employ another person as music reviewer, but considers 'the short
warning as far from handsome treatment'. SW wants Jones to know why he will
not receive 'any matter for the press' from SW 'in this month as heretofore', and
thanks him for his past 'kind assistance'.

Sarah→Thomas Maurice **17/1/1817**

MA DDWF/14/33 My Mother with Charles & Myself wish to make known
📧 17/1/1817

When Thomas Maurice [historian and author, 1754–1824, from 1798 assistant
keeper of manuscripts in the British Museum] visited SGW in Buckingham
Street [a few years earlier], he told her that CW III had said that 'all his family
were prejudiced against him'. SGW mentioned this to 'the other boy' [JWW]
and remarked on CW III's 'ingratitude' to the family that had 'fostered' him.

CW III never visited or asked about SGW. He 'caricatured' SW, he sent
anonymous letters, and he spoke of Sarah as 'that old devil'. For many years
Sarah and her family have had no communication from CW III, except for two
apologetic letters.

Sarah recounts how CW III 'was placed under our roof on the first great quarrel
and separation' of SW and CLW, how she accompanied him 30 miles to a
country school [at Wateringbury], and how, through her interest, he was placed
at St Paul's School, from which he could have proceeded with financial security
to university had SW and CLW not taken him away precipitously, leaving Sarah
with some bills to pay. CW III then was 'articled to an apothecary' [Mr Rivers,
see Sarah→Mr Bingham, 26/6/1812].

Sarah believes that SW and CLW prevented CW III from 'coming to us',
thereby destroying his gratitude. An effect of this folly is that SW now may
'class' CW III 'at the head of his enemies'.

---

[376] The recipient seems likely to have been either James Asperne, the publisher,
or Stephen Jones, the editor, of the *EM*.

[377] A reproduction of this ltr faces p 8.

CW III's 'timid nature', his inclination 'to servile acquiesence' and his 'peculiar talent for flattery' may derive from his having to please both SW and CLW, 'who were always quarrelling and opposing each other'. CW III has now taken 'a decided part' against SW. Sarah regrets that SW has 'given reason to his children of complaint', even though he paid £300 to apprentice CW III, placed JWW 'in a good situation', and allows CLW £130 per annum.

When SW is 'unable to pay this allowance regularly' CLW sends him a writ. Without assistance from Sarah and her 'far from affluent' family, SW would have been 'taken to prison long ago'. Sarah fears that this will be SW's 'end'. She is striving to persuade SW to give up the ruinous, dishonourable 'manner of life he now leads'. He can have no 'extrication from his pecuniary embarrassments if he continues to have two families'. He can never support CLW if he is 'obliged to go to the King's Bench' [prison]. CLW is 'a fool' to add lawyers' bills to his expenses.

SGW has been told that CW III 'always urges the attorney to send the writ'. Sarah urges Maurice to endeavour to convince CW III that this course of action is wrong. CW 'always prognosticated misery' from SW's attachment to CLW, 'who had a most unprincipled extravagant father' and 'belonged to a stock where there was no truth'. Fortunately, CW did not live to see 'the calamities which vice has brought' upon SW.

SW→VN   **4/1817?**
BL Add 11729 f 152; *O*   You guess the purport of this: I am again
⊡ 'Tuesday morning'[378]
   SW requests VN's 'candid and unreserved opinion' on SW's present state, 'both mental, public, and domestic', and on the 'probable, possible, or more immediate causes' of SW's 'general and permanent discomfort' that VN has witnessed. SW's 'upper story' is 'still far from in patient order'. He requests a lift tomorrow.

Sarah→Joseph Benson   **14/4/1817**
MA DDWes/7/104   I wished & intended to have called & thanked You
⊡ 14 April; pmk 15/4/1817
   Joseph Benson [Methodist minister, 1748–1821] will be happy to hear that Sarah's 'poor brother' SW is 'awakening to a sense of his past conduct'. Sarah asks for Benson's prayers.

---

[378] Ltr placed here because of the context of SW's impending breakdown. No evidence is available for a more precise dating.

Sarah memorandum   6/5/1817
Hamptons International catalogue   He precipitated himself out of the Window
22/5/1998 lot 548[379]
Hamptons International (Godalming, Surrey) catalogue

SW 'precipitated himself' out of a window 'in a fit of frenzy'. He thought he was pressed by creditors as 'writs were issued against him' by CLW and he had received threats from his landlord. SW's life was preserved 'miraculously'.

WL→Sarah   2 York Buildings   8/5/1817
WBRR v 3 (Dec 1851) p 446   I am just returned from Pimlico
WBRR

WL has just returned from Pimlico [CLW's home] but was unable to see CLW. He left a 'short but strong note' with SW's 'little daughter' [Emma] and then called on Mr and Mrs King [not identified] to give them the 'melancholy intelligence' [of SW's condition]. Mrs King promised to see CLW immediately and to bring her and her children to York Buildings [Sarah's home, where SW was staying] as soon as possible.

WL's nerves have been 'shaken', but he has the 'painful satisfaction' of knowing that he has seen SW once more according to SW's wishes. WL is grateful to Mr [John] Heaviside [surgeon, 1748–1828, from 1790 surgeon extraordinary to King George III] for transmitting these wishes. Heaviside and Sarah's other 'medical friends' have 'acted with great humanity'.

If SW 'departs easily' and 'without any bitter pain, either of mind or body', it will give WL 'great consolation' to hear this. Seeing CLW and their children, and the reconciliation that WL hopes will then happen, will prepare SW's mind for 'the last and most sacred consolation of religion'. WL recommends that this be administered to SW 'before it is too late'.

---

[379] According to notes (now in WHS, Wesley Historical Society Manuscript Journal v 3 p 187) written on 18/9/1904 by Robert Thursfield Smith, a collector of Methodist books and manuscripts who formerly owned this memorandum, Sarah wrote this memorandum on the back of a 7/- ticket to SW's annual benefit concert scheduled for 24/5/1817 in the Theatre Royal, Covent Garden. Smith states that this ticket, for admission to a box, was signed by SW. The present location of this item is not known.

Sarah journal entry[380]   2 York Buildings   **8/5/1817**

WBRR v 3 (Dec 1851) p 445   [not known]
WBRR

It was pronounced today that SW had but a few hours to live. He was perfectly in his senses today. When Elizabeth Mortimer [née Ritchie, 1754–1835, *see* note to JW→SW, 29/4/1790] arrived today to comfort SGW, SW exclaimed 'O! Miss Ritchie do you know me?', calling her by her maiden name rather than by her married name. Mrs Mortimer said that she was sorry to see SW in this situation and wanted to read to him a hymn by CW which was a prayer for mercy. She asked SW if he wished for mercy and he said 'yes'. She said that SW had resisted Jesus' mercy and had provoked His wrath. SW agreed that he had been a blasphemer and feared that it was too late for him to repent, and that his repentance would be 'not of the right sort, arising more from the fear of punishment than from hatred to sin'.

SW added that if his life were spared he hoped he would not live as he had done. He wished to see several persons, 'particularly his wife and children', and confessed that he had been a great sinner, an undutiful son, and had 'sadly abused the talents that God had given him'. Some days previously he had felt 'as though surrounded by evil spirits' and had feared that 'it was a foretaste of Hell and his companions there'. In reply to Mrs Mortimer's inquiry SW admitted that he wished to live 'another kind of life' than that which he had lived up to now.

Sarah→William Wilberforce   2 York Buildings   **12/5/1817?**

GEU in box 7   We should have presented our Congratulations
ltr undated[381]

On 'Saturday sevennight' [3/5/1817] SW left 'his mistress' [SS, presumably at 4 Gower Place] and came to SGW's house [2 York Buildings], his mind so deranged 'that we were obliged to have a keeper'. A lodging for SW was

---

[380] *WBRR*'s text was taken from Sarah's 'copious diary'. Presumably this was one of the 'Forty-five Ladies Pocket Diaries, with MS. Notes by Miss S. Wesley' which were offered for sale by Sothebys in lot 266 of their 10/7/1906 sale of 'important letters and relics of the Wesley family'. According to the auctioneer's record (BL S.C. Sotheby 1308), lot 266 was not sold, and the present location of Sarah's diaries is not known.

[381] Assigned to 12/5/1817 for the following reason. Ltr says SW leapt from a window 'last Tuesday' and has now survived 'for more than five days'. The leap appears to have happened on Tuesday 6/5/1817, as CW Jr noted in his diary entry for that day (MA DDWF/23/15) that SW 'was wonderfully preserv'd thro' Providence' and 'had a most Providential escape'. Ltr assigned to 12/5/1817, six days after the leap, on the presumption that if ltr had been written on 13/5/1817 then Sarah would have said that SW has survived for more than six days. Ltr <14/5/1817 as 6/5/1817 then would not be 'last Tuesday'. The statement in ltr that SW's recovery is now thought possible is consistent with CW Jr's diary entry for 11/5/1817 that SW is 'pronounc'd [by a physician] to be mending'.

arranged in the neighbourhood. 'Last Tuesday' [6/5/1817], while SGW was sitting beside him, SW 'flung up the window, and himself out of it', landing on stones 25 feet below. Sarah found that SW was alive. His 'senses returned soon after' and he became 'sensible of the horrid injection of Satan'. [The Rev.] Mr [Basil] Woodd [clergyman and hymn-writer, 1760–1831] then came and prayed with SW, who 'earnestly entreated mercy'.

Sarah told SW that he had probably 'but a few hours' to live. She was grateful that he was not 'left to die with a wicked woman' [SS] but was 'brought to his family', with pious people around him. 'Against all the judgement of the physicians' SW now has survived for 'more than five days', and his recovery is 'thought possible'. Sarah removed SGW to the lodging that had been obtained for SW and continues to care for him at 'our house' [2 York Buildings]. SGW regards his survival as an 'unspeakable blessing' and feels 'that God has not cast out her prayers'. Sarah fears, however, that this incident may 'hasten' SGW's demise and asks William Wilberforce [philanthropist, member of parliament and campaigner against slavery, 1759–1833] to call upon SGW, as this may be the last time that SGW can thank him for his friendship.

SGW is gratified by Sarah's reports of SW's 'looks' and 'words'. Sarah hopes that SW may 'live to be an illustrious penitent'.

CW III→'Dear Sir'[382]   19/5/1817

GEU in box 6   It is fortunate for your Patience that a Multiplicity of Thanks is
▪ Mon 19 May={1817}[383]

CW III cannot thank the recipient sufficiently for rescuing SW 'from ignominy and perdition' and showing 'regard for his soul as well as his body', notwithstanding the censure and abuse that the recipient has received. CW III understands that SW 'clamours exceedingly after his spurious children' [SSW and Rosalind, his children with SS]. This greatly distresses Sarah, especially because SW's 'two surgeons[384] are solicitous to comply with his demands' and say that if SW were moved to his own lodgings he could see whomever he liked. Such licence would be lamentable because it would cut off 'all hope of reconciliation' between SW and 'his lawful family'. CW III believes that SW is insane. If this licence were given to him, his insanity would be 'permanent and incurable'.

Everyone agrees that SW 'must be moved from his present abode'. CW III

---

[382] Ltr presumably sent to one of RG, WL or Kingston, who together took charge of SW's affairs after his leap (*see* Sarah→Kingston, 26/8/1817).

[383] Assigned to 1817 from context of CW III's belief in SW's insanity and the need for SW's family to make decisions regarding his abode.

[384] From CW Jr's diary, MA DDWF/23/5, it appears that the physicians attending SW at this time were Sir William Bagshawe [William Chambers Darling, 1771–1832, who assumed the surname 'Bagshawe' in 1801 and was knighted in 1806] and Mr John Heaviside, *see* WL→Sarah, 8/5/1817.

seeks the recipient's advice on this matter and also on how SW, CLW and Emma are to be supported until it pleases God to restore SW's reason. The incomes of CW III and JWW are too limited to provide this support. CW III and his family 'could not concur in any proposal' to transfer SW that was not sanctioned by the recipient, whose recommendations CW III awaits.

Richard J. S. Stevens diary entry   29/5/1817

Camb Add 9110   Smith informed me that Saml Wesleys friends were to have diary entry dated 29/5/1817

Smith [not identified] told R. J. S. Stevens that SW's friends would meet today to decide whether SW 'should be placed in St Luke's Hospital [for Lunatics], or in a private madhouse'.[385]

SW→VN   Chapel St[386]   31/5/1817

BL Add 11729 f 154; *O*   Here I am in the greatest Agonies of Mind & Body
☑ 'Saturday morning 30 May', an incorrect date, pmk 31/5/1817[387]

SW is in 'the greatest agonies of mind and body', although the agonies of his mind are greater. He begs VN to visit him this evening. SW asks why everyone has forsaken him. Even his 'little ones' [SSW and Rosalind] are kept from him.

---

[385] In July 1817 (*see* Sarah→RG, 7/7/1817), SW was placed under the care of Alexander Robert Sutherland, medical doctor, *c*1780–1861. As Dr Sutherland was physician to St Luke's Hospital for Lunatics from 1811 to 1841, he may have seen SW as early as May 1817.

[386] According to CW Jr's diary (MA DDWF/23/15), SW was 'removed to Chapel Street' on 23/5/1817 'by order' of his 'two physicians', Sir William Bagshawe and Mr John Heaviside, who attended him until his health improved sufficiently for him to go to Southend on 3/6/1817. Sarah→CW III, 4/3/1818?, notes that, 'through the means' of Sir William, Sarah's family were able to 'rescue' SW from SS [i.e., to keep him from returning to her at Gower Place].

[387] Assigned to Saturday 31/5/1817 on the presumption that SW mistook the date but not the day of the week.

Sarah memorandum 6/1817?

WBRR v 3 (Dec 1851) p 445 [not known]
>SW's 3/6/1817 departure to Southend; presumably <Sarah→RG, 7/7/1817[388]

Sarah thanks God that she was able to convey SGW to 'a neighbouring lodging' [so that SW could be accommodated near Sarah at 2 York Buildings in May 1817, *see* Sarah→William Wilberforce, 12/5/1817?] and to revive SGW's 'despairing, fainting spirit' with assurances of SW's continued life. Although Sir William Bagshawe had told Sarah that 'not one in a million' in SW's 'desperate state' ever lived, Sarah did not mention this to SGW. Sarah reasoned 'even then' that SW 'might be the one of that million'; if not, who was she 'to repine' at God's sovereign will? SW appeared 'penitent' and 'deeply sensible of his state', and she hoped that 'he would be a monument of mercy at the last hour'. While not mentioning SW's 'imminent danger' to SGW, Sarah visited him 'with the idea that every hour might be his last'.

'At length, to the astonishment of the physicians [presumably Sir William Bagshawe and Mr John Heaviside] themselves', SW was pronounced out of danger, and 'enabled to remove to Southend [on 3/6/1817] for change of air and scene'.[389]

CW III→Sarah 5/6/1817

GEU in box 6 The Mole-eyed Goddess of Misprision seems particularly
☞ Thu 5 Jun={1817}[390]

Sarah has drawn a false conclusion from a letter [not preserved] that CW III wrote to WL. AFCK, 'in the handsomest manner', interested himself in CW III's family by proposing a benefit concert to raise money to provide better support for SW and to relieve CLW's 'exigencies', and made several 'applications with success'. As WL had 'taken upon himself the charge' of SW's person, it was appropriate that WL should be approached in this connection, and CW III was 'considered the most proper person' to approach him. Although WL's response to CW III's approach [not preserved] was extraordinarily 'ungentlemanly', CW III's reply to WL cannot be considered 'vulgar or impertinent', as Sarah had suggested.

WL alluded, in his letter to CW III, to a letter [not preserved] that CW III wrote to SW [some time earlier, when SW and SS were living together]. CW III

---

[388] Memorandum is presumed to precede Sarah's 7/7/1817 letter because it records the physicians' pronouncement that SW was out of danger, whereas that letter indicates that she and SGW then considered SW to be in sufficient danger to require confinement in an asylum.

[389] CW Jr recorded in his diary (MA DDWF/23/15), about 28/5/1817, that Mr Heaviside thought that SW would recover 'through Providence' if he was 'kept quiet'.

[390] Assigned to 1817 from ref. to WL being in charge of SW (*see* Sarah→Kingston, 26/8/1817).

acknowledges that his letter was written with greater 'asperity' than was appropriate. However, he had been provoked by a 'cruel, abusive, false and unfatherly' charge from SW. The severest parts of CW III's letter were 'levelled at the odious woman' [SS] who then was SW's 'prime minister', and who 'incited' SW to 'any unjust or contemptible action' that could gratify 'her diabolical passions and propensities'.

Legal proceedings [against SW] were undertaken only 'after every mild application had been made and treated with contempt'. SW slighted CLW's 'solicitations' that he 'furnish her with the means of living'. He sent a 'myrmidon (Mr Swan)' to prevent shopkeepers in Pimlico [where CLW and her children lived] granting her credit [*see* SW→SGW, 24/10/1811]. SW even authorised her landlord to evict her while he was 'maintaining a strumpet' [SS] with 'a separate family and establishment'. As neither CW III nor his brother [JWW] could support CLW, it was their duty to ensure that she 'derived succour from the right quarter' [i.e., from SW]. All that they did was to write, in CLW's name, to her lawyer and to her trustee, [George] Oliver, asking them to take appropriate measures. Oliver agreed to take SW's 'bill at two months'. The prospect of SW going to jail 'was never considered'.

It seemed impossible to CW III and JWW that someone of SW's eminence, 'who boasted of the frugality of his new housekeeper' [SS], would be 'distressed' by paying the £130 annuity [to CLW]. If so, why did he not retrench?

If either of their parents was in need, CW III and JWW would provide aid. They are sorry if SW's feelings were injured by actions they were obliged to take because SW 'wantonly deprived' CLW of necessaries while he 'lavished' the means of procuring them 'upon the indulgencies of a worthless prostitute' [SS]. No epithet that SGW directed at CW III would surprise him.

CW III acknowledges Sarah's kindness and expressions of friendship, and looks forward to visiting her soon. He cannot come tomorrow [6/6/1817] because of other commitments, nor can Emma, who has a 'very severe cold'.

Sarah→RG[391]   **7/7/1817**

GEU in box 8   Mr Kingston being ill, my Mother Earnestly requests you
▣ 'Monday 7'[392]

Because Kingston [who, together with RG and WL, was in 'charge' of SW, *see*
Sarah→Kingston, 26/8/1817] is ill, and as Sarah is leaving town,[393] SGW
'earnestly requests' RG to act for her [concerning SW]. Sarah has told WL that
'he must give up his charge' [of SW] not to Sarah but to SGW, as she alone
assigned SW 'over to' WL.

RG is requested to let Dr [Alexander Robert] Sutherland know that SGW
entrusts SW to Dr Sutherland's care, 'with the kind superintendence of' RG and
Kingston. Dr Sutherland 'must obtain the advice of' Dr [George Leman] Tuthill
[physician to Bethlem Hospital and other institutions, 1772–1835], whose fee is
to be paid out of SW's finances. Dr Sutherland is 'to appoint the place' where Dr
Tuthill will see SW [presumably to sign a certificate attesting to SW's lunacy,
required for his admission to an asylum].

Sarah's family will be obliged 'if Dr Sutherland will manage this for us', as
they live 'at too great a distance to have oral communication' with him, and 'the
whole affair had better be arranged' before SGW 'hears anything more about it'.

Sarah is sure that her health will improve after she leaves this 'scene of
trouble'. She looks forward to hearing from RG 'after all is settled', but wants
the place of SW's abode [i.e., the place where SW will be kept] not to be
mentioned to SGW without Sarah 'knowing it first'. Sarah hopes that SGW can
be satisfied without 'precise knowledge', as 'it [the place of confinement] must
not be talked about'.

---

[391] Ltr addressed to 'My dear Sir'. RG assigned as recipient because he,
Kingston and WL were in charge of SW (*see* Sarah to Kingston, 26/8/1817) and
after WL's resignation Kingston and RG remained in charge of SW.

[392] Assigned to 7/7/1817 for the following reason. 'Monday 7' in ltr is taken to
mean 'Monday the 7th'. Ltr >6/5/1817, the date of SW's leap, and <24/8/1817
when SW was at Blacklands, the place where he would be kept, *see*
Kingston→Sarah, 24/8/1817. In 1817, after 6/5/1817, July was the only month
when Monday occurred on the 7th.

[393] According to CW Jr's diary (MA DDWF/23/15), Sarah went to Hillingdon
(Middlesex) on 12/7/1817 and returned to London on 17/7/1817.

CW Jr→RG[394]   **about 8/7/1817**
BL Add 39168I f 65   I enclose you Mr Linley's Letter just received
▣ ltr undated[395]

CW Jr encloses a letter [not preserved] from WL. SGW begs RG to call on WL tomorrow so that she may 'settle' according to WL's 'wish' expressed in his letter [presumably regarding WL's relinquishing the charge of SW, *see* Sarah→RG, 7/7/1817]. CW Jr and SGW hope that RG will thank WL for the trouble he has taken [regarding SW].

SW now must be left to the 'judicious decision' of Dr [Alexander Robert] Sutherland. It is 'grievous' that the bill [presumably for SW's treatment] should fall on WL and RG. A 'cheap abode' should be found for SW so that part of SW's 'scanty income' can go to them [as compensation for payments they have made on SW's behalf]. It is hard for WL and RG to suffer for their generosity; CW Jr would repay them if he could. Sarah is too weak to call on Dr Sutherland.

CW Jr and Sarah hope that Kingston is better and send their regards to him.

Kingston→Sarah   Blacklands   **24/8/1817**
GEU Wesley Coll. ltr 98   I was with your brother five hours of yesterday
▣ 24/8/1817

Kingston spent five hours with SW [at Blacklands] yesterday [23/8/1817] afternoon. Although he has never seen SW look healthier he certainly has seen him look happier. Mrs Bastable, the proprietress [of Blacklands], discussed SW's case with Kingston and showed him the extensive 'entirely enclosed' gardens of 'the establishment'. After making tea for SW and Kingston, which SW 'ate heartily', she departed.

SW immediately, 'with great calmness and self-possession', questioned Kingston on 'many points' of his letter [to SW, not preserved]. SW 'did not deny the soundness' of Kingston's reasoning; however, Kingston was unable to persuade SW to consent to his recommendations.

SW says that 'he has no business' [at Blacklands]. He feels 'that his conduct does not justify his being treated as an insane person'; he 'is not touched by the interference of his friends' and does not think what they have done or are doing is for his good. He is provoked exceedingly by the knowledge 'that his own funds pay for his own imprisonment'; whereas if he were 'of sound mind and

---

[394] RG not named in ltr but assigned as recipient because ltr indicates that the recipient is someone other than WL or Kingston who took responsibility for SW's affairs and, according to Sarah→Kingston, 26/8/1817, RG was the only such person.

[395] Ltr placed here because it appears to have been written soon after Sarah→RG, 7/7/1817: RG (the presumed recipient of ltr) appears to have acceded to SGW's request in the earlier letter that he act for her; WL, who at the time of the earlier letter had been told that he must resign his charge of SW to SGW, has now written a letter presumably doing this; and Kingston, who was ill at the time of the earlier letter, is hoped in this ltr to be better.

proper feelings' he would prefer the present arrangement to his 'being an object of charity'. SW's hopes, fears and wishes 'are all extravagant' and 'encumber the efforts of his reason'.

SGW desired Kingston to tell SW that 'his little boy' [SSW] was 'about to be provided for in the way proposed' [presumably the letter from Kingston to SW contained a proposal that SSW be sent to the Heywood Hall school near Manchester, *see* Sarah→Kingston, 26/8/1817]. SW 'greatly objected' to the [school's] distance. He stated, with increasing agitation, that this was a plan to send SSW out of SW's reach so that SW should never see SSW again. SW implored Kingston to prevent or at least to delay this plan. Kingston said he would not do this 'without some reasonable objection' to the plan.

Then, as the 'allotted time' for the interview was passed, Mrs Bastable came in with 'the keeper'. Kingston said he would promise only to make SW's family aware of his 'aversion' to the plan and his 'desire for at least its delay'. SW angrily replied that this was not what he had expected from Kingston, and left the interview dissatisfied and irritated.

Kingston believes that Dr [Alexander Robert] Sutherland permitted Kingston to see SW 'too soon'.[396] SW's 'short, dry' acknowledgement [not preserved] of his receipt of Kingston's letter had caused Kingston to think this, even before he went [to Blacklands]. He understands that SW has written [not preserved] to Mr [Joseph] Major and perhaps to other friends to come to visit. Kingston thinks SW 'will never recover' if he is 'trifled with, deceived or injudiciously soothed', and considers that SW should have no interviews with friends at present. However, SW's friends 'must do as they please'.

The inventory of SW's wardrobe that Sarah had delivered to Kingston has been numbered to show the items 'now in the possession of Mrs Bastable' and is enclosed [not preserved]. He has asked Mrs Bastable to procure additional clothing [for SW] and to see that necessary mending is done. Kingston proposes to discuss his interview [with SW] with Dr Sutherland 'as soon as possible'.

Sarah→Kingston[397] **Blacklands** **26/8/1817**
GEU Wesley Coll. ltr 85 I have been favor'd with two letters
26/8/1817

On behalf of her family, Sarah thanks Kingston for his two letters [Kingston→Sarah, 24/8/1817, and another letter not preserved]. Unlike SW, who has surrounded himself with 'sycophants and flatterers', Sarah is a sincere person. Accordingly she is not offended by Kingston's candour.

SW 'never could endure an unpleasant truth' nor 'suppose a person could love him who uttered it to his face'. 'All his misfortunes' originated from this, including his hatred of Sarah and CW. By opposing SW's will, CW lost SW's

[396] On 20/8/1817 Dr Sutherland had called on CW Jr (and presumably SGW and Sarah) with 'tidings' of SW 'being better' (CW Jr diary, MA DDWF/23/15).

[397] Ltr addressed to 'Dear Sir'. Kingston identified as recipient because ltr is a reply to Kingston→Sarah, 24/8/1817.

affection. CW never regained this until long after he 'removed to a happier world'.

It would be unreasonable to expect Kingston to neglect his own affairs for those of SW. However, Kingston 'kindly undertook the charge' of SW with RG and WL 'without the name of it' [i.e., without being a legally appointed guardian] and, 'after the resignation' of WL, continued 'unwearied attentions' to SW's interest. As RG was out of town, and Mr Swan 'did not appear', Kingston was the only person to whom the family could apply 'in such an exigency'.

If the family had appeared [before SS], 'the woman' [SS] would have become fixed 'in her refusal to promote her child's establishment' [the education of SSW according to the plan of Sarah and her family]; moreover, an appearance by the family 'would have irritated poor' SW 'to the highest degree also'. The plan [for SSW's education] 'now has failed' but the family 'used every proper method to present it'. CW Jr twice called on Mr Swan (before and after Sarah's letter [not preserved] to Kingston), and also presented the plan to Mr Swan in writing. Swan did not reply in writing but called one morning and said he would 'use all his interest' with SS 'not to stand in her own light'. As Sarah heard nothing further she concluded that SS 'did not choose to send' SSW. He therefore 'will remain with his unprincipled mother to be trained up with the vicious, and incorporated with the vulgar'.

Sarah has advised 'the ladies' who would have 'taken care' of SSW that he is not coming to Manchester. She has written to Mr Bridge [not identified], who would have escorted SSW from Manchester to Heywood Hall [school] 12 miles away, but he cannot receive Sarah's letter before he leaves for Manchester.

The defeat of this plan means that SW's children 'are likely to be involved in the misfortunes of their father' and 'probably' will become 'sad memorials' of SW's 'misspent youth'. If SSW is to be sent to a school 'it must be at the expense of others', as the family's plan has failed.

Sarah is grieved but mostly is not surprised by Kingston's 'interesting and circumstantial' account of SW [in Kingston→Sarah, 24/8/1817]. SW's indignation 'at not being a burden on society' indicates that 'his mind is less sane than ever'. If Sarah had seen Kingston when he called she would strongly have opposed SGW's wish that SW be 'acquainted with the intention of placing' SSW at the school. SW's entire insanity 'has proceed from this vile connection' [with SS]. The 'death of one of the children' [SW's 'little boy' mentioned in SW→VN, 7/8/1816] 'drove him frantic on the road to Norwich' [about 10/8/1816, see SW→VN, 1/8/1816]. Seeing another child 'tormented his mind to fury the night [5/5/1817] before the fatal accident' [SW's jump from a window on 6/5/1817]. The 'idea of all of them', including 'the woman' [SS], 'perpetuates his malady'.

Unless SW was 'in a state to be grateful for' Kingston's 'friendly letter' [not preserved, see Kingston→Sarah, 24/8/1817], 'any mention of these unhappy beings' [SS and her children] 'must have revived his perverseness and violence'. Dr [Alexander Robert] Sutherland 'surely was too sanguine' by thinking SW to be far better than he is. Sarah agrees with Kingston that SW's 'insanity is chiefly self will'. If SW were at liberty he might 'only evince' his insanity 'in going again' to SS and, 'on the first contradiction from her', destroy himself.

SGW→SW Blacklands **29/8/1817**
WHS[398] I thank you for your letter; wch I shd answer myself but my Eyes
▣ '29 August' & 📫→ⅈ

SGW thanks SW for his letter [not preserved]. Her eye troubles oblige her to use her friend Mrs [Elizabeth] Mortimer as amanuensis. SGW hopes that SW continues 'to derive benefit' [at Blacklands] and is glad to hear 'great hopes' that SW will again come 'amongst' [us]. She is thankful that God has established SW's health 'so much', and 'above all' that He 'averted the greatest of evils' [presumably SW's premature death]. She prays that SW will keep his mind 'tranquil', as 'patience will hasten' his cure. 'We all unite in love and prayers' for SW's restoration, as SGW hopes to see SW again 'in this world'. Sarah will send SW 'the things' [of his] left here [at 2 York Buildings], and Mrs Bastable 'will procure the rest'.

In a postscript, Mrs Mortimer hopes that SW often calls upon God for the help he needs.

SW→William Hawes **28/11/1817**
BL Music Ms Loan 79.10/3; *O* Pray accept my best Thanks for your extremely
▣ 28/11/1817

SW thanks William Hawes [musician and music publisher, 1785–1846, from 1/7/1817 Master of the Children of the Chapel Royal] for offering to take his 'little boy' [SSW, as a chorister at the Chapel Royal]. SSW is a 'very apprehensive child' [i.e., he learns readily] and is 'very fond of music'. SW is confident that Hawes will treat SSW with kindness. RG will look after the necessary arrangements.

SGW→SW Blacklands **18/12/1817**
Drew Wesley Family Letters, SGW series I am alive—but nearly Blind.
ltr dated in another hand (Sarah's?) 'Thursday 18/12/1817'[399]

SGW is 'alive, but nearly blind'. Her love keeps SW where he is [at Blacklands]. She hopes that SW 'will soon come out well' to his 'ever affectionate mother'.

---

[398] Ltr is signed by SGW but otherwise is in the handwriting of Elizabeth Ritchie Mortimer.

[399] This date is confirmed by CW Jr's 18/12/1817 entry in his diary (MA DDWF/23/15): 'I...took a note to Mr Fox [not identified] to carry from my Dear Mother to my Brother'.

CW Jr→RG   **27/12/1817**

GEU in box 8   Powlett hath just now sent to say He is going to Peckham

☞ '27 December'[400]

   Mr Powlett [for a time deputy organist to CW Jr at Chelsea College] is going to
Peckham Chapel 'to perform for the vacant appointment'. If he does not obtain
this post he probably can 'attend the following Sunday' for SW at K[entish]
T[own] Chapel. CW Jr unites with RG in hoping that SW, 'at this time of need',
will not be deprived of the situation [of organist at Kentish Town Chapel]. CW
Jr sends season's greetings from 'us all'.

SW→RG   Blacklands[401]   **3/1/1818**

MA DDWF/15/23; *O*   Upon Examination, the Little Book you were so kind as

☞ 3/1/1818

   The book which RG kindly brought to SW was not the right one: SW wanted
the *Ordo Recitandi Officii Divini* and asks RG to obtain it for him as soon as
possible. SW longs for his 'great music book' and asks RG to bring it. As RG
desired, SW has composed 'a movement'. He asks RG to visit him on
Wednesday [7/1/1818] if possible.

CW III→Sarah   Blacklands   **27/2/1818**

GEU in box 6   As I never expressed any Suspicion that you were desirous of

☞ Fri 27 Feb & 🖎→ⓘ

   Mrs Bradshaw [not identified], who conveyed [to Blacklands] a letter [not
preserved] that CW III wrote to SW 'some time ago', told CW III that the
'Mistress of the Blacklands Establishment' [Mrs Bastable] allows anyone
recommended by Sarah to visit SW. The financial affairs both of SW and of his

---

[400] Assigned to 1817 for the following reason. SGW→Mr Hornby, 15/5/1818,
says SW's salary for 18 months at Kentish Town Chapel was due on 24/6/1818,
indicating that he was organist there in December 1816 and December 1817. No
additional information is known about SW's appointment to or tenure at that
chapel. 1817 is preferred to 1816 because SW→'Dear Sir', 26/12/1816, and
surrounding letters do not suggest that SW then had extraordinary needs or was
likely to be deprived of an organist's situation, whereas in December 1817 SW
was confined at Blacklands and therefore was unable to carry out the duties of
an organist except by having others deputise for him. In addition, CW Jr was
dismissed as organist of Chelsea College about 1/8/1817, where Powlett
frequently had carried out the organist's duties as CW Jr's deputy, as the college
governors no longer wanted those duties to be fulfilled by a deputy (CW Jr diary
entries, MA DDWF/23/15). Hence Powlett appears more likely to have been
seeking work in December 1817 than in December 1816.

[401] SW notes that ltr is to be transmitted to RG 'by favour of Dr [Alexander
Robert] Sutherland'.

'legal family', by which CW III means CLW and her 'little daughter' [Emma], are in a very reduced state, and CW III is 'endeavouring to get up a benefit concert' to provide relief.

CW III does not consider his family to be litigious. However, CLW regards neither SGW nor Sarah as friends. A letter [not preserved] from WL indicates that he volunteered to approach CLW [regarding SW]; CW III never suspected that SGW requested WL to make such a visit. If SW wishes to see CW III and if such a visit is approved by SW's physician, CW III would like to see SW. However, CW III would not 'press the matter' unless both conditions are met. He regrets that other business has prevented him from visiting Sarah recently but hopes to visit her at 'the first opportunity'.

SGW will   3/3/1818
PRO PROB 11/1665[402]   I Sarah Wesley of York Buildings New Road
will dated 3/3/1818

SGW bequeaths all her household furniture to CW Jr and her clothes, plate, linen and trinkets to Sarah. The residue of SGW's property is bequeathed in equal portions to CW Jr, SW and Sarah. SGW appoints CW Jr and Sarah executors of her will. SGW signs this will in the presence of James Pettit of the Bank of England and of William Thornton and [her relative] Frances Baldwyn, the latter two of 2 York Buildings, Marylebone, the same address as SGW's.

Sarah→CW III   Blacklands   4/3/1818?
GEU Wesley Coll. ltr 86   Mr Cook has written to my Brother Charles to offer
ltr so dated but not in Sarah's autograph[403]

'Mr Cook' [possibly Matthew Cooke, who probably had deputised for SW earlier, *see* SW→George Smith, 23/4/1809] has written [not preserved] to CW Jr, offering to take SW as a boarder for £2/2/- a week. CW Jr forwarded this offer 'to the gentlemen who have the whole management of' SW and his affairs [RG and Kingston].

Before 'the last unfavourable accounts' [of SW], Sarah had asked RG why SW's doctors 'thought it so very unsafe' to give SW liberty. RG replied that, because 'the patients [considered by their doctors to have similar conditions to SW's] have rarely recovered in less than a twelve months trial', the doctors did not wish 'to risk their reputation', or expose SW to the outside world, before a year had elapsed.

RG and Kingston also thought that, the longer SW was confined, the greater the 'chance of his mistress [SS] disposing of herself' [i.e., going away], which 'she doubtless would do'. 'It would be very horrible' if SW wished to return to her,

---

[402] Document is the Prerogative Court of Canterbury copy of the original will, which was proved on 11/1/1823.

[403] This date is plausible because ltr is a reply to CW III→Sarah, 27/2/1818.

although Sarah has 'no voice' in this matter. SGW would not permit SW 'to continue in confinement' unless she dreaded 'his returning to the same scene of disorder and misery' [living with SS], which would 'induce' SW to end his life.

SW would never have hated Sarah if she had not 'dropped' AD's 'acquaintance' upon realising that AD 'was the sole cause' of SW's 'conjugal infidelity'. Sarah's action 'might have convinced' CLW that Sarah was CLW's especial friend, but SW 'sought to make' CLW 'believe the contrary'. When Sarah discovered this, she 'had a full explanation' with CLW, who promised to tell her 'every future insinuation tending to separate us'. CLW kept her word for some time but, after all intercourse ceased, 'ill conjunctions' were made.

CW III should not forget that Sarah sent to acquaint him 'with the melancholy situation' of SW [after SW's leap from a window]. Sarah was anxious for CLW to see SW and for SGW to give her blessing to CW III and JWW. Sarah cherished CW III in his early childhood and feels partial towards him. He and JWW have conducted themselves well since SW's malady, except in one case when JWW was contemptuous of CW Jr's kindness. Sarah scarcely knows 'little Emma' but feels 'much interest in her welfare as a child flung out of her prospects and necessitated to earn a livelihood' by the music profession which has been 'so fatal' to SW.

SS must be the person who 'gave out' that Sarah could admit people [to see SW at Blacklands]. SS 'can bear no good will' to Sarah's family who 'rescued' SW from SS 'through the means of Sir W[illiam] Bagshaw[e] and Mrs Knapp' [not identified]. Sarah will inquire how Mrs Bastable [the Blacklands proprietress] could say Sarah 'gave tickets of admission' [for visitors to Blacklands]. Even SGW cannot admit persons without approval from Dr [Alexander Robert] Sutherland.

Sarah asks if CW III has called on Dr Sutherland. Dr Sutherland refused CW Jr's proposal that Mr Glover see SW, saying that 'it agitated' SW to see old friends. Even Sarah is not to see SW until 'he is more controlled'.

SGW shares Sarah's dread of SW's returning to his 'vile course of life'. SW's and SS's 'illegitimate children do not come to us'. 'The boy' [SSW] 'should never have borne' SW's name if Sarah 'could have prevented it'.

SW→RG   **23/3/1818**

BL Add Ms 35013 f 73; *O*   I trust that you will give me the Comfort of a Visit
▣ 23/3/1818

SW asks RG to visit him as soon as possible, and inquires about the safe arrival of the Psalm which he entrusted to Kingston several days ago. SW hopes that it will suit RG's purpose. SW remarks that [John Bernard] Logier 'has raised a hornet's nest about him' [presumably a reference to the publication or impending publication of *An Exposition of the Musical System of Mr Logier; with Strictures on his Chiroplast...by A Committee of Professors in London* (London, 1818), in which SW's praise of Logier's chiroplast, *see* SW→John Bernard Logier, 1/9/1814, is criticised].

SGW→Mr Hornby   **5/1818**
MA DDWF/27/4A   Rec'd May 1818 of __ Hornby Esqr Treasurer
⊟ 'May 1818'[404]
SGW has received £45 [the amount has been altered from £47/15/-] from Mr
Hornby, treasurer of the Kentish Town Chapel organ committee, as payment for
SW's salary as organist of that chapel for 18 months. This sum was due on
'midsummer day next' [24/6/1818].

Sarah→'Dear Madam'[405]   Blacklands   **26/6/1818?**
GEU Wesley Coll ltr 91[406]   My Mother joins me in grateful Acknowledgments
ltr undated[407]
SGW and Sarah thank the recipient for her 'friendly attentions' to SW.
Yesterday [25/6/1818] Dr [Alexander Robert] Sutherland told SGW that SW had
recovered safely. SGW has written [not preserved] to Mrs Bastable [the
proprietress of Blacklands], so there is now no obstacle to SW changing 'his
place of abode' whenever he likes. SW's friends doubtless will find suitable
apartments for him. 'An excursion to the country' would compose SW's mind
'on his first emancipation', but a companion would be necessary 'to attend to his
health and comforts', whom SW would have to choose.
SGW, CW Jr and Sarah have made extensive financial sacrifices at various
times to assist SW and to save him from CLW's arrests. He has never been able
to repay SGW. This assistance has reduced the family's 'scanty principal', and
Sarah has had 'much difficulty' to provide the comforts to which SGW is
entitled and without which her life might soon end. The 'late fatal accident
which happened under our roof' [SW's leap from a window on 6/5/1817] caused
considerable expense, including hiring a keeper [for SW] and removing [SGW]
to another house [*see* Sarah→William Wilberforce, 12/5/1817], which Sarah
defrayed personally. It is utterly impossible for SGW, CW Jr or Sarah to assist
[SW] any more.

---

[404] This receipt bears SGW's signature but is otherwise in another hand. The
date in May is not stated.

[405] An annotation, not by Sarah, on ltr asserts that the recipient was 'Miss Ogle'.
For Susannah Ogle *see* SW→VN, 12/9/1825.

[406] Ltr is an incomplete draft.

[407] Assigned to 26/6/1818 because ltr says that Dr Sutherland called on SGW
'yesterday' to tell her that SW had recovered safely, and CW Jr's pocket-book
entry for 25/6/1818 (Dorset) reads 'Dr Sutherland call'd pronouncing my poor
brother thro' mercy well of his late malady' (*Matthews* p 1111).

Sarah memorandum   1/10/1818
MA DDCW/8/5(f)   My Spirit was much discomposed and irritated yesterday
memo dated 1/10/1818
 Sarah's 'spirit' was considerably irritated yesterday [30/9/1818] 'by an account
of poor Sam's [SW's] aversion and calumny'. SW denies that she ever did him
'good or kindness'. Sarah restrained herself from revengeful thoughts and
prayed to God that she may bear these false accusations in a spirit acceptable to
Christ Jesus. She believes that she has 'only done good' with respect to SW and
has 'requited evil with kindness'.

SW→VN   17/11/1818
BL Add 11729 f 106; *O*   Will you call to meet at Ball's on Thursday next
▣ Tue 17 Nov={1812,1818,1829}[408]
 SW asks VN to meet him at [James] Ball's on Thursday [19/11/1818] between
12 and 1 pm. SW is surprised at the terms that [Samuel] Chappell mentions for
'scoring' a symphony [for the Philharmonic Society, *see* Philharmonic Society
Minutes of Directors' Meeting, 15/12/1818], and had thought that Sir George
Smart had intended a 'civil and different kind of engagement' by nominating
SW for the job. In SW's recollection, 1/6 per sheet is no more than what was
'charged for common copying many years ago'. If SW's legs were what they
had been he could get 'a dozen fold' more by running errands. He presumes that
VN concurs and thanks him for his present.

Philharmonic Society Minutes of Directors' Meeting   15/12/1818
BL Music Ms Loan 48.2/1   Mr Novello's note read.
minute dated 15/12/1818
 VN's note to the directors of the Philharmonic Society [not preserved,
presumably requesting a higher fee for SW] was read. It was moved by
[William] Ayrton and seconded by WH that SW 'be requested to finish the two
scores he has begun, at the rate of 3/- per sheet'. The motion was carried.

SW→Hodges   Duke St   2/1819
Hodges p 199–200; *O*   In answer to the favour of your letter, for which I
Hodges quotes 'February 1819' from Hodges's diary [not preserved]
 SW thanks Hodges for his letter [not preserved] and commends his invention [a
contrivance, which Hodges called a 'typhus pedal', that enabled organ keys to be

---

[408] Ltr assigned to 1818 because SW then spent considerable time at Ball's
(SW→Hodges, 2/1819, is written from there) and SW's complaint about the low
· fee offered for scoring a symphony apparently led to the Philharmonic Society
doubling their offer (*see* Philharmonic Society Minutes of Directors' Meeting,
15/12/1818). Not 1829 because SW then had no contact with James Ball.

held down] as being 'extremely ingenious'. However, the invention will achieve its full effect only in the hands of performers who 'understand the entire management of an organ'. As they are 'comparatively few', SW wonders how generally useful the invention will be.

SW→VN   1/3/1819?
BL Add 11729 f 52; *O*   If you can manage at such short notice
⬛ Mon 1 Mar={1813,1819,1824}[409]

SW asks VN to visit him this evening. 'Honest James Ball of Duke Street' is expected and no one else. SW asks VN to bring with him a book into which he copied some of SW's 'pot-hooks and hangers' [musical compositions], as the originals are 'a little astray' in various corners of SW's 'palace'.

SW→RG   17/3/1819?
BL Add 35013 f 74; *O*   If it be agreeable for you to assist me on Friday next
⬛ Wed 17 Mar={1819,1824,1830}; wmk 1817[410]

SW asks if RG will assist him next Friday [19/3/1819] [presumably by turning pages at the Covent Garden Oratorio concert at which SW was organist]. If RG agrees, SW will expect him 'in that odious den of banditti, the Green Room' at 6.30 pm on that evening.

Sarah→SW   24/3/1819
GEU in box 7   I write to you in kindness, and because I hear you are well
⬛ 24/3/1819

Sarah hears that SW is well. She writes to him 'in kindness'. She believes that 'evil minded persons' have misrepresented her, and asks SW to tell her candidly why he has expressed hateful words.

When SW, fearing and fleeing from his creditors, arrived 'that evening' [3/5/1817, *see* Sarah→William Wilberforce, 12/5/1817], Sarah did not expect him, although she had assured him that 'we would shelter you whenever you

---

[409] Ltr presumably <1824 because SW→VN, 29/8/1820, says that Ball insulted SW and he does not like to go there, and Sarah→Mr Probyn, 19/8/1822 says that Ball is less in SW's favour than previously, suggesting that SW and Ball had little or no contact after 1820. However, no reason has been found to prefer 1813 to 1819 as the year of ltr, which accordingly has been entered ambiguously under both dates.

[410] Assigned to 1819 because it is the closest of these three years to the watermark year, and because SW is known, from advertisements in *The Times*, to have been organist at the Covent Garden Oratorio Concert on 19/3/1819, when Handel's *Messiah* was performed. No evidence has been found that SW performed in the 19/3/1824 Covent Garden concert.

came'. She sent Miss [Esther] Coope away at 10 pm to accommodate him. Sarah remembers SW saying that her conduct then 'could proceed from nothing but love'.

However, from a fever which 'seized' his head, SW 'took a violent antipathy' to Sarah and desired to be placed under his 'own friends' [WL, RG and Kingston] who 'came to require' SGW to 'sign her consent' to this action. WL and SW's friends can assure SW that Sarah did not obstruct SW's release [to them].

When Sarah heard that SW planned to place himself 'in the power' of people who SW had said had treated him ill, she tried to dissuade him from going to his 'enemies'. Her intention was to bring SW to lodgings she had taken and to 'sacrifice' her 'whole time' to his care. If he had not taken a 'strange aversion' to her 'every subsequent evil might have been avoided'.

Sarah has never reproached SW for subjecting her, without her knowledge, to WL's debt, which she satisfied in case of [SW's?] decease. She is certain that 'some persons' have an interest in prejudicing SW against her.

SGW is pained that SW harbours 'such ill will' towards Sarah. Sarah will absent herself if SW does not wish to see her when he calls. If they do meet, disagreeable subjects will not be mentioned. Sarah is 'so thankful' that SW is alive that 'all other considerations' are surmounted. She trusts that God has 'good in store' for him.

CW III→Sarah   3/4/1819
GEU in box 7   My Friend, Mr Maurice, having informed me
▣ 3/4/1819

[Thomas] Maurice has conveyed that 'some displeasure' was lately expressed at Sarah's house against CW III on account of his 'long absence'. CW III believes that a lengthy explanation is in order.

Notwithstanding Sarah's opposition, CW III has resolved 'to become a member of one of the universities' [he was admitted to Christ's College, Cambridge on 20/4/1819] and then 'to take the clerical office'. She has argued against this calling because he has been 'educated in strife'. However, the 'almost painful impression' that the 'unhappy disputes' of SW and CLW made on his 'infant mind' have made him fearful of giving offence and desirous to promote harmony.

Sarah has unjustly and evilly represented CW III to Maurice as 'a brutal and malicious son' who caused SW's arrest, without mentioning the circumstances of CLW's scanty meals, threadbare clothing and exhausted patience while her husband [SW] maintained 'an abandoned mistress [SS] and a spurious family'. Furthermore, Sarah showed CW III a letter [not preserved] that she wrote to Sir William Bagshawe, in which she attributed SW's calamities to 'arrests urged by his wife and sons'. Such one-sided reports can greatly diminish the regard in which CW III is held, as well as his future prospects. Although he does not think that Sarah was deliberately malicious, he cannot believe that her actions were 'friendly'.

Commenting upon Sarah's 'favourite accusation' against him and JWW, CW III admits to writing to CLW's solicitor, in CLW's name and on her behalf, 'to procure the necessary relief' from SW so that she could pay her landlord for lodging and food that were months in arrears. CW III acted when SW was in 'the full exercise of his professional talents' and was supporting SS and her 'offspring' in 'comparative elegance'. CW III realises that his action was 'a grievous sin', but believes that his repentance can atone for this. He asks whether 'the mutual kindness' which subsists between himself and SW is not evidence of 'mutual forgiveness'.

CW III, however, has little hope, of being able to change Sarah's views of him. He requests that 'the extreme diversity of sentiment' existing between them 'may induce us both to avoid opportunities of mentioning each other's name'. If, however, Sarah persists in propagating 'misstatements' of his 'character and conduct', he will 'offer a full defence' to his friends and the public.

SW→Richard Mackenzie Bacon   Euston St   5/6/1819
Camb Add Ms 6247 ltr 130; *O*   Having been informed by Mr Horsley that you
☐ 5/6/1819

WH has informed SW that Richard Mackenzie Bacon [1776–1844, editor of the *Norwich Mercury* and the *QMMR*] requires an assistant in his 'musical publication' [presumably Bacon's projected encyclopaedia or dictionary of music, in the subsequent preparation of which both SW and WH were involved, *see* Thomas Moore journal entry, 2/11/1821].[411] SW has WH's recommendation and requests further information from Bacon.

Latrobe→Sarah   20/8/1819
Baker Box 8 (Wesley Family)   Last Week I returned from Holland
☐ 20/8/1819

Latrobe found Sarah's note [not preserved] on his return last week from Holland. He was uncertain of SW's situation and finds her comments 'highly interesting'. Latrobe joins with Sarah in hoping that the prolongation of SW's 'life on earth is meant to afford him time to return' to his Saviour. Latrobe sends his respects to SW, 'if he will accept' them, and to SGW and CW Jr.

---

[411] The *QMMR* reported in 1820 that a dictionary of music was in preparation, and a prospectus for it, identifying WH and SW as contributors to 'the extended plan' of the work, was included with the *QMMR* in 1822. However, it does not appear to have been published, and the extent of SW's contribution to it is not known. *See Kassler Science* v 1 p 48–49.

SW→VN   Euston St   **28/10/1819**
BL Add 11729 f 71; *O*   The enclosed will perhaps prove some Apology
☛ Thu 28 Oct={1813,1819,1824}[412]
The enclosed letter [not preserved] explains why SW sent to VN's house to
inquire after birds sent by [Thomas] Pymar [*see* SW→Pettet, 29/9/1815]. The
enclosure is dated 26 September [1819], but SW received it last Monday
[25/10/1819]; it must have been detained at [James] Ball's for over a month. SW
apologises for his handwriting: he has broken his thumb.

SW→?[413]   **16/11/1819**
Puttick & Simpson catalogue 26/6/1884 lot 125[414]   [not known]
Puttick & Simpson catalogue
  Ltr concerns the use of pedals.

SW→VN   **3/12/1819**
BL Add 11729 f 73; *O*   I have long since done with all musical Controversy
☛ Fri 3 Dec={1813,1819,1824}[415]
SW suggests that 'the best and shortest way' with the 'Norwich Nibbler'
[James Taylor, musician and writer, 1781–1855, whose 3/8/1819 letter to the
editor of the *QMMR*, published in *QMMR* v 2 no. 5 (1819) p 15–22, commented
on consecutive fifths in VN's *A Collection of Sacred Music*, the first volume of
which was published in 1811] is to refer him to [John Freckleton] Burrowes's
[The Thorough-Base] Primer [published in 1819] for instruction about fifths.
  SW is glad that VN and WL have understood each other about 'the Shakspere
book' [probably WL's *Shakspeare's Dramatic Songs*, first published in 1815 and
1816, for which SW arranged the 'Music in Macbeth']. WL is 'a very excellent
man' who has the highest respect for VN. SW has been dining with his friend
[Rev. Christopher] Jeaffreson and his family.
  [William] Behnes [sculptor, 1795–1864] of Newman Street wishes to be
known to VN. He and 'the brothers' are 'sensible lads' [Henry Behnes Burlowe,
sculptor, 1802–1837, and Charles Behnes, artist, *d*1840]. SW calls at their house
almost daily.

---

[412] Assigned to 1819 because SW's Euston St address rules out 1813 and VN's
Oxford St address rules out 1824.

[413] Hodges is a conceivable addressee, as SW→Hodges, 2/1819, is concerned
with organ pedals.

[414] Ltr, sold as part of the Julian Marshall collection, was purchased at this
auction by the collector William Hayman Cummings. The present location of ltr
is not known.

[415] Assigned to 1819 because of ref. to 1819 *QMMR* review of VN's
publication.

SW has heard that VN has thoughts of living towards Camden Town. SW 'wants sadly to see' VN and requests information about their meeting. If SW is to arrange a concert he needs VN's advice. F[rançois] Cramer, [John] Braham and [Thomas] Vaughan have promised their help.

SW→VN Euston St **9/12/1819**
BL Add 11729 f 296; *O* The following are my Notions about the Progressions
▣ Thu 9 Dec={1819,1824}[416]

SW comments on the [musical] progressions objected to [in a review of VN's *A Collection of Sacred Music*, see SW→VN, 3/12/1819]. The effect is 'by no means harsh or unpleasant to the ear' and 'in some of the best writers' there are numerous examples of the same progression. SW gives an example from Handel's *Messiah*.

SW wishes to discuss with VN the possibilities of 'earning a few halfpence by a concert' and invites VN to meet him at the home of [Rev. Henry Francis Alexander] Delafite [lecturer at Covent Garden Church and foreign secretary to the Royal Society of Literature, 1772?–1831], 40 Clarendon Square, Somers Town, on Saturday evening [11/12/1819] between 6 and 8 pm. Delafite 'is a very kind friend' to SW.

SW→VN **23/12/1819**
BL Add 11729 f 45; *O* No news from Miss S. Perhaps a little more Urgence
▣ Thu 23 Dec={1813,1819}[417]

'Miss S' [possibly the soprano Catherine Stephens] has not replied to SW's letter [not preserved, presumably a request that she perform in his proposed concert]. SW does not like to write again but dislikes being 'trifled with' where money is concerned. He asks VN to leave his 'kind cobble' of SW's 'blunderbuss canon' [not identified] at [William] Behnes's house as soon as possible. SW's letter [not preserved] to the ambassador [presumably Pedro de Sousa Holstein, 1781–1850, Ambassador of Portugal] 'has been committed to safe hands'. SW hopes that 'it may produce justice to the right party' [not identified].

---

[416] Assigned to 1819 because VN's Oxford Street address rules out 1824.

[417] Ltr <1821 because addressed to VN at 240 Oxford Street. Assigned to 1819 because SW→VN, 23/12/1813 is on a completely different subject and SW→VN, 3/12/1819, the first mention of Behnes in SW's extant correspondence, says that SW visits Behnes's home almost every day.

Thynne Gwynne→Sarah   **21/1/1820**
MA DDWF/22/37   Accept my thanks for your obliging letter
☑ 21/1/1820
   Replying to Sarah's letter [not preserved], Thynne Gwynne [SGW's cousin]
hopes that Sarah and CW Jr will 'bear the unfavourable prospect' of SW's future
comfort 'with Christian fortitude'.

SW→Robert William Elliston   Euston St   **19/5/1820**
Bristol Watkinson album p 68, ltr 835; *O*   Concerning young Mr Goadby, the
☑ 19/5/1820
   Mr Goadby, the bearer of this letter, has 'attended and drilled' many pupils of
Corri [presumably Domenico Corri, composer, publisher and teacher, 1746–
1825] for nearly three years. Goadby's own low tenor voice 'is but indifferent,
and not sufficiently smooth for glee singing', but he reads music well and has
some knowledge of the piano and a 'firmness of finger'. SW thinks that Robert
William Elliston [actor and theatre manager, 1774–1831, from 1819 lessee of
Drury Lane Theatre] would find Goadby useful in assisting 'choral
practitioners', and would be obliged if Elliston placed Goadby in his 'musical
department' [at Drury Lane Theatre].

SW→VN   Euston St   **29/8/1820**
BL Add 11729 f 156; *O*   It is as false as mischievous to tell you that I never
☑ Tue 29 Aug & 📷→{1820,1826}[418]
   VN's impression that SW never inquires after him is false. SW has not been to
[James] Ball's for many weeks because he does not like to be insulted, and sees
[Joseph] Major only about once every four to six weeks. SW sends condolences
[on the death of VN's son Sidney Vincent Novello, 1816–1820]; he has been
similarly bereaved 'many times'. SW is 'very low and ill' and is concerned
about his childrens' future. He would meet VN 'anywhere but in Duke Street'
[Ball's address]. The music at the Chapel [presumably the Portuguese Embassy
Chapel] is 'too overwhelming' for SW to stand. He asks that any
communications be sent to him at [William] Behnes's home in Newman Street,
which is 'always open' to SW.

---

[418] Assigned to 1820 because ltr addressed to VN at Percy Street where he lived
during the years 1820–1823.

SW→VN   **20/11/1820**
BL Add 11729 f 158; *O*   Can you give or obtain for me, any Copying
▣ Mon 20 Nov={1809,1815,1820,1826}[419]
SW writes from the house of Mr [Stephen Francis] Rimbault [organist and composer, 1773–1837], 9 Denmark Street, Soho, which SW visits 'almost daily' and where any reply should be sent. He asks if VN can 'give or obtain for' him 'any copying, literary or musical'. He has not forgotten VN's request for 'the Ossian recit' [possibly SW's 1784 song 'Alone on the sea-beat rock'], but must write it out from memory as he does not have the book in which it is contained. He thinks that the book is in the possession of Rev. [Henry] Delafite, who is away in the country.[420]

Sarah→SW   **5/12/1820**
GEU in box 7   Could you believe that Affection induced me to address you
▣ 5/12/1820
Sarah has no motive other than SW's welfare. She is affected by SW's misery. Mr Worgan [possibly Thomas Danvers Worgan, composer and theorist, 1774–1832, son of CW Jr's teacher Dr John Worgan] has told her that he 'pressed' SW to accept 'a situation' which would have extricated him from his 'present difficulties', but that SW declined because he would lose the assistance of his 'charitable friends' in London. However, SW had told Sarah that 'those friends had withdrawn their aid', and that he now had 'no resources but the Chapel [possibly the Portuguese Embassy Chapel] and casual employment'. SW's poverty therefore 'seems inevitable'.
SW's life has been 'miraculously preserved'. He should repent, like the Prodigal Son. While he continues 'in evil' there can be no hope for him. SW's duty is to pay his debts 'and not contract more'. He should assist CLW and not leave his 'present connection' [SS] destitute. This cannot be done if he refuses 'an advantageous offer' which would enable him to be just.
Money would enable SW to procure some one to take care of him 'in a strange place'. SW is unhappy now 'and may be more miserable as age advances'. Sarah cannot do much for SW if he becomes sick or destitute: she is 'strained and encumbered' taking care of SGW. She has had to hire another servant to attend SGW, whose apothecary bills 'we can ill afford'. Little money will remain at

---

[419] Assigned to 1820 because of SW's despondency and need for menial work; these circumstances do not fit the other listed years.

[420] VN added a long endorsement to ltr, stating that he wished 'to place this affecting note on record, as an eternal disgrace to the pretended patrons of good music in England', who had 'the contemptible bad taste to undervalue & neglect the masterly productions of such an extraordinary musician as Sam Wesley' and 'the paltry meanness of spirit, to allow such a real genius...to sink into such poverty, decay and undeserved neglect, as to be under the necessity of seeking employment as a mere drudging copyist to prevent himself from starvation'. VN hoped that 'such unfeeling brutes meet their just reward'.

SGW's death. The family have 'sunk' [i.e., realised investments of] nearly £300 to assist SW. Sarah is now managing CW's stock so that what is left can be shared amongst CW Jr, Sarah and SW.

Sarah grants that 'many men are more immoral than' SW: 'they leave to poverty the women they seduce' and do not care for their offspring. But when an opportunity arises [for SW] 'to provide for all', it is 'contrary to reason' to refuse it 'from personal fears of not being taken care of'.

Sarah invites SW to come to her home for dinner. However, because of his present 'rooted and deep enmity' against Sarah, it would not be appropriate for them now to live in the same house.

SW seems to think Sarah has 'an abhorrence of the poor woman' [SS]. This is not so, but SS cannot know peace while she violates the Golden Rule. SW has injured SS's principles and has made her 'reconciled to a disgraceful mode of life'. If he gave SS an allowance she could 'go on' and be able to maintain herself and her children [without SW's presence]. SW then might have the children with him 'when they grow older'. Such a course of action would be 'acting right in the sight of God'.

SW→George, 3rd Baron Calthorpe   Euston St   4/8/1821
Hampshire 26M62/F/C285; *O*   I trust that I shall not be deemed too
✉ 4/8/1821

SW asks Baron Calthorpe [1787–1851] to support SW's application for the organist's post at the 'New Church of St Pancras'.

SW→Thomas Preston   21/9/1821
BL Add 63814 item 137[421]   Received of Mr T. Preston five pounds for
receipt dated 21/9/1821

SW acknowledges receipt of £5 from T[homas] Preston [music publisher] for the copyright of SW's *24 Short Pieces or Interludes for the Organ*.

SW→VN   2/10/1821
BL Add 11729 f 159; *O*   Will you tell me whether the short Magnificat
✉ Tue 2 Oct={1810,1821,1827}[422]

SW asks if the 'short Magnificat' that VN requires may be composed like one of [Samuel] Webbe [Sr] 'in little duets and solos with an occasional chorus', and

---

[421] This receipt is signed by SW but not written by him.

[422] Assigned to 1821 because a Magnificat by SW that VN planned to have printed is known to have been written in October 1821, and no such Magnificats are known to have been written by SW in October 1810 or October 1827. Also, no evidence has been found that SW and VN were in correspondence either in 1810 or in 1827.

for what voices it should be written. [SW's autograph score of this Magnificat, dated 6/10/1821, is at Texas Finney 13; VN's manuscript copy of this composition, with instructions for the engraver, is at BL Add 65455.] SW fears that his best efforts will prove to be 'a very poor job', as all his 'inventive spirit' unfortunately has 'long evaporated'.

SW→VN **9/10/1821**
BL Add 11729 f 160; *O*   If any Thing I can write please You, it is well
☞ 9/10/1821
   SW is glad that he has written something [his Magnificat, *see* SW→VN, 2/10/1821] that pleases VN, as SW will 'never more write anything that will please' himself. He regrets that he cannot find the score of his *Confitebor*, which he regards as 'the least incorrect' of his compositions and the one most likely to benefit his descendants if published. SW is conscious that he is 'totally undeserving' of a Christian burial.

Thomas Moore journal entry **2/11/1821**
Dowden v 2 p 500–501   Arrived in St James's Place at eight
Dowden
   Thomas Moore [Irish poet and musician, 1779–1852] dined 'at Power's' [the office or home of Moore's music publisher James Power, 1766–1836] to meet [Henry Rowley] Bishop [composer, 1786–1855, *later* Sir Henry] 'upon musical matters'. Bishop and 'three others, (Horsley [WH], Wesley [SW] and someone else [Muzio Clementi])' are employed 'on a musical dictionary' [*The Encyclopaedia of Music, or General Dictionary of Music*].[423] [Heinrich Christoph] Koch [German musical theorist, 1749–1816], whose work [his *Musikalisches Lexikon* (1st edition, 1802; 2nd edition, 1817) or his 1807 abridgement *Kurzgefaßtes Handwörterbuch der Musik*] 'has been translated for them', is 'their great resource'.

---

[423] In a prospectus included with vol. iv (1822) of the *QMMR*, it was announced that 'Part I' of this four-part encyclopaedia, involving 'the combined talents and experience' of 'Clementi, Henry R. Bishop, Horsley and Wesley', would be published under the superintendence of [Richard Mackenzie] Bacon 'early in 1823'. However, this projected publication apparently never appeared.

SW→VN   Euston St   **27/11/1821**
BL Add 11729 f 162; *O*   Can you recommend me to a Pennyworth of writing
🔲 27/11/1821
SW asks VN to recommend him for 'a pennyworth of writing of any sort,
whether of music or words'. As a composer SW is 'a cripple', but as a copyist he
believes he is as accurate though not as fast as he formerly was. He desires a
speedy reply.

John Harding→Sarah   **16/1/1822**
MA DDWF/26/58   Mr Harding presents his compliments to Miss Wesley
🔲 16/1/1822
John Harding [a medical doctor from Kentish Town] regrets the 'disagreeable
circumstances' that compelled Sarah to address him regarding SW. Harding is
friendlily   disposed   towards   SW   and   would   happily   relieve   SW's
'embarrassments' if he could. However, as he is 'exerting himself to endeavour
to procure an appointment' worthy of SW, 'it would be unreasonable and
degrading' for him simultaneously to solicit a loan to SW of the 'trifling sum' of
£10. Harding suggests that SW's relatives should assist him, and is horrified by
Sarah's suggestion that 'moral and pious people' refuse to assist SW 'while he
lives with Mrs —' [SS], although they would assist him if he were in jail.
   Harding is glad to hear that SW 'is likely to be assisted by the Musical Fund'
and hopes that he may obtain the appointment he is soliciting in 'the new
church' [St Pancras Parish Church]. However, 'elections are very uncertain
things'.
   Harding saw CLW this morning and lent her £5 towards 'the bill which was
due'. He hopes that Sarah will contribute 'the other moiety' so that SW is not
'embarrassed with legal proceedings for so small a sum'.

Sarah→Sarah Tooth   **17/1/1822**
MA DDWF/14/38A   I know it will afford you pleasure to hear
🔲 17/1/1822
Sarah Tooth will be pleased to hear that SGW is well 'after her attack', but
since then the family have had 'a painful scene'. 'Poor Sam' [SW] came to
request the family to let him have £50 from SGW's 'little remaining stock'. He
wanted this sum from the 'remainder' which will come to him at SGW's decease
but which will come to CW Jr and Sarah if SW dies before SGW [*see* CW will,
28/5/1785]. Showing a resolution that Sarah did not expect, SGW asked SW
'with tears' if he 'would starve her in her latter days'. CW Jr, 'moved to anger',
denounced SW's 'cruelty' and declared that he, CW Jr, would never consent to
sink [to withdraw] any more of SGW's property.
   Sarah could not have supposed that CW Jr would stand forth 'so energetically'.
When SW said 'he would be arrested if he did not obtain £10 by Wednesday'
[presumably 16/1/1822, *see* John Harding→Sarah, 16/1/1822], she 'was so
weak' as to say she would not oppose his request if CW Jr and SGW consented.

In this respect Sarah lacks 'the firmness of man'. The thought of SW going to prison 'in his state of mind' overpowered her principles of justice. She had told SW that his proposed action [to get money from SGW's stock] was wrong, and happily SGW and CW Jr did not consent to it.

Sarah's weakness had, however, the 'good effect' of giving her influence to prevail upon SW 'to rise from his knees to' SGW and to depart. Sarah walked out with him and took the opportunity to set before him 'the consequences of his course of life'. She told him that 'far better men' than SW had been imprisoned and that, if he were 'within the rules of the Bench' [i.e., confined to the area controlled by the King's Bench prison], many people would aid him 'who would not assist him to live on in evil' [with SS].

CW Jr has written 'to the Musicians Fund' in SW's favour, and 'we [CW Jr and Sarah] have got a subscription' amongst SW's acquaintances to take up a £10 bill by tomorrow [18/1/1822]. This will give SW 'some space to collect the rest' of the money he needs, and also will not deprive him 'of the chance of a church' [St Pancras Parish Church] that would pay him £100 a year 'if he can obtain it'. [The 21/2/1822 minutes of the church trustees report that SW's application for the post of organist was unsuccessful.]

This is 'a critical moment' for SW. Sarah would 'lament an imprisonment which might bring back a mental malady' if this can be avoided without doing 'wrong actions', such as withdrawing SGW's property. Sarah's mind and time have been 'anxiously employed'. She trusts that she will have Divine support in these trials and knows that the family will have Sarah Tooth's prayers.

Sarah→Adam Clarke   13/2/1822
Wcoll D6/1/288(a)   Your little note, my worthy friend, arrived last night
☐ 13/2/1822

Sarah will write about 'poor Sam' [SW] in her next letter. 'He is a heart sore.' God grant that he be restored.

Sarah→Adam Clarke   25/3/1822
Wcoll D6/1/292   I have been looking over Dr Whitehead, and a manuscript
☐ 25/3/1822

For SW's sake, Clarke perhaps ought to suppress [in his forthcoming book *Memoirs of the Wesley Family; Collected Principally from Original Documents* (London, J. Kershaw, 1823)] 'some affecting instances' of CW's 'suffering' when SW 'turned to the Romish Church'. Sarah can relate these instances to Clarke when she sees him, although they are 'harrowing' to her memory.[424]

---

[424] In this book Adam Clarke reports SW's composition of a Mass for Pope Pius VI but does not mention CW's reaction to SW's interests in Roman Catholicism.

Sarah→Adam Clarke   6/4/1822
Wcoll D6/1/294(a)   I know you will do justice to my honoured father
▣ 6/4/1822
   Sarah hopes that Clarke will remember all her family in his prayers, including
'poor Sam' [SW]. SW always comes to Sarah in his tribulations, which she
thinks is 'a good sign'. He 'is indeed wretched' but he 'cannot break his bonds'
and still continues to live with 'that mistress' [SS]. CLW drove SW 'to
desperation by spending his property and then refusing to live with him'. He 'did
not seduce' the 'present woman' [SS]. SW's 'head is restored', but 'his mind' is
'disordered'. 'One legitimate son [CW III] is in orders' [he was ordained in
Salisbury in 1821]. Sarah's opinion of him is not high, although he visits and
'behaves decently'.

SW→'Dear Sir'[425]   Euston St   11/5/1822
Argory; *O*   I rely much on your Indulgence to pardon the Liberty
▣ Sat 11 May & 🔧→①
   SW must pay an 'acceptance for £12' today. He cannot honour it because of
'an unexpected disappointment'. He seeks 'assistance' from the recipient.

Sarah→Adam Clarke   24/5/1822
Wcoll D6/1/296   I return with thanks your interesting, your invaluable
▣ 24/5/1822
   Sarah fears that 'one of the family' [SW] 'will become quite dependent on
bounty'. 'Only affliction' is likely to 'turn' SW's heart. Sarah pities SW.

Sarah→Mr Probyn   19/8/1822?
GEU in box 7   It is long since we had the pleasure of seeing you
▣ '19 August'[426]
   SW 'drank tea' with SGW 'a fortnight ago' and 'brought his daughter [Emma]
and the best of his two sons [JWW]—(not saying much for him either)'. CW Jr

---

[425] Walter McGeough is a likely recipient because ltr is now kept with other
letters from SW to him and SW did ask him for financial assistance five months
later (SW→Walter McGeough, 12/10/1822). However, other possible recipients
have not been ruled out. Ltr's request for £12 today suggests that the recipient
was then in London.

[426] Assigned to 1822 for the following reason. The ref. to SW's application to be
organist of St Pancras Church suggests ltr written in 1821 or 1822, but MEW's
birth on 19/4/1821 rules out SS's 'near lying in again' in August 1821. An 1822
date for ltr presumes that Sarah had not heard that SW's application to St
Pancras Church was unsuccessful. Such a presumption is consistent with SW
and Sarah having little contact at this time.

and Sarah absented themselves 'as it would have caused useless agitation' on both sides. Sarah hears SW 'is as well as he ever was since his alliance with that woman [SS] who is near lying in again'. SW's 'insanity certainly is of a peculiar kind': although 'its paroxysm admitted no doubt', 'all the rest' of SW's behaviour 'partook more of malignity than madness'. Sarah has always considered SW's 'perverse will' to have been 'the source of his mental malady'. She 'cannot but pity him'.

People say that SW 'may have [the organist's position in St] Pancras Church' if he wishes, but he will have to 'convert himself' and not spend time 'in lamentations and abuses of his friends instead of active exertions'. CW Jr has written to SW with this advice and also has spoken 'to different persons', but Sarah supposes that CW Jr's 'kind advice' affronted SW. [James] Ball is less in SW's favour than usual, Sarah believes 'from the same cause'. No one who values SW's favours 'must dare to point out the right path to him'.

SW→John Fane, Lord Burghersh   Euston St   2/9/1822
K; *O*   Permit me to return my grateful Acknowledgements to Your Lordship
2/9/1822

SW is flattered to accept the honour of being named a[n Honorary] Member of the Royal Academy of Music [of which Burghersh, 1784–1859, 11th Earl of Westmorland, was the principal founder and the first president].

SW→Walter McGeough   Euston St   12/10/1822
Argory; *O*   I feel it my Duty to explain to you the State of Matters
12/10/1822

SW explains the 'state of matters' concerning the organ being built [by James Davis] for Walter McGeough [1790–1866, later Walter McGeough Bond, at The Argory, County Armagh, Northern Ireland]. McGeough specified 33 pieces for SW to arrange; 11 of these have been found to take up eight barrels. As McGeough originally ordered only six barrels, SW seeks McGeough's authorisation to increase their number. SW is 'suffering not only from bodily infirmity' but is 'harassed by tormenting applications in consequence of vexations and unexpected pecuniary disappointments'. He is faced with an immediate demand for a bill for £15 and requests financial assistance from McGeough. [James] Davis will write to McGeough in the coming week.

CW Jr→Langshaw Jr   17/10/1822
GEU W/L; *Wainwright* p 73–74   I would not wait for the intelligence
17/10/1822

CW Jr sees SW 'very seldom' but hears that he is well.

SW→Walter McGeough   11/11/1822

Argory; *O*   Pray forgive me for not having more immediately returned
⌐ 11/11/1822
SW belatedly thanks McGeough for his letter [not preserved] and its contents
[presumably part or all of the £15 requested in SW→Walter McGeough,
12/10/1822], which 'proved a very material benefit and reasonable assistance'.
As McGeough requested, SW has seen the Behnes's [William Behnes and his
brother, the sculptor Henry Behnes Burlowe] about the bust [William Behnes's
bust of McGeough, completed in 1823]. SW also has seen [James] Davis
regarding McGeough's organ.
SW now has arranged 14 pieces for this organ, which he lists, including
'Wesley's March'.[427] By using the metronome, SW has obtained 'the correct
division of the time of each piece'. As Davis will explain soon to McGeough,
none of these pieces has yet been set on barrels because they would take up more
room than is available on the six barrels that he ordered. SW awaits
McGeough's instructions on this matter.

Sarah memorandum   about 10/12/1822

MA DDWF/14/68/3   On his Entrance he was much affected
memo undated but headed 'Her last words to Samuel'[428]
When SW entered SGW's bedroom [at 14 Nottingham Street, presumably on
10/12/1822], he was 'much affected' by the change in her countenance. Sarah
told SGW that SW had come. He knelt down by SGW's bedside and begged her
to forgive him. SGW blessed him and his children and expressed satisfaction
that they were prospering. She told him that he had a good sister [Sarah]. When
he mentioned his favourite son [SSW], SGW said 'God bless all your children'.

---

[427] Three barrels originally supplied for this organ survive at The Argory
(County Armagh, Northern Ireland), but none of the three contains 'Wesley's
March', probably the march from the overture to SW's 'Begin the noble song'.
It is not known how many barrels were commissioned, nor what the lost
barrels—presumably destroyed in a fire at The Argory in 1898—contained. The
extant barrels have the following works, all of which are listed by SW in ltr:
Fischer's Minuet with Mozart's Twelve Variations; the Overture and March
from Mozart's *Die Zauberflöte*; the Overture to Arne's *Artaxerxes* and 'See the
Conqu'ring Hero Comes' from Handel's *Judas Maccabaeus*. The innovative
barrel registrations embodying SW's arrangements are discussed in Stephen
Bicknell, *The History of the English Organ* (Cambridge, *c*1996) p 221.

[428] This memorandum, describing SGW's last words to SW from her deathbed,
is assigned to 12/1822 because SGW died on 28/12/1822 and, according to
Stevenson p 444, 'took to her bed on December 1st [1822], from which she
afterwards rose but once'. It was written presumably on or shortly after
10/12/1822, as GW Jr recorded in his 1822 diary, MA DDWF/23/16, that SW
called on 10/12/1822 and did not record that SW called on any other day of that
month.

Then, suddenly recollecting who 'the mother of Samuel' [SSW] was, SGW said 'but she [SS] is an impudent baggage [a strumpet] to take my name' [i.e., to take the name 'Sarah Wesley']. SW 'then arose and soon quitted the room'. SGW hoped that he 'would be led into the right way'.

CW Jr→Langshaw Jr   3/4/1823

GEU W/L; *Wainwright* p 77–78   I begin to think you have not received a Letter
◨ 3/4/1823

CW Jr hears that SW is well, although CW Jr and Sarah 'do not often see him'.

SW→VN   Euston St   4/7/1823

BL Add 11729 f 164; *O*   My old Friend Mr Jos. Barret
◨ 4/7/1823

SW's 'old friend' Joseph Barret, of 50 Upper Berkeley Street, Edgware Road, has promised to look after SW's burial arrangements if he outlives SW. SW wishes to be buried near the remains of his 'transcendent and inestimable friend' [AD] in the Paddington churchyard. SW requests that VN meet Barret to discuss the matter.

John Berridge→[Proprietors of the   30/9/1823
Biographical Dictionary of Musicians][429]

Euing R.d.88/195   Mr C Wesley of 14 Nottingham St near Baker St gave me
◨ 30/9/1823

John Berridge [a collector of information for the *Dictionary of Musicians* printed in 1824 for Sainsbury and Co.] visited CW Jr, who said that he had no time 'to draw up a sketch of his biography', adding that most of his compositions were '30 years old and now out of date'. He told Berridge that 'a good account' of himself, SW, Crotch and perhaps Lord Mornington [Garret Wesley] was given by Daines Barrington in the *Philosophical Transactions* [*of the Royal Society of London*], which is at the British Museum. [CW Jr was mistaken: only Barrington's account of Crotch was published there.] CW Jr, 'a man in years but apparently vigorous', though 'quite grey', will not give Berridge any further information.

---

[429] The sender, whose name is given in ltr only by the initials 'J. B.', is identifiable as John Berridge because his full name appears in another letter (also in Euing) concerning the 1824 *Dictionary of Musicians*, for which he gathered information. Leanne Langley recounts the evidence for this identification in 'Sainsbury's *Dictionary*, the Royal Academy of Music, and the Rhetoric of Patriotism' in Christina Bashford and Leanne Langley, eds., *Music and British Culture, 1785–1914* (Oxford, 2000, p 86 footnote 66). The recipient's name is not stated in ltr.

SW→VN   Euston St   **26/11/1823**
BL Add 11729 f 166; *O*   Pray give me a Line informing me when and where
⊟ '26 November'; pmk 1823
   SW requests an opportunity for a short 'confidential chat' to get VN's advice
on 'a point relative to a society' [probably the Glee Club, *see* SW→Richard
Clark, 4/12/1823] that consists of 'fools, knaves, and musicians'.

SW→VN   **4/12/1823?**
BL Add 11729 f 168; *O*   Tell me promptly & bluntly whether you approve
⊟ 'Thursday 6/12/1823', an incorrect date, pmk ?/12/1823[430]
   SW requests VN's prompt and blunt opinion of the annexed letter
[SW→Richard Clark, 4/12/1823?]. He suggests that VN [who had moved about
8/1823 to Shacklewell Green, Stoke Newington] should agree 'for once' to sleep
in London, after their mutual engagement on Wednesday [12/12/1823].

SW→Richard Clark[431]   **4/12/1823?**
BL Add 11729 f 169; *O*   As I no longer now attempt to sing
ltr undated[432]
   SW no longer attempts to sing, although 'in years past' he found it 'an
amusement'. Moreover, he has grown 'weary' of glees. He therefore advises
[Richard] Clark [writer and singer, 1780–1856, at this time secretary of the Glee
Club] that he resigns from the Glee Club. As the club recently has acquired a
'skilful extemporaneous pianist' [not identified], no 'chasm' will result from
SW's future non-attendance. He wishes the society well.[433]

---

[430] The day in the postmark is illegible. Assigned to Thursday 4/12/1823 on the
presumption that SW mistook the date rather than the day of the week.

[431] Ltr addressed to 'Mr Secretary Clark'.

[432] Assigned to 4/12/1823 because ltr (a draft) enclosed with SW→VN,
4/12/1823?; ltr accordingly has the same dating reason as that letter.

[433] SW was a 'perpetual visitor' to the Glee Club, *see* 'The Catch and Glee
Clubs', *QMMR* v 2 no. 7 (1820), p 324. John Parry, 'The Glee Club', *MW* no.
103 = n.s. no. 9, 1/3/1838, p 140–142, recalled (p 142) that 'the late Samuel
Wesley used to delight the company with his matchless execution of Sebastian
Bach's Fugues on the pianoforte, or an extemporaneous effusion on a given
subject, frequently some conspicuous passage in a glee recently sung'.

SW→VN   **19/12/1823**
BL Add 11729 f 171; *O*   As a formidable Bunch of musical Amateurs are
⏹ 19/12/1823
   SW's Magnificat and Nunc Dimittis [from his Morning and Evening Service]
are to be performed [at St Paul's Cathedral] on Thursday next [Christmas Day,
25/12/1823]. SW asks VN to bring the score on Sunday [21/12/1823] to Percy
Street [VN's former address, possibly still used as his business premises], where
SW will be able to get it. SW respects VN's musical judgement much more than
that of any other professional man in the United Kingdom and hopes that VN
has fulfilled his promise to suggest any changes to the score.

BJ→Editor, *Biographical Dictionary of Musicians*   **15/1/1824**
Euing R.d.86/111   According to your desire I send you some of the
⏹ 15/1/1824
   BJ sends information about himself for the 'new Biographical Dictionary of
Musicians' that was printed for Sainsbury and Co. later in 1824. He notes that, in
1809 [presumably on 29/11/1809], he united with SW in performance, 'playing
alternately the fugues' of JSB and Handel, with 'many of his choruses'. 'About
3000 persons of the highest respectability, and many of the first rank professors
and amateurs, were present' [at the Surrey Chapel], and sat 'with the greatest
attention through a four hour's performance on the organ'.

WL→CW Jr   **2/2/1824**
Wcoll D6/1/378(a)   My best thanks, my dear Mr Wesley, for myself
⏹ 2/2/1824
   On behalf of himself and his friend Pettet, WL thanks CW Jr for his
composition. WL thinks that CW Jr's composition is 'exceedingly appropriate'
[for Pettet's forthcoming collection entitled *Original Sacred Music*] but suggests
that a passage be changed. SW, who called upon WL yesterday [1/2/1824],
concurs with WL's opinion of CW Jr's composition. WL will send CW Jr 'the
work' [Pettet's collection] when it is published.

SW→VN   Euston St   **17/2/1824**
BL Add 11729 f 173; *O*   'The Gossip Report' is seldom 'an honest Woman
⏹ 17 Feb; pmk 1824
   SW asks if VN, as rumoured, will be an 'umpire' at the 'approaching digital
contest among the psalm tune combatants' at St George's, Hanover Square. SW
has been persuaded to apply, in competition with [George] Mather [organist,
*d*1854], 'Mr J. Sale' [presumably John Bernard Sale, composer and organist,
1779–1856] and others, and is 'tolerably philosophical' about the result. SW
wishes to disprove the 'pretty successfully circulated' falsehood that he is
'averse from all musical employment'. However, he 'hates music as a source of
great misery'. He would like to chat with VN for half an hour.

WL→CW Jr   22/2/1824?
MA DDWes/1/109   Have the kindness to inform me if your brother is aware
▣ '22 February'[434]

WL asks if SW is aware that the £5 which WL forwarded to CW Jr for SW was
a loan. If SW knows this, WL has a proposal which, if SW agrees to it, will wipe
out the loan and will make WL indebted to SW for £5. WL knows that SW's
lectures [at an unidentified venue] begin in March but forgets the day appointed
for the first lecture. WL asks if CW Jr has heard from Pettet about WL's hymn
[presumably WL's contribution to Pettet's *Original Sacred Music*]. 'Sam' [SW]
has not called upon WL 'this age'.

CW Jr→John Trevor   24/2/1824
Stevenson p 464[435]
Stevenson

CW Jr writes to 'Lord Hampden' [John Trevor, 3rd Viscount Hampden, 1749–
1824] on behalf of SW [presumably to solicit a subscription to SW's Morning
and Evening Service].

CW Jr→Richard Edgcumbe   24/2/1824
Stevenson p 464[436]
Stevenson

CW Jr writes to Mr [Richard] Edgcumbe, [musical amateur, 1764–1839, 3rd
Earl of Mount Edgcumbe] on behalf of SW [presumably to solicit a subscription
to SW's Morning and Evening Service].

SW→James Chapman Bishop   Euston St   28/2/1824
Argory; *O*   I presume you are already informed that the Organ
▣ Sat 28 Feb & 🖎→{1824,1829}[437]

SW informs James Chapman Bishop [organ builder, 1783–1854] that the order
for Walter McGeough's organ, which originally was to be built by [James]

---

[434] Assigned to 1824 on the presumption that ltr discusses the compilation of
Pettet's *Original Sacred Music*, see SW→Pettet, 8/3/1824.

[435] Stevenson quotes CW Jr's diary entry for 24/2/1824 (Dorset), which
mentions ltr. The present location of ltr is not known.

[436] Stevenson quotes CW Jr's diary entry for 24/2/1824 (Dorset), which
mentions ltr. The present location of ltr is not known.

[437] 1829 ruled out because McGeough's organ was not completed when ltr
written but was completed by September 1824 (*Elvin*, p 99). Also, ltr before
SW→VN, 8/3/1824, in which SW says that he was swindled out of 50 guineas
by Davis and Bishop.

Davis and now is to be 'finished' by Bishop, was obtained as a consequence of SW's recommendation of Davis to McGeough. Davis agreed to pay SW a commission of 50 guineas [£52/10/-]. This payment is now Bishop's responsibility 'when the organ is completed'.

SW→Pettet   Euston St   8/3/1824
BL Eg. 2159 f 76; *O*   I am aware that I ought (in friendly Propriety) to have
▣ Mon 8 Mar; pmk 1824

SW should have acknowledged Pettet's letter [not preserved] and gift earlier, but letter-writing has become irksome. SW wrote [in 1798] a little anthem in four parts on the first two verses of Psalm 65 ['Te Decet Hymnus']. He proposes to adapt this to English words as a full anthem and hopes that it will suit Pettet's purpose [i.e., that it will be suitable for inclusion in Pettet's *Original Sacred Music*].

SW is planning to publish his Morning and Evening Service. Proposals have already been issued and the 'said tunes are promised to make their appearance for judgement and execution' in May. If Pettet is interested, SW can send some proposals [for people to subscribe to the publication], together with Pettet's book and the anthem. SW thanks Mrs [Harriot] Pettet for her gift of sausages.

SW→VN   8/3/1824
BL Add 11729 f 175; *O*   I hasten to forward the Enclosed
▣ 8/3/1824

SW 'forwards the enclosed' [presumably one or more proposals for his Morning and Evening Service, *see* SW→Pettet, 8/3/1824] and asks how many additional copies VN would like. Attwood would like to perform the Service at St Paul's [Cathedral] on a Sunday, when the congregation is likely to be largest. 'Honest' [James] Davis and [James Chapman] Bishop 'together have just swindled' SW out of 50 guineas [£52/10/-] [presumably by declining to pay SW a commission in respect of Walter McGeough's organ, *see* SW→James Chapman Bishop, 28/2/1824].

'Little Evans' [presumably Charles Smart Evans, composer, singer and organist, 1780–1849, who was of small stature] told SW that VN has formally resigned from the 'South Street drudgery' [the organist's position at the Portuguese Embassy Chapel]. SW seeks confirmation of this from VN before giving 'any decisive answer to the engravers' [presumably regarding the list of subscribers to SW's Service].[438]

---

[438] VN, who is identified as 'Organist to the Portuguese Embassy' in the printed list of subscribers to SW's Morning and Evening Service, subscribed for six copies of this publication.

SW→Pettet   Euston St   **18/3/1824**
Drew Wesley Family Letters, SW series; *O*   I thank you for your kind Letter
▣ 18/3/1824

SW thanks Pettet for his letter [not preserved] and regrets that the manuscript he designed for Pettet [*see* SW→Pettet, 8/3/1824] is not yet ready. It will be ready shortly. SW encloses the prospectus of his intended publication [his Morning and Evening Service] and trusts that Pettet and [the organists] [John] Eager and [Thomas] Pymar will 'aid its progress' in Pettet's part of the world [i.e., in Norfolk and Suffolk; Eager, Pettet and Pymar all subscribed]. SW's Service is 'soon to be performed at St Paul's' [Cathedral].

SW→VN   **23/3/1824**
BL Add 11729 f 53; *O*   Thanks.—Do you chuse that the Words 'Organist to
▣ '23 March'[439]

SW thanks VN [for agreeing to subscribe to SW's Morning and Evening Service] and inquires if VN wishes to be identified as organist to the Portuguese Embassy in the 'printed list' [of subscribers]. SW seeks VN's advice about forms of address for the subscription list. SW has been told that his Service is to be rehearsed [i.e., performed] on Saturday next [27/3/1824] at St Paul's.

SW→VN   **25/3/1824**
BL Add 11729 f 55; *O*   Attwood has postponed the Day of Trial to Saturday
▣ Thu 25 Mar={1813,1819,1824,1830}[440]

Attwood has postponed the 'day of trial' [the first performance of SW's Morning and Evening Service] to 'Saturday week' [3/4/1824] because the Philharmonic Society rehearses its concert [to take place on 5/4/1824] that day. Attwood judges that many of his friends will be in London for that reason and will come to St Paul's [Cathedral] for the morning service before the [Philharmonic Society] rehearsal and possibly for the afternoon service afterwards. An anthem by Attwood also will be sung at St Paul's.

---

[439] Assigned to 1824 because of ref. to preparation of list of subscribers to SW's Morning and Evening Service.

[440] Assigned to 1824 because of ref. to Attwood's first performance of SW's Morning and Evening Service at St Paul's Cathedral, which took place on 3/4/1824 (*see* SW→RG, 1/4/1824).

SW→RG **1/4/1824**

BL Add 35013 f 80; *O*   My Service is to be tried at St Pauls on Saturday next
📧 Thu 1 Apr; pmk 1824

SW's Service is to be 'tried' [i.e., performed for the first time] at St Paul's
[Cathedral] next Saturday [3/4/1824] in the morning and afternoon [at Matins
and at Evensong].

SW→Pettet Euston St **6/4/1824**

Drew Wesley Family Letters, SW series; *O* ·   There is a good Latin Proverb
📧 6/4/1824

SW apologises to Pettet and to Pettet's engraver for the delay in supplying
SW's [enclosed] anthem ['Thou, O God art praised in Sion', the English version
of Te Decet Hymnus, *see* SW→Pettet, 8/3/1824]. SW has transcribed its Canto
part from the original C clef to the treble clef, which is better suited for 'female
amateurs'. The delay was caused solely by SW's having to transcribe the voice
parts of his Morning and Evening Service at St Paul's [Cathedral], where it was
'very respectably' first performed last Saturday [3/4/1824]. It will be repeated on
a Sunday.

SW→VN **19/4/1824**

BL Add 11729 f 177; *O*   On Sunday next (25th) it is purposed among their
📧 19/4/1824

SW's Morning and Evening Service is to be repeated next Sunday [25/4/1824].
VN is rumoured to have played his last high Mass at South Street [the
Portuguese Embassy Chapel] yesterday [18/4/1824], and so may have the leisure
to attend 'that comfortless paragon of empty magnificence' [St Paul's Cathedral]
on Sunday, either in the morning or the afternoon. SW would like 'a little
confab' with VN. SW invites VN to spend an evening with him and 'Joey'
M[ajor], and to stay overnight in London.

SW→VN **23/4/1824**

BL Add 11729 f 180; *O*   Voici des Propositions!—You have indeed been
📧 23/4/1824

SW encloses copies of proposals [for subscriptions to the publication of his
Morning and Evening Service]. VN has been 'very generally successful' in
distributing them. If more are needed SW will leave them at [Joseph] Major's
for VN. SW asks when he can meet VN there. SW now thinks that his Service
may not be performed at St Paul's [Cathedral] on Sunday [25/4/1824], and
suspects [William] Hawes to have had a hand in this matter. SW comments on
the low standard of the earlier performance [on 3/4/1824]: if the composition
cannot be sung with 'a little more feeling and precision', he would rather that it
not be performed there. In a choir 'made up of half-schooled musicians and
dignified parsons' a composer is uncertain of hearing his music performed well.

SW→VN   **26/4/1824**

BL Add 11729 f 182; *O*   Is the second Chord in the enclosed Scrap a false
▣ Mon 26 Apr={1824,1830}[441]

SW asks if 'the second chord in the enclosed scrap' [a progression from the
Jubilate of SW's Morning and Evening Service] is a 'false harmony'. If it is, he
wishes to know why; if not, he wishes to know the correct figuring to use for this
chord.

SW→VN   **12/5/1824**

BL Add 11729 f 180; *O*   You know there is much squabbling at present
▣ 12/5/1824

SW suspects that VN is guilty of 'musical high treason' by his comments on
'plodding pedants' and 'tasteless drones' [the critics of SW's Morning and
Evening Service], as Attwood, a 'personage high in royal favour and musical
office', is one of them. He has criticised SW's 'unfortunate appoggiatura'
[presumably the progression mentioned in SW→VN, 26/4/1824], which both
VN and SW think to be unexceptionable. SW insinuates that Attwood's lessons
with Mozart have done him little good, and relates an anecdote of a nobleman
who claimed in [Felice de] Giardini's presence to have learnt the violin with him
for many years, to which Giardini replied that he had certainly tried to teach the
nobleman, but the nobleman had learnt 'notting at all'.

SW→VN   **20/5/1824?**

BL Add 11729 f 185; *O*   I never more regretted the Difficulty of being in two
▣ Thu 20 May={1813,1819,1824,1830}[442]

SW will be out of town both today and tomorrow, otherwise he would have
'accepted the challenge on St Ann's account' [possibly a reference to a church of
that name or, alternatively, to a further performance of JSB's 'St Anne' fugue,
BWV 552; SW and VN had performed SW's organ-duet introduction to this
fugue and VN's organ-duet arrangement of it at the Foundling Hospital Chapel
on 15/6/1814].

---

[441] Ltr not before 1824 because of ref. to SW's recently composed Morning and
Evening Service; assigned to 1824 because of discussion of that composition;
also, no 1830 correspondence known between SW and VN.

[442] Assigned to 1824 for the following reason. 1813 excluded because ltr says
SW will be out of London on 20 May but on 20/5/1813 he played at St Paul's
Cathedral (*see* SW→VN, 26/5/1813). 1830 considered unlikely because no
1830 correspondence between SW and VN is known. 1824 is preferred to 1819
because 1824 was much more active in 1824 and hence more likely to be going
out of town for two days, but 1819 has not been ruled out.

SW→VN **14/6/1824**

BL Add 11729 f 137; *O* The Words of the vocal Ditty herewith were nearly
▣ Mon 14 Jun={1824,1830}[443]

SW encloses the score of his *Carmen Funebre*, a 'vocal ditty' whose words are nearly the last that his 'excellent father' [CW] addressed to SW before his death. SW has long wanted to set these words to music. He hopes that this composition will be sung at his own funeral as a testimony of his veneration for the 'dictates' of CW, 'whose value was utterly unknown' to SW until after his death. SW seeks VN's opinion of the composition.

SW would like to introduce [Joseph] Barret to VN in connection with 'a last request' [SW's burial; *see* SW→VN, 4/7/1823]. SW has known Barret for 20 years and can vouch that he is 'a sensible man', although he knows nothing of music.

SW→VN **about 1/7/1824**

BL Add 11729 f 192; *O* Herewith are the separate Parts of the *Carmen*
ltr undated[444]

SW encloses the 'separate parts' of his *Carmen Funebre*. As this composition is new, and his motet 'Exultate Deo' [composed in 1800] is familiar to their friend Street, SW recommends that VN give the *Carmen Funebre* to VN's 'well-drilled corps' so that it will be ready for the evening when he wishes SW to join his 'vocal party'. SW promises to make a score of the *Carmen Funebre* for VN soon. In the meantime, VN may like 'to sketch out sufficient score from the parts to rehearse it' with the least proficient of his choir. It is 'lucky' that [Angelica] Catalani is not the '1st canto': she would need to learn the 116 bars by heart, as she cannot read music. [Brigida Giorgi] Banti [Italian soprano, *c*1756–1806] also could not read music but was 'one of the best singers, the finest actress, and the stoutest swallower of brandy in the operatic annals of England'.

---

[443] Assigned to 1824 from ref. to SW's *Carmen Funebre* as ltr indicates that this work was recently composed and an autograph of this work (at Texas Finney 13), bearing VN's note that the manuscript is in SW's handwriting, is dated 11/6/1824.

[444] Ltr >SW→VN, 24/6/1824, when SW apparently first mentions his *Carmen Funebre* to VN, and <SW→VN, 1/8/1824 (first letter of this date), when SW sends VN a score of this work that he promises in ltr to make for VN.

SW→VN   **1/8/1824**

BL Add 11729 f 189; *O*   I know't not whether the sudden Death of your
☑ Sun 1 Aug={1824,1830}[445]

SW does not know whether the death of VN's 'maître d'hôtel' [not identified]
has upset plans for VN's musical meeting 'this week'. If SW was not engaged to
be away from London [in Margate] until next Saturday [7/8/1824], he would
come to the meeting to see VN. SW encloses the score and parts of his *Carmen
Funebre*. He is sorry if VN was disappointed at not being told the date of the
opening of the 'new ecclesiastical theatre' [the 15/7/1824 consecration of
Camden Chapel, of which SW had been appointed organist] but had not thought
that VN would be interested in 'such a clumsy mimicry of the Mass'. VN is
always welcome in the organ loft [of Camden Chapel] on a Sunday, 'either
morning or afternoon'.

SW→VN   **1/8/1824**

BL Add 11729 f 191; *O*   Since I wrote the enclosed there is a young Person
☑ 1/8/1824

A young man approached SW following the [Camden] Chapel service today
for 'a few hints upon the organ', after SW had written the enclosure [SW→VN,
1/8/1824, the first letter of this date]. This man, a stranger, will be in London
only for a fortnight, during the time when SW plans to be on holiday. SW
encouraged him to approach VN [for lessons].

SW→SS   Margate   **3/8/1824**

BL Add 35012 f 51   We are here safe and sound, after a very pleasant Voyage
☑ Tue 3 Aug; pmk 1824

SW and SSW arrived in Margate after a pleasant journey yesterday [2/8/1824].
They and Mr Tinney [a bass singer] have taken lodgings: two rooms at 12/- per
week. SW intends to return to London on Saturday [7/8/1824] by the boat which
arrives at 6 pm; he will then take the stage[coach] from the Bank to Camden
Town. He asks SS to tell Staples [not identified] to be at the [Camden] Chapel
by 7, and to let Gardner, the clerk, know SW's plans.

SW hopes that the children are well and wishes that they were all with him.
Sam [SSW] is 'very useful and attentive, and as stingy as you can wish him'.
SW hopes that 'Fish' [MEW] is reconciled to his absence, and that SS will look
after his dogs. SW assumes that SS has 'managed something' about his letter
and parcel for VN, and asks her to send to [Robert Thomas] Skarratt about the
proofs [presumably of SW's Morning and Evening Service]. If Skarratt sends

---

[445] Ltr not before 1824 because of ref. to SW's *Carmen Funebre*. Assigned to
1824 because no 1830 correspondence known between SW and VN; also, ref. to
the opening of the 'new ecclesiastical theatre' fits the 15/7/1824 consecration of
Camden Chapel; and SW is not known to have participated in a similar opening
in July 1830.

the proofs to SS by Saturday morning [7/8/1824], SW will correct them while he is in London. He has not yet met RG or Mrs J [not identified]. SW and SSW may go to Ramsgate tomorrow [4/8/1824] or Thursday [5/8/1824]. SW met Mr Bond the wine-merchant this morning, to whom he owes a large bill; Bond was 'exceedingly civil'. SW hopes to find 'Fish' [MEW] no worse on his return, and hopes that SS and Dr 'Gally Pot' [presumably the nickname of a medical doctor] have cured MEW's arm and his cough.

SW encloses some letters of the alphabet for MEW to learn, and a prayer that SS should 'drill' Rosalind to memorise. SS should tell Rosalind that if she learns all her [multiplication] tables and the Collect for next Sunday [8/8/1824, the 8th Sunday after Trinity] by the time SW arrives on Saturday, he and her brother [SSW] will bring her 'something pretty' on the following Saturday [14/8/1824].

Frances Burney d'Arblay→	**17/8/1824 or 24/8/1824**
Charlotte Francis Barrett	**or 31/8/1824**
Berg letters of Mme d'Arblay;	I am quite consternated—in the phrase of my
Hemlow v xi p 543–549	
Hemlow[446]	

Frances Burney d'Arblay [novelist, 1752–1840, CB's daughter] describes the 15/7/1824 consecretation of Camden Chapel, of which her son Alexander d'Arblay [minister, 1794–1837] was perpetual curate. At the consecration William Howley [1766–1848, from 1813 to 1828 Bishop of London] 'was met at the portico' by Rev. James Moore [1769?–1846, vicar of St Pancras New Church] and others, including the organist, SW, 'who mounted [the organ] instantly after' to give a welcome 'of sweet harmony'. SW subsequently 'ran and re-ran over the keys with fugish perseverance' during a wait for Alexander d'Arblay to appear.

SSW→SW	**10/9/1824**
BL Add 35019 f 3r	Your proofs have gone to Mr Ridge
☞ 10/9/1824	

SSW has sent SW's proofs [presumably of SW's Morning and Evening Service] to Mr Ridge [not identified] and has given SW's 'others' [presumably some of SW's arrangements of Handel's duets, *see* SW→VN, 13/9/1824] to [William] Hawes [SSW's master at the Chapel Royal and a director of the Royal Harmonic Institution, the publisher of SW's arrangements]. Hawes says that he is not in a great hurry but would like to have them one by one so that he can publish them separately.

---

[446] According to *Hemlow*, ltr was written between c16/8/1824 and 2/9/1824; the portion of ltr concerning SW is dated 'Tuesday evening'; hence ltr assigned to one of the three Tuesdays within the range that *Hemlow* gives.

SW→VN   Euston St   **13/9/1824**

BL Add 11729 f 194; *O*   From my Smattering of Latin I just venture to guess
☞ 13/9/1824

SW is arranging Handel's *13 [Celebrated Italian] Duets* [published in London
in 1777] for publication by the Royal Harmonic Institution at the solicitation of
'that royal quondam culinary artist, but now the supreme disposer of minstrelsy
and minstrels in London' [apparently William Kitchiner, who had acquired the
nickname 'royal cook' from entertaining George IV when Prince Regent,[447] and
whose *The Loyal and National Songs of England* and *The Sea Songs of Charles
Dibdin* had been published in 1822 and 1823 respectively], whom VN may
remember meeting at Joseph Gwilt's house.

SW can guess at the meaning of Italian sentences from his knowledge of Latin.
However, he has no Italian dictionary and asks VN to 'sketch out the meaning'
of the enclosed lines [not preserved].

SW regrets not having met VN on the occasion when Burgh [presumably Rev.
Allatson Burgh, *bap*1770, author of *Anecdotes of Music* (1814), from 1815 vicar
of St Lawrence Jewry] had said VN might be at Hampstead. SW knows that VN
objects to visiting the Burghs because of the 'vitriolic and acetous qualities of
the hostess' [Mrs Burgh]. However, these qualities are more than compensated
by the 'frankness and cordiality' of the Burghs' child, who is VN's pupil;
moreover, SW is much diverted by Burgh.

SW is arranging the names of his 'cústomers' [subscribers to his Morning and
Evening Service] in alphabetical order. He asks VN for the names of subscribers
whom VN sent to SW's 'shop' [presumably to Camden Chapel, which SW
describes as a 'shop' in SW→VN, 3/5/1825].

SW→VN   Euston St   **18/9/1824**

BL Add 11729 f 196; *O*   For the first Time in my Life, I do not believe your
☞ Sat 18 Sep; pmk 1824

SW doubts VN's claim not to know Italian, and again requests a translation
[*see* SW→VN, 13/9/1824]. If VN will not make one, perhaps his brother
[Francis Novello] will.

SW promised to take his friend John Harding, 'a medical man' of Kentish
Town, to see the Savoy [Lutheran] Church organ, and has arranged this
provisionally for the following Wednesday [22/9/1824]. SW inquires if VN
would like to come too. SW called on 'Dr Steinkoffph' [Carl Friedrich Adolph
Steinkopff, 1773–1859, from 1801 minister of the German Lutheran church in
the Savoy] but found him away. SW also called on the 'minister' (whose name
he has forgotten), who told SW that he would need to contact the clerk [not
identified], who is also the organist, to see if Wednesday is clear.

SW and VN have been invited by Harding to dine afterwards with him and his
assistant, a former sailor. Mr Dowling [not identified], whom SW met at

---

[447] Bridge, Tom and Colin Cooper English, *Dr William Kitchiner: Regency
Eccentric* (Lewes, Sussex, 1992) p 16.

Harding's and who is now Harding's patient, is a delightful companion but is 'not equal to dining out'. VN can expect to hear from SW by Tuesday [21/9/1824].

SW→VN　　　　　　　　　　　　　　　　　**20/9/1824**
BL Add 11729 f 198; *O*　　　On Wednesday, at 12, the Clerk of the German
📧 20/9/1824
SW asks VN to bring some 'scraps of the musical Leviathan' [JSB], 'perhaps the 30 [Goldberg] Variations', to their meeting at noon on Wednesday [22/9/1824] at the [Savoy] German Church when the clerk/organist has agreed to receive them [*see* SW→VN, 18/9/1824]. SW will bring the accompanied violin sonatas [by JSB], which will produce a novel effect as organ trio sonatas. He hopes that the arrangements for the day will be suitable. [John] Harding hopes that Dowling [his patient, *see* SW→VN, 18/9/1824] will be present. VN may bring any other suitable music by 'Mozart or other such pygmy composers' but should not 'overstuff his pockets with Rossini'. VN is welcome to stay overnight with SW afterwards.

SW→VN　　　　　　　　　　　　　　　　　**25/9/1824**
BL Add 11729 f 200; *O*　　　I learn that the perambulating Biographers
📧 sat 25 Sep; pmk 1824
The guides at [Westminster] Abbey object to the organ being played 'out of church hours', as it interrupts their work. SW has arranged to meet [George] Cooper [organist, *c*1783–1843] at noon on Wednesday [29/9/1824] at his church, St Sepulchre's, near Newgate. Cooper will bring 'some tunes of the old wig', which is how John Christian Bach referred to his father [JSB]. SW hopes that [VN's pupil Edward] Holmes [organist and music critic, 1799–1859] will bring and play his [Holmes's] fugue. SW is glad that VN enjoyed his evening at [John] Harding's in Kentish Town. Harding's hospitality is 'no faint antithesis' to that of their former host in Stamford Street [Joseph Gwilt, who had lived at 8 Stamford Street, Southwark between 1810 and 1812].

SW→John Harding[448]   **27/9/1824**

Gloucester Acc. 15019;[449] *O*   I find that those Vagabonds who shew the Tombs
🖅 27/9/1824

The 'vagabonds' who guide people about [Westminster] Abbey object to the
organ being played, except during 'church hours'. Consequently, SW has
arranged with [George] Cooper to meet on Wednesday [29/9/1824] at St
Sepulchre's, where the organ is excellent and they will not be interrupted. SW
asks Harding to inform their 'Hampstead host' [presumably Burgh] of this
arrangement, leaving him to decide whether to attend. SW hopes that Harding
will dine with them on Wednesday. VN enjoyed his day [with Harding] at
Kentish Town.

SW→VN   **28/9/1824**

BL Add 11729 f 202; *O*   Your Letter has quite metagrobolized me
🖅 Tue 28 Sep; pmk 1824

VN's letter [not preserved, expressing his unwillingness to meet George
Cooper] has perplexed SW. He does not know 'what to do for the best'. Without
incivility, he cannot now cancel the arrangement to meet Cooper at his church
tomorrow [29/9/1824]. [John] Harding has been informed of this meeting [*see*
SW→John Harding, 27/9/1824] and is likely to attend. However, an enclosed
letter [not preserved] shows that there is 'a pull another way', and SW hopes to
'hedge the business'. SW now proposes to see Cooper at noon and to get to Mr
B[urgh]'s about 4 pm tomorrow when VN's 'fair pupil' [Burgh's daughter, *see*
SW→VN, 13/9/1824] can suggest an activity for them. The Burghs never dine
before 5 pm.

SW→Editor, *The Times*   Euston St   **11/10/1824**

The Times, 12/10/1824   That truth and accuracy ought to characterize
The Times

The article on SW in the new biographical and historical dictionary of
musicians published by Messrs Sainsbury and Co. asserts that 'he died about the
year 1815'. This 'departed musician', however, has 'lately composed' a Church
Service which is 'now in the press' and 'about to be ushered speedily into public

---

[448] Ltr addressed to 'Dear Sir'. John Harding identified as the recipient on the
basis of SW→VN, 25/9/1824, in which SW says he is glad that VN enjoyed his
evening in Kentish Town [i.e., with Harding], and SW→VN, 28/9/1824, in
which SW states that Harding has been informed [i.e., by ltr] of the 29/9/1824
meeting with George Cooper.

[449] The item which contains ltr is described in H. Diack Johnstone, 'Treasure
trove in Gloucester: a grangerized copy of the 1895 edition of Daniel Lysons'
History of the Three Choirs Festival', *Royal Musical Association Research
Chronicle* no. 31 (1998) p 1–90.

notice'. Sainsbury and Co. would oblige the world by giving details of SW's funeral and tomb. His 'living address' is in Euston Street.

Sainsbury and Co.→Editor, *The Times*   12/10/1824
The Times, 13/10/1824   The humorous letter of Mr. S. Wesley in your paper
The Times

SW's humorous letter [SW→Editor, *The Times*, 11/10/1824] ought properly to have been addressed to Sainsbury and Co. rather than to *The Times*. SW evidently wishes to injure the reputation of the new biographical dictionary of musicians, which took 16 months of painstaking work to compile. SW 'refused, or at least neglected' to supply 'any data respecting his musical career' to the compilers, who therefore had to compose an article about him from 'the best previously published authorities'. A compiler later was told of a confusion of CW Jr with SW, and that SW had 'died about the year 1815'; to support this, the compiler was shown an article on CW Jr in *Public Characters* [*of all Nations*, London, 1823, v 3 p 599] which refers to CW Jr's 'own brother the late Mr S. Wesley'. The 'isolated error' adduced by SW 'is no imputation on the general accuracy' of the dictionary, and SW has been 'somewhat ungrateful towards Messrs Sainsbury' whose article about him, notwithstanding this error, contains a 'very warm' and 'very just' eulogy of his merits.

SW→Editor, *The Times*   Euston St   14/10/1824
The Times, 16/10/1824[450]   When people make public blunders, it is more
The Times

Sainsbury and Co. say [Sainsbury and Co.→Editor, *The Times*, 12/10/1824] that SW refused or neglected to supply them with data about his career. SW received one request for such data about 12 months ago but felt no obligation 'to furnish gratuitously to utter strangers materials for their own publication'. He holds 'egotism to be generally nauseous and disgusting' and considers it 'both indelicate and in bad taste to publish the history of any living artist'. SW had no desire to injure the reputation of the Sainsbury and Co. *Dictionary* but rather 'to contradict and refute an injurious report' of himself. Sainsbury and Co. are in a dilemma. Either they believed SW died about 1815 or they did not. If they did, why did they ask him 'to write his own life' eight years later? If they did not, 'where was the honesty' of stating that he died about that year? SW has nothing more to say on this subject.

---

[450] Printed ltr dated 'Thursday October 13', an incorrect date, as 13/10/1824 was a Wednesday. Date amended to Thursday, 14/10/1824, on the presumption that SW wrote an incorrect date rather than an incorrect day of week.

Sainsbury and Co.→Editor, *The Times*   **16/10/1824**

The Times, 18/10/1824   We must request the favour of a very few more lines
The Times

SW [in SW→Editor, *The Times*, 14/10/1824] evidently desires to strengthen 'his first attack' on Sainsbury and Co.'s biographical dictionary of musicians [SW→Editor, *The Times*, 11/10/1824] 'by accusing the compilers of a want of honesty in fixing the date' of his decease. The compilers personally knew that SW was alive in 1814. However, they were 'out of England' for 'the whole of 1815' and of course 'never saw his decease announced'. They 'consequently' concluded that SW died in 1815, but qualified their opinion 'by the word "about"'. They do not consider that their action 'can be construed into want of honesty'.

SW→VN   **18/10/1824**

BL Add 11729 f 204; *O*   I trust that Illness was not the Occasion
☞ 18/10/1824

SW hopes that illness was not the cause of VN's non-appearance at Kentish Town last Sunday week [10/10/1824]. SW's [Morning and Evening] Service is to be 'troublesome' to 'our royal composer' [Attwood] in the course of the following week. SW asks what is to become of his *Carmen Funebre*.

SW→Thomas Simpson Cooke   Euston St   **19/10/1824**

BL Add 33965 f 103; *O*   You will much oblige me by an immediate Line
☞ 19/10/1824

SW asks [Thomas Simpson] Cooke [composer and singer, 1782–1848, from 1813 leader of the orchestra at Drury Lane Theatre] whether Fuller [not identified], whom SW recommended to [the Drury Lane Theatre manager Robert William] Elliston as a member of Cooke's 'theatrical chorus', has been engaged.

SW→Editor, *The News of Literature*   Euston St   **20/10/1824**
and Fashion

News of Literature and Fashion   The 'Ghost extraordinary', which (strange as
no. 20 (23/10/1824) p 309[451]   it may sound) is at present very materially
News of Literature and Fashion

SW comments on 'the very curious, but most incontrovertible, statement of facts' in the article 'Ghost Extraordinary' in last Saturday's *News of Literature and Fashion* [no. 19 (16/10/1824) p 293, which reported the statement in the Sainsbury and Co. dictionary that SW died about 1815, and SW's response, SW→*Editor, The Times*, 11/10/1824]. SW advises that 'the said ghost' [i.e.,

---

[451] *The News of Literature and Fashion* prints ltr under the title 'A voice from Charon's boat'.

SW] is 'at present very materially occupied', and hopes to establish, by alchemical experiment, 'that music-paper may be infallibly transmuted into gold'.

SW→Editor, *The Harmonicon* Euston St **about 24/10/1824**
Harmonicon v 2 no. 23 (Nov 1824) p 210 I transmit to you a Correspondence
ltr undated in *The Harmonicon*[452]
SW transmits correspondence from himself and from Sainsbury and Co. that lately appeared in *The Times* [SW→Editor, *The Times*, 11/10/1824 and 14/10/1824; Sainsbury and Co.→Editor, *The Times*, 12/10/1824 and 16/10/1824], together with commentary on this subject 'from a very respectable weekly publication' [the article 'Ghost Extraordinary' in the 16/10/1824 *News of Literature and Fashion*] and his response to that commentary [SW→Editor, *The News of Literature and Fashion*, 20/10/1824].

SW→Editor, *The Examiner*[453] Euston St **25/10/1824**
The Examiner no. 874 (31/10/1824) p 697 I have heard of an individual who
The Examiner
The Examiner of last Sunday week [17/10/1824] confirmed that SW was alive, contrary to 'the public declamation of those learned biographers' [the dictionary published for Sainsbury and Co.] who stated that he 'died about 1815'. However, *The Examiner* went on to say that CW Jr is no longer alive. SW assures the editor that this 'also is a mistake', unless CW Jr has happened to die within the last fortnight. Had this happened, SW surely would have heard.

Sarah→Henry Moore **30/10/1824**
MA DDWes/6/16 On the death of Mr Collinson my Mother had it in her
pmk 30/10/1824, a Saturday; ltr incorrectly dated 'Saturday 29 October'
On the death of [Edward] Collinson [Methodist businessman, c1730–1803], SGW was able to sell out of 'the stocks'. All her 'fortune' was sold out, as was part of the money paid in by the trustees, which would have made 'a pretty income'. The situation of Sarah's 'unhappy brother' SW led all the family to help him, 'perhaps more largely than prudence required'. Were it not for a 'providential legacy', the family would have been 'much straitened', even in SGW's lifetime.
Sarah now has £50 annually, which she hopes will prevent her asking for assistance, and her brother [CW Jr] has his church [i.e., his position as church

---

[452] Ltr presumably ≥23/10/1824, when SW→*Editor, The News of Literature and Fashion* was printed in that journal. As ltr was printed in the November 1824 *Harmonicon* it presumably was written on or very shortly after 23/10/1824.

[453] SW signs ltr with the name 'Redivivus'.

organist], which enables them to 'board comfortably, though not keep up an establishment'.

SW→CW Jr   Euston St   **6/11/1824**
GEU Wesley Coll. ltr 58; O^{454} At last you herewith receive the long promised
⊡ 6/11/1824
SW 'at last' encloses the 'long promised copies' of his [Morning and Evening] Service. The engraver 'performed his task well' although he was nearly late. SW seeks to borrow Handel's 'Italian duets'. He is now arranging [for publication by the Royal Harmonic Institution, *see* SW→VN, 13/9/1824] 'an accompaniment' for these 'in lieu of the figured bass'. He has completed the arrangement except for 'the last page of the 13th duet' which was deficient in the score from which he worked.

SW has had 'much employment' from the [Royal] Harmonic Institution, arranging 'a multitude' of oratorios and songs, and believes that his arrangements have made these compositions 'more practicable and useful'. Comparatively few people possess the previously published scores and perhaps fewer can readily accompany correctly from a figured bass. The editions [of Handel's music] of [John] Bland [music publisher, *c*1750–*c*1840] 'and other quack publishers' were 'quite futile and contemptible'.

SW→VN   **12/11/1824**
BL Add 11729 f 206; *O*   Harding called yesterday to tell me that neither he
⊡ Fri 13 Nov[455]
Neither [John] Harding nor the Burghs can come tomorrow [13/11/1824] to St Lawrence, Jewry [of which Allatson Burgh was vicar]. SW suggests postponing this meeting to next Saturday '21 November' [in fact, to Saturday 20/11/1824] and asks if VN agrees. VN's copies [of SW's Morning and Evening Service] have been 'in King Street' [Joseph Major's premises in Holborn] for some days past. SW believes that VN has heard from WL.

---

[454] Ltr is incomplete; only the first page has been preserved.

[455] Ltr addressed to VN at Shacklewell Green where he lived between 1823 and 1825. The dates Friday 13 November and Saturday 21 November, stated explicitly in ltr, occurred in 1818 and 1829 but not in any intervening year and therefore must be incorrect dates. Ltr assigned to Friday 12 November 1824 because SW proposes in ltr to meet VN at St Lawrence, Jewry next Saturday rather than tomorrow, and SW→VN, 23/11/1824, mentions VN's non-appearance at St Lawrence on Saturday 20/11/1824. This assignment is consistent with SW mistaking the date but not the day of the week when he wrote ltr.

SW→VN Euston St **23/11/1824**
BL Add 11729 f 208; *O* I know that you are not much frightened at Rain
☞ Tue 23 Nov; pmk 1824
SW is puzzled at VN's non-appearance at St Lawrence's [Jewry] last Saturday
[20/11/1824] and wonders if a headache was the cause. SW asks VN to explain
and invites him to join SW in the organ loft [at Camden Chapel] next Sunday
[28/11/1824].

CW Jr→Langshaw Jr **24/11/1824**
GEU W/L; *Wainwright* p 80–81 Yesterday your Friend call'd, when I was out
☞ 24/11/1824
CW Jr had informed SW that Langshaw Jr and Mr Heaton [of Lancaster]
subscribed to SW's 'work' [his Morning and Evening Service] and is surprised
that only one copy was delivered. Sarah will send Langshaw Jr her copy. CW Jr
will tell SW about the missing copy when they next meet. CW Jr thinks that
SW's composition is 'plain and elegant'.

SW→VN **29/11/1824**
BL Add 11729 f 210; *O* Sam shall have Mr Holmes's Composition to study
☞ 29/11/1824
Sam [SSW] shall have [Edward] Holmes's composition to study as soon as
possible. Sir Robert Peat [c1771–1837, Perpetual Curate of Brentford], an 'old
acquaintance' whom SW last saw a fortnight ago, is 'agog' to hear SW's
[Morning and Evening] Service and has asked for a performance at his
parsonage. SW proposes to bring SSW [to sing the treble part] and to engage
two people to perform the alto and tenor parts. SW will sing the bass part and
VN will play the piano. SW asks VN to suggest a suitable day. Sir Robert will
secure beds for the party. Although VN dislikes meeting new people SW's
introduction of [John] Harding to VN proved agreeable. VN's copies [of SW's
Service] are at [Joseph] Major's, who also is an old acquaintance of Sir Robert's
and has been invited to join the party.

SW→VN Euston St **3/12/1824**
BL Add 11729 f 212; *O* I much fear that the same Cause of your Absence
☞ Fri 3 Dec; pmk 1824
SW fears that the reason for VN's absence last evening [2/12/1824] from Lisle
Street is the same as that which prevented him from being with SW today in
Brunswick Square [where VN taught at a school, *see Cowden Clarke VN* p 21].
SW's Brentford arrangements [*see* SW→VN, 29/11/1824] are still not settled.
[The tenor Henry] Robertson has volunteered; James Elliott could not be
bettered for accuracy of intonation. SW requests a line from VN, unless he
prefers to see SW at church [Camden Chapel] on Sunday [5/12/1824].

SW→VN   Euston St   **6/12/1824**
BL Add 11729 f 214; *O*   I wish you could have given me a better Account
▣ 6/12/1824

SW hopes that VN's health is improving and asks if 'next Thursday week'
[16/12/1824] would suit him for the Brentford excursion [*see* SW→VN,
29/11/1824]. SW welcomes VN's suggestion of Mr Frank [as a singer] and
suspects that [William] Hawes [SSW's master at the Chapel Royal] will not
allow SSW to be present [at Brentford]. SW asks for the names and addresses of
all who have received their copies [of SW's Morning and Evening Service] from
VN.

SW→VN   **12/12/1824**
BL Add 11729 f 216; *O*   I did not answer you sooner, because I could not
▣ Sun 12 Dec; pmk 1824

SW was unable to answer VN's letter [not preserved] sooner. Only last night
SW received a letter [not preserved] from [Sir Robert] Peat who expects them at
Brentford on 22/12/1824. Sir Robert can either provide accommodation or
obtain vehicles to transport the party back to London afterwards, whichever is
required. As SW has already asked James Elliott to take part in a 'ludicrous trio'
for the next meeting of Somerset House Lodge, VN should approach Elliott
about [singing at] Brentford. SW wishes VN to repeat the request to [Henry]
Robertson [to sing at Brentford] and wants to secure the service of VN's brother
[Francis Novello, as bass singer].

SW→VN   Euston St   **13/12/1824**
BL Add 11729 f 218; *O*   Your second Letter reached me soon after I had
▣ 'Monday morning'; pmk 13/12/1824 (a Monday)

VN's second letter [not preserved] arrived shortly after SW had replied to
VN's earlier letter [not preserved]. SW is concerned about VN's health and
hopes that it will soon improve. He recommends that VN see [John] Abernethy
[surgeon, 1764–1831]. SW has told WL many times that Rev. Henry Delafite
lives at 35 Clarendon Square, Somers Town.

In response to VN's request for a composition, SW suggests his 'Ave Regina
cælorum' for two 'cantos' [soprano voices], written about 40 years ago, which
should be suitable, as it is easy [a revised version of this composition
subsequently appeared in volume 2 of VN's publication *Convent Music*]. If VN
advises the nature of other pieces he requires, SW will search for anything
suitable in his 'dunghill' of manuscripts. He proposes to defer the Brentford visit
until VN is in better health, but needs to hear from him as the party currently is
expected there on 22/12/1824.

The money [presumably for copies of SW's Morning and Evening Service]
arrived safely.

Robert Peat→SW **19/12/1824**

BL Add 11729 f 223   I went to Town on Friday, for the express purpose

☞ 19/12/1814

Sir Robert Peat went to London on Friday [17/12/1824] 'for the express purpose' of seeing SW to arrange for [the visit to Brentford on] Wednesday next [22/12/1824]. Sir Robert had a serious fall *en route* and must therefore postpone the visit. He now expects SW, VN and their party some time in the following week.

SW→VN Euston St **20/12/1824**

BL Add 11729 f 220; *O*   I have resolved to defer the Brentford Expedition

☞ Mon 20 Dec; pmk 1824

SW has decided to postpone the Brentford trip until they can be more confident of VN's participation, and suggests Wednesday [29/12/1824] as a possible date. SW will write to [Sir Robert] Peat. He encloses the composition ['Ave Regina cælorum'] that he wrote about in his last letter [SW→VN, 13/12/1824]. VN is welcome to the other compositions that he desires. SW recollects that [his composition] 'Ecce panis [angelorum]' is in D minor and remembers that he omitted one line in the hymn, which he now must supply. He will write again when he receives Sir Robert's reply.

VN should 'bring in his bill' on 27/12/1824 for the many threepenny letters that SW has lately posted to him [at Shacklewell Green]. 'Everyone' joins SW in commending the 'acumen and sagacity' of [the surgeon John] Abernethy [*see* SW→VN, 13/12/1824]. SW wishes that VN would see Abernethy.

SW→VN Euston St **21/12/1824**

BL Add 11729 f 222; *O*   By the enclosed you will find that the Party

☞ Tue 21 Dec; pmk 1824

SW encloses Sir Robert Peat's letter [Robert Peat→SW, 19/12/1824]. SW has proposed Wednesday 29/12/1824 for the visit to Brentford, but the date is provisional upon VN's health. If VN is confident of being well enough, perhaps he will let his brother [Francis Novello] and [Henry] Robertson know. [James] Elliott can participate that day.

SW→VN **22/12/1824**

BL Add 11729 f 225; *O*   Your sending me your last, post paid, induces me

☞ 'Wednesday night 22nd'; pmk 23/12/1824 (a Thursday)

SW is glad that VN is going to Cambridge. VN should find the change of air beneficial to his health and will be 'gratified by an examination of the numerous curiosities in the libraries'. He also will see the 'miracle' of King's College Chapel which has an organ by [John] Avery, the best [organ] builder since 'old [Bernard] Smith' [organ builder, 1630?–1708]. During an earlier visit to Cambridge [about 1788], SW corrected the Trinity College librarian who identified as a missal a manuscript that SW recognised was a breviary. SW is going to Brentford on 29/12/1724, taking only SSW. Sir Robert Peat has not seen SSW before and is fond of children.

SW→VN   Euston St   **8/1/1825**
BL Add 11729 f 227; *O*   Mr Holmes gave me much Gratification
◻ 8/1/1825

[Edward] Holmes told SW on Wednesday [5/1/1825] that VN's Cambridge trip has been beneficial. Although SW hates 'the [medical] faculty' almost as much as he hates lawyers, he nevertheless wishes that VN would consult [John] Abernethy, who has exceptional honesty and skill. SW's [Morning and Evening] Service has been 'nibbled by rats' in *The Harmonicon* [January 1825, whose anonymous reviewer discerned faults in SW's composition], and SW feels obliged to 'accommodate them with a kick'.

SW has stated that the 'new [in fact, second-hand] organ at Camden Chapel' is 'very imperfect'. Since, as 'a madman', SW's word is considered unorthodox, [Thomas] Adams [organist and composer, 1785–1858] and [James] Davis are to 'tell the real truth' about the organ next Wednesday [12/1/1825]. SW thought it best not to be present at this 'solemn mockery of common sense' but will be pleased to accompany VN if VN wishes to go.

SW→VN   **17/1/1825**
BL Add 11729 f 229; *O*   Your sudden Reverse of Purpose yesterday
◻ Mon 17 Jan; pmk 1825

SW and [John] Harding were disappointed by VN not appearing yesterday [16/1/1825]. SW must have his 'Ecce panis [angelorum]' [*see* SW→VN, 20/12/1824] in order to supply the omitted line. SW saw WL this morning and reassured him that the 'black ball against him' [presumably regarding his election to the Classical Harmonists' Society, *see* SW→VN, 15/2/1825] was a mistake. SW told WL that he might expect to receive a message to the same effect from VN soon.

WL denies all knowledge of the identity of SW's 'sapient judge' [the reviewer of SW's Morning and Evening Service in *The Harmonicon*]. WL believes that the review was written with 'friendly intention' and is anxious lest SW should reply in 'other than gentle terms'. SW is scornful about this. SW and VN know that once upon a time WL considered SW 'as a fit inhabitant for Dr [Alexander Robert] Sutherland's madhouse [Blacklands]'. WL's 'decision in the present instance' almost tempts SW to ask if Dr Sutherland has a vacancy in his asylum [for WL]. SW will proceed to finish his reply to the review and will seek VN's opinion of it then.

SW plans to write to [Sir Robert Peat at] Brentford and asks what he should say regarding VN. SW comments scurrilously on WL's enthusiasm for a 'party of fusty bachelors' to be held at Dulwich.

SW→VN **20/1/1825**

BL Add 11729 f 229; *O*   I discover that after all, I have been hypercritical
☞ Thu 20 Jan={1825,1831}[456]

SW finds that he had not omitted a line in his 'Ecce panis [angelorum]' after
all. He is not overly anxious to take issue with his critic in *The Harmonicon* but
feels that he should do so as a matter of principle. He will submit what he has
written to VN when finished, which should be by the end of the week. He cannot
invite VN to 'that box of catcalls' at the [Camden] Chapel on Sunday
[23/1/1825] but they could meet afterwards and compare notes at [John]
Harding's [home]. SW wants to hear about VN's visit to Cambridge and
comments on his own experiences there. SW recalls CW's frequent command to
him, 'Sam, do as thou wilt, or I'll make thee'.

SW→VN **27/1/1825**

BL Add 11729 f 233; *O*   Should you be minded to take a Stroll to Kentish
☞ Thu 27 Jan; pmk 1825

If VN desires to stroll to Kentish Town on Sunday [30/1/1825], SW will gladly
'jog on' with him. SW has finished his reply to *The Harmonicon* review [of his
Morning and Evening Service] and will give it to VN if he sees him on Sunday.
SW expects that the 'gentlemen of *The Harmonicon*' will not accept his reply.
He has resolved not to have anything more to do with this 'junto of mere book-
making blunderers'. SW is informed that one of those involved [in *The
Harmonicon*] is [William] Ayrton 'of operatical notoriety' [who was in fact the
editor] and that 'our royal and metropolitan organist' [Attwood] is another.
'Crotch could hardly write such nonsense as the others' but 'loves money better
than real reputation'. SW has lately completed a new vocal composition.
[Robert William] Elliston's brains ought to be blown out: 'he would have
extorted £2000 from [Edmund] Kean if he had not risked his, and 5000 more
people's lives on Monday night' [24/1/1825]. [SW alludes to a report that
Elliston had insisted that Kean appear that night at Drury Lane Theatre
notwithstanding fears of a riot; if he did not appear it was incorrectly supposed
that Kean would have to pay a £2000 penalty.]
SW asks VN's opinion on a rate of £1/1/- for 'copying and arranging' six pages
of manuscript music.

SW→VN **31/1/1825**

BL Add 11729 f 235; *O*   Harding has desired me to request that you will dine
☞ 31/1/1825

[John] Harding invites VN to dine with him after SW's 'work of penance' [his
organist's duties at Camden Chapel] next Sunday afternoon [6/2/1825]. On

---

[456] Assigned to 1825 because of ref. to SW's *Harmonicon* review mentioned in
preceding letters. No such review appeared in *The Harmonicon* in 1831.

Thursday [3/2/1825] SW plans to bring his revised reply to his review in *The Harmonicon* and hopes that VN will find it 'less exceptionable' than a previous version. SW will try to obtain Sam [SSW] for Thursday evening [to sing at a concert of the Classical Harmonists' Society at the Crown and Anchor Tavern], but hints that [William] Hawes may be unwilling to release him [from the Chapel Royal]. SW desires to look at the Te Deum by [Carl Heinrich] Graun [German composer, 1703?–1759] before Thursday.

SW→'My dear Sir'   31/1/1825

K; *O*   I have just received the enclosed, which I am quite sure is written
⊟ 'Monday evening 1 Feb 1825', an incorrect date[457]

SW has just received the enclosure [not preserved] and is 'quite sure' that it was sincerely written. The writer of the enclosure proposes that he and SW should make 'an afternoon call' on Sunday [6/2/1825] at Kentish Town [presumably at John Harding's house, *see* SW→VN, 31/1/1825].[458]

SW→VN   15/2/1825

BL Add 11729 f 237; *O*   I trust that your Daughter is out of Danger
pmk 15/2/1825

SW trusts that VN's daughter [not identified] is out of danger. He seeks VN's early opinion on the enclosure [not preserved], but thinks that their opinions will be the same. WL is 'in high spirits' at being elected to the [Classical Harmonists'] Society and wishes VN to dine with him at Furnival's Inn [WL's address] at a date of VN's choice, when 'very good' music by WL's brother [presumably Thomas Linley Jr, composer and violinist, 1756–1778] will be played. SW alludes cryptically to imperfections in a female singer or singers [not identified] and thinks that some songs in [Handel's] *Judas Maccabaeus* [to be performed at the first Oratorio concert at Covent Garden on 18/2/1825, at which SW was the organist and 'conductor'] will 'suffer no slight metagrobolization' as a result.

---

[457] Assigned to Monday evening 31/1/1825 on the presumption that SW mistook the date but not the day of the week.

[458] If so it is plausible that Harding was the recipient of ltr and that VN had written the enclosure.

SW→VN   22/2/1825

BL Add 11729 f 239; *O*   I shall expect you to take some Coffee
☞ Tue 22 Feb={1825}[459]

SW invites VN to take coffee with him in his 'rabbit hatch of a parlour'
tomorrow [23/2/1825] at 5.30 pm. SW thinks that the order of items in the
[Oratorio] concert [at Covent Garden on 23/2/1825] is unwise. Although
Mozart's *Requiem* as 'the best music' ought to come last, [Haydn's] *The
Creation* should have formed the second part and not the first. SW has just had
'the mulligrubs' caused by 'cold air rushing in front of the organ for four hours'
at the [Oratorio] concert [at Covent Garden, at which SW played the organ] last
Friday night [18/2/1825]. He is grateful that he can earn money in a better way
than by such 'theatrical slavery'.

SW→RG   17/3/1825

BL Add 35013 f 82; *O*   I hope that this finds You quite recovered
☞ Thu 17 Mar; pmk 1825

SW hopes that RG has recovered his health and can be with SW tomorrow
evening [18/3/1825, at the Covent Garden Oratorio concert]. Handel's *Messiah*
will be their evening task.

SW→VN   25/3/1825

BL Add 11729 f 240; *O*   Your Cambridge Business is of urgent Importance
☞ Fri 25 Mar={1825}[460]

SW returns VN's letters [not preserved] immediately, as VN's 'Cambridge
business is of urgent importance'. If SW's reply to [William] 'Ayrton's
nonsense' [the review in *The Harmonicon*] is to appear at all, it should appear
soon.

SW recalls that VN said that publication in *The Examiner* should be 'given up'.
Monthly publications are often 'greedy of controversy', and SW desires VN's
advice about which monthly would be most likely to print his reply. SW
understands that *The Gentleman's Magazine* 'refuses nothing, good, bad or
indifferent' and therefore has lost much of its original respectability, but,
'according to our infallible dogma of the infallible Lutheran pope' AFCK, 'it
must do as well as it can'.

---

[459] Assigned to 1825 because the advertisement in *The Times* for the 23/2/1825
Covent Garden Oratorio concert states that Mozart's *Requiem* and Haydn's *The
Creation* were on the programme of that concert.

[460] Assigned to 1825 because of ref. to SW's reply to the review of his Morning
and Evening Service in the January 1825 number of *The Harmonicon*. 'Mr.
Samuel Wesley's reply to the critique on his Church Service, in *The
Harmonicon*' ultimately appeared in the *Literary Chronicle and Weekly Review*,
v 7 no. 317 (11/6/1825) p 377–380.

Attwood was at Covent Garden on Friday [18/3/1825], praising the 'sublimities' of [Carl Maria von] Weber [German composer, 1786–1826]. SW wonders if Attwood was equally complimentary about the 'profundities' of [Joseph Augustine] Wade [Irish composer, 1801?–1845]. Attwood and [William] Hawes are 'sworn conscientious brothers'.

SW→VN   **29/3/1825**

BL Add 11729 f 242; *O*   I have deposited my Panegyric upon the *Harmonicon*
▣ Tue 29 Mar={1825}[461]

SW has sent his reply to his *Harmonicon* critics to [Edward Dixon] Pouchée, publisher of the *News of Literature and Fashion*.[462] 'The Ghost Extraordinary', which first appeared in that paper [*see* SW→Editor, *News of Literature and Fashion*, 20/10/1824], 'evidently' was written by 'some occult friend', whom SW conjectured was [Edward] Du Bois, but Pouchée denied this. Pouchée seemed unconcerned when SW told him that music type was needed [for SW's reply]. Several musical quotations, including some from Boyce, are a necessary part of SW's argument.

SW→VN   Euston St   **12/4/1825**

BL Add 11729 f 243; *O*   So I am to have the Honour of firing the first
▣ 'Tuesday 12th'; pmk 13/4/1825 (a Wednesday)

At last night's [Philharmonic Society] concert [11/4/1825], [Joseph] Major told SW that VN had returned [from Cambridge]. SW awaits news of VN's 'academic discoveries'. Major showed SW a copy of the 'Norwich Musical Review' [i.e., the *QMMR*, v 7 (1825) no. 25] containing another review of SW's [Morning and Evening] Service.

[Edward Dixon] Pouchée says that he cannot insert [in the *News of Literature and Fashion*] SW's reply to the *Harmonicon* review [*see* SW→VN, 29/3/1825], because the reply 'is too long for a newspaper'. 'Joe Street junior' [Joseph Edward Street, son of Joseph Payne Street] told SW that he will send SW's reply to 'one of the monthly journals'.

---

[461] Assigned to 1825 for the same reason as SW→VN, 25/3/1825.

[462] Although Pouchée is identified in the *News of Literature and Fashion* only by the initials E. D. Pouchée, he presumably was the Edward Dixon Pouchée who published in 1824 a prospectus of a serial called *The European Review*, and who is listed as a printer under the name 'Edward Dixon Pouchie' in Todd, William B., *A Directory of Printers and Others in Allied Trades, London and Vicinity, 1800–1840*, London, 1972, p 153.

SW→Mary Ann Russell[463]   Euston St   **16/4/1825**

BL Add 11729 f 245; *O*   I delayed an earlier Reply to the Favour of your
📧 16/4/1825

SW apologises for his delayed reply to the letter [not preserved] from Mary Ann Russell [1781–1854, widow of William Russell, the late organist of the Foundling Hospital]. Publication of the oratorio [William Russell's *Job*] has been agreed, and it is important to proceed quickly. An arrangement of the score for the pianoforte is essential but could not be prepared by one person in less than a month. SW today suggested to his friend, [William] Drummer, that the task be divided amongst several people. SW knows at least six persons competent to make the arrangement but considers that it is best done by three, which will save time and expense. He is too busy making other similar arrangements to be able to do this work himself but proposes that Mrs Russell apply immediately to 'two or three men of high musical eminence'. SW is prepared to assist in the 'revision' of the arrangement and in the correction of proofs, without fee.

SW→VN   **19/4/1825**

BL Add 11729 f 179; *O*   You will see the Drift of the enclosed.
📧 Tue 19 Apr; pmk 1825

SW encloses an 'application' [not preserved] from [Robert] Williams [1794–>1846, from 1816 to 1842 organist of St Andrew by the Wardrobe].[464] Williams, whom SW believes VN knows, is 'clever and worthy' and will write to VN directly. VN can safely give Williams a favourable word. SW adds jocularly that, if VN doubts whether SW is 'a sensible man', VN can ask Mrs Bastable [the Blacklands proprietress] or Dr [Alexander Robert] Sutherland.

Sarah→Maria Cosway   **22/4/1825**

MA DDWF/14/45   I wrote nearly a year ago in answer to your most kind letter
📧 22/4/1825

Sarah's 'poor brother' SW is 'quite restored to himself'. As proof, he now considers Sarah as 'his friend, whom disease made him regard as an enemy'. Sarah can never forget the kindness that Maria Cosway [miniature-painter and musician, *c*1760–1838] showed to SW.

---

[463] Ltr addressed to 'Dear Madam'. Mary Ann Russell designated as addressee because VN annotated ltr, identifying the recipient as 'the widow of Mr Russell, org.' of the Foundling'.

[464] Williams presumably was applying for testimonials to support his candidacy for the position of organist at St Matthew's, Brixton, *see* SW→Robert Williams?, 10/5/1825.

SW→VN   **27/4/1825**

BL Add 11729 f 247; *O*   I am paying great Attention to my Judge or Judges
⬛ Wednesday; pmk 27/4/1825 (a Wednesday)

SW has 'little doubt' that WH is the 'Lord Chief Justice' of the review [the
QMMR review of SW's Morning and Evening Service] and has written him an
'inquisitorial line' [not preserved] on this subject. WH is a musician of
'abundant merit' which is 'lamentably counterbalanced by an exuberance of
envy'.

SW→VN   Euston St   **2/5/1825**

BL Add 11729 f 249; *O*   I expected you to have looked in here on Friday
⬛ 2/5/1825

SW expected VN to come on Friday evening [29/4/1825], when they could
have discussed the enclosed letter [not preserved]. SW will not reply until he
sees VN on Thursday [5/5/1825], when he hopes that VN will be able to place
his orchestra better than on the 'last evening' when SW deputised for him [at the
Classical Harmonists' Society on 7/4/1825], as about two-thirds of the
performers could not see the piano then. SW suggests that VN call in tomorrow
[3/5/1825].

SW→VN   **3/5/1825**

BL Add 11729 f 251; *O*   Thank you for your Letter, but not much for
⬛ 'Tuesday evening'; pmk 4/5/1825 (a Wednesday)

SW thanks VN for his letter [not preserved], but not for the news of VN's ill
health.

SW doubts that he will be able to attend the [Classical Harmonists'] Society at
the Crown and Anchor [Tavern] on Thursday [5/5/1825]. His 'loving wife'
[CLW] has caused him to be arrested for non-payment of £25, which he cannot
advance all at once, and he is going to prison tomorrow [4/5/1825].[465] He will
write again soon, either from home or from prison. His sudden release is 'hardly
probable' and he wonders how he can be in jail and in church [Camden Chapel]
simultaneously. His church duty must be fulfilled somehow; otherwise he fears
that his reputation at that 'shop' [Camden Chapel] 'for general punctuality' will
suffer. VN should not keep secret [from the Classical Harmonists' Society] the
real cause of SW's absence on Thursday.[466]

---

[465] The annuity of £130 that SW agreed to pay for CLW's maintenance in their
25/3/1812 Deed of Separation had been reduced by this time to £25, *see*
CLW→CW Jr, about 21/5/1825, and Sarah→Thomas Marriott, 27/5/1826.

[466] The text summarised by this last sentence has been scratched out in ltr. It is
not known whether this erasure was made by SW before he sent the ltr or by
someone else subsequently.

SW→Sarah   Euston St   **8/5/1825**

MA DDWes/6/36   This is a better Place to date from than the King's Bench

⌨ Sun 8 May; pmk 1825

Euston Street [SW's home] is a better address from which to write than the Rules of the King's Bench Prison [the area in which SW was confined, for non-payment of debt, in a spunging house in Cursitor Street off Chancery Lane]. SW was released yesterday afternoon [7/5/1825] and was unable to advise Sarah of this earlier. He is well aware of, and truly grateful for, her exertions. Mr Fuller [probably Frederick James Fuller, special pleader], who proved a true friend, has done wonders: he mollified and astonished [George] Oliver 'by a just statement of facts' and frightened SW's 'amiable family banditti'. John [JWW] behaved well from filial affection, despite the efforts of CLW and his 'holy inquisitorial brother' [CW III]. Sarah is correct in saying that SW is a coward when the sufferings of those he loves are incorporated with his own. He is pleased to be able to attend his organ 'in person' [at Camden Chapel] today. If next Saturday [14/5/1825] suits, SW may visit and 'con over' CW Jr's oratorio.

SW shortly will fulfil his promise regarding the only portion of the book [not identified] which could have disturbed SGW. Only one article in this book refers to freethinking on religious matters.

SW→Charles Smart Evans   Euston St   **9/5/1825**

BL Add 11729 f 253; *O*   In reply to your Letter, allow me to state candidly

⌨ Mon 9 May; pmk 1825

Replying to Charles Smart Evans's letter [not preserved], SW advises that he has 'taken no benefit [concert] during the last nor the present season' and has decided not to play in public 'except in the way of a professional engagement'. He has made this decision generally known and therefore must decline Evans's request to play at his benefit [concert]. SW recently refused a similar request from another person who had not rendered SW as much 'active service' as Evans has. If SW should live for another year, he will be glad to offer his services to Evans again.

SW→Robert Williams?[467]   Euston St   **10/5/1825**

MA DDWF/15/26; *O*   I presume that you read the bouncing Paragraph

⌨ Tue 10 May={1825}[468]

SW invites his correspondent to visit this evening between 8 and 9 pm to chat about the 'bouncing paragraph in last night's [9/5/1825] *Courier*'. [This

---

[467] Ltr addressed to 'Dear Sir'. Robert Williams presumed as the recipient because SW had promoted his candidacy for the Brixton position (*see The Courier*, 9/5/1825, and SW→VN, 19/4/1825).

[468] Assigned to 1825 because the relevant 'bouncing paragraph' was published in *The Courier* on 9/5/1825.

paragraph is about the choice of William T. Ling as organist at St Matthew's, Brixton instead of SW's pupil Robert Williams, who had been recommended by SW as 'umpire'; letters 'published by Mr S. Wesley and Mr Williams' on this matter are mentioned in the *Courier* article but have not been located]. The trustees or vestry of the [Brixton] church 'are no better than a bunch of swindlers' and SW's correspondent should expose them. SW believes that there should be 'an entirely new election' [of an organist for this church].

SW→VN   Euston St   **10/5/1825**
BL Add 11729 f 255; *O*   Here I am, safe (which I was when locked up
⬚ Tue 10 May; pmk 1825

SW has been released but is not yet 'well recovered from the effects of close air' and the 'scenes of misery' that he witnessed last week [at the spunging house]. He has agreed to help Mrs [Mary Ann] Russell by arranging the oratorio [William Russell's *Job, see* SW→Mary Ann Russell, 16/4/1825]. If her patrons are true to their promise she should gain from the publication.

Palmer [possibly the W. H. Palmer Esq. who subscribed for two copies of SW's Morning and Evening Service, or his son] wishes to meet VN soon at the Savoy [German] Chapel or somewhere else where a large organ is available, and hopes that VN will dine with him afterwards at his home. Palmer's mother is a 'frank charming woman'; his father, a lawyer, is a 'frank blunt honest man'.

SW→Sarah   Euston St   **10/5/1825**
MA DDWF/15/28   There is no Doubt that John is the best of that bad Bunch
⬚ 'Tuesday morning'[469]

SW thinks that John [JWW] is 'the best of that bad bunch' [his children by CLW] but is cynical about the motives for his 'filial affection'. SW has seen [William] Drummer, who 'recounted all that passed between them' before JWW intervened 'in the affair' [SW's incarceration in the spunging house]. SW will relate the story to Sarah and hopes to be with her on Saturday [14/5/1825] at 3 pm. He sends love to CW Jr.

---

[469] Assigned to Tuesday 10/5/1825 because ltr, which discusses JWW's filial affection and mentions SW's hope to be with Sarah on Saturday 14/5/1825, appears to follow SW→Sarah, 8/5/1825, which also mentions SW's hope to see Sarah on Saturday 14/5/1825 and JWW's 'filial affection' when SW was confined in the spunging house.

SW→CW Jr Euston St **10/5/1825?**

MA DDWes/6/45 When Miss Ince called here, her Communication was not

☞ Tue 10 Apr[470]

Miss Ince [not identified] called at SW's Euston Street home, but her message was not clear. SW understands that Sarah desires his 'statement of facts relative to the spunging house incarceration', not the account of 'good Mrs W.' [CLW]. He understands that his 'evangelical son' [CW III] claims to have been 'the engine' of SW's liberation. This is false. RG 'first interfered'; then, together with Sarah, he 'frightened' JWW 'into some exertion for extricating' SW in order 'to save his own reputation from atrocious ingratitude' in the opinion of Messrs Scott [Sir Claude Scott, 1742–1830, who was JWW's 'master' in the coal-merchant business, *see* SW→Sarah, 20/4/1827] and Benson, JWW's partner [in that business].

SW was arrested on a Monday [2/5/1825] and was 'not liberated till the Saturday following' [7/5/1825]. His 'dutiful son' [CW III] 'was literally hunted into something like decency at last', which consisted of 'the advancement of £5', which he promised 'on the day when he first saw' SW 'in the place' [probably Wednesday 4/5/1825, when SW first was brought to the spunging house]; instead, CW III never came near the spunging house 'for three days after'.

RG will provide 'you both' [CW Jr and Sarah] with 'a true account' of CW III's 'unfeeling conduct throughout the whole affair'. For the Reverend CW III to maintain that he was 'an efficient cause' of SW's emancipation 'demands more logic than the University of Cambridge and more sophistry than the Society of Jesus' can furnish. RG, who 'came forward like a sincere friend', was 'the sole person' to whom SW owes 'any cordial gratitude in the business'.

SW now is afflicted by rheumatism which has affected both his knees 'for some days past'. Chronic diseases such as rheumatism and gout cannot be cured, only palliated; one or the other is a 'general concomitant of declining mortality'. Today SW had planned to be at Dulwich with 'our old friend' Ozias Linley [who from 1816 was organist of Dulwich College], but the 'embargo' on SW's legs has prevented this.

SW asks to be remembered to Sarah. He thought that she would be saved 'some trouble' if SW wrote this letter to CW Jr rather than to her.

---

[470] Ltr >7/5/1825, when SW was released from the spunging house. Tuesday & 10 April & Sarah alive→1827, but 10/4/1827 seems an unlikely date for ltr as the events discussed took place almost two years earlier. Ltr accordingly has been assigned (with some doubt) to Tuesday 10 May 1825, on the presumption that SW wrote ltr shortly after his release from the spunging house and got the day of week and the date-within-month right but wrote down the wrong month.

Wait→SW   Euston St   **11/5/1825**
BL Add 11729 f 258   I did not immediately reply to your letter
⌨ 11/5/1825

Before replying to SW's letter [not preserved], Wait took 'due steps to set our project on a certain basis' by seeing the vice-chancellor [of the University of Cambridge, Thomas le Blanc, *c*1773–1843] on this subject. The vice-chancellor thinks that the [university] senate cannot act [to give SW permission to publish his transcriptions from the Fitzwilliam manuscripts] until after VN has completed his own selection. SW 'will be at liberty by grace' [from the university] to publish after then. When VN has published, he should make it clear, by giving letters of recommendation to his friends, that SW's publication is not in opposition to VN's publication.

Wait is confident that there is much in manuscript [in the Fitzwilliam collection] which would reflect well on SW's labours and would be 'of the most lucrative nature' [if published]. Wait will be in London next week for a week or two and will call upon SW when he arrives. He suggests that SW return with him to Cambridge to examine the collection and to select all that he considers most valuable. SW can settle his plans of publication in Cambridge where he can obtain the interest of both VN's and Wait's friends. Wait is 'confident' that SW's plans can be realised.

SW→Robert Williams?[471]   Euston St   **12/5/1825**
MA DDWF/15/27; *O*   On my Return from Hampstead I found the enclosed
⌨ 12/5/1825

SW forwards a letter [not preserved, presumably concerning the Brixton Church organ affair] and desires to hear personally from his correspondent how his affairs 'are going on'. SW has been giving a lesson to his correspondent's 'rival's friend' [not identified, possibly a friend of William T. Ling who was Williams's rival for the organist's post at Brixton, *see* SW→Robert Williams?, 10/5/1825]. SW will be at home tomorrow [13/5/1825] between 3 and 5 pm if his correspondent wishes to call in.

---

[471] Ltr addressed to 'Dear Sir'. Robert Williams presumed as recipient because SW signs ltr as 'your hoaxed and belied umpire', presumably a reference to SW's role in selecting the organist for the Brixton church.

SW→CW Jr   12/5/1825?

Fitzwm ltr 18   The sending of Boxes to your House was an entire Mistake

🖃 'Thu 12 Nov', an incorrect date[472]

Sending boxes to CW Jr's house 'was an entire mistake'. The bearer [of this letter] 'is ordered to bring them back immediately'. SW is not surprised that both his sons [CW III and JWW] deny 'having been privy to' SW's arrest [on 2/5/1825], as CLW 'has practised them long enough in the art of lying and effrontery'. SW will visit when he can but CW Jr can hardly believe how much SW suffers when he comes 'into the vicinity of Paddington', even though he hopes and trusts to be buried there [next to AD]. He sends love to Sarah.

CW Jr→Emma   about 14/5/1825

SW's copy of ltr at GEU in box 7[473]   I wished my sister to write to you

SW's copy of ltr undated[474]

Sarah refused CW Jr's suggestion that she write to Emma regarding the 'cruel treatment' of SW [in the spunging house] and commissioned CW Jr to write his sentiments directly. CW Jr is 'shocked' that SW was put in a spunging house, where he nearly died. He 'could not breathe there in such hot weather' and people there 'thought he was suffocating in the night'. Regardless of any claim of [SW's] 'barbarous treatment' of CLW, a 'lasting stigma' would have been brought upon 'all of you' and on the 'universally respected' Wesley family if SW 'had died or lost his senses' there. How could SW 'exercise the profession' by which he earns his living if he were 'immured all his days'? Sarah thinks, and CW Jr hopes, that CW III 'did not know' [that SW would be arrested and incarcerated] but Emma, who was at home, 'must have known it'. SGW 'would not have used' a child of CLW 'in such a cruel manner'. CLW 'cannot love her children to bring such a reflexion upon you all'.

---

[472] The date is incorrect because ltr is addressed to CW Jr at 49 Gloucester Place, and hence is >4/5/1824 (when CW Jr was at 14 Nottingham Street) and <1/11/1825 (when CW Jr was at 1 New Street, Dorset Square); however, Thursday did not occur on 12 November between 1818 and 1829. During the period of CW Jr's residence at 49 Gloucester Place, the only known arrest of SW took place on 2/5/1825, prior to his incarceration in the spunging house (*see* SW→VN, 3/5/1825 and SW→CW Jr, 10/5/1825?). Ltr assigned, with considerable doubt, to Thursday 12 May 1825, the only Thursday the 12th in 1825, and a time when CW Jr and Sarah were actively concerned to learn the circumstances that led to SW's arrest and incarceration. If this dating is correct, SW wrote down the correct date and day-of-week in ltr but wrote down the wrong month.

[473] The location of the original letter is not known.

[474] Ltr >7/5/1825 when SW was released from the spunging house and placed here because apparently after SW→CW Jr, 12/5/1825?, which mentions CW III's denial that he knew SW would be arrested before this happened.

SW→VN   Euston St   **15/5/1825**
BL Add 11729 f 257; *O*   You will perceive, by perusing the enclosed, that
☞ Sun 15 May; pmk 1825

SW requires VN's comments on the enclosed letter [Wait→SW, 11/5/1825] and would like to have his reply before Wait's imminent visit. Wait is 'desirous of combining propriety with benevolence'. SW is considering coming on Tuesday [17/5/1825] to St Paul's [Cathedral, at the Festival of the Sons of the Clergy] for 'a slice of [William] Boyce's immortal anthem' ['Lord, Thou hast been our refuge']. SW fears that this is a day in which VN is 'delivered over to the tormentors' [i.e., is teaching] until evening, so they will be unable to meet.

Sarah→SW   **16/5/1825**
GEU in box 7[475]   I have diligently searched for the Letter, and without success
☞ 16/5/1825

Sarah has searched unsuccessfully for a letter [not preserved] from Mr Benson [JWW's partner in the coal-merchant business]. Benson said in this letter that he called upon CLW with a letter [not preserved] by 'Mrs S. Wesley' [i.e., Sarah, *see* Sarah→SW, about 28/5/1825]. However, CLW 'refused to receive any communications in her own private concerns' or to look at this letter.

Sarah has never been indifferent to SW's welfare and asks whether SW seriously thinks that his present life is right. Does he consider that his afflictions result from his way of living? Sarah knows that SW has felt 'the miseries' devolved upon himself and his children. God alone 'can enlighten the understanding, which the will clouds'. Life is short, and the lives of Sarah and SW are 'nearly terminated'. Sarah sees SW 'on a precipice'. She trusts that his sufferings will be ended when he returns to his Heavenly Father, who alone can teach SW 'the right way' and enable him 'to walk in it'.

CLW→CW Jr   **about 21/5/1825**
MA DDWF/25/7   I beg to assure you that you shall have all the credit due
ltr undated[476]

CLW responds to CW Jr's 'late heroic letter' to Emma [CW Jr→Emma, about 14/5/1825], which CW Jr's 'amiable sister' [Sarah] dared him to write. By criticising, 'with coarse and ruffianly language', those [CLW and her children] who were 'compelled, for self-preservation, to become the ministers of punishment' [of SW], CW Jr upholds 'crime', regardless of the hypocrisy with which he pretends 'to discountenance it'.

SW, to whom CW Jr has 'of late grown so wonderfully affectionate', has had ample and repeated notice that CLW 'should be driven to proceed to extremities' if he refused to pay her 'the trifling pittance' which she consented to accept [an

---

[475] Ltr appears to be incomplete.

[476] Ltr placed here because it is a reply to CW Jr→Emma, about 14/5/1825.

annual payment of £25, *see* Sarah→Thomas Marriott, 27/5/1826] instead of her 'due' [the £130 annuity provided in their Deed of Separation]. CLW will not gratify CW Jr's 'impertinent curiosity' by stating whether CW III knew of CLW's 'determination to enforce' her claim.

CW III's sentiments regarding CW Jr's letter to Emma are (1) that 'it was unmanly and contemptible', and (2) that CW Jr should 'espouse the cause of the widow [CLW] and the fatherless [Emma]', rather than 'abusing the one [CLW], and hectoring the other [Emma]'. Although Sarah and CW Jr 'are, no doubt, greatly shocked' at SW's wicked behaviour, it 'is not so "universally" known' as they seem to imagine. CLW 'will take care that truth shall have its way'.[477]

CLW has enjoined Emma to deliver to her, unread, any future letters from CW Jr to Emma. When he talks 'of bringing "wretched reproaches" in the Wesley family', CW Jr should think of [SW's] 'drunkenness, adultery, and blasphemy'; 'of evil speaking, lying and slandering; of hypocrisy, vanity, and Mr Banks' [a married man with whom Elizabeth Ellison, granddaughter of SW's aunt Susanna Wesley, lived].

Sarah→John Gaulter   23/5/1825

GEU in box 7   The Interest you have always taken in our Family

📧 23/5/1825

The interest that John Gaulter [Methodist minister, 1765–1839] has 'always' taken in the Wesley family 'induces' Sarah to detail some circumstances relating to her 'poor dear brother' SW, in whose concerns Gaulter 'may be essentially useful'.

Gaulter's son 'received' SW in his home at some previous time [presumably in the second half of 1818, *see* WBRR v 3 (December 1851) p 446], when SW had recently 'been restored [at Blacklands] from a frenzy fever'. Before and occasionally long after the onset of this illness, its effects caused him to have 'strong antipathies to those who loved him'. However, following SGW's death [in 1822], SW seems to be 'quite recovered, and able to pursue his profession'.

Sarah supposes that SW's success was 'exaggerated' to CLW. Although he had recently sent CLW 'some monies', he was arrested without notice by [George] Oliver 'at her suit', as the lawyer 'refused to wait' [for more money]. SW was 'carried to the spunging house in Cursitor Street, Chancery Lane' on Wednesday 4/5/1825, when the weather was extremely hot. 'As usual in all troubles', SW told Sarah of his situation, but his friends advised him to 'go to the [King's] Bench' [the prison to which the spunging house was attached] rather than to be 'continually harassed'.

While SGW was alive, CW Jr and Sarah sold 'much of our little property' to assist SW and to avoid distressing SGW, 'but now the case is different'. CW Jr

---

[477] On a copy of ltr in SW's hand (in Baker, Box 8 (Wesley Family)), SW notes that 'truth shall have its sway' makes better sense than CLW's phrase 'truth shall have its way', and suggests that when CLW wrote ltr she miscopied CW III's 'original'.

and Sarah would 'impoverish themselves' by further assistance to SW 'without essentially aiding him', as CLW says that she 'will always arrest him for arrears' while he lives [with SS] 'in a manner we all regret'.

CLW is 'of a cruel, vindictive spirit'. She refused to live with SW and flung 'temptation in the way' by admitting SS, 'whom she knew was not good', to wait upon SW 'many years ago'. On 4/5/1817 SW's 'dread of arrests' issued by CLW and her children 'drove him frantic'. He 'leapt out of the window [on 6/5/1817] thinking they were coming to take him to execution'. SGW feebly endeavoured to hold SW.

Sarah believes that Oliver has a kind nature but has acted each time by order of CLW or her children. It was 'particularly cruel' to seize SW without warning, as he is 'industriously labouring to support his two families' and willingly allows CLW what he can. Sarah wrote [not preserved] to her nephew the coal-merchant [JWW] saying that 'he would never know happiness' if SW perished from confinement. She also wrote to JWW's partner in the coal-merchant business [Mr Benson, *see* SW→CW Jr, 10/5/1825?], pointing out the disgrace that would fall upon JWW and CW III, who 'has lately married well' [he married Eliza Skelton on 7/12/1824], if SW should die in the spunging house. For whatever reason, SW was liberated on 7/5/1825, and Sarah understands that Oliver was 'softened'.

Sarah wants Gaulter to use his influence with Oliver, in Oliver's capacity as CLW's trustee, so that in future he does not 'proceed to such inhuman measures'. Although they [CLW and her children] will say SW never sends money 'without being dunned', this is untrue: 'he often has none to send'. Oliver knows SW's 'mental malady'. However, only Sarah—whom SW treated ill 'when under its influence'—takes pity. Gaulter should tell Oliver that 'it will be a standing dishonour' if SW is 'consigned to prison' by a Methodist. If Oliver says that CLW and her children have made him arrest SW again, Oliver should 'give up the trusteeship of this furious wife'.

'We' [presumably Sarah and CW Jr] hope to visit Gaulter next Monday [30/5/1825] if he is free.

John Gaulter→Sarah   26/5/1825

GEU in box 7   I am disposed to think that my young friend has not heard
▣ 26/5/1825

Gaulter has received Sarah's letter [Sarah→John Gaulter, 23/5/1825]. He now knows 'the whole case'. He called upon [George] Oliver, who was not at home, and will call on him again. 'To the utmost of his little influence', Gaulter will press Oliver to meet Sarah's 'forgiving and most sisterly regard for a great mind' [SW].

Sarah→SW   **about 28/5/1825**
GEU in box 7[478]   This (as nearly as we can recollect) was the Letter
ltr undated[479]

Sarah encloses a copy [not preserved], made from her and CW Jr's memory, of
CW Jr's heartfelt letter to Emma [CW Jr→Emma, about 14/5/1825]. Sarah
supposes that the passage in that letter which gave CLW 'greatest umbrage' was
the accusation that, by exposing her children to 'the reproach' [that confining
SW to a spunging house would discredit the Wesley family, would prevent his
earning a living, and might cause his death or insanity], she did not love her
children. They [CLW and her children] possibly 'did not imagine' that SW
'would have resolution to go to the spunging house', which was 'a severe blow
to us' [Sarah and CW Jr]. Until 'Mr [William] Drummer wrote to your son
[presumably CW III]; and I, to Mr Benson [JWW's partner], it is at least a
charitable conjecture that they [CW III and JWW] did not know' of SW's
incarceration, but to have left SW there 'one instant beyond the time they could
extricate' him was 'most barbarous treatment'.

CLW's allusion [in CLW→CW Jr, about 21/5/1825] to Banks must have been
meant as a 'reproach to poor Lizzy [Elizabeth] Ellison' who 'lived with him', as
SW knows. Because CW Jr mentioned [in CW Jr→Emma, about 14/5/1825] the
'respectability' of the Wesley family, CLW ungenerously 'pointed to this
undeniable fact'.

SW→VN   **10/6/1825**
BL Add 11729 f 261; *O*   I do not know whether you are aware that a certain
pmk 10/6/1825

SW sends four lines of derisive doggerel that he has written about WH and
suggests that VN might send this on to his 'loyal friend' [Leigh] Hunt. SW
intends to set out for Cambridge on Tuesday [14/6/1825], despite his 'horror of
stage coaches'.

SW→VN   **11/6/1825**
BL Add 11729 f 263; *O*   The following, I think is a better Reading
☞ 11/6/1825

SW sends a revised version of his doggerel on WH [*see* SW→VN, 10/6/1825].
Wait dined with SW at home yesterday evening [10/6/1825]. Wait and SW plan
to travel to Cambridge together, probably on Wednesday [15/6/25].

---

[478] Ltr is torn and appears to be an incomplete draft.

[479] Ltr placed here because it was written presumably soon after CLW→CW Jr,
about 21/5/1825, to which it refers.

CW Jr→a sister of Wait[480]   **14/6/1825**

GEU in box 7[481]   I am much obliged by the kind Letter I received from you.

☞ 14/6/1825

'Dr Daniel' [Wait], the recipient's brother, called on CW Jr at his church [St Marylebone] last week. Wait expects SW at Cambridge 'to examine the Handelian music' and the 'curious' manuscripts that Lord [Richard] Fitzwilliam [7th Viscount Fitzwilliam, 1754–1816] left to the University of Cambridge. Lord Fitzwilliam [years ago] granted CW Jr permission to publish many compositions by [Domenico] Scarlatti [which appeared as Scarlatti's *Thirty sonatas, for the harpsichord or piano-forte...from manuscripts in the possession of Lord Viscount Fitzwilliam* published *c*1800 by Robert Birchall], but this music is only for 'real judges' who can appreciate 'such high composition'.

SW→'My dear Sir'   Euston St   **14/6/1825**

MA DDWF/15/30; *O*   When I found Webb at his Door this Morning, he told

ltr 'Tuesday evening'[482]

This morning, when SW visited Webb [possibly the Rev. Richard Webb, *c*1770–1829, minor canon of St Paul's Cathedral and Westminster Abbey, to whose 1808 *A Collection of Madrigals* SW had subscribed], Webb told SW that SW's correspondent had recently left him and was on his way to SW's house. SW is sorry that his correspondent feels that he is too late in the 'promulgation' of his 'lithographic apparatus'. SW had heard of such a thing only a few nights earlier from Wait, but does not feel that because one person has 'hit upon' an invention, another similar one need be abortive, since 'every mechanical invention' can be improved. Wait's reference was to the Typolithographic Press [established by William Ross] in White Lion Court, Wych Street, Drury Lane [printers of the lithographed journal *The Parthenon*].

SW today met Mr Warren, father of a young organist [Joseph Warren, 1804–1881], of whom SW's correspondent has probably heard. Mr Warren Sr wishes to have 'all the rights and wrongs of the Brixton [church organist] squabble' [*see* SW→Robert Williams?, 10/5/1825]. SW has promised to show Warren his correspondent's papers on this subject, and asks his correspondent to send them to Warren at his home at Upper Lark-Hall Place, Clapham. SW's

---

[480] Ltr addressed to 'Dear Madam'. Wait is identified in ltr as the addressee's brother but her identity has not been further established.

[481] Ltr is torn with slight loss of text.

[482] Assigned to 14/6/1825 for the following reason. Ltr says SW heard of the Typolithographic Press a few nights ago from Wait and will travel to Cambridge within a day. SW dined with Wait in London on 10/6/1825 (*see* SW→VN, 11/6/1825) and arrived in Cambridge after a slightly delayed departure (*see* SW→VN, 15/6/1825) on Saturday 18/6/1825 (*see* SW→SS, 19/6/1825); 14/6/1825 is the only intervening Tuesday. Also, the first issue of *The Parthenon*, printed by the Typolithographic Press, is dated 11/6/1825.

correspondent's 'spirited stir' has done much good, and musicians will thank him secretly for it. SW will travel to Cambridge 'within a day or so'.

SW→VN   Euston St   **15/6/1825**
BL Add 11729 f 264; *O*   Our late Duke of Cumberland, the Brother of
☞ 15/6/1825

SW is still in London rather than in Cambridge as planned. Wait was obliged to go to Hertfordshire to settle some business and will not return home [to Cambridge] until Friday [17/6/1825]. SW will join him there on Saturday [18/6/1825]. SW's 'humble apology' for the mortal sins in his [Morning and Evening] Service [SW's 'Reply to the critique on his Church Service, in *The Harmonicon*'] was printed in last Saturday's [11/6/1825] *Literary Chronicle*.

Every new reader of WH's letter to SW [not preserved] confirms SW's belief that WH was the 'faithfully yours with his stiletto in the dark' [i.e., the anonymous *QMMR* reviewer of SW's Service].

SW→CW Jr   Euston St   **16/6/1825**
MA DDWF/15/29   Inadvertently I marched off with the elegant Scroll
☞ Thu 16 Jun & 🖙→🗓

SW inadvertently went off with the 'elegant scroll' [not identified] which he now encloses. He also left behind the paper [the 11/6/1825 *Literary Chronicle and Weekly Review* containing SW's reply to his critic in *The Harmonicon*] in which his 'apology' for all his 'imputed false harmony' is contained. He asks CW Jr to return this by post as soon as possible. CW Jr did not mention when he intends to leave for Wales; if this is after 25/6/1825, SW may be able to see him before he leaves.

SW sends his love to Sarah. He is sorry that she was 'abused' by his 'unworthy wife' [presumably by CLW's refusal to read Sarah's letter to her, *see* Sarah→SW, 16/5/1825]. The affair is 'too contemptible to justify a moment's disquietude'. SW feels certain that Sarah would never meet with disrespect (much less calumny) from 'one of the illegitimate part' of his family.

SW→SS   Regent St, Cambridge   **19/6/1825**
BL Add 35012 f 53   You now see that I am alive: I am safe and sound
☞ 19/6/1825

SW arrived by coach in Cambridge at 5 pm yesterday [18/6/1825] safe and sound, where he is likely 'to be killed with kindness'. Wait has not yet arrived, but is expected at 4 pm today. SW wants SS to take particular care of herself in her 'present situation' [her pregnancy with their son John Wesley, born before 2/7/1825, *see* SW→VN, 2/7/1825] and not to spend long hours at a wash-tub or to lift heavy weights. She is to write by return.

SW is pleased with his reception in Cambridge and enjoys the pure air and the conversation of the place. Mrs [Eliza] Wait is charming and hospitable; she invited a clergyman, 'a very great scholar' [not identified], to meet SW, and SW found him a 'glorious companion'. SW will return on Saturday [25/6/1825]. He hopes that [Edward] Rowlands [organist, 1802–1844] performed what was required of him [presumably by deputising for SW at Camden Chapel].[483]

SW→VN   Regent St, Cambridge   **21/6/1825**
BL Add 11729 f 266; *O*   According to your Command I pester you
⊡ 21/6/1825

SW is trying to make the most of his time in Cambridge and is reluctant to think of his return to London next Saturday [25/6/25]. Wait, his host in Cambridge, looks after him well. SW wishes VN to list as soon as possible the names of all composers that he intends to use [in his compilation of music from the Fitzwilliam collection] so that they may avoid clashes. SW has heard that VN has not 'meddled' either with [the Italian composers Domenico] Paradies or [Alessandro] Scarlatti and concludes that VN intends to leave these composers to another hand.

SW is very pleased with the organs in Cambridge. He grieves at the mischief done to the Trinity College organ by 'that brace of quacks, Flight and Robson'. The organ at Peterhouse is a 'sweet little instrument', and that at St Mary's 'utters the true ecclesiastical sounds'. He has not been able to try the organ at King's College, having been refused access by the provost [George Thackeray, 1777–1850].

SW→SS   Cambridge   **23/6/1825**
BL Add 35012 f 55   If you promise to take a Coach, but not otherwise
⊡ Thu 23 Jun={1814,1825,1831}[484]

If SS undertakes to take a coach, SW will permit her to meet him on his arrival at the Angel, Islington, on Saturday [25/6/1825]. He is coming by the Telegraph stage, which arrives at 4 pm. SS and 'Fish' [MEW] can travel on the Paddington stage, but they are not to ride outside. SW has written [not preserved] to Mr Fuller [not identified], whom he has charged to look after SS, and who SW thinks will not permit SS to walk any part of the distance [because of her pregnancy]. SW asks SS to get him some fish for Saturday. He has been living 'on the fat of the land'; the people at Cambridge have made him 'as vain as a peacock'. SS did not pack his *Confitebor* for him, 'but it does not much signify now'.

---

[483] SW→SS, 9/9/1825, indicates that Rowlands deputised for SW there.

[484] Assigned to 1825 because ref. to MEW rules out 1814 and SW known to be planning to return from Cambridge to London on 25/6/1825 (*see* SW→VN, 21/6/1825) but not known to have been in Cambridge in June 1831.

SW→VN Euston St **25/6/1825**
BL Add 11729 f 268; *O* I am just imported to the 'Seat of Confusion and
📧 'Saturday evening 26 June'[485]
SW has just returned to London, the 'seat of confusion and noise', from the 'terrestrial paradise' of Cambridge. King's College Chapel, Cambridge, 'might dignify the New Jerusalem'. VN should say when he will visit and dine with SW the following week. SW will serve him one mutton chop and a gallon of porter. SW has a letter for VN from Wait.

SW→VN Euston St **2/7/1825**
BL Add 11729 f 269; *O* You know that Paradox, 'take one from one
📧 Sat 2 Jul; pmk 1825
SW indirectly announces the birth of his child [his son John], on account of which he is obliged to postpone his 'chop and porter' dinner with VN [*see* SW→VN, 25/6/1825] until after next Tuesday [5/7/1825].

SW→Sarah Euston St **6/7/1825**
GEU Wesley Coll. ltr 59 I enclose a Copy of the two letters you wished
📧 6/7/1825
SW forwards three letters [not preserved] to Sarah, including one received yesterday from Mr Porter. He has received a 'civil' notice [not preserved] from [George] Oliver that £15/2/6 is required by 'Saturday next' [9/7/1825].
SW 'can get no answer from the baronet' in Hampshire [presumably Sir James Gardiner, 1785–1851, who shortly after replied with an invitation to SW to spend a week with him in Hampshire, *see* SW→VN, 12/8/1825]. He is not hopeful of receiving a satisfactory answer by Saturday from the baronet, who owes him money. SW intends to approach others 'by tonight's post'.
SW is 'fully aware' of the importance of gettng the money. He does not want to move from Hampstead Hill to Castle Street, Holborn [presumably a debtors' prison], although such a move might delight 'the Christian spirit' of CLW and her 'evangelical son' CW III. SW hopes that 'John' [JWW] was truly surprised by the letter, and continues to think that his 'heart is made of better stuff' than that of his brother CW III.
SW is due to receive money today from 'the [Camden] Chapel' but must devote this sum to his tax obligations. He is pursuing several subscribers who owe him 'for their copies' [of his Morning and Evening Service]. If all amounts owing to SW had been paid he would be 'in a comparatively easy position'.

---

[485] The date Saturday 26 June={1824,1830} has been rejected because SW is not known to have been in Cambridge in either of those years; also, his first known contact with Wait was in 1825 and no 1830 correspondence between SW and VN is known. Ltr assigned to Saturday 25/6/1825 when SW is known from preceding letters to have planned to return from Cambridge to London on the presumption that SW wrote down the correct day of week but an incorrect date.

Saturday's debt 'is the only one' from which he feels 'actually harassed at this moment'.

SW will call on Sarah before she leaves London if he can. He hopes that CW Jr is well.

SW→SSW   Regent St, Cambridge   **1/8/1825**
BL Add 35012 f 109; *O*   I have written to Harding (& I think your Mother
◻ 1/8/1825

SW has written to [John] Harding and is certain that he will come forward with the requisite £5. SSW should buy a 1/- or 1/6 penkife. SSW says nothing about 'the poor girls' [Rosalind and EW] or whether the baby [John Wesley] has caught the measles. Mrs [Eliza] Wait is not yet confined [for the birth of Sydenham Wylde Wait *d*1828] but the house is in some agitation and SW dines with the Waits only on special invitation.

VN and SW played over SW's *Confitebor* at Trinity College chapel today. Everyone is urging him to publish it by subscription. Mrs [Mary] Frere [wife of William Frere, Master of Downing College, 1775–1836] is 'a great patroness of all musical schemes' and will procure SW a long list of subscribers. Wait would not encourage SW in any risk or allow him to proceed until he is sure of a 'very liberal subscription'.

SW is likely to turn to good account the manuscripts [from the Fitzwilliam collection] that he is copying. If [William] Hawes has 'any guts in his brains' he will make SW a 'liberal offer' for a share in the concern.

SW asks SSW to write fully about news from home. SSW should transcribe WH's letter [not preserved] if it is not too long. SW does not want SSW to enclose it, as this will incur double postage.

SW is anxious about money. He does not want to borrow from VN and would not, under any circumstances, ask Wait for money. SW's lodging costs 18/- for the fortnight, which he considers reasonable.

SW corrects SSW's spelling and encourages him to become a good English scholar. He could become a Latin scholar also if he made 'good use of the most valuable article in life, which is time'.

SW→VN   **9/8/1825**

BL Add 11729 f 271; *O*   According to Command I have sounded my own
☞ Tue 9 Aug={1814,1825,1831}[486]

As commanded, SW has 'sounded his own trumpet' in the enclosure [not preserved: it presumably included or suggested the paragraph on SW's *Confitebor* which appeared in *The Examiner* on 14/8/1825]. SW mislaid his penknife and SSW's copy of 'Bach's *Exercises*', and asks if VN knows their whereabouts. SW wonders if they were left 'in the Museum' [perhaps in the Fitzwilliam Museum area of the Cambridge University Library, as SW and VN had both been in Cambridge the preceding week; *see* SW→SSW, 1/8/1825].

SW inquires whether 'the queen bee' [VN's wife Mary Sabilla Novello] has returned from Boulogne.

SW→VN   Euston St   **12/8/1825**

BL Add 11729 f 272; *O*   Major has lent me the Quarterly No. 26.
☞ 'Friday night'; pmk 13/8/1825 (a Saturday)

[Joseph] Major has lent SW no. 26 of the *QMMR*. It includes the plates [headed 'Wesley's Service'] of 'incipient scraps' [i.e., musical examples of the beginnings of sections of SW's Morning and Evening Service] to which reference was made in the review [of SW's Service] in no. 25 of that magazine. SW plans to send his 'retort courteous' to [Richard Mackenzie] Bacon [editor of the *QMMR*]. SW thinks that Bacon is unlikely to accept it for publication, as he is a 'professed friend of the canonist' [WH].

Major is engaged 'for a fortnight to come'. On 21/8/1825 VN and SW have agreed to dine with 'friend Pug' [not identified] at his villa in Kentish Town at 5 pm.[487] SW has received 'a most obliging invitation' to spend a week with Sir James Gardiner in Hampshire at his expense.

SW asks whether 'our puff' will appear on Sunday [14/8/1825; when *The Examiner* published a paragraph about the performance of SW's *Confitebor* in Cambridge, *see* SW→VN, 9/8/1825].

SW encloses a copy of JW's 'Apology for answering fools according to their folly', which VN liked so well. It exhibits 'simple but masterly style of

---

[486] Assigned to 1825 for the following reason. 1814 rejected because SW was ill on 9/8/1814 and first advised VN of this two days later (SW→VN, 11/8/1814) whereas ltr gives no hint of SW being ill. 1831 presumed unlikely because no 1831 correspondence between SW and VN survives. Also, 1825 is about the time when VN's daughter Mary Victoria Novello, 1809–1898, from 1828 Mary Cowden-Clarke, was sent to school in Boulogne, *see Cowden-Clarke Life* p 25, and ref. to SW sounding his 'own trumpet' is consistent with the appearance of a paragraph in *The Examiner* on 14/8/1825 regarding SW's *Confitebor, see* SW→VN, 12/8/1825.

[487] Although SW earlier had used the nickname 'Mr Pug' to refer to himself, at this time 'Pug' clearly refers to someone else who has not been identified.

argumentation'.[488] SW is convinced that he and VN are not far apart on essential matters of religion.

SW→VN   Euston St   **17/8/1825**
BL Add 11729 f 274; *O*   The enclosed will increase your Respect
☞ Wed 17 Aug; pmk 1825
   SW encloses a letter [not preserved] just received from the 'egregious ass' WH. SW sends VN a 'new parody upon the favourite old song Sweet Willie O', directed at WH. As VN did not call yesterday [16/8/1825] SW is unlikely to see him before Sunday [21/8/1825]. Sarah [SS] inquires if VN wishes to stay overnight then.

SW→William Hone[489]   Euston St   **18/8/1825**
MA DDWes/6/103; *O*   'Ingratium si dixeris, omnia dicis!'—and I should
☞ 18/8/1825
   SW thanks William Hone [author, 1780–1842] for 'the singularly kind remark' with which he ended his short memoir of SW [published in the 28/7/1825 weekly instalment of Hone's periodical *The Every-Day Book*]. Hone has flattered SW by describing him as one 'without guile' but has nonetheless given him the highest praise. SW would have made a 'wretched' lawyer and a worse courtier, as experience has taught him that nothing is worth a lie. Hone has pronounced him 'a good man': SW lays no claim to goodness in 'what is usually called a moral sense', but feels gratification at any opportunity to relieve mental or bodily pain and abhorrence at inflicting it without necessity. In the religious sense, however, he 'shrinks into self-annihilation', which he can best express by quoting 'a consoling verse' ('Might I in thy sight appear') by his 'late dear and inestimable father' [CW]. CW Jr is alive and in good health; at present he is either at Bristol or in Wales.

SW→VN   Euston St   **19/8/1825**
BL Add 11729 f 277; *O*   I am not worth the 30 Variations at this present
☞ 'Friday night'; pmk 19/8/1825 (a Friday)
   At this moment SW is not worth the '30 Variations' [JSB's *Goldberg Variations*]. He 'willingly made over' his only manuscript copy to VN and has mislaid his [presumably printed] French copy. VN should bring anything that he

---

[488] The enclosure possibly was the document in SW's handwriting now at BL Add 11729 f 302, which SW headed 'In one of the numerous controversies between John Wesley and his puny antagonists, being accused of evasion and shifting, he thus replies:'.

[489] Ltr addressed to 'Dear Sir'. Hone identified as recipient because he published the short memoir of SW mentioned in ltr.

thinks palatable. SW will bring the song he spoke to VN about, which he prefers to the song 'in A' [not identified] that tickled VN's fancy. SW cannot agree with the 'regal organist' [Attwood] that the piano is emperor of all keyed instruments and wishes that 'Mr Pug's organ were half as good as his piano'.

SW wrote [not preserved] to the editor [Richard Mackenzie Bacon] of the 'Quarterly' [*QMMR*] to ask if he will insert SW's reply [to that magazine's review of his Morning and Evening Service] but has not yet had an answer. SW suspects that 'H' [WH] has put Bacon up to evasion or refusal. In any case SW will give his paper to VN's friend [Charles Cowden] Clarke [author, 1787–1877, from 1828 VN's son-in-law], as SW feels obliged to call attention to WH's 'extraordinary conduct'.

Sam [SSW] will be with SW and VN on Sunday [21/8/1825]. SSW's voice 'betrays symptoms of anti-vellutism' [breaking, a reference to Giovanni Velluti, Italian castrato, 1781–1861, who made his London début in the King's Theatre on 3/6/1825] and he soon will need to start shaving. VN should bring his song 'If in that breast so good and pure', which is a great favourite of SW and which SSW could sing if transposed. [John] Harding is fond of vocal music. They will need to 'cackle him out a stave or two' if they wish to be invited again.

SW→VN   **about 26/8/1825?**

BL Add 11729 f 281; *O*   As I mean to leave town on Thursday for my trip
ltr undated[490]

Since SW last saw VN, Sir James Gardiner has sent SW an 'irresistible invitation' [not preserved]. SW means to leave London on Thursday [1/9/1825] for his trip, returning 'tomorrow fortnight' [he appears to have returned to London from Winchester on Saturday 10/9/1825]. He conveys this information exclusively to VN as he does not like to 'prate' about his whereabouts.

SW encloses 'two more prime proofs of the pot calling the kettle black arse'. They are examples, supplied by SSW, of harmony from [WH's] canon 'Audivi vocem', commemorating Parson [Thomas] Rennell [1787–1824] who died 'a few months ago' [in fact, on 30/6/1824].

SW has seen [Henry] Phillips [bass singer, 1801–1876] and has 'initiated' him in the air 'Confessio et Magnificentia' from SW's *Confitebor*. Phillips is delighted with it. SW hopes to 'get him at the Oratorio' [concert]. [Henry] Robertson says Phillips asked too much last season, but the Oratorio managers should be able to 'squeeze out' an extra £10/10/- or £21 'for the credit of a

---

[490] Ltr presumably >SW→VN, 12/8/1825, in which SW says that he has been invited by Sir James Gardiner to spend a week in Hampshire. SW visited Gardiner in September 1825 and again in October 1825. It has not been determined to which one of these visits ltr refers, so ltr has been entered ambiguously both at about 26/8/1825 (referring to a planned departure on Thursday 1/9/1825 and a planned return to London about 10/9/1825), and at about 7/10/1825 (referring to a planned departure on Thursday 13/10/1825 and a planned return to London about 22/10/1825).

national concern'. Robertson thinks that 'Confessio et Magnificentia' and [Mary Anne] Paton's 'Fidelia' [a soprano aria from *Confitebor*] would form a 'Jachin and Boaz' [the two pillars of King Solomon's temple]. One of the [*Confitebor*] choruses might be heard 'with patience' even after the hunting chorus from [Weber's] *Der Freischütz*. It is lamentable that [George Eugene] Griffin says that SW cannot write and that WH 'pisses upon' what SW has written.

SW→VN   Euston St   **31/8/1825**
BL Add 11729 f 279; *O*   You will find the enclosed to be another damning
▣ Wed 31 Aug; pmk 1825
SW encloses a letter [not preserved] from WH declaring that he has 'no interest whatever' in the *QMMR*. SW regards this as 'another damning proof' of WH's falsehood in declaring that he had nothing to do with the review [there of SW's Morning and Evening Service]. SW has decided not to submit an article for the consideration of the editor of that magazine [Richard Mackenzie Bacon]. VN's friend [Charles Cowden] Clarke is the 'only man' to give SW's paper to the world, and SW will send it to him. SW met Miss Jennings, an 'agreeable old maid', at [William] Drummer's yesterday [30/8/1825]. She boasts of VN's 'acquaintance and approbation'.

SW→SS   Winchester   **9/9/1825**
BL Add 35012 f 57   Well Pexy, I could not be as good as my Word
▣ 9/9/1825
SW was not able to return today as he had hoped, as he could not book an inside place in either of today's stagecoaches. He is thus obliged to stay another day. He writes from the house of a 'very excellent clergyman', where [Sir James] Gardiner's sons are at school, and where they all dined and passed yesterday evening [8/9/1825]. SW expects to come [to London] tomorrow [10/9/1825] by the telegraph stagecoach. SS should meet him at the White Horse Cellar at 4 pm. In case of any accidents, she should instruct [Edward] Rowlands to go to the [Camden] Chapel [to substitute for SW as organist] on Sunday morning and afternoon [11/9/1825].

SW→VN   Euston St   **12/9/1825**
BL Add 11729 f 283; *O*   Send me the Norwich Editor's foolish Letter as soon
▣ Mon 12 Sep & 🖎→①
VN should send SW as soon as possible 'the foolish letter' [not preserved] from the 'Norwich editor' [Richard Mackenzie Bacon] as SW 'must quote a part of it'. SW enjoyed himself and was kept busy at [Sir James] Gardiner's and had little leisure to prepare his 'retort courteous to the worthy Mus. Bac.' [WH]. Gardiner knows WH and believes that SW is right to expose him.
On the journey to Winchester SW heard that SW and VN's 'excellent friend'

Miss [Susannah] Ogle [c1761–1825] had died.[491] SW desires confirmation of this [in fact, she had died on 19/2/1825]. WL is out of town, but could have given SW the address of one of her brothers [John Savile Ogle, 1767–1853, or Henry Bertram Ogle, 1774–1835].[492] SW fears that Miss Ogle may have died ranking him 'among the many ungrateful wretches whom she had served essentially'.[493]

Sir James introduced SW to several 'prime sensible folk' including the Rear Admiral of the Navy, Earl Northesk [William Carnegie, 1758–1831]. SW played two services at [Winchester] Cathedral in the absence of [George William] Chard [organist, singer and composer, 1765–1849] who had gone to the [Three Choirs Festival] meeting at Hereford. SW had met Chard previously and found him to be 'much less disagreeable than musicians in general'. Next Sunday [18/9/1825] SW dines at 5 pm with 'Mr Pug' [not identified] at Kentish Town. They would be delighted to have VN join them.

SW→VN Euston St **14/9/1825**
BL Add 11729 f 285; O[494] As you jaw me for my Gentility I send you some
📧 Wed 14 Sep & 🖂→ⅰ

SW's 'classical brethren' [members of the Classical Harmonists' Society] have ordered three of his 'books' [copies of SW's Morning and Evening Service], which have been sent. SW asks how he should approach them for payment, as he still owes money to his engraver.

SW will now turn his attention to his 'train of compliments to the Mus. Bac.' [WH], and asks the name of the magazine in which [Charles Cowden] Clarke is concerned. SW intends to preface his reply to the *QMMR* with a short address explaining why he is submitting a paper [to Clarke's journal] that was originally intended for another publication.

---

[491] Susannah Ogle, of Bath, had subscribed for six copies of SW's c1806 corrected edition of George Frederick Pinto's *Four Canzonets and a Sonata* and for the SW/CFH edition of the '48' and VN's 1811 *A Collection of Sacred Music*. A manuscript of her 1811 adaptation 'to English words' of five airs by Beethoven, which she made for the Bath violinist John David Loder and subsequently presented to the Bath composer and pianist James W. Windsor, is at RCM Ms 33/1.

[492] Susannah Ogle's sister Esther Jane Ogle, c1775–1817, was the second wife of Richard Brinsley Sheridan, whose first wife, Elizabeth Ann Linley, was WL's sister.

[493] An annotation on Sarah→'Dear Madam', 26/6/1818?, suggests that that letter may have been written to Miss Ogle; if so, she may have assisted SW in some way after his release from Blacklands.

[494] The address portion of ltr is at EUL Dk 7.38 3.

[495] SW may be referring to Byrd's antiphons in the Fitzwilliam collection that he subsequently proposed to publish by subscription; *see* SW→RG, 4/4/1826.

SW has had a 'rich treat in chewing the cud' of musical examples by [William] Byrd [English composer, c1540–1623].[495] They turn out to be full of SW's own 'errors and heresies', according to 'his holiness Pope Horsley' [WH].

SW→VN   Euston St   **19/9/1825**
BL Add 11729 f 286; *O*   I have just received the enclosed.—You must instruct
⌨ Mon 19 Sep & 📖→⬛
SW has just received the enclosed letter [not preserved, evidently from Wait] and wants VN's instructions on how to deal with it. It appears preferable that VN write to Cambridge about it, as 'Dr W' [Wait] indicates that the matter is urgent. SW missed VN yesterday [18/9/1825, at the dinner in Kentish Town, *see* SW→VN, 12/9/1825]; 'Pug' and [John] Harding were 'in high order'.

SW→VN   **22/9/1825**
BL Add 11729 f 288; *O*   If either you or I had chosen to play 'Life's subtle
⌨ Thu 22 Sep; pmk 1825
If either SW or VN had chosen to be underhanded, they might now be half as rich as [William] Hawes. SW is inclined to agree with VN that Wait 'voted for the manoeuvring system' merely to defeat the self-serving actions of 'Clarke' [John Clarke-Whitfeld, from 1821 professor of music at Cambridge University]. SW does not object to putting the question directly to the University [of Cambridge] and will not hesitate to do so.
[Henry] Robertson invited SW to meet VN tomorrow [23/9/1825] to see 'the organ intended for the [Covent Garden] theatre'. SW will bring his *Confitebor* with him to notify Robertson that he intends to bring [a performance of] it forward. SW is going shortly to Brentford and will give VN's compliments to [Sir Robert] Peat.

SW→VN   Euston St   **3/10/1825**
BL Add 11729 f 290; *O*   A Perusal of the enclosed, just now received, will
⌨ Mon 3 Oct; pmk 1825
VN's perusal of the enclosure [not preserved, evidently from Wait] will 'put matters in a new light concerning the necessary plan of operations' [regarding SW's obtaining authorisation from Cambridge University to copy Fitzwilliam manuscripts]. SW is sure that VN will understand Wait's arguments and hopes that the plan will be satisfactory to VN; otherwise SW will 'stumble at the threshold and never be able to enter the house'. He hopes to come to VN by 7 pm on Thursday [6/10/1825] but desires VN's immediate reply. [Sir James] Gardiner has invited SW to Winchester next week. SW is uncertain whether to accept.

SW→VN   **about 7/10/1825?**

BL Add 11729 f 281; *O*   As I mean to leave town on Thursday for my trip
ltr undated[496]

Since SW last saw VN, Sir James Gardiner has sent SW an 'irresistible invitation' [not preserved]. SW means to leave London on Thursday [13/10/1825] for his trip, returning 'tomorrow fortnight' [he appears to have returned to London from Winchester on Saturday 22/10/1825]. He conveys this information exclusively to VN as he does not like to 'prate' about his whereabouts.

SW encloses 'two more prime proofs of the pot calling the kettle black arse'. They are examples, supplied by SSW, of harmony from [WH's] canon 'Audivi vocem', commemorating Parson [Thomas] Rennell [1787–1824] who died 'a few months ago' [in fact, on 30/6/1824].

SW has seen [Henry] Phillips [bass singer] and has 'initiated' him in the air 'Confessio et Magnificentia' from SW's *Confitebor*. Phillips is delighted with it. SW hopes to 'get him at the Oratorio' [concert]. [Henry] Robertson says Phillips asked too much last season, but the Oratorio managers should be able to 'squeeze out' an extra £10/10/- or £21 'for the credit of a national concern'. Robertson thinks that 'Confessio et Magnificentia' and [Mary Anne] Paton's 'Fidelia' [a soprano aria from *Confitebor*] would form a 'Jachin and Boaz' [the two pillars of King Solomon's temple]. One of the [*Confitebor*] choruses might be heard 'with patience' even after the hunting chorus from [Weber's] *Der Freischütz*. It is lamentable that [George Eugene] Griffin says that SW cannot write and that WH 'pisses upon' what SW has written.

SW→VN   **about 8/10/1825**

BL Add 11729 f 303   I send what I promised, & what I hope you may approve.
ltr undated[497]

SW encloses what he promised [evidently a draft of a letter, not preserved, to Thomas le Blanc, vice-chancellor of Cambridge University] and hopes that VN will approve it. SW believes it would appear better if the letter were enclosed in a frank and asks if VN can procure one. If Wait is displeased by SW

---

[496] Ltr presumably >SW→VN, 12/8/1825, in which SW says that he has been invited by Sir James Gardiner to spend a week in Hampshire. SW visited Gardiner in September 1825 and again in October 1825. It has not been determined to which one of these visits ltr refers, so ltr has been entered ambiguously both at about 26/8/1825 (referring to a planned departure on Thursday 1/9/1825 and a planned return to London about 10/9/1825), and at about 7/10/1825 (referring to a planned departure on Thursday 13/10/1825 and a planned return to London about 22/10/1825).

[497] Ltr placed here because it was written presumably while SW was awaiting Wait's response to SW's suggestion that SW write to le Blanc. Wait's favourable reply presumably received 10/10/1825 and mentioned in SW→VN, 10/10/1825.

approaching le Blanc directly, SW cannot help it. He thinks, with VN, that it is the most honest thing to do, and that le Blanc 'will prefer openness of conduct'.

SW→VN   **10/10/1825**

BL Add 11729 f 292; *O*   Wait accedes to my addressing the Vice Chancellor
☞ 'Monday night'; pmk 11/10/1825 (a Tuesday)

Wait [in a letter to SW, not preserved] accedes to SW addressing the vice-chancellor [of Cambridge University, Thomas le Blanc]. Wait wants VN to inform his friend [John Lucius] Dampier [1793–1853, barrister and fellow of King's College, Cambridge; his 18/1/1825 letter to VN regarding VN's catalogue of the Fitzwilliam manuscripts is in the Brotherton Library, University of Leeds] that VN will let SW transcribe music from composers [in the Fitzwilliam collection] that VN does not plan to edit himself. Wait's letter was kind and encouraging: Wait thinks that SW's 'point at Cambridge will be carried without any material opposition'.

SW leaves tomorrow [11/10/1825] for Winchester and hopes to return by 'the latter end of next week'. VN should write to him at the Winchester post office.

SW has finished 'his work with Horsley' [SW's reply to WH]. SW lent the manuscript to [Rev. Henry] Delafite, who promised to pass it on to VN at Miss Campbell's [not identified] on Friday [15/10/1825].

SW→SS   Winchester   **20/10/1825**

BL Add 35012 f 59   I hope that nothing bad has prevented my receiving
☞ Thu 20 Oct={1814,1825,1831}[498]

SW hopes that no bad reason prevented him from receiving a letter from SS yesterday [19/10/1825]. He was displeased not to receive one today. He leaves Winchester tomorrow [21/10/1825] about 9 am and hopes to reach Bagshot [Surrey] by 1 pm to meet 'Pug', who is likely to reproach him for not being there earlier, as they will have little time to see Windsor Castle. SW does not know at what time on Saturday [22/10/1825] he will return to London; it will be as early as he can.

---

[498] Assigned to 1825 because SW planned to be in Winchester on 20/10/1825 (*see* SW→VN, 10/10/1825). 1814 can be excluded because SW was in Norwich on 20/10/1814 (*see* SW→SS, 16/10/1814). 1831 considered unlikely as no information is available to suggest that SW travelled in October 1831.

SW→VN   Euston St   **24/10/1825**
BL Add 11729 f 232; O^{499} I this day received the enclosed, and you will find
☞ 'Monday 24th'[500]
SW today received the enclosed letter [not preserved] from Wait, who SW believes 'states accurately the real fact'. Whether SW is to receive any benefit from, or should continue his visits to, [the Fitzwilliam collection in] Cambridge now depends greatly upon VN.

SW→Street   **30/10/1825**
MA [uncatalogued]; O   I know of nothing at present likely to prevent
☞ '30 October'; pmk 1825
SW is unaware of anything which would prevent him meeting Street and Mr Lewis [not identified] on 8/11/1825, 'the vigil of Lord Mayor's Day' [9/11/1825], at George's Coffee House [in the Strand] at 5 pm.

CW Jr→Langshaw Jr   **1/11/1825**
GEU W/L; *Wainwright* p 83–84   Mr Mason last Sunday brought me your Letter
☞ 1/11/1825
CW Jr would have sent Langshaw Jr 'the set of Lord Fitzwilliams's Scarlatti' [CW Jr's edition of Domenico Scarlatti's *Thirty sonatas, for the harpsichord or piano-forte...from manuscripts in the possession of Lord Viscount Fitzwilliam* published *c*1800 by Robert Birchall, *see* CW Jr→a sister of Wait, 14/6/1825], but Birchall unfortunately destroyed the plates because the publication did not have a good sale. CW Jr had great trouble in selecting the sonatas. All [Lord Fitzwilliam's] 'curious musical library' is left to King's College, Cambridge. SW and [William] Hawes 'mean to publish' this library 'by subscriptions'.

SW→VN   Euston St   **23/11/1825**
BL Add 11729 f 294; O   I hope by this Time you are become convalescent
☞ Wed 23 Nov; pmk 1825
SW considers VN's 'utter aversion from all medicine' to be 'extreme' and hopes that VN is convalescing. Wait's 'long silence' puzzles SW. It would be

---

[499] Ltr lacks SW's signature and appears to be incomplete.

[500] Assigned to 24/10/1825 for the following reason. The context of Wait and SW writing to VN about visits to Cambridge limits ltr's possible years to 1825 and 1826. In 1825 Monday was the 24th in January and October; and in 1826 Monday was the 24th in April and July. Ltr presumably >Wait→SW, 11/5/1825, which preceded SW's visits to the Fitzwilliam collection in Cambridge, and <'Jubal'→Editor, *The Harmonicon*, 25/4/1826, by when VN's and SW's different collections entitled *The Fitzwilliam Music* had been announced.

'vexatious' if SW were to be denied 'all advantage' resulting from his labour of copying 100 pages of [Fitzwilliam] manuscripts and his waiving other important engagements. SW wishes to avoid appearing disrespectful of Wait but will be gratified if VN's friend [John Lucius] Dampier [*see* SW→VN, 10/10/1825] could use his influence so that SW's 'original intention may be carried into effect'. SW leaves to VN and Dampier the choice of mode to follow so that SW can realise the rewards of his efforts.

After what VN's friend [Charles Cowden Clarke] said to SW at one of VN's [Classical Harmonists'] concerts, SW is 'a little surprised' by the apparent difficulty of having his commentary upon WH's 'panegyric' [the *QMMR* review of SW's Morning and Evening Service] inserted in November's *London Magazine*. Clarke's negotiations with the magazine's anonymous editor [Henry Southern, 1799–1853] to print SW's commentary apparently were unsuccessful. SW's understanding from VN that Clarke had 'paramount authority' over the magazine [the firm of Hunt and Clarke were the magazine's publishing agent] clearly is erroneous.

SW→VN   Euston St   **12/12/1825**
BL Add 11729 f 298; *O*   Do you feel any Objection to declare in writing
◻ Mon 12 Dec & 🖘→⬚
SW asks if VN has any objection to declaring in writing that he intends to publish, in his selection from the Fitzwilliam collection, only compositions by 'the Italian masters', and that publishing other works in the collection is open to anyone who obtains 'a grace' [from Cambridge University] for that purpose. Such a declaration should remove all obstacles to the attainment of SW's object [to publish a selection himself], to which VN always has been well disposed. SW thinks that VN would have supplied such a declaration months ago if he had realised that it would have been SW's 'infallible passport to the library'. SW is preparing parts for the chorus 'Magna Opera Domini' [from his *Confitebor*] for VN's 'next evening' [of the Classical Harmonists' Society, on 5/1/1826], and will forward them [to VN] in due course.

SW→VN   **29/12/1825**
BL Add 11729 f 300; *O*   This is the first moment I could secure for noticing
◻ Thu 29 Dec={1814,1825,1831} & VN at Shacklewell Green[501]→⬚
SW presumes that VN intends to 'muster' [members of the Classical Harmonists' Society] next Thursday [5/1/1826] 'selon la règle' and encloses the orchestral parts of 'Magna Opera Domini' [*see* SW→VN, 12/12/1825]. He assumes that two copies of each part will suffice.

SW has been entrusted for the next three years with the musical education of a 'lad' [presumably Thomas Francis, 1812–1887; *see* SW→Sarah, 29/5/1826] who has a good soprano voice. This commitment will take SW up to his

---

[501] VN lived at Shacklewell Green in the years 1823–1825.

climacteric, if he survives that long. As yet his pupil sings mostly by ear, but can get through two or three songs, including 'Angels ever bright' [from Handel's *Theodora*], which suggests that he is capable of 'high improvement'. SW plans to bring him on Thursday.

SW dined with Burgh [presumably Rev. Allatson Burgh] on Christmas Day and was sorry to hear that VN's 'indisposition' prevented him from joining them.

SW→'Sir'[502]   Euston St   **23/1/1826**
MA DDWF/15/31; *O*   I hasten to acquaint You that several of my Friends
☙ 23/1/1826

Several friends of SW and friends of his 'young pupil' [presumably Thomas Francis] particularly wish that the pupil may be permitted to sing twice at the concert on the '6th inst' [i.e., the New Choral Fund's 6/2/1826 Annual Concert at the English Opera House, Strand]. 'Parties are forming' to come to hear this pupil; they expect to hear him sing two songs. SW asks the recipient to convey this information to the committee. SW is prepared to contribute [to the concert] an 'extemporaneous piece' on the organ.

SW→CW Jr   **2/2/1826**
MA DDWes/6/46; *O*   Here are two Tickets—the Committee have behaved as
☙ 2/2/1826

SW encloses two tickets [for the New Choral Fund concert on 6/2/1826]. 'The committee have behaved as committees always do, pitifully and shabbily' in allowing SW only four tickets, each to admit two people to the pit. SW asks CW Jr to return the tickets if he decides not to attend.

Sarah→John Hall   **3/2/1826**
MA DDWes/6/98   I have received thro the medium of my good friend
☙ 3/2/1826

Sarah gives news of CW Jr. It is 'a great blessing' that he is 'so strongly attached' to the Methodists. Their hearts 'yearn' for her 'other brother' [SW] but rejoice that he is no longer a Roman Catholic and that he often has 'deep convictions'. SW was 'the child of many tears and prayers'. If he 'had had a good wife with any sense of religion, he would not have fallen into the evils we deeply lament'. Wait, who is John Hall's cousin, called the other day with 'a very bad account' of Mrs Wait [apparently Wait's mother, as Sarah→Mrs Roberts, 8/3/1826, MA DDWF/14/50, states that 'Dr Wait called some time ago with a very unfortunate report of his poor dear mother'].

---

[502] A plausible recipient is John Eames, who was secretary of the New Choral Fund.

Sarah will   **26/2/1826**

MA DDWF/14/49[503]   Being thro the Mercy of God in my Senses & Health
will dated 26/2/1826

Sarah appoints CW Jr her sole executor and bequeaths to him all that she dies
possessed of 'in the stocks and out of them'. She desires that CW Jr give £50 to
'William John Wesley [JWW] for having once released his poor father [SW] out
of a spunging house'. [Sarah does not explicitly revoke her will of 24/7/1804
and expresses no other wishes.]

William Holmes→SW   Euston St   **10/3/1826**

BL Add 35019 f 130   The Bishop of London is not a musical Man
▣ 10/3/1826

The Bishop of London [William Howley], who is 'not a musical man', has
asked William Holmes [clergyman, c1768–1833, at this time Sub-Dean of the
Chapel Royal] to state what he knows of SSW. Holmes is pleased to do this and
hopes that SSW may be successful [in his application to be organist of St
James's Chapel, Hampstead Road, according to EW's annotation on ltr]. Holmes
encloses a letter [not preserved] recently received from [William] Hawes and
suggests that SW should take this letter to Mr Ward [not identified].

SSW→Emett   **25/3/1826**

BL Add 35019 f 131   I write to let you know I have been appointed Organist
pmk 25/3/1826

SSW has been 'appointed organist of St James's Chapel, Hampstead Road'.
SW goes to Cambridge on Monday [27/3/1826].

SW→Sarah   Euston St   **27/3/1826**

MA DDWF/15/32   At last I have obtained the Address of the three Individuals
▣ Mon 27 Mar & 📷→{1820,1826}[504]

Parson [Alexander] d'Arblay [of Camden Chapel] had quite forgotten SW's
written request [not preserved] until SW chanced on him last Friday [24/3/1826]
but now has supplied the addresses that Sarah requested. They are: Mrs
[Charlotte Francis] Barrett [1786–1870], 1 Bellevue Place, Richmond; Miss
Burney, 28 Clipstone Street, Fitzroy Square; and Mme [Frances] d'Arblay,
Bolton Street, Mayfair.

SW is just setting off for Cambridge. He hopes that Sarah and CW Jr are well
and means to call on them on his return from Cambridge, which he anticipates
will be next Saturday [1/4/1826].

---

[503] This document appears to be a draft or a copy.

[504] Assigned to 1826 because ltr addressed to Sarah at New Street, Dorset
Square, where she lived from 1825 until her death in 1828.

SW→RG   **4/4/1826**
BL Add 35013 f 84; *O*   I returned Yesterday from Cambridge
☐ 4/4/1826

SW returned yesterday [3/4/1826] from a busy but pleasant visit to Cambridge.
He received 'the most flattering encouragement' towards his intended
publication of [William] Byrd's 'excellent antiphons' [SW's transcriptions of
motets from Byrd's *Gradualia*]. SW is anxious to know how Mr Lawrence [not
identified] is getting on with his copying of the choral parts [of SW's *Confitebor*]
for the [first] performance on 4/5/1826. SW hopes that Mr Lawrence will 'name
an early day' for assembling those of his friends who had promised SW their aid.

R. Carter→SW   Euston St   **11/4/1826**
BL Add 35027 f 89   It was my intention not to play in a public orchestra
☐ 11/4/1825 or 11/4/1826[505]

Carter had not intended to play orchestrally in public until he had made his
appearance as a 'public performer', but the desire to serve SW [by playing in
SW's benefit concert on 4/5/1826 in the New Argyll Rooms] has outweighed
other considerations. If Mr [Charles] Saust [German flautist and composer,
*b*1773, who arrived in London in 1800] is to be SW's other flautist, Carter will
willingly play second flute to him; if the other flautist is to be [Charles]
Nicholson [1795–1837], it perhaps will be 'prudent' for Carter not to play at all,
and if it is anyone else, not to play a secondary part. Carter hopes that SW will
not think him 'fastidious' and is convinced that SW knows the 'tender thread on
which the reputation of a young man entering the world hangs'. In expectation
of SW's answer, Carter holds himself in readiness for 4/5/1826.

SW→George Smart   Euston St   **13/4/1826**
DLC Mss Div, M F Hales Coll.,   I find that as I should not require the Services
Acc. 10,735, v 1 p 29; *O*   of your Pupils till the second Act
☐ Thu 13 Apr & ✉→{1820,1826}[506]

As SW will not require Sir George Smart's pupils to perform until the 'second
Act' [in the chorus of SW's *Confitebor* at SW's concert on 4/5/1826], when the
pupils' performance at the theatre [probably in Weber's *Oberon* at Covent

---

[505] The handwriting of the last digit of the year is unclear. Ltr assigned to
11/4/1826 because of ref. to SW's concert on 4 May. Such a concert took place
on 4/5/1826 but no such concert is known to have taken place on 4/5/1825.

[506] Assigned to 1826 because ltr presumably concerns SW's 4/5/1826 concert, of
which (according to the review in *The Harmonicon*, v 4 no. 42 (June 1826)
p 131) the second act, consisting entirely of SW's *Confitebor*, included a chorus
in addition to the orchestra that performed in the first act. No event is known to
have taken place about April or May 1820 that would have caused SW to
require Sir George Smart's pupils to perform.

Garden] will have ended, he presumes that Smart will have no objection to SW announcing Smart's pupils [in press advertisements]. SW desires a prompt reply, as he is 'scolded' by his friends that his advertisements are not 'in greater forwardness'.

SW→Sarah   Euston St   27/4/1826
MA DDWF/15/33; *O*   Your Hint is very friendly, and I accept it as such
⬛ Thu 27 Apr & 🖳→{1820,1826}[507]

SW thanks Sarah for her hint, but she has been misinformed: he has no expectation of receiving as much as one third of £300 by his first publication from the Fitzwilliam collection [of his edition of Byrd's antiphons]. He would consider even £100 a tolerable sum, although he hopes that efforts will be made at the University [of Cambridge] to promote future publications from this source. He asks her to divulge the author of 'so vague and silly a report'.

SW will write immediately to Lord Pomfret [George Fermor, 1768–1830, third Earl of Pomfret]. SW does not know how far the Earl's generosity may extend to SW, but he doubts, from an anecdote told to him by 'Sam' [SSW], that Pomfret will be over-generous. However, Pomfret's influence may be 'serviceable'.

CW Jr should not worry that SW is unversed in the etiquette that titled men 'expect and insist on'. Sarah is aware that SW 'preaches sermons' [gives lectures] on Fridays [at the Royal Institution] among great lords and ladies, and is therefore serving his time to 'the propriety of Ps and Qs'.

SW is 'besieged on all sides' with preparations for [his concert] next Thursday [4/5/1826]. He wishes to be remembered to CW Jr and asks Sarah to tell CW Jr that SW desires to have CW Jr's glee 'Arno's Vale' copied out as soon as possible [possibly so that it can be performed as part of one of SW's Royal Institution lectures, *see* CW Jr→Elizabeth Isabella Spence, 4/7/1827].

Sarah memorandum   1/5/1826
MA DDWF14/51   Attended the Missionary Meeting at the City Road!
memo dated 1/5/1826

Sarah attended the meeting of the Wesleyan Missionary Society in the City Road [Methodist] Chapel [on 1/5/1826]. Revisiting this chapel produced mixed feelings. Her 'distracted family' presents 'a melancholy wreck': her 'poor brother' SW, his 'unprincipled legitimates' and his 'forlorn illegitimates', his 'unhappy wife and pitiable mistress'. All of SW's family seem to pursue 'silly implacable and undeserved hatred'. This is in contrast to the love Sarah received from her 'pious and tender ancestors' and the kindness with which 'we' [presumably Sarah and CW Jr] 'were hailed by the dear Methodists on our entering'. Sarah still has friends amongst the Methodists. 'Poor dear Charles' [CW Jr] is 'esteemed by them'.

---

[507] Assigned to 1826 because of ref. to SW's first publication of music in the Fitzwilliam collection.

SW→**Domenico Dragonetti** 4/5/1826

BL Add 56411 f 18; *O*   I hope and trust that you will favour me
ref. to SW's 4/5/1826 concert 'this evening'; pmk 4/5/1826

SW hopes that Domenico Dragonetti [Italian double bass player, 1763–1846, from 1794 resident in London] will play in this evening's performance of SW's *Confitebor*. Otherwise it will 'lose a very material part of good effect'.

SW→**'The Musical Public'**   Euston St   8/5/1826

Russell preface   Having long been on the most friendly and intimate terms
Russell

Having 'long been on the most friendly and intimate terms' with the late 'excellent and ingenious composer' William Russell, SW accordingly embraced 'with equal pleasure and alacrity' the opportunity of serving his widow [Mary Ann Russell] by adapting the instrumental parts of William Russell's oratorio [*Job*] for the organ or pianoforte [*see* SW→Mary Ann Russell, 16/4/1825]. Because it is impossible 'to produce upon the organ the effect of stringed instruments', SW has had to alter many violin passages. He trusts that his adaptation will be found easy to perform.

'Jubal'→Editor, *The Harmonicon* 20/5/1826

Harmonicon v 4 no. 42 (June 1826) p 113   I am a subscriber to Mr Vincent
Harmonicon

'Jubal' [the pseudonym of a correspondent who writes from Hampstead] is a subscriber to VN's *The Fitzwilliam Music, being a Collection of Sacred Pieces, selected from Manuscripts of Italian Composers in the Fitzwilliam Museum.*[508] The 'peculiar nature' of this work, the first volume of which was praised in the February 1826 *Harmonicon*, 'could hardly be expected to repay' VN financially for 'the time, labour and expense' he consumed in preparing it for publication. 'Jubal' and others therefore 'read with surprise the announcement of another publication [presumably SW's printed proposal for an edition of Byrd's antiphons], compiled from the same source, and to be ushered forth' by SW 'under the same title' [i.e., under the title *The Fitzwilliam Music*, which SW used later in 1826 for his edition of Handel's *Three Hymns*].

'Jubal''s surprise was enhanced by his knowledge that VN 'had long been the intimate, the active, the tried friend' of SW. As 'Jubal' could not believe that 'mercantile rivalry' had arisen between VN and SW, he 'was at a loss to understand how two musical works of so confined a nature could be produced'

---

[508] The printed subscription list of VN's *The Fitzwilliam Music* does not give Hampstead as the address of any subscriber. The identity of 'Jubal' has not been discovered but may have been VN or one of his friends, as the next extant letter from SW to VN, SW→VN, 10/6/1830, appears to allude to their having been 'violently at variance', presumably regarding the subject that 'Jubal' brought to public attention in ltr.

advantageously to their editors at the same time. He 'took some pains' to inquire into the situation.

'Jubal' found that, although the Oxford and Cambridge agents for VN's work are the same as those announced for SW's work, VN 'has no concern whatever' with SW's work. It also appears that VN, in addition to his other 'acts of friendship', introduced SW to 'the university' [of Cambridge] and 'acquiesced in the grace' by which SW 'acquired the power of copying any part of the Fitzwilliam Manuscripts'. It 'need scarcely be added' that VN's friendly actions were undertaken 'in utter ignorance of the steps' that SW intended to follow to produce 'a rival publication'.

'Jubal' forbears to comment whether SW's actions are 'worthy of a respectable member of an enlighted profession', but trusts that the editor of *The Harmonicon* [William Ayrton] will 'submit the facts of the case to the musical public'.

SW→Sarah — Euston St — 26/5/1826

Dorset D/C00:G/C6   Mr Bond's Trustees it seems meditate Hostility.
☑ Fri 26 May & 🖼→{1820,1826}[509]

The trustees [in bankruptcy] of Mr Bond [SW's wine-merchant] seem to 'meditate hostility'. The man who called on Sarah [Mr Griffiths, *see* Sarah→Thomas Marriott, 27/5/1826] does not believe that SW cannot pay the £80 he owes to Bond. Griffiths says that Bond is prepared to swear that SW promised payment when they met in Margate [on 3/8/1824, *see* SW→SS, 3/8/1824]. SW made no such promise but told Bond that he would do all he could, as soon as possible. It is absurd to expect SW to be able to pay such a bill except 'in very small and slow quantities'. Mr Porter, who unwittingly brought SW 'into dire mischief', and whom SW has already consulted, will 'leave no quirk of law untried' to avoid bad consequences.

SW fears that Sarah gives the 'Methodist professor' [Griffiths] 'too much credit for Christian forbearance': SW has 'never found much open profession of piety, without abundance of deceit'. Prompt action is required to check the people who are 'bent upon summary proceedings' against SW.

Sarah→Thomas Marriott — 27/5/1826

MA DDWF/14/52   I should have been happy to see you when I called
☑ Sat 27 May; pmk 1826

Sarah seeks the address of Mr Griffiths, 'the son of the worthy minister', who visited the other day and is 'employed to collect the debts of Mr Bond the wine merchant'. Bond has 'stopped payment' and 'put his affairs in the hands of a Mr Jones'. 'We' [Sarah and CW Jr] paid the balance due Bond for purchases from SGW's time which Bond had neglected to send to her. However, Bond 'has a large debt due of ten years standing' from Sarah's 'unfortunate brother' SW.

---

[509] Assigned to 1826 because ltr >SW→SS, 3/8/1824, which mentions SW meeting Bond at Margate.

Bond had said that he would 'never trouble' SW, as Bond had been assured that if SW ever became prosperous he had 'the honesty to defray' the debt.

Sarah told Griffiths that it was 'utterly impossible' for SW to repay this debt: he has great difficulty paying CLW £25 per annum. Moreover, Griffiths would not get the money if he went 'to law', although SW might go 'to the Bench' [a sponging house or prison], which could 'bring back his malady' and 'shorten his days'. Griffiths assured Sarah that 'no such measures would be taken' against SW; however, Sarah has just received a letter from SW [SW→Sarah, 26/5/1826] in which he says that 'they intend to proceed against him'. This would be 'as cruel as it would be useless', as SW is 'really unable to do anything just now'.

Sarah grieves that, while SW lives in a sinful way, God 'may see fit to bring this evil' upon him. Until SW 'returns to the path of righteousness misery must follow'. Sarah nevertheless wants 'to avert the dreadful recurrence' of SW's malady. She asks Thomas Marriott [1786–1852, at this time a retired businessman with antiquarian interests concerning Methodism, brother of William Marriott Jr] if he has any influence with Jones that could soften his demands. SW's arrest 'at this moment would so overset his shattered nerves' that he would be 'totally disqualified for his profession', which he pursues indefatigably.

It would be 'a great disgrace to the cause of Methodism' if SW were imprisoned. Sarah fears that SW's head 'would immediately be affected' and implores Marriott's assistance.

SW→Sarah Euston St 29/5/1826
MA DDWF/15/34   I am sorry you should suspect me of an illiberal Sneer

▣ Mon 29 May & 🖂→{1820,1826}[510]

SW is sorry if Sarah suspects him of sneering at any religious body. His remark [that he 'never found much open profession of piety, without abundance of deceit', in SW→Sarah, 26/5/1826] was a general observation and the result of 'no very pleasant experience'. He has found that those who made the least profession of piety were more candid and honest than those who 'had the law and the gospel perpetually' in their mouths. He reminds Sarah of their 'sagacious father's contempt and abhorrence of cant and extraordinary professions of sanctity', and also how severely CW criticised the hypocrisy of the lay preachers, to whom he attributed the breach between himself and JW. [George] Oliver's conduct is enough to prove how little gospel words are necessarily followed by gospel deeds.

SW has seen Mr Glover and, if he is right, SW has little to fear. Mr Porter is not so sanguine, but SW thinks that he [SW] knows more of the law than Porter. If the worst happened, it would result in the necessity of paying half the debt [owed to Bond, the wine-merchant, *see* SW→Sarah, 26/5/1826] and allowing two years [to pay the balance], which would reduce the debt from £80 to £40.

---

[510] Assigned to 1826 because ltr addressed to Sarah at New Street, Dorset Square, where she lived from 1825 until her death in 1828.

SW is glad that 'young [Thomas] Francis' has entertained Sarah and CW Jr. Francis has a good voice, of which the most must be made while it lasts, which SW fears will not be for long. If SW had had him [as a pupil] three years ago, he would have sung SW out of debt long ago.

SW has been copying the hymn that Sarah wanted and has almost finished it. Mrs Bradshaw's address is 4, 5 or 6 Lower Eaton Street, Pimlico, where 'old Attwood' [Thomas Attwood, Attwood's father, *see* Elizabeth Waller→SGW, 12/9/1782], 'another among my uncle's black sheep', lived for many years [at 20 Lower Eaton Street].

SW→Sarah   Euston St   **10/6/1826**
WBRR v 3 (Dec 1851) p 453   Here is the song you signified your wish to have.
WBRR: 'Saturday 10/6/1827', an incorrect date[511]
SW sends Sarah the song she desired [*see* SW→Sarah, 29/5/1826]. He thinks she said that the author was Sir John Suckling [poet, 1609–1642]. SW 'offered to play the Requiem' for [Carl Maria von] Weber [who died in London on 5/6/1826] on 'Friday next' [16/6/1826] at Moorfields [Roman Catholic] Chapel, but shall be 'neither surprised nor disappointed' if his offer is refused 'through the jealousy of S— and A—' [Sir George Smart, at whose home Weber died, and Attwood, who in fact presided at the organ in the Moorfields Chapel requiem service, which took place on 21/6/1826]. SW now is surprised only 'when people do right'.

SW→Sarah   Euston St   **14/6/1826**
MA DDWes/6/38   I have not the slightest Objection to appropriate
▪ Wed 14 Jun & 📷→{1820,1826}[512]
SW has no objection to using any revenue gained by Sarah securing subscriptions for his [proposed] publication [of Byrd's antiphons] to 'the lessening' of Mrs B's [not identified] demands. He pities the claimant but there is not much excuse for 'those two base legitimates' [CW III and JWW] who refused to assist when they could, and when they knew that SW could not. Sarah should ask Mrs [James] Ball of Duke Street, Grosvenor Square about the sums that he was robbed of by CLW's tradesmen, which 'sank every penny' that SW had in the Bank [of England].

SW will circulate news of CW Jr's 'robbery' by [the organ builder William] Allen, who has an infamous reputation for everything except voicing the reed stops of an organ. SW already is under a financial obligation to [William] Drummer and Street; otherwise he would apply to them for a loan and send Sarah the money.

---

[511] Assigned to Saturday 10/6/1826 because of ref. to Weber's death which occurred on 5/6/1826.

[512] Assigned to 1826 because of ref. to Weber's funeral that year.

SW is glad that [Thomas] Francis sang out well [*see* SW→Sarah, 29/5/1826]. Francis did not expect money for the engagement but probably would accept £1. The matter should rest with Mr Edmonds [not identified], as it was his party. [William] Hawes always used to get £3/3/- whenever SSW performed, and gave him nothing, not even thanks. SSW has 'a pretty good prospect' at being able to earn a good living, although in a profession that SW hates and despises.

The 'musical honours intended the German', the performance of Mozart's *Requiem* [at Moorfields Chapel for Weber's funeral], have been superseded by [the Rev. William] Poynter [1762–1827, at this time Vicar Apostolic of the London district], who will not allow more than 20 performers in the chapel at a time.

SW→Sarah   **8/7/1826?**

Fitzwm ltr 26   I have thrown out one 'silly', and trimmed a Word or two
📧 'Saturday noon'[513]

SW has made minor revisions to what he wrote [presumably the initial version of his response to 'Jubal'→Editor, *The Harmonicon*, 20/5/1826] and thinks that it is now more to Sarah's taste than before. He has retained the 'jest' that if his antagonist wishes to 'accompany his harp [Jubal was a harpist], perhaps only few would forbid the bans'. Sarah rightly supposes that SW does not want his libeller to hang himself: hanging is unjust except in cases of murder and 'infantile rape', where no mercy should be shown. SW puns that his 'squib' should now 'explode'.

SW→Sarah   Euston St   **29/7/1826**

Dorset D/C00:G/C6   I write to you in sorely perplexing Plight.
📧 29/7/1826

SW is in a 'sorely perplexing plight'. Nearly £40 is owed to him but he can get none of it. The organ builder [John] Gray owes him £10; £15 due to SSW is

---

[513] Assigned to 8/7/1826 for the following reason. Ltr presumably >1/7/1826 when the contents page of the July 1826 *Harmonicon*, no. 43, acknowledges receipt of SW's reply to 'Jubal' [not preserved] and announces its deferral 'till next month', noting that 'in the interim he shall hear from us'; and <1/8/1826 when the contents page of the August 1826 *Harmonicon*, no. 44, says that SW's 'letter does not appear, as promised, in the present number' because 'we wished him to abridge his communication, and to moderate some of his expressions, but he has declined complying with our request, in terms that do not shew much discretion'. Also ltr before SW→Sarah of Saturday 29/7/1826 on other subjects (although mentioning the attack on SW in the 'rascally *Harmonicon*'). Assigned to 8/7/1826 on the presumption that SW would have responded as soon as possible to *The Harmonicon*'s presumed request that he shorten and moderate his original letter replying to 'Jubal', and that ltr tells Sarah that SW has made some changes. However, the two following Saturdays have not been ruled out.

postponed; the 'ruffian' [Robert William] Elliston owes SW £4/4/- 'for lessons to a man whom he and his have used villainously'. SW would pay up to £2/2/- of 'usurious interest' to anyone who would advance him £20 for two months. He is now 'in utter distress, even for quotidian expenses', and SS is in 'so anxious and perturbed a state' that SW fears 'for her brain'. He wonders if Mr Gregory [*see* SGW→RG, 18/11/1812] would advance money 'on any terms', but an application to him could not come from SW, to whom Gregory has been 'rude'.

SW had planned to leave London for Cambridge on Monday [31/7/1826]. This is now out of the question: with all the assistance he needs, he 'must be detained' [in London] for another week. Some 'very unpleasant conclusions' are likely to be drawn from SW's failure to arrive in Cambridge 'on account of the jealousy' of VN's friends, who will attribute SW's absence to 'cowardice on account of the attack' on him 'in the rascally *Harmonicon*' ['Jubal'→Editor, *The Harmonicon*, 25/5/1826].

SW→SS   Castle Inn, Cambridge   **13/9/1826**
BL Add 35012 f 61   Where's my Tea & Sugar that you were to pack up
✉ 'Wednesday evening'; pmk 14/9/1826 (a Thursday)

SW did not find the tea and sugar that SS had agreed to pack to save expense. He wants to hear how their children are. He is making good progress in Cambridge and has already 'copied six famous fine hymn tunes from Handel's own manuscript' that are set to words by CW.[514] SS should send SW half a quire of 14-stave manuscript paper, as he wishes to transcribe a 'capital Mass of [Alessandro] Scarlatti' which, if it were to be copied on 12-stave paper, would lose 'half a sheet of paper all through'. Fish [MEW] will explain this.

The librarian [at Cambridge University] desires that 'a good bundle of proposals' [for the publication of SW's transcriptions of Byrd's antiphons in the Fitzwilliam Collection, *see* SW→Street, 25/5/1830] be sent immediately, as new arrivals [to the library] are expected daily, and many more proposals were wanted [for prospective subscribers] than were in the first bundle. The librarian feels that much may be done 'with expedition', and is 'much pleased' with the 'respectable list' [presumably of subscribers] that SW brought.

The oratorio *Gideon* [compiled by John Christopher Smith Jr, composer, 1712–1759, from his own and Handel's music, and first performed at Covent Garden on 10/2/1769] is not 'among the music in the library', but SW is sure that every note of Handel that he hopes to bring out has never been engraved, and will thus prove 'an entire novelty'.

SW has written [i.e., has transcribed music] today for eight hours without fatigue, and has decided not to dine on any day until the evening, in order to make the most of the light. By the time this letter arrives, SW hopes that some salmon or a dish of trout will be 'on the road' towards his two very attentive and

---

[514] As SW and Sarah subsequently (e.g., SW→Jackson, 8/11/1826, Sarah→John Gaulter, 25/10/1826) refer to three hymns that Handel set to CW's texts, SW's use of the word 'six' here appears to be a mistake.

obliging assistants. They are pleased that SW has decided not to work at the [Fitzwilliam] Museum on Sunday; it has done VN more harm than he is aware of. SW comments on the adverse consequences of sabbath-breaking.

SW expects that SS is doing her best with his 'cursed duns'. Some of these 'barking dogs'—including [William] Hodsoll, Powlett, Wright, and Tully the printer at 67 or 76 Fleet Street—have a better claim [for payment] than others.

SW is contented in Cambridge. The air is good, although not so good as in Gravesend, to where he promises that SS and the family will go in the Christmas holidays, if not before. He is inquiring about obtaining a goose to bring back to London with him on Saturday 23/9/1826. He asks SS to write with good news about 'the babes'; he is 'comparatively indifferent concerning other things'.

SW→SS   Cambridge   20/9/1826
BL Add 35012 f 63   I send the Bill as you wished, dated at 15 Days
☞ Wed 20 Sep; pmk 1826

SW encloses the bill. It is dated at 15 days from the present, so will need to be paid by 5/10/1826. SW now has only £1/6/- remaining. He has had more expense than if Wait or the 'young man' had come, but that would have interrupted his working day and he could not have transcribed half of what he has now done. Because SS failed to pack tea and sugar, he has been obliged to drink tea at his landlady's charge. SW breakfasted once at the home of 'Captain Henslow' [Edward Prentice Henslowe, who had married Cecilia Maria Barthélemon, composer, daughter of François-Hippolyte Barthélemon], and dined once at Mr Key's, the procurator of the [Fitzwilliam] Museum.

Cambridge is an expensive place for inns, and it was not until yesterday that Ridgeway [not identified] found an eating place where SW dined for half the amount he paid elsewhere. He does not think he will be able to bring any food back with him. Geese are likely to be as expensive as in London; pork is far more reasonable and is of particularly good quality.

Richard Broderick→SW   Euston St   14/10/1826
BL Add 35013 f 31   With the assistance of my friend Mr Silveira we have
pmk 14/10/1826

Richard Broderick [Irish priest, 1771–1831, from 1809 a priest at the Sardinian Chapel, London] and his friend Mr Silveira have found 'the entire' of the verse 'Ab ortu solis usque ad occasum, magnus est...', which SW had partly written out on the back of this letter. The whole verse is in the *Missale Romanum*.

Sarah→John Gaulter   25/10/1826
MA DDWF/14/53   We are returned thro a gracious Providence) safely,
☞ 25 October; pmk 1826

Sarah's 'poor brother' SW, when looking over manuscripts at Cambridge which he is permitted to publish, found three of CW's hymns set to music by

Handel, in Handel's autograph. Sarah can 'easily account' for this. Mrs [Priscilla] Rich [actress, c1713–1783] was 'imprest with seriousness' by hearing CW preach at West Street Chapel and consequently 'quitted the stage' [the Covent Garden Theatre] of which Mr [John] Rich [theatre manager, c1691–1761] 'was proprietor'. Mr and Mrs Rich were friends of Handel, who taught 'Mr Rich's daughters'. CW and SGW thus heard Handel's 'fine performances'.

SW intends to publish 'these three hymns' which, he says, are 'fitted for a chapel congregation'. Sarah knows that John Gaulter will aid SW in this matter if he can.

SW→'Sir'   Euston St   **27/10/1826**
MA DDWF/15/35; *O*   I have taken the Liberty to enclose the Prospectus
☞ 27/10/1826

SW takes the liberty of enclosing the prospectus of 'a musical work, now preparing for publication' [his proposed edition of Byrd's antiphons]. He expects that it will be 'a useful volume' to those who value and study church music and can 'safely' recommend it 'as such'. The name of the author alone 'is likely to excite respect and attention'.

SW→Tooth   Euston St   **31/10/1826**
MA DDWes/6/22; *O*   Mr Samuel Wesley presents best Compliments to Miss
☞ 31/10/1826

SW believes that Sarah informed Tooth that SW intends to publish Handel's hymns to words by CW and that Sarah has told Tooth some of the background. The hymns are 'eminently appropriate to congregational singing'. They are in a 'beautifully simple style', and should 'speedily attract notice and encourage general zeal to join in them'. To make them universally useful, they need only sufficient publicity; when established in the Wesleyan Connexion, they will soon also be adopted by the dissenting congregations. SW hopes that he may be 'instrumental in assisting and increasing the energies of vocal devotion'.

SW→Jackson[515]   Euston St   **8/11/1826**

MA DDWes/6/26; *O*   I take the Liberty of addressing you upon a Subject

▣ 'November'[516]

SW writes on a subject that is likely to be 'of interest and utility to the Wesleyan Connexion generally'. The University of Cambridge has granted SW a grace, authorising him 'to transcribe and publish any portions of the very valuable musical manuscripts in the library of the Fitzwilliam Museum'. There he discovered three hymn tunes ('Sinners, obey the gospel word', 'O Love divine, how sweet thou art' and 'Rejoice! The Lord is King') that Handel composed to words by CW. SW describes the metrical scheme of each hymn and remarks that the melodies are applicable to any hymns in these metres and thus will be 'a valuable acquisition in all congregations where similar metres are in use'. The style of the music is 'simple, solemn, and easy of execution to all who can sing or play a plain psalm tune'.

SW has decided to publish these hymns, as refraining from publishing them would be a 'culpable neglect'. The plates are already engraved and the hymns will be 'inscribed to the Wesleyan Society'. That CW's son and JW's nephew should chance on this manuscript after a lapse of '80 or 90 years at least' is 'a circumstance of no common curiosity'. SW hopes that this letter will engage Jackson's attention to a publication which is 'slight only in price', as 'the tunes are comprised in three pages'.

SW→Tooth[517]   Euston St   **8/11/1826**

MA DDWes/6/64; *O*   It is only within two Hours that I received the Favour

▣ 8/11/1826

SW has only just received Tooth's letter of 4/11/1826 [not preserved] in response to his note [SW→Tooth, 31/10/1826]. He thanks her for her 'energetic interest' in his publication [his edition of the Handel hymns from the Fitzwilliam Collection]. At her suggestion he has written [SW→Jackson, 8/11/1826] to [the Rev. Thomas] Jackson, who probably received his letter six hours ago. Mr [John] Jackson [artist and Methodist, 1778–1831], of Newman Street, wants to

---

[515] Ltr addressed to 'Reverend Sir'. Jackson identified as addressee because SW→Tooth, 8/11/1826 (evening), says that he has written to Jackson about the hymns at her suggestion (i.e., for the first time), and Jackson subsequently published ltr (to SW's surprise, *see* SW→Thomas Roberts, 6/1/1827) with minor changes in the December 1826 number of the *Wesleyan Methodist Magazine*, p 817–818, which he edited.

[516] Assigned to 8/11/1826 because SW→Tooth, 8/11/1826 (evening) says that Jackson probably received SW's letter six hours ago, suggesting that SW wrote or at least posted ltr on the morning of 8/11/1826.

[517] Ltr addressed to 'Dear Madam'. Tooth identified as addressee because ltr is on same subject as SW→Tooth, 31/10/1826, and SW is not known to have corresponded with any other Methodist woman on this subject at this time.

promote the hymns. SW suggested, in his last letter to him [not preserved], that the two Jacksons were relatives, and presumes [mistakenly] that this is so, as [John] Jackson did not deny it in his reply [not preserved].

SW wishes the 'whole [Methodist] Society' to know his excitement at discovering the Handel hymns. He 'cannot anticipate a greater musical gratification' than 'hearing chaunted by a thousand voices, and in the strains of Handel, "Rejoice! The Lord is King"'. SW is waiting for 'a line' from [John] Jackson regarding the title page; this is all that remains to be done [before printing], as the plates are finished. 500 copies can be struck off in a few days. Copies could be circulated even before any announcement is printed. However, publicity is 'of the utmost consequence' to promote the publication widely.

SW→Sarah   Euston St   **13/11/1826**
MA DDWes/6/21   I have just now received the enclosed letter, which is a Proof
☞ 13/11/1826
SW has just received the enclosed letter [from Jackson, not preserved, presumably his reply to SW→Jackson, 8/11/1826], which proves that 'the cause of the hymns will not be languid among the [Methodist] Society'. SW has not met Jackson, but his style of writing shows that he is well disposed towards SW.

SW→Sarah   Euston St   **14/11/1826**
Dorset D/C00:G/C6   I am in no small Perplexity from a Disappointment
☞ Tue 14 Nov & ✍→{1820,1826}[518]
Wait had volunteered to obtain a loan [for SW] of £50 for four months, which would have 'set matters straight' and enabled SW to 'proceed comfortably in the very busy career' that he has ahead of him this winter. Wait has let SW down, to SW's 'perplexity'.

SW has been invited by the West[ern] Literary [and Scientific] Institution in Leicester Square to read a course of lectures. Unless his mind is kept 'tolerably quiet and easy' he will be 'incapacitated for any methodized exertions of brain'. [George] Oliver has sent a threatening letter [not preserved] and SW expects a further letter from Oliver's lawyer.

SW's failure of what he 'had rationally reckoned on' is a '*coup de foudre*' [a sudden calamity]. He feels like a spider that is about to be swept away. SW never had the prospect of more profitable engagements than now, and it would be lamentable if he were to be interrupted in them by legal coercion. He asks to be remembered to CW Jr.

---

[518] Assigned to 1826 because ltr refers to Wait as 'Dr Wait', and he received the LL.D. degree from Cambridge in 1824.

Sarah memorandum[519]   **about 15/11/1826**

MA DDWes/6/18   Mr Rich was the proprietor of Covent Garden
memo undated[520]

Mr [John] Rich, proprietor of Covent Garden Theatre, offered it to Handel for
the performance of his oratorios. Handel also taught 'Mr Rich's daughters'. Mrs
[Priscilla] Rich was one of the first to attend West Street Chapel, where she was
deeply impressed by CW's preaching. He became her intimate friend and she
gave up the stage entirely.

CW, SGW and Sarah visited Mrs Rich frequently when Sarah was young.
Through their connection with the Riches, CW and SGW used to hear 'Handel's
fine performances' and Handel was 'doubtless led to set to music' the hymns by
CW that are now at Cambridge with Handel's annexed tunes. This is the work
that SW has received permission 'to copy and print'.

---

[519] This memorandum was printed in the *Wesleyan Methodist Magazine*,
December 1826, p 818, where the editor, Jackson, characterises it as a note by
'Miss Wesley' [Sarah] 'now before us'. Its content is substantially similar to a
portion of Sarah→John Gaulter, 25/10/1826.

[520] Ltr placed here on the assumption that Jackson requested information about
the CW/Handel *Hymns* after receiving SW→Jackson, 8/11/1826 and after
deciding to publish SW's letter in the *Wesleyan Methodist Magazine*. In the
December 1826 number of that magazine, Sarah's memorandum is printed just
below that letter.

SW→Emett   Euston St   **23/11/1826**

BL Add 35013 f 90; *O*   As you were so kind as to promise me the Procuration

☐ Thu 23 Nov & wmk 1825 & 🖾→⬛

SW takes up Emett's promise to procure a frank, and would like to have it for Monday 27/11/1826, for a letter [not preserved] that SW will send to Sir James Gardiner, Roche Court, Fairham, Hants.

SW has 'perused Forkel's *Life of Sebastian Bach* with some satisfaction'. JSB cannot be praised too highly, but AFCK's clumsy, Germanic and 'often nearly unintelligible' English is 'a grievous disparagement of its subject'. Forkel himself is dogmatic and pedantic at times, and sometimes shows 'audacious ignorance', as when he asserts that 'Handel's melodies will not remain in remembrance like those of' JSB. The contrary is true: to affirm that JSB's melodies are as good as Handel's is to bestow 'high praise'upon JSB. AFCK should blush at 'inserting such libellous nonsense' in 'a work containing so many interesting memoirs of the prince of harmonists'.[521]

When Emett next is in the area SW will be glad to see him.

SW→John Jackson   Euston St   **29/11/1826**

Berg Acc. 368539B; *O*   At last I have obtained a few Copies of the Hymns

☐ Wed 29 Nov & 🖾→{1820,1826}[522]

SW has obtained 'a few copies of the *Hymns*' [*The Fitzwilliam Music...Three Hymns...Words by...Charles Wesley...Set to Music by George Frederick Handel...transcribed...by...Samuel Wesley*], slightly late from the printer, hence the delay in John Jackson receiving a copy. The *Hymns* were printed without wrong notes, which is a rare occurrence.

SW→Jackson   Euston St   **19/12/1826**

MA DDWes/6/27; *O*   I trust that you will pardon a short Trespass on your Time

☐ 19/12/1826

SW writes about the 'circulation' of *The Fitzwilliam Music...Three Hymns*, which already are being mentioned by people outside the Methodist Connexion. Mr [John] Kershaw [Methodist minister, 1766–1855, from 1823 to 1827 steward of the Methodist Book-Room] tells SW that their publication is as yet scarcely known, and that early notice should be given of the fact. SW suggests that they

---

[521] Commentators have interpreted SW's remark as a claim that AFCK made the English translation of Forkel's biography that was published by T. Boosey and Co. in London in 1820. However, that translation was apparently not by AFCK, and the words quoted by SW in ltr do not appear in it. SW's remark is discussed extensively in Michael Kassler, 'The English translations of Forkel's Life of Bach', in Michael Kassler (ed.), *Aspects of the English Bach Awakening* (Aldershot, 2002, forthcoming).

[522] Assigned to 1826 because of ref. to SW's edition of Handel's hymns.

be announced in 'your Magazine' [the *Wesleyan Methodist Magazine*, of which Jackson was editor] of the 'approaching month, and new year' [the January 1827 number]. He encloses a slip relative to another work which he is publishing by subscription [presumably his proposed edition of Byrd's antiphons] and asks that it be added to the announcement. He feels ashamed for not having sent Jackson a copy of the *Hymns* earlier.

CW Jr→Thomas Roberts   1/1/1827
MA DDWF/20/14 (photocopy)   We remitted your kind note to our Brother
⊟ 1/1/1827

The note [not preserved] written by Thomas Roberts [Methodist itinerant preacher, c1765–1832] has been passed to SW, who appeared 'much gratified' by it and by Roberts's attention. SW truly values Roberts's gift of JW's portrait. CW Jr is glad that SW has made contact with the 'dear Methodists' and hopes that their prayers for him will 'ascend to the Throne of Grace'.

SW may yet be 'an illustrious penitent'. CLW drove him to 'his present irregularity' [with SS]. Martin Madan's book [*Thelyphthora*] 'confirmed him in the lawfulness of polygamy' when CLW 'refused to live with him and spent all his property'. CW Jr hears that SW was 'much affected' by the Methodist meeting the other day. SW sent his piano [to the meeting] and accompanied the Methodists 'with his masterly performance'.

SW→Thomas Roberts   Euston St   6/1/1827
Cheshire; *O*   I beg you to accept my very cordial Thanks
⊟ 6/1/1827

SW thanks Roberts for the print of JW, which SW has framed, and gives Roberts a copy of *The Fitzwilliam Music…Three Hymns*. SW's letter regarding these hymns [SW→Jackson, 8/11/1826] was published in this month's *Wesleyan Methodist Magazine* [in fact, in the December 1826 number], contrary to SW's intention [i.e., SW had not written to Jackson for this purpose].

SW→Sarah   Euston St   **8/1/1827**

Fitzwm ltr 19   I have at last discovered what you perservered in pronouncing

📧 8/1/1827

SW has found that the 'true word' for Sarah's eye complaint is 'amaurosis' rather than 'amorosis'. He describes the disease, quoting from [Samuel] Johnson's *Dictionary*. [John] Harding told SW 'yesterday' [7/1/1827] that the disease 'is obstinate but not incurable'. SW would starve if his own eyes failed unless he could pay 'an accurate amanuensis'. He hopes that CW Jr is well.

SW is not quite well. He has sent £7 to [George] Oliver [as part payment of maintenance for CLW], who 'was perfectly civil'.

SW will call on Sarah soon. He asks if she knows of the wonderful 'Jew Christian Wolf' [Joseph Wolff, missionary, 1795–1862, whose *Missionary Journal and Memoir* was published in London between 1824 and 1829].

CW Jr→Langshaw Jr   **11/1/1827**

GEU W/L; *Wainwright* p 86–87   I have thought it a long time since I have

📧 11/1/1827

George Langshaw [clergyman, 1806–1848, Langshaw Jr's son] told CW Jr that Langshaw Jr has heard of SW's publication *The Fitzwilliam Music...Three Hymns*. The words that Handel set from CW's poems 'are charming in the true Church German style'.

SW 'is engaged to lecture at the Royal Institution this season' and also at the 'Leicester Institution' [the Western Literary and Scientific Institution, *see* SW→Sarah, 14/11/1826]. Accordingly 'he will have full employment'.

SW→Sarah   Euston St   **13/1/1827**

Fitzwm ltr 20   I find it impossible to be with You to Day

📧 Sat 13 Jan & 📧→{1821,1827}[523]

SW cannot be with Sarah today but 'will attend to the troublesome linen draper' [George Oliver] as SW 'can manage to pay the remainder of the alimony [for CLW] on Tuesday' [16/1/1817]. CW Jr is 'sadly mistaken' to suppose that SW could wish Sarah to be worried on his account.

SW would never ask WL for 'another pecuniary favour', even to keep SW from jail. WL 'is a very stingy, selfish, rich man', about whose character SW made up his mind long ago. SW 'can perhaps forgive', but never can forget, WL's delivering him 'to the tormentors at Dr [Alexander Robert] Sutherland's court of inquisition' [Blacklands].

---

[523] Assigned to 1827 because ltr addressed to Sarah at New Street, Dorset Square, where she lived from 1825 until her death in 1828.

SW→Sarah   Euston St   **22/1/1827?**

Fitzwm ltr 22   I am going this Morning to the Book Room

☙ 'Monday morning'[524]

SW is going to the [Methodist] Book-Room this morning, where 'several pounds are due for hymns' [i.e., for the sale of copies of *The Fitzwilliam Music...Three Hymns*]. He will forward the amount forthwith to [George] Oliver, who was not paid last week the £6 that SW owes him. This happened because of an 'unforeseen disappointment' and not from neglect.

SW 'cannot stoop to ask any favour of' WL. SW told Sarah in a recent letter [SW→Sarah, 13/1/1827] his real opinion of WL's mind, which is 'little and interested'. Moreover, WL is 'most ridiculously vain and conceited'.

SW fears that Sarah has not been able to read with her own eyes [because of her eye disease] his book on [George Gordon] Byron [poet, 1788–1824] by [Sir Samuel Egerton] Brydges [bibliographer, 1762–1837; either his *Letters on the Character and Poetical Genius of Lord Byron*, London, 1824, or his *An Impartial Portrait of Lord Byron*, Paris, 1825]. SW is sure that Sarah would approve 'the judgement and candour that pervade every page' and asks if anyone has read parts of it to her. Brydges is 'manifestly a very superior man'.

SW comments on the 'splendid panegyrics' [presumably the obituary in the *Literary Gazette* no. 521, 13/1/1827, p 27] on Sarah's late friend [Elizabeth] Benger [writer, 1778–1827].[525] He was grieved to learn that she died [on 9/1/1827] in straitened circumstances. SW has 'lost a week at the [British] Museum' by the death [on 5/1/1827] of the Duke [Frederick, Duke of York, whose funeral took place on 20/1/1827]. He asks to be remembered to CW Jr.

SW→Jackson   Euston St   **12/2/1827**

MA DDWes/6/28; *O*   Several Persons who are zealous in promoting

☙ 12/2/1827

Several persons have suggested to SW that it would be good to publish the Handel hymns [in *The Fitzwilliam Music...Three Hymns*] in parts for four voices, thus making the hymns available for choirs who sing in harmony as well as for those who sing in unison. SW has followed this advice and has placed his four-part version in the hands of the engraver, who promises to produce the plates without delay. It has also been observed that the hymns would be more useful if all the verses were included below the tune; this SW has also done. He

---

[524] Assigned to 22/1/1827 for the following reason. Ltr refers to SW's 'late letter' to Sarah giving his 'real opinion' of WL's mind: that letter is presumed to be SW→Sarah, 13/1/1827, in which SW says he will pay remainder of CLW's alimony on Tuesday 16/1/1827. SW says in ltr that this was not paid last week, hence ltr presumed to be written on the Monday after 16/1/1827.

[525] This obituary notes (p 28) that Miss Benger was 'ushered' into London society about the year 1802 'principally through the zealous friendship of Miss Sarah Wesley'.

understands that the hymn 'Rejoice the Lord is King' [the third of the three hymns] was omitted, by 'some unaccountable negligence', from the latest edition of the Hymn Book [JW's *A Collection of Hymns, for the Use of the People called Methodists*, 'corrected edition', London, J. Kershaw, 1825].

SW feels himself 'truly honoured' in his role in publishing 'those sacred strains so appropriate to the sublime poesy' of CW. A large assortment [of the choral arrangement of the hymns] will be ready for delivery on 1/3/1827 [*see* SW→Thomas Roberts, 8/3/1827].

CW Jr→Marianne Francis   late February 1827
BL Eg. 3707 f 38[526]   We have had a most miraculous
ltr undated[527]

SW lectures 'not only for the Royal Institution' but also for the [text missing, presumably the Western Literary and Scientific Institution, *see* CW Jr→Langshaw Jr, 11/1/1827].

SW→Thomas Roberts   Euston St   8/3/1827
Cheshire; *O*   I embrace the earliest Opportunity afforded me of proving
🖃 8/3/1827

SW gives Roberts a copy of his 're-publication' of the CW/Handel Hymns [*Handel's Three Hymns from the Fitzwilliam Library, Arranged in Score* by SW] 'ramified into a score for four voices' for choir use. Roberts had advised SW to make this arrangement. SW is 'in hourly expectation' of receiving 'a large lot' of copies of the arrangement from the printer.

Samuel Benson→Sarah   12/4/1827
MA DDWF/26/12   I hope you will not forget your very kind promise
🖃 12/4/1827

Any original papers' which Sarah could procure for the *Literary Chronicle* 'would be extremely acceptable'. Samuel Benson [clergyman and writer, 1779–1881, for many years chaplain of St Saviour's Church, Southwark] 'rather expected this week some original anecdotes of Handel which Mr Wesley [presumably CW Jr] promised to copy out'. The *Literary Chronicle* now pays £8/8/- per sheet 'for original matter'. Benson has asked SW to write 'reviews etc.'. Although the journal has 'no want of help', Benson prefers 'transactions with those of whom I know something and who would write *con amore*'.

---

[526] Ltr is torn with considerable loss of content.

[527] Assigned to late February 1827 because ltr says that the fire in CW Jr's and Sarah's New Street, Dorset Square home took place 'a few Sundays ago' and *Stevenson* p 465 states that this fire (or perhaps the Methodist thanksgiving service at City Road Chapel following the fire) occurred on Sunday 11/2/1827.

SW→Sarah   Euston St   **20/4/1827**
MA DDWes/6/37   'Between us two let there be Peace.'
▣ 20/4/1827
SW seeks reconciliation with Sarah. He feels increasingly averse to controversy of any kind and finds it 'uncommonly painful' to enter into disputes concerning his 'own flesh and blood'. He thinks it best to avoid argument where the parties differ completely in judgement and opinion.

Sarah's censure of SW's conduct concerning SSW results from her imperfect knowledge of the facts. It is 'notorious' that several years ago the King [George IV] showed particular pleasure in the vocal talents of SSW, who was announced to him as 'the son of Samuel Wesley, the musical celebrity'. After this, and many other occasions when SSW's name has appeared in a concert bill, it would be absurd and impossible to attempt to conceal that he is SW's son. Nobody cares about his parentage.

Sarah is mistaken in her suppositions about prejudice concerning SSW's illegitimacy: [Sir Claude] Scott, the former 'master' of SW's son JWW in the coal trade and an active member of the Royal Institution, invited SSW to the 'conversazione' [popularised discussions and demonstrations of scientific subjects] on Friday evenings there, and sent him a ticket of admission for the whole season. SW assumes that Sarah would not claim that Scott, knowing from [William] Drummer the 'whole story' of JWW and SSW, and knowing SW's separation from JWW's mother [CLW], could suppose that they were both children of the same mother.

The Methodists all know SW's 'matrimonial story', and knew this long before the publication of the [CW/Handel] *Hymns*.

SW→Sarah   Euston St   **29/4/1827**
Fitzwm ltr 21   I hoped to have seen you before now, but it could not be.
▣ 29/4/1827
SW had hoped to see Sarah earlier, but this was not possible. Sarah's worry about [George] Oliver was without cause, for when SW sent him a bill for a month later, he was 'all civility'. The threat of CLW's brother [perhaps Captain Martin, *see* CLW→Sarah, undated, 1805–1809] was 'ridiculous'; he realises that the Deed [of Separation] is 'not worth half a pinch of snuff'.

The enclosed letter [an invitation, not preserved, to attend the breakfast for the children of Methodist preachers][528] will show Sarah that her 'good people' are 'not disposed to quarrel' with SW. He will attend the *déjeuner* at the 'extraordinary hour' of 7 am. He must leave home at 6 am to get there in time, as it is more than three miles away.

SW hopes that CW Jr is well. If he wants to come to SW's lecture [at the Royal Institution], which has become a 'very fashionable lounge', he should let SW know some days in advance, as SW's 'power of giving admissions is limited'.

---

[528] This breakfast took place annually in May. *See Stevenson City Road* p 192.

SW→CW Jr   **1/5/1827**
Fitzwm ltr 23   I can only promise to call on Friday Evening
▢ 1/5/1827

SW promises to call some time between 6 and 9 pm on Friday evening [4/5/1827]. He is worried for reasons other than [George] Oliver's demands: he has three bills overdue, and probably will receive a writ. SW seems destined to live on Earth 'in hot water'. He will see CW Jr's friend Edmonds [*see* SW→Sarah, 14/6/1826] when he can [presumably to ask for money], but remembers that he had to remind him many times about his subscription to SW's Morning and Evening Service [his name does not appear on the printed list of subscribers].

SW has been at the [British] Museum for five hours. 'Poor' [Elizabeth] Benger is supposed to have 'accelerated her dissolution' [*see* SW→Sarah, 22/1/1827?] by taking cold there. It is a perilous place for a tender constitution. SW's constitution must be of brass or iron.

SW→CW Jr   Euston St   **4/5/1827**
Fitzwm ltr 24   Yesterday was indeed not an idle one but I was enabled
▢ 'Friday morning'[529]

Yesterday [3/5/1827] was a busy day but SW fulfilled all his engagements 'with alacrity'.[530] CW Jr should advise SW soon if he wants to go next Thursday [10/5/1827] to Albemarle Street [SW's lecture at the Royal Institution]. If so, SW will reserve tickets (of which he is allowed only six) for CW Jr and Sarah.

The breakfast yesterday [for the children of the Methodist preachers, *see* SW→Sarah, 29/4/1827] was interesting. SW is glad that he did not miss it. The preacher prayed 'lustily' for all of CW's children and was 'hugely delighted' when SW's name was announced. A note from CW Jr was read, apologising for his non-appearance. It is a pity that he did not attend.

CW III's courtesy 'is not of the right breed'; there is 'not a grain of sincerity among the whole bunch' [of the children of SW and CLW]. SW thinks that

---

[529] Ltr annotated 4/5/1827 by Tooth. Her annotation is corroborated by the circumstance that, during SW's residence in Euston Street, he lectured at the Royal Institution only in 1826, 1827 and 1828 (*Kassler* p 17–20), and of these years Miss Reece (who, according to Tooth's annotation, was the young lady who chatted to SW at the Methodist breakfast) is listed in the minutes of the Royal Institution as a 'special subscriber' only in 1827 (*ibid.* p 23). Also, SW→Sarah, 29/4/1827, mentions SW's invitation to the Methodist breakfast and asks if CW Jr is interested to attend SW's lecture; both subjects are treated in ltr; and both letters contain SW's statement that Sarah should not fear that George Oliver will act against SW. The extant correspondence does not indicate that SW attended the Methodist breakfast in any year other than 1827.

[530] Besides the Methodist breakfast, SW's engagements on 3/5/1827 included lecturing at the Royal Institution.

[George] Oliver is 'now inclined to be civil' and will not 'tease' Sarah again.[531] Oliver is 'a mere tool of his [Oliver's] wicked wife, and shows teeth which cannot bite'. The Deed [of SW's and CLW's separation] is 'not worth a louse, and can hurt nobody'.

SW will call as soon as he can. He asks if the tall, sensible, well-informed lady who comes to his [Royal Institution] lectures and chatted to him at the Methodist breakfast was Miss Urling. [In an annotation on this letter, Tooth identifies the lady as Miss Reece.[532]]

CW Jr→Marianne Francis 5/5/1827

BL Eg. 3707 f 40   I am the voice of my Sister, who cannot face white Paper.
☞ 5/5/1827

CW Jr writes for Sarah, 'who cannot face white paper'. Marianne Francis will be pleased to hear that SW is 'restored' and behaves to Sarah as he should. She attributes 'all' to a fall SW had 'a few years ago' [presumably his May 1817 jump from a window] which 'certainly injured his head as he was not blooded'. Also, the 'cruel treatment' of CLW, who prejudiced his children against him, 'drove him wild'. SW teaches at the Royal Institution 'with approbation'. He 'is no longer a Deist'.

SW→RG Euston St 15/6/1827

BL Add 35013 f 78; *O*   Sunday the 24th is fixed for the Debut
☞ Fri 15 Jun & 🖎→{1821,1827}[533]

Sunday 24/6/1827 is fixed for the inauguration of the organ at Somers Town Church [consecrated on 11/5/1827, now St Mary the Virgin, Eversholt Street]. SW asks RG to call tomorrow evening [16/6/1827] to arrange 'the vocal preliminaries'.

---

[531] CW Jr→Tooth, 1/3/1830, refers to a letter [not preserved] by SW, in which he said that Oliver 'often intruded' on Sarah until she eventually sent word that 'if he troubled her again with his letters, she would give no reply'.

[532] Probably Dorothea Buxton Reece [*b*1805], daughter of Rev. Richard Reece [Methodist minister, 1765–1850] and at some time a pupil of CW Jr (*see* CW Jr will, 18/5/1831). Another of Mr Reece's daughters, Mary [1799?–1852], had married Mr George Frederic Urling in 1821 [*Stevenson City Road*, p 394–395], presumably accounting for SW's confusion.

[533] Assigned to 1827 because ltr >11/5/1826, when the Somers Town church was consecrated.

CW Jr→Elizabeth Isabella Spence   **4/7/1827**
Gloucester Acc. 15019   We hope you are well—& soon to see you here
☞ 'Wednesday 4 July' & CW Jr at 1 New Street, Dorset Square→⊡
  CW Jr asks Elizabeth Isabella Spence [author, 1768–1832] to obtain a copy of
his glee 'In Arno's Vale', which SW 'had performed' at the Royal Institution
[presumably as part of one of SW's lectures there, *see* SW→Sarah, 27/4/1826].

SW→Crotch[534]   Euston St   **7/7/1827**
Norfolk in Ms 11244; *O*
☞ 7/7/1827
  SW asks Crotch to accept 'a few old-fashioned bars' [probably SW's 'Tu es
sacerdos [II]', of which the autographs, RCM 2141c and RCM 4022, are dated
6/7/1827], which are in the style of those whom Crotch terms 'the minority'. SW
is likely to remain with that minority, despite the 'fashionable mania for
operatical adulteration of church descant'. He thinks that some of the later
Masses ascribed to Mozart that VN has published are forgeries.

SW→Mary Hind   Euston St   **6/10/1827**
DLC Music Div., ML95.C89   Mr Samuel Wesley has heard Miss Hind
☞ 6/10/1827
  SW has heard Mary Hind perform on the organ and believes that she is 'amply
qualified' to be a church organist. [Accompanying documents at DLC indicate
that she used this mechanically copied testimonial together with one from Crotch
when she applied for the post of organist at St Mary, Islington in January 1828.]

SW→SS   15 Marlborough Place, Brighton   **10/10/1827**
BL Add 35012 f 65   If you do not send me an Answer to this by return of Post
☞ Wed 10 Oct={1821,1827,1832}[535]
  SW and SS 'blundered devilishly' about the coach: he did not arrive in
Brighton until after 10 pm. He is to find his own accommodation in Brighton,
and will pay 10/- per week. SS should send him all the money she can.
  The 'parson of the parish' [Henry Michell Wagner, 1792–1870, from 1824
vicar of Brighton] received SW courteously when he delivered the letter [not
preserved] from [Joseph] Robson [of the organ builders Flight and Robson], and
asked SW to play the organ on Sunday [14/10/1827] and to dine with him on

---

[534] Ltr addressed to 'My dear Sir'. Crotch identified as addressee because ltr is
preserved in the Crotch papers at Norfolk; also, SW's ref. to musical style is
consistent with Crotch's interests.

[535] Assigned to 1827 because SW in Brighton then and ltr mentions Lanza and
Wellings who also are mentioned in SW→SS (from Brighton), 14/10/1827; SW
not known to have been in Brighton in October 1821 or October 1832.

Monday [15/10/1827]. He also behaved 'in the kindest manner' upon 'the point that Robson suggested concerning' SSW. SW hopes that SSW does not continue to 'annoy and worry' SS. As SW cannot know the truth of the matter [not identified] from SSW himself, SW asks SS to 'employ' her sister to write to him about this.

SW is anxious to hear how everyone—including his 'dear Fish' [MEW] and 'the parson' [SW's son John]—is. Mr Wellings, his wife and sister are 'elegant creatures', and Barr<et> [text missing; perhaps Joseph Barret, *see* SW→VN, 4 July 1823] could not have gratified SW's feelings more than by introducing him to 'so truly polished and sensible a family'. SW hopes that Wakefield [his doctor] is paying attention to SS [who is shortly expecting a child, *see* SW→SS, 16/10/1827] and will keep her safe and sound until SW returns. SW intends to bring some game for Wakefield as a reward.

SS should let [Gesualdo] Lanza know that SW will give up the performance of his *Confitebor* song as there is no time for Lanza's [female] pupil to learn it to the perfection that SW requires. Lanza should announce Miss Mayor's song 'I've been roaming'; Lanza's pupil will do his concert credit by performing it.

SW→SS   Brighton   **14/10/1827**
BL Add 35012 f 67   You know that I am very anxious about you all
▢ 14/10/1827

SW is anxious to hear news about everyone, including 'my dear Parson' [John], 'my Fish' [MEW] and 'Master Sam' [SSW], and asks SS to reply by return of post. SW received the trousers and the sovereign [£1] safely. He has two scholars [in Brighton]; both are delightful women who take a lesson daily. He started with one on Wednesday [10/10/1827] and with the other on Friday [12/10/1827]. Mr Wellings bargained to pay SW £10/10/- to instruct his sister. By Friday [19/10/1827] the other pupil will have had seven lessons; eight if SW can teach her early on Saturday [20/10/1827] before returning to London. He fears this will not be possible: he would then arrive in London late on Saturday night, and [Gesualdo] Lanza's lecture is not yet rightly arranged. SW will have £10/10/- if Wellings pays him; from the other pupil at 15/- a lesson (which is what he will demand, as he has to walk a mile and a half) he will have £5/5/- [as payment for seven lessons].

SW has had been well treated in Brighton: if he had about 2/- from everyone who was 'courting and caressing' him, he would return with 'a good lumping pennyworth of cash'. He believes that Wellings thinks well of him and is sure that Wellings's sister, a 'most amiable widow', does. She has a 'wonderful genius' for music: SS is to tell SSW that Wellings's sister showed SW three pages of her composition in which he could not alter more than three notes for the better.

Brighton is 'a most bewitching place', but what place will not be bewitching to one who is 'muched and cuddled' from morning to night? The parsons are more anxious to hear his voluntaries than to preach their own sermons, and SW was unable to play the people out of church today [i.e., they were reluctant to leave until he had finished his voluntary]. Wellings told SW that he was robbing half the congregation of their dinner.

SW has written [not preserved] to [William] Drummer. He has read dreadful accounts of a thunderstorm and hopes his 'poor girls' [Rosalind and EW] are not 'scorched to cinders' by the lightning. Tomorrow [15/10/1827] he is to be at the parson's house. Tuesday [16/10/1827] is uncertain. On Wednesday [17/10/1827] he will be at a 'most elegant scholar's house (Dr Price, a physician)'. Thursday [18/10/1827] is uncertain; on Friday [19/10/1827] he will be with the parson again. He asks SS to find a safe way of sending him some money. He does not like to be without money until he is paid. He asks for the name of [John] Braham's present wife before she married him [it was Frances Elizabeth Bolton].

SW→SS   Brighton   **16/10/1827**
BL Add 35012 f 69   I still remain in much Anxiety about you
⊟ 16/10/1827

SW still is anxious about SS. Attwood is to have the whole order for the erection of the church organ [at St Peter's Church] in Brighton; they want it to be put up by 'next December' [December 1827], but it will be impossible to install anything more than a 'mere box of whistles' in so short a time. It is said that Attwood is recommending an organ already in existence. SW thinks that this might be the organ from St Katharine's Church, which was taken away when the church was demolished.

SW asks SS to send money: she would not like him to appear penniless in a strange place. He is 'pretty sure' of being paid from each quarter before he leaves; nonetheless, he would feel nervous if he were not able to pay his way in Brighton and his return fare to London, without presuming on the money due to him. He is to pay £1 for his lodgings, and should pay 2/- to each of the two persons attending him; his fare will be £1/1/-, with an additional 1/- payable to the coachman.

He means to come by the 3 pm stage on Saturday [20/10/1827] which will arrive about 9 pm at the Golden Cross, Charing Cross. SW therefore will not be able to help [Gesualdo] Lanza until Sunday [21/10/1827]. Someone should meet the coach to carry SW's portmanteau. SW will not bother himself with anything at 10 pm, especially if he finds SS 'in the straw' [presumably for the birth of Thomasine] and the house at 'sixes and sevens'. He cannot joke about anything until he personally sees SS's condition.

SW now has exactly 16/- in hand; as he writes, the person who took his booking for his return journey demanded half of it in advance, so he now has only 6/- left. SS should send down another sovereign [£1]. She should wrap it up and book it as a parcel; it will then come safe. He longs to see 'Parson Rooke' [their son John].

SW→Sarah   Euston St   **13/11/1827?**
Fitzwm ltr 25   I expect to be with my Friend Mr Drummer tomorrow
▣ Tue 13 Nov & 🖾→{1821,1827}[536]
SW expects to be with his friend [William] Drummer tomorrow [14/11/1827].
Drummer is considering a plan to render SW 'some really essential service' by
'alleviating some of the pressure' he has from creditors. If SW's mind had not
'regained a tone of strength', which he could not have 'believed possible, but
from experience', the daily 'pestering' for money he receives 'from so many
sides' would have 'produced madness or idiocy' long before now. SW is 'pretty
certain' that Drummer will broach the subject. SW will not show any *mauvaise
honte* but will acknowledge that 'pecuniary assistance' from 'any friendly
quarter' will be welcomed. There are some from whom SW would not accept
aid, even if this meant that he had to sweep the streets during the rest of his days.
Amongst 'such benefactors' SW places his 'reverend son' [CW III] 'first, and
chief'.
SW thought it best to mention this to Sarah before writing to Mrs Bradshaw.
Sarah should let Mrs Bradshaw know that he has 'a fair prospect' of doing her
some good shortly. If Sarah can come forward with £2, SW thinks that he may
be able, in a few days, to add another £3 or possibly £5. None of SW's creditors
deserves half the consideration of 'this poor woman'. SW will give Sarah the
earliest news of the result of his visit to Drummer, as he is anxious to confer his
'mite upon the widow' whenever he can.

Sarah will   **16/11/1827**
Drew Wesley Family Letters, Sarah series[537]   In the name of God Amen, I
will dated 16/11/1827
Sarah [without explicitly revoking her will of 24/7/1804 which included
provisions for SW, CW III and JWW, or her will of 26/2/1826 which included a
provision for JWW] appoints CW Jr as her 'whole and sole executor' and
bequeaths all she has 'or shall die possessed of' to him. CW Jr is to deliver those
of Sarah's 'manuscripts' that he does not wish to retain to the Rev. Mr [John]
Gaulter 'in the Methodist Connexion'. This will was signed by Sarah in the
presence of James Graham 'advocate Edinburgh' and Susanna Mullins.

---

[536] Assigned to 1827 because ltr appears to follow SW's recent writing to
Drummer (*see* SW→SS, 14/10/1827); in addition, no 1821 correspondence
between SW and Sarah is extant nor is any 1821 contact between SW and
Drummer known. SW's 'strength of mind' also suggests 1827 rather than 1821.
However, 1821 has not been proved impossible: CW III was ordained before
13/11/1821.

[537] This will is signed by Sarah but otherwise is not in her handwriting.

SW→William Pepys[538]   Euston St   **23/11/1827**
K; *O*   In Reply to your Application upon the Subject of Lectures
▣ 23/11/1827
SW has no objection 'to repeat [at the London Institution] a course of lectures similar to that delivered at the Royal Institution last season'. An organ and piano were used there and 'vocal assistance was also rendered in numerous examples'. In addition, [Nicholas] Mori [violinist, *c*1796–1839] occasionally played the violin. There were eight lectures, and SW was paid £6/6/- per lecture.

SW→William Brande   Euston St   **10/12/1827**
BL Add 56411 f 28; *O*   I know not how to attempt any Excuse
▣ 10/12/1827
SW apologises for not having earlier thanked [William] Brande [1788–1866, from 1813 Professor of Chemistry at the Royal Institution] for his letter of 17/11/1827 [not preserved]. SW has been extremely busy. In reply to Brande's inquiry, SW states that he no present plan to part with the copyright of his lectures [at the Royal Institution]. If he decides to do so he will consult with Brande before disposing of the copyright elsewhere.

SW→William Pepys   Euston St   **19/12/1827**
Fitzwm ltr 27; *O*   I think I can safely engage to provide Singers at two Guineas
▣ Wed 19 Dec & ▣→{1821,1827}[539]
SW can supply singers [for his lectures at the London Institution] at £2/2/- per head, but not for less. The bass [Henry] Phillips will not sing for less than £3/3/-. It is not necessary to hire three or four singers for every lecture but an organ must be hired for the whole course [of lectures]. SW cannot state the cost until he has haggled with some of the [organ] builders; he pledges to do his best and to 'proceed upon the most economical plan possible'. Pepys is anxious to have a statement of the total charge, but SW is unable to provide this until he knows the cost of hiring the organ and how many of the lectures will require singers.

---

[538] Ltr addressed to 'Sir'. William Hasledine Pepys [1775–1856], a manager of the London Institution, is presumed as the recipient because (1) he proposed to the 8/11/1827 meeting of the Institution's Board of Management that 'Westley' be engaged to deliver eight lectures on music (Guildhall Library, Corporation of London ms 3076 v 3 p 131; the Board approved Pepys's proposal and referred the matter to the Lecture Committee), and (2) subsequent letters from SW regarding his lectures there are addressed explicitly to Pepys.

[539] Assigned to 1827 because SW discussed lecturing at the London Institution in 1827 but not in 1821.

SW→William Pepys   Euston St   **1/1/1828**
Fitzwm ltr 28; *O*   Herewith is an Estimate of the lowest Terms on which
⬛ 1/1/1828

SW provides a detailed estimate of a minimal budget for his course of lectures [at the London Institution], presuming that three singers are to be engaged for five attendances. Pepys and his [Lecture] Committee should decide what is required. Pepys had remarked that Crotch's earlier course [of lectures in the London Institution in 1827] had been entirely instrumental, and that 'therefore the more vocality, the better'. SW's itemisation specifies £37/16/- for 6 lectures at £6/6/- each; £31/10/- for 3 singers at 5 lectures at £2/2/- each; £10/10/- to hire the organ; and £3/3/- to hire the piano; making the total cost £82/19/-. Pepys should inform SW speedily if he feels that any 'retrenchment' can be made. SW does not see how his vocal group can be 'brilliant' without a treble voice, a *sine qua non* if any four-part pieces are to be sung.

SW→Secretary, Russell Institution[540]   Euston St   **2/1/1828**
ROM 934.43.277; *O*   The lowest Terms upon which I can read Six Lectures
⬛ 2/1/1828

SW's 'lowest terms' for reading six lectures [at the Russell Institution] are £31/10/-. He is engaged this season at the Royal Institution and the London Institution, at both of which 'vocal additions' to his lectures are provided at extra cost. He asks whether the Russell Institution requires such additions. He notes that 'the general good effect' of his lectures will be enhanced by the hire of an organ and pianoforte, which also are extra expenses. SW regrets that he has mislaid his correspondent's name and title.[541]

---

[540] At this time the Secretary was Edward Wedlake Brayley [topographer and archaeologist, 1773–1854]. SW did not remember his name.

[541] The Russell Institution presumably accepted SW's terms, as a course of six lectures by SW in that Institution, commencing Wednesday, 30/1/1828, was advertised in the *Literary Gazette* no. 574 (19/1/1828) p 46.

SW→William Pepys   Euston St   **12/1/1828?**
BL Add 56411 f 30; *O*   If convenient to You I will attend you on Thursday at 2
☞ 'Saturday night'[542]
If convenient SW will call on Pepys on Thursday at 2 pm to look at the lecture
room [at the London Institution] and to settle finally 'the point relative to the
organ' [presumably whether an organ can be accommodated during SW's
lectures]. An organ is 'a desideratum of no slender importance, and ought to be
admitted, if possible'.

SW→William Pepys   Euston St   **1/2/1828**
Fitzwm ltr 13; *O*   Be so kind as to favour me, as soon as possible
☞ Fri 1 Feb & ✍→{1822,1828}[543]
SW asks Pepys to let him know, as soon as possible, the day and hour at which
he is 'expected to mount guard' at his 'new station' [i.e., to lecture at the London
Institution].

Richard J. S. Stevens diary entry   **11/3/1828**
Camb Add 9110/4   Attended Mr S. Wesley's 2[d] Lecture
journal entry dated 11/3/1828
On 11/3/1828 R. J. S. Stevens attended SW's second lecture at the London
Institution. The subject was 'the proper management of sacred musical
performance, wherein a full vocal and instrumental band is employed'. Stevens
found SW's method of accompaniment 'too boisterous' and disliked his 'striking
the note for the singer in recitative'. A lady sang 'Let not rage' which, though
much applauded, Stevens considered 'horrid squalling'. In the lecture, SW
recommended 'the education of females as sopranos'. He played Handel's 'Then
round about the starry throne', but not very well. Then he played an
'introduction and fugue' by JSB. The introduction was 'extraordinary', with 'no
definite modulation'. The fugue, on a complicated subject, was 'excessively well
played'. However, very few of SW's audience could understand it.

---

[542] Ltr presumably after SW→Pepys, 1/1/1828, which gave SW's budget that
included an amount for organ hire and asked for Pepys's suggestions of any
retrenchment. Ltr assigned to 12/1/1828 on presumption that it follows Pepys's
reply [not preserved] to the 1/1/1828 letter, and that this reply suggested that the
London Institution lecture room might be unable to accommodate an organ. Ltr
presumably before SW→Pepys, 1/2/1828, by which time the performance
arrangements for SW's lectures appear to have been settled. However, other
Saturdays in January 1828 have not been ruled out as possible dates for ltr.

[543] Assigned to 1828 because SW lectured at the London Institution in 1828 but
not in 1822.

SW→Joseph Fincher   Euston St   **17/3/1828**

BL Add 38071 f 32; *O*   Mr Scott, having expressed himself so zealous
☐ Mon 17 Mar & 📷→{1823,1828}[544]

[Sir Claude] Scott [at this time vice-president of the Royal Institution] is
'zealous for the introduction of the Jew's Harp Artist' [Charles Eulenstein,
German jew's harp player, 1802–1890]. SW is 'anxious to know immediately'
from Joseph Fincher [Assistant Secretary of the Royal Institution] whether the
arrangements for Eulenstein's performance [presumably in a lecture by SW at
the Royal Institution] are settled. It will be necessary for SW to interview
Eulenstein at SW's home on Wednesday [19/3/1828].

SW→'Dear Sir'[545]   Euston St   **29/3/1828?**

BL Music Ms Loan 79.10/3; *O*   I find that no Plates of my Madrigal were ever
☐ Sat 29 Mar & 📷→{1823,1828}[546]

The plates of SW's madrigal ['O sing unto mie roundelaie'], which [Robert
Thomas] Skarratt engraved [*see* SW→VN, 17/2/1813], never were 'sent home'
to SW. [Joseph] Gwilt was so 'disgusted' that this madrigal failed to win the
[Madrigal Society] prize [in 1812] that he published it at his own expense. SW
received only a few copies of this publication and thinks that the plates were sent
to Gwilt. If SW's correspondent cannot 'recover the plates' by inquiring of
Gwilt (an erratic man with whom SW has had no communication 'for several
years past' and from whom he can gain 'no information'), SW 'will republish
the tune, in that cheap and clever way' that Willis [presumably the Dublin music
publisher Isaac Willis who established a London business about 1824 and in the
1820s was one of the few printers of lithographed music in England] exhibited
yesterday [28/3/1828] to SW and his correspondent.

SW memorandum   **11/4/1828**

GEU Wesley Coll. ltr 78   Samuel Wesley, Son of the late Revd Charles Wesley
memo dated 11/4/1828

SW, a son of CW and nephew of JW, was born 'at Bristol, in Charles Street
King's Square' on 24/2/1766 and is 'consequently entering his 63rd or
climacteric year'. He is now organist of Camden Town Chapel, Hampstead
Road.

---

[544] Assigned to 1828 because SW lectured at the Royal Institution in 1828 but
not in 1823.

[545] William Hawes appears likely to have been the recipient because ltr is
preserved with other correspondence to him and concerns music publishing.

[546] Assigned to 1828 because the Dublin music publisher Isaac Willis
established his business in London *c*1824; however, 1823 has not been ruled
out.

SW→Jackson[547]   Euston St   **21/4/1828**

MA DDWes/6/31; *O*   I have had in Contemplation for some Months past

📭 21/4/1828

For some months, SW has contemplated composing 'a few tunes' appropriate to CW's hymns in the [Methodist] Collection [JW's *A Collection of Hymns, for the Use of the People called Methodists*, 'corrected edition', London, J. Kershaw, 1825], with each tune suiting 'a separate metre'. Several of SW's musical friends think that such a publication would be an acquisition to the psalmody of the [Methodist] Connexion. SW desires Jackson's comments.

SW→Jackson   Euston St   **17/5/1828**

MA DDWes/6/32; *O*   According to your Suggestion, I address a few Words

📭 17/5/1828

SW writes about the hymn tunes which he has composed and adapted to the various metres in the [Methodist] 'Collection edited in 1825' [*see* SW→Jackson, 21/4/1828]. He has tried to make the tunes as appropriate to the poetry as possible and will be gratified if they 'hereafter prove a vehicle of impressing more strongly and effectively the grand truths which pervade the whole volume'. He has shown the tunes to various men of good judgement in church music, and they have said that the melodies he invented will be easily learned and are appropriate to the words. Whether sung in separate parts (as they will be printed) or in unison, the effect will be 'powerfully devotional'.

SW considers it his duty to offer the copyright of the manuscript to the [Methodist Book-Room] Committee before offering it elsewhere. He has consulted 'a few impartial men' about a 'fair and moderate price', and they tell him that £150 is an 'undeniably just requisition'. If only 'a moiety' of the new tunes become popular there is little doubt that the demand for the book will become general. SW 'disposed of full 1800 copies of the three tunes from the Fitzwilliam Library'[548] and afterwards sold the plates 'for a liberal sum'. He intends to prefix an explanatory preface to the new tunes.

---

[547] Ltr addressed to 'Dear Sir'. Jackson identified as addressee because ltr refers to 'your collection' of hymns and the subject raised in ltr is pursued in SW→Jackson, 17/5/1828.

[548] Ltr is unclear whether '1800 copies' refers to one or both SW publications of his arrangements of the three CW/Handel *Hymns*.

SW→CW Jr   Euston St   **20/5/1828**
BL Add 35012 f 120   I should have enumerated among my manifold Sins
▣ Tue 20 May & 🖃→{1823,1828}[549]

SW apologises for not previously sending the melody [not preserved] he now encloses. He leaves for Birmingham tomorrow [21/5/1828, to direct and to play at two concerts on 23/5/1828 marking the opening of the organ at St Peter's, Dale End] and trusts that he will return safe and sound to his children. Arrangements concerning the 'immediate annoyance' have been 'smoothly managed', but he knows that 'the furnace of affliction' will be 'his portion on earth'. He sends kind regards to Sarah and is glad that she has partly recovered her sight.

SW→SS   Birmingham   **22/5/1828**
BL Add 35012 f 71   I got hither safely last Night, but not till half after 9
▣ Thu 22 May; pmk 1828

SW arrived safely in Birmingham at 9.30 pm last night [21/5/1828]. The pretence that the journey takes only 12 hours is false. He means to return on Sunday morning [25/5/1828] by the coach that leaves at 6.45 am and should reach Islington by 7.30 pm. Joe [not identified] should arrive there by a little after 7 pm. The weather is poor for SS's 'Gravesend sail', but she should remember that air upon the water is equally beneficial whether it rains or shines.

Mr Hands's sister and brother-in-law [not identified] are 'excellent people', and SW is well looked after. He is invited to dine with Mr [Thomas] Freer, one of the churchwardens, before the rehearsal at 6 pm this evening. Mr Greaves, the leader of the 'band' [the orchestra], has engaged SW for the same time tomorrow.

It seems that [Joseph] Moore is no longer the 'high and mighty' that he was: SW's host Mr Tolly [not identified] told SW that he believes that Moore does not have more than £100 a year to live on. SW doubts the truth of this.

SW is 'very anxious about the brats' [his children]. If SS takes 'Fish' [MEW] with her tomorrow she will leave 'the parson' [their son John] behind. SW is anxious that SS will not be 'well and properly managed', especially if she does not take Mr Baker [not identified] and 'the little rat'. SW will not forget SS's 'commissions', but has had to spend 6/6 in gratuities to the coachmen and the guard. He wishes SS a pleasant sail tomorrow.

---

[549] Assigned to 1828 because ltr addressed to CW Jr at New Street, Dorset Square, where he lived from 1825.

SW→William Upcott   20/8/1828

Bath A.L. 1523; *O*   I feel it right to announce to you, that a Set of 30 Hymn
✉ Wed 20 Aug={1828}[550]

SW's set of 30 *Original Hymn Tunes, Adapted to Every Metre in the Collection
by the Rev. John Wesley, A.M.* has just been published and may be had from the
[Methodist] Conference Office. SW thinks that the tunes are good and
commends them to the many friends and acquaintances of William Upcott
[antiquary and autograph collector, 1779–1845, from 1806 to 1834 assistant
librarian of the London Institution, from where SW writes this letter].

SW→Jackson   Euston St   2/9/1828

MA DDWes/6/29; *O*   As the recent Publication (concerning which you have
✉ 2/9/1828

SW's recent publication [*Original Hymn Tunes*] has involved 'heavy expense',
for which remuneration can 'be only expected'. As he wishes that the money
advanced by 'you' [presumably the Methodist Book-Room Committee] should
be repaid as soon as possible, he cannot resist requesting great efforts in
promoting the new publication. SW acknowledges that the success of publishing
the three CW/Handel *Hymns* was the 'primary stimulus' for his present
undertaking. He was further impelled by the knowledge that tunes were not
available for every metre in the current hymn book [JW's *A Collection of
Hymns, for the Use of the People called Methodists*, 1825 edition].

SW fears that [the Rev. John] Mason [Methodist minister, 1781–1864, from
1827 steward of the Methodist Book-Room] and others may have mistaken his
motive in seeking a further advance of money: it was to promote the circulation
of copies which would most quickly ensure the return of the money. SW's
printer cannot proceed without ready money. 100 copies are immediately
wanted. The shops to which SW has sent title-pages object to displaying them
because, when asked for a copy of the publication, they have none to produce.

No objection was voiced when SW proposed his publication; if it had been,
SW would have dealt with the objection, and possibly would have abandoned
the project. As it is, he has prepared for the press a work which is sure to be
popular, but which 'stagnates for the immediate lack of £30'. SW cannot expect
success for the hymns in 'the church', but he thinks that the dissenting
congregations will give them great encouragement: they are fond of new tunes,
and these tunes are 'fairly entitled to become old, and yet never obsolete'. He is
pleased that the 'former advertisement' remains in the number [of the *Wesleyan
Methodist Magazine*] for the current month. Great progress might be made if
every preacher informed of SW's publication at the [Methodist] Conference
were disposed to aid it.

---

[550] Assigned to 1828 because the preface of SW's *Original Hymn Tunes* is dated
10/7/1828.

SW→Charles Britiffe Smith   Euston St   **4/9/1828**
BL Add 31764 f 27; *O*   It appears to me that the English translation
▣ 4/9/1828

SW quotes a Greek epigram and an English translation of it [by CW III, used in SW's 1807 glee 'Life is a jest'], and comments that this translation is 'far superior to the original'.

SW→SS   Nottingham   **10/9/1828**
BL Add 35012 f 50[551]   This night's post was gone to London long before
▣ 'Wednesday night'[552]

SW promised to write as soon as he got to Nottingham. Tonight's London post left before he arrived, so SS probably will not receive this letter before Friday [12/9/1828]. They [SW and Master Bennet, not identified] expect to leave for Leeds tomorrow [11/9/1828] and to get there between 4 and 5 pm. SW will send a letter on Friday [12/9/1828] which SS will receive on Sunday [14/9/1828]. He longs to know how SS and their 'dear babes' get on but thinks it is not worthwhile for her to write, as he intends to return on Tuesday [16/9/1828] unless 'some very profitable reason' detains him. In his next letter he will draw the picture he promised 'the parson' [their son John]. SW is anxious about all his family and hopes that 'that sneaking Miss R' [not identified, conceivably Rosalind] has sent SS SW's 'pitiful sum'.

SW hopes that he will not be 'done' in the 'organ concern' [his performance at the opening of the organ at Brunswick Methodist Chapel, Leeds]; if so, 'the whole [Methodist] Connexion' should be publicly exposed for it. However, he believes that the affair will be conducted 'fairly and handsomely'. 'Little B' [Bennet] is very attentive. They are getting on as well as may be expected. [Remainder of text missing.]

SW→SS   Leeds   **13/9/1828**
BL Add 35012 f 73   All is going on smoothly to every Appearance here
▣ Sat 13 Sep={1828}[553]

All is going well [in Leeds]. The performances at the [Brunswick Methodist] Chapel yesterday [12/9/1828] gave 'universal satisfaction'. The [Methodist] people make more of SW on account of his name than they would of [Napoléon] Bonaparte. SW wishes he had £1/1/- for every time he has shaken hands since

---

[551] Ltr is incomplete.

[552] Assigned to Wednesday 10/9/1828 because ltr says SW leaving for Leeds tomorrow and the 11/9/1828 *Leeds Intelligencer* (according to *Lightwood* p 207) reported that 'A Mr Wesley is on his way to Leeds. He slept at Nottingham last night, and will be here today'.

[553] Assigned to 1828 because the Brunswick Methodist Chapel organ was 'opened' by SW in that year.

his arrival last Thursday [11/9/1828]: then 'we [SW and SS] might go to Gravesend every week for twelve months without feeling the expense'.

'Our Yorkshire Bile' [not identified] has not yet appeared, and there is no danger of his 'running away to Hull' with SW. It has been recommended that SW go to York to see the Cathedral, but he does not intend to incur the expense of a 24-mile journey. He prefers quietness to 'jumbling in a coach'. SW plans to return [to London] on Tuesday morning [16/9/1828] but does not know on what coach. The Smiths are a delightful family. 'Little Bennet' has been helpful to SW.

SW longs to see [his son] Johnny and hopes that Rosalind is getting on and that his 'dear Fish' [MEW] is not 'ill-used because his rascally master shuts him out of doors'. SW will say nothing about the Hymns [presumably SW's *Original Hymn Tunes*, see SW→Jackson, 2/9/1828], but thinks that SS will be glad that he did not sell the copyright. He has been working very hard [in Leeds] and hopes that his remuneration 'will be done handsomely, or justly at least'. He feels that the consequences of this trip are likely to solve many of SW's and SS's 'present troubles about vile money'. He does not know what sort of 'grub' he can bring to SS but intends to buy a Yorkshire goose.

CW Jr→SW   **18/9/1828**
MA DDWF/20/22[554]   In great Affliction, but I hope in resignation to God
WBRR v 3 (Dec 1851) p 452

CW Jr [who is in Bristol with Sarah] informs SW that Sarah is near 'a crown of glory' [i.e., is near death; she died on 19/9/1828]. She became ill [in Slough] at the home of Lady [Mary] Herschel [1750–1832, widow of Sir William Herschel, astronomer and musician, 1738–1822], and for five weeks has been unable to eat. Sarah's 'life has been exemplary'. SW and CW Jr should follow her as she followed Christ Jesus.

CW Jr supposes that SW went to Leeds. The ministers there of CW Jr's 'uncle's people' [the Methodists] wanted him [to perform at the opening of the new organ in Brunswick Methodist Chapel, Leeds], but this 'was impossible'. CW Jr accordingly directed the ministers to send for SW.

CW Jr hopes that he and SW will meet again. CW Jr asks God to bless SW and implores SW to 'follow the things which make for everlasting peace which this world cannot give'.

---

[554] The bottom of ltr is torn, but the only text that appears to be missing is the date. The date is taken from *WBRR*, where ltr is printed with unacknowledged additions.

SW→Emett 21/9/1828

BL Add 35013 f 92; *O*   I will prepare the Papers in the Way you require
☞ 'Sunday night'[555]

SW will prepare the papers [not identified] as soon as possible in the way that Emett [who was blind] requires. However, on the advice of Wakefield, his doctor, SW is going to Gravesend tomorrow [22/9/1828] because his intestines are 'yet unsettled'.

SW must return [to London] on Saturday next [27/9/1828]. He will be glad to see Emett on Sunday [28/9/1828], whether or not Sarah [of whose 19/9/1828 death in Bristol SW presumably had not yet heard] is still alive.

CW Jr→RG 21/9/1828

MA DDWF/20/23   It has pleased God to take my beloved Sister to Glory
☞ 21/9/1828

CW Jr informs RG of Sarah's death. CW Jr does not remember where she had placed her will but thinks that it is safe 'with an old friend' and that she had asked RG to be one of her executors. CW Jr has written to SW [CW Jr→SW, 18/9/1828, or a subsequent letter not preserved], and plans to return to London [from Bristol] as soon as possible after Sarah's funeral.

SSW→Emett 22/9/1828

BL Add 35019 f 133   Although I much regret the cause of your not being able
☞ 'Monday evening'[556]

SSW regrets that Emett's bowel complaint prevents him from visiting but is not sorry that he is not coming, as SW 'is gone to Gravesend' and Emett 'would have been disappointed of his company'. SSW informs Emett that Sarah is dead, and that SW 'together with his [intestinal] illness [*see* SW→Emett, 21/9/1828] is greatly distressed about it'.

---

[555] Assigned to Sunday night 21/9/1828 on the presumption that SW had received CW Jr→SW, 18/9/1828, which advised that Sarah was near death, but had not yet heard that Sarah had died on 19/9/1828. This dating assignment is consistent with SW travelling to Gravesend on the day when news of Sarah's death reached him, as indicated in SSW→Emett, 22/9/1828. (14/9/1828 is not a possible date for ltr because SW was in Leeds then.)

[556] Assigned to Monday evening 22/9/1828 because ltr conveys news of Sarah's death, not known to SW or SSW the previous night (*see* SW→Emett, 21/9/1828), and confirms that SW went to Gravesend on 22/9/1828 as he had planned the previous night.

CW Jr→Joseph Entwisle   **29/9/1828**

MA DDWF/20/24   I need not say to you, my old rever'd Friend Mr Wood
🖃 29/9/1828

CW thanks the Rev. Joseph Entwisle [Methodist minister, 1767–1841] and others for their assistance to his 'beloved sister' [Sarah] and for their prayers. He asks Entwisle to pray also for his 'poor dear brother' SW, to whom CW Jr thinks that God will come. CW Jr expects to remain in Bristol for another week.

SW→SS   Gravesend   **1/10/1828**

BL Add 35012 f 75   Your Letter certainly brought but little good News
🖃 1/10/1828

SS's letter [not preserved] brought little good news, but SW is glad to know that she is well. SS considers 'Master Sam' [SSW] mad 'to advise reconcilement' with a blackguard [not identified] who wants to imprison SW. SW will 'write to appoint' Suter [not identified, presumably a relative of SS] on Monday [6/10/1828].

SW is being very economical, but complains about the high cost (2/6) of a warm bath. He describes the meals he has eaten; yesterday [30/9/1828] he and 'Ros' [Rosalind] dined with Mr and Mrs Porter. The 'ghost joke' was a great success. Everyone was disappointed by SS's absence. They all went to Cobham House yesterday morning and were shown round the 'magnificent mansion'. SW begs SS to come, despite difficulties. Rosalind sends her love. SW complains that SS did not put up his [razor] strop.

CW Jr→SW   Euston St   **9/10/1828**

MA DDWF/20/24A   I hope to hear you are perfectly recover'd.
pmk 9/10/1828 (Bristol)

CW Jr hopes that SW has recovered from his malady [*see* SW→Emett, 21/9/1828]. CW Jr's spirits understandably have not yet got well, following the great loss [of Sarah]. SW's son John [JWW] visited a few days ago [in Bristol] and also went to Kingswood [the school established by JW]; 'his Christian name was a passport to him with the good Methodists'.

CW Jr hopes to be in London on 31/10/1828. He recently visited Hannah More [writer of religious tracts, 1745–1833] who is 'a walking library' of the past age, remembering Sir Joshua Reynolds [artist, 1723–1792], [Samuel] Johnson, CB and other talents of the time.

CW Jr is 'surrounded' with Methodist preachers and good friends. He prays that SW and CW Jr will make 'religion the first thing, which only can give comfort at the last'.

SW→Jackson   Euston St   **10/10/1828**

MA DDWes/6/30; *O*   I cannot but again express to you the strong Reluctance
✉ Friday 10/10/1828; pmk 10/10/1828[557]

SW is reluctant to write regarding money, which he values no more for its own
sake than CW and JW did. SW lost £60 within the last three months because an
organ builder [not identified] refused to pay it [presumably in commission for
the sale of an organ] as no formal legal agreement had been written. This amount
would have enabled SW to proceed with his printer so that there would have
been no scarcity of copies of his 'late work' [his *Original Hymn Tunes*]. At
present there is 'a stagnation', as each 100 copies cost SW nearly £12, for which
his 'poor typographer can afford no credit'.

SW and Jackson are agreed that SW's unique 'tune book' will eventually be
popular, but this may take considerable time. SW suggests that it may be better
for him to dispose of the copyright altogether 'at a fair valuation', rather than to
be faced by financial worries of this sort from time to time. He seeks Jackson's
early thoughts on this matter.

SW→RG   Euston St   **10/10/1828?**

MA DDWF/20/24A   So you see that Master John was for 'making Hay while
Ltr written on CW Jr→SW, 9/10/1828, which bears 10/10/1828 London pmk[558]

Forwarding CW Jr→SW, 9/10/1828, SW notes that 'Master John' [JWW] was
for 'making hay while the sun shines'. SW thinks that it is 'high time' for him
also to become active [possibly regarding what he believes are his entitlements
from Sarah's estate].

SW→RG   Euston St   **30/10/1828**

MA DDWes/9/21; *O*   My Brother has written to inform us that he expects
✉ 30/10/1828

CW Jr has written [not preserved] to inform SW and RG that he intends to be
in London on Saturday [1/11/1828]. SW plans to call on CW Jr on Sunday
[2/11/1828], and thinks that RG should see CW Jr on Monday [3/11/1828], as
'nothing but evil can result from delay' [presumably regarding SW's
entitlements from Sarah's estate, *see* CW Jr→RG, 11/11/1828].

---

[557] The address portion of ltr has 'Friday 9 October', an incorrect date.

[558] Assigned to 10/10/1828 because CW Jr's 9/10/1828 letter was delivered on
10/10/1828 and SW presumably forwarded ltr to RG that day or soon thereafter.

CW Jr→RG   **11/11/1828**

BL Add 35038 f 2   I shall be obliged to you to call directly on me
⬚ 11/11/1828

  CW Jr asks RG to call on him directly to do what is necessary concerning
Sarah's will [of 16/11/1827], and suggests that they meet early afternoon
tomorrow [12/11/1828].

CW Jr→RG   **15/11/1828**

MA DDWF/14/55   I send you a Copy of my dear Sister's will
⬚ 15/11/1828

  CW Jr transcribes Sarah's will of 16/11/1827 in full. He found this will [in
which SW is not mentioned] 'in her pocket book'. He asks RG to appoint a time
and place where they can meet to 'administer'.

CW Jr→Sarah Tooth   **17/11/1828**

MA DDWF/20/25   You and your Daughters are not out of my thought
⬚ 17/11/1828

  CW Jr asks Sarah Tooth [Tooth's mother, widow of Samuel Tooth] to pray for
him and for his 'poor brother' [SW]. SW has been 'very ill' since his return from
Leeds [about 16/9/1828, *see* SW→Emett, 21/9/1828], but is now a little better.
Sarah's will [of 16/11/1827], 'signed by Mr [James] Graham', an Edinburgh
advocate, finally was found a few days ago.

Henry John Gauntlett→RG   **27/11/1828**

MA DDWF/15/38A   Mr Samuel Wesley has communicated to me a wish
⬚ 27/11/1828

  SW saw Henry John Gauntlett [lawyer, organist and composer, 1805–1876]
this morning and asked him to make contact with RG concerning Sarah's will.
SW believes it 'highly necessary that some decisive steps should be immediately
taken' to secure his property interests. Gauntlett understands that CW Jr has
given RG 'written authority to collect together all the property belonging to the
family'. Gauntlett fears that, without possession of Sarah's will, any steps that
RG might take would 'excite suspicion in the minds of the parties' with whom
CW Jr resides. They, in turn, 'might poison' CW Jr's mind regarding SW and
RG, which would 'prove injurious to all parties'.
  This morning Gauntlett, accompanied by SW, interviewed [Elizabeth]
Mortimer, who 'holds the will'. She is willing to give up the will to RG or to
SW, but her legal adviser has informed her that she cannot 'resign possession' of
it without written authority from [Sarah's] executor, CW Jr. SW wants RG to
obtain this authority and has asked Gauntlett to consult with RG regarding the
best way of accomplishing this. Gauntlett proposes to draw up the required
authority and to go with RG to CW Jr's home. Gauntlett suggests that RG ask to
see CW Jr 'alone for a minute or so', when RG 'must prevail' on CW Jr to sign

the authority. Once SW possesses the will, 'the distress and anxiety of mind' that he 'now undergoes' will cease, and RG will be 'enabled' to make terms 'with the party at present possessing' CW Jr that are 'consistent' with Sarah's wishes.

Gauntlett fears that, unless speedy action is undertaken, 'the other party' will prevail upon CW Jr to obtain the will from Mrs Mortimer. At SW's desire, Gauntlett is 'drawing up a case for the perusal and opinion of Mr Porter'.

CW Jr→Tooth   29/12/1828
MA DDWes/6/86   How inadequate I am to express the lasting obligation
☞ 29/12/1828

CW Jr has had no more annoyance from SW and SW's 'associate' RG [presumably regarding Sarah's will]. Yesterday [28/12/1828] CW Jr heard that 'the lady [possibly Elizabeth Mortimer] at K[entish] T[own]' made Mrs Ince write four letters to different persons abusing CW Jr and his maternal relations [probably including his cousin Elizabeth Greene, at whose home CW Jr was living].

SW→Emett   Euston St   15/1/1829
BL Add 35013 f 95; *O*   Particular business will detain me from Home
☞ Thu 15 Jan; pmk 1829

SW will not be at home for most of tomorrow [16/1/1829]. SSW also will be absent. SW asks Emett to name a day next week when SW and SSW can receive him.

SW→William Hawes   Euston St   24/1/1829
BL Music Ms Loan 79.10/3; *O*   Nearly a Month ago Mr S. Wesley addressed
☞ 24/1/1829

Nearly a month ago SW addressed a note [not preserved] to Hawes, inquiring whether he would be disposed to engage SW's services at the ensuing Oratorios [concerts]. Hawes replied orally that he would write to SW to let him know. Today SW saw [Thomas] Adams advertised as the organist. SW asks if Hawes's behaviour exhibits 'the attentive punctuality of a man of business, or the polished manners of a courtier'.

CW Jr→Tooth   26/1/1829
MA DDWes/6/84   You have given me a task, which I feel inadequate to fulfil
☞ 26/1/1829

Mr Taylor [possibly Rev. Joseph Taylor Jr, later president of the Methodist Conference] called today and says he will get Mr [Rev. Henry] Moore to speak to CW Jr's 'poor deluded brother' [SW, probably regarding Sarah's will]. 'God grant that it may have the intended effect.'

SW→William Bird   Euston St   **27/1/1829**
Bird preface   Mr Samuel Wesley has carefully perused the Hymn Tunes
Bird

SW has 'carefully perused' the hymn tunes [in the publication *Original Psalmody*] composed by [William] Bird [composer, of Watford, Hertfordshire] and thinks that several of the melodies are 'extremely smooth and pleasing'. 'Inaccuracies' in the harmonies have been corrected [by SW], and the work 'is likely to become very useful to the lovers and students of psalmody'.

SW→RG   Euston St   **31/1/1829**
MA DDWF/15/39; *O*   I fully proposed to have been with you this Day
☐ 31/1/1829

SW intended to be with RG today but two scholars dropped in whom SW had to teach. Furthermore, he is 'closely pressed for time' to prepare a lecture for 'Tuesday next' [3/2/1829]. This is the day that the 'lousy lawyer's bill' is due to be paid, so SW is in a 'true, proper and orthodox dilemma'. If RG is able to procure for him a loan of either £20 or £30, he will receive SW's note payable on 25/3/1829 and also 'property to the amount of the sum advanced'. SW asks RG to look in this evening. He would not be so troublesome to RG if the affair were not urgent and the impending danger imminent.

SW→'Dear Sir'[559]   Euston St   **7/3/1829**
BL Add 31764 f 28; *O*   The ingenious & profligate Author of 'Lacon'
☐ 7/3/1829

SW comments on a 'paper' [not identified] written by his correspondent and given to SW at their last Masonic 'lodge night'. SW remains convinced that 'no multitudinous addition of instruments' can ever add to the solemnity of tone possessed by the organ, which unites with the human voice in a 'similarity of effect vainly attempted by any other instrument except the flute'. Some voices

---

[559] The recipient's identity has not been determined. Ltr was owned by the collector Thomas Mackinlay and appears as lot 356 in the posthumous 12/7/1866 sale of his library by the auctioneers Puttick and Simpson, where it is described as a 7-page letter on organ and pianoforte playing dated 7/3/1829. The 1846 privately printed *Catalogue of Original Letters and Manuscripts, in the Autograph of Distinguished Musicians...Collected by Thomas Mackinlay* (a copy is in the British Library, shelf-mark S.C. 950(4)) lists a 'long letter' by SW 'to T. B. Smith, dated March 7, 1837'. No 7/3/1837 letter by SW is extant, and all the surviving letters that he wrote in the last months of his life are short. If the long SW letter said in the 1846 Mackinlay catalogue to have been written on 7/3/1837 is in fact ltr then the recipient can be identified as T. B. Smith. 'T. B. Smith' could be conjectured to be a misprint for Charles Britiffe Smith, to whom SW wrote on 4/9/1828, but no evidence has been found that Charles Britiffe Smith was a Mason.

do resemble the reed stops of organs but in these cases the tone of the human voice is 'either naturally bad, or vitiated by a false mode of exerting it'; the latter is true of [John] Braham. The nearer the tone of the human voice approaches that of a 'fine diapason', the closer it comes to perfection.

SW's correspondent's paper states that 'the introduction of stringed instruments may increase the flow of harmony'. This is not altogether correct: stringed instruments 'strengthen the force of the tones, but not the power of the radical and constituent harmony'. They 'much embellish and diversify' the general effect, but that effect is 'theatrical' rather than 'ecclesiastic'. SW therefore agrees with his correspondent's critique that requiems sung to the organ without instruments are most 'consistent with perfect taste'.

Anyone who plays the piano, even if he can execute 'the marvellous difficulties' of [Johann Nepomuk] Hummel [Austrian composer and pianist, 1778–1837] and [Ignaz] Moscheles [German composer and pianist of Czech birth, 1794–1870], soon will discover his incompetency if he attempts to play a psalm tune on the organ. Even if these pianists are harmonists—in other words, if 'they know how to modulate'—they are sure to treat the organ, 'the noblest of all instruments', in the 'most awkward and barbarous way'. When striking a chord, they do not put the keys down simultaneously, but one after the other, starting from the lowest, which SW illustrates diagrammatically. The effect of this is 'perfectly ludicrous'. Pianists also forget that the sound of an organ pipe is 'continuous, not fleeting', so that if the performance of a passage is not 'extremely nice, and accurate' and if notes are protracted, even for half a second beyond their proper duration, the result will be 'false harmony'. Those who imagine that the piano needs more delicate management than the organ are mistaken: 'the direct reverse is the truth'. He who wishes to be a good player on both the piano and the organ must learn the organ first; otherwise, he will never deserve to be called an organist.

SW turns to 'a little Masonic confidence'. He suspects that his correspondent suggested SW's 'right and title' to all the 'finery' in which he came to the banquet on the other Monday. If so, SW thanks him; if it were some other Mason that 'made the motion', SW asks to know his name. SW believes that his correspondent is aware that SW's mind is 'not that of a mere musician'. From boyhood SW has loved more of the alphabet than its first seven letters [the names of the musical notes]. Had he not been an 'idle dog', he might, under the instruction of CW (whose loss he feels daily, more than forty years afterwards), have been long ago qualified to 'bandy Latin and Greek' along with [Samuel] Parr [pedagogue and Latin scholar, 1747–1825] and [Richard] Porson [Greek scholar, 1759–1808]. SW's trade is music, but he wishes that music had been destined only for his amusement. This would have happened had he taken the opportunities offered in his youth to enter one of the learned professions. Unfortunately 'it was otherwise ordained', and he attended to the cultivation of only one talent, which 'unluckily' cost him little effort: had there been any 'up-hill work' for him in music, he would have soon have given it up.

SW's motive for 'pestering' his correspondent with 'egotism' is this: although SW is 'closely occupied in drumming the intrinsic value of minims and semibreves' into impenetrable skulls, he would 'feel no objection' to making himself useful to those engaged in literary pursuits. SW suggests that he might 'lend a helping hand' in some critical work where he understands the language and the subject, and asks his correspondent to 'think a little' on this proposal.

SW→'Sir'[560]   Euston St   **24/3/1829**
MA DDWF/15/37; *O*   In reply to your Note I have to inform you
◻ Tue 24 Mar & 🖾→①

Replying to his correspondent's note [not preserved], SW states that the three hymns which he transcribed from the Fitzwilliam Museum are 'unquestionably' in Handel's handwriting, with which SW is well acquainted. SW also knows the history of this composition, which Handel undertook at the request of a particular friend of CW. Handel composed only the hymns' melody and a figured bass. SW 'ramified' Handel's composition 'for a choir'.

SW→Stephen Francis Rimbault   **30/3/1829**
Schoelcher p 51–52   [not known]
Schoelcher

[John] Rich, 'the most celebrated Harlequin of his time', was proprietor of Covent Garden Theatre when Handel conducted his oratorios there [*see* Sarah→John Gaulter, 25/10/1826]. His wife [Priscilla Rich], 'who became a serious character after having formerly been a very contrary one', requested Handel to set to music the three hymns that SW transcribed in the Fitzwilliam Library from the autograph and subsequently published.

SW→RG   Euston St   **10/4/1829**
GEU Wesley Coll. ltr 79; *O*   Dr Wait delivers this to You, & is very anxious
◻ Fri 10 Apr & 🖾→①

Wait urgently seeks to confer with RG regarding a matter of vital importance to Wait and his family. RG, who is 'so deeply versed in affairs of urgent business', will recognise that it is necessary to proceed immediately.

CW Jr→Tooth   **19/5/1829**
MA DDWes/6/94   A thousand thanks for the long and repeated Trouble
◻ 19/5/1829

Mrs [Elizabeth] M[ortimer] of K[entish] T[own] 'accosted' CW Jr at the meeting today and gave him a letter [not preserved] from SW, who again is in

---

[560] Although a pencilled annotation on this letter states that the recipient was [the violinist Nicholas] Mori, the circumstance that SW→Stephen Francis Rimbault, 30/3/1829, deals with a similar subject, suggests that he could have been the recipient.

danger of being arrested [for debt]. CW Jr has never beheld such a letter, which is full of accusations against the 'dear departed saint now hymning in glory' [Sarah]. He does not wish to entrust this letter to the post but will show it to Tooth if she calls next Saturday [23/5/1829].

SW→'Sir'   Euston St   23/5/1829
MA DDWF/15/40; *O*   I must have appeared very remiss, & inattentive
📧 Sat 23 May & 📧→i

SW has been busy with other correspondence and apologises for his delay in replying to the recipient's 13/5/1829 letter [not preserved]. SW regrets his inability to supply information desired by the recipient's friend regarding the Annesley family. [Adam] Clarke and [Henry] Moore have been 'sedulous in the Wesleyan genealogy'. If they cannot assist, SW fears that any future research he might do on the subject would be 'altogether ineffectual'. He does not believe that his late sister [Sarah] would have been able to bring forth documentary evidence. He has not found in [Robert] Southey's *Life of [John] Wesley* [published in 1820] mention of 'that collateral relationship which is wanted in the present instance'.

SW→CW Jr   Euston St   1/6/1829
Drew Wesley Family Letters, SW series   I thank you for your punctual
📧 1/6/1829

SW thanks CW Jr for his 'punctual attention', which has 'just in time' prevented a 'personal attack' on SW. Tooth visited SW on Saturday afternoon [30/5/1829]. She is interested in SW's and CW Jr's welfare. SW will seek information regarding CW Jr's 'property in the Funds'. Contrary to CW Jr's information, CLW is alive, and her annual £25 alimony remains 'a drawback' on SW's 'scanty income'.

SW→Editor, *The Harmonicon*   29/6/1829
PC–London[561]   Having repeatedly noticed in your widely extended
📧 29/6/1829

SW, using the pseudonym 'Scrutator', transmits 'the following extraordinary and curious fact which has lately occurred', noting that 'anecdotes of musical characters' often have appeared in *The Harmonicon*.

An organist, when driving a gig near London, was overturned; the fall severely bruised his head and brought on delirium. He subsequently was 'restored to reason and health' but, during his confinement in bed, he dreamt that he was in Heaven where 'the situation of organist was vacant'. He volunteered his

---

[561] Ltr is in SW's handwriting but does not mention his name. It was not published in *The Harmonicon*.

services. 'All the celestial judges of fine performance', particularly Handel and JSB, 'were enraptured' and he therefore obtained the position. The organist claims to remember 'every bar of the voluntary' he played and 'means shortly to commit the whole to paper' and to publish it on this planet.

The story that [Giuseppe] Tartini [Italian composer, 1692–1770] dreamt that Satan played a violin solo for him 'is too trite to need repetition'. SW/'Scrutator' may have seen this solo in print, but well remembers hearing Thomas Linley Jr, brother of 'that beautfiul vocalist' [Elizabeth Ann Linley] 'the first Mrs [Richard Brinsley] Sheridan', 'inimitably' perform Tartini's 'diabolical' composition [his violin sonata in G minor, of which the last movement, a representation of the composer's dreams, includes a section called 'the devil's trill']. Although this piece is eccentric in style, 'the rules of our terrestrial harmony' are never 'violated or neglected'. The circumstance that the devil took up the violin 'as his musical instrument' should not depreciate the instrument's 'intrinsic value' which has been delightfully demonstrated by performers such as [Nicholas] Mori, [Louis] Spohr [German violinist and composer, 1784–1859] and [Charles-Auguste de] Bériot [Belgian violinist, 1802–1870].

SW/'Scrutator' hopes that the anecdote he related 'will not be long withholden' from readers on Earth. They will then be able to compare 'the strains elaborated in Tartarus' [the abyss below Hades] with 'those inspired in Olympus' [home of the Greek gods].

SW→Rosalind   2/7/1829
BL Add 35012 f 111   Your Mother, myself & Doctor Gallipot all intend
⊟ Thu 2 Jul={1818,1829,1835}[562]

SW, SS and 'Doctor Gallipot' [presumably a medical doctor, *see* SW→SS, 3/8/1824] intend to visit Rosalind [in Gravesend] and to come by the morning boat on Monday [6/7/1829]. They had planned to have come several days ago but were prevented.

CW Jr→Tooth   1/8/1829
MA DDWes/6/91   I take it very kind your writing again.
⊟ 1/8/1829

At the invitation of Mrs [Elizabeth] Greene [CW Jr's cousin, at whose home he lodged], SW dined here [20 Edgware Road] yesterday [31/7/1829] 'in high glee'. It hurt CW Jr to hear SW speak against 'the good Methodists' because Mr Morley [possibly David Morley, *c*1759–1837, for many years a Methodist class

---

[562] Assigned to 1829 for the following reason. Ltr addressed to Rosalind Wesley in Gravesend. 1818 excluded because Rosalind then would have been about four years old, too young to be living away from home. 1835 excluded because Rosalind then was married to RG and accordingly would have been addressed by her married name.

leader] and Jackson would not give SW £200 for his *Hymns*.[563] SW is 'much pleased' with Tooth and means to present a copy of the *Hymns* to her.

CW Jr asks Tooth, whom SW respects, not to tell SW of CW Jr's intended journey [to Bristol]. SW talks of going to Bristol, but CW Jr hopes that this is 'not to get a paltry 5/- benefit concert'.

CW Jr generally meets Mrs [Elizabeth] M[ortimer] of K[entish] T[own] at the Hind Street Chapel meetings. She 'always speaks' of SW.

James Townley & Robert Newton→SW   10/8/1829

MA M-PLP 107-6-19   Your offer to dispose of the copy-right of the improved
☞ 10/8/1829

On behalf of the [86th annual] Conference [of the Methodist Church], [Rev.] James Townley [Methodist minister], president [of this Conference], and Robert Newton, secretary [of this Conference], advise SW that 'his offer to dispose of the copyright of the improved edition' of 'Sacred Harmony' for £105 was read to the Conference.[564] Conference thanked SW for 'his consideration of their interest', but it is not their policy to negotiate in such cases, and they have referred SW's letter [not preserved] to the Book [Room] Committee for their consideration.

SW→John Thomas Smith   Euston St   11/9/1829

BL Add 45102 f 137; *O*   I have encouraged young Mr Bennet to enquire
☞ Fri 11 Sep & 🔍→ ⓘ

SW has encouraged 'young Mr Bennet' [who had accompanied SW to Leeds, *see* SW→SS, 13/9/1828] to ask John Thomas Smith [antiquary, 1776–1833, from 1816 keeper of prints and drawings in the British Museum] if he is acquainted with any of the '24 personages' on the list that Bennet will present. Bennet has been informed that any one of them is authorised to appoint 'whomsoever comes well recommended for integrity and steadiness, and that no pecuniary security is requisite for the election of the candidate'.

---

[563] The 11/12/1828 and 8/1/1829 minutes (MA) of the Methodist Book-Room committee record that SW had written [not preserved] an offer to sell the copyright and plates of his [*Original*] *Hymn Tunes* for £150 or 150 gns = £157/10/-. The committee declined SW's offer on the grounds that their stock of this publication was sufficient for present and anticipated sales.

[564] Possibly this is a mistaken reference to SW's offer to sell the copyright of his *Original Hymn Tunes* for £150, *see* note to CW Jr→Tooth, 1/8/1829.

SW→SS   Blagdon [Somerset]   **18/9/1829**
BL Add 35012 f 77   You may guess that if I could have let you hear of me
⬛ Fri 18 Sep={1818,1829,1835}[565]

SW would have written before if he could. He is sorry for the disappointment, but it was unavoidable. Bennet will tell SS all the details. SW has the promise of a recital at [St Mary] Redcliffe [Bristol], where 'an advantageous performance' is virtually certain, and also of three other recitals, one of them at Wells Cathedral. SS is to sound out [George] Cooper immediately on his terms for coming down. SW hopes that all the children are well, and asks for news. He will not write more, as Bennet will answer all of SS's questions.

Wait & SW→SS   Blagdon   **23/9/1829**
BL Add 35012 f 78   *Wait:*   Everything goes on beyond expectations
                         SW: According to Mr B's Letter you have been
⬛ Wed 23 Sep; pmk 1829

Wait: Everything is going well, and Wait expects that SW's performances will be successful. CW Jr's playing every day in Bristol—where he was mistaken for SW—has been a problem, but this mistake was corrected in the newspapers yesterday [22/9/1829]. SW will begin in Bristol with a 'grand performance' at St Mary Redcliffe, where he tried the organ last night. He should not be hurried home, as it seems that he is to be offered several more organ recitals.

SW sleeps at the Waits' home at Blagdon [where Wait was rector] every night; if SW stayed at Bristol he would have to play to all the principal people every evening. SW's health is much improved. Sam [SSW], not [George] Cooper, should come down to Bristol. Cooper would take from SW's receipts and would not be half as useful as SSW; in addition, he would be introduced into SW's 'ground', which should be avoided, as SW otherwise may be able to make money from organ recitals in Bristol every year. SS should ask Bennet to find out how long an attorney must present his bill before he can exact payment. He asks SSW to bring the books that were sent for Wait from Gauntlett's office.

SW: According to Mr B[ennet]'s letter, SS should have been at Gravesend by now. SW wishes that she could remain at Gravesend for a week. As soon as he can send the money he will enable her to do this. He is sure that his journey will prove financially worthwhile. Even if he should clear only £100 SS should not be discontented. He expects to make more, but it may take a further week, and he must reconcile himself to not seeing all his 'dear young fry'.

Mrs [Eliza] Wait gave birth to a daughter [Leila Kennedy Wylde Wait] on Monday [21/9/1829]; both are well. SS should not let Wait's statement prevent Cooper from stating the terms on which he proposes to come to Bristol. SW should be the person who decides whether or not he should come. Wait and SW went to Bristol yesterday to try the St Mary Redcliffe organ and to talk to the

---

[565] Assigned to 1829 because SW was in Blagdon in September 1829 (*see* SW→SS, 23/9/1829) and is not known to have been there in 1818 or 1835; also, SW's promised Bristol recital took place within a fortnight after ltr.

churchwardens. It was agreed that SW should have use of the church, and that a share of his profits should go to defray the expenses of the recent repairs and additions to the organ.

They are to dine tomorrow with the churchwardens, the organist [Cornelius Bryan, c1775–1840, from 1818 organist of St Mary Redcliffe, *see* Wait & SW→SS, 25/9/1829], the organ builder and some members of the vestry. SW must write to Mr Thiselton [not identified] to say that he cannot remit the £10 due until after SW's first performance. Thiselton must therefore allow SW several days later than next Monday [28/9/1829].

SS should tell Bennet that SW is vexed that he had to walk so far on Saturday [18/9/1829]. Wait thanks Bennet for his kind offer of service, which he is likely to need. SW asks SS to kiss 'Nancy Dawson' [their daughter Thomasine], 'Fish' [MEW], 'Calf' [presumably their son John] and 'poor Roz' [Rosalind]. SW supposes that SSW has acquired 'the scale of the hurdy gurdy and the salt box under his learned instructor and companion in the Fisherman's Hotel'.

Wait's sister has sent £5 to Wait, who has had an offer to 'conduct a review' which should bring him £30 per month [part 1 of *The Repertorium Theologicum: or, a Critical Record of Theological Literature*, edited by Wait, was published in London in 1829; apparently no further parts appeared]. SS should say nothing about this.

Wait & SW→SS		Blagdon	**25/9/1829**
BL Add 35012 f 80	*Wait:*	Do not hurry Mr Wesley back	
	SW:	If I were not to write today, you would have	

▣ 25/9/1829

Wait: SS is not to hurry SW back, for 'the harvest will be rich beyond his expectations'. SW will have three recitals at St Mary Redcliffe, some at Clifton church and some elsewhere. They have had difficulties because of CW Jr, to the extent that SW's identity has been disputed [*see* Wait & SW→SS, 23/9/1829]. SS should not mention SW's success to anyone, lest others 'try the experiment on this rich ground'. Wait has a promise from the vestry [of St Mary Redcliffe] that SW will have three recitals there next summer. The church holds 4,000 people and the parish bears the expenses of advertisements and singers. SW will send SS a Bristol newspaper with the accounts.

CW Jr gave a recital on St James's organ yesterday [24/9/1829], 'doubtless to injure his brother' [SW]. Wait was right in his conjecture that Hodges is 'close' to CW Jr's 'backside'. Hodges 'now shows his cloven hoof'.

SW: SS would have no letter before Monday [27/9/1829] if SW did not write today. He reiterates Wait's request not to publicise SW's success at Bristol. The first 'morning music' at St Mary Redcliffe will take place next Thursday [1/10/1829]. He has permission to have two further meetings [i.e., concerts] at that church. 'Bryant' [Cornelius Bryan], the organist, is so 'civil and attentive' that SW thinks it will be unnecessary to ask [George] Cooper to come down. SW has not received Cooper's letter [not preserved], and comments on the unreliability of the posts and delays in receiving mail.

SW has heard that the Duke of Wellington [Arthur Wesley, from 1798 Wellesley, field marshal, 1769–1852, at this time Prime Minister], has brought into parliament a bill allowing proof sheets to be sent free of charge.[566] If the proofs of the 'Scotch songs' [not identified, *see* SW→SS, 11/10/1829] are ready, they can be forwarded to SW without expense. If SS can get all the copies of the hymns that 'that rascal [Rev. John] Mason [steward of the Methodist Book-Room] has got', SW will be able to sell them. If they [the Methodist Book-Room committee] want more, they must print them themselves.

CW Jr has been trying to prevent SW's interest in Bristol, and SW has had great difficulty in persuading people that he is 'the real Samuel Wesley' and not an impostor. SS should write by Monday's post, if she cannot by tomorrow's: SW is anxious to know how they all get on. He will send the money as soon as he can. SS should explain to all those who are impatient at SW's absence that he is 'scraping up the blunt' to prevent them complaining of him when he returns.

Abbot's bill for £9/19/- is due on Friday 9/10/1829, and SW should be able to send the amount at the beginning of the week after next [5/10/1829]. SSW must go immediately to Lovelace, the printer in Osnaburgh Street, Clarence Garden, and tell him that Mrs [Eliza] Wait is confined to her bed, and that he will receive a letter and an enclosure next Monday [28/9/1829]. This is 'of the greatest consequence'.

Hodges journal entry   Bristol   1/10/1829

Hodges p 48–49   I proceeded with my brother Archelaus to Redcliff Church
Hodges

Hodges and his brother Archelaus Hodges [*bap*1808] proceeded to St Mary, Redcliffe [Bristol] where they heard SW's 'really outstanding performance' on the church organ. This was the most wonderful organ performance that Edward Hodges had ever heard or had conceived possible: he was 'knocked off his stilts'. After a duet performed by SW and SSW, 'the concluding fugue was sublime'. Many professional organists attended 'and were doubtless carried into the third Heaven'. After the performance, Hodges 'exchanged a few words with the old man' [SW] and with SSW. Hodges then wrote 'a paragraph for the [Bristol] *Mirror*' lauding SW. Words cannot praise SW too highly: 'he is the prince of musicians and emperor of organists'.

Hodges journal entry   Bristol   4/10/1829

Hodges p 49–50   I performed two or three movements out of Sebastian Bach
Hodges

Hodges played a few movements by JSB on his piano but disliked the result. 'God has made one man a Wesley [SW], another a Hodges.' Perhaps SW's visit to Bristol was 'ordered by divine goodness' to teach Hodges humility. Hitherto

---

[566] The Duke of Wellington was a son of Garret Wesley, Mus. Doc., 1st Earl of Mornington and hence a distant relative of SW.

Hodges thought himself 'something in music at least', but even that is now 'taken' from him. Somehow he got through his organist's duties at St Nicholas's in the morning and at St James's in the afternoon and evening, but [after hearing SW play on 1/10/1829] he will not say that he 'played the organ'.

CW Jr→Tooth   Bristol   5/10/1829
MA DDWF/20/32   Through a kind Providence, here we are again.
▣ 5/10/1829
   CW Jr has just returned [to London] from Bristol. SW is at Bristol, 'performing in public' at St Mary, Redcliffe [church]. He 'is to be remunerated'.

Hodges journal entry   Bristol   5/10/1829
Hodges p 50   At one o'clock I hastened to Redcliff Church to witness
Hodges
   At 1 pm Hodges hastened to St Mary's, Redcliffe to hear SW play again. Hodges was delighted by the performance but was 'not completely carried away', as he had been on the earlier occasion [on 1/10/1829].

SW→SS   Blagdon   7/10/1829
BL Add 35012 f 82[567]   I got your Letter late last Night
▣ 7/10/1829
   SW received SS's letter [not preserved] late last night [6/10/1829] and was not able to write before now. He encloses the receipt as required. Scadding [not identified] advanced £5 and therefore must send SS £10/15/- [the balance due].
   SW hopes that SS will get to spend two or three days at Gravesend, getting 'good air before the winter'. SW wishes to be home. If it were not for the necessity of making what he can in Bristol, he would 'stick his bum' into the London coach.
   There has been 'infernal opposition' from the fools that Charles [CW Jr] has been 'humbugging so many years', and his lies have done a great deal of mischief. SW could not live in Bristol: it is as bad as the worst part of London. The places around Bristol are very pleasant, but Blagdon is better than them all. He wishes he could have sent money earlier, but has not yet received any.
   Today is the third and last performance at St Mary Redcliffe, and he will then 'row them for a settlement'. If he can arrange one good [musical] meeting elsewhere, the 'total result will not be to be sneezed at'.

---

[567] Ltr is incomplete.

Hodges journal entry   Bristol   **7/10/1829**
Hodges p 50–51   I spent a very rattletrappish sort of morning
Hodges

SW set forth between noon and 1 pm to hear SW's 'third and last' organ performance at St Mary, Redcliffe. This time Hodges did not 'experience so much gratification as upon either of the former occasions'. He is uncertain whether this was due to 'satiety' or whether SW's performance had fallen off. Hodges now regards his article about SW, published in the 4/10/1829 *Bristol Mirror*, as 'somewhat bombastic and stiltified' [he had written that SW's effect was 'literally superhuman' and that his 'splendid extemporaneous effusions left his hearers perfectly astounded']; however, this was how he felt at the time.

Now that Hodges has heard SW a few times he is able to analyse how SW produces his effects. Although initially surprised by SW's 'exceedingly full' and seemingly incomprehensible harmonies, on subsequent hearings Hodges has understood that SW's harmonies were 'either diatonic or chromatic mixtures'. Hodges attributes his initial surprise to his lack of familiarity with 'the precise pitch of that particular organ'; now that he has analysed what SW did, his performances have been lowered, in Hodges's estimation, 'to the ordinary range of mortal ability'. Although SW's modulations were initially 'astounding, because mysterious', they soon became familiar. Nevertheless, SW's merit cannot be totally 'frittered down to the ordinary level of humanity' or he would have many equals. SW's 'grand forte is confessedly extempore fugue' but the fugue subjects seem merely 'illegitimate offsprings' of SW's idol JSB. Doubtless SW has 'well studied' the opening of each fugue in advance of his extempore performance.

SW→SS   Blagdon   **11/10/1829**
BL Add 35012 f 83   It was impossible to answer the last Letter sooner
▪ 11/10/1829 and 12/10/1829

SW was unable to answer SS's last letter any sooner. He supposes that their letters will cross. He did not write to [George] Cooper, as his letter to SS [SW→SS, 25/9/1829] was sufficient to inform Cooper that he was not expected, and SW cannot imagine that he would be offended. Cooper need not fear that SW's return [to London] could be as late as 4/11/1829. SW intends to stay in Bristol no longer than is necessary, and hopes to be back [in London] in the week after next at the latest.

SW is anxious about the 'Scotch songs' [*see* Wait & SW→SS, 25/9/1829]. He anticipates a 'row' at their not coming out, and that the Lees will blame him [George Alexander Lee, composer, music publisher (with Henry Lee, as 'Lee & Lee') and theatre manager, 1802–1851, whose song 'Blue bonnets over the border', arranged from the 'celebrated national air' of Scotland, had been published in late 1828 or early 1829]. SW has been ready to correct and return the proofs whenever he receives them in Blagdon. The Bristolians are 'a shabby scabby set'. At St Mary Redcliffe they are trying to cheat him as much as they can, but he and Wait are fighting them and if necessary will expose them. Tomorrow [12/10/1829] is the day appointed to settle with the churchwardens. If SW gets any money worth sending, he will inform SS immediately.

He does not require SS to send further clean linen. He calculates that two more shirts will be as many as he needs, in addition to the one he has already.

All the Waits are well. They send their best wishes. Wait must be in London during this week, but asks SS not to tell anyone. She is to tell Bennet that SW received his letter [not preserved] today, and that SW and Wait will forward the testimonial to him. SSW probably will go back [to London] tomorrow night. He will tell SS 'a rum story of the Bristol hogs'.

SW→SS Blagdon **18/10/1829**

BL Add 35012 f 85   You forget that the delivery of Post Letters here is often
◼ 18/10/1829

The postal delivery of letters to Blagdon often is uncertain. SS should not imagine that SW ever neglects an opportunity for replying as soon as it is possible to forward a letter. SW is angry that SSW did not give her all the cash (after paying his travelling expenses) that he took from SW. SSW's tailor's bill could have waited until after SW's return.

SW finds that SSW has tried to alarm SS about SW's success. This is 'very wicked and foolish'. Although SW has been 'ill-used' by the 'shabby scabby churchwardens of Redcliffe', he can certainly make money in two or three places elsewhere, and Wait is 'piping all hands' to help him. It is wrong of SSW to suggest that Wait has been culpable or inattentive. The Bristolians are not to be managed by kindness but by fear.

SW is 'vexed' about the bills, but cannot get rid of them until he has earned the money by the exertions he is now making. The lies and misrepresentations of CW Jr and his friends have been the main obstacle to SW's success, but there is good reason now to expect 'a triumph over their villainous and treacherous proceedings'. It is now accepted on all sides that SW is SW, and CW Jr is not, and the Bristolians now realise how much they had been 'gulled and humbugged'. This 'proves that cheating play is always sure to fail at the last'.

SW longs to see his 'chickens' although he has been well looked after at Blagdon. He was grieved to hear of Mr Middleton's loss [of his son], especially as he had seemed 'so wrapt up in the fate of that little fellow' [SW→Rosalind, 2/7/1829, is addressed to her at 'the builder Mr Middleton's, Windmill Square, Gravesend']. SW will send news as soon as there is anything good to communicate.

SW→SS Blagdon **21/10/1829**

BL Add 35012 f 87   All Matters with me are presenting a favourable Prospect
◼ 21/10/1829

SW's prospects are favourable. He has secured a performance at the Moravian Chapel [in Bristol] which will take place soon, and expects one evening to give concerts in two churches, each of which will hold 700 people. Hodges has behaved 'in the most handsome and liberal manner' and is doing his utmost to repair the disappointment caused by the [St Mary] Redcliffe churchwardens, the organist [Cornelius Bryan], and CW Jr's party. Now that the truth has emerged, the tide is running in SW's favour. SW longs to see all his family, and nothing but his determination to do all he can for them prevents his earlier return. SS will certainly receive some money next week.

SW is anxious to hear about SS. She should get Bennet to write to him immediately with all the news. SW will commission Bennet to receive the money for her. SW is aware of the 'teasing state' in which she is placed but is sure that she has made the best of things. She cannot be arrested, and SW hopes that those who are troublesome will be pacified for a week or two longer, knowing that he is working at Bristol to earn the money to pay them all. He hopes that SSW does not worry SS by his failure to help. If SSW ever has a family of his own he will know what his duty to them is.

SW is now setting out for Bristol to make arrangements about the Moravian Chapel. Latrobe has done him much good by the way he has promoted SW's interest amongst his own people [the Moravians] in Bristol.

SW→SS   Blagdon   **25/10/1829**
BL Add 35012 f 89   I got the Letter dated the 20th only last Night
▣ 25/10/1829

SW was in Bristol from Thursday [22/10/1829] until last night [24/10/1829], so did not get SS's letter of 20/10/1829 [not preserved] until last night.[568] Wait will deliver the present letter to SS and will tell her the news.

SW has secured [recitals at] two churches with the possibility of a third, as well as the Moravian Chapel, where he is to play tomorrow [26/10/1829]. He is confident of being able to send £20 to SS on Tuesday [27/10/1829]. She can be sure of more money later, but her disappointment up to now has been caused by the rascality of the [St Mary Redcliffe] churchwardens, which SS will have heard about from Wait and from SSW.

Wait asks SW to add that Wait's failure to call on SS again is not a mark of 'slight or inattention', but is because 'the G—s' [the Gauntletts, i.e., Henry John Gauntlett and his brother Edward Ebenezer Gauntlett (*bap*1808), both of whom were lawyers: *see* SW→SS, 29/10/1829], knowing Wait's friendship with SW and SS, will be lying in wait for Wait at their house. Long though SW's struggle has been, he hopes that SS will have no cause to be dissatisfied in the end. She should get some money from the father of [the singer] Miss Mayor. SW is determined not to lose money anywhere 'for an absurd delicacy'.

SS will hear from SW again when he has good news to report.

---

[568] Presumably SW left Blagdon for Bristol on 22/10/1829, as a copy of his duet 'Phere moi kupellon' (BL Add 35005 f 118ᵛ) bears Wait's annotation that it was written at Blagdon Rectory on 22/10/1829.

SW→SS   Cloisters, Bristol   **27/10/1829**

BL Add 35012 f 91[569]   You must know that the only Reason of your not

☞ 27/10/1829

The only reason why SS did not receive a letter today is that SW did not have the right news; but if she goes to the banking house of Grote, Prescot[t], and Co., St Mildred's Court in the Poultry, Cheapside, she will find a post bill for £30 waiting for her. SW will have more money for her shortly. All is going well; when he writes next he will be able to fix the date of his return journey, which he longs to do.

Hodges [with whom SW is staying] has shown himself a good friend: he and some others have done great things, in a short time, to help SW. SS will have seen 'the poor doctor' [Wait], whom she should tell about SW's visit [to Bristol]. She should write by return of post. SW will not return to Blagdon until Friday morning [30/10/1829].

Hodges journal entry   Cloisters, Bristol   **28/10/1829**

Hodges p 54   Between eight and nine Wesley came to breakfast

Hodges

Between 8 and 9 am, SW came to breakfast. Hodges showed some of his musical compositions to SW before and after the meal. SW 'flattered and encouraged' Hodges, commended the strength of his style [of composition], and said that Attwood never could have written such a chorus as Hodges's 'Thou O King, art a King of Kings'.

SW→SS   Cloisters, Bristol   **29/10/1829**

BL Add 35012 f 93[570]   I expect to move towards London either on Monday or

☞ 29/10/1829

SW expects to start out [for London] in a day coach, either on Monday [2/11/1829] or on Tuesday [3/11/1829]. The Clifton affair [a recital at Clifton Church] is not to be, as the churchwardens feel that it is 'too soon after Topliff's nonsense' [Robert Topliff, organist and composer, 1793–1868] to be sufficiently productive. Yesterday [28/10/1829] SW played at St Nicholas's Church; today he is going to St James's.

Hodges has managed the whole affair 'in a very clever, and a very delicate manner'. Many friends of Hodges and of 'Mr Frip' [Edward Bowles Fripp, organist and composer, 1787–1870] have come forward with subscriptions. All have given a guinea [£1/1/-], and many three or four, so SW may depend on at least £50 more to come. The account of all the receipts is to be done tomorrow [30/10/1829]. It will be found that SS need not repent of SW having made his 'experiment' here. The results will certainly improve if he returns next year.

---

[569] Ltr is incomplete.

[570] The end of ltr is damaged.

SW will write in due course regarding the business concerning [William Henry] Kearns [Irish violinist and conductor, 1794–1846, from 1817 resident in London]. [Thomas] Greatorex is an 'old brute', with whom SW does not consider the business likely to succeed. SSW's letter [not preserved] is 'a specimen of a very curious manuscript', but SW managed to get his meaning. As the Clifton meeting is not to take place, SSW need not worry about himself or [George] Cooper providing music.

The Dean of Bristol [Henry Beeke, 1751–1837] gave Hodges £2 on SW's account. They might have had the use of [Bristol] Cathedral 'if the application had been skilfully made'. SW will explain more on his return home. He assures SS that he has made several good friends in Bristol who are intent on promoting his interest whenever he returns.

SSW has written [not preserved] nothing about 'our learned little Doctor' [Wait] who, in 'the utmost agitation', fearing that he could not escape his pursuers, left SW on Sunday night [25/10/1829]. The Gauntletts [Henry John Gauntlett and Edward Ebenezer Gauntlett, *see* SW→SS, 25/10/1829] are 'a brace of hell hounds'.

Wait wrote to his wife [Eliza] after SW had arrived in Bristol. SW goes back to Blagdon tomorrow.

SW→SS   Cloisters, Bristol   **30/10/1829**
BL Add 35012 f 95   The same Trouble that you complained of before
☞ 30 Oct[571]

SS should go to the same banking house as previously [Grote, Prescott and Co., *see* SW→SS, 27/10/1829], where she will receive £50. SW has just received letters [not preserved] from Wait and from SSW. The calculation about the churches in SW's last letter [SW→SS, 29/10/1829] was mistaken. They [SW and SS] have done as well as they could, and much better than could have been expected.

SS is to pay none but the most urgent bills before she sees SW. She can expect him on Monday [2/11/1829] or Tuesday [3/11/1829]; Tuesday is more likely. He longs to return home.

SW is now going back to Blagdon. He will write to [William Henry] Kearns but does not expect the least success. [George] Cooper's £5 'proposal' is 'cursedly shabby'.

---

[571] Assigned to 1829 because SW was at The Cloisters, Bristol (Hodges's home) only in October 1829.

SW→Tooth   Euston St   **17/11/1829**
MA DDWF/15/41; *O*   It is not without much Reluctance that I am obliged
ltr undated[572]

A tradesman with whom SW has dealt for more than seven years has issued a
writ against him for £22. 'Several officers', from whom SW had a very narrow
escape, 'besieged' his house last night [16/11/1829]; he now is harbouring 'in
the house of a friend'. He asks Tooth to approach CW Jr to lend him £25 to
cover the writ and legal expenses. SW is going later today to Watford. He is
preparing a concert there that he expects will be profitable; indeed, his financial
prospects look better than they have been for many years. He can 'get out of
town safely today and remain until Saturday morning' [21/11/1829], so if the
matter can be 'adjusted' tomorrow [18/11/1829] he 'may return without danger'.

SW→SS   Watford   **17/11/1829**
BL Add 35012 f 97   I am here safe and sound, & found Bird at Home
▣ 'Tuesday 17 November'; pmk 1829

SW arrived in Watford today in haste; he is safe and sound. He found
[William] Bird at home studying the letter [not preserved] that Bird received
from [Daniel] Wait on SS's account. It would have been absurd to disguise the
truth about SW's personal danger [of arrest, *see* SW→Tooth, 17/11/1829]. SW
presumes that SSW informed SS of what passed between Madden [not
identified] and Robson [possibly Joseph Robson of the organ builders Flight and
Robson]. SS must tell SW 'directly' all that she has done since SW's departure,
and all that she is now doing and intends to do 'in this infernal business'.
  Bird is 'in a peck of troubles about his tunes' [presumably his *Original
Psalmody, see* SW→William Bird, 27/1/1829] but is 'a good honest dog'. SW
asks SS to send some clothes and his pills in a parcel by coach. She should
comfort the children, to whom he sends love, and take comfort herself. He fears
nothing: his trust in the mercy and protection of God is 'perfect, and boundless'.
SS is to write and let SW know how 'Prophet Daniel' [Wait] gets on. She is to
show Wait this letter and to get him to answer [George] Oliver and Tomkison
[not identified].

CW Jr→Tooth   **23/12/1829**
MA DDWes/6/85   My dear and respected friend Miss Tooth will pardon my
▣ 23/12/1829

  CW Jr sends 'a most curious letter [not preserved] from the old quarter' [SW].
SW 'ought to be satisfied' with 'two church organs', with SSW 'being appointed

---

[572] Assigned to 17/11/1829 because ltr says SW is going to Watford today, and
SW→SS, 17/11/1829, presumably written very soon after his arrival there, says
that SW arrived safely in Watford. SW is not known to have taken any other trip
to Watford during the time that he lived at Euston Street.

to Waterloo organ' [i.e., as organist of St John's, Waterloo Road], and the '£50 lecture at Camberwell' [not identified].

CW Jr wishes to follow Sarah's example of owing 'no man anything'. He 'cannot do more for' SW. CW Jr suspects that SW worded the anonymous letter. Mr Hopwood [not identified] is certain that the letter is in SW's style and wondered 'if we have the name of Wagster among the good Methodists'. CW Jr thinks that the writer of the anonymous letter 'wishes to be thought a minister'. He seeks Tooth's 'wise judgement' regarding the letter and hopes that she can return it to him during the approaching holidays, when they can talk about it.

SW→SS   Park St, Bristol   **10/1/1830**
BL Add 35012 f 99   We arrived both safe & sound tho' not until half past 9
▣ 10/1/1830

'We' [SW and Joseph Collyer, a singer who performed at SW's 1830 lectures to the Philosophical and Literary Society of Bristol, at the Bristol Institution] arrived safely [in Bristol] at 9.30 pm last night [9/1/1830]. They dined with Hodges and have good lodgings at Park Street. SW will write to Parson Storie [not identified], so 'dutiful master Sam' [SSW] need not worry SS.

SW is anxious to learn how SS's mouth 'gets on' and suspects that Wakefield [her doctor] gave her too strong a preparation containing too much mercury. SW asks SS to write by return to let him know whether [William] Bird has called and has given any hopes of 'squaring matters in the Watford affair'. If [John] Capel [1767–1846, MP for Queenborough, 1826–1832, from 1828 president of the Glee Club] does not come forward, he is not the gentleman that SW took him for. Collyer has refused to take any money beyond his expenses.

SW→SS   62 Park St, Bristol   **14/1/1830**
BL Add 35012 f 101   I would have gladly returned you a Letter
▣ 14/1/1830

SW was too busy to answer SS's letter [not preserved] immediately. [Joseph] Collyer has caught a cold, but is on the mend and should be able to 'tickle the ladies' ears' as successfully as he did on Monday [11/1/1830, at SW's first lecture]. SW's lectures are very popular, and he should get more for them than 'the mere bargain for delivering them'. The Manager of the [Bristol] Institution tells SW that the Parson at Frome has agreed to allow SW to perform there. This should be a source of further profit.

None of the Waits should be able to 'pick another halfpenny' out of SW's pocket: it is a 'grievous thing that a man so fitted to make his fellow creatures happy should exert the powers of such a head only to deceive and plunder them'. Wait's brother, William Wait, called to invite SW to dinner.

SW is anxious to know about SS and the children, and hopes that she is better. Mr Badham, who worked hard for SW at the Moravian Chapel [in Bristol] previously, called in five minutes after the books arrived. SW made him accept a book [probably SW's *Original Hymn Tunes*], and he bought another two. SW gave another to Hodges, who SW thinks will 'puff the work in every direction'. SW must present a copy to [Edward Bowles] Fripp [*see* SW→SS, 29/10/1829], who gave SW a copy of his *Psalms*. 12 copies [of SW's publication] then will be left, which SW is sure he will sell. He cannot decently ask for money [for his lectures] before Saturday [16/1/1830], but he and Collyer agree that there can be no objection to asking for an advance then. Collyer is 'devilishly indignant' at Thiselton's behaviour [*see* SW→SS, 23/9/1829].

SW hopes that SS is not 'worried and teased' by 'a certain organist related to you' [SSW]. SW insists that Bennet should tell him all about SSW's behaviour.

SW is well and has not needed to take a single pill. He will be in better spirits when he learns that SS's health is improved. He promises that they will visit Gravesend before the end of the summer. If they can get a new house 'well stuffed with lodgers who will pay and not run away' [remainder of sentence scored out]. SW encloses a sovereign [a £1 coin].

SW→SS   Park St, Bristol   **17/1/1830**
BL Add 35012 f 103   I trust that this will find you well enough to venture
☑ 17/1/1830

SW hopes that SS is well enough to venture into the parlour without danger from the draughts of wind which have troubled them in 'Carnes's infernal den' [their Euston Street house] ever since they have been there. He sends £5 and will send £5 more when he can. He is sorry to hear of Rosalind's malady and asks that she be well nursed. Bennet writes favourably [not preserved] of the manners of 'the pedalist' [presumably SSW] to SS. SW will certainly give 'the young sprig' lessons, if he will pay 50 guineas [£52/10/-] on the nail.

SW will write tomorrow to the Gauntletts. His 'partner Joe' [Collyer] is so much better that he is expected to perform tomorrow [at SW's 18/1/1830 lecture]. The Curator of the [Bristol] Institution has written to the Parson at Frome. The wife of Mr Badham [*see* SW→SS, 14/1/1830] is a Methodist and will be interested in SW's *Hymns*. Mr Badham advised SW to appear at the Methodist Chapel this evening, where he thinks that SW will be able to sell some copies.

SW asks for news about the children. He must write a few lines [of recommendation] for 'Master Bennet' to [Gesualdo] Lanza, and hopes that they may be of use. SW has little confidence in Lanza's schemes, as Lanza always has too many irons in the fire.

SW→SS   Bristol   **22/1/1830**
BL Add 35012 f 104   I was delighted to find that you are getting about a bit
▣ Fri 22 Jan={1819,1830}[573]

SW is glad that SS is better, but will never forgive [her doctor] Wakefield for
'poisoning' her [*see* SW→SS, 10/1/1830]. SW's lectures continue to be well
attended in spite of the severe weather. The Parson at Frome has not replied, and
it is thought that a church performance would not be successful until the weather
has become warmer. In addition, it seems from SSW's statement that there is a
'general outcry' against SW in London, and that he is to be 'starved directly' if
he does not return next week. [Joseph] Collyer thinks they should set out on
Thursday [28/1/1830].

The people at Bath have been trying to persuade SW to lecture there, but on
terms which would make him out of pocket. He cannot ask the [Bristol]
committee for more money this week: the whole fee is to be paid immediately
after the last lecture [on 27/1/1830]. SS should write on Saturday [23/1/1830].
Otherwise he will not get her reply before Tuesday [26/1/1830].

SW→SS   Bristol   **26/1/1830**
BL Add 35012 f 106[574]   We mean to be stirring our Stumps towards our Dens
▣ 26/1/1830

'We' [SW and Joseph Collyer] mean to set off on Thursday morning
[28/1/1830]. If all goes well, SW should be home by 10 pm. He will take a
hackney carriage from the inn [where the stagecoach arrives]. There is still no
answer from Frome, but in the present cold weather a concert there or in any
other church would be 'a losing concern'.

SW has had 35 of the of 50 guineas [£36/15/- of £52/10/-] promised for his
course of lectures [in Bristol] and thinks he may get between £15 and £20 in
addition to the 15 guineas [£15/15/-] still owed him. He is sorry that Sam [SSW]
has not taken 'his roosting perch' with Atkins [not identified]. SW supposes that
there will be no profit from 'the Oratorio affair'. If he could have lived on
honours and flattery SW would be richer than Rothschild or any Jew.

SW knew Tom Lawrence well [Sir Thomas Lawrence, artist, 1769–20/1/1830,
from 1820 president of the Royal Academy], and also his 'foolish father'
[Thomas Lawrence] who, when he was an inn-keeper [of the Bear Hotel,
Devizes], used to force his guests to listen to him reciting poetry.

SW and Collyer had a pleasant day at [William] Wait's home on Saturday
[23/1/1825]. SW and William Wait [Wait's brother] talked confidentially about
'the Doctor' [Wait]. William Wait pities Wait's case but 'cannot excuse' Wait's
conduct and 'fears that it is out of human power to serve him or save him'.

---

[573] Assigned to 1830 because ltr refers to people (Collyer, the Frome parson)
and events (Wakefield's poor treatment of SS) that are mentioned in SW's
immediately preceding 1830 letters.

[574] The end of ltr is missing.

CW Jr→Tooth   29/1/1830
MA DDWes/6/92   Indeed I have thought it long since I have heard, or seen you.
🖅 29/1/1830

Miss Jones of Bristol [*see* Sarah→SGW, 7/8/1786] informs CW Jr that SW is 'showing off' to a large audience [i.e., he is lecturing at the Bristol Institution].

Yesterday [28/1/1830] Mrs Dalton [not identified] and Miss Jane Jeffreys took CW Jr to St Martin's Lane to perform on a capital organ made for the Honourable Mr Pigot [John Hugh Smyth-Pigott, *d*1831] at Brockley [Hall] near Bristol. The makers [Flight and Robson] did not wish SW to 'get in with' that rich gentleman.

SW→EW   15/2/1830
BL Add 35012 f 112   I wished to have come over to you before now
🖅 15/2/1830

SW hoped to visit EW earlier [at South Clapton] but was unable to find a half-day free. He will certainly see her in the coming week. It is a long time since he has visited his friend [William] Drummer, who probably feels neglected by SW's absence and will gladly receive SW whenever he can manage to come.

CW Jr→Tooth   1/3/1830
MA DDWF/20/34   On my return today from His Majesty's Antient Musick
🖅 2/3/1830

Tooth has had 'a curious letter' [not preserved] from SW, saying that [George] Oliver 'often intruded' on Sarah. Sarah eventually sent word that 'if he troubled her again with his letters, she would give no reply'. 'We [CW Jr and Sarah] sold out' [from their investments] for SW, 'which did no good'.

SW should pay CLW the £25 per annum [maintenance]. CLW brought SW money on her marriage. Dr [James] Price left SW £1000 and a house in Guildford which, as Tooth's father [Samuel Tooth] knew, SW sold for £500. CW Jr cannot give SW any more. SW has had £100 from CW Jr; Mrs [Elizabeth] Mortimer has blamed him for giving this to SW. CW Jr heard today from Bristol that SW 'received £70 for his lectures' [at the Bristol Institution].

CW Jr does not wish to think about this subject again. If Tooth sees SW she should not tell him what CW Jr has written.

SW→'Dear Sir'   **1/3/1830?**
Drew Wesley Family Letters, SW series; *O*
▣ Mon 1 Mar & wmk 1825 &🖎→①[575]

SW is not 'disposed to hypercriticise'. It is better to discover beauties than to point out faults. However, the individual 'whose blunder in accentuation' SW noticed 'with a little asperity' [presumably in a lecture or in a published review] is 'one of the most rancorous musical hypercritics in existence'. The addressee probably heard 'long ago' that SW had quarrelled with this hypercritic, who had 'assassinated' SW's 'church service' anonymously [presumably a reference to the unsigned review, which SW attributed to WH, of SW's Morning and Evening Service in the *QMMR*]. When SW 'cross examined' the hypercritic and demanded to know whether he wrote the criticism, the hypercritic refused to answer but said that he fully agreed with the criticism's 'truth'. [SW had asked WH if he had written the *QMMR* review (see SW→VN, 27/4/1825); people to whom SW showed WH's reply believed that it indicated indirectly that WH was the author of the review (*see* SW→VN, 15/6/1825).]

SW apologises for the apparent 'irritation' with which he criticised the hypercritic's placement of 'a strong musical stress upon grammatical particles'. However, the addressee knows that such a practice demonstrates 'illiterate education'.

SW→Emett   Mornington Pl   **23/4/1830**
BL Add 35013 f 97; *O*   Henry Gauntlett has promised to be here this Evening
▣ Fri 23 Apr & 🖎→①

Henry [John] Gauntlett has promised to be at SW's home tonight and wishes to meet Emett. SW would be glad if Emett could attend.

SW→William Henry Kearns   Mornington Pl   **1/5/1830**
Sotheby catalogue 21/11/1978 lot 392[576]   [not known]
Sotheby catalogue

SW asks Kearns to return the manuscript copy of 'Bach's violin solos' as he will need this next week.

---

[575] An attempt was made to alter the date of ltr after it was written. The word 'Monday' and what appears to be a flourish after the '1' have been scratched out and now are almost illegible without special illumination. SW appears to have dated ltr 'March 1', but the possibility that he originally wrote some numeral after the '1' has not been ruled out. As our dating reason presumes the authenticity of the March 1 date, a question-mark has been placed after the assigned date. Ltr has been marked 'No 38' by an unknown hand. The significance of this mark has not been determined.

[576] Ltr was sold by Sotheby's to the antiquarian book dealer Richard Macnutt. The present location of ltr is not known.

SW→Street   Mornington Pl   **25/5/1830**

Osborn file folder 17958; *O*   If I know aught aright of my own Heart

☑ 25/5/1830

Before the end of his 'mortal and sorrowful career', SW wishes to pay all his 'pecuniary obligations', not only those where 'legal demand' may be made but also the claims of 'kindly accommodating friends'. His greatest 'debt of honour', for which he is eternally grateful, is to Street, who on numerous occasions has given him prompt assistance and has never pressed for repayment. Street and 'a few other friends' know that many years of SW's existence have been spent amid 'much domestic turbulence and persecution', and that some of his 'bitterest foes' have been of his 'own household'. For a time he was 'rendered responsible for heavy debts' that were contracted [by CLW] without his knowledge and were 'vilely exaggerated by tradesmen', who often presented excessive bills.

However, SW never has had 'any propensity towards idleness' and still wishes to work hard in 'whatever department' he may be capable. He has long regretted that the '15 fine Latin anthems' [i.e., antiphons] by [William] Byrd which he transcribed from the Fitzwilliam Collection remain unpublished. Proposals [seeking subscribers to this publication] were printed in 1826 [*see* SW→SS, 13/9/1826], a list of about 200 subscribers appeared long ago in the [Cambridge University] Library and at several principal music shops, and nine of the plates have been engraved, but the project did not succeed because of lack of financial support, possibly because SW 'omitted to mention in the printed proposals' that a publication of this extent required 'auxiliary encouragement in the necessary expenses incurred by the editor' [SW].

SW has raised the matter with several 'principal music sellers'. They all acknowledge that the manuscript [i.e., Byrd's music], which SW was granted a grace from the University [of Cambridge] to copy, is a 'treasure'. Nevertheless, they are unwilling to take on the cost of publishing so large a work, even though SW estimates that 'it will not extend beyond 80 pages' and has offered to make over the amount due from subscribers. As SW believes that Byrd's *Cantiones Sacrae* are in 'your [the Madrigal Society's] collection', he asks if Street thinks it would be proper 'to turn over' the planned publication of the 15 Byrd anthems to the Madrigal Society, in return for a 'certain consideration' to be paid to SW.

SW has met with 'several trying disappointments' recently, including 'the loss of £60 in a professional concern' [possibly his organ recitals at St Mary Redcliffe, Bristol]. He is concerned about the well-being of his children, whom he probably must leave 'long long before the period at which they can be in a condition to provide for themselves', and is anxious to explore every possibility of earning 'an honest penny'. He is confident that Street will provide the benefit of his advice.

SW→'My dear Madam'   Mornington Pl   **29/5/1830**
McGee   You must have believed that I had forgotten my Promise
☞ Sat 29 May & 🖼→🛈

Although SW has tried his best, he has been 'unable to procure an admission for the Oratorio' [concert] tonight.

SW→VN   Mornington Pl   **10/6/1830**
BL Add 11731 f 17; *O*   Two certain parties having been violently at Variance
☞ 10/6/1830

In response to VN's letter dated 11/5/1830 [not preserved], which SW received 'not before' 4/6/1830, SW recounts an anecdote by JW that ended 'at once' the quarrel between two persons who had been 'violently at variance'. One of the two had considered himself 'very deeply aggrieved' and 'vindictive' towards the other.[577]

SW [presumably replying to VN's request for information about Purcell in connection with a forthcoming publication] has rummaged through his old lectures and has found only two 'scraps concerning Purcell', a 'transcendent' genius on whose works 'an elaborate course' of lectures might be given. One scrap notes that Purcell's 'immortal' church service in B♭ is rarely if ever sung at St Paul's [Cathedral], at Westminster Abbey or at the Chapel Royal, whereas 'all the harmless and hackneyed chords of [the composers Charles] King [1687–1748] and [James] Kent [1700–1776]' are in constant demand at cathedrals all over England. The other compares Purcell to Shakespeare 'in his rare faculty of exciting mental emotions of every kind, by his magical and marvellous modes of expression on all occasions'. If SW comes across other material on Purcell, he will forward it.

SW did not know that the tune 'Burford' was attributed to Purcell, nor can he inform VN whether there are other tunes in 'the English psalmody' that Purcell is known to have written. The '104th' has been supposed to be a melody of Corelli but SW does not know on what authority. SW asserts that 'all the really good old psalm tunes are Gregorian melodies in a metrical form'.

---

[577] VN's letter apparently marks his resumption of communication with SW following its presumed break in 1826, when 'Jubal'→Editor, *The Harmonicon*, 20/5/1826, publicised that SW planned to use for one of his publications the same title, 'The Fitzwilliam Music', that VN had previously employed. No SW/VN correspondence is known to have been exchanged between SW→VN, 29/12/1825 and VN→SW, 11/5/1830, mentioned in ltr. Accordingly, SW's statement in ltr about two parties who have been 'violently at variance' seems to be a reference to VN and himself. The delay in SW's receipt of VN's 11/5/1830 letter is consistent with the hypothesis that VN did not know, when he wrote, that SW had moved from Euston Street to Mornington Place.

CW Jr→Tooth   **10/6/1830**

MA DDWF/20/36   I hope your Dear Mother and Family are all better.

⬛ 10/6/1830

Mrs Bayley of the Hind Street Chapel called upon CW Jr 'from Mrs [Elizabeth] Mortimer' of Kentish Town, with the news that SW 'is seriously ill'. CW Jr fears that 'drink is the cause' and asks Tooth to investigate. He is 'not able to give' more cash to SW, which he thinks SW wants. Mrs Bayley thinks that SW has removed to 1 Fred[e]rick Place, New Road [in fact, SW had removed on 22/3/1830 to Mornington Place], but CW Jr suggests that Tooth get 'proper direction' from Mrs Mortimer.

CW Jr→Tooth   **31/7/1830**

WMM   Mrs Greene hath been again far from well

⬛ 31/7/1830

CW Jr supposes that SW has not sent a girl to Tooth. CW Jr wishes him well 'in the best way'. 'We' [CW Jr and Tooth] must pray for him.

CW Jr→Tooth   **5/8/1830**

MA DDWF/20/37   I think it proper to acquaint you

⬛ 5/8/1830

'The person with whom' SW resides [SS] sent a lad to CW Jr, saying that 'Mrs Wesley' [SS] desired him to 'come immediately' because SW 'was seriously ill, deranged, and strapped down'. Mrs [Elizabeth] Greene [CW Jr's cousin, in whose home he was lodging], who hears 'that drink hath again been the cause', said that such a visit would not be useful and that she and CW Jr were about to go to Brighton. The lad then said that SW was better now, as the doctor had bled him. The lad added that 'the woman' [SS] indulges SW by letting him have his own way with no resistance.

It is deplorable that one of the Wesley family has had 'such a wretched life'. Tooth should 'get the good People [the Methodists] to pray for him'. Sarah was very kind to SW 'and his legitimate children', 'selling repeatedly out of her little property but it has done no good'. CW Jr supposes that SW 'wants more money' but CW Jr has done more than he could afford. Friends counselled him to give nothing to SW, but CW Jr could not be 'an unkind brother'. CW Jr depends upon Tooth finding out, and informing him by letter, 'the real state' of SW's condition.

CW Jr→Tooth   27/8/1830
MA DDWes/6/81   I am well pleased allways to hear from you.
📧 27/8/1830
CW Jr heard from Dr Emerson, who called at SW's house but did not go in, that SW is suffering from 'repeated fits of convulsion'. CW Jr was told that SW is being attended by Dr Penkard but does not know if this is true. CW Jr would be obliged if Tooth can obtain news of 'the real state' of SW's health, and implores that SW may turn to God.

CW Jr→Tooth   1/9/1830
MA DDWF/20/38   I am obliged to trouble you again, not having heard
📧 1/9/1830
CW Jr inquires about money 'kindly granted' to him by Tooth's friends. He has had a letter [not preserved] from a friend of SW's 'entreating for money on loan', which CW Jr 'positively refused'.

SW→Richard Akers   15/3/1831
BL Add 29261 f 12   Received of Mr Richard Akers Seven Pounds for Rent
receipt dated 15/3/1831
SW has received £7 rent due from Richard Akers [presumably a lodger].

Richard J. S. Stevens memorandum[578]   3/1831
Camb Add 9111 v 2 p 21   A Collection was made for Mr Samuel Wesley
Memo refers to a March 1831 event[579]
A collection was made for SW in March 1831. VN was the receiver. [John] Capel [president of the Glee Club, *see* SW→SS, 10/1/1830], [Stephen] Groombridge [singer, a former president of the Glee Club] and [presumably R. J. S.] Stevens each sent £5. According to RG, 'the bailiffs' were in possession of SW's house and furniture. SW was 'thought to be mad in May 1817'.

---

[578] Stevens called the two volumes of this manuscript 'Anecdotes. Occurrencies. [sic] Extracts. Opinions, and Observations.'.

[579] An undated printed circular 'To the friends of Mr Samuel Wesley, in general, and the members of the Glee Club, Madrigal Society, and Somerset House Lodge in particular', presumably issued about this time, appeals for 'pecuniary contributions' to assist SW. The circular (a copy is at BL Add 56411 f 34) states that SW faces 'total ruin'. Without financial assistance, he is unable to settle himself 'on an establishment which, there is every reason to hope, would prevent a recurrence of his present annoyances'. Donations to help SW will be 'thankfully received' by VN, WL and John Capel.

CW Jr will[580]   Mornington Pl   **18/5/1831**

PRO PROB 10/5485   This is the last Will and Testament of me Charles Wesley
will dated 18/5/1831

CW Jr revokes all prior 'wills and testamentary papers' [including CW Jr will,
11/1828–11/1830]. He bequeaths £300 to his 'dear brother' SW, £10 to CW III,
£50 to JWW, and £50 to SW's 'only daughter' Emma, who is 'now married'
[she married Frederick Newenham, artist, 1806–1859, on 5/11/1830]. CW Jr
gives, amongst other bequests, £200 and specified books to his cousin Frances
Baldwyn, and £200 and all his other books, manuscripts, music and musical
instruments to his cousin Mrs Elizabeth Greene. He leaves 'the eldest Miss
Tooth' [Eliza Tooth] £5 for a ring [but a 24/5/1832 codicil to this will voids this
bequest to Tooth and leaves £5 instead to CW Jr's former pupil Dorothea
Reece]. CW Jr appoints Edward Glover and Elizabeth Greene executors of his
will.

CW Jr→Thomas Allan   **8/5/1832**

MA DDWF/20/41   It would give me much pleasure to hear you, Mrs Allan
🖃 8/5/1832

CW Jr seeks the assistance of Thomas Allan [a solicitor] in finding
employment for JWW. JWW is industrious, but his work in the coal trade 'did
not answer, having met with bad debts'. CW Jr cannot support him, and SW
'does not care for that part of his family'.

SW→Jackson   **26/6/1832**

Bristol Watkinson album, ltr 661; *O* I hope you will forgive my applying to you
🖃 Tue 26 Jun & SW's late style of handwriting→ i

SW hopes that Jackson will forgive him for applying today [presumably for
money], but a 'pressing occasion' has made this unavoidable.

---

[580] Both this will and the 24/5/1832 codicil are signed by CW Jr but are written
in another hand. The will with that codicil was proved in the Prerogative Court
of Canterbury on 21/7/1834.

SSW→SW   Pentonville   **17/10/1832?**
BL Add 35019 f 6   I write to inquire some intelligence respecting your
☞ 'Wednesday October'[581]

SSW seeks news of SW's 'proceedings at Islington' [SW's home in King's Row, Pentonville, a short distance from the Angel, Islington] and asks whether SW now has got 'people' [presumably lodgers] in his house [at Pentonville]. SSW is anxious to learn what was done since SW's last letter [not preserved], how the family are and what SW's prospects are for 'a more comfortable life in the future'. Summers [not identified, perhaps SW's Pentonville landlord] has 'no claim' upon SW until his lodgings are taken.

SSW cannot now send what SW requires [presumably money], but hopes to be able to send money in about three months, after he begins teaching. 'Of course' SSW would have been pleased 'to have lived quietly without this tiresome and somewhat degrading occupation' [of teaching], but the salary at Hereford Cathedral, where he begins duty [by 'reopening' the enlarged organ] on 6/11/1832, is insufficient. He is lodging near the Cathedral and may travel to Wales before then. He describes a concert in which he played the pianoforte. He asks SW to advise when he wants poultry sent. SW should remind SS to think of SSW's knives, forks and other things [that presumably are to be sent to Hereford].

Mr Hunt [not identified] of Grafton Street owes SSW £2/12/6. If SW can get payment he may keep 'all above' £1/1/-, which SSW needs to settle an account.

SSW→SS   **25/10/1832**
BL Add 35019 f 10   Tell Ros I dont write to her this time
☞ 'Thursday'; pmk 26 October[582]

SSW is 'glad that the cottage is let' [presumably a lodging associated with SW's Pentonville home, *see* SSW→SW, 17/10/1832?]. SS should ensure that she is paid promptly for it. SW should write a 'civil note' to Hunt [*see* SSW→SW, 17/10/1832?], telling him that SSW has many bills to pay. SW 'may order tea and sugar' now from Kemp [not identified], but should be careful

---

[581] Ltr assigned to 1832 because of ref. to SSW beginning duty at Hereford Cathedral: he was appointed on 10/7/1832 and 'reopened' the reconstructed organ there on 6/11/1832 (*Elvin* p 167–168). Information has not been found to determine on which Wednesday in October 1832 ltr was written. Ltr placed tentatively at 17/10/1832 because SSW says that he has found lodgings at Hereford and has time to travel to Wales before his Cathedral duties start; also, ltr precedes SSW→SS, 25/10/1832 and plausibly could have been written eight days earlier, during which time a response [not preserved] could have been sent to SSW from SW or his family in London.

[582] Assigned to 1832 because SSW is in Hereford and ltr refers to Mr Hunt (who is mentioned in SSW→SW, 17/10/1832?) and to the St Dunstan's organ vacancy and states that Hereford Cathedral is not open. Ltr accordingly assigned to Thursday 25/10/1832, the day before the postmarked date.

when giving lessons to 'the girl'. SW cannot teach her much, but Mrs Kemp is 'very particular' and 'a great fool'. SS's account [with Kemp] for tea should not exceed SW's fees for lessons. If SW 'chooses' he can use 'a great deal of music', which will add considerably to the profit.[583] Kemp owes SSW 'a good sum of money' [presumably for teaching Kemp's daughter], but perhaps it is best if SSW gets someone other than SW to ask for it.

SSW asks if SW has settled with [John] Dean [music publisher and seller] regarding music,[584] and inquires who has got the [organist's] post at St Dunstan's.[585] SSW wants to have, soon, a copy of SW's church service [Morning and Evening Service] 'to perform at the [Hereford] Cathedral'. He asks how SW is and remarks that SW should write 'better letters' to SSW. He notes that SW did not correct all the 'faults' in Rosalind's letter [not preserved] to SSW, and advises SS that Rosalind should get a dictionary.

SSW→SS   **15/12/1832**

BL Add 35019 f 12   Call on Monday Morning at the coach office for a parcel.
▣ Sat 15 Dec & Wait a doctor→{1827,1832}[586]

SS is to call at the coach office on Monday morning [17/12/1832] for a parcel. It will contain SSW's anthem ['The Wilderness and the Solitary Place', composed for the 6/11/1832 re-opening of the Hereford Cathedral organ] that SSW is submitting for the [Gresham] prize in London. The anthem must be delivered that Monday. SSW will send a letter to RG with the parcel. SS should keep SW at home to write a motto in Latin for SSW.

SSW exclaims about his 'escape' from [Henry John] Gauntlett [perhaps a reference to the anonymous review of SSW's canzonet 'When we two parted' in *The Harmonicon* no. 59 (November 1832) p 259, which praises this composition but notices two errors in it]. SSW asks SS to visit 'poor Dr' Wait [who became bankrupt in 1833].

---

[583] *See* SW→Miss Matthews, 19/11/1833, in which SW acknowledges payment for music as well as for musical instruction.

[584] Dean had published SSW's 'An original air [for piano]' and SSW's arrangement 'O when do I wish for thee'; both works are advertised in the November 1831 *Harmonicon*. SW's relationship with John Dean apparently continued to the end of SW's life; *see* SW→Jackson, 24/4/1837.

[585] According to *Dawe* p 41, a 28/9/1832 plan to appoint judges to select a new organist for the church of St Dunstan in the West was abandoned on 12/10/1832, and Thomas Adams was elected organist on 25/10/1832.

[586] Assigned to 1832 because of ref. to SSW's anthem; also, SSW is known to have been away from London (in Hereford) in December 1832 but is not known to have been away from London in December 1827.

SSW→SS   **31/12/1832**
BL Add 35019 f 14   I write to tell you that Mr Bishop will leave London
pmk (Hereford) 1832; pmk (London) 1/1/1833[587]

SSW thinks that SW and RG should catch [George] Cooper in St Paul's
[Cathedral, where he was Assistant Organist]. They should tell Cooper that they
have a coach waiting and want the manuscripts [not identified] directly. Cooper
should be given no knowledge of their intention or he would 'smuggle' half the
manuscripts away.

SSW wants to have SW's *Confitebor* performed at the [Three Choirs] festival
[in Hereford in 1834]. SW 'shall come here [to Hereford] to conduct his music'.
SSW asks how SW is and requests that SW or Eliza copy, in a letter, a message
from SSW to W[illiam] H[enry] Kearns.

Felix Mendelssohn→RG   **26/7/1833**
BL Add 35027 f 54[588]   Excuse my not having answered your kind letter
▣ 26 July

Because of his father's illness, Felix Mendelssohn [German composer, 1809–
1847] declines RG's 'offer of playing the organ at Christ's Hospital' [where RG
was organist] and particularly regrets that he therefore will be deprived 'of the
pleasure of being introduced to Mr Wesley' [SW].

SW→Miss Matthews   **19/11/1833**
MA DDWF/15/44   £2/9/- for musical instructions & music
receipt dated 19/11/1833

SW has received £2/9/- from Miss Matthews for musical instruction and music.

---

[587] Accordingly ltr assigned to Monday 31/12/1832.

[588] Assigned to 1833 because ltr, written from 103 Great Portland St, London
says that Mendelssohn's father Abraham Mendelssohn is ill; and Fanny
Horsley→Lucy Hutchins Callcott, 25/7/1833 (printed in *Gotch* p 42–47), states
that the Mendelssohns then were lodging at this address and that Abraham
Mendelssohn, who had broken his shin, was confined to a sofa (*Gotch* p 45–46).

SW→John Fane, Lord Burghersh   Pentonville   **6/3/1834**
BL Add 56411 f 32; *O*   Understanding that there will be a grand Performance
▣ 6/3/1834
SW, an old member of the music profession known to Burghersh,[589]
understands that there will shortly be a 'grand performance' at [Westminster]
Abbey in commemoration of Handel. SW offers to 'preside at the organ' on this
occasion.

SSW→SS   Pentonville   **2/4/1834**
BL Add 35019 f 16   I am surprised at not having heard from you
▣ 2/4/1834
SSW is surprised not to have heard from SS and surmises that something 'very
unpleasant' must have happened. He supposes that he is not expected at his
sister's [Rosalind's] wedding [to RG, on 26/5/1834]. SSW's presence 'could
effect no good object', and he cannot afford the journey's expense [from
Hereford] for 'mere personal amusement'.
SS has complained of SW's 'misconduct' again. SSW had hoped that 'every
bad effect' of SW's 'dreadful illness' had gone away, and grieves to learn
otherwise.
SSW has received permission to marry [he married Marianne Merewether,
1808–1888, in Herefordshire on 4/5/1835].

Edward Glover→SW   **23/5/1834**
MA DDWF/15/38B   As Executor with Mrs Greene I have the melancholy Task
▣ 23/5/1834
Edward Glover, CW Jr's co-executor with Mrs [Elizabeth] Greene [*see* CW Jr
will, 18/5/1831], informs SW that CW Jr died about 3 am today.

SSW→SS   **2/10/1834**
BL Add 35019 f 20   I have not sent the poultry
pmk (Hereford) 2/10/1834
SSW is delighted to hear 'on all sides' that SW is so much better and trusts that
SW finds 'some proper amusement, somewhere'. SSW thinks that SW, if he is
'careful with that most dangerous thing, the tongue', might pass much pleasant
time at RG's home. SSW wonders why SW does not write to him.

---

[589] Besides knowing about SW's musical achievements (*see* SW→John Fane,
2/9/1822), Burghersh would have been aware of his distant relationship to SW.
Lord Burghersh's wife Priscilla Anne Fane (artist, 1793–1879) was the daughter
of William Wesley *later* Wellesley-Pole (1763–1845, *later* 1st Baron
Maryborough and 3rd Earl of Mornington) and therefore was a granddaughter of
Garret Wesley, 1st Earl of Mornington (and a niece of the Duke of Wellington).

SSW→SS   **16/10/1834**
BL Add 35019 f 22   Don't think because I have not written lately that I don't
pmk (Hereford) 16/10/1834
SSW has been to the 'very gay' Birmingham Music Meeting and has been
spoken of very highly in a newspaper. He recalls that SW once conducted 'those
meetings' and wonders how SW came to 'let that slip out of his hands'. SSW
asks why SS does not get all the books from [George] Cooper and why 'that
person [is] to enjoy all the best fruit' of SW's existence.

SW→Jackson   **3/1/1835**
MA DDWF/15/45; *O*   You will much oblige me by a Pound toDay
⌦ 3/1/1835
SW desires £1 today [3/1/1835] rather than 'next Friday' [9/1/1835], as he is
'pushed to make up a little payment'.

SW→Emett   **27/2/1835**
BL Add 35013 f 99; *O*   I rec'd the enclosed To Day,—from Sam.
⌦ 27/2/1835
SW has received the enclosed letter [not preserved] from SSW but does not
share SSW's opinion regarding SW's *Confitebor*: SW thinks that he should have
£200 for it. All the parts are copied. 'Mrs W' [SS] has been ill but is better. SW
asks Emett to see VN tomorrow if he can, and to tell him what SSW says about
the performance [*see* SW→Emett, 3/3/1835].

SW→Emett   Pentonville   **3/3/1835**
BL Add 35013 f 101; *O*   I really think the Confitebor with all the Parts worth
⌦ 3/3/1835
SW thinks that his *Confitebor* with all the parts is worth £200. If VN will not
give more than £150 then this is the least that SW will accept. It may be
advisable to try [the music publishers] Birchall, Chappell and Cramer, but VN
most knows the value [of *Confitebor*]. SW asks whether Emett mentioned [to
VN, *see* SW→Emett, 27/2/1835] that SSW would have *Confitebor* performed if
this would be advantageous [to VN]. SW would not be so 'urgent' in raising this
matter if he did not have 'several little bills pressing' him.
     SW has 'the books' [volumes of printed music] from Hart's [presumably the
London music engraver and publisher Joseph Hart, or possibly Joseph Binns
Hart, organist, composer and music seller, 1794–1844, of Hastings]. The books,
which SW lists, are more valuable than Emett had supposed. If Emett can
recommend anyone to buy them, SW will sell them for 2½ guineas [£2/12/6].
     MEW mentioned to RG that SW intended to sell *Confitebor* and RG said that
he would 'give a little money now' for it and then publish it after SW's death.
SW thinks RG would offer only about £10, 'which would do no good'. 'We'
[SW, SS and their children at home] are glad to hear that Frederica [probably

Emett's daughter, who subsequently died, *see* SSW→Sarah Harriet Emett, 5/4/1835] is getting better. They hope to see the Emetts 'in a day or two'.

SSW→Sarah Harriet Emett   5/4/1835
BL Add 35019 f 135   Your Melancholy information arrived here
☞ 'Sunday'; pmk (Hereford) 5 – 1835; pmk (London) 6/4/1835[590]
  SSW sympathises with Sarah Harriet Emett [Emett's daughter] on the death of her sister. He is grateful that EW was able to assist the Emetts. SSW never obtains 'any intelligence' respecting SW.

SW→Jackson   9/5/1835
Baker Box 8 (Wesley Family); *O*   Ill health obliges me to become again
☞ Sat 9 May={1829,1835}[591]
  SW has been 'confined to the house' all week owing to ill health, and requests Jackson's 'kind assistance' now rather than next Friday [15/5/1835].

SW→J. Simpson   Pentonville   16/7/1835
WCL LDWMM 1999/7561/1   [not available]
☞ 16/7/1835
  SW is obliged by the kindness of Simpson [possibly John Simpson, music seller and musical instrument maker] concerning the bill. SW has found examples of CW's and SGW's handwriting for Simpson.

Crotch→SW   3/8/1835
BL Add 35027 f 8   It gratified me much to receive another note from you
ltr dated 3/8/1805, apparently by mistake[592]
  Crotch was glad to receive another note from SW [not preserved], as SW's notes are 'so valuable'. Crotch encloses a copy of his *Elements* [presumably the 1833 edition of his *Elements of Musical Composition*] for the use of SW's 'little daughter' [Thomasine]. SW will find it 'dry enough'. If there is any merit in it, it is that Crotch insists upon knowing the key before giving a name to a chord or discord. JSB is still Crotch's delight. He asks SW to excuse his long note: there is generally one in all good fugues near the end. He thanks SW for inquiring

---

[590] The month in the Hereford postmark is illegible, but the remaining postmark data are sufficient to assign ltr to Sunday 5/4/1835.

[591] Assigned to 1835 because of SW's late handwriting style.

[592] Ltr written from 10 Holland Road, Kensington, where Crotch lived from October 1832 to July 1836 (*Rennert* p 71, 73). Assigned to 3/8/1835 because ltr answered by SW→Crotch, 5/8/1835.

after his health, which is very good. Crotch hopes that SW also is enjoying good health.

SW→Crotch   Pentonville   **5/8/1835**
RCM pasted in LXXVIII.D.19; *O*   Accept my cordial Thanks for your very
✉ 5/8/1835

SW and his daughter [Thomasine] thank Crotch for his letter [Crotch→SW, 3/8/1835] and present [of Crotch's *Elements*]. SW thinks that he has not been 'much mistaken' in his opinion of JSB and is glad that Crotch has not given up 'old Bach' [JSB]. SW is happy to hear of Crotch's good health; of his own he cannot boast.

SW→Jackson   Pentonville   **12/11/1835**
MA DDWes/7/45; *O*[593]   In the Edition of Cowper's Works published by
✉ 12/11/1835

SW asks Jackson to allow him to correct [in the *Wesleyan Methodist Magazine*, of which Jackson was editor] a false assertion on p 292 [of v 1, published in 1835] of [the Rev. Thomas Shuttleworth] Grimshawe's edition of the *Works* of [William] Cowper [1731–1800], which is 'said to have allusion to' CW under the title of 'Occiduus'. [On that page is printeda previously unpublished 9/9/1781 letter from Cowper to Rev. John Newton, clergyman, 1725–1807, discussing the Sunday concerts of 'Occiduus'.]

SW states that CW Jr's 'occasional performances' of 'some portions of sacred music on Sunday' were never, as Cowper claims, 'desecrated' by the inclusion of 'song tunes' or other airs. Cowper's 'additional representation' that CW forgot his 'uniform objection to such places of fashionable resort as Vauxhall or Ranelagh' is likewise 'flagrantly untrue'. SW would not have troubled to deny these claims had they not originated from Cowper himself.

SW→Street?[594]   **about 2/1836**
BL Add 56228 ltr 11; *O*   You will exceedingly oblige me, if you can possibly
ltr undated[595]

SW requests £1 because of 'very urgent necessity'. He is 'preparing some work for the press, with some anecdotes' of his life [presumably the work of which a

---

[593] Ltr not in SW's handwriting but signed shakily by him.

[594] Ltr addressed to 'My dear Sir'. Street, to whom most other letters in this manuscript are explicitly addressed, is a plausible recipient, but no other evidence that he was the recipient of ltr has been found.

[595] Ltr, written in SW's late style of handwriting, is placed here on the assumption that ref. to SW's work in preparation for the press is to SW's article that appeared in the 18/3/1836 *MW*.

small initial portion was published as 'A Sketch of the State of Music in England, from the Year 1778 up to the Present', *MW* v 1 no. 1, 18/3/1836, p 1–3; the remainder of SW's *Reminiscences*, now BL Add 27593, of which the first part is dated 8/4/1836, was not published during SW's lifetime]. However, SW cannot get paid for this work until 'the whole is finished'.

SW's son [presumably MEW], who has been 'educated in the Blue Coat School' [probably the Bluecoat School 'for educating poor children', in Caxton Street, Westminster], is about to quit school 'with a very good character' and seeks a job as a youth in an office.[596] SW will be obliged if the recipient can recommend SW's son—who will be delivering this letter—to a potential employer.

SW→Crotch   Pentonville   30/3/1836
BL Add 31764 f 32; *O*   My Son requests me to forward to you a Copy
☞ 30/3/1836

At SSW's request, SW forwards a few compositions and a 'manuscript' by SSW which SSW submits as his 'exercise for the degree of Bachelor in Music' [from Oxford University, where Crotch was the Professor of Music]. SSW fears that his submission is not exactly what is required by the university statutes but would be greatly indebted if it can be accepted. Crotch will have heard that SSW's abilities have been extraordinary from childhood. SSW has been organist at Camberwell, Waterloo and Hereford Cathedral, and is now 'organist and sub chanter at Exeter Cathedral'. SW is sure that Crotch will do what he can to help SSW.

SW→Henry John Gauntlett   16/6/1836
JRUL Eng. Ms. 386 (3045); *O*   I conclude that by this Time you have examined
☞ Thu 16 Jun={1825,1831,1836}[597]

SW expects that Gauntlett has examined 'the music' [possibly SW's motet mentioned in SW→Gauntlett, 30/9/1836]. SW proposes to see him tomorrow [17/6/1836] to discuss what needs to be done regarding it, as SW presently is 'sadly hampered for the want of a little ready cash'.

---

[596] SSW had attended the Bluecoat School for a year 'at about the age of six', i.e., about 20 years earlier (*Stevenson* p 544). Although Christ's Hospital, of which RG was music master, was known as a 'bluecoat school' from the uniform worn by its boys, neither SSW nor MEW is listed in the Christ's Hospital children's registers for the years 1815 to 1835 (Guildhall Library ms 12818/14–15). We are grateful to Stephen Freeth, Keeper of Manuscripts, Guildhall Library, for this information.

[597] Assigned to 1836 on the basis of SW's late handwriting style.

SW→Jackson   31/8/1836
Bristol Watkinson album p 71, ltr 839; *O*   Will you be so kind as to spare me a
▣ 31/8/1836
  SW is 'much embarrassed' and asks Jackson to 'spare him' £1 this morning.

SW→Attwood   Pentonville   1/9/1836
BL Add 35013 f 103; *O*[598]   I send you my Daughter's Album, who is making
▣ Thu 1 Sep={1831,1836}[599]
  EW is compiling an album [now BL Add 35026] of musical autographs of
'talented musicians'. SW asks Attwood to contribute 'a few bars' to the album,
which SW's son [probably MEW] is bringing.

Crotch→SW   2/9/1836
BL Add 35027 f 9   I have kept your son so long while I transcribed
▣ 2/9/1836
  Crotch has transcribed 'a little composition' [a fugue] into EW's album. He
kept SW's son waiting while doing this.

Crotch→SW   Pentonville   7/9/1836
BL Add 35027 f 8   I perceive it has escaped your memory
▣ 7/9/1836
  SW has forgotten that, for the past three years, Crotch has refused to write
testimonials. For the sake of consistency he must refuse to write one for EW.
However, she may show Crotch's letter if this is helpful to her.

Thomas Adams→SW   Pentonville   14/9/1836
BL Music Library Dep. 1995/19 ltr 1   In promoting by any means in my power
▣ 14/9/1836
  Thomas Adams undertakes to write a testimonial for EW. He will be at [St
George's] Camberwell next Sunday morning [18/9/1836] and in the City [at St
Dunstan's-in-the-West, Fleet Street; he was organist of both churches] in the
evening, and will be glad to hear EW play at either church. If the matter is
urgent he will gladly come to St Dunstan's next Friday [16/9/1836]. He does not
doubt EW's capability but, 'as a point of conscience', he feels that he should
hear her play before writing a testimonial for her.

---

[598] The portion of ltr containing SW's signature has been cut away.

[599] Assigned to 1836 from the context of EW compiling her album (*see*
Crotch→SW, 2/9/1836) and the circumstance that SW is not known to have
lived at Pentonville as early as 1831.

Thomas Adams→SW   **17/9/1836**
BL Music Library Dep. 1995/19 ltr 2   I beg that your daughter, when she arrives
☐ 17/9/1836
Adams asks EW to come immediately to the organ loft on her arrival at St
Dunstan's [on Sunday evening 18/9/1836, *see* Adams →SW, 14/9/1836], and
not to wait to meet him at the door. The service begins at 6.30 pm and usually
ends after 8.30 pm. Adams will be glad to see EW at any stage of the service.

Thomas Adams→SW   **18/9/1836**
BL Music Library Dep. 1995/19 ltr 3   I have very sincere satisfaction in
☐ '18 September'[600]
Adams encloses a testimonial [not preserved] for EW. He has a 'highly
favourable opinion' of her performances.

Thomas Adams→SW   **20/9/1836**
BL Music Library Dep. 1995/19 ltr 4   I cannot resist the desire of saying that
☐ '20 September'[601]
Adams thanks SW for his letter [not preserved] in reply to Adams's testimonial
for EW [enclosed with Thomas Adams→SW, 18/9/1836]. SW's letter has given
Adams much pleasure. He hopes that EW's application will be successful. He is
happy to see her in his organ loft at any time.

Attwood→SW   Pentonville   **30/9/1836**
BL Add 35027 f 15   I am but this moment arrived in town
☐ 30/9/1836
Attwood agrees to hear SW's daughter [EW] at St Paul's [Cathedral] tomorrow
[1/10/1836] at 3 pm, after the service.

---

[600] Assigned to 1836 because ltr follows on from the immediately previous
Thomas Adams→SW letters.

[601] Assigned to 1836 because ltr follows on from the immediately previous
Thomas Adams→SW letters.

SW→Henry John Gauntlett   **30/9/1836**

MA [uncatalogued]; *O*   I suppose you will think I am always troubling you
☑ Fri 30 Sep & SW's late style of handwriting→{1831,1836}[602]

SW is 'most dreadfully embarrassed'. He apologises for troubling Gauntlett,
but asks for 'the other pound' for the motet [possibly SW's 'Tu es sacerdos [II]',
composed in 1827].[603] SW inquires whether Gauntlett has seen Davison
[presumably Frederick Davison, organ builder, c1815–1889, to whom SW wrote
on 24/5/1837] concerning the 'Psalms and Chants' [not identified], and asks if
Gauntlett thinks that Davison has 'done anything with them'.

For the last month, SW's picture [not identified] has been lying at the
Leadenhall Street premises of [William John] Huggins [artist, 1781–1845].
There were several gentlemen to whom Huggins wished to show the picture, but
it will be brought to Gauntlett by 'Erasmus' [MEW] 'in his dining hour if he can
find time'. SW desires to see Gauntlett.

Ignaz Moscheles→SW   Pentonville   **1/10/1836**

BL Add 35027 f 49   [not preserved]
pmk 1/10/1836
   [Only the envelope is preserved.]

John Goss→SW   Pentonville   **8/10/1836?**

BL Add 35027 f 17   I very much regret that I did not get your note till 10
☑ 'Saturday 7.30 am'[604]
   John Goss [organist and composer, 1800–1880] regrets that he received SW's
letter [not preserved] only late last night. Attwood [Goss's teacher] visited Goss
last night and will 'enclose this apology'. Goss can meet SW's daughter [EW] at
'Chelsea Church' [St Luke's, of which Goss was organist] at 5 pm today.

---

[602] Assigned to 1836 because MEW presumably was more likely to have carried
out this errand in 1836, when he was 15 years old, than in 1831, when he was
only 10.

[603] VN's copy of Gauntlett's arrangement of this anthem (to the English words
'He is our God and strong salvation') [RCM Ms 5253] bears VN's annotation
that Gauntlett had purchased the copyright of 'Tu es sacerdos' from SW.

[604] Ltr placed here conjecturally on the presumption (1) that ltr precedes EW's
16/10/1836 trial for an organist's position (*see* SW→Mr Davison, 12/10/1836);
(2) that Attwood heard her play on 1/10/1836 (*see* Attwood→SW, 30/9/1836) in
order to provide a reference for her; and (3) that SW would have approached
Attwood for a reference for EW before he approached Attwood's pupil Goss.
Ltr accordingly assigned to Saturday 8/10/1836, the only Saturday after
Attwood heard EW when there was still time for Goss to write an additional
reference for her.

SW→Mr Davison[605]   12/10/1836?

BL Add 35013 f 107; *O*   If I can be useful to you To-morrow I can be with you
▣ Wed 12 Oct & late SW handwriting style→{1831,1836}[606]
SW can be with Davison [presumably Frederick Davison] tomorrow morning
[13/10/1836] and asks him to call this evening. SW's daughter [EW] has to play
the organ tomorrow in the West End [of London] and would be happy for
Davison to go with her. If she succeeds on Sunday [16/10/1836], she will 'have
the place'. The service begins at 7 and she must leave [home] at 6.

SW→Jackson[607]   28/1/1837

Bristol Watkinson album p 71, ltr 840; *O*   You would much oblige me by
▣ 28/1/1837
SW asks for 'half a sovereign' [10/-] this morning rather than next week. SW's
son would have requested this yesterday [27/1/1837] but did not see Jackson.

SW→Governors, Royal Society of Musicians   about 1/2/1837

[not known][608]   [not known]
Royal Society of Musicians minutes of the 5/2/1837 Governors' Meeting
SW thanks the governors of the Royal Society of Musicians [perhaps for some
financial assistance, although SW was not a member of this society and the
minutes identify him as a non-claimant].

Ignaz Moscheles→SW   Pentonville   1/3/1837

BL Add 35027 f 49   If there is anything to tempt you in the enclosed
▣ 1 March; pmk 1837
Moscheles encloses a programme for his forthcoming 'soirée' [at the King's
Concert Room, Hanover Square] on 'Saturday next' [4/3/1837] and warmly
invites SW and 'Miss Wesley' [presumably EW] to attend as his guests.

---

[605] The likely recipient is Frederick Davison, to whom SW wrote on 24/5/1837.

[606] Assigned to 1836 because EW would have been only 12 years old in 1831
and therefore would have been unlikely to have been considered at that time for
an organist's position.

[607] Ltr addressed to 'My dear Sir'. Jackson presumed as addressee because SW
known to have addressed similar requests to him (e.g., SW→Jackson,
31/8/1836) and not known to have addressed similar letters to anyone else.

[608] The minutes of the 5/2/1837 Royal Society of Musicians Governors' Meeting
say that 'letters of thanks from the following non-claimants were presented'; the
list that follows includes SW's name. The current location of SW's letter is not
known.

Ignaz Moscheles→SW   Pentonville   **11/3/1837**
BL Add 35027 f 49   I regret that indisposition should have deprived me
⌑ 11 March; pmk 1837
    Moscheles regrets that SW's indisposition deprived Moscheles of the pleasure
of seeing SW at his 'soiree' [on 4/3/1837, *see* Ignaz Moscheles→SW, 1/3/1837].
SW's 'friend' remains on the list [of admissions]. Moscheles hopes to see SW or
at least 'Miss Wesley' [presumably EW] in future.

SW→John Barnett   Pentonville   **15/3/1837**
BL Add 35013 f 108; *O*   Mr Wesley presents his Compliments to Mr Barnett
⌑ Wed 15 Mar & 🖂→[i]
    SW sends EW's album to John Barnett [composer, 1802–1890] and asks him to
contribute to it. [Barnett contributed his Andante for String Quartet on f 20 of
EW's album, now BL Add 35026.]

SW→Jackson[609]   **17/3/1837**
Bristol Watkinson album p 71, ltr 838; *O*   Can you oblige me To Day with a
⌑ Fri 17 March={1826,1837}[610]
    SW asks for £1 today, instead of 10/-, and 'will not trouble' Jackson next week
[for money].

Thomas Vaughan→SW   Pentonville   **17/4/1837**
BL Add 35027 f 113   It will give me the greatest pleasure to see you at my
pmk 17/4/1837
    Vaughan invites SW to attend his concert 'on Wednesday next' [19/4/1837]
and has put the names of SW and SW's 'friend' [not identified] on his free list.

---

[609] Ltr addressed to 'My dear Sir'. Jackson presumed as addressee because SW
is known to have addressed similar requests to him (e.g., SW→Jackson,
31/8/1836) and is not known to have addressed similar letters to anyone else.

[610] Assigned to 1837 because ltr written in SW's late style of handwriting.

SW→Jackson   24/4/1837
Bristol Watkinson album, ltr 660; *O*   Excuse my sending again on this Subject
▣ Mon 24 Apr={1826,1837}[611]
  SW apologises for writing again on the same subject [his earlier letter is not
preserved]. The address 'had better be to X Y Z at Mr [John] Dean's Music
Library, 148 New Bond Street, London'.[612]

Ole Bull→SW   5/5/1837
BL Add 35027 f 83   Mr Ole Bull presents his Compliments to Mr Wesley
▣ 5 May[613]
  Ole Bull [Norwegian violinist, 1810–1880] is pleased to comply with SW's
request [by contributing a fragment of solo violin music, dated 5/5/1837, in
EW's album] and hopes that SW will accept the enclosed 'admissions for his
farewell concert' on Friday evening 19/5/1837 at the King's Theatre concert
room.

SW→Frederick Davison   24/5/1837
BL Add 35013 f 105; *O*   Be so obliging as to send my violin Pieces
▣ 24/5/1837
  Frederick Davison should send SW's violin pieces, as SW has 'an opportunity
to dispose of them'. Ole Bull 'is coming in a day or two to try some of them
over'.

---

[611] Assigned to 1837 because ltr written in SW's late style of handwriting; also,
SW→Sarah, 13/11/1826 indicates that SW was not in contact with Jackson in
April 1826.

[612] John Dean had published some of SSW's music. *See* SSW→SS, 25/10/1832.

[613] Assigned to 1837 because Bull's farewell concert took place on 19/5/1837
and his contribution to EW's album is dated 5/5/1837.

Felix Mendelssohn→Cécile Mendelssohn   14/9/1837

ltr partly quoted in Cécile Mendelssohn→Lea Mendelssohn   [destroyed]
Bartholdy, 21/9/1837; *Ward Jones* p 192–194[614]
The Mendelssohns' 'honeymoon diary' entry for 14/9/1837[615]

About 1,000 people filled the church [Christ Church, Newgate Street] for Felix Mendelssohn's organ performance [at 1 pm on 12/9/1837]. He had to push his way to reach the organ bench where SW, the most famous organist in London, was sitting. SW had been brought there by his daughters [EW and presumably Rosalind].[616] He was 78 [in fact, he was 71] years old and weak.

At Mendelssohn's request, SW played the organ. His performance was so moving that his daughter [probably EW] cried and had to be led down [from the organ] to the sacristy.[617] Then Mendelssohn played for a long time, to great acclaim.[618]

---

[614] Felix Mendelssohn's original ltr, together with almost all the other letters that he wrote to his wife Cécile, was burnt after her death in accordance with her request (*Ward Jones* p xxiii).

[615] Ltr assigned to 14/9/1837 for the following reason: (1) Ltr after Felix Mendelssohn left London on 13/9/1837 for Birmingham; (2) ltr before Cécile Mendelssohn's 21/9/1837 letter to Felix Mendelssohn's mother Lea Mendelssohn, in which ltr is quoted; and (3) in the Mendelssohns' 'honeymoon diary' (Bodl MDM c.6), the only reference to a letter from Felix to Cécile Mendelssohn in this interval is one he wrote from Birmingham on 14/9/1837 (*Ward Jones* p 106).

[616] However, many years later, EW told Frederick George Edwards that her friend Sarah Harriet Emett had come with her to the church on this day. *See* F. G. E[dwards], 'Samuel Wesley 1766–1837', *Musical Times* v 43 (1/12/1802) p 800.

[617] EW later told Frederick George Edwards that SW's performance had so moved her that she had to leave the church. *Ibid.*

[618] In 1839 (*Ward Jones* p xxv), therefore more than a year after the event, Felix Mendelssohn wrote another account of his meeting with SW at Christ Church, Newgate on 12/9/1837. According to the latter account, in Mendelssohn's 'honeymoon diary' entry for 11–12/9/1837 (*Ward Jones* p 102–105), 'old Wesley, trembling and bent', shook hands with Mendelssohn and, at Mendelssohn's request, sat down to play the organ, for the first time in many years. Despite his frailty, SW improvised admirably, 'with great artistry and splendid facility'. His daughter [probably EW] was so moved that she fainted and could not stop crying, as she believed that she would never hear him play like that again. Alas, Mendelssohn learned soon after he returned to Germany that SW had died [on 11/10/1837].

Mendelssohn's 1839 account is corroborated by a contemporary report ('Mendelssohn as an organist', *MW* v 7 no. 79, 15/9/1837, p 8–10) of the event: 'Mr Samuel Wesley, the father of English organists, was present and remained not the least gratified auditor, and expressed his delight in terms of unmeasured approbation. At the express desire of M. Mendelssohn, who wished that he could hereafter say he had heard Wesley play, the veteran took his seat at the instrument and extemporised with a purity and originality of thought for which he has rendered his name ever illustrious. The touch of the instrument, however, requires a strong and vigorous finger, and Mr Wesley, who is at present an invalid, was unable to satisfy himself, although he could gratify those around him' (*op. cit.*, p 10).

CALENDAR OF UNDATED
CORRESPONDENCE

SW→Dr Ford   **6/1771–6/1776**
WMM   I wrote according to my promise
SW's handwriting style is that of a child; each letter in ltr is printed[1]
   SW fulfils his promise to write. He hopes that Dr Ford and SW's London
friends are well. SW was very glad to see his friends at Bristol and wants very
much to see Ford. Sarah sends her love and desires Ford to write to her.

SW→Prudence Box   Charles St, Bristol   **16/7/1771–16/7/1775**
Fitzwm ltr 1   I Promis'd to write to you (when I was in London)
📧 16 July[2]
   SW could not write immediately to Prudence Box on his arrival [in Bristol] as
he had promised when he was in London. They [SW and his family] did not
arrive [in Bristol] until after 2 pm and then had to go to Mrs Anne Stafford's
who was 'in a sad taking', as they had brought Harley [a dog] with them. As she
refused to let it in the kitchen, they were obliged to take Harley to Mrs Farley's
house. Mrs Farley received the dog gladly.
   Prudence's silk handkerchief that SW used to wear round his neck is lost or
stolen, but SGW says that she will buy Prudence a replacement. He will give
Prudence's letter to Mr May tomorrow. He sends his love to various animals.
Friends send their love to Prudence.

---

[1] Ltr not before SW's first visit to London believed to be in the latter part of
May 1771. April 1773 is a plausible date as SW→CW Jr, 20/4/1773, says that
SW who then was in Bristol has not received a letter from Dr Ford who then
was in London, and in both letters SW's handwriting style is that of a child, in
which each letter is printed. Ltr <26/6/1776, as SW→SGW, 26/6/1776 and
SW→CW Jr, 26/6/1776 are both written in a script handwriting style.

[2] Ltr not before SW's first visit to London believed to be in the latter part of
May 1771. Ltr <Prudence Box's death on 9/1/1777. 16/7/1776 is ruled out
because SW was at Guildford then. SW's handwriting style in ltr is that of a
child; each letter is printed.

CW→James Hutton   1776
Baker p 112   [not known]
Baker dates ltr 1776

CW informs James Hutton [founder of the Moravian church in England, 1715–1795] that Mr M [possibly Martin Madan] plans to take CW Jr and SW on Wednesday to Mr Southwell [possibly Edward Southwell, 1738–1777, from 1763 to 1776 MP for Gloucestershire, *see* Daines Barrington→CW, 24/2/1777], where [Daines] Barrington is to bring [John Christian] Bach [German composer, 1735–1782, from 1762 resident in London, JSB's son] and 'a troop of connoisseurs'.

Tryphena Bathurst→Daines Barrington   1776–1777
MA DDWes/1/88   Lady Tryphena Bathurst's Compts to Mr Barrington
⬚ 'Monday'; CW corresponded with Daines Barrington in 1776–1777

Lady Tryphena Bathurst [*b*1760, daughter of Henry 2nd Earl Bathurst, Lord Chancellor] thanks Daines Barrington for securing CW's permission for CW Jr and SW to play music to her. She would like to put off the performance until next week so that [her mother] Lady Bathurst [Tryphena Bathurst, 1730–1807, wife of Henry 2nd Earl Bathurst, Lord Chancellor] can attend.

Sarah→Penelope Maitland   9/1783—1794
Bodl Ms Eng. Misc. c.502 f 39[3]   There is no haste for the return
ltr after, but presumably not immediately after, James Price's 3/8/1783 death[4]

Dr [James] Price, 'who poisoned himself' and showed signs of late repentance, lived at Guildford. 'We [the Wesley family] knew him intimately.' At his death he left SW 'a small independence'. Price was talented but, although 'a religious boy', committed when only 24 [i.e., in 1776–1777] the 'fatal act' of becoming 'a professed Deist', who openly despised the truth.

---

[3] Ltr is a torn sheet, lacking salutation and signature.

[4] Ltr presumably not after 1794 because all the dated correspondence of Penelope Maitland in this manuscript was written during the years 1780 to 1794.

SW→Shepherd   **18/4/1784–12/1784**

AdF S4619 dossier 5   My Father has shown me a Letter which he received

📧 'Sunday evening'[5]

CW has shown SW a letter [not preserved] that CW received from Shepherd. CW did not see Shepherd in the coach when she came with Lady Traquair [Mary Stewart, wife of Charles Stewart, 1746–1827, 7th Earl of Traquair]. CW asked SW to tell Shepherd 'verbatim' CW's observations on Shepherd's letter, which are: that no one has 'endeavoured to widen the breach'; that CW bears no enmity to anyone and in particular harbours no animosity towards Shepherd; and that CW never would explain verbally his position, as 'he was not disposed to enter into the merits of either's cause'. SW acknowledges that Shepherd has made 'every possible advance towards friendly terms', but sees that there is no more to be said.

SW looks forward to seeing Shepherd as soon as possible. Mr [Rev. Joseph] Ferrers [Carmelite friar, 1725–1797] has returned from the country and hopes to see her soon.

SW→?[6]   **1784–1792**

BL Add 35013 f 110 (copy)[7]   Many and unavoidable interruptions having

copy of ltr has no date

SW replies to his correspondent's last letter [not preserved] that gave answers to SW's queries on various theological subjects that were posed in a prior letter [not preserved]. The answers given to SW's first, second, fifth and sixth queries are 'completely satisfactory'. However, SW takes the opportunity to discuss further, in considerable detail, the answers given to his third and fourth queries:

---

[5] Ltr assigned to 1784 for the following reason. It is addressed to 'Mrs Freeman Shepherd' at 13 Leicester Square, where SW→Shepherd, 19/3/1784 also is addressed; whereas SW→Shepherd, 26/12/1783, is written to 'Miss Freeman' at Dr Sharps, Leigh Street, Red Lyon Square; hence ltr presumably >1783. SW→Shepherd, 16/1/1785? is addressed to 'Mrs Freeman Shepherd' at 416 Strand; hence ltr presumably <1785. Ltr presumably not before Sunday 18/4/1784, the first Sunday after Easter, as it refers to a 'breach' between CW and Shepherd, which presumably arose after CW learned from the Duchess of Norfolk, after Easter 1784, that SW had converted to Roman Catholicism (*see* Chronology, 4/1784), for which CW and JW blamed Shepherd (*see* JW→SW, 18/3/1788; Sarah→JW, 4/4/1788; Shepherd→Adam Clarke, 1810–1813). Also, SW→Shepherd, 19/3/1784, suggests that Shepherd then was still a welcome guest in CW's home.

[6] According to an annotation on ltr by EW, the recipient was Dr Alexander Geddes [1737–1802]. Neither the source of her information nor its accuracy is known.

[7] Ltr is a copy in an unknown hand.

'What are the true means of salvation for him who knows and believes the Church revelation?' and 'What is true morality?'.

SW hopes that his correspondent will not consider him 'captious and disputatious', or of having 'intentionally sophisticated' any scriptural text by giving a 'whimsical opinion' of it. He has written 'rather for love of truth than of argument'. He conjectures that, on most subjects, one must be content with having reached the probability of truth.

Sarah→?   1784–3/1796
GEU Wesley Coll. ltr 87[8]   a Person [tear] Roman Catholic, asked me if I ltr presumably written when SW openly professed Roman Catholicism[9]

Someone asked Sarah if she thought that SW 'could be a Christian who deemed it right to utter curses so bitterly on the least occasion'. Sarah replied that SW would not behave so 'had he not belonged to that cursing Church' [the Roman Catholic Church]. Any 'pious pastor' in any [Protestant] sect would have admonished SW that such behaviour 'brought sin upon the soul', disqualified the soul from receiving 'the spirit of love', and was opposite to the example of Christ Jesus. But could SW be so admonished by a priest when 'his anathemas were esteemed part of duty'?

Sarah's interlocutor said that Catholics held it as much a duty as Protestants to pray for enemies, not to curse them, and wished that some friend would speak to SW on the subject. Sarah answered that she has spoken to him on this subject. She is convinced that SW's membership of the [Catholic] Church prevented him from seeing his behaviour to be 'a sin', for if SW perceived his behaviour as sinful he would 'own it', even to a Protestant.

---

[8] Ltr is a torn fragment with considerable text missing.

[9] Ltr presumably >SW→Shepherd, 26/12/1783, in which SW says that he does not wish to profess Catholicism openly. Sarah→Penelope Maitland, 29/7/1789, says that SW still is a Roman Catholic. SW→Shepherd, 26/4/1792, says that his views now are very different from Catholic doctrine; it is up to the Catholics whether they wish to retain him. Presumably <SW→Sarah, 12/3/1796, in which SW tells Sarah that he is a Deist.

SW→Shepherd

10/9/1784–15/4/1785

AdF S4619 dossier 5   My Letter to Mr Gordon was sent on Tuesday last
◻ 'Friday'[10]

SW wrote last Tuesday to Mr Gordon [not identified], according to the mode that Shepherd prescribed. SW advised him that, although Bishop [James] Talbot would not object to writing to [William] Gibson [1738–1821, from 1781 to 1790 president of Douay College in France], the Papal Nuncio was just about to depart from Paris [for Rome] and could not object to having 'the tin case' [containing SW's *Missa de spiritu sancto*] 'packed with his luggage' if Gordon were to desire it. SW apologised for again troubling Gordon, who has 'honoured the music' [SW's Mass] by 'receiving it into his custody'.

If Gordon agrees 'to ask the Nuncio's leave', Bishop Talbot will write to Dr [Monsignor Christopher] Stonor [1716–1795, the English agent of the Roman Catholic Church in Rome] to inform him that the book [i.e., SW's Mass] is on its way to Rome. Stonor would receive it and probably would present it to the pope.

Shepherd should advise SW if he has committed any procedural errors.

Mr & Mrs Robert Udny→CW Jr

10/1787–10/1792

MA DDWes/1/112   Mrs Udny presents her best respects to Mr Wesley
◻ 'Friday'; written from Teddington where the Udnys had a home[11]

Mr and Mrs Udny [Robert Fullerton Udny, 1722–1802, and his wife Martha Jordan Udny, 1761–1831],[12] invite CW Jr and SW to visit them at Teddington on Sunday and to stay overnight. If SW is unable to come, CW Jr is welcome to come on his own.

---

[10] Ltr concerns the conveyance of SW's Mass to the pope. Hence ltr >SW→Shepherd, 6/9/1784, in which SW says that his Mass is bound and seeks her advice on the best way of conveying it to the pope and ltr <15/4/1785 as Gianangelo Braschi→James Talbot, 4/5/1785, states that the Mass has been received in Rome.

[11] Ltr presumably written after the Udnys' marriage on 18/10/1787 and when CW Jr and SW were living in the same house, i.e., before SW's move to Ridge about 10/1792 (*see* Latrobe journal entry, 18/10/1792).

[12] Mrs Udny later was employed as sub-governess to the Princess Charlotte and assisted CW Jr in matters relating to his organ performances for the Prince Regent.

SW→Sarah   1789–1790

GEU Wesley coll ltr 74   I shall never offer any arguments to convert
ltr presumably written when SW 'took up' the subject of polygamy[13]

SW will never offer arguments to convert Sarah to polygamy or to any other
doctrine. He asks only that she regard [Martin] Madan justly. She should read
his book [*Thelyphthora*] again carefully and then tell SW if Madan's 'chief
design' was not to save women from ruin and 'to make those honourable and
happy whom the world delights to crush and to destroy', however erroneous this
design may be 'in point of religion'.

SW→SGW & Sarah   1791–1792

MA DDWF/15/4   I would wish to have it believed
ltr written when SW had known CLM for about nine years[14]

SW asserts that no part of his conduct concerning 'Miss Martin' [CLM] has
resulted from 'a love of rebellion or an impatience of parental authority'. His
experience 'of nine years' has been that every unfavourable report of her has
been 'breathed from the breast of envy, and uttered by the tongue of slander',
and that 'her crime was not want of virtue, but excess of beauty'. He is
convinced that she has remained 'solely and inviolably attached' to him. Were
he to desert her, he would 'deserve and expect the last punishment due to the
darkest ingratitude'.

CLW→SW[15]   after 5/4/1793

Drew Wesley Family Letters, CLW series   You[r] letter has so affected me
ltr signed 'C. L. Wesley' so after her 5/4/1793 marriage to SW

CLW has been so affected by SW's letter that she cannot answer it at present
but will answer it shortly. She has received the £6/13/6 safely. She wishes and
prays daily for SW's 'every comfort'. She writes 'in sorrow'.

---

[13] Sarah→SW, 2/9/1807 says that SW took up the subject of polygamy in 1789.
This appears to be an early letter in the discussion. Sarah is addressed as 'Sally';
SW's handwriting has a youthful style.

[14] SW→SGW, 7/11/1792, says that SW and CLM first met in October 1782.

[15] Ltr addressed to 'Mr Wesley'. SW presumed as the addressee because CLW
is not known to have written to CW Jr and presumably would have addressed
her sons by their first names.

SW→? 1794–1799

GEU Wesley Coll. ltr 76[16]   [text missing]...his aid in future.
presumably not much before CW Jr's first public appearance on 19/3/1794[17]

If, by a few public appearances, he [presumably CW Jr] 'should be hereafter
established in a capital concert', the sacrifice should not be regretted, as this is
the only prospect 'likely to be lastingly advantageous'. Circumstances require
that 'he must play' and SW 'must teach, or starve'.

CLW→SGW 1794–1809

Drew Wesley Family Letters, CLW series   The things have but just come
ltr >CW III's 25/9/1793 birth and <final parting of SW and CLW

CLW sends 'Mr Wesley's [SW's] last shirt'. He now has had his four shirts.
She sends love to SW and will answer his letter [not preserved], but cannot make
promises that no sensible human being can make.

SW says that CLW 'must implicitly obey' his demands, 'however
unreasonable' they may be, but CLW could obey some demands only from 'a
God'. She would never 'give up a friend for any mortal or cringe to a foe'. She
thanks SGW for her kindness to CLW's son.

CW Jr→John Preston 2/1794–1797

BL Add 63814 item 98   Received of Mr Preston the Sum of five Pounds five
presumably after 24/1/1794 first performance of Shield's song *Old Towler*[18]

On behalf of SW, CW Jr acknowledges receipt of £5/5/- from the music
publisher [John] Preston for the copyright of SW's *Rondo with Variations from
Mr [William] Shield's 'Old Towler'*.

---

[16] Ltr is incomplete; only the last page is preserved.

[17] *See* SW→SGW, 18/1/1794. Ltr presumably <1800 as by then CW Jr had
made more than a few public appearances.

[18] At Covent Garden.

Shepherd→SW→Shepherd[19]   **3/1794–1797**
MA DDWes/7/40   *Shepherd:*   Did not MFS one day and desiring
                            SW: Ferrers was not his confessor
wmk 1794; <Ferrers's 1797 death[20]

Shepherd: Had not Shepherd informed SW that she had been assured by Lord and Lady Traquair [Charles and Mary Stewart] that SW's confessor Mr [Rev. Joseph] Ferrers had told them that SW was a 'profound and received' member of the Church of Rome? Did not Shepherd say that, if this were so, then CW would soon hear of it? Did not SW say that he dreaded this? Did he not ask Shepherd to approach Lord and Lady Traquair and all [Roman] Catholics whom he knew, to ask them not to speak of the matter, as the consequences would cause grief to CW and to SW?

SW: Ferrers was not SW's confessor. If Shepherd does not believe SW she should ask Ferrers who, 'although a priest, is not a liar'.

Shepherd: Does SW not know that, to spare CW's feelings, Shepherd went to Lord and Lady Traquair and to Ferrers, and persuaded them not to talk of the matter? Did not Shepherd also go to [Stephen] Paxton [Roman Catholic composer and 'cellist, 1735–1787; *see* Shepherd→Adam Clarke, undated, 1810–1813, where Paxton is identified as a famous viol-da-gamba performer], who had boasted of the convert [SW], and beg him never to speak of this in the presence of Protestants? Was it not then that CW Jr came home from Dr Shepherd's [not identified] house, 'all vexations and astonishment', and told SW that it had been said 'in the presence of the musical gentry there assembled' that SW had been seen in one of the 'Popish Chapels' giving the cup and attending the priest at Mass? Did not Shepherd, expecting that news of the matter would come 'from mouth to mouth' to CW, then press SW to divulge the news to CW, as this would be less shocking than having it conveyed [to him] 'by public report'? Did not SW say that he lacked the courage, and ask her to do this herself? Did she not answer that it would seem 'an impropriety' coming from her, and be interpreted [by CW] as a 'bravado and insult'?

SW: Yes.

Shepherd: Did Shepherd not go with SW to Bishop [James] Talbot and ask Talbot's advice? Did not Talbot propose sending [Rev. Arthur] O'Leary to inform CW that SW was a Catholic? Did not Shepherd reply, 'as wounded to the quick', in regard to CW's feelings as a father and as a clergyman of the Church of England, 'so would you send as a Dymock to insult him [CW] the man [O'Leary] who had written so bitterly' of his brother JW? [*see* Shepherd→Sarah, 12/3/1794].

SW: Yes.

---

[19] Ltr is written in two columns. In the left column Shepherd poses questions to SW. He replies and comments in the right column.

[20] Ltr >SW→Sarah, about 16/3/1794, when SW encourages Sarah to meet his 'quondam friend' Shepherd.

Shepherd: Shepherd summons SW to say 'before God' whether or not he heard her say that as the Duchess of Norfolk [Catherine Howard, 1718–21/11/1784, wife of Charles Howard, 1720–1786, 10th Duke of Norfolk] was 'the first Catholic in the Kingdom', it would be fittest, and much more respectful of CW, for the Duchess to break the news to him, especially as she had felt 'the anguish of a parent's heart on a similar occasion' [her son Charles Howard, 1746–1815, from 1786 11th Duke of Norfolk, had converted from Roman Catholicism to the Church of England] and therefore could better sympathise with CW's situation.

SW: Yes.

Shepherd: Did not Shepherd send to SW, for his consent, a letter [not preserved] that she wrote to the Duchess of Norfolk, expressing respect and tenderness to CW?

SW: Yes.

Shepherd: Was not SW consulted in these negotiations?

SW: Yes, although Shepherd 'very well knows' that it was only with the 'utmost reluctance' that he consented to the Duchess of Norfolk's visit, regarding it as the lesser of two evils.

Shepherd: Did not SW write to Duchess of Norfolk himself, asking her to break the news to CW?

SW: SW certainly copied a letter [not preserved] 'indited' by Shepherd to the Duchess of Norfolk, as another letter begun by Patterson, the Duchess's learned chaplain, making no sense and in bad English, was judged to be 'somewhat improper'.

Shepherd: Did not Shepherd send a letter [not preserved] to SW by express messenger, advising SW that the Duchess would be visiting CW? Did not SW know the day and almost the hour of her visit?

SW: SW did not know the hour of the Duchess's visit. He went to Shepherd's house early that morning, and Shepherd told him to return home immediately as the Duchess was there.

Shepherd: Did not Shepherd through this whole affair show her regard, respect and goodwill to CW, SGW and SW?

SW: Yes.

Shepherd: In what way did Shepherd speak to the Catholics of CW, SGW and JW?

SW: Always respectfully. At Lord Traquair's house, Shepherd wrote an account [not preserved] for SW of her philippic to O'Leary, in which 'her writ was much more than a match for his billingsgate'.

Shepherd: Did not Shepherd urge SW never to allow any Catholic to speak slightingly of CW or JW in SW's presence?

SW: Yes.

Shepherd: Did not Shepherd tell SW that, in return for CW's 'kind liberalism', SW owed to him the grateful return of every act of duty and love, and in particular to play the organ for CW when he preached charity sermons in Protestant churches?

Did not Shepherd say that SW should not heed what Catholic bigotry might urge to the contrary?

SW: Yes, but 'Catholic bigotry' is as proper a conjunction of words as 'wide contraction' or 'extended closeness'.

Shepherd: Did Shepherd not urge as a motive to persuade SW to learn Greek that it would please CW?

SW: Yes, although it did not in fact do so. CW laughed at SW for attempting Greek and SW consequently was discouraged.

Shepherd: Did not Shepherd send SW the Pope's letter to Talbot containing the honourable mention of the Pope's having received SW's Mass [Gianangelo Braschi→James Talbot, 4/5/1785], that SW might show this letter to CW and give 'a father's partial heart' the delight of his son's prowess?

SW: Yes.

Shepherd: Did not Shepherd encourage SW to live a good life? Did not the withdrawing of his friendship date from the time of CW's complaint to Bishop Talbot, Talbot's communication of these complaints to Shepherd, and her remonstrances with SW [about 7/1785, *see* Shepherd→SW, 7/1785?]? Did SW fairly and honestly tell CW every aspect of Shepherd's behaviour before the Duchess of Norfolk's visit, and represent things as they really were? Did he not, on the contrary, seek to 'envelop himself in a cloud of concealment'?

SW: Shepherd tried to instil in SW 'her own notions of sinless perfection'. She appeared to want him to become a priest, expressing at the same time her fear that he should rush into orders precipitately, without the 'experimental certainty' of being able to 'live the life of angels' [the ideal life towards which Shepherd desired SW to aspire, *see* Shepherd→Sarah, 5/8/1795, and Shepherd→SW, 17/11/1802]. SW had an 'experimental certainty' that he had not got 'into that latitude', and chose not to hamper himself with a vow that he knew he could not keep.

CW's complaints [about SW] to Talbot were 'not only unkind, but principally false'. Shepherd told SW that the principal complaint against him was that he had 'frequent intercourse with women'—what in 'English cant' is called 'criminal intercourse'. This charge was untrue. SW visited 'a young woman at Kensington' who has been 'most falsely traduced' [possibly CLM; SW→CLM, 27/3/1788 is addressed to CLM at Kensington], but at that time there was nothing that Shepherd would term 'criminal intercourse' between them. CW therefore was 'a dupe to bad people' who, by their 'malignant and unfounded conjectures', robbed him of SW's confidence and affection [Sarah→SW, 27/5/1791, notes that CW required SW to break off his connection with CLM, but that SW continued this connection as an 'amour'].

The 'true and only cause' of SW's alienation from Shepherd was her insisting on his yielding a point and, when he had done so, her insistence that he should now consider himself 'the weakest and wickedest of his sex'. Shepherd used all her influence to persuade him to give up a woman whom he loved, merely to remove the scandal which it was pretended that his 'ill example' had given to the 'pious members of Holy Mother [Roman Catholic] Church'. Shepherd even begged on her knees that SW should 'sacrifice' an innocent victim to calumny, but he was 'for once obstinately just', and he chose rather to sacrifice Shepherd.

Shepherd's last query appears unworthy of her. She acknowledges that SW always was fearful of communicating anything relating to how he became a Catholic to CW. How, therefore, could SW present to CW Shepherd's conduct on a subject that SW did not dare mention to CW? SW sought only to avoid 'the strife of tongues'. He knew CW's 'violence of temper' and tried to 'hinder the introduction of any topic that might tend to excite it'.

SW→Sarah   **11/1794–5/1798**
MA DDWes/6/39   He who resolves hastily, usually repents
ltr undated[21]

SW is weighing arguments for and against separating from CLW. When he has done this to the best of his 'coolest judgement', his decision will be firm. He would not wish to part from CLW if there were any chance of living with her 'on decent terms'; affectionate terms are out of the question. But 'daily experience' proves this to be impossible. Her conduct towards him becomes worse and worse: 'tenderness will not touch her, and to reason she is deaf'. Unless a miracle happens within the next six months and he receives 'the repentance, the respect, and the kindness' which he deserves, he is determined that his 'lively moments shall not run down to waste'. If SW's separation were to result in his imprisonment followed by disease and death, he would still prefer this to 'a life of continual vexation and insult'.

Sarah may press on him 'the obligation of a vow', to which he could give twenty good answers; but 'a sufficient answer to any reasonable person' is that a vow to love anyone to the end of life, whether or not the person deserves it, is 'preposterous and absolutely impossible to be fulfilled'. SW knows from experience that 'ceremonies bind not hearts'; it is 'a law of nature, and therefore of God, that nought but love can answer love and render bliss secure'.

All that SW could hope for is to live in peace with CLW. 'Friendship, confidence, esteem are all vanished into nonentities', but if CLW were to be 'truly kind' in her future behaviour, SW could forgive, although he could not forget, 'the savage expressions and horrid epithets she has applied to the most amiable of women' [presumably AD]. SW would be grieved to see CLW destroy herself, but he cannot prevent it. Although he has been her protector there is no reason why he should be her dupe, and he will not 'tamely bear the yoke of matrimony without honour, profit or pleasure'. He will give her six months to amend, but will not 'drag on existence with an ungrateful shrew'.

---

[21] Presumably not before 1/11/1794 because, in SW→Sarah, 26/10/1794, SW tells Sarah, apparently for the first time, that CLW was not designed to be SW's 'second self'. Presumably not after 23/5/1798, as SW→Sarah, 23/5/1798, says that SW has decided to pursue separate maintenance for CLW without delay.

## CLW→Sarah				1/10/1795–1799

Drew Wesley Family Letters, CLW series		I trust my dear Sally, you will keep
>Sarah with CLW in Bristol (9–10/1795); <Rebecca Gwynne's death in 1799

CLW trusts that Sarah will stay as promised at St Albans for a day or two, when CLW will meet her with 'little Charles' [CW III] and will give her [the *Descriptive Catalogue of*] *Rackstrow's Museum* to read. SGW's servant Molly is 'a deceitful hussy' and 'a sad lying woman', as proved by what she said about Mrs Foot[e]. SW 'should have checked' Molly for 'speaking to him so of his cousin' and SGW's boarder [not identified].

SW told CLW that Sarah was 'overheard speaking ill of him' but CLW replied that she never heard Sarah speak ill of him. On the contrary, the only quarrels that CLW and Sarah had at Bristol were caused by Sarah 'not so harshly treating the infamous conduct of Mrs Deane' [AD], which CLW knew AD 'merited'. Sarah recommended [in Bristol] that CLW should suffer calmly, advising that time would 'restore' SW to her if she conducted herself properly.

CLW has never discussed family details with servants. She loves SW dearly, 'better than mortal!'. SW was the love of her youth. He 'has taken too strong root ever to be otherwise than loved by' CLW. Yet some actions of SW 'disgrace him'. Mrs Cooper, a charwoman employed 'here' in CLW's absence, says that SW told her that CLW 'had a child before marriage and many other unpleasant things' which are unworthy of being told. CLW still wishes that Sarah and her brother [SW] 'were on [speaking] terms', as CLW dearly loves both of them. Sarah should 'call in' Miss Browne [not identified].

CLW sends her 'love and duty' to SGW and to Sarah's aunt [Rebecca Gwynne].

## SW→Sarah				1796–1/4/1806

GEU Wesley Coll. ltr 77[22]		I have only to say that there seems a Fatality against dating range from context[23]

Fate seems to be against SW and Sarah discussing any subject temperately. Sarah is very wrong to consider SW an enemy. He has several obligations to her and is unlikely to forget her kindnesses. He alludes to certain [unspecified] 'delicacies'. SW's condition is 'a series of heavy judgements' that are breaking him down, as Sarah may perceive. He believes himself 'as much belonging to the Devil' as Sarah 'pronounces' him to appear.

---

[22] Ltr is incomplete.

[23] SW's reference to Sarah's kindnesses (presumably her endeavours to mediate between SW and CLW and her looking after CW III), his mention of delicacies (perhaps regarding his *c*1804 amour with a servant girl, *see* Sarah→SW, 2/9/1807), and his feeling that he is breaking down, suggest a date for ltr after Sarah's being with CLW in Bristol and prior to SW's move to Camden Town.

SW→?[24]   **1797–8/1801**

MA DDWF/15/9   I have reason to think the Time not far distant
presumably not much earlier than SW→James Kenton, 18/1/1797[25]

SW thinks it will not be long before 'absolute necessity' obliges him to leave
CLW. It would be impossible as well as disagreeable to go into details about her
'insufferable behaviour'. It should suffice to say that she has determined to be
'totally useless, uniformly insultive and thoroughly disgusting'. CLW is
considering leaving SW suddenly, which he would regret, as it would cause
considerable confusion. He wishes for a 'sober, quiet, rational separation'.

SW→Sarah   **1797–6/1805**

GEU Wesley Coll. ltr 62   As I am seriously setting about a few Arrangements
presumably >SW→James Kenton, 18/1/1797 & <SW reunited with CLW[26]

SW's 'present precarious state of health and circumstances' necessitates that he
arrange his affairs. He wishes to prevent, as far as possible, the 'mischief' that
might result if his letters or papers were to be read by a third party following an
accident or a 'sudden change' in his condition. He has collected his
correspondence with Sarah, which he re-read today with mixed feelings, and
advises her to destroy it now or later. SW thinks that one of his letters shows that
he never disputed with her for the sake of argument but only from 'conviction of
the truth' of his position. Of course he is not infallible.

The date of a letter from SW to James Kenton [possibly SW→Kenton,
18/1/1797] establishes SW's claim to have been patient [with CLW]. One letter,
which SW has 'christened an important letter', describes 'poor Mrs W's
[CLW's] sad conduct' that led to SW's unguarded quotation of a phrase, an act
that Sarah described as 'treacherous' [*see* SW→Sarah, 3/3/1796, in which he
denies having been treacherous]. SW never intended evil at that moment but
remembers 'having been thoroughly exasperated at the time'. He thinks,
'without any exaggeration', that 'most other men would have risked their trial
for murder in a similar case'.

---

[24] Ltr has no salutation. SW says in ltr that his relationship to the recipient is an
'affectionate ill-acting well-meaning friend'.

[25] SW→James Kenton, 18/1/1797, says that SW recently came to the conclusion
that it is necessary for him to separate from CLW. Ltr presumably not much
after Sarah's 28/7/1801 memorandum stating that the separation is about to take
place. SW also discusses an impending separation from CLW in SW→Sarah,
23/5/1798. SW's handwriting style in ltr places it in this dating range rather than
*c*1810 when he again separated from CLW.

[26] A plausible date for ltr is November 1804: *see* SGW→SW, 12/11/1804,
regarding SW's fears of his speedy dissolution. SW and CLW presumably were
reunited before July 1805 as Emma was born in January or February 1806.

All this is past, and SW would be pleased if this 'imprudence' was 'among the worst' of his 'many *faux pas*'. He wishes to conclude his 'felicitous career in good-will' towards everyone who may feel themselves to have been injured by him. With the exception of CLW, he knows of no one alive who feels personal enmity towards him. God best knows how SW will fare 'in another state of existence'.

SGW→SW   **1800–1812**

MA DDWes/1/55   The child of my latest care, whom my heart has yearn'd ltr presumably >1800 because SGW describes herself as aged[27]

SW's 'aged mother' SGW has 'yearn'd over' him 'in the various and afflicting vicissitudes of life'. She trusts that he is 'earnestly concerned' to turn to God, 'who alone can give pardon, and peace to the troubled mind'. She entreats SW to 'train up' his children 'in the fear of God which is true wisdom', and 'to depart from evil'.

SW→SGW   **1800–1815**

VUQ   I hope to call upon You To=morrow about 2 o'clock wmk '180-'; last digit of wmk not legible[28]

SW hopes to call on SGW tomorrow about 2 pm. He cannot stay for dinner tomorrow.

CLW→SGW   **1801–1805**

Drew Wesley Family Letters, CLW series   I am ashamed at not having ere this >1800 as JWW talking; <1806[29]

CLW apologises for her delay in replying to SGW's letter [not preserved] enclosing a letter [not preserved] from CW III, who CLW is happy to hear is well. CLW rejoices in SGW's 'providential escape' from danger and longs to see her. 'Johnny' [JWW] is 'always talking of his grandmamma' [SGW]. Both CW III and JWW love SGW; otherwise 'they would be two little ungrateful beings'. All of SW's relations have been very good to both children.

---

[27] SGW's handwriting is legible and firm, hence ltr not after 1812 when her eyesight was deteriorating. November 1804 is a conceivable date for ltr as SW's mental troubles then gave SGW great concern.

[28] Ltr probably after SW's 1806 move to Camden Town when he no longer lived in the same house as SGW.

[29] <1806 because CW III described as 'little' so presumably under 12; also, no mention in ltr of Emma, who was born in January or February 1806.

John Braham→Mr Hammond   1801–1837

BL Add 35027 f 111   I regret I cannot have the pleasure of securing you

🖃 16 August; presumably not before Braham's 9/12/1801 debut as an adult

John Braham regrets that he has no vacancy in his theatre company for Mr Hammond [not identified; ltr is addressed to him at the English Opera House], but asks that his compliments be given 'to the distinguished and inimitable' SW.

Shepherd→Sarah   1802?

MA Letters Chiefly to Wesleys v 1 ltr 36   I was ever delighted with our good

Ltr mentions the year 1802

Shepherd sends Sarah a copy of the letter, Shepherd→SW, 24/4/1792, that she wrote soon after she arrived in England from France. She also sends a copy of SW's reply, SW→Shepherd, 26/4/1792. As Shepherd was in France [from August 1785 until about April 1792], she was 'utterly ignorant' both of the charges that she tried to set SW against his family and of CW's 'charitable deathbed prayer' that was printed in the *Arminian Magazine* [*see* Sarah→JW, 4/4/1788].

Sarah→SW   7/5/1802–9/7/1811

Baker in box 8[30]   I was witness to the agreement before the last Concert

>6/5/1802, the last concert in Hyde's Rooms, Tottenham Street[31]

Sarah witnessed 'the agreement before the last concert' [in Hyde's Rooms, Tottenham Street on 6/5/1802]. When this agreement was made, SW said that he would accept remuneration of £10 or £20, according to the concert's success. SW 'had much trouble in the course of' the concert, which was not profitable. Nevertheless, SW received £18, and Sarah remembers him saying that he would not demand any more to prepare 'the final settlement of the accounts belonging to the concert', which he never did. SW 'had no right' to any additional remuneration. CW Jr said that Mr Stevens [*see* SW→SGW & Sarah, 8/9/1802] was satisfied for CW Jr to allow 'the 10 per cent', so Sarah did not witness that separate agreement.

---

[30] Ltr is incomplete or a draft. It has no salutation or close.

[31] Ref. to Stevens indicates that ltr refers to matters arising from the accounts of these concerts. Ltr presumably <SW→SGW, 10/7/1811, in which SW says that no family member is prepared to pay back what he thinks he is still owed in respect of these concerts.

CW III→Sarah   1803–1805

GEU Wesley coll. ltr 92   I was very glad to receive your Letter & more so
CW III at school in Wateringbury between 1803 and 1805

CW III was very glad to learn from Sarah's letter [not preserved] that he has a
chance to see her before he goes home. He suggests that she visit him at
Wateringbury, as SW does not want him to leave school before the holidays.

SW→CLW   5/1803–6/1805

Baker Box 8, in folder 3   My Symptoms of corporal Infirmity & mental
⊡ 'Tuesday night'; presumably >1/5/1803 when SW still was visiting CLW[32]

SW's 'symptoms of corporal infirmity and mental distraction' increase daily.
He writes in 'a moment's interval of calm'. He plans shortly to make his will, in
which he hopes to do justice to CLW and their children. As CLW knows, his
assets consist of £1,000 in the 5 per cents [government stock bequeathed to SW
in James Price will, 6/2/1783], a legacy of £100 from [Rebecca] Gwynne to CW
III and SW that is payable on SGW's decease [*see* Rebecca Gwynne will,
9/8/1799], and 'a reversion of a part of £2400' [the numerals are overwritten] in
case SW outlives SGW, CW Jr or Sarah, which SW hopes will not happen [the
money to be distributed to SW from CW's estate after SGW's death, *see* CW
will, 28/5/1785].

'A series of imprudent and vulgar violence' has destroyed SW's health. Even if
he were to live longer, he would lose £200 a year 'in consequence of the
annihilation of one establishment' [AD's school] caused by 'the cruel
persecution of its support and original [AD], whose health is now so impaired
that it will be absolutely necessary [for her] to seek rest shortly' from work.

SW believes that CLW is well qualified to earn money when he becomes
incapable of providing for her, as he has done willingly up to now. He accepts
that CLW wants a true friend, but fears that she would scorn the friend's advice.
SW would have been her best friend had she allowed this. Now he can only
wish, but not act, to do her much good.

---

[32] *See* SGW→Sarah, 30/4/1803. Ltr <SW and CLW reunited.

SW→Sarah?[33]   1804–1808
GEU Wesley Coll. ltr 63   I have just read your note
perhaps about 1/6/1804[34]

SW has just read the recipient's note [not preserved] by chance. He thinks that he would not have found it if SGW had realised the effects it would have upon his 'irritable temper'. 'Mr W' [CW Jr] has behaved in this matter 'as usual', in a false, treacherous and mischief-making manner. SW is unaware that he ever applied the word 'pet' to his [male] child [presumably CW III] or to the recipient's conduct towards this child. 'Mr W' is 'excessively mad' that SW has told him that 'little is to be expected at Bath', and consequently is wreaking his 'vengeance' by 'trying to render' SW and the recipient 'inveterate enemies'.

SW pities and forgives CW Jr. SGW tells SW that CW Jr and the recipient 'continually' communicate words which SW has said that 'may be construed' unfavourably to SW.

CLW→Sarah   1805–1809
Drew Wesley Family Letters, CLW series   And so you of all people, are
ltr undated; >1804 from ref. to JWW's schooling

CLW wishes Sarah well on her journey and asks her to kiss CLW's 'darling' [presumably CW III] for CLW. CW III speaks 'not higher to' Sarah than of her. The 8/- for JWW's schooling is not yet due. CLW frequently speaks of Sarah as a friend and is convinced from Sarah's conduct that Sarah is her friend. Sarah should not have been offended by CLW writing to her 'in the third person'.

CLW is 'too ill to write two letters' today and wants to write also to Captain Martin, her brother. SW once called CLW's letters 'washerwoman's letters'.

SW→Mr Freebairn   9 Arlington St   1806–6/1808
NN *MNY; *O*   I take the Liberty of informing you that Mr Stokes has been
✉ 'Sunday 5 o'clock'; wmk 1806[35]

Mr Freebairn [not identified], whom SW has not met, had planned to visit Stokes this evening. Since Stokes is dining with SW today, SW asks Freebairn to

---

[33] The addressee is not identified in ltr. Sarah presumed as addressee because she was in continual communication with CW Jr and regularly wrote to SGW.

[34] This dating suggestion is based upon SGW→Sarah, 24/5/1804, which reports SW's opposition to CW Jr going to Bath; also, SW had an irritable temper at that time. However, SW says in SW→SGW 6/11/1807, that he is personally estranged from CW Jr who is entirely influenced by Sarah. SW→CW Jr, 28/10/1808, suggests that they then were on good terms. Ltr presumably not >1809 as there is no evidence of friendship between CLW and Sarah after then.

[35] Ltr <23/6/1808, when SW's address had recently become 27 Arlington Street, as evidenced by SW underscoring the numerals '27' in SW→CB, 23/6/1808.

come to SW's house. As SW understands that Freebairn is 'partial to music', SW and Stokes may be able to provide him with 'some little amusement'.

SW→Sarah   1806

GEU Wesley Coll. ltr 67[36]   You may safely believe me sincere
presumably after SW's move to Camden Town[37]

SW has never designed to 'meddle' with Sarah's principles or with her conduct on any subject. On the contrary, he has carefully avoided using words, 'particularly of late', that might 'introduce any dispute upon religious prejudices'. If Sarah had children SW would consider it highly unjust and uncivil to interfere in their education unless she desired this.

SW may be obliged to hear SGW's talk when he is with her but he is not obliged to regard it. SGW is 'welcome to quit the world' with her motley 'contradictory principles and laughable absurdities' but is not welcome to 'inspire' them into SW's children. As long as SW has the power to influence his children 'they shall reason and judge for themselves upon all mental and disputable subjects'. He 'cannot understand' the contents of Sarah's last note [not preserved].

SW→Robert Birchall   Camden Town   1806–13/1/1810

BL Add 34007 f 45; *O*   If convenient to you to settle for the Copy-right
🖼→dating range[38]

SW asks [Robert] Birchall to pay the bearer, SW's son, for the copyright of SW's [*Variations on a*] *Polish Air* [which Birchall printed and sold before April 1806, when the publication was reviewed in *MM*]. SW, in the 'midsummer holidays', will adjust the balance due to Birchall.

---

[36] Ltr is a torn fragment.

[37] Ltr presumably written (1) when JWW was of sufficient age to be 'inspired' by words spoken by adults (hence not before 1804), and (2) when SW was no longer living in SGW's home (therefore after his move to Camden Town). May 1806 appears to be a likely time for ltr to have been written as CW III was removed then, to Sarah's dismay, from St Paul's School (*see* Sarah memorandum, 3/8/1806), presumably causing a dispute between Sarah and SW about CW III's education. SW and Sarah are not known to have discussed SW's children's education in later years.

[38] If (as seems likely) Birchall acquired the copyright about the time when this work was published ltr can be dated 1806, and SW's son can be identified as CW III, as JWW was under seven years of age in April 1806.

SW→SGW   Camden Town   **1/12/1807–1/12/1809**
Fitzwm ltr 12   I presume by your Invitation that the Coast is Clear
☞ '1 December' & wmk 1807 & 🖾→dating range
From SGW's invitation SW presumes that his children can visit SGW today.
'Mrs Wesley' [CLW] will come at 3 pm with SW's 'dear little idol' [Emma] and
'Jacky Dandy' [JWW]. CW III would come but is going with SW and 'a
dignified clergyman' [not identified] to the Westminster [School] play tonight.

SW→RG   **1808–1817**
BL Add 35013 f 50; *O*   I never was laid under Contribution to any of
☞ 'Saturday night'; wmk 1808[39]
SW 'never was laid under contribution' to any of the 'stringed instrument
gentry' before, but if a second violinist cannot be found for love [presumably to
perform at a benefit concert], it had better be for money. 'We' should therefore
have Mr Betts [probably Arthur Betts, violinist and composer, 1776–1847].
   However, SW's 'great difficulty' concerns the wind instruments and the
violoncellos. If SW cannot procure these instruments, the concert must be
postponed, to his 'great additional expense, disadvantage, and future risk' as
well as the disappointment of the public and of his friends.

CW Jr→Charlotte Ann Broome   **4–12/1808**
BL Eg. 3700A f 179   Pray accept my best thanks for your kind card
ltr docketed 1808. Not before SW and CB became reacquainted >1/4/1808[40]
   CW Jr has to take leave this morning of 'a very old friend going to
Lincolnshire' [not identified] and thus regrettably is prevented from waiting
today on 'the man of genius and taste' [CB]. However, CW Jr hopes to go with
Charlotte Ann Broome [CB's daughter, 1761–1838] to see CB at another time.
CW Jr is obliged to CB for his 'kind zeal' to SW, 'who is rather more in the
musical way' than CW Jr is.

---

[39] The end of this dating range presumes that ltr was not written on paper ten or
more years old. SW's first extant dated letter to RG is SW→RG, 24/7/1812.
According to an advertisement in *The Times*, 3/6/1812 p 2, Arthur Betts or a
member of his family was a seller of tickets to SW's 5/6/1812 benefit concert.
SW's concern about recruiting orchestra members for his 4/5/1813 benefit
concert is noted in SW→VN, 30/4/1813 and SW→VN, about 1/5/1813.
However, insufficient information is available to identify the particular concert
to which ltr refers.

[40] *See* CB→SW, 23/3/1808?

SW→BJ   7/1808–12/1809
EUL Dk.7.38.3; O^{41} [text missing] ...a word to any of my Friends.
presumably written during the main period of SW's correspondence with BJ[42]

SW promises to send BJ, in a few days, a full account of the 'musical hurly-burly' going on 'here' round the clock, and conveys regards to BJ's wife [Mary] and 'young friends' [presumably BJ's children].

Shepherd→Adam Clarke   1810–1813
Adam Clarke p 126–127   The bearer is come to me as a servant
Adam Clarke p 124 says Clarke introduced to Shepherd by Sarah in 1810[43]

Shepherd cannot help 'disculpating' herself from a belief spread amongst Methodists that she made 'young' SW a Papist. SW was converted to [Roman] Catholicism two years before she first met him, by a Frenchman who went to CW's house [possibly Mr Chouquet, *see* CW→SGW, 23/9/1778]. Shepherd heard of SW's conversion from the famous viol-da-gamba performer 'Mr Payton' [a misprint for Stephen Paxton, *see* Shepherd→SW→Shepherd, 3/1794–1797] and persuaded SW 'not to live in criminal hypocrisy and deception', but to tell CW honestly of his conversion.

SW lacked the courage to do this and begged Shepherd to break the news to CW. She thought that this would be 'indecorous' and persuaded 'the late Duchess of Norfolk' [Catherine Howard] to inform CW 'in all the delicacy of Christian charity'. Shepherd considered that the duchess 'would best sympathise' with CW in 'tenderness of feeling' because her son [Charles Howard] also had left the 'religion of his ancestors' [by converting from Roman Catholicism to Protestantism]. The Duchess, who 'went in person' to see CW [between Easter and Whitsunday 1784, *see* Shepherd→Sarah, 14/3/1794], also would show CW 'all possible honour'.

Shepherd had no further involvement in this matter other than 'endeavouring to persuade this two years' old convert [SW] to live soberly, temperately and piously'. For this effort she has done 'ample penance'. It has been her unwanted fate to be heavily burdened by ingratitude and 'scourged with defamation'.

---

[41] Ltr is a torn fragment.

[42] Ltr apparently written when SW was outside London, possibly when he was in Bath in early 1809.

[43] *Adam Clarke* p 133 says that Shepherd survived the date of these letters by 'about two years'. *Etheridge* p 459 says that Shepherd died in 1815, hence ltr presumably <1814.

SW→Sarah   1810–9/1828
MA DDWF/15/48   I have been obliged to scrape all the Money I could
▣ 'Monday night'[44]

SW writes to Sarah in an 'agitated state'. He has been 'obliged to scrape all the money' he could in order to get out of town, and has been able to leave at home only a few shillings. He asks Sarah to lend him £2, which he promises to pay on his return [to London]. He is 'much wounded in spirit', and the 'sorrows' of his heart are enlarged, yet he has always believed that one, and only one, person [Sarah] can bring him out of his troubles.

SW→Sarah   15/8/1810–5/1811
GEU Wesley Coll. ltr 72[45]   I must confess that I was much surprized
ltr undated[46]

When SGW visited 'the other evening', SW was surprised by her 'requisition', of which Sarah apparently had foreknowledge. He already has given 'convincing proof' of his 'readiness to assist' SGW as much as possible without ruining himself and his dependents. £100 advanced in SW's 'very precarious circumstances' is equivalent to £300 from a person whose income is certain, and 'everybody knows' that SW's income 'must ever be irregular'.

It is 'very long' since SW 'yielded up' £100, for which Sarah and CW Jr gave a 'note of hand' [a promissory note]. SW parted with this £100 even though it 'extremely' inconvenienced him, especially after what he had lost by the failure of the concerts [in Hyde's Rooms, Tottenham Street in 1802, *see* SW→CW Jr, 31/5/1811]. Sarah knows that SW has never pressed her or CW Jr for repayment [of the £100], even though SW has been 'frequently very seriously embarrassed' and obliged to borrow money from friends.

Having already 'exceedingly straitened himself' on SGW's account, SW now is required by SGW and Sarah to suffer another £100 'to be sunk' [i.e., realised]

---

[44] Ltr <Sarah's 19/9/1828 death and presumably not before 1810, when the possibility began that SW could be arrested for not paying money due to CLW or to her creditors. Ltr conceivably could have been written on Monday evening 2/5/1825, as SW was arrested that day but was not incarcerated in the spunging house until Wednesday 4/5/1825, and Sarah→John Gaulter, 23/5/1825, notes that 'as usual in all troubles' SW told Sarah of his situation, but his friends advised him to 'go to the [King's] Bench' [the prison to which the spunging house was attached] rather than to be 'continually harassed'. However, other Monday evenings within this dating range can be conjectured.

[45] Ltr is torn at bottom, with some loss of text.

[46] Ltr presumably after SSW's 14/8/1810 birth (on the assumption that SSW is one of the six persons mentioned in ltr that SW has to support in addition to himself) and presumably <SW→CW Jr, 31/5/1811, in which SW says he no longer has property in the funds.

from the provision left by CW, even though Sarah knows that the restitution of this sum is 'improbable'. SW 'is at a loss to determine' how this request can be reconciled 'with justice and propriety'. He does not know 'why a man [SW] with six persons to provide for (beside himself)' [presumably CLW and her three children, SS and SSW], and 'possessed of so precarious a property', can be 'expected to sacrifice sum after sum in consequence of very imprudent conduct of others' [CW Jr and Sarah], who keep two houses and 'perpetually' travel 'hundreds of miles for the honour of attending kings and concerts gratis'.

Since Sarah has such extensive connections with 'persons of rank and independence', SW suggests that she try borrowing £100 from them, giving appropriate security and interest.

SGW 'urges that the money she wants out of the Bank [of England]' is truly hers, and that CW had no right to restrict her access to it [CW will, 28/5/1785, gave SGW the interest but not the principal of the money he left to her]. However, CW well knew that if the money had been left exclusively to her it would have 'gradually melted away to non-existence'. 'Generosity' has been a 'characteristic principle' of SGW, but it needs to be 'counterpoised' by prudence.

William Seaman Stevens→SW   1811
Stevens p iii   In offering the following Treatise to your notice and protection
Stevens published 1811

William Seaman Stevens [author, *b*1778] offers his *Treatise on Piano-Forte Expression* to SW's 'notice and protection'. Because SW's musical talents are 'known and superior', his name will 'shield' Stevens from attacks on the treatise, and SW's 'established reputation and erudite character' will grant it 'a safe conduct to the world'. As both the treatise and SW's 'public labours as musical lecturer to the Royal and Surry Institutions' have been directed towards 'improvement of the musical art', Stevens trusts that his treatise [which includes an 'exercise' for piano that SW composed 'expressly for this work'] will be found worthy of SW's patronage.

SW→VN   1811–8/1820
BL Add 11729 f 109; *O*   Pon Honour you are a funny Man.
⬛ 'Friday morning'[47]

SW was 'detained at Paddington' for an extra hour and therefore could not return home when he had intended. [James] Ball will confirm that SW was at Duke Street [Ball's premises] before 8 pm, with two 'books of tunes', but VN

---

[47] SW's extant correspondence with VN begins in 1811 so ltr presumably not before then. Ltr presumably <SW→VN, 29/8/1820, when SW says that James Ball has insulted him and that SW would meet VN 'anywhere but' at Ball's premises; no later contact between SW and Ball is known to have occurred.

had left by that time. In contrast to VN, Stokes and Samuel Webbe [Jr] would have waited for SW to arrive. SW humorously suggests that VN should be more patient.

SW→VN   Duke St?[48]   **1811–8/1820**
Add 11729 f 108; *O*   Mr Ball lives at the above directed Place
📧 'Sunday 24th'
SW will remain at [James] Ball's home with three JSB motets until 9 pm. Two pianos there [probably in Ball's piano manufactory, at the same address] are in tune with one another.

SW→George Smart   **1811–1832**
Cary W514.S636; *O*   S Wesley was at Sir G. Smart's Door exactly at 20
📧 'Monday morning'; >George Smart knighted on 1/1/1811[49]
SW was at Sir George Smart's house at 8.40 am today but Sir George had already left. SW is informed that there is no chance of his meeting with Sir George before next Sunday.

Lucius Coghlan→SW   **6/1812–1814**
Lightwood p 168   [not known]
ltr after but presumably not long after SW became Grand Organist on 13/5/1812
'In a very short time and without any expense', SW obtained a 'blue apron' [worn by the Grand Organist and other Grand Officers of the Freemasons]. Moreover, SW obtained this honour 'to the extreme mortification and utter disappointment of another [not identified] for whom it was actually intended'. By 'steady application' to his profession, and by cultivating 'rationally the high friends' he may make as Grand Organist, SW soon must be repaid 'twelve times over' the £12/12/- that he is now out of pocket from his Masonic activities.
   Rev. Lucius Coghlan [*c*1750–1833, Chaplain of the Grand Lodge] has raised SW 'to a point of elevation' [the Grand Organist's position], from which he

---

[48] At the top of ltr, where a return address normally is placed, SW has written out James Ball's address, 27 Duke Street, Grosvenor Square. If the placement of this address signifies that SW lived there when ltr was written, ltr can be assigned to 24/1/1819, the only Sunday that occurred on the 24th of a month during the time when SW is conjectured to have lived at Ball's premises. If, however, SW's statement of this address indicates only where he and VN were to meet that evening, the dating range of ltr begins at 1811, when SW's extant letters to VN start, and ends before SW→VN, 29/8/1820, in which SW states that he has been insulted by Ball, after which their contact apparently ceased.

[49] SW's handwriting style is earlier than that of his last years.

'may shine with present lustre and future emolument'. Already SW earns more money than Coghlan. Nevertheless, Coghlan will grant SW a free ticket if he participates tomorrow and, if SW still desires this, will provide that His Royal Highness [the Prince Regent, Grand Master of the Freemasons until 12/5/1813, or his successor, the Duke of Sussex] shall 'forbid the secretaries' to require SW to pay for his ticket 'at any time'.

If SW still believes that the time he spends on Masonic activities is wasted then Coghlan will have no objection if SW resigns.

SW→SGW   **1813–4/1815**
BL Add 35012 f 17   Be assured that I will make any possible reasonable
ltr undated[50]
SW assures SGW that he will make 'any possible reasonable sacrifice' of his feelings to avoid giving her pain. He has no intention of stopping to see her, despite the circumstances.

SW→'Dear Sir'   Gower Pl   **10/1813–5/1817**
MA DDWF/15/24B; *O*   Pray come & breakfast with me on Sunday Morning
🕮→dating range
SW invites the addressee to breakfast with him next Sunday at 9 am. SW has undertaken to perform VN's 'whole duty for the day at the popish Mass-House' [to substitute for VN as organist at the Portuguese Embassy Chapel] and needs someone to turn pages, 'as the morning service is all in score for the organ'. SW remarks that the music is 'just as good as the [Roman Catholic] religion is bad', which pays the music 'the greatest of all possible compliments'.

SW→VN   Gower Pl   **10/1813–5/1817**
BL Add 11729 f 77; *O*   You will give me Credit (I think) for not intentionally
🕮→dating range[51]
SW humorously asks for VN's attention to 'the business relative to the bottom of a certain printed paper [not identified] generally circulated in times like the present'. SW's only reason for 'pressing the motion' is that the point gained would be a 'knock-down blow to a few malicious opponents'.

---

[50] The dating range is the time that SGW lived in Buckingham Street, to where ltr is addressed.

[51] The ref. to a printed paper conceivably is to the printed sheet which SW had prepared when applying for the position of organist to the Foundling Hospital; if so, ltr would date from about the same time as William Kitchiner→Christopher Idle, 10/11/1813, which is written upon a copy of that printed sheet.

Sarah→SW   **2/1817–1822**

GEU in box 6   It is painful to me to write upon a subject
>Sarah left Percy Street in late 1816 & >Sarah→Thomas Maurice, 17/1/1817[52]

Sarah is pained by having to write about a matter which she hoped was settled 'long ago'. She does not regret any tenderness shown to 'a poor little boy [SSW] who could not possibly offend', nor is she 'insensible to the hardships to which he is exposed' through no fault of his own. However, CW's name is and should remain 'honourable', and respect is due the [Methodist] Society which allows SGW a salary, 'without which she could not live in any comfort'.

CW III visits 'us' [SGW, CW Jr and Sarah] and is expected daily. But if SW's children [SSW and Rosalind] by 'Mrs Suitor' [SS] were received by 'us' [SGW, CW Jr and Sarah] while SW lived with SS, SGW's 'salary would be withdrawn' if it were reported that she 'countenanced vice'. Also, SW's 'other children' [by CLW] would find it hard 'to have rivals and supplanters'.

Sarah would 'rejoice' to aid 'the amiable little boy' [SSW] 'individually considered', but his 'unhappy parents' [SW and SS], who 'violate decency and the laws of society' by 'continuing their intercourse', deprive their poor children of the notice that they otherwise would obtain, 'notwithstanding the misfortune of their birth'. When Sarah wrote [not preserved] to SW from Percy Street, a member of Parliament to whom SGW is very much indebted [probably William Wilberforce] was anxious that we [SGW, CW Jr and Sarah] 'support the credit' of CW and JW by 'not patronising an evil course of life' and by not injuring CW's grandchildren 'by the wife' [CLW].

Reports [about SW's conduct] had reached him [Wilberforce] that, if corroborated, would have been 'highly detrimental' to SGW's interest. Sarah has 'often supported' SW's credit. Why should our [SGW's, CW Jr's and Sarah's] credit be destroyed, for 'no essential benefit' to SW?

Sarah 'could take notice of the poor children' [SSW and Rosalind] if SW adopted 'a different course of life', but she cannot 'uphold evil', disoblige her best friends or disrespect CW's name, 'which is disgraced' [by SW's actions]. Although SW may 'scorn' these sentiments now, a time may come when he shares them.

---

[52] In that letter Sarah tells Thomas Maurice that she has not seen CW III for many years, whereas ltr says that Sarah expects CW III daily. Ltr probably <1819, as CW III→Sarah, 3/4/1819, mentions his long absence from Sarah's house and their extreme diversity of sentiment, implying that he did not visit her daily at that time.

SW→RG   Euston St   **1819–3/1830**
BL Add 35013 f 76; *O*   If you can help me forth with the Accommodation of
🖃 'Saturday morning'; 📧→dating range[53]
SW asks RG for the 'accommodation' of 'one small portrait of our invalid
monarch' [a sovereign coin, valued at £1, first minted in 1817]. SW promises
that Pexy [SS] will refund £1 to RG next Tuesday if RG calls.
SW is 'all in a bustle'.

SW→RG   Euston St   **1819–3/1830**
BL Add 35038 f 1; *O*   Do pray contrive to call in here
🖃 'Friday afternoon'; 📧→dating range
SW asks RG to call in during the evening. If the business were not urgent, SW
would not be so 'importunate'. RG soon will learn that SW needs RG's advice.

SW→Mr Dunn   Euston St   **1819–3/1830**
NN *MNY; *O*   Mr S. Wesley begs leave to acquaint Mr Dunn
🖃 '2 o'clock Tuesday'; 📧→dating range
SW waited at Drury Lane Theatre for several hours yesterday and today,
hoping to meet Mr Dunn [probably William Nathaniel Dunn, 1782–1855, for a
time deputy treasurer of Drury Lane Theatre]. SW asks Dunn to write to him.

SW→Emett   **1820–9/1828**
BL Add 35013 f 94; *O*   I was obliged to send a Porter with this
🖃 'Thursday morning'; addressed to Emett at 25 Ebury St, Pimlico[54]
SW was obliged to send a porter [with the matter, not preserved, accompanying
this letter] and could not do this until late last night.

SSW→SW   Euston St   **1820–3/1830**
BL Add 35019 f 4   I called at Mr Allcroft's but he was not at home
📧 & presumption that SSW did not run errands before 1820→dating range
SSW called at 'Mr Allcroft's' [probably the premises of Robert Allcroft,
engraver of Dean Street, Soho], but he was not at home. A boy at the shop said
he thought it [not identified] would cost about 5/- per plate. If so, it will be much

---

[53] The 'invalid monarch' mentioned in ltr is either George III (in which case ltr
<George III's 29/1/1820 death) or George IV *d*26/6/1830.

[54] Ltr before SSW→Emett, 22/9/1828, which is addressed to 2 Elizabeth Street,
Chelsea. No contact between SW and Emett is known to have taken place
before the 1820s.

cheaper than SW expected. SSW saw [George] Cooper this afternoon and told him about it. SSW hopes that SW will not forget to spend SSW's evenings at home. SSW has not seen 'that bandit' [not identified] yet, and would be very glad never to see him again.

Sarah memorandum   10/1822–11/1824

GEU in box 8   Shuddered at hearing S— called & behaved with a Shew of kind memo on paper bearing a torn address that probably is 14 Nottingham Street[55]

Sarah shuddered when she heard that SW had called [at the home she shared with CW Jr] and had expressed 'kind interest' about her. The thought of SW 'returning affection to his injured sister' has 'harrowed' up all her resentments. She told CW Jr that she 'never wished to see' SW or to 'remember him or recognise him in any world'. She would never persecute or defame him, and 'would do him any service possible', but she loathes 'the idea of intercourse'. Only religious principle restrains her from invoking judgements [against SW].

She prays that God will keep her from sinning and will make her love even her enemies.

SW→'Esq.'   Euston St   13/3/1825–13/3/1828

MA DDWF/15/38; O^{56} That imperious Tyrant called Necessity, is the sole
⌨ '13 March'; <Sarah's 19/9/1828 death[57]

SW apologises that his addressee has not received the balance of the bill; he will have it in a week's time. SW cannot at present answer the query about his

---

[55] Sarah and CW Jr lived at that address from 10/1822; by 24/11/1824 they had moved to 49 Gloucester Place.

[56] The address panel of ltr is torn and considerable text is missing. The address of the recipient is identifiable only as a Street in a place whose name ends in 'side', probably Cheapside. According to *Clarke's New Law List* for 1834, Henry John Gauntlett and his brother Edward Ebenezer Gauntlett practised law at 73 Queen Street, Cheapside then, and SW→Henry John Gauntlett, 16/6/1836, is addressed to Queen Street, Cheapside. But as Henry John Gauntlett→RG, 27/11/1828, concerned with Sarah's will, is written from 15 Serjeants Inn, Fleet Street, and as neither Gauntlett is listed in *Clarke's New Law List* for 1825 or 1828, it would be unsafe to conclude that ltr's recipient was a Gauntlett. It is not known that SW had financial dealings with either Gauntlett before the matter of Sarah's will, and this matter presumably did not arise until after her death.

[57] Ltr presumably after SGW's 22/12/1822 death, as SW probably would have asked SGW rather than Sarah and CW Jr about family history if SGW had been alive. Ltr also presumably after Sarah's *c*1825 recognition of SW's 'restoration' and the resumption of their dining together (*see* Sarah→Maria Cosway, 22/4/1825).

grandmother's maiden name but will ask CW Jr and Sarah tomorrow when he dines with them.

CW Jr will   11/1828–11/1830

GEU in box 8   In the name of GOD. Amen. I Charles Wesley of the Parish will >Sarah's 19/9/1828 death & presumably <Emma's 5/11/1830 marriage[58]

CW Jr names Tooth as his 'residuary legatee and sole executor' and leaves her £600. He leaves £100 to each of Emma, CW III and JWW and gives Emma the 'oval picture' of SW. To SW, CW Jr bequeaths his musical instruments, books and 'little monumental bust of Handel', and also the portrait [of CW Jr] drawn by [John] Russell [artist, 1745–1806]. CW Jr gives his 'large bust of Handel' to Christ Church, Oxford. He leaves money and other things to his 'dear friend' Mrs [Elizabeth] Greene [his cousin] and to her sister Fanny [Frances] Baldwyn.

SW→Joseph Alfred Novello   7/1830–1834

Sotheby catalogue 15/5/1996 lot 148   [not known]
Sotheby catalogue dating range: *c*1830–1834[59]

SW assigns the copyright of his 'Six short voluntaries' and his 'Variations on Jessy of Dunblane'[60] to Joseph Alfred Novello [music publisher, 1810–1896, VN's son, who established the Novello music publishing company in 1829].

SW→John Capel   Pentonville   1832–1837

MA DDWF/15/46; *O*   I have but this Moment received the enclosed
▪ '27 April' & ⟶dating range

SW has just received 'the enclosed' [not preserved]. SW's address was left before the beginning of the season at 'the Tavern' [possibly the Crown and Anchor Tavern, where the Glee Club, of which Capel was president, met]. SW cannot tell why the letters were sent to Mr Cooper and not to SW.

---

[58] The will mentions Sarah's place of burial and presumably was written after CW Jr moved about 20/11/1828 to 20 Edgware Road; Emma is named 'Emma Wesley'. This will was revoked by CW Jr's 18/5/1831 will.

[59] Presumably not before 7/1830, as SW resumed writing to VN on 10/6/1830 after communication between them had lapsed for several years. Both works mentioned are advertised by J. Alfred Novello on the wrapper of the 13/10/1837 *MW*, where they are said to be 'in the press'. From the Sotheby catalogue description it is unclear whether the two assignments of copyright were given in one or in two documents.

[60] 'Dunblane' is so spelt on SW's autograph (RSCM), but the name appears in several variant spellings in contemporary reports of this composition.

SW→Christopher Lonsdale   Pentonville   **1832–1837**

BL Add 34007 f 44; *O*   Mr Wesley's Compts to Mr Lonsdale & begs to return
🖎→dating range

SW thanks Mr Lonsdale [presumably Christopher Lonsdale, music publisher, 1795?–1877] for the fugues [possibly Lonsdale's publication of the SW/CFH edition of JSB's '48']. SW has the organ duet [presumably SW's *Grand Duet for the Organ*, which Lonsdale published] but has not seen the 'additional fugues'. He accepts Lonsdale's 'kind offer'. If Lonsdale should ever require anything in SW's line, SW will be happy to 'make some little recompense'.

VN→SW   Pentonville   **10/1832–7/1834**

BL Add 35027 f 35   I was speaking the other day, about old times, with your
☷ 'Monday morning'[61]

VN spoke recently with SW's former student [Marmaduke Charles] Wilson. Wilson recalled with pleasure his playing, with SW, [John Baptist] Cramer's *Studio* [*per il Pianoforte*, composed between 1804 and 1810], to which SW had added a violin accompaniment. VN asks to see a copy of this accompaniment. He anticipates buying it for his own 'portfolio' if he can afford the price, which he asks SW to set.

VN hopes that SW intends to have his *Confitebor*, which does great honour to his 'musical genius', performed at the 'Hereford Festival' [the Three Choirs Festival, held in Hereford 9–11/9/1834], either under SW's direction or that of his son [SSW]. If SW sends a copy of the 'beautiful solo' 'Fidelia' [from *Confitebor*], Clara [Novello, soprano, 1818–1908, VN's daughter] will 'study it very attentively' and will endeavour 'to do justice to it'. If SW agrees to have this solo published so that copies are 'ready by the time of the Hereford Festival', its performance there probably would promote a sufficient sale to make the publication 'rather advantageous' to SW. VN will be happy to 'revise the proofs' of this publication, to spare SW 'as much trouble as possible'. SW's early reply is requested.

SW→'Reverend and Dear Sir'   **1835–1837**

MA DDWes/6/57; *O*   The following Answers are I know perfectly correct
ltr undated; wmk 1835[62]

SW answers a request [not preserved] for information about his family history. SGW's family estate at Garth, Breconshire, Wales 'still remains', and SW

---

[61] Ltr presumably after Clara Novello's debut in October 1832. Ltr bears twopenny post paid stamp (*Willcocks/Jay* L493) of the Westminster Office, which closed in July 1834.

[62] The recipient possibly was Jackson, who edited the *Wesleyan Methodist Magazine* and collected information about Methodist history in this context.

understands that it 'will at some time devolve' to him. Besides CW Jr, Sarah and SW, CW had five children, 'all of whom died very young'. Two of the five were boys named 'John'. The elder John 'showed an extraordinary propensity to music' at the age of two by waving his hands 'in just time' to played or sung measures, but he died aged 2½.

CW was educated at Westminster School and Christ Church, Oxford, where he studied 'for orders'. He went, as JW's 'coadjutor', to America with General [James Edward] Oglethorpe [1696–1785]. CW was well versed in Latin, Greek and Hebrew and he read German. He came to London from Bristol, where all his children had been born, when SW was about eight years old and lived at [Chesterfield Street,] Marybone until his death in 1787 [in fact, he died in 1788].

CW Jr went to Mr Needham's grammar school in Bristol where he learned Latin. On leaving, CW Jr, whose musical talent was apparent from the age of 2¾, 'was devoted entirely to music'. The Bristol organist Mr [Edmund] Broderip heard CW Jr 'in petticoats' and said that he would make a great player. He was taught first by Mr Rooke in Bristol and then in London by Mr [Joseph] Kelway, Queen Charlotte's harpsichord master, and in harmony and composition by Dr [William] Boyce, 'a most amiable man, and a profound master'.

Sarah was educated at Miss Temple's school in Bristol and was taught some Latin by CW. She also had 'some talent' for singing, but the 'musical genius' in the Wesley family seemed to originate in SGW. JW's wife [Mary] once said 'invidiously' that 'the Methodist Cages (Houses)' seemed not to be 'fine enough' for this 'singing bird'. Although SGW frequently attended Methodist meetings, she 'was not a regular member of the [Methodist] Society'.

CW Jr and Sarah received 'the greater part of their education at school'. SW is 'obliged' to CW for teaching him Latin.

SW identifies some distinguished people with whom CW was acquainted. Lord Mornington [Garret Wesley], father of the present Duke of Wellington [Arthur Wesley later Wellesley, field marshal, 1769–1852, from 1814 Duke of Wellington], for several years came weekly to CW's house to breakfast and to play 'quartettos' for hours. Lord Mornington brought 'his tenor violin [i.e., viola] under his arm and said that he should never be ashamed at being mistaken for a musician'. Dr [Samuel] Johnson was not musical but said that he envied CB's 'sixth sense', his 'relish for music' [*see* Thomas Green journal entry, 28/6/1813]. CW also was 'well acquainted with' the Countess of Huntingdon [Selena Hastings, 1707–1791], General [Pascal] Paoli, Daines Barrington and 'his brother, the Earl' [William Wildman Barrington, statesman, 1717–1793, 2nd Viscount Barrington].

CW was not visited often by Methodist preachers, but JW often brought two or three with him when he came. When at Bristol, CW preached at the New Room in the Horse-fair; when in London, he 'had no constant duty' but usually preached on Sundays at West Street Chapel, which his family also 'generally attended'. He was very fond of music and, long before SW's time, played the flute a little. SW does not know that CW would have chosen the profession of music for him and CW Jr. CW once asked Lord Chesterfield [presumably Philip

Dormer Stanhope, statesman and writer, 1694–1773, 4th Earl of Chesterfield] what he should make his sons, and Chesterfield replied 'whatever nature seems to have designed them for'.

SW does not remember when the CW Jr/SW concerts started but thinks that he was about 14 or 15 years old at the time [in fact, SW was 12 years old at the first concert in 1779]. The concerts continued for several seasons. The room in Chesterfield Street admitted from 60 to 80 persons and was generally filled. Members of the nobility attended. Once JW came with some [Methodist] preachers and said, 'I do this, to show that I consider it no sin'. JW 'loved music much, but was no performer'. He was extraordinarily punctual. When he first preached in Ireland he was much persecuted, but he 'had the happy art of gaining the hearts of his hearers'.

Ebenezer Blackwell [banker, *d*1782] was for many years 'intimate' with the Wesley family, but SW does not recall 'any interesting particulars' about him. SW undertakes to try to answer any other questions that his correspondent may ask.

Ole Bull→SW   >4/1836
BL Add 35027 f 83   Mr Ole Bull presents his best Respects to Mr Wesley
ltr written from London where Bull arrived in May 1836
Ole Bull is 'extremely obliged' to SW for his kindness and is 'highly flattered' by SW's compliments. Bull feels much better but is following his doctor's advice to stay in bed.

SW→Domenico Dragonetti   ≥1/7/1836
BL Add 56411 f 23; *O*   I have sent you my Daughter's Album, as she is
ltr in SW's late style of handwriting[63]
SW encloses his daughter's [EW's] album. She would value 'a few bars' from Dragonetti, whom SW sincerely admires.

---

[63] Dragonetti's undated contribution to EW's album (BL Add 35026) follows SW's contribution dated 1/7/1836 to this album; hence ltr not before then.

CALENDAR OF DOUBTFUL CORRESPONDENCE

SW→Sarah   **10/5/1797**
Sotheby catalogue 10/7/1906 lot 279[1]   [not known]
Sotheby catalogue
  [No information is known about ltr beyond the Sotheby catalogue entry.]

Shepherd→Sarah[2]   **14/12/1809**
SMU   I like your Quaker much.
☑ 'Thursday 14 December' & wmk 1808→{1809,1815}[3]
  Shepherd breathes '*vendetta ultionem* to that she fiend Boswell and her male associate in malice, Sam Belial' [i.e., Sam the Devil].

---

[1] Ltr is entered here because a number of the descriptions in this catalogue are inaccurate. Ltr was purchased at this sale by Robert Thursfield Smith, but does not appear to be at GEU, which acquired much of Smith's collection of Wesley family letters.

[2] Ltr is relevant to SW only if 'Sam Belial' refers to SW, as asserted by Tooth in a note (at SMU) which accompanies ltr. Tooth states that ltr 'alludes to some plotting' by Euphemia Boswell [1774–1837, daughter of James Boswell, the biographer of Samuel Johnson] and SW 'to injure' Sarah and CW Jr 'with Lord and Lady Moira' [Francis Rawdon-Hastings, 1754–1826, created 2nd Earl of Moira in 1793, and his wife Flora, Countess of Loudon, 1780–1840]. Confirmation of Tooth's claims has not been found.

[3] 1815 excluded because Tooth, in her note accompanying ltr, says that Shepherd died on 29/6/1815. (*Etheridge* p 459 corroborates that Shepherd died in 1815, but does not give the month or day.)

SSW→Advertiser in *The Times*[4]   Mornington Pl   **26/4/1831**

RSCM; *O*   Mr S Wesley informs the Advertiser in the 'Times' of yesterday
▣ 26/4/1831

SSW, using the name 'S. Wesley', informs the advertiser in *The Times* of
25/4/1831 [in fact, the advertisement appeared in *The Times* of 26/4/1831] that
he is selling an organ which was built a short time ago 'expressly for himself'. It
is nine feet high, possesses 1½ octaves of pedals, and has 'a powerful quality'.
The price is £126.

---

[4] Ltr is relevant to SW only if SSW wrote ltr on SW's behalf. At this time both
SW and SSW lived in Mornington Place, and SSW sometimes used the name
'S. Wesley' with no middle initial to refer to himself. It is not known whether
the organ described in ltr was owned by SSW or by SW, nor that either had the
financial ability to purchase an organ in 1830 or 1831 (*see* Richard J. Stevens
memorandum, 3/1831, which records RG's statement that, in 3/1831, 'the
bailiffs' were in possession of SW's house and furniture). The records of the
organ builders Elliot & Hill (now in the Birmingham City Archives, Central
Library, Birmingham) show that in November 1830 'Mr Gauntlett' (presumably
Henry John Gauntlett) was charged £5 'for removing the organ from Mr
Wesleys to Tottenham Court [the firm's premises] fixing up & tuning & from
there to Mr Gauntlett's house'. As the organ mentioned in ltr was built 'a short
time ago', it presumably was not the organ that had been repaired and removed
by Elliot & Hill five months earlier.

~ 4 ~

MUSICAL WORKS

INTRODUCTION

The list of Samuel Wesley's musical works which follows describes some 550 compositions, most of which have never been published. It includes works that are lost or incomplete but excludes brief fragments and sketches of compositions. The list is organised according to the following categories:

Sacred Vocal Music	works 1–177
Secular Vocal Music	works 201–330
Orchestral Music	works 401–424
Chamber Music	works 501–531
Organ Music	works 601–679
Harpsichord and Pianoforte Music	works 701–827

Within each category compositions are listed by function (e.g., Roman Catholic sacred music, Anglican sacred music), by kind (e.g., secular choruses, secular songs, symphonies, concertos), or—in the case of keyboard music—by whether a work was printed before 1839. Secular vocal music (other than oratorios) and smaller sacred compositions are ordered alphabetically by the first line of their text, with initial articles 'a' and 'the' considered in the ordering. All other works are presented alphabetically by title, with initial articles disregarded in the ordering.

The category 'organ music' includes music for the Royal Seraphine, an instrument invented by John Green about 1830.[1]

Works incorrectly attributed to Samuel Wesley also have been entered in the following list, with the tilde sign '~' given in place of a work number. Unless otherwise indicated, the misattributions are made in the British Library catalogue.

Music by other composers that SW edited or arranged is listed in a separate enumeration (works 901–929). Manuscript copies by SW of other composers' music are entered only where he altered a work substantially or is known to have had plans to publish it.

---

[1] See the note to work 601 below.

Prior Lists of SW's Musical Works. The first known catalogue of Samuel Wesley's compositions and arrangements was published in *The Musical World* in 1837, immediately following his obituary.[2] Henceforth referred to as *MW list*, it enumerates some 90 works, although its numbering is erratic—e.g., four different works are given the number 52, and the first item is not numbered at all.

In 1849 Vincent Novello presented a manuscript volume to the British Museum 'as a tribute of respect and a token of veneration for the memory of his beloved friend, Samuel Wesley, who, in the donor's estimation, was one of the greatest musical geniuses that England has ever produced'. This manuscript, now BL Add Ms 17731, includes at folio 41 VN's list of many printed and manuscript compositions by SW (and a few by CW Jr) that VN's 'esteemed friend' Thomas Hawkins had collected.

VN's list was printed in 1874 by William Winters as part of his account of the musical talents of the Wesley family,[3] and was reprinted the following year by Eliza Wesley in an appendix to her *Jacobs* book of 24 SW letters, where she also republished much, but not all, of *MW list* (without its numbers).[4]

Several other lists of SW's compositions have appeared subsequently, notably as supplements to articles about SW in the successive editions of *Grove's Dictionary of Music and Musicians*.

The list of SW's musical works presented here is substantially larger than any of its predecessors. Its compilation accordingly has resulted in the identification of numerous works not known to prior bibliographers. Of particular interest is the discovery of an SW edition of the first three of J. S. Bach's *Six Little Preludes*, work 903, which has not previously been taken into account by Bach scholars.

---

[2] 'Catalogue of Mr Wesley's compositions', *MW* v 7 no. 86 (3/11/1837) p 117–118.

[3] Winters, William, *An Account of the Remarkable Musical Talents of Several Members of the Wesley Family*. London, 1874, p 86–91.

[4] Eliza Wesley, 'The musical works of Samuel Wesley', in *Jacobs* p 51–60. Because *Jacobs* is much more accessible than either VN's manuscript or Winters's publication, *Jacobs* page numbers are given in this book for works in VN's list.

Structure of the List. Each entry for a work comprises several rows of data. The first row contains a number which we have given to the work, a short title (for secular and smaller sacred vocal music the title is the first few words of text) and, when this can be stated or estimated with confidence, the year or a range of years during which SW composed, edited or arranged the work. Unless SW wrote the year explicitly on a surviving autograph of the work, the date is enclosed in square brackets and has been assigned editorially, for reasons given either in the entry or in supporting footnotes. The evidence for these assignments includes, where available: dates on non-autograph sources; dates on other works in the same manuscript source; references to the work in letters; watermarks; SW's handwriting style; and the date when printed copies of the work were first published or reviewed.

If contemporary manuscripts of a work are known they are listed in the next row of the entry, headed '*ms*'. Any autograph mss are presented first, in roman type, followed by non-autograph manuscripts (if any) in italic type, with the full or abbreviated name of the copyist given in parentheses where known. The folio number of the beginning of a work is provided where a manuscript contains many items or where this otherwise aids identification: for instance, to distinguish pieces with the same or similar titles. Information relevant to our dating of a particular manuscript—such as a stated date of composition, or a watermark containing the year when paper in a ms was made—is mentioned, together with other descriptive data such as whether a source is incomplete.

If a work was printed before 1839, or was first printed after 1838 in an edition either by SW's friend Vincent Novello (VN) or by SW's children Samuel Sebastian Wesley (SSW) or Eliza Wesley (EW), details of this publication (including a short title, the publisher's name and other information relevant to its dating) are provided in the next row, headed '*pr*'. Reviews of these publications that have come to our attention are indicated here if the reviews appeared during SW's lifetime. If a different publisher is known to have reissued the publication during SW's lifetime this also is noted.

(Music publications during SW's lifetime usually were printed in very small quantities. It is not uncommon for no copy, or only a single copy, of a publication to have survived if the publisher failed to deposit copies at Stationers' Hall.)

Publication dates in square brackets are editorial, and derive from one or more of the following: the date of the publication's entry at Stationers' Hall (abbreviated ESH);[5] dated watermarks on a copy of the publication; dates on prefaces; SW's home address at the time of publication; references to the publication in SW's correspondence; publishers' catalogues; publishers' names and addresses;[6] publishers' plate numbers;[7] and dates of a publication's reviews. A number preceded by the acronym 'RISM' indicates that the publication has been so catalogued in the Répertoire International des Sources Musicales. The abbreviation '*facs*' followed by the name of a modern edition signifies that the publication has been reproduced in facsimile there.

Where a work comprises numerous individually titled subsidiary works they are itemised in the next row of its entry, headed *cont.*

If an edition or arrangement of the work published after 1950 has come to our attention, this is noted in the next row, headed *ed.* Particular effort has been made to find modern editions of SW's many organ pieces, but the information presented here must be regarded as selective rather than comprehensive.

Other remarks about a work, such as the voices or instruments for which it is composed, its genre if explicitly stated on a manuscript

---

[5] Many publications of works by SW and his contemporaries which claim on their title-pages to have been entered at Stationers' Hall in fact were not entered on the Stationers' Hall registers. As entry required deposit of printed copies, the date of entry cannot have preceded the date of first publication and, to achieve the legal protection provided by entry, generally was very close to that date. An ESH date therefore generally is a reliable estimate of a publication date. For a discussion of this matter see Alan Tyson, *The Authentic English Editions of Beethoven* (London, 1963), appendix I, p 131–143.

[6] As given in Humphries, Charles and William C. Smith, *Music Publishing in the British Isles from the Earliest Times to the Middle of the 19th Century* (Oxford, 2nd edition with supplement, 1970).

[7] As given in Neighbour, O. W. and Alan Tyson, *English Music Publishers' Plate Numbers in the first Half of the 19th Century* (London, [1965]) and Deutsch, O. E., *Musik Verlags Nummern; Eine Auswahl vom 40 datierten Listen 1710–1900* (Berlin, 2nd edition, 1961).

source (e.g., 'A hymn.'), the author of the text if known, and the date and place of the work's first performance during SW's lifetime if known, are given in the last row, headed *rmk*. If the work appears in *MW list* its number there is given.

If SW dedicated a work to a person or a collection of people this information also is noted here. Brief notes about each dedicatee is given in a separate section which follows the list of SW's musical compositions.

The symbol '♫' designates that a recording of the work has been released commercially. Details of these recordings are given in the discography section.

The following two abbreviations are used in entries:

LPS	Temperley, Nicholas (ed.), *Works for Pianoforte solo by late Georgian Composers: Samuel Wesley and Contemporaries (The London Pianoforte School 1766–1860, v 7)*. New York and London, 1985.
The Symphony	Divall, Richard and John I. Schwarz (eds.), *The Symphony 1720–1840, Series E v 3*. New York and London, 1983.

HISTORY OF THE MUSIC MANUSCRIPTS

The two most important collections of Samuel Wesley's music manuscripts, comprising a very large proportion of his compositions, are at the British Library and the Royal College of Music. Both collections originated principally from two sources: manuscripts that SW possessed at the time of his death, which then passed to members of his family; and manuscripts owned by Vincent Novello or the music publishing firm that he founded.

BRITISH LIBRARY. *MSS THAT PASSED TO SW'S FAMILY.* The largest group of these manuscripts is in the Eliza Wesley Collection, bequeathed to the British Museum by EW in 1895 and now catalogued as BL Add Ms 34496–35027.[8] This bequest contained a large number of autographs of works by SW which, for one reason or another, were not published in his lifetime: his earliest compositions, including his oratorios *Ruth* and *The Death of Abel*; music associated with the CW Jr/SW concerts (including scores of SW's early symphonies and concertos); and sacred vocal music arising from SW's involvement with Roman Catholicism and the embassy chapels, including the working score of the *Missa de spiritu sancto* and the score of the *Confitebor*. Three other manuscripts in EW's bequest are among those that VN presented to the Musical Antiquarian Society in 1843, and are discussed below.

BL Add Ms 35038–35040, containing anthems, songs and a volume of early harpsichord and organ pieces, some by SW, were presented to the British Museum in 1896 by Robert Glenn Wesley, SW's youngest son.

MSS OWNED BY VN OR THE NOVELLO FIRM.[9] These mss—autographs as well as copies by VN and others—fall into three categories: (1) mss which VN presented directly to the British

---

[8] EW's bequest also included numerous letters described in the section above on History and Prior Publication of the Correspondence.

[9] For further information on this subject, see Chris Banks, 'From Purcell to Wardour Street: A Brief Account of Music Manuscripts from the Library of Vincent Novello now in the British Library', *British Library Journal* v 21 no. 2 (autumn 1991) p 240–258.

Museum on several occasions between 1840 and 1849; (2) mss which he gave to friends or institutions, and which subsequently were acquired by the British Museum; and (3) mss—many of them copies used in preparation for printing—which remained with the Novello firm until recently. A portion of this firm's archive was presented to the RCM in 1964 (see below); another portion, now called the Novello Collection, came to the BL in October 1986 and comprises Add Ms 65382–65499; and a third portion, the Supplementary Novello Collection, came to the BL in May 1987 and is catalogued as Add Ms 69851–69854.

Mss in the first category include five volumes of SW autograph compositions, now Add 14339–14444, which VN presented in 1843. Add 14339 is the score of *Begin the noble song (Ode to St Cecilia).*[10] An 1849 donation included Add 17731, a volume containing Latin sacred music by SW.

The main items in the second category are mss that VN presented to the Musical Antiquarian Society in the 1840s, some bearing his instructions that they were to be given to the British Museum in the event of the Society dissolving, which indeed occurred about 1849.[11] Included in this category are three pieces in Add 33240, as well as a number of works forming parts of Add 35003, 35005 and 35024 which somehow found their way to EW when the Society was wound up but which later came to the British Museum as part of her bequest.

Included in the third category are manuscripts of many works subsequently published by the Novello firm, some of which evidently were used as printer's copy. They include the autograph of SW's hitherto unknown sonata of 1797 for violin and piano, written for Johann Peter Salomon (now Add 69854), and an album (now Add 69859), apparently compiled by Rosalind Eleanor Esther Glenn (*b*1835), daughter of RG and of SW's daughter Rosalind, which contains an organ voluntary in D minor by SW not present in any other source.

---

[10] VN also presented to the British Museum at this time SW manuscript copies of works by J. S. Bach. Add 14330 includes the '48' and three of the six trios that SW published with CFH; Add 14344 is a copy of the *Goldberg Variations.*

[11] Banks, *op. cit.*

OTHER SW MSS. The British Library acquired an important SW autograph ms from the antiquarian music dealers Travis and Emery in 1992. Entitled 'Harmony 1800', and now Add Ms 71107, it provides the only source of two pieces ('Beati omnes qui timent Dominum' and an organ fugue in D), and for many other pieces it provides the only autograph source.

Manuscript Eg. 2571 includes copies of six sacred and three secular vocal works by SW in the hand of his friend Joseph Payne Street.

ROYAL COLLEGE OF MUSIC.[12] *MSS THAT PASSED TO SW'S FAMILY.* Mss 3073, 4016–4018, 4020–4022, 4025–4029 and 4038 were bequeathed to the RCM by SSW's third son, Francis Gwynne Wesley (1840–1921). They had apparently belonged to SSW, although he made no mention of them in his will. Not all of these mss were in the family continuously since SW's death. Ms 4018, for instance, was given to VN by the widow of Charles Stokes in 1839, and appeared as lot 855 in the sale of part of VN's library by Puttick and Simpson on 4 September 1862, where it was purchased by SSW for 9/6. Ms 4038, an album in the hand of Marianne Merewether (1808–1888), includes music by SW that she copied before her marriage to SSW in 1834.

MSS OWNED BY VN OR THE NOVELLO FIRM.[13] An important set of SW's music manuscripts—now mss 639, 1039 and 1040—was presented to the Sacred Harmonic Society by VN's son Joseph Alfred Novello. These manuscripts passed to the Royal College of Music in 1883 after the Society was wound up.[14]

Ms 640 was presented by VN to James W. Windsor of Bath on 10 January 1849, and came to the RCM in 1890 as part of the Windsor Collection, bequeathed by Windsor's daughter Elizabeth.

---

[12] We are grateful to Dr Peter Horton of the RCM library for information regarding the history of the library's collection.

[13] See Jeremy Dibble, 'The RCM Novello library', *Musical Times* v 124 (1983) p 99–101.

[14] Ms 2130, containing letters by SW to BJ and others, also passed from the Novello firm to the RCM via the Sacred Harmonic Society; see the section above on the History and Prior Publication of the Correspondence.

Ms 4582 (originally part of ms 5253), and mss 5235, 5237, 5238, 5249, 5251 and 5253, are part of the large quantity of Novello-firm working copies that were presented to the RCM in 1964. They are counterparts of manuscripts now in the Novello Collection and the Supplementary Novello Collection at the BL.[15] Ms 5235, consisting of a score and four vocal part-books, appears to have come originally from the music library of the Portuguese Embassy Chapel.

The following repositories hold smaller quantities of significant SW music manuscripts:

FITZWILLIAM MUSEUM. The presentation copy of SW's *Missa de spiritu sancto* is now Ms 730. This ms was sent by SW to Pope Pius VI in 1784[16] and presumably was then deposited in the Vatican library. It was acquired in 1885 by the Roman Catholic antiquary Hartwell de la Garde Grissell (1839–1907) and brought back to England. Subsequently it was owned by the collector Ralph Griffin, who presented it to the Fitzwilliam Museum in 1936.[17] The Museum also possesses the sole source of SW's anthem 'O praise the Lord, ye that fear him' (Ms 624), an autograph copy of the organ *Preludes in All the Keys throughout the Octave* (Ms 699), and a few other ms items.

BODLEIAN LIBRARY. The autograph score (Ms Mus. c.31) of the Kyrie of SW's harmonisation of the *Missa pro angelis* was presented by VN on 14 July 1848. The Bodleian also possesses a nineteenth-century set of parts of 'Tu es sacerdos' [II] and 'Omnia vanitas' (Mss Mus. Sch. D375 a–j). Three mss from the library of St Michael's College, Tenbury were acquired recently:[18] an autograph volume (Ms

---

[15] The division of Novello firm mss between the BL and the RCM seems to have been made on an *ad hoc* basis.

[16] See SW→Shepherd, 6/9/1784?.

[17] See Philip Olleson, 'Spirit voices', *Musical Times* v 138 (1997) p 4–10, and 'Samuel Wesley and the *Missa de Spiritu Sancto'*, *Recusant History* v 24 (1999) p 309–319.

[18] These mss are described in Edmund Fellowes, *The Catalogue of Manuscripts in the Library of St Michael's College Tenbury* (Paris, 1934).

Tenbury 1246) inscribed 'Libro del Samuel Wesley 1783', containing the only known source of an early setting of 'Dixit Dominus' [I] and manuscripts of five pieces of secular vocal music, one of which ('One kind kiss before we part') is unknown in any other source; a volume (Ms Tenbury 621) formerly owned by CW Jr and containing a copy, probably in CW Jr's hand, of SW's 'O Lord God most holy'; and a volume (Ms Tenbury 874) containing a mid- or late- nineteenth-century copy of 'Omnia vanitas'.

PIERPONT MORGAN LIBRARY. The Mary Flagler Cary Music Collection purchased in 1976, from the antiquarian music dealer Richard Macnutt (catalogue 107, item 125), an important collection, now ms 499, of 24 autograph glees and part songs written in the late 1770s and early 1780s. All these compositions are known from other sources, but for one piece ('The world, my dear Mira, is full of deceit') the Cary manuscript is the only known autograph, and for another ('Harsh and untuneful are the notes') it is the only known complete autograph.

METHODIST ARCHIVES AND RESEARCH CENTRE. Besides their large collection of Wesley family letters and papers, the Methodist Archives hold some SW autograph music manuscripts: three early sonatas for violin and keyboard, a duet for two violins, the variations for piano on 'A favorite Italian air', and two other short piano pieces.[19]

A few autograph musical compositions are in other libraries. The Library of Congress has autographs of SW's D major fugue for organ, his organ voluntary op. 6 no. 9, and 'Deus majestatis intonuit', 'Gloria et honore' and 'Life is a jest'; all were formerly owned by the music collector William Hayman Cummings (1831–1915).[20] The Harry Ransom Humanities Center, University of Texas purchased in

---

[19] Barry Cooper, 'Catalogue of pre-1900 music manuscripts in the John Rylands University Library of Manchester', *Bulletin of the John Rylands University Library of Manchester* v 79 no. 2 (summer 1997) p 27–101.

[20] Of these, only 'Life is a jest' appears (as lot 199) in the catalogue of the 17–24/5/1917 Sotheby sale of items from Cummings's library, where it was bought by B. F. Stevens for £1.

1970 'Omnia vanitas' and Magnificat [II] from the American musicologist Theodore M. Finney (1902–1978). The Royal School of Church Music possesses autographs of the glees 'The glories of our birth and state' and 'While others, Delia, use their pen' and the variations for piano on 'Jessy of Dunblaine'.[21] 'Dixit Dominus' [III], and 'While ev'ry short liv'd flower of sense' are in the Euing Collection, Glasgow University Library.

SW autograph compositions now in private collections include the score of the original version of the organ concerto in C, the trio for three pianofortes, the glee 'Tobacco's but an Indian weed', the song 'When all around grew drear and dark', two early organ voluntaries, the fugue from the organ voluntary op. 6 no. 3, a fugue for piano in D, and a march for wind band in B♭.

---

[21] The RSCM also possesses SW's transpositions of three JSB preludes and fugues from part 2 of the '48' into 'more commodious keys'. See SW→VN, 30/3/1813.

SACRED VOCAL MUSIC

1. ROMAN CATHOLIC MASSES

1	**Missa defunctorum 6 Toni**	[1811–1812]

ms BL Add 14342

pr *Gregorian Mass for the Dead, from Mr S. Wesley's Arrangement, the Organ Accompaniment by V. Novello* in VN, *Twelve Easy Masses* (London, [1816]).

rmk Plainchant, bc. *See* SW→VN, 27/3/1812, 4/2/1814.

2	**Missa de sanctissima Trinitate 5 Toni**	[1812]

ms BL Add 35001

rmk SATB. Incomplete: Kyrie, Gloria, part of Credo only. *See* SW→VN, 5/12/1812.

3	**Missa de spiritu sancto**	1784

ms BL Add 35000 (dated 22/5/1784), Fitzwm 730 (presentation copy to Pope Pius VI, dated 1/9/1784)

ed Francis Routh (London, 1997)

rmk SATB, SATB chorus, orchestra. *See* SW→Shepherd, 6/9/1784?, Gianangelo Braschi→James Talbot, 4/5/1785.

4	**Missa in duplicibus 6 Toni**	1789

ms BL Add 34007 (dated 20/11/1789)

pr in VN, *Twelve Easy Masses* (London, [1816]).

rmk Plainchant, bc.

5	**Missa pro angelis**	[1811–1812?]

ms Bodl Ms Mus. c.31 (Kyrie only, dated 28/11/1812), BL Add 17731 (lacks Kyrie, dated 21/12/1812), BL Add 35001 (dated 21/12/1812), *BL Add 14342 (VN, lacks Kyrie), BL Add 69852 (VN), RCM 674 (J. W. Windsor), RCM 679* (Kyrie only, incomplete), *RCM 4028* (lacks Kyrie), *RCM 1143* (Kyrie only), *RCM 5251* (VN)

pr Kyrie in VN, *A Collection of Sacred Music* (London, [1811]).

rmk SATB, org. acc. Probably the 'Missa Solennis' described in *MW list* 3 as 'a Grand Mass, every movement of which is founded on a Gregorian phrase which runs throughout the composition'. *See* SW→VN, 5/12/1812, 11/8/1814.

2. ROMAN CATHOLIC MASS MOVEMENTS

6   Agnus dei
ms   RCM 5235 a–e (VN)
rmk   AT, bc

7   Christe eleison   1810
ms   BL Add 14342 (short score dated 10/9/1810)
rmk   SATB

8   Credo in unum Deum   *Doubtful*[1]
ms   BL Add 35024, *BL Add 14341 (VN)*
rmk   SAB

9   Hosanna in excelsis   *Lost*
rmk   *MW list* 10: 'choral motet'

10   Kyrie eleison   [*c*1780][2]
ms   BL Add 31222
rmk   SATB, bc. 'Quattro voci designatum pro Missa de Sancta Cruce.'

11   Requiem æternam dona eis Domine   1800
ms   RCM 4020, RCM 4582, *BL Add 14342* (dated 18/5/1800), *RCM 5251*
rmk   SAB (RCM 4020); SATB (RCM 4582). 'Introitus in Missa Solemnis
                pro defunctis.'

12   Sanctus Dominus Deus sabaoth
ms   RCM 5235a–e (VN)
rmk   SATB

---

[1] EW noted on BL Add 35024 that this ms was 'written out [by SW] at a very early age', but a name at the end of ms suggests that the composer was Pietro Gugliemi [1728–1804].

[2] Date proposed from other works in ms.

3. OTHER LATIN WORKS

~ **Ab ortu solis** *by Byrd → 920*

Ad Offertorium → 37

~ **Alleluia! Cognoverunt discipuli** *by Byrd → 920*

13 **Amavit eum Dominus** [*c*1781][3]
ms BL Add 31222
rmk SA, bc. 'Antifona ad Magnificat in Communi Confessionis non Pontificis.'

14 **Anima nostra erepta est** [1798]
ms BL Add 14340, RCM 4020 (first item in ms entitled 'Harmony 1798'), RCM 4021, *RCM 5235a-e (VN)*, BL Eg. 2571 (Street)
rmk SSATB

15 **Ave maris stella** 1786
ms BL Add 35001 (dated 1786), *BL Add 14342 (VN)*
ed John Marsh (London, 1977); Francis Routh (London, 1984)
rmk SS, str. 'A hymn.'

16a **Ave Regina cælorum [I]** *c*1781
ms BL Add 31222, BL Add 65454
rmk SS, bc. 'Antifona a Purificatione usque ad feria Quinta in Cœna Domini. A due soprani.' On BL Add 14340 (a source for work 16b), SW noted 'composed originally as a duet only, about the year 1781'.

---

[3] Date proposed from other works in ms.

16b   Ave Regina cælorum [II]   [1824]
ms   BL Add 14340 (noted by VN as made in 1824), BL Add 65454, *RCM 5235a-e (VN)*
pr   in VN, *Convent Music*, v 2 (London, [c1840]).
ed   Geoffrey Webber (Oxford, 1997)
rmk   SSATB, bc. An arrangement of 16a. See SW→VN, 13/12/1824, 20/12/1824. ♫

17a   Ave verum corpus [I] [F]   1781
ms   BL Add 31222 (dated 1781)
rmk   SS, bc. 'Ad Sanctissimo Christi Corpore. Ad Missam. A due voci.'

17b   Ave verum corpus [II] [B♭]   1812
ms   BL Add 14340 (dated 6/7/1812), *RCM 5235a-e (VN)*
pr   In VN, *A Collection of Motetts for the Offertory*, book 1 [1818]. Announced as 'recently published' in *English Musical Gazette*, 1/1/1819, p 14.
ed   Roger Wibberley (http://ludwig.gold.ac.uk/Rwibberley/swesley) (1996)
rmk   ATB, org. A substantial revision of 17a. See SW→VN, 7/7/1812.

18   Beati omnes qui timent Dominum   1801
ms   BL Add 71107 (dated 19/8/1801)
rmk   AT, bc.

19   Benedicamus Deo   [<1811]
ms   BL Add 14340 (dated '30 September')
pr   In VN, *A Collection of Sacred Music* (London, 1811).
rmk   SATB.

Carmen funebre → 54

20	**Confitebor tibi, Domine**	1799

ms   BL Add 35002 (dated 14/8/1799), *RAM 106 (EW), RCM 4016, RCM 4121 (SSW)*

ed   John Marsh (London, 1978, *Musica Britannica* v 41); Francis Routh (London, 1984)[4]

rmk   SATB soloists, SSATB, orch. Text from Psalm 111. *MW list* 1. First performance 4/5/1826. *See* SW→Street, 6/10/1799, 18/10/1799; SW→CB, 28/11/1799; SW→VN, 9/10/1821; SW→ SSW, 1/8/1825; SW→VN, 26/8/1825, 12/12/1825; SW→RG, 4/4/1826; SW→George Smart, 13/4/1826; SW→Domenico Dragonetti, 4/5/1826; SW→Emett, 27/2/1835, 3/3/1835.

21	**Constitues eos principes**	1814

ms   BL Add 14340 (dated 9/11/1814)

ed   John Marsh (in SW, *Two Motets*, London, 1974, *Novello Early Church Music* no. 28)

rmk   SSATB. 'Pro Festis SS Apostolorum.'

22	**De profundis clamavi**	[1800–1807?][5]

ms   BL Add 71107, *BL Add 14341*

ed   Partly printed as 'Si iniquitates observaveris' in Peter le Huray *et al*, *Anthems for Men's Voices* (New York, 1965)

rmk   ATB. Text from Psalm 130. ♪

23	**Deus majestatis intonuit**	1799

ms   BL Add 35001 (parts), BL Add 71107 (dated 26/9/1799), DLC Music Div. ML96.W49 Case, *RCM 1040 (VN)*

ed   John I. Schwarz Jr (Sevenoaks, *c*1984)

rmk   SSAATTBB, org, str. 'Antiphona a duplici choro cantanda cum instrumentis.' *See* SW→Street, 9/11/1799.

24	**Deus noster refugium**	1807

ms   BL Add 14341 (dated 7/9/1807), BL Add 71107 (dated 7/9/1807)

rmk   SSB. 'Mottetto.'

---

[4] EW, 'John Wesley' [presumably JWW], SSW and RG advertised in 1838 for subscribers to a publication of a vocal score of *Confitebor*, with a keyboard accompaniment arranged by SSW (*MW* no. 102 = n.s. no. 8, 23/2/1838, p 134), but this proposed edition apparently did not eventuate.

[5] Dating range proposed from other works in BL Add 71107.

~   **Dies sanctificatus illuxit nobis**   *by Byrd → 920*

25   **Dixit Dominus [I] a 4**   1782
ms   Bodl Tenbury 1246 (dated 14/10/1782)
rmk   SATB.

26   **Dixit Dominus [II] a 8**   1800
ms   BL Add 71107 (dated 13/1/1800), RCM 639 (dated 13/1/1800), *BL Add 14341 (VN)*
rmk   SSAATTBB. 'Antiphona duobus choris cantanda.' *See* SW→Street, 3/5/1800?. ♫

27   **Dixit Dominus [III] a 3**   1806
ms   BL Add 14340, BL Add 35001 (parts), BL Add 71107, Euing R.d.66(5) (dated 25/12/1806), *BL Eg. 2571 (Street), RCM 4583b (BJ), RCM 5251 (VN, includes instructions to engraver)*
rmk   ATB. 'Mottetto a tre voci.' First performed 27/12/1806 at Concentores Society.[6] *See* SW→CW Jr, 15/1/1807. Probably *MW list* 6.

28a   **Domine salvam fac reginam nostram Mariam [I]**   [*c*1811]
pr   In VN, *A Collection of Sacred Music* (London, 1811). An arrangement for organ of the 'Sicut erat in principio' section printed in VN, *Select Organ Pieces* [*c*1830], p 132.
rmk   SATB, obbl org. *MW list* 14. ♫

28b   **Domine salvam fac reginam nostram Mariam [II]**
ms   *RCM 5235a–e (VN)*
rmk   A different setting of the same text as 28a.

29   **Domine salvum fac regem nostrum Georgium [I]** [*c*1780][7] [C]
ms   BL Add 31222 f 13[v]
rmk   SAT, bc.

---

[6] This performance is noted on BL Add 14340 and BL Add 71107.

[7] Date proposed from other works in ms.

30   Domine salvum fac regem nostrum Georgium [II] [C] 1780
ms   BL Add 31222 f 16^v
rmk   SA, bc. 'Antifona ad Vesperas.'

~   **Ecce, advenit dominator**   *by Byrd → 920*

31a   Ecce iam noctis [I]   1801
ms   BL Add 71107 (dated 21/8/1801), BL Add 65454, MA (fragment), *BL Eg. 2571 (Street)*
pr   arr. as 'Hymnus matutinus' in VN, *Short Melodies for the Organ* [1848–1858]
rmk   ATB. 'Hymnus matutinus, e Breviaro Romano.'

31b   Ecce iam noctis [II]   1808
ms   BL Add 14340 (dated 1808), *RCM 5251 (VN)*
rmk   SSATB, org. An arrangement of 31a.

32   Ecce Maria genuit nobis   1780
ms   BL Add 31222 (dated 9/11/1780)
rmk   SSA, bc. 'Antifona in festo Circumcisionis Domini nostri.'

33   Ecce panis angelorum   1813
ms   BL Add 14340 (dated 31/3/1813), Bl Add 35001 (alto part only), *RCM 5235a–e (VN), RCM 5238 (VN, includes instructions to engraver)*
pr   In VN, *The Evening Service*, book 9 p 19.
ed   Geoffrey Webber in *Bread of Heaven: Five Communion Anthems for SATB Choir* (Oxford, 1998)
rmk   SATB. 'Sequence for Corpus Christi.' *See* SW→VN, 31/3/1813, 2/4/1813, 20/12/1824, 17/1/1825, 20/1/1825. ♫

34   Ecce, sic benedicetur homo   1801
ms   *BL Add 14341* (dated 19/8/1801)
rmk   ATB.

~   **Ego sum panis**   *by Byrd → 920*

35	**Emitte lucem tuam**	[*c*1781][8]

ms   BL Add 31222

rmk   SS, bc. 'Post Antiphonam. Introito ad Missam.'

36	**Exultate Deo**	1800

ms   BL Add 17731, BL Add 35001 (short score and parts), BL Add 71107 (dated 28/6/1800), *BL Add 14341*

pr   In VN, *Collection of Anthems*, book 12 no. 250.

ed   As 'Sing aloud with gladness' (London, 1951).

rmk   SSATB, org. Text from Psalm 81. *MW list* 5. *See* SW→VN, about 1/7/1824. ♫

37	**Gloria et honore**

ms   DLC Music Div. ML96.W49 Case (entitled 'In Festo Transfigurationis D.N. Jesu Christe. Ad Offertorium.')

pr   In VN, *A Collection of Motetts for the Offertory*, book 2 p 19 [1818].

ed   John I. Schwarz Jr as 'Ad Offertorium for tenor (or soprano) and keyboard continuo' (London, 1988)

rmk   T, org. 'In Festo Transfigurationis D. N. Jesus Christe.'

38	**Gloria Patri [I]** [F]	[*c*1780][9]

ms   BL Add 31222 f 4[v]

rmk   SATB, bc. 'A quattro voci.'

39	**Gloria Patri [II]** [F]	[*c*1780][10]

ms   BL Add 31222 f 20[v] (dated '27 October')

rmk   SA, bc. 'In festo Transfigurationis Domini Nostri Jesu Christe ad Missam.'

40	**Gloria Patri [III]** [B♭]	1780

ms   BL Add 31222 f 18[v] (dated 14/12/1780)

rmk   SA, bc. 'In festo S. Petri ad Vincula ad Vesperas.'

---

[8] Date proposed from other works in ms.

[9] Date proposed from other works in ms.

[10] Date proposed from other works in ms.

41   Gloria Patri [IV] [D minor]   [*c*1800][11]
ms   BL Add 14341, BL Add 71107
rmk   ATB.

42   Hodie beata Virgo Maria   1780
ms   BL Add 31222 (dated 10/11/1780)
rmk   SSA, bc. 'Ad Magnificat in festo Purificationie BM Virginie.'

~   **Hodie Christus natus est**   *by Byrd → 920*

        Hymnus matutinus → 31a

43   In exitu Israel   1810
ms   RCM 4022 (dated 3/5/1810)
ed   Philip Brunelle (Fort Lauderdale, Florida, US, *c*1989)
rmk   SSAATTBB, org. Text from Psalm 114. 'Antiphona duobus choris
        cantandis, organo comitante.' First performance, Hanover Square
        Rooms, 19/5/1810. Performed at Three Choirs Festival, Hereford,
        9/1834, directed by SSW. *MW list* 4. ♫

44   In manus tuas, Domine   [1810–1814?][12]
ms   BL Add 14340, *RCM 5235a–e (VN)*
rmk   SATB. 'Responsorium breve. Ad completorium.'

45   In te, Domine, speravi   1798
ms   BL Add 14340 (dated 28/7/1798), *RCM 5235a–e (VN)*
rmk   S, bc.

~   **Jesu, nostra redemptio**   *by Byrd → 920*

---

[11] Date proposed from other works in BL Add 71107.

[12] Dating range proposed from oter works in BL Add 14340.

46   Justus ut palma florebit
ms   *BL Add 14341 (VN), BL Add 65455 (VN, includes instructions to engraver)*
rmk   SAB, org. 'A motet.'

47   Levate capita vestra   1798
ms   BL Add 14340 (dated 16/2/1798), RCM 4020, *RCM 4028, RCM 5235a–e (VN), RCM 5249 (VN), BL Eg. 2571 (Street)*
pr   In VN, *A Collection of Motetts for the Offertory*, book 12 p 15 [1818].
ed   Roger Wibberley (http://ludwig.gold.ac.uk/Rwibberley/swesley) (1996)
rmk   AATB. 'Antiphona quatuor vocibus cantanda, sine organo.'

48   Magna opera Domini   [*c*1825]
ms   BL Add 35001 f 145 (incomplete, wmk 1825)
rmk   SATB, orch. Text from Psalm 111.

49   Magnificat anima mea [I]   1783
ms   RCM 2141c (dated 27/12/1783)
rmk   SSS, org. 'Canticum beatæ Mariæ virginis.' ♩

50   Magnificat anima mea [II]   1821
ms   Texas Finney 13 (dated 6/10/1821), *BL Add 14341 (VN), BL Add 65455 (VN, includes instructions to engraver)*
rmk   SATB, org. *See* SW→VN, 2/10/1821, 9/10/1821.

51   Miserere mei, Deus   1792
ms   BL Add 14342 (dated 7/4/1792), *BL Eg. 2571 (Street)*
rmk   AB, bc. *See* SW→Street, 21/2/1797.

52   Nocte surgentes   1801
ms   BL Add 71107 (dated 16/9/1801), *BL Add 14341 (VN, dated 10/9/1801)*
rmk   ATB. 'Hymnus e Breviario Romano.'

~   **Notum fecit Dominus**   *by Byrd* → *920*

~   **O admirabile commercium**   *by Byrd* → *920*

~   **O magnum mysterium**   *by Byrd* → *920*

53   **Omnes gentes plaudite**
ms   BL Add 35033, *Add 65455 (VN, includes instructions to engraver)*
rmk   SSA, bc. 'A motet.'

54   **Omnia vanitas (Carmen funebre)**   1824
ms   RCM 4022 (noted by VN as the original manuscript), Texas Finney 13
      (dated 11/6/1824 by SW, noted by VN as a copy in SW's hand), BL
      Add 35033, *Bodl Ms Mus. Sch. D375 a–j, Bodl Tenbury 874*
pr   In SSW, *A Few Words on Cathedral Music* (London, 1849)
ed   Stainton de B. Taylor (London, 1952)
rmk   SSATB. 'Carmen funebre.' *MW list 7. See* SW→VN, 14/6/1824, about
      1/7/1824, 1/8/1824 (1st ltr), 18/10/1824. ♫

~   **O quam suavis est, Domine**   *by Byrd* → *920*

55   **Ostende nobis, Domine**   1827
ms   RCM 2141c (dated 8/9/1827)
rmk   SATB. 'Antiphona quatuor vocibus cantanda.' ♫

56   **Pro peccatis suæ gentis**   1792
ms   BL Add 14340, RCM 4025 (two copies, one noted as composed in
      1792), *RCM 5235a–e*
rmk   ATB. 'Motett for 3 voices.' Text from Stabat Mater.

~   **Quia illic interrogaverunt**   *by Byrd* → *920*

57   **Qui tollis peccata mundi**   1781–1782
ms   BL Add 14232 (dated 'Anno 1781 vel 1782'), RCM 4020, *RCM 4583b*
      (BJ), RCM 5251 (VN)
rmk   SS, bc. 'Pro feria sexta in Parasceve.'

~   **Regis Tharsis et insulæ**   *by Byrd* → *920*

58   Sacerdos et pontifex   [*c*1780][13]
ms   BL Add 31222
rmk   SATB. 'Antifona a Quattro Voci.'

59   Salve Regina, mater misericordiæ [I] [F]   1799
ms   RCM 4020 f 34ᵛ and f 41ᵛ (two copies, both dated 10/9/1799), BL Add
         33240, *RCM 4583b (BJ), RCM 5238 (VN), BL Eg. 2571 (Street)*
pr   In VN, *The Evening Service*, book 7 p 18 [1822]
rmk   ATB. 'Antiphona.'

60   Salve Regina, mater misericordiæ [II] [D minor]
ms   BL Add 35003 f 19 (incomplete, contains score of first movement for
         ST and part of S solo 'Ad te clamamus')
rmk   ST soloists, str.

61   Salve Regina, mater misericordiæ [III] [B♭]
ms   BL Add 35001 f 148 (Canto primo principale and Tenore coro parts
         only), BL Add 35003 f 11 (Alto principale, Basso principale, Canto II
         coro parts only); incomplete—no other surviving sources known

Si inquitates observaveris → 22

62   Sit nomen Domini benedictum   1801
ms   BL Add 14341 (dated 12/6/1801), BL Add 71107 (dated 12/6/1801)
rmk   SAB. 'A motet.'

63   Sperate miseri   1783
ms   BL Add 35025 (dated 9/10/1783)
rmk   SA, org.

64   Stabat mater
ms   *RCM 5235a–e (VN), RCM 5238 (VN, who notes that only the soprano
         and bass parts are by SW)*
rmk   SATB, org. Described by VN as a chant.

---

[13] Date proposed from other works in ms.

~ **Surge, illuminare Jerusalem** *by Byrd* → *920*

65 **Tantum ergo** [*c*1788]
ms RCM 5235a–e (VN, who notes work 'composed about the year 1788')
pr In VN, Twelve Easy Masses [1816].
rmk SATB. Text by St Thomas Aquinas.

66 **Te decet hymnus** 1798
ms RCM 4020 (dated 19/9/1798), *RCM 4028, RCM 4583b (BJ)*
rmk SATB. 'Antiphona quatuor vocibus cantanda sine organo.' *MW list* 9.
Text from Psalm 65. Adapted in 1824 to English words 'Thou O God
art praised in Sion', work 114. *See* SW→Pettet, 8/3/1824.

67 **Tota pulchra es** 1812
ms BL Add 14340 f 33 and 35 (rough and fair copies, dated 24/10/1812),
RCM 5235a–e (VN)
rmk SB, chorus. 'Prosa de BM Virgine.'

68 **Tu es sacerdos [I]** 1814
ms BL Add 14340 (dated 5/1/1814)
ed John Marsh (in SW, *Two Motets*, London, 1974, *Novello Early Church
Music* no. 28)
rmk SATB. ♫

69 **Tu es sacerdos [II]** 1827
ms RCM 2141c (dated 6/7/1827), RCM 4022 (dated 6/7/1827), *Bodl Ms
Mus. Sch. D375 a–j*
pr in SSW, A Few Words on Cathedral Music (London, 1849).
ed J. V. Roberts (London, 1905)
rmk SAATTB. 'Antiphona sex vocibus cantanda.' Probably *MW list* 8. For
probable references to work *see* SW→Crotch, 7/7/1827, SW→Henry
John Gauntlett, 16/6/1836, 30/9/1836. Gauntlett's arrangement of work
as 'He is our God and strong salvation' is at RCM 5253. ♫

~ **Tui sunt cœli** *by Byrd* → *920*

70   Ut queant laxis   [1812?]
ms   RCM 4025, RCM 5235a–e (VN)
rmk   ATB. 'Hymnus in Festo Nativitatis S. Johannis Baptistæ.' Probably the
         work composed for 24/6/1812 mentioned in SW→VN, 22/6/1812.

~   **Viderunt omnes fines terræ**   *by Byrd* → *920*

~   **Vidimus stellam**   *by Byrd* → *920*

4. MUSIC FOR ANGLICAN SERVICES

71   Morning and Evening Service [F]   [1824][14]
ms   *See* 71.1–71.6 for the mss of each movement
pr   *Te Deum, Jubilate, Sanctus, Kyrie Eleeson, Magnificat and Nunc
         Dimittis. A Morning and Evening Church Service for four Voices, with
         an accompaniment for the organ or piano forte.* (London, James Balls,
         for the author [SW], [1824].) RISM W919a. Reviewed *The
         Harmonicon* v 3 (1/1825) p 10; QMMR v 7 no. 25 (1825) p 95.
rmk   SATB, org or pf. First complete performance St Paul's Cathedral,
         3/4/1824, *see* SW→VN, 25/3/1824, SW→RG, 1/4/1824., SW→Pettet,
         6/4/1824. Published 11/1824, *see* SW→CW Jr, 6/11/1824; SW→VN,
         12/11/1824.

71.1   Te Deum [F]   [1808]
ms   RCM 4025 (partly autograph, includes instructions to engraver), *BL
         Add 14342* (dated 1808)
pr   *See* 71.
rmk   SATB, org. First performance St Paul's Cathedral, 30/10/1808, *see*
         SW→CW Jr, 28/10/1808. Performed there again on 25/12/1808, *see*
         SW→CW Jr, about 20/12/1808.

---

[14] This composition was first performed in its entirety and was first published in
1824. The individual movements were composed earlier; see the entries below
for 71.1–71.6.

71.2   **Jubilate** [F]   [1808]
ms   The same ms as 71.1.
pr   See 71.
rmk   SATB, org. Performed with 71.1 on 30/10/1808 and 25/12/1808. ♩

71.3   **Sanctus** [F]   [1822?][15]
ms   BL Add 34999 (wmk 1821) f 122ᵛ, *RCM 4025*
pr   See 71.
rmk   SATB, org.

71.4   **Kyrie eleeson** [F]   [1822?][16]
ms   BL Add 34999 (wmk 1821) f 122, BL Add 35007 f 88
pr   See 71.
rmk   SATB, org. Text is the responses to the Ten Commandments in the
        Anglican Communion Service.

71.5   **Magnificat** [F]   1822
ms   BL Add 14341 (dated 8/11/1822), RCM 4025 f 15 and f 25 (two copies,
        one dated 8/11/1822; the other with instructions to engraver)
pr   See 71.
rmk   SATB, org. First performance St Paul's Cathedral 25/12/1823, *see*
        SW→VN, 19/12/1823.

71.6   **Nunc Dimittis** [F]   [*c*1823]
ms   RCM 4025 (with instructions to engraver)
pr   See 71.
rmk   SATB, org. First performance 25/12/1823 with 71.5, *see* SW→VN,
        19/12/1823. ♩

---

[15] 1822 proposed on the presumption that work composed about the same time
as 71.5 and 71.6.

[16] 1822 proposed on the presumption that work composed about the same time
as 71.5 and 71.6.

72   Evening Service [G]
ed   C. Vincent and C. W. Pearce (London, 1897)[17]
rmk   SATB, org.

73   Doxology [A minor]
ms   BL Add 34999 f 119 (dated 'May 2')
rmk   SATB.

74   Jubilate Deo [D]
ms   BL Add 34999 f 108 (incomplete)
rmk   SATB, 2 vlns.

75   Nunc dimittis [G]
ms   BL Add 34999 f 124 (sketch)

76   Responses to the Litany [A]   1806
ms   BL Add 34999 f 117 (alto principale part, dated 20/11/1806, and
              annotated by SW 'Revd Mr Webb'[18]), *BL Add 14341, RCM 4583b (BJ)*
rmk   SB and SATB. First performance at St Paul's Cathedral initially
              planned for 25/12/1806 but postponed to Easter Sunday 29/3/1807. *See*
              SW→SGW, 12/1806, SW→CW Jr, 15/1/1807, 21/3/1807. Performed
              again at St Paul's Cathedral on 17/4/1808. *See* Latrobe→Joseph Foster
              Barham, 18/4/1808.

5. ANGLICAN ANTHEMS

**A Funeral Anthem on the Death of the late
Charles Wesley Esq.** → 77

---

[17] Stated to be published, for the first time, 'by permission of [SW's son]
R[obert] Glenn Wesley...from mss in the possession of Dr Vincent and Dr
Pearce'. The present location of these mss is not known.

[18] Presumably a reference to the Rev. Richard Webb [c1770–1829, minor canon
of St Paul's Cathedral].

77	**All go unto one place**	[1834][19]

ms   BL Add 34999 (alto part only)

pr   *A Funeral Anthem on the Death of the late Charles Wesley Esq.* (London, J. A. Novello, [1834][20]). Reviewed *MW* v 6 no. 72 (28/7/1837) p 109.[21]

rmk   SATB, org. acc. *MW list* 11. First performance, Sacred Harmonic Society, 7/8/1834. Dedicated to Jackson.

78	**All the earth doth worship thee**	1801

ms   BL Add 71107 (dated 8/8/1801), *BL Add 14341 (VN)*

ed   Roger Wibberley (http://ludwig.gold.ac.uk/Rwibberley/swesley) (1996)

rmk   SATB. 'An anthem.'

79	**Behold, how good and joyful [I] [G]**	[1774–1775]

ms   BL Add 34998 (SW's 'pasticcio book, 1774–1775') f 3

rmk   SSB, org, with indications for fl, vns, va, vc. 'An anthem.' Text from Psalm 133.

80	**Behold, how good and joyful [II] [B♭]**	1813

ms   BL Add 33240 (dated 12/5/1813), *BL Add 14341 (VN)*

pr   In VN, Services and Anthems for Men's Voices, no. 103.

rmk   ATB. 'An anthem composed for the installation of the RWGM' [i.e., the 12/5/1813 installation of Augustus Frederick, Duke of Sussex, as Right Worshipful Grand Master of the Freemasons]. ♫

81	**Behold, how good and joyful [III]**	*Lost*

rmk   *MW list* 13, where said to be 'with organ obligato accompaniment', thus presumably not works 79 or 80. Possibly the same as 82.

82	**Behold, how good a thing it is**	[1813]; *Lost*

rmk   For male voices, written to celebrate the 12/1813 union of the Masonic two Grand Lodges of England. *See* SW→VN, 23/12/1813, 26/12/1813? and *EM* v 65 (1814) p 6–12, 49–52.

---

[19] >CW Jr's 23/5/1834 death; <7/8/1834 first performance.

[20] A printed announcement (copy at WCL) of the first performance states that the anthem 'will be published in a few days by J. A. Novello, 67 Frith-street, Soho, and may be had of J. Mason, 14, City-road, and 66, Paternoster-row'.

[21] The reviewer notes that this review has been delayed.

83   **Behold, I was shapen in wickedness**   [1774–1775]
ms   BL Add 34998 (SW's 'pasticcio book, 1774–1775') f 17
rmk   S, bc.

84   **Be pleased, O Lord, to deliver me**   [*c*1802]
ms   BL Add 34999 (wmk 1802)
rmk   SAB. 'An anthem.'

85   **Go not far from me, O God**
ms   BL Add 31239, RCM 4025 (two copies)
rmk   SS, bc. 'A short verse anthem.'

86   **Hear, O thou shepherd of Israel**   [*c*1775]²²
ms   BL Add 34999
ed   Ralph Greaves (London, *c*1925)
rmk   SA solo, chorus, org.

He is our God and strong salvation → 69

87   **Hide thy face from my sins**   [1774–1775]
ms   BL Add 34998 (SW's 'pasticcio book, 1774–1775') f 18
rmk   S, bc. 'A slow anthem.'

88   **How are thy servants blest, O Lord**
ms   BL Add 34007 f 38
rmk   S solo, SAB, vn, bc. Accompanied recitative and three-part chorus.
            Text by Joseph Addison.

I am well pleased → 90

89   **In the multitude of the sorrows**   [1801]
ms   BL Add 71107, *BL Add 14341 (VN, work said to be composed on
            12/6/1801)*
rmk   ATB. 'A verse for three voices.'

---

²² Ms is in SW's very early handwriting. The names of the original soloists,
Miss Jack and Mr Sand, are given.

90   **I said, I will take heed**   [1776, revised 1797]
pr   in John Page, *Harmonia Sacra* (London, [1800]), noted as 'composed in the year 1776, revised and enlarged by the author, 1797'.
rmk   Alto solo, SATB chorus, bc. 'Solo anthem.' *MW list* 12, where the title is mistakenly given as 'I am well pleased'.

91   **I will arise and go to my Father**   [c1837][23]
ms   BL Add 35006
rmk   S, acc. 'An anthem.'

92   **Lord of the earth and heavens sublime**   [c1834][24]
ms   BL Add 35039 f 51^v and f 53 (two copies)
rmk   S, S chorus, bc. 'An anthem.'

93   **Mansions of Heav'n, your doors expand**   1835
ms   BL Add 35039 f 61 (dated 28/2/1835)
rmk   S solo, SA, org. 'A chorus.'

94   **My delight shall be in thy statutes**   1816
ms   BL Add 34999 f 103 (dated 11/4/1816)
rmk   S, bc in compressed score. 'An anthem.'

95   **Now the strife of death is over**   [1837?][25]
ms   RCM 4028
rmk   S, S chorus

96   **O deliver me**
ms   RCM 4025
pr   in SSW, *The European Psalmist* (London, 1872) p 529.
rmk   SAB, org.

---

[23] Date proposed from other works in ms.

[24] Date proposed from other works in ms.

[25] Date proposed from SW's very late handwriting.

97   O give thanks unto the Lord [I] [E]   [*c*1835][26]
ms   BL Add 35039 f 66
rmk   SS, org.

98   O give thanks unto the Lord [II] [D]   1837
ms   RCM 4025 (dated 14/7/1837)
rmk   SATB, org acc. 'A coronation anthem.'[27]

99   O Jesus our King   1777
ms   BL Add 34999 (noted 'composed in 1777')
rmk   S, bc. 'Song.'

100   O Lord God most holy   *c*1800
ms   MB **M.408.2, item 6 (SW states work written about 1800), BL Add
         71107, *BL Add 14341 (VN), Bodl Tenbury 621 (CW Jr?), RCM 5237
         (Stokes)*
rmk   SATB. 'From the burial service.' Note on MB manuscript by 'J. S.'
         (Street?) states that work was performed at a Gray's Inn 'musical party'
         on 17/6/1819 and again on 22/1/1820. ♪

101   O Lord God of hosts   [<1781]; *Lost*
rmk   *Barrington* p 307 describes work as an anthem in three sections, the
         first 'for a single tenor', the second 'a duet for two boys', and the third
         'a chorus'. *Barrington* adds that this work was performed at the Chapel
         Royal and at St Paul's Cathedral, and that the tenor singer 'frequently'
         was the Rev. [Samuel] Mence [Chapel Royal gentleman, *d*1786].

102   O praise the Lord, all ye heathen   [1774–1775]
ms   BL Add 34998 (SW's 'pasticcio book, 1774–1775') f 62[v]
rmk   S, bc. 'A solo anthem.'

103   O praise the Lord of Heaven   [1774–1775]
ms   BL Add 34998 (SW's 'pasticcio book, 1774–1775') f 62[v]
rmk   Solos and chorus. 'An anthem.'

---

[26] Date proposed from other works in ms.

[27] Victoria acceded to the throne on 20/6/1837. Her coronation, on 28/6/1838,
was after SW's death.

104 O praise the Lord, ye that fear him
ms   Fitzwm 624
rmk   SATB, org. 'An anthem.'

105 O remember not our old sins   1821
ms   BL Add 35008, RCM 4025 (two copies, one dated 16/8/1821)
pr   in SSW, *The European Psalmist* (London, 1872) p 533
rmk   SAB.

~   **O sing unto the Lord**   *by William Boyce*[28]

106 O ye that love the Lord   [1774–1775]
ms   BL Add 34998 (SW's 'pasticcio book, 1774–1775') f 19^v
rmk   S, bc. 'A solo anthem.'

107 Praise the Lord, O ye servants   [1774–1775]
ms   BL Add 34998 (SW's 'pasticcio book, 1774–1775') f 18^v
rmk   S, bc. 'A solo anthem.' Text from Psalm 113.

108 Praise the Lord, ye servants [B♭]
ms   BL Add 57919
rmk   T solo, SATB chorus, org. 'An anthem.' Text from Psalm 113.

109 Praise ye the Lord, ye immortal quires   1775
ms   BL Add 34998 f 71 (dated 27/2/1775)
rmk   S, bc. 'A solo anthem.'

Sing aloud with gladness → 36

110 Sing praises to the Lord
ms   BL Add 57918
rmk   ATB solo, SATB chorus, org. 'Anthem for three voices.'

---

[28] Misattributed in Fitzwm catalogue.

111   The Lord is my shepherd [I] [F]   1774
ms   BL Add 34998 f 62 (dated 'June 1774')
rmk   S, bc. 'A solo anthem.' Text from Psalm 23.

112   The Lord is my shepherd [II] [B♭]   1834
ms   BL Add 35039 f 55 and f 58 (two copies, one dated 6/12/1834)
rmk   SA, chorus. 'An anthem.' Text from Psalm 23.

113   This shall be my rest forever   1800
ms   RCM 4020 (dated 4/7/1800), BL Add 33240, *RCM 5251*
rmk   ATB. 'An anthem.' Text from Psalm 132.

Thou art a priest for ever → 69

114   Thou, O God, art praised in Sion   [1824]
ms   RCM 4028
pr   in Pettet's *Original Sacred Music* (London, [1825]).
rmk   SATB. 'An anthem.' Text from Psalm 65. SW's adaptation, for Pettet's
        publication, of work 66 ('Te decet hymnus') to English text. *See* SW→
        Pettet, 8/3/1824, 18/3/1824, 6/4/1824.

115   Thou shalt make me hear of joy and gladness   [1774–1775]
ms   BL Add 34998 (SW's 'pasticcio book, 1774–1775') f 17ᵛ
rmk   SSB. 'An anthem.'

116   Who can tell how oft he offendeth?   1823
ms   BL Add 34999 (dated 4/7/1823)
rmk   S, bc. 'An anthem.' Text from Psalm 19.

6. ANGLICAN HYMNS IN COLLECTIONS

117 Original Hymn Tunes [1828]

ms   RCM 4027 (except where otherwise noted)

pr   *Original Hymn Tunes, Adapted to Every Metre in the Collection by the Rev. John Wesley, A.M....newly composed and arranged for four voices, with a separate accompaniment for the organ or piano forte.* Preface dated 10/7/1828. Published for SW.

cont A fountain of life and grace; All thanks be to God; Behold the saviour of mankind; Come and let us sweetly join; Come Holy Ghost all quick'ning fire; Come let us anew our journey pursue; Come Lord from above, the mountains remove; Come on my partners in distress; Come O thou traveller unknown; Come thou all-inspiring spirit; Come thou everlasting spirit; Come ye that love the Lord [RIDGE];[29] Father in whom we live; Father of all whose powerful voice; Glorious saviour of my Soul; Glory be to God on high; God of all grace and majesty; Hail! Father, Son and Holy Ghost; Happy the souls that first believed; Happy the souls to Jesus joined (also *BL Add 34999 f 127*); Jesu my saviour, brother, friend; Jesus thy blood and righteousness; Lamb of God who bear'st away; Lo! He comes with clouds descending; Love divine, all loves excelling; Maker saviour of mankind; Messiah full of grace; My God the spring of all my joys (also BL Add 34999 f 128); O God! thou bottomless abyss; O heavenly King look down from above; O Jesus my hope, for me offer'd up [NAZARETH]; Our friendship sanctify and guide; Stand th'omnipotent decree; Thee O my God and King; Worship and thanks and blessings; Ye servants of God your master proclaim (not in RCM 4027); Ye simple souls that stray (in RCM 2227, not in RCM 4027); Young men and maidens, raise

rmk   SATB, org or pf. Published before SW→William Upcott, 20/8/1828. *See* SW→Jackson, 17/5/1828, 2/9/1828, 10/10/1828.

---

[29] This hymn tune subsequently became known as RIDGE (hymn 410 in the *Methodist Hymn Book*, London, 1933), *see* Lightwood, James T., *The Music of the Methodist Hymn-Book* (London, 1935) p 272–274.

118   **Hymns in VN's collection *The Psalmist***   1834–1837[30]
pr   VN, *The Psalmist. A Collection of Psalms and Hymn Tunes suited to all the Varieties of Metrical Harmony*. (London, 4 vols., 1835–1842)
cont   Hymns composed by SW:
AMERSHAM, ARNSBY, AZOTUS, BATH, BETHLEHEM,[31] BLANDFORD, BRIDGEWATER, BRISTOL ('He's blest whose sins have pardon gain'd': *see* 131), CESAREA, CHERTSEY, CHICHESTER, CHRISTCHURCH, CLIFTON, COLCHESTER, DAMASCUS, DERBY, DUNSTABLE, DORKING, EPWORTH, FALMOUTH, GALATIA, GALILEE, GIBEON, HARLOW, HERTFORD ('O Lord my rock, to Thee I cry': *see* 143), HIERAPOLIS, JOPPA, LAVENDON, LINCOLN COLLEGE, LYCAONIA, KINGSLAND, LLANBERRIS, NORWICH, PHILLIPI, RAMAH, READING, RICHMOND, ROMSEY, SALAMIS, SALISBURY, SHELFORD, SMYRNA, SNOWDON, SYRIA, TARSUS, THESSALONICA, THYATIRA, TIVERTON, TROAS, WALTHAM ABBEY, WALWORTH, WATFORD, WEYMOUTH, WOODFORD

Arrangements by SW of Gregorian melodies
or of hymns by other composers:
ARIMATHEA, BEDFORD, BERKSHIRE, BETHANY, CAERNAVON, CYRENE, CANTERBURY, CHESTERTON, EVERSLEY, GILEAD, HEBRON, KEDRON, KETTERING, LEICESTER, LOUGHTON, LYSTRA, MADELEY, NORTHAMPTON, PHILADELPHIA, PORTSEA, PRAGUE, ST DIONIS, ST DAVID'S, ST MARY, WESTMINSTER NEW, YORK
rmk   SATB.

7. INDIVIDUAL ANGLICAN HYMNS

119   **And now another day is gone**   [1774–1775]
ms   BL Add 34998 (SW's 'pasticcio book, 1774–1775') f 44
rmk   S, bc. 'A hymn.' Text by Isaac Watts.

---

[30] Many original SW hymns in this collection are dated 1834, 1835, 1836 or 1837. GILEAD and KEDRON, published in VN's collection after SW's death, were taken from work 913 arrangement II., published in 1827.

[31] This hymn was published in John Bernard Sale, *Psalms and Hymns for the Service of the Church* (London, 1837), and subsequently became known by the alternative name 'DONCASTER' (hymns 685 and 807(i) in the *Methodist Hymn Book*, London, 1933). *See* Lightwood, James T., *The Music of the Methodist Hymn-Book, op. cit.*, p 394, 435.

120	**ASCENSION**	[<1823]
pr	in J. S. Holmyard, *The Psalms, Hymns and Miscellaneous Pieces, as sung at the Episcopal Chapel of the London Society for Promoting Christianity amongst the Jews.* (London, [<1823])	
rmk	SATB.	

121	**Awake my glory, harp and lute**	1827
ms	RCM 2141b (dated 25/10/1827)	
rmk	S, bc. 'A hymn. Composed for Mrs Stirling of Brighton.' Text from Psalm 78.	

~	**BERKSHIRE** *by CW Jr, arranged by SW → 118*[32]	

122	**CHELMSFORD**	
pr	in Matthew Cooke, *Select Portions of the Psalms of David.* (London, c1795)	
rmk	SATB.	

123	**Come, Lord, from above**	[1774–1775]
ms	BL Add 34998 (SW's 'pasticcio book, 1774–1775') f 5^v	
rmk	SS, bc. 'A hymn.'	

124	**Eternal father of mankind**	1799
ms	RCM 4020 (dated 17/8/1799), *RCM 4583b (BJ)*	
rmk	SS, bc. 'A hymn composed for the Cheshunt [Hertfordshire] Charity children.'	

125	**Far above their noblest songs**	c1792
ms	BL Add 14340 f 38 (noted as composed 'about the year 1792'), *RCM 5251 (VN)*	
rmk	SATB. 'A hymn.' Text by CW.	

---

[32] Incorrectly attributed to SW in the *Methodist Hymn-Book* (London, 1933). *See* Lightwood, James T., *The Music of the Methodist Hymn-Book, op. cit.*, p 46.

126   Father, I know my day is nigh
ms   BL Add 34999 f 124^v
rmk   S, bc. 'Hymn.' Text from Deuteronomy xxxi 14: 'Behold thy days approach when thou must die.'

Father of light and life → 214

127   Father of me and all mankind   [*c*1825][33]
ms   RCM 4025
rmk   S, bc. 'Hymn 251.'

128   Gentle Jesus, meek and mild   [1808]
ms   *BL Add 14341 (VN, who noted 'Composed May 8 1808 (an exquisite gem by Master Sammy)')*
ed   Robin Langley in SW, *Two Sacred Songs* (Oxford, 1997)
rmk   S, pf. Text by CW.

129   God of almighty love   [1774–1775]
ms   BL Add 34998 (SW's 'pasticcio book, 1774–1775') f 79
rmk   S, bc. 'A hymn.'

130   Hark! in the wilderness a cry   [1774–1775]
ms   BL Add 34998 (SW's 'pasticcio book, 1774–1775') f 9
rmk   SSB. 'A hymn.' Text by Walter Shirley.

---

[33] Date proposed from other similar works in ms.

131   **He's blest whose sins have pardon gain'd [BRISTOL]**[34] 1806
ms   BL Add 14341 (dated 15/8/1806), BL Add 71107 (dated 15/8/1806),
        BL Add 59873, BL Eg. 2512 f 6 (Matthew Cooke), RCM 4583b (BJ),
        RCM 5251.
pr   in Matthew Cooke, *A Collection of Psalm and Hymn Tunes for the Use*
        of the Lock Hospital (London, [1808]); in BJ, *National Psalmody*
        (London, [1817]);[35] in Thomas Cahusac, *A Collection of Psalms,*
        Hymns, Chants and other Pieces, as sung at the Bentinck Chapel,
        Paddington (London, [c1820]); in J. S. Holmyard, *The Psalms, Hymns*
        and Miscellaneous Pieces, as sung at the Episcopal Chapel of the
        London Society for Promoting Christianity amongst the Jews (London,
        [<1823]); VN, *The Psalmist*, work 118.
rmk   S, bc. Text from Psalm 32. *See* SW→BJ, 15/2/1816.

HOOKER → 162

132   **I have longed for thy salvation**
ms   RCM 4028 f 49
rmk   1v, bc.

133   **In dreary waste where horror dwells**   [1774–1775]
ms   BL Add 34998 (SW's 'pasticcio book, 1774–1775') f 8
rmk   SSB. 'A hymn.'

Invocation to the Deity → 214

134   **Jesus, at thy command**   [1837]
ms   BL Add 34999 f 175 (noted by EW to have been composed a few days
        before SW's death)

---

[34] BRISTOL is alternatively named WESLEY in some later hymn books.

[35] BJ listed this work in his 'table of the new compositions' published in
National Psalmody, apparently unaware that it had been previously published
elsewhere.

135 Let all that breathe Jehovah praise [*c*1828][36]
ms RCM 4027
rmk SB.

136 Let earth and hell their powers employ
ms BL Add Ms 35040
rmk S, bc.

137 Lord, if with thee part I bear [1774–1775]
ms BL Add 34998 (SW's 'pasticcio book, 1774–1775') f 6
rmk SSB. 'A hymn.'

138 Meet and right it is to praise God [*c*1828][37]
ms RCM 4027
rmk S, bc.

139 Might I in thy sight appear 1807
ms BL Add 14340 (dated 1807), BL Add 71107, *RCM 640 (VN), RCM 4038 (Marianne Merewether*[38]*), RCM 5251 (VN)*
pr arranged as 'The sinner's only plea' in VN, *Short Melodies for the Organ* [1848–1858]; ed. by SSW in *The European Psalmist* (London, 1872)
ed Geoffrey Bush and Nicholas Temperley, *Musica Britannica* v 43 p 16; Geoffrey Webber, *Samuel Wesley, Two Sacred Songs* (Oxford, 1997)
rmk S, bc. Text by CW. *See* SW→BJ, 17/11/1808?, 21/11/1808?; SW→ William Hone, 18/8/1825. ♫

140 Music as first by heaven designed [1774–1775]
ms BL Add 34998 (SW's 'pasticcio book, 1774–1775') f 37
rmk S, bc, with indications for tutti and solo. 'A hymn.'

---

[36] Date proposed from other works in ms.

[37] Date proposed from other works in ms.

[38] Marianne Merewether (1808–1888) married SSW in Hereford on 4/5/1835. She compiled RCM 4038 before her marriage.

141 **No more to earth's low scenes confined** [1830–1836][39]
ms BL Add 34999 f 132
rmk SATB.

142 **O for a shout of sacred joy** [1830–1836][40]
ms BL Add 34999 f 129
rmk SATB. Text from Psalm 47.

143 **O Lord my rock, to Thee I cry [HERTFORD]** 1806
ms BL Add 14341 (dated 15/8/1806), BL Add 71107 (dated 15/8/1806),
BL Eg. 2512 f 5ᵛ (Matthew Cooke), RCM 4583b (BJ)
pr In VN, *The Psalmist*, no. 118.
rmk S, bc. Text from Psalm 28.

144 **O Lord our Lord**
ms BL Add 34999 f 129ᵛ
rmk SATB. Text from Psalm 8.

145 **Once more my soul the rising day**
ms *BL Add 34999 f 182 (SSW, noted as transcribed by him when a boy)*
rmk S, pf. 'Morning song.' Text by Isaac Watts.

146 **O Thou to whom our lips are taught**
ms BL Add 34999 f 130
rmk SATB (ms is a compressed score).

147 **O 'tis like ointment on the head**
ms RCM 4028
rmk AT, org.

148 **Praise God from whom all blessings flow** [1774–1775]
ms BL Add 34998 (SW's 'pasticcio book, 1774–1775') f 45ᵛ
rmk S, bc. Text by Thomas Ken.

---

[39] Dating range proposed on the basis of watermarks in BL Add 34999.

[40] Dating range proposed on the basis of watermarks in BL Add 34999.

149   Praise the Father for His love   [1774–1775]
ms   BL Add 34998 (SW's 'pasticcio book, 1774–1775') f 55
rmk   S, bc.

PROTECTING LOVE → 164

RIDGE → 117

150   Shepherd of souls, with pitying eye   [1774–1775]
ms   BL Add 34998 (SW's 'pasticcio book, 1774–1775') f 5
rmk   S, bc. 'A hymn.' Text by JW or CW.

151   Shout, sons of heaven, your voices raise
ms   BL Add 35038
rmk   S, bc.

152   Supremely good, supremely great   [1807]
ms   *BL Add 14341 (dated 23/3/1807)*
rmk   S, bc.

153   Sweet were the sounds of heavenly love   [*c*1835][41]
ms   BL Add 35039 f 67
rmk   S, bc.

154   The Lord of glory   [1830–1836][42]
ms   BL Add 34999 f 129^v
rmk   SATB. Text from Psalm 27.

155   The sacred minstrel plays and sings   [1774–1775]
ms   BL Add 34998 (SW's 'pasticcio book, 1774–1775') f 38
rmk   S, bc, with indications for tutti and solo

---

[41] Date proposed from other works in ms.

[42] Dating range proposed in BL catalogue.

| 156 | **Thou Jesu art our King** | 1798 |

ms BL Add 14340 (dated 11/4/1798), BL Add 65454, RCM 4020, *RCM 4583b (BJ), RCM 5251*

rmk SATB. 'A hymn.' Text by JW, after Johann Scheffler.

| 157 | **Thus saith the Lord of earth and heaven** | [*c*1825][43] |

ms RCM 4025

rmk S, bc. 'Hymn 90.' Text by JW or CW.

| 158 | **Thy royal seat, O Lord** | |

ms *BL Add 35008, RCM 4025 f 114^v*

rmk SATB.

| 159 | **To all the listening tribes** | [1830–1836][44] |

ms BL Add 34999 f 129

rmk SATB. Text from Psalm 108.

| 160 | **To God the Father, God the Son** | 1774 |

ms BL Add 34998 (dated 29/10/1774)

rmk 3 voices. 'A hymn.'

| 161 | **To Thee great Author of all good** | [1774–1775] |

ms BL Add 34998 (SW's 'pasticcio book, 1774–1775')

rmk SS, bc.

| 162 | **We sing the wise, the gracious plan [HOOKER]** | [*c*1826][45] |

pr In Joseph Major, *A Collection of Sacred Music for Churches & Chapels* (London, [*c*1826]). Reviewed *The Harmonicon* v 4 no. 48 (1826) p 244.

rmk SATB. 'A hymn.'

WESLEY → 131

---

[43] Date proposed from other works in ms.

[44] Dating range proposed in BL catalogue.

[45] According to the title-page of Major's *Collection of Sacred Music*, SW wrote this hymn 'expressly for' this publication.

163 **What hymns, O Lord, of grateful joy** [*c*1835][46]
ms   BL Add 35039 f 64ᵛ
rmk S, bc. 'A Christmas hymn.'

164 **What tho' my frail eye lids refuse [PROTECTING** 1807
LOVE]
ms   RCM 4021 (dated 12/10/1807)
rmk S, bc.

165 **When shall the poor, the child of grief, a place** 1807
of refuge find?
ms   BL Add 14341 (dated 23/3/1807)
rmk S, bc.

166 **Who is the trembling sinner** 1821
ms   RCM 2141b (dated 14/12/1821), RCM 4022 (dated 14/12/1821)
pr   in SSW, *The European Psalmist* (London, 1872) p 536.
rmk S, bc (with accompaniment in RCM 4022). 'A hymn.' Text by CW.

167 **Hymn tune [A]**
rmk SATB, bc. Ms of 18 bars, with VN's annotation, sold at Sotheby's
       21/5/1998 lot 408, to the music antiquarian dealers J. & J. Lubrano.
       Now in a private collection.

168 **Hymn tunes**
ms   Other untitled hymn tunes at BL Add 34999 f 163–175 and in RCM
       2141b, 2227, 4020, 4025, 4027 and 4028.

Hymn tunes with interludes → 633

---

[46] Date proposed from other works in ms.

8. ANGLICAN CHANTS

169   A Chant for the Litany
ms   *RCM 5238 (VN, who states that ms is copied from SW's autograph, includes instructions to engraver)*

170   Chants for the Somers Town Church   [c1827]
ms   RCM 2141b
rmk   S, bc. Chants for Jubilate, Gloria and Psalms. SW opened the organ at this newly built church on 24/6/1827, *see* SW→RG, 15/6/1827.

171   Glory be to the Father [I–III]   [1774–1775]
ms   BL Add 34998 (SW's 'pasticcio book, 1774–1775') f 16
rmk   Three double chant settings: SATB, SB, SATB.

172   Glory be to the Father [IV]
ms   RCM 4021
rmk   SATB. 'From a Jubilate.'

173   Lord have mercy upon us   1827
ms   RCM 2141b f 26^v (dated 22/6/1827)
rmk   S, bc.

174   Nunc Dimittis   [c1837][47]
ms   BL Add 35006
rmk   SATB.

---

[47] Date proposed from other works in ms.

175   Te Deum
pr   In BJ, *National Psalmody* (London, [1817]).
rmk   Double chant. S, T, SATB, org. *See* SW→BJ, 15/2/1816.[48]

176   Venite, exultemus   [1807]
ms   RCM 4021
rmk   SATB. SW→CW Jr, 21/3/1807, quotes the soprano and bass parts and
         states that work was composed for a performance at St Paul's Cathedral
         on Easter Sunday, 29/3/1807.

177   Chants
ms   BL Add 14342 f 62^v, Add 31239 f 4^v–10, 11^v, 12^v, Add 34996 f 16–19,
         Add 34998 f 39^v, 60, Add 34999 f 176^v–178, Add 35006 f 16, 47, Add
         35040 f 26; RCM 2141b, 4020, 4021, *5238*, *5249*, 5251
rmk   Miscellaneous single and double chants, mostly untitled.

---

[48] BJ stated in *National Psalmody* that this was a 'new composition', suggesting
that SW had written the work shortly before enclosing it in SW→BJ, 15/2/1816.
However, as BJ also published SW's hymn BRISTOL (work 138) as a new
composition in *National Psalmody*, apparently unaware that it was written in
1806 and previously published, his claim regarding the newness of Te Deum
cannot be used to date this work without corroboration.

SECULAR VOCAL MUSIC

1. ORATORIOS

201   **The Death of Abel**   [1777–1779?]

ms   BL Add 34999 (incomplete, includes score of Act 2 and part of Act 3, and parts for the Overture to Act 2; the Overture is dated 1779; annotated by EW as composed when SW was 11 years old)

202   **Ruth**   [1772–1774][1]

ms   BL Add 34997 (has various dates between 8/9/1774 and 26/10/1774), BL Add 34998 f 21 (part of scene beginning 'Naomi, dry those tears'), BL Add 34998 f 46 (airs)

rmk   Text by Thomas Haweis (*see* SW→CB, 4/9/1809). *See* William Boyce →SW, 28/10/1774?

203   **Oratorio fragments and sketches**   [1774–1775]

ms   BL Add 34998, SW's 'pasticcio book, 1774–1775', includes, besides portions of *Ruth* (work 75), 'With pleasure I obey' (f 29) and 'Like a bright cherub' (f 41), both apparently from SW's otherwise lost oratorio *Gideon*

2. DRAMATIC WORKS

204   **Clara**   *c*1799

ms   BL Add 35005 f 39, 72 (fragments of songs only, dated 1799), BL Add 35003 f 42 (fragments of songs only)

---

[1] According to CW (*Barrington* p 293), 'the airs of *Ruth*…[SW] made before he was six years old, laid them up in his memory till he was eight, and then wrote them down'.

205   **The Misanthrope**   *Lost; Doubtful*
rmk   Listed as a manuscript opera in the biographies of SW in Brown, James
D., *Biographical Dictionary of Musicians* (London, 1886, p 612) and
also in Brown, James D. and Stephen S. Stratton, *British Musical
Biography* (London, 1897, p 440). No reference to this work has been
found in documents written during SW's lifetime.

3. CHORUSES, GLEES AND PART-SONGS
(WITH AND WITHOUT ACCOMPANIMENT)

206   **Adieu ye soft scenes of delight**   1781
ms   BL Add 31222 (dated 1781), Cary 449 (dated 1781), *BL Add 35028
(EW), MB Catch Club mss xx 20*
rmk   SSB. 'A serious glee.'

A new glee, for three voices → 248

~   **Arise, awake ye silly shepherds**   *by Thomas Morley*

207   **Begin the noble song (Ode to St Cecilia)**   1794
ms   BL Add 14339 (score, dated 21/10/1794), BL Add 35003 (fragments),
BL Add 35005 f 1 (parts), BL Add 35008 (score of the Allegro from the
overture), RCM 4017 (score, dated 14/7/1837, written out by SW from
memory), *BL Add 35008 ('cello part of the Allegro and March from the
overture), BL Add 35004*
ed   Francis Routh (London, 2000)
rmk   Text by Samuel Wesley Sr [clergyman and poet, 1662–1735, from 1695
rector of Epworth, CW's father]. First performance Covent Garden
22/2/1799. *MW list* 2, as 'An Ode to St Cecilia's Day'. March from the
overture arranged as last movement of work 623 and as *Grand
Coronation March* (work 737).

208 Beneath, a sleeping infant lies [1797]²

ms RCM 4020, *RCM 5237 (Stokes), BL Add 14343 (VN)*

rmk SAB. 'Epitaph on Susanna Wesley. Aged 3 years.'³ Text by Samuel Wesley Jr [schoolmaster and poet, 1691–1739, brother of CW and JW].

209 Beneath these shrubs 1800

ms RCM 4020 (dated 7/6/1800), *RCM 4583b (BJ)*

rmk ATB. 'Epitaph on a favourite dog.'

210 Beneath yon grassy hillock 1818

ms BL Add 35038 (dated 1818)

rmk ATB.

211 Blushete me Carolos 1798

ms RCM 4020 (dated 1798), *RCM 4583b (BJ), RCM 5237 (Stokes), BL Add 14343 (VN), BL Add 35003 (Stokes)*

rmk SSB. 'On Mr [Charles James] Fox & Parson Horne Tooke, imitated from Horace's ode Bk II ode 4.'

212 But if his teeth so far are gone 1824

ms RCM 4025 f 104 (dated 17/11/1824), *RCM 4583b (BJ), RCM 5237 (Stokes), BL Add 14343 (VN)*

rmk SSB. 'Epist. ad Corinth, translated by Martin Madan.' The text is a continuation of 'When down his throat', work 249.

Carmen Bacchanale: Dum vivimus vivamus → 226

213 Circle the bowl with freshest roses 1782

ms BL Add 31222 (dated 7/9/1782), Cary 449 (dated 7/9/1782), *BL Add 35028 (EW)*

rmk SSAB (BL Add 31222); SSSB (Cary 449). 'A glee.'

---

² Susanna Wesley, daughter of SW and CLW, died before SW→SGW, 22/12/1797.

³ This annotation appears on a copy of this song offered for sale as item 153 in catalogue XVI of the Leamington Book Shop, Washington DC, c1958. The present location of this copy is not known.

Death's final conquest → 239

Epitaph on Susanna Wesley → 208

214	**Father of light and life**	1801

ms BL Add 71107 f 76 (dated 22/3/1801), BL Add 34999 f 81 (vocal and string parts of final section), *BL Add 14343 (VN)*

pr *Father of Light. Invocation to the Deity.* (London, Regent's Harmonic Institution [plate no. 363, 1820], ESH 3/5/1820).

rmk SATB, str. BL Add 71107: 'Invocation of the Deity'. Text from James Thomson's *The Seasons*.

215	**Glee, performed…at the Literary Society**[4]	[1799]

pr *Glee, perform'd at the Anniversary Meeting of the Literary Society, May 2nd 1799. Composed for the Occasion.* (London, Robert Wornum, [1799].) RISM W914.

rmk First performance 2/5/1799 at the 7th annual festival/dinner of the Literary Fund, held at Freemasons Tavern, Great Queen Street, Lincolns Inn Fields.

216	**Goosy goosy gander**	*c*1781

ms Cary 449 (noted as composed around 1781), BL Add 31222, BL Add 35005, *BL Add 14343 (VN)*, RCM 5237 (Stokes), BL Add 35028 (EW)

pr *Goosy Gander. A Favorite Glee.* (London, Robert Birchall, 133 New Bond Street [1800?]). RISM W916.

rmk SSB (printed source has pf acc). 'A favorite glee.' SW→CW Jr, 15/1/1807, mentions that work had been sung by Miss Abrams.

217	**Happy the man and happy he alone**	1800

ms RCM 4020 (dated 14/3/1800), *BL Add 14343 (VN)*, RCM 4583b, RCM 5237 (two copies)

rmk ATB; SAB (RCM 5237); TTB (RCM 5237). 'From Dryden's translation of Horace, book 1, ode 29, strophe 4.'

---

[4] SW was a member of the Society for a Literary Fund, *see* SW→Thomas Busby, 3/6/1800.

218	**Harsh and untuneful are the notes**	1783
ms	Cary 449 (dated 31/5/1783), RCM 2141c (lacks beginning, dated 31/5/1783), *BL Add 35028 (EW)*	
rmk	SSB. 'A trio.' Text from Laurence Sterne's *Tristram Shandy.*	

219	**Here shall the morn her earliest tears bestow**	[c1800–1810][5]
ms	BL Add 35005, RCM 4021	
rmk	SATB. 'A glee.'	

220	**Hilaroi piomen oinon**	1800
ms	BL Add 65454 f 8 (draft score, dated 3/11/1800), BL Add 71107 f 21^v, *BL Add 14343 f 11^v, BL Add 35005*	
rmk	ATB. 'A glee in Greek, the words from Anacreon.'	

221	**Hurly burly blood and thunder**	[1810]
ms	*BL Add 65488 (Stokes, dated 17/5/1810), RCM 5251 (VN)*	
rmk	SSB. 'An ode for the birth day of the King by Edward Lord Thurlow, from *The Asylum for Fugitive Pieces.*'	

222	**If in fighting foolish systems**	1807
ms	BL Add 14340 (dated 30/5/1807)	
rmk	SSB or TTB.	

~	**I follow to the footing** *by Thomas Morley*[6]

223	**I walked to Camden Town**	[1809?]
ms	RCM 4021	
rmk	ATB. 'A burlesca for three voices: Messrs Wesley, Salomon and Saust.'[7] *See* SW→Tebaldo Monzani, 4/10/1809.	

---

[5] Dating range proposed from other works in RCM 4021.

[6] The correct title of Morley's composition is 'I follow, lo, the footing'.

[7] Charles Saust [German flautist and composer, *b*1773, who arrived in London in 1800] was a close friend of Salomon; *see* Alan Tyson, 'Salomon's will', *Beiträge zür Rheinische Musikgeschichte* v 3 (1965) p 43–45.

224   **Integer penis**   [*c*1798][8]
ms   RCM 4020
rmk   SAB. 'Imitation of Horace.' Text by Martin Madan.

Invocation of the Deity → 214

225   **Life is a jest**   1807
ms   BL Add 71107 (dated 17/1/1807), DLC Music Div. ML96.W49 Case
        (dated 17/1/1807), *BL Add 14340 (Matthew Cooke), Eg. 2571 (Street)*
rmk   ATTB. 'A glee with words translated from Greek by Charles Wesley
        Jr.'[9] Text attributed to Palladas (4th century AD) from *Anthologia
        Palatina* 10.72. *See* SW→Charles Britiffe Smith, 4/9/1828.

226   **Mihi est propositum in taberna mori**   1784
ms   BL Add 35003 (dated 1/11/1794), BL Add 71107 (with title 'Mihi fit
        propositum…'), *BL Add 14343 (VN, with autograph translation by
        Leigh Hunt), RCM 5237 (Stokes)*
rmk   SATB, bc; 1v, bc in RCM 5237. 'Dum vivimus vivamus, Carmen
        Bacchanale.' Text by Walter Map.

227   **Nella casa troverete**   [*c*1781]
ms   Cary 449, BL Add 31222 (two versions), RCM 822 (Benjamin Cooke),
        BL Add 35028 (EW), MB Catch Club mss xx 41
rmk   SSS. 'A glee.' 'Written at an inn.'

228   **Now the trumpet's martial sound**   1815
ms   BL Add 35003 (dated 15/1/1815), *BL Add 14343 (VN)*
rmk   SATB. 'A glee on the Peace of 1814.' Text by Kingston.

---

[8] Date proposed from other works in ms.

[9] The translator presumably was CW III, as SW is not known to have called his
brother CW Jr 'Charles Wesley Jr'.

229   O Delia, ev'ry charm is thine   [1811?]
ms   *RCM 4028 f 50ᵛ* (with dedication in SW's hand to Miss Stotherd)
rmk   SATB. 'Glee for 4 voices, from a melody the author of which is
        unknown. Words adapted by Peter Pindar.' Probably the glee to
        Pindar's words first performed at SW's benefit concert on 27/4/1811,
        see the Chronology entry for that date.

230   Old King Cole   1813
ms   BL Add 14342 (dated 9/8/1813), *RCM 5251 (VN)*
rmk   ATB.

231   On the salt wave we live
ms   BL Add 35003
rmk   3 v. 'A glee.'

232   O sacred bird, let me at eve   1800
ms   RCM 4020 (dated 4/4/1800), *RCM 5237 (Stokes), BL Add 14343 (VN),
        BL Eg. 2571 (Street)*
rmk   ATB or SSB. 'Part of Akenside's Ode to a Nightingale.'

233   O sing unto mie roundelaie   1812
ms   BL Add 14342 (dated 27/2/1812), BL Add 35005 (noted by EW as a
        copy written out by SW for her in 1837), *BL Music Ms Loan Madrigal
        Society B1–10 item 48, BL Music Ms Loan Madrigal Society J item 51*
pr   *O sing unto mie roundelaie. A madrigal for five voices.* (SW,
        Tottenham Ct, [1813])[10]
ed   Paul Hillier in *English Romantic Partsongs* (Oxford, 1986); Geoffrey
        Bush and Michael Hurd in *Invitation to the Partsong* v 5 (London,
        c1990)
rmk   SSATB. 'Madrigal.' Text by Thomas Chatterton. Dedicated to Joseph
        Gwilt. *See* Timothy Essex→SW, 14/1/1812 (inviting SW to compose
        for the Madrigal Society competition), SW→VN, 17/2/1813,
        Chronology 9/3/1813, SW→'Dear Sir', 29/3/1828?. ♫

---

[10] The printed composition states: 'This was a candidate for the prize cup, lately
given by the Madrigal Society'.

234   **Qualem ministrum**   [1785]
ms   BL Add 35005 f 127, 150 (score, two copies), *BL Add 35005 (S1, S2, A1, A2, B2 parts)*
rmk   SSAABB. 'Drussi Laudes. From Horace, Ode IV, 4.' *See* SW→CW, 22/8/1785.

235   **Roses, their sharp spines being gone**   [1798]
ms   BL Add 14343 f 43ᵛ,[11] RCM 4020, *BL Add 14343 f 53 (VN), BL Add 35003, BL Add 65460 (VN, an arrangement)*
pr   Arranged as 'Madrigalian Melody' in VN, *Short Melodies for the Organ* [1848–1858], p 288
rmk   SSB. 'A part song.'

236   **Say, can pow'r or lawless wealth**   1791
ms   BL Add 35003 (partly autograph, dated 3/1/1791), *RCM 5237 (Stokes), BL Add 14343 (VN), BL Eg. 2571 (Street)*
rmk   SSB.

237   **Sol do re mi**   [1800–1807][12]
ms   BL Add 71107, *RCM 5237 (Stokes), BL Add 14343 (VN)*
rmk   SSB. 'A fantasia.'

238   **Take, O take those lips away**
ms   RCM 4025 (incomplete)
rmk   1v, pf. Text from Shakespeare's *Measure for Measure*.

239   **The glories of our birth and state**   1799
ms   RCM 4020 (dated 15/10/1799), RSCM (dated 15/10/1799), BL Add 35005, *BL Add 14341 (VN), RCM 5237 (Stokes)*
pr   In VN, Novello's Part-Song Book (London, [1850])
rmk   SATB. 'Death's final conquest.' Text adapted from James Shirley.

---

[11] The copy at BL Add 14343 f 43ᵛ is unsigned but includes, in lieu of a signature, a distinctive symbol at the end. The copy is marked 'Received Aug 29 98. R. L.', and VN annotated it as probably a competition entry. It bears SW's address, probably added later, 'Hornsey Lane, near Highgate'.

[12] Dating range proposed from other works in BL Add 71107.

240   **The Macedon youth**   [1800]
ms   BL Add 71107, BL Add 33240 (incomplete), *RCM 5237 (Stokes, includes instructions to engraver), RCM 5251 (VN, includes instructions to engraver)*
rmk ATB or SSB. 'A brisk part song.' Performed at Concentores Society, 27/11/1800.

241   **There are by fond mama supplied**   *c*1778
ms   Cary 449 (dated 'about the year 78'), BL Add 35003, *BL Add 35028 (EW)*
rmk SSA, bc. 'A trio.'

The rights of man → 254

242   **Thou happy wretch**   1783
ms   Cary 449 (dated 25/9/1783), RCM 2141c, *BL Add 35028 (EW)*
rmk SAB. 'A serious glee.' Text from Thomas Young's *Night Thoughts*.

243   **Three bulls and a bear**   [1774–1775]
ms   BL Add 34998 (SW's 'pasticcio book, 1774–1775'), *Euing R.d.27*
rmk 3vv. 'A catch.'

244   **Thus through successive ages stands**
ms   BL Add 35003
rmk SATB, tpts, timp, hns, str, bc.

245   **Tobacco's but an Indian weed**   [1800][13]
ms   Private UK collection, *BL Add 35005 (EW), RCM 5251 (VN)*
pr   *A 3 Part Song* (begins 'Tobacco is an Indian weed'; the title, the date 'Sunday June 1800', and SW's signature are engraved from SW's handwriting).
rmk SAB. Text from Thomas d'Urfey, *Wit and Mirth, or, Pills to Purge Melancholy* v 3 p 291.[14]

---

[13] Assigned to 1800 on the presumption that the date on the printed music is the date of composition.

[14] The text was reprinted in the 1781 *Vocal Magazine*, from which SW set several poems to music.

246   **Unde nil maius**   1810
ms   BL Add 14340 (dated 29/3/1810), *RCM 5251 (VN, includes instructions to engraver)*
rmk   ATB. 'Eulogium de Johanne Sebastiano Bach, ab Horatio absumptum.'

247   **What bliss to life can autumn yield**   1807
ms   BL Add 14340 (dated 19/12/1807), BL Add 35005 (dated 19/12/1807), *RCM 723 (J. W. Windsor)*
rmk   ATB. 'A glee.' Text by Samuel Johnson.

248   **When Bacchus, Jove's immortal boy**   1806
ms   BL Add 71107 (dated 6/9/1806), *BL Add 14343 (VN)*
pr   *A New Glee, for Three Voices, The Words translated from the 27th Ode of Anacreon...by Thomas Moore, Esq. Composed, Presented & Performed at the Society of Harmonists, on Thursday Decr 18th, 1806, & respectfully Inscribed to the Translator.* (London, Walter Turnbull, [c1807].) Reviewed *MM* v 23 no. 1 = no. 153 (1/2/1807) p 76. RISM W915.
rmk   SSB. Text from no. 49 of Thomas Moore's versions of Anacreon in his *Epistles, Odes and Other Poems* (London, 1806). First performance 18/12/1806. *See* SW→CW Jr, 15/1/1807.

249   **When down his throat**   [c1798][15]
ms   RCM 4020
rmk   SSB. The text continues as 'But if his teeth so far are gone', work 212, and perhaps also was translated by Martin Madan.

250   **When first thy soft lips**   1783
ms   Cary 449 (dated 24/6/1783), RCM 2141c, *BL Add 35028 (EW)*
rmk   SSB, bc. 'A glee.'

251   **When friendship, love and truth abound**
ms   *BL Add 35003*
rmk   SAT or TTB. 'A glee.' A Masonic text.

---

[15] Date proposed from other works in ms.

252   **When Orpheus went down to the region below**   [1781?]
ms   Cary 449 (noted 'supposed to be 1781'), BL Add 31222, *BL Add 35028 (EW), MB Catch Club mss xx 23*
rmk   SSB. 'A glee.' Text from *Vocal Magazine*, 1781.

253   **While ev'ry short liv'd flower of sense**   [1822]
ms   BL Add 35003, BL 35005, Fitzwm 697, Euing R.d.68(1), *BL Add 14343 (VN, who dates composition 5/3/1822)*
rmk   ATTB, pf. 'Serious glee. Candidate for the prize cup given by the Glee Club 1822.'

254   **While others, Delia, use their pen**   1800
ms   BL Add 71107 (dated 14/9/1800), RSCM (dated 14/9/1800), BL Add 35003, *RCM 5237 (Stokes), BL Add 14343 (VN)*
rmk   ATB (SSB in RCM 5237). 'The Rights of Men, an Address to a Lady.' Performed at Concentores Society, 27/11/1800.

255   **While Prussia's warlike monarch blusters**   1782
ms   BL Add 31222 f 41 (dated 1782)
rmk   4 vv.

256   **Whoes there? a granidier**   [1774–1775]
ms   BL Add 34998 f 34 (SW's 'pasticcio book, 1774–1775')
rmk   S, bc. 'A catch.' 'The soldier and the houseman.'

257   **Why should we shrink from life's decline?**   1813
ms   BL Add 35005 (dated 24/5/1813), *BL Add 14342*
rmk   ST, fls, obs, hns, bns, str. 'A harvest cantata for Mr and Mrs [Thomas and Elizabeth] Vaughan.'[16]

258   **You are old, Father Dennis**   1799
ms   RCM 4020 (dated 9/8/1799)
rmk   ATB. 'The old man's complaints and how he gained them.' Text adapted from Robert Southey's 'You are old, Father William' (first published in *The Morning Post*, 17/1/1799).

---

[16] Possibly written for, but apparently not performed at, the Vaughans' benefit concert at Hanover Square Rooms on 28/5/1813.

4. SONGS AND DUETS

259   **Adieu ye jovial youths**   1783
ms   Cary 449 (dated 27/2/1783), Bodl Tenbury 1246 f 1 (dated 27/2/1783), *BL Add 14343 (VN), BL Add 35028 (EW)*
rmk   S, bc. 'An arietta.' Text by William Shenstone, from *Vocal Magazine,* 1781.

260   **Alack and alack, the clouds are so black**   [1774–1775]
ms   BL Add 34998 (SW's 'pasticcio book, 1774–1775'), BL Add 35005
rmk   S, chorus, str, timp, org. 'Derdham Downs, a cantata.'

261   **Alone on the sea-beat rock**   1784
ms   Cary 449 (dated 7/5/1784), BL Add 35005, *BL Add 35028 (EW)*
rmk   S, 2 vln, bc. 'Armin's lamentation for the loss of his daughter, from the *Sorrows of Winter* by Ossian.' *See* SW→VN, 20/11/1820, for a possible reference.

262   **And is he then set free?**   1782
ms   BL Add 35003 (dated 30/5/1782)
rmk   SA, 2 vlns, bc. 'On the death of Mr William Kingsbury.'

263   **An election's a comical plan**   [*c*1777]
ms   BL Add 34999 (on verso of work 99, dated 1777), BL Add 35005
rmk   S, bc.

Armin's lamentation for the loss of his daughter → 261

264   **As on fam'd Waterloo the lab'ring swain**   [1816]; *Lost*
rmk   B, acc. 'Waterloo battle song, recitative and air.' Text by the Rev. John Davies. Dedicated to Henry William Paget, 1st Marquess of Anglesey. Performed from manuscript, possibly for the first time, by the bass singer Thomas Bellamy [1770–1843] at the New Musical Fund concert, 24/4/1817 [New Musical Fund programmes, BL c.61.g.20.(5)]. *See* SW→VN, 28/6/1816; SW→'Dear Sir', 23/7/1816.

265	**Autumnus comes with sickly brow**	$[c1777]^{17}$
ms	*BL Add 35003*	
pr	*Barrington* p 309–310	
rmk	S, bc. 'Song.' Text by Thomas Percy.	

266	**Behold where Dryden's less presumptuous car**	
ms	BL Add 31217, RCM 4025 (incomplete)	
rmk	B, pf (BL Add 31217 also has 2 vns, vc). Text by Thomas Gray. *MW list* 70.	

Chanson d'Henri IV → 282

267	**Come all my brave boys who want organists' places** [1798]	
ms	BL Add 35005, Fitzwm 697	
pr	*The Organ Laid Open. Or, The true Stop discovered. A new song.* RISM W913.	
rmk	S, bc, SATB chorus. The text, by Martin Madan Jr, relates to SW's unsuccessful 1798 application for the organist's position at the Foundling Hospital, and is written out by SW in SW→William Seward, 16/6/1798.	

268	**Come Stella, queen of all my heart**	1801
ms	BL Add 71107 (dated 29/7/1801), *BL Add 14343 (VN)*	
rmk	T, bc. Text by Samuel Johnson, from his *Ode to Summer*.	

Derdham Downs → 260

269	**Election squib**	*Lost*
rmk	*MW list* 79. Presumably a different work from 263, which was composed when SW was very young.	

270	**England, the spell is broken**	
ms	BL Add 35005 f 107	
rmk	S, pf, chorus. 'A song.'	

---

[17] *Barrington*, published in 1781, states (p 308) that the text was written when Thomas Percy, who was born on 13/9/1768, was nine years old.

| 271 | **Eyes long unmoisten'd wept** | [1836] |

pr *Recitative & Air from an Elegy on the Death of Malibran de Beriot* (London, J. Alfred Novello, [1836]). Reviewed *MW* v 4 no. 43, 6/1/1837, p 45.

rmk S, pf. 'The composer is indebted to the *John Bull* newspaper of 2d October for the words.' The mezzo-soprano Maria Malibran de Bériot died on 23/9/1836 at the age of 28.

272   **Fairy minstrels**

ms *BL Add 14343 (VN)*

rmk S, pf. Text by Kingston. The music is the same as 276.

273   **Farewell! If ever fondest prayer**

ms BL Add 35003 (written in SW's late handwriting style)

rmk S, pf. 'A song, the words by Byron.' Text first published in *The Corsair*, 2nd edition, 1814.

| 274 | **Flutt'ring spread thy purple pinions** | 1783 |

ms Cary 449 (dated 21/6/1783), RCM 2141c (dated 21/6/1783), *BL Add 35028 (EW)*

rmk S, bc. 'A love song, the words by Swift, and in the modern taste.'

275   **Gentle breath of melting sorrow**

ms BL Add 35005

rmk S, str. 'A song.'

| 276 | **Gentle warblings in the night** | 1799 |

ms BL Add 35005 (dated 3/2/1799), *BL Add 35003 (VN)*

rmk S, 2 fl, bass for pf. The music is the same as 272.

| 277 | **Go, minstrel, go** | [1835][18] |

ms BL Add 35005 f 112 (original, wmk 1834), f 96 (copy)

rmk S, pf. 'A song composed on J. B. Cramer's leaving England.'

---

[18] Assigned to 1835 because John Baptist Cramer left England then and did not return to live there until 1845. A printed programme of the *Dinner given by the musical Profession to Mr J. B. Cramer before his Departure from England, Freemason's Tavern, July 15, 1835* is at BL Add Ms 38071 f 43.

278 Hark! his hands the lyre explore
ms BL Add 35003, BL Add 35005, RCM 4020 f 16^v
rmk S, pf. Text from Thomas Gray's *Ode on the Progress of Poetry*.

279 Hope away! Enjoyment's come 1793
ms BL Add 35003 (dated 7/5/1793)
rmk S, 2 vlns, bc. 'Aria.'

280 In gentle slumbers
ms BL Add 35005
rmk S, 'violetti', bass. 'A song.' Text by Martin Madan.

281 In radiant splendor 1816
ms BL Add 35005 (dated 15/8/1816)[19], RCM 2141b, *BL Add 14343 (VN)*
rmk S, pf. 'On the nuptials of Princess Charlotte, the words by the Rev. John Davies.'

282 La belle Gabrielle 1792
ms BL Add 35003 (dated 11/2/1792), BL Add 71107, *BL Add 14343 (VN)*
rmk SS, bc. 'Chanson d'Henri quatre.'

283 Little tube of mighty pow'r 1798
ms RCM 4020 (dated 12/7/1798)
rmk S, bc. 'Address to a pipe.' Text from *Vocal Magazine,* 1781.

284 Looking o'er the moonlight billow [1831?]; *Lost*
pr London, Zenas T. Purday (advertised *The Harmonicon*, August 1831)
rmk 'Song.' Text by M. Crawford, Esq. *MW list* 74.

285 Louisa view the melting tears c1783][20] [
ms BL Add 31222, Cary 449, *BL Add 35028 (EW)*
rmk S, bc. 'An arietta.'

---

[19] BL Add 35005 is annotated by Stokes as given to him by SW on the day this work was composed, and by VN as given to him by Stokes's widow.

[20] Date proposed from other works in the three manuscripts.

286   Love and folly were at play
pr   *Love and Folly. Song.* (London, W. Hodsoll, [*c*1800].) RISM W917.
rmk   S, pf. 'A favorite song.' Text from *Vocal Magazine*, 1781.

287   Love, like a cage-contented bird
ms   RCM 4025 (sketch)
rmk   S, kbd.

288   Love's but a frailty of the mind   1783
ms   Cary 449 (dated 4/4/1783), Bodl Tenbury 1246 (dated 4/4/1783) f 14ᵛ,
        BL Add 35028 (EW)
rmk   S, bc. Text from *Vocal Magazine*, 1781.

289   Near Thame's fam'd banks   1799
ms   BL Add 56411 f 2 (dated 22/12/1799)
rmk   A, 2 vlns, bc. 'Composed for the performance of Mr [Thomas] Carter
        and for the use of the Ad Libitum Society to whom it is respectfully
        inscribed.'

290   Not heav'n itself   [1804]
ms   *BL Add 14343 (VN, who noted that work was composed on 10/12/1804)*
rmk   S, bc. 'A song, the words from Dryden's translation of Horace.'

291   Of all the joys were e'er possest   1801
ms   BL Add 71107 (dated 22/1/1801), *BL Add 14343 (VN, dated
        22/1/1801), RCM 5237 (Stokes)*
rmk   SB. 'A duet.'

292   O how to bid my love adieu   1783
ms   Cary 449 (dated 14/7/1783), RCM 2141c, *BL Add 35028 (EW)*
rmk   S, bc. 'An arietta.'

293   One kind kiss before we part   [*c*1783]
ms   Bodl Tenbury 1246 (volume entitled 'Libro del Samuel Wesley 1783')
rmk   1v, bc.

On music → 317

294   Orpheus could lead the savage race   1836
ms   BL Add 35026 (the first item in EW's album, dated 1/7/1836)²¹
rmk   1v, pf. Text from Dryden's *A Song for St Cecilia's Day*.

295   O that I had wings like a dove   [1800?]
ms   RCM 4020 (on verso of work 113, which is dated 4/7/1800)
rmk   S, bc.

296   Pale mirror of resplendent light   1783
ms   Cary 449 (dated 9/1783), RCM 2141c (dated 9/1783), *BL Add 35028
        (EW)*
rmk   S, kb. 'An arietta.'

297   Parting to death we will compare   1783
ms   Cary 449 (dated 12/7/1783), BL Add 71107, BL Add 35005, RCM
        1111, RCM 2141c, *BL Add 14343 (VN), BL Add 35028 (EW)*
rmk   S, bc. 'An arietta.' Text from *Vocal Magazine*, 1781.

298   Phere moi kupellon   1797
ms   BL Add 35003 f 34 (dated 11/1/1797), BL Add 35003 f 33, BL Add
        35003 f 118ᵛ²²
rmk   AB or TB.

**Recitative & Air from an Elegy on the Death
of Malibran de Beriot → 271**

299   See the young, the rosy spring   [c1809]²³
ms   BL Add 71107, RCM 4028, *BL Add 14343 (VN), BL Add 35003 (VN)*
rmk   SS, pf. 'A duetto from an ode of Anacreon.' Translated by Thomas
        Moore.

---

²¹ For this album of musical autographs *see* SW→Attwood, 1/9/1836.

²² BL Add 35003 f 118ᵛ is annotated by Wait as 'composed' by SW at Blagdon
Rectory on 22/10/1829; however, it is the same composition as the 1797 work.
SW presumably wrote it out from memory at Blagdon.

²³ Date proposed from other works in BL Add 71107.

300   **Since pow'rful love directs thine eye**   [*c*1783][24]
ms   Bodl Tenbury 1246 f 5ᵛ (volume entitled 'Libro del Samuel Wesley 1783'), Cary 449, *BL Add 35028 (EW)*
rmk   SS, bc.

301   **Sweet constellations mildly bright**   1782
ms   Cary 449 (dated 1782), BL Add 31222, *BL Add 35028 (EW)*
rmk   SS, bc. 'Address to the Evening Star.'

302   **Tergi il pianto idolo mio**   [*c*1785][25]
pr   *Tergi il pianto idolo mio. A Rondo.* London, Wm Napier, [*c*1785]. RISM W918.
rmk   S, obs, hns, str.

303   **The autophagos**   *Lost*
rmk   *MW* list 78.

The organ laid open → 267

304   **There was a little boy**   [*c*1800]
pr   *There was a Little Boy. A New Duet.* (London, Robert Birchall, [*c*1800].) RISM W919.
rmk   SS, pf.

305   **The rising sun of freedom**   [*c*1798][26]
ms   RCM 4020, *BL Add 14343 (VN)*
rmk   S, SATB chorus, pf. 'A song for Mr Fox's birthday' [presumably Charles James Fox, politician, 1749–1806].

---

[24] The proposed dating is consistent with the dates of other compositions in Cary 449.

[25] Date proposed by RISM for the publication.

[26] Date proposed from other works in RCM 4020.

306   The standard of England still floats on the waves
ms   BL Add 35003 (incomplete)
pr   *True Blue and Old England for ever!* (London, Willis, [1830])
         Reviewed *The Harmonicon*, n.s. no. 35 (11/1830) p 478.
rmk   S, pf, SATB chorus. 'True Blue and old England for ever.' Text by
         Thomas H. Bayly. *MW list* 72.

307   The white robed hours   1783
ms   Cary 449 (dated 24/9/1783), RCM 2141c, *BL Add 35028 (EW)*
rmk   S, bc. 'An arietta.'

308   The world, my dear Mira, is full of deceit   1784
ms   Cary 449 (dated 1784), *BL Add 35028 (EW)*
rmk   S, bc. 'Aria.' Text from *Vocal Magazine*, 1781. SW wrote on Cary 449:
         'This song was composed in 1784 at the desire of the Duchess of
         Norfolk.[27] I should not otherwise have set words so full of trite and
         worn out expressions, and so totally destitute of poetical elegance.'

309   Think of me   [1837]
ms   BL Add 35005 (contains EW's note that SW composed this in 1837)
rmk   S, pf. 'A song.'

310   This is the house that Jack built   [1809?]
ms   BL Add 35038, BL Add 35005 (partly autograph), *BL Add 65454*
pr   According to *Jacobs* p 55, this work was published by 'Monro', i.e.,
         John Monro, who published music in London from *c*1815 to *c*1823, or
         possibly the successor firm Monro & May, who published music from
         *c*1823 to 1848. No copies of this publication have been located.
rmk   S, bc. 'A song on the Opera riot.'[28]

311   Too late for redress   1783
ms   Cary 449 (dated 13/9/1783), RCM 2141c, *BL Add 35208 (EW)*
rmk   S, bc. 'An arietta.' Text from *Vocal Magazine*, 1781.

---

[27] Catherine Howard, 1718–21/11/1784, *see* Shepherd→Sarah, 12/3/1794;
Shepherd→SW→Shepherd, 3/1794–1797.

[28] There were riots at Covent Garden in the autumn of 1809, following an
attempt by management to raise ticket prices.

True blue, and old England for ever → 306

312   **Twas not the spawn of such as these**   1825
ms   BL Add 65454 (dated 28/9/1825), RCM 4028 (dated 28/9/1825)
rmk S, pf. 'Horatii Carm. VI Lib. III.'

Waterloo battle song → 264

313   **What folly it is**   1836
ms   BL Add 35003 (dated 11/8/1836)
rmk S, pf. 'Composed for Mark Howell Esq. previous to his leaving England.'

314   **What are the falling rills**
ms   BL Add 35005
rmk Solo v, fl, str. 'A cantata.'

315   **What shaft of fate's relentless pow'r**
ms   BL Add 14340, RCM 4020, *RCM 4028 (SSW), RCM 5251 (VN, includes instructions to engraver, and VN's note that this song was a favourite of the tenor Thomas Vaughan)*
ed   Geoffrey Bush and Nicholas Temperley, *Musica Britannica* v 43 p 10
rmk S or T, pf. 'A sonnet.' Text by Martin Madan.

316   **When all around grew drear and dark**   1837
ms   Private UK collection (dated 1/8/1837)
rmk 1v, pf. Ms bears SW's inscription: 'Composed for Eliza [EW] to present to her friend Miss [Sarah] Emett [Emett's daughter] on her birthday as a token of her sincere regard'.

317   **When thro' life unblest we rove**   [1835][29]
ms   BL Add 35005 f 95 (original, wmk 1834), f 94 (copy)
rmk S, pf acc. 'On music.'

---

[29] Although EW noted on the ms that this work was composed in 1837, it is assigned to 1835 because it is written in the same ink, and on the same sheet, as work 277, which has been assigned to 1835 for reasons given in that entry.

318   **When we see a lover languish**   1783
ms   Cary 449 (dated 1783), RCM 2141c, *BL Add 35028 (EW)*
rmk S, bc. 'An arietta.'

319   **Within a cowslip's humble bell**   [*c*1808]
ms   BL Add 35003 (wmk 1808)
rmk S, bc.

320   **Yes, Daphne, in your face**   1781
ms   Cary 449 (dated 1781), BL Add 35005, Bodl Tenbury 1246 f 12ᵛ, *BL
       Add 14343 (VN), BL Add 35028 (EW)*
rmk S, kbd acc. 'An arietta.'

5. CANONS

321   **As pants the heart**
ms   BL Add 34999
ed   Roger Wibberley (http://ludwig.gold.ac.uk/Rwibberley/swesley) (1996)
rmk 3 v. 'Canon 3 in 1.'

322   **Collaudate Dominum Deum**   1830
ms   RCM 4022 (dated 27/3/1830)
ed   Roger Wibberley (http://ludwig.gold.ac.uk/Rwibberley/swesley) (1996)
rmk ATB. 'Canon in quinto et octavo.'

323   **Diligam te Domine in toto corde meo**   [*c*1825–1826][30]
ms   BL Add 31239, Add 34999 f 29
ed   Roger Wibberley (http://ludwig.gold.ac.uk/Rwibberley/swesley) (1996)
rmk SAT (BL Add 31239); SAB (BL Add 34999). 'A canon at the 5th and
       8th.'

324   **God shall bless us**   [1774–1775]
ms   BL Add 34998 (SW's 'pasticcio book, 1774–1775') f 36ᵛ
ed   Roger Wibberley (http://ludwig.gold.ac.uk/Rwibberley/swesley) (1996)
rmk SA.

---

[30] Dating range proposed from other works in Add 31239.

325   Hallelujah, Amen   [1774–1775]
ms   BL Add 34998 (SW's 'pasticcio book, 1774–1775') f 19
pr   Roger Wibberley (http://ludwig.gold.ac.uk/Rwibberley/swesley) (1996)
rmk   2 v.

326   He maketh the barren woman to keep house   [1774–1775]
ms   BL Add 34998 (SW's 'pasticcio book, 1774–1775') f 36ᵛ
ed   Roger Wibberley (http://ludwig.gold.ac.uk/Rwibberley/swesley) (1996)
rmk   SS.

327   Kyrie eleison
ms   *BL Add 14341 (VN)*
ed   Roger Wibberley (http://ludwig.gold.ac.uk/Rwibberley/swesley) (1996)
rmk   SATTB. 'Canon upon a subject in Mozart's "Kyrie".' [from Mozart's
         Missa Brevis in F, K 192/186f]

328   Laudate Dominum, omnes gentes
ms   *Fitzwm 697*
rmk   'A canon.'

329   O sing unto the Lord   [1774–1775]
ms   BL Add 34998 (SW's 'pasticcio book, 1774–1775') f 36ᵛ
ed   Roger Wibberley (http://ludwig.gold.ac.uk/Rwibberley/swesley) (1996)
rmk   SA.

330   Praise Him upon the well tun'd cymbals   [1774–1775]
ms   BL Add 34998 (SW's 'pasticcio book, 1774–1775') f 36ᵛ
ed   Roger Wibberley (http://ludwig.gold.ac.uk/Rwibberley/swesley) (1996)
rmk   SA.

ORCHESTRAL MUSIC

1. OVERTURES

401	**Overture** [G]	1775
ms	BL Add 34998 f 27 (dated 9/1/1775)	
rmk	On two staves, with indications for scoring.	

402	**Overture** [D]	1778
ms	BL Add 35010 f 1 (score, dated 11/12/1778), f 7 (parts)	
rmk	Obs, hns, str, org.	

403	**Overture** [C]	1780
ms	BL Add 35010 f 20 (score, dated 26/10/1780), f 29 (parts)	
rmk	Hns, str.	

~   **Overture** [E] (1832)   *by SSW*

~   **Overture,** *The Dilosk Gatherer*   *by SSW*

2. SYMPHONIES

404	**Sinfonia Obligato** [D]	1781
ms	BL Add 35011 f 1 (score, dated 27/4/1781), f 26 (parts)	
ed	Richard Divall in *The Symphony*, p 157	
rmk	Solo vn, solo vc, solo org, hns, timp, str. ♫	

405	**Symphony** [A]	[c1781]
ms	BL Add 35008 f 186 (first and second vn parts only)	

406	**Symphony** [A]	[c1784]
ms	BL Add 35011 f 140 (score), f 153 (parts)	
ed	Richard Platt, as *Symphony 5* (London, [1974])	
rmk	Hns, str. ♫	

407   **Symphony** [D]   1784
ms   BL Add 35011 f 42 (score, dated 6/2/1784), f 54 (parts)
ed   Richard Platt, as *Symphony 2* (London, 1976)
rmk   Hns, str. ♫

408   **Symphony** [E♭]   1784
ms   BL Add 35011 f 59 (score, dated 25/4/1784), f 74 (parts)
rmk   Hns, str. ♫

409   **Symphony** [B♭]   1802
ms   BL Add 35011 f 91 (score, dated 27/4/1802)
ed   John I. Schwarz Jr in *The Symphony*, p 221
rmk   Fls, obs, bns, hns, timp, str. ♫

3. CONCERTOS

410   **Harpsichord concerto** [G]   [1774–1775]
ms   BL Add 34998 (SW's 'pasticcio book, 1774–1775') f 50 (harpsichord part only)

411   **Harpsichord concerto** [F]   [1774–1775]
ms   BL Add 34998 (SW's 'pasticcio book, 1774–1775') f 53 (harpsichord part only)

412   **Piano concerto**   [1813][1]; *Lost*
rmk   First performance by Marmaduke Charles Wilson at SW's benefit concert, Argyll Rooms, 4/5/1813 (programme advertised in *The Times*, 22/4/1813). *MW list* 76.

Organ concerto [A] → 529

---

[1] Marmaduke Charles Wilson's autobiographical entry in the *Dictionary of Musicians* (London, printed for Sainsbury and Co., 1824, v 2 p 541) states that this concerto was completed on 3/5/1813.

413   **Organ concerto [B♭]**   [1800]
pr   Finale arranged in VN, *Select Organ Pieces* [c1830], p 650, where it is dated 21/3/1800 and described as 'a Purcellian air with variations from the ms Organ Concerto in B♭'.
rmk   All but the Finale lost. Possibly first performed 31/3/1800 at an oratorio concert directed by François-Hippolyte Barthélemon at Hatton House, Cross Street, Hatton Garden (advertised in *The Times*, 27/3/1800).

414   **Organ concerto [D]**   1800, revised 1809
ms   BL Add 35009 f 80 (score, original version, dated 22/3/1800), f 95 (parts, original version)
pr   Last movement arranged for keyboard as *The Hornpipe and Variations from a favorite Organ Concerto*, work 711.
ed   Revised version arranged for organ solo by W. J. Westbrook in *Arrangements for the Organ*, books 15–16; last movement arranged for organ solo by G. Allanson Brown as *Allegro for Organ* (New York, 1961).
rmk   Org, str; revised version for larger orchestra. The revised version incorporates as its penultimate movement an arrangement of JSB's D major fugue from part 1 of the '48' (BWV 850/2). Original version probably performed with SW as soloist at King's Theatre, 21/4/1800. Revised version first performed, with SW as organist, at Tamworth Festival on 22/9/1809. *See* SW→BJ, 4/9/1809, 25/9/1809. *MW list* 22.

415   **Organ concerto [B♭]**   1813
ms   BL Add 35009 f 135 (some parts only, violino principale part dated 1813)
rmk   Org, str (organ part not extant). First performance 17/3/1813 (*The Times*, 17/3/1813).

416   **Organ concerto [G]**   1813
ms   BL Add 35011 f 159 (last page of score only, dated 31/10/1813), BL Add 35010 f 106 (hn, bn, string parts of last movement)
pr   Last movement arranged as second movement of 607.
rmk   Org, hn, bn, str. *MW list* 21.

417   **Organ concerto** [C]   1814
ms   Private UK collection (score of original version, dated 5/3/1814), BL
       Add 35009 f 162 (incomplete set of parts of second version, including
       the 'Rule Britannia' movement)
rmk   Org, 2 fl, 2 ob, 2 tpt, 2 hn, 2 bsn, timp, str. First performance by SW at
       Covent Garden oratorio concert, 9/3/1814. Finale of original version,
       adapted from last movement of no. 2 of 621, replaced in subsequent
       version by new movement based on 'Rule Britannia'. First performance
       of the second version at Covent Garden, 1/6/1816. *MW list* 20. *See*
       SW→RG, 8/3/1814; SW→VN, 1/6/1816.

418   **Violin concerto** [C]   1779
ms   BL Add 35008 f 60 (score, dated 13/11/1779), f 165 (parts)
rmk   Vln, str.

419   **Violin concerto** [A]   [1780?]
ms   BL Add 35008 f 129 (score, dated '24 February')
rmk   Vln, hns, str.

420   **Violin concerto** [D]   1781
ms   BL Add 35009 f 2 (score, dated 10/4/1781), f 83 (parts)
rmk   Vln, hns, str. ♫

421   **Violin concerto** [E♭]   [*c*1781]
ms   BL Add 35009 f 63 (score), f 79 (two horn parts)
rmk   Vln, hns, str.

~   **Violin concerto** [E]   *by Giornovichi* → *922*

422   **Violin concerto** [B♭]   1782
ms   BL Add 35009 f 22 (score, dated 12/9/1782), BL Add 35008 f 149
       (parts)
rmk   Vln, hns, str.

423   **Violin concerto [G]**   1783
ms   BL Add 35008 f 104 (score, entitled 'Concerto 6' by SW,[2] dated
        15/12/1783), f 114 (parts)
rmk   Vln, hns, str.

424   **Violin concerto [B♭]**   1785
ms   BL Add 35009 f 42 (score, dated 4/3/1785), f 58 (one horn part)
rmk   Vln, obs, hns, str.

---

[2] This is the only violin concerto that SW numbered on his autograph score.

CHAMBER MUSIC

1. Violin and Keyboard

501   **Sonata [F]**   [1774–1775]
ms   BL Add 34998 f 56 (SW's 'pasticcio book, 1774–1775')

502   **Sonata [A]**   1778
ms   BL Add 35008 f 44 (dated 8/3/1778)
rmk   Vln, bc. 'Solo per violino con accompanato per basso.'

503   **Sonata [E♭]**   1778
ms   BL Add 35008 f 43 (dated 25/7/1778)
rmk   Vln, bc. 'Sonata a violino solo.'

504   **Sonata [B♭]**   1781
ms   MA MAM P12C (dated 14/11/1781)
rmk   Vln, bc.

505   **Sonata [D]**   [c1781][1]
ms   MA MAM P12C
rmk   Vln, bc.

506   **Sonata [A]**   [c1781][2]
ms   MA MAM P12C
rmk   Vln, bc.

---

[1] Date proposed because work 504, dated 1781, is in the same ms.

[2] Date proposed because work 504, dated 1781, is in the same ms.

507   **Two Sonatas** [G and C], op. 2   [c1786][3]
pr   *Two Sonatas for the Piano Forte or Harpsichord; with an*
       Accompanyment for a Violin...Op. 2. (London, SW, Chesterfield St.)
       RISM W921.
rmk   Vln, pf or hpschd. 'Composed and dedicated to the public.'

508   **Sonata** [F]   1797
ms   BL Add 69854 f 1 (dated 19/2/1797, with annotation by VN that ms
       was presented to him by Stokes)
rmk   Vln, pf. 'Composed for Salomon.'

2. TWO VIOLINS

509   **Duet for two violins** [D]   1785
ms   MA MAM P12C (dated 20/1/1785)
rmk   'Duetto a due violini.'

3. TWO VIOLINS AND BASS

510   **'Catherine Hill'**   1776
ms   BL Add 35008 f 45 (dated 28/1/1776)

511   **'Warwick's Bench'**   1776
ms   BL Add 35008 f 45[v] (dated 28/1/1776) 'Composed for Mr W. Russell'
       [i.e., for William Russell, musician, 1755–1839].

512   **Three movements** [C, D and C]
ms   BL Add 35008 f 47 (parts)
rmk   Incomplete.

---

[3] The printed edition was sold also at J. Dale's Music Library, 132 Oxford
Street. Joseph Dale was at this address from January 1786 to early 1791 *(H&S)*.
This work presumably predates SW's op. 3 sonatas, work 702, which were
published before May 1789.

4. OBOE, VIOLIN AND VIOLONCELO

513   Trio [A]
ms   BL Add 35007 f 168ᵛ
rmk   Apparently composed jointly by SW, CW Jr and Reinagle[4].

5. TWO FLUTES AND PIANO

514   Trio for pianoforte and two flutes [F]   1826
ms   BL Add 48302 f 1, dated 10/1/1826
pr   *Trio, for the Piano Forte & two Flutes.* (London, J. Alfred Novello, c1830.)[5]
ed   Hugh Cobbe (London, 1973)
rmk   *MW list* 46. Dedicated to George Rudall. ♫

6. THREE UNSPECIFIED INSTRUMENTS

515   Alla breve [F]
ms   BL Add 35007 f 165ᵛ
rmk   For two treble instruments and bass.

516   Brisk Tune [C]   [*c*1825–1826][6]
ms   BL Add 31239 f 18ᵛ (score)
rmk   One part written in soprano clef, one in alto clef, one in bass clef.

517   Fragment [G minor]
ms   BL Add 35007 f 180
rmk   For two treble instruments and bass.

---

[4] Several members of the Reinagle family were composers. The particular Reinagle involved in this composition has not been identified.

[5] This publication includes an advertisement for SW's *An English Air, arranged as a Rondo*, which was composed in March 1830. See the entry for work 728.

[6] Date proposed from other works in ms.

518   **Movement** [A minor]
ms   BL Add 35007 f 165
rmk   For two treble instruments and bass. Noted by EW as 'a very early composition'.

519   **Mrs Mills's Minuet** [C]   [1774–1775]
ms   BL Add 34998 (SW's 'pasticcio book, 1774–1775') f 34^v (score)
rmk   For two treble instruments and bass.

520   **Quodlibet** [B minor]   [1824]
ms   BL Add 65454 f 2 (score, dated 26/8/1824 by VN)
rmk   For two treble parts and bass.

521   **Three short movements** [B♭]
ms   BL Add 35007 f 167
rmk   The movements are marked 'Fuga', 'Imatazione [sic] (Mesto)' and 'Grave'. The first two movements are for two treble instruments and bass; the third is for three treble instruments and bass.

7. FOUR VIOLINS

522   **Glee for four violins**   [*c*1774][7]
ms   BL Add 31763 f 38^v

8. STRING QUARTETS

523   **String quartet** [G]   1779
ms   BL Add 35007 f 181 (dated 29/11/1779)
rmk   'Quartetto a due violini, viola e violoncello—violino primo, viola, e violoncello obligati.'

---

[7] Date proposed from other works in ms.

524	**String quartet** [E♭]	[*c*1825?]
ms	*BL Add 35007 f 196* (parts)	
ed	Francis Routh (London, 2000)	
rmk	♫	

525	**Andante con espresso** [C]	1780
ms	BL Add 35008 f 54 (dated 1/1/1780)	

526	**Fugue** [B♭, on a subject from Haydn's *The Creation*][8]	1800
ms	BL Add 71107 f 15 (score, dated 31/8/1800), BL Add 35007 f 187 (parts)	

527	**Minuet** [C minor]	1807
ms	BL Add 14340 f 67 (dated 1807), RCM 4021, *RCM 5251 (VN, who describes work as 'in the German style')*	

528	**Minuet** [F]	[1800]
ms	BL Add 71107 f 24ᵛ, RCM 5251 (VN, dated 1800)	
rmk	'A minuet in Haydn's manner.'	

9. TWO VIOLINS, VIOLA, BASS AND ORGAN

529	**Quintet** [A]	1787
ms	BL Add 35007 f 213 (dated 17/4/1787)	
rmk	'Quintetto.' 2 hns included in finale. Listed as an organ concerto in the article on SW in *The New Grove Dictionary of Music and Musicians* (London, 1980).	

---

[8] The subject, 'Blessed be his name for ever', is from Haydn's chorus 'Achieved is the glorious work'. In the ms SW identifies various contrapuntal techniques that are used in this elaborate fugue.

10. WIND BANDS

530   **March [D]**   1777

ms   BL Add 35007 f 237 (dated 24/6/1777)

rmk   2 hns, 2 obs, 2 bsns, serpent. Facsimile of ms printed in Max Hinrichsen (ed.), *Music Book v 7*, London, *c*1952, plates 6–8.

531   **March [B♭]**

rmk   Ms, undated, offered for sale in Sotheby catalogue 15/5/1996 lot 557.[9] Perhaps the ms of the wind band version of 783.

---

[9] This ms did not sell at this auction. Its present location is not known.

ORGAN MUSIC

1. Works Printed before 1839

601   **Characteristic Airs for the Seraphine**   [1830–1837]

pr   *Characteristic Airs for the Seraphine.* (London, J. Green, ≥1830.)[1] No copies located.

rmk   *Jacobs* p 54 lists three airs by SW ('nos. 4, 5, 6'). BL catalogue lists five SW *Characteristic Airs for the Royal Seraphine*, but the BL copy apparently was destroyed in World War II.

602   **Fantasy [F]**   [1809]

pr   In VN, *Select Organ Pieces* [c1830] 'from an unpublished ms in the possession of the editor', dated 14/6/1809.

ed   Robin Langley, *14 Short Pieces* (Oxford, 1981), p 14.

rmk   ♫

Fugue [C minor] → fugue of 606

603   **Fugue [D]**   1800

ms   BL Add 71107 f 26ᵛ (dated 16/2/1800), DLC ML96.W Case, *RCM 4583b (BJ)*

pr   In VN, *Select Organ Pieces* [c1830] p 259.

ed   Robin Langley, *Six Voluntaries and Fugues* (Oxford, 1981), p 20.

---

[1] The Seraphine was advertised on the wrapper of the December 1830 *Harmonicon* by its inventor and manufacturer, the music publisher John Green, as 'a new patent musical keyed instrument with sustained sounds of extraordinary force and sweetness'. It was advertised as having a royal patent in the January 1831 *Harmonicon* and as a new kind of organ in the January 1833 *Harmonicon*.

604   **Grand Duet [I]** [C]   1812

ms   BL Add 14344 (dated 24/5/1812)

pr   *Grand Duet for the Organ.* (London, Lonsdale, [≤1837].) *MW list* 17.[2]
No copies located. A 'new edition', published by Lonsdale, reviewed
MW no. 101 = n.s. no. 7 (16/2/1838) p 100. Also published as *Grand
Duett, in three movements, for the Pianoforte or Organ.* (London, J.
Dean, plate no. 540, [1836–1837].) Reviewed *MW* v 4 no. 51
(3/3/1837) p 166.

ed   Walter Emery, *Early Organ Music*, no. 19. (London, 1964)

rmk   Org or pf. Dedicated to Frederick Marshall. First organ performance at
Hanover Square Rooms, 5/6/1812, by SW and VN. *See* SW→VN,
6/5/1812, 14/12/1812, about 1/5/1813, 5/10/1814; SW→Christopher
Lonsdale, undated, 1832–1837. ♪

605   **Largo** [F]   [1808 or 1800]

ms   BL Add 69851 f 1 (dated '9 September', year missing)

pr   In VN, *Select Organ Pieces* [*c*1830] p 555, as 'Diapason Movement',
annotated 'composed by Samuel Wesley, Sep 9 1808 (from the original
manuscript)'; in VN, *Short Melodies for the Organ* [1848–1858], p 220,
as 'Slow Movement for the Organ', annotated 'from an original ms
dated 9 September 1800'.

ed   Robin Langley, *14 Short Pieces* (Oxford, 1981), p 12; Christopher
Tutin, as 'Diapason Movement for Organ' (London, 1982).

606   **Prelude and Fugue [I]** [C minor]   *c*1826

ms   RCM 4022 f 35ᵛ (fugue, dated 24/7/1826)[3]

pr   *Preludes and Fugues for the Organ, intended as Exercises for the
improvement of the hands, and suitable as Voluntaries, for the Service
of the Church....No. 1.* (London, Goulding and D'Almaine, [<1835]. No
copies located. Published by D'Almaine & Co., 1837.)[4]

ed   Robin Langley, *Six Voluntaries and Fugues* (Oxford, 1981), p 28
(preludium and fugue only)

rmk   Work comprises three movements: preludium, arietta and fugue. *MW
list* 19. Dedicated to Thomas Adams.

---

[2] *MW list* calls this work 'the greatest composition for the organ which has
appeared since the days of Sebastian Bach'.

[3] SW's shorter, C♯ minor version of the arietta, dated 1/8/1826, is entered below
as 654.

[4] The D'Almaine & Co. edition, probably reprinted from the original plates, is
entered in the 'weekly list of new publications', *MW* v 7 no. 83 (13/10/1837)
p 80, and reviewed in *MW* no. 101 = n.s. no. 7 (16/2/1838) p 100.

607   **Prelude and Fugue [II]** [G]
pr   *Preludes and Fugues for the Organ, intended as Exercises for the improvement of the hands, and suitable as Voluntaries, for the Service of the Church....No. 2.* (London, Goulding and D'Almaine, [<1835]. No copies located. Published by D'Almaine & Co., 1837.)[5]
rmk   Fugue an arrangement of last movement of work 416. *MW list* 19. Dedicated to Thomas Adams. ♫

608   **A Short and Familiar Voluntary** [A]   [1827?]
pr   *A Short & Familiar Voluntary, for the Organ.* (London, W. Hodsoll, ESH 3/2/1827). Subsequently published by Zenas T. Purday.
rmk   *MW list* 39.

609   **Six Desk Voluntaries**   *Lost*
pr   London, J. A. Novello, *c*1837. Advertised as 'in the press' on wrapper of 13/10/1837 *MW*. No copies located.
rmk   Presumably different from work 613, which was published by another firm.

610   **Six Introductory Movements** [D, E, F, A, C,   1797–1830?
      E minor] **and a Loud Voluntary** [D]
ms   BL Add 35007 f 51–52ᵛ (no. 1, called 'Desk Voluntary 5', dated 6/9/1797; no. 3, called 'Desk Voluntary 3', dated 27/8/1830; no. 6, called 'Desk Voluntary 4'), BL Add 35008 ('Loud Voluntary', dated 6/9/1830)
pr   *Six Introductory Movements for the Organ, Intended for the Use of Organists as Soft Voluntaries, to be Performed at the Commencement of Services of the Established Church, to which is added a Loud Voluntary with Introduction and Fugue.* (London, Clementi, Collard & Collard, plate no. 3472, [1831].) Reviewed *The Harmonicon* (7/1831) p 171. Published from later in 1831 by Collard and Collard.
ed   Nos. 1, 3 and 6 in Robin Langley, *14 Short Pieces* (Oxford, 1981), p 6, 13, 11; no. 1 in Gwilym Beechey, *Three Short Pieces* (Ely, 1996) p 1; Loud Voluntary in Kenneth Simpson, *Voluntary in D* (London, 1941)
rmk   *MW list* 43, as 'Six introductory movements or soft voluntaries, to which is added a fugue in D'.

---

[5] The D'Almaine & Co. edition, probably reprinted from the original plates, is entered in the 'weekly list of new publications', *MW* v 7 no. 83 (13/10/1837) p 80, and reviewed in *MW* no. 101 = n.s. no. 7 (16/2/1838) p 100.

611   **Six Short Toccatas**   *Lost*
pr   *Six Short Toccatas, Intended as Short Voluntaries for the Use of*
       Organists. (London, Collard & Collard, [1832].) No copies located.
rmk   A work with this title was advertised by Collard & Collard on the
       wrapper of *The Harmonicon*, March 1832, as 'new music...for the
       piano-forte' [sic]. This advertisement presumably was for a work other
       than 610, *Six Introductory Movements*, which also was published by
       Collard & Collard.

612   **Six Short Voluntaries** [D, B♭, F, F, E♭, C]   [*c*1830–1834][6]
ms   RCM 4025 f 65–76, entitled 'Six fugues with introductions, for young
       organists'.
pr   Presumably the work advertised by J. A. Novello under the title 'Six
       short voluntaries for the organ' on the wrapper of the 13/10/1837 *MW*,
       where it is said to be 'in the press'. No copies located.

613   **Six Voluntaries [F, A, G, B♭, D, C] for**   [1831–1832?]
       Young Organists
ms   RCM 4025 f 78–85
pr   *Six Organ Voluntaries, composed for the use of Young Organists, op.*
       36.[7] (London, J. Dean, plate no. 120, [1831–1832]. Published 1837 by
       D'Almaine & Co.[8])

614   **Slow Air [D]**   [1794]
pr   In VN, *Select Organ Pieces* [*c*1830] p 646, dated 5/10/1794.

---

[6] SW's assignment of copyright in 'Six short voluntaries' to J. Alfred Novello
appeared in Sotheby catalogue 15/5/1996 lot 148, as part of a lot dated *c*1830–
1834 by the cataloguer.

[7] This opus number presumably was chosen by the publisher, as SW's known
numberings of his own compositions do not go beyond op. 6.

[8] The D'Almaine & Co. reprint is entered in the 'weekly list of new
publications', *MW* v 7 no. 83 (13/10/1837) p 80, where it is listed as SW's 'op.
56'.

615   **Three Voluntaries [1st set]** [D, F, D;   [c1824]
      ded. John Harding]
pr   *A First Set of Three Voluntaries for the Organ Composed & Inscribed*
       to John Harding Esq. (London, Preston, wmk 1824.)
ed   Last two movements of first voluntary in John Scott Whiteley, *An*
       Organ Album for Manuals Only (York, 1983).
rmk *MW list* 37.

616   **Three Voluntaries [2nd set]** [E minor, C, B♭;   [c1824][9]
      ded. John Harding]
pr   *A Second Set of Three Voluntaries for the Organ Composed &*
       Inscribed to John Harding Esq. (London, Preston, [c1824].)
       Subsequently published by Coventry and Hollier.
ed   No. 1 as 'Introduction and Aria cantabile' in Ewald Kooiman, *Incognita*
       Organo v 14 (Hilversum, 1981).
rmk *MW list* 38.

617   **Twelve Short Pieces with a Full Voluntary added**   1816
ms   RCM 4025 f 57 (all the short pieces and fragmentary sketch of the Full
       Voluntary, dated 10/7/1816)[10]
pr   *Twelve Short Pieces, for the Organ, with a Full Voluntary Added,*
       Composed & inscribed to Organists in General. (London, Clementi,
       ESH 7/6/1817.) Subsequently published (London, c1830–1834) by
       Collard and Collard. Also published, according to *Jacobs* p 54, as
       Twelve short pieces for the Organ, with full Voluntary added, inscribed
       to Performers on the Seraphine and Organists in general (London, J.
       Green, ≥1830; no copies located).[11] Nos. 1–12 published as *Zwölf kurze*
       und leichte Orgelstücke (Leipzig, Hofmeister, plate no. 649, [c1820],
       RISM W924a.). No. 13 and Full Voluntary published as *Drei leichte*
       Orgelstücke (Leipzig, Hofmeister, plate no. 660, [c1820], RISM
       W924b).
ed   Nos. 1–13 and Full Voluntary in Gwilym Beechey, *Twelve Pieces and a*
       Full Voluntary (Ely, 1998); nos. 1–13 in Gordon Phillips, *Twelve Short*
       Pieces for Organ or Harpsichord (*Tallis to Wesley* v 7, London, 1957);
       Full Voluntary in Robin Langley, *Six Voluntaries and Fugues* (Oxford,

---

[9] Date proposed on the presumption that SW composed his two sets of
voluntaries dedicated to John Harding at about the same time. The publisher's
address on printed copies of the two works is the same: '71 Dean Street, late of
the Strand'.

[10] The first of these pieces is reproduced facing p 9.

[11] See the note to work 601.

1981); nos. 6, 8, 9 arr. by John E. West, *Three Short Pieces (Old English Music* v 12); nos. 6, 7 in Basil Ramsey, *Early Organ Music for Manuals* book 1 (London, 1982); nos. 8, 9 arr. Basil Ramsey as *Air and Gavotte* (London, 1969); nos. 4, 5, 11 arr. Martin Ellis as *Three Pieces* (Sevenoaks, 1981).

rmk   Work comprises 13, not 12, Short Pieces [G, G, G, A, A, A, F, F, F, D, D, D, D] followed by the Full Voluntary [D minor]. Nos. 8 and 9 subsequently known as 'Air and Gavotte'. *MW list* 40, as 'Twelve short pieces, to which is added a grand fugue composed at the request of Muzio Clementi'. *See* SW→VN, 28/6/1816, 15/7/1816. ♫

618   **Twenty-four Short Pieces or Interludes**   [*c*1821]

pr   *A Book of Interludes for Young Organists.* (London, Preston, [*c*1821].) No copies located. Published from 1834 by Coventry and Hollier. No copies located.[12]

rmk   Two pieces each in C, G, D, A, E, F, B♭, E♭, E minor, A minor, D minor, G minor. *MW list* 44. *See* SW→Thomas Preston, 21/9/1821 (a receipt for copyright assignment to Preston).

619   **Variations on 'God save the King'**

ms   RCM 4022 f 32ᵛ

pr   In *Beauties for the Organ* (London, [1820?])

620   **Variations on 'Rule, Britannia'**

ms   RCM 4022 f 34ᵛ

pr   In *Beauties for the Organ* (London, [1820?])

rmk   ♫

---

[12] The music is preserved in a *c*1851 edition (London, R. Cocks & Co., plate no. 9551).

621 **Voluntaries** [D, C, C minor, G, D, C, E♭, D,   [*c*1801–1817]
           G minor, F, A, F], op. 6

ms   Private UK collection (no. 3, fugue only), DLC Music Div. ML96.W49 Case (no. 9), BL Add 35008 f 1 (no. 10, dated 1/1814)

pr   Nos. 1–12 initially published individually as *No. [] A Voluntary for the Organ, op. 6.*, and then also in two sets as *Six Voluntaries for the Organ, op. 6.* (London, W. Hodsoll, [*c*1802–1817].) RISM W924. Individual voluntaries and the two sets subsequently published by Zenas T. Purday. Some imprints, apparently from the same plates, also published by Robert Birchall. *Facs* of nos. 1–12 from individual Hodsoll and Birchall imprints as *Voluntaries for the Organ* (Williamstown, Massachusetts, Broude Brothers, 2000). No. 3 fugue in VN, *Select Organ Pieces* [*c*1830] p. 6. No. 6 'andante larghetto' in VN, *Short Melodies for the Organ* [1848–1858], p 209.

ed   Nos. 1–12 arr. Francis Routh (St Louis, Missouri, 4 vols., 1982–1983); nos.. 1–12 ed. Geoffrey Atkinson (Ely, 2 vols., 2000); no. 1 in Robin Langley, *Classical Organ Music* v 1 (Oxford, 1986); nos. 1, 11 ed. Geoffrey Atkinson (Ely, 1998); no. 3 ed. Peter Williams (*Tallis to Wesley* v 24, London, 1961); nos. 3, 6 in Robin Langley, *English Organ Music: An Anthology* v 6 (London, 1988); nos. 7, 12 in Gwilym Beechey, *Two Voluntaries* (Ely, 1996); no. 9 in Ewald Kooiman, *Incognita Organo* v 14 (Hilversum, 1981); nos. 9, 10 in Robin Langley, *Six Voluntaries and Fugues* (Oxford, 1981, p 1, 7).

rmk   *MW list* 23–34. No. 1 reviewed *MM* v 13 (July 1802) p 601; no. 10 reviewed *New Monthly Magazine* v 3 no. 14 (1 March 1815) p 153 and *GM* v 85 part 1 (June 1815) p 445. Nos. 7, 8 advertised on work 705 [published before June 1808]. ♫

622 **Voluntary** [B♭, ded. Attwood]   1829
ms   RCM 4028 f 69, dated 27/2/1829
pr   *A Voluntary for the Organ, Composed and Inscribed to Thomas Attwood, Esq.* (London, W. Hodsoll, ESH 27/4/1830.) Subsequently published by Zenas T. Purday.
ed   Francis Routh (St Louis, Missouri, 1984)
rmk   *MW list* 36, as 'Fugue in B flat, dedicated to Mr Attwood'. ♫

623 **Voluntary** [D, ded. William Drummer]   [*c*1828]
pr   *A Voluntary for the Organ, Composed and Inscribed to William Drummer.* (London, I. Willis & Co., Egyptian Hall Piccadilly, plate no. 'Royal Musical Repository 456' [1828].)
rmk   Three movements: largo, fugue and march, the latter from the overture to 'Begin the noble song' (work 207). *MW list* 35, as 'Grand fugue, dedicated to W. Drummer Esq.'. ♫

624   Voluntary [G minor, ded. WL]
pr   London, Monro & May, *c*1823–1837. No copies located.[13]
rmk   *MW list* 42.

625   Voluntary [G, ded. Henry John Gauntlett]
pr   London, Monro & May, *c*1823–1837. No copies located.[14]
rmk   *MW list* 41.

626   Voluntary [B♭]
pr   In VN, *Select Organ Pieces* [*c*1830], p 422. Also (presumably the same work, issued singly) London, J. A. Novello, *c*1837, advertised as 'in the press' on wrapper of 13/10/1837 *MW*. No copies of the latter edition located.
rmk   In two movements.

2. VOLUNTARIES, FUGUES AND OTHER LARGER WORKS NOT PUBLISHED IN SW'S LIFETIME

627   Andante Maestoso and Presto [D]   1788
ms   BL Add 14340 f 61 (dated 16/5/1788)
ed   *Andante Maestoso* in Robin Langley, *14 Short Pieces* (Oxford, 1981), p. 4
rmk   C. W. Pearce, 'A notable eighteenth-century organ concerto', *The Organ* v 7 (1927) p 38–41, mistakenly identifies work as a concerto.

628   Four Fugues [D, D minor, G, B♭]   1774
ms   BL Add 34998 ('Four fugues for organ', dated 11/1774)

629   Fugue [C]   [*c*1800][15]
ms   BL Add 71107 f 26, DLC ML96.W Case, *BL Add 35007 f 63*
ed   John Scott Whitely, *An Organ Book for Manuals Only* (York, 1982)

---

[13] The music is preserved in a later edition published in London by R. Cocks & Co.

[14] The music is preserved in a later edition published in London by R. Cocks & Co.

[15] Date proposed from other works in BL Add 71107.

630   **Fugue** [D]   1801
ms   BL Add 71107 f 31ᵛ (dated 4/1/1801)

631   **Fugue** [B minor] **on a theme by Mendelssohn**   1837
ms   BL Add 35007 f 99ᵛ (dated 9/9/1837)
ed   Gordon Phillips, in *Three Organ Fugues...published for the first time*
        (*Tallis to Wesley* v 14, London, 1962)
rmk   'Composed expressly for Dr Mendelssohn.' On the theme that Felix
        Mendelssohn wrote in EW's album (BL Add 35026 f 66) on 7/9/1837.

632   **Grand Duet [II]**   *Lost*
rmk   *MW list* 18, described as 'A second grand organ duet, unpublished; the
        composer preferred this to the other [i.e., work 607], and considered it
        his best composition for the organ'. Perhaps the 'complicated' duet for
        two organs mentioned in SW→CB, 9/3/1802?.

633   **Hymn tunes with interludes**   [1830–1836?]
ms   BL Add 34999 f 133–162, RCM 4025 f 54, RCM 4028
cont BL Add 34999: ABINGDON, ADVENT HYMN, ANGELS' HYMN,
        BEDFORD, BURFORD, CAMBRIDGE NEW, CAREY'S, CHISWICK,
        DARWELL'S, DEVIZES, EVENING HYMN, HANOVER, HOTHAM, HOWARD,
        IRISH, ISLINGTON, LONDON NEW, MILES'S LANE, MOUNT EPHRIAM,
        MORNING HYMN, NEWCOURT, OLD 100TH, OXFORD, PORTUGAL, ST
        ANN'S, ST BRIDE'S, ST DAVID'S, ST GEORGE'S, ST MATTHEW'S,
        SHELDON, WAREHAM, WESTMINSTER NEW, WINDSOR and YORK.
        RCM 4025: CANTERBURY, GREAT MILTON and WAREHAM.
        RCM 4028: two different interludes to WINDSOR.
rmk   Some of these hymn tunes or interludes may have been printed in book
        1 of *Parochial Psalm Tunes and Interludes* (published by Willis, no
        copies located), which is listed in *Jacobs* p 54 as containing SW
        compositions.

634   **Introduction and Fugue** [D minor]   [1836–1837]
ms   BL Add 35006 f 4ᵛ
rmk   Possibly for piano.

635   **Introduction and Fugue** [G]   [1836–1837?]
ms   BL Add 35006 f 2
rmk   Possibly for piano.

636 **Preludes in All the Keys throughout the Octave**   1797
ms   BL Add 35007 f 68–81 (dated 10/5/1797–5/11/1797), BL Add 35006 f 18^v–25, f 26^v–28^v (incomplete), Fitzwm 699, *BL Add 65497 f 2 (VN)*
rmk   Org or pf. BL Add 35007 has 34 preludes, two in each of C, D, E, F, G, A, B♭, B, E♭, A♭, C minor, D minor, E minor, F minor, G minor, A minor and B minor.

637 **Voluntary [C]**   [1774–1775]
ms   BL Add 34998 (SW's 'pasticcio book, 1774–1775')

638 **Voluntary [C]**   [*c*1817?]^{16}
ms   BL Add 34089 f 9, BL Add 69859 f 32^v

639 **Voluntary [D]**   1775
ms   Private UK collection (dated 18/11/1775)

640 **Voluntary [D]**   1817
ms   BL Add 34089 f 1 (fugue dated 8/10/1817), *BL Add 69859 f 30^v*
ed   Christopher Tutin, as *Introduction and Fugue in D* (London, 1982); first movement in Robin Langley, *Six Voluntaries and Fugues* (Oxford, 1981), p 19
rmk   'Voluntary & Fuga.' This and 641 may form a single voluntary.

641 **Voluntary [D]**   [1817]
ms   BL Add 34089 f 3, *BL Add 69859 f 30^v* (dated 20–21/10/1817)
rmk   This and 640 may form a single voluntary.

642 **Voluntary [D minor]**   [*c*1817?]^{17}
ms   *BL Add 69859 f 21*
rmk   In two movements, the second a fugue.

643 **Voluntary [G]**   1784
ms   Private UK collection (dated 24/5/1784), annotated by 'J. L.' [i.e., Langshaw Jr] as having been written for him

---

^{16} Date proposed from other works in BL Add 34089.

^{17} Date proposed from other works in BL Add 69859.

644 **Voluntary '12th'** [B♭] 1817
ms BL Add 34089 f 4 (dated 5–6/11/1817), *BL Add 69859 f 22ᵛ*
ed Robin Langley, *Six Voluntaries and Fugues* (Oxford, 1981), p 23
rmk In two movements. SW's title suggests that work may have been initially intended as no. 12 of work 621.

3. SMALLER WORKS NOT PUBLISHED IN SW'S LIFETIME

645 **Adagio** [E minor]
ms BL Add 35007 f 84

646 **Air** [C]
pr In VN, *Short Melodies for the Organ* [1848–1858], p 209, described as composed by SW with additions by VN.

647 **Air** [C minor] [≤1808]
ms RCM 640 f 5, *RCM 1151 f 73 (J. W. Windsor, compiled in 1808)*
pr In VN, *Short Melodies for the Organ* [1848–1858], p 105
ed Robin Langley, *14 Short Pieces* (Oxford, 1981), p 2. ♫

648 **Air** [F] 1806
ms BL Add 71107 f 99ᵛ (entitled 'Aria—Andante espressivo', dated 10/6/1806), *BL Add 65497 f 15ᵛ (VN), RCM 4038 (Marianne Merewether)*
pr In VN, *Short Melodies for the Organ* [1848–1858], p 10, as 'An old English air, harmonised with additions by Samuel Wesley, June 1806'.
ed Arr. A. E. Floyd (for organ), *An Old English Melody* (London, 1955).

649 **Air** [F]
ms BL Add 65497 f 17 (VN)
pr In VN, *Short Melodies for the Organ* [1848–1858], p 59, as 'Simple Air', noted as being from an unpublished ms.

650   **Andante** [G] ('Scraps for the Organ, no. 3')   [≤1808]
ms   RCM 4021 f 13ᵛ, *RCM 1151 f 45ᵛ (J. W. Windsor, compiled in 1808,*
        this work designated as 'Scraps for the Organ' and noted as 'copied
        from the author's ms in the possession of Miss [Susannah] Ogle')
pr   In VN, *Short Melodies for the Organ* [1848–1858], p 252, as 'Simple
        melody for the organ', described as being 'from an unpublished ms by
        Samuel Wesley formerly in the possession of Miss Ogle of Bath'.
ed   Robin Langley, *14 Short Pieces* (Oxford, 1981), p 15.

651   **Andante** [B♭]   1827
ms   Private UK collection (dated 29/11/1827)

652   **Aria** [D minor] ('Scraps for the Organ, no. 1')   [≤1808]
ms   RCM 4021 f 12ᵛ, *RCM 1151 f 40ᵛ (J. W. Windsor, compiled in 1808,*
        this work designated as 'Scraps for the Organ')
pr   In VN, *Short Melodies for the Organ* [1848–1858], p 277, as 'Simple
        melody for the organ', described as being 'from an unpublished ms by
        Samuel Wesley formerly in the possession of Miss Ogle of Bath'.

653   **Aria** [G]   [1823]
ms   *BL Add 35007 f 49 (EW, dated 1823)*
rmk   'Aria, poco vivace.' A longer version of 654.

654   **Arietta** [G]   1792
ms   BL Add 71107 f 95 (dated 20/3/1792), *BL Add 65497 f 16 (VN), RCM
        4038 f 115 (Marianne Merewether)*
rmk   653 is a longer version of this work.

655   **Diapason Melody** [F]
pr   In VN, *Short Melodies for the Organ* [1848–1858], p. 159, 'from the
        original ms in the editor's possession'.

656   **Diapason Movement** [C]
ms   BL Add 35007 f 56
ed   Robin Langley, *14 Short Pieces* (Oxford, 1981), p 1; Gwilym Beechey,
        Three Short Pieces (Ely, 1996), p 2.

657 Diapason Movement [D]   1797
ms   BL Add 35007 f 83 (dated 6/9/1797)
ed   Robin Langley, *14 Short Pieces* (Oxford, 1981), p 7; Gwilym Beechey,
       Three Short Pieces (Ely, 1996), p 3.

658 Diapason Movement [D]   [1836?][18]
ms   BL Add 35007 f 54
ed   Robin Langley, *14 Short Pieces* (Oxford, 1981), p 6.

659 Diapason Movement [D]   *[1836?][19]*
ms   BL Add 35007 f 55

660 Diapason Movement [D]   [1836?][20]
ms   BL Add 35007 f 57
rmk 'Slow.' In 3/2 time.

661 Diapason Movement [D]   [1836?][21]
ms   BL Add 35007 f 57ᵛ
rmk Fugal, in 4/4 time. Possibly a continuation of 661.

662 Diapason Movement [D]   1836
ms   BL Add 35007 f 60ᵛ (dated 1836)

663 Diapason Movement [F]   [1836?][22]
ms   BL Add 35007 f 59
rmk 'Cheerful.' In 6/8 time, incorporating a fugue.

---

[18] Date proposed from Diapason Movement [D], work 662, which is dated 1836 and is located near this diapason movement in BL Add 35007.

[19] Date proposed from Diapason Movement [D], work 662, which is dated 1836 and is located near this diapason movement in BL Add 35007.

[20] Date proposed from Diapason Movement [D], work 662, which is dated 1836 and is located near this diapason movement in BL Add 35007.

[21] Date proposed from Diapason Movement [D], work 662, which is dated 1836 and is located near this diapason movement in BL Add 35007.

[22] Date proposed from Diapason Movement [D], work 662, which is dated 1836 and is located near this diapason movement in BL Add 35007.

664   Diapason Movement [A]   [1836?]²³
ms   BL Add 35007 f 53

665   Diapason Piece [C]
pr   In VN, *Short Melodies for the Organ* [1848–1858], p. 176, from SW's
          'original manuscript'.

666   Diapason Piece [G]
pr   In VN, *Short Melodies for the Organ* [1848–1858], p. 162, 'from an
          original unpublished manuscript'.

667   Duets [D, G, F, A, G, B♭, A, G, 'for Eliza Wesley']   [c1830]
ms   BL Add 35007 f 1–19 (the last duet incomplete; annotated by EW in
          1895 'composed for me & I used to play them with my dear father
          when a little girl')
ed   Nos. 3, 6 and 8 in *Robin Langley, English Organ Music: The Duet
          Repertory 1530–1830* (London, 1988).
rmk   ♫

668   Effusion [G minor]
ms   *BL Add 65497 f 1 (VN)*

669   Introduction to *J. S. Bach, Fugue* [E♭] (*'St Anne'*)   [1814]
ms   BL Add 14344 f 53 (with information about the first performance noted
          by VN), BL Add 14340 f 58, *RCM 640 (Charles Smith), RCM 1151 (J.
          W. Windsor), RCM 4029*
rmk   Organ duet. First performance by SW and VN at Foundling Hospital
          Chapel, 15/6/1814.²⁴ ♫

---

²³ Date proposed from Diapason Movement [D], work 662, which is dated 1836
and is located near this diapason movement in BL Add 35007.

²⁴ On this occasion SW and VN also played VN's arrangement of JSB's 'St
Anne' fugue [BWV 552] for organ duet. SW's copy of this arrangement is at BL
Add 14344 f 55.

670 **Larghetto** [B♭] ('Scraps for the Organ, no. 2')   [≤1808]
ms   RCM 4021 f 13, *RCM 1151 f 46 (J. W. Windsor, compiled in 1808, this work designated as 'Scraps for the Organ')*
pr   In VN, *Short Melodies for the Organ* [1848–1858], p 227, as 'A Melody for the Organ: Smoothly-flowing Style'.
ed   Robin Langley, *14 Short Pieces* (Oxford, 1981), p 8.

671 **Lento** [F]   1810
ms   RCM 4021 f 15^v (dated 1810), Gloucester Acc. 15019
ed   Robin Langley, *English Organ Music: An Anthology* v 6 p 49 (London, 1988).
rmk   The two mss vary slightly.

672 **Melody** [C♯ minor]   1826
ms   BL Add 31239 f 23 (dated 1/8/1826)
ed   Robin Langley, *14 Short Pieces* (Oxford, 1981), p 3.
rmk   An expanded version in C minor constitutes the arietta of 606.

673 **Melody** [D] 'for M. B.'[25]   *Doubtful*[26]
ms   Private UK collection
ed   Robin Langley, *English Organ Music: An Anthology* v 6 p 50 (London, 1988).

674 **Movement** [C]   [>1829][27]
ms   RCM 4025 f 65 (untitled)

675 **Movements** [D, D minor, B minor]   [1774–1775]
ms   BL Add 34998 (SW's 'pasticcio book, 1774–1775') f 25
rmk   For the cornet stop of the organ.

---

[25] 'M. B.' conceivably refers to SW's pupil Mary Beardmore. *See* SW→CW Jr, 15/1/1807; SW→SGW, 15/1/1807; SW→Mary Beardmore, 7/7/1808, 31/8/1809.

[26] According to Robin Langley's edition.

[27] Dating range proposed from other similar works in ms.

676   Movements [D]   [1774–1775]
ms   BL Add 34998 (SW's 'pasticcio book, 1774–1775') f 19
rmk   Adagio, Moderato, Pomposo.

677   Pastoral Melody [D]   [1831]
pr   In VN, *Short Melodies for the Organ* [1848–1858], p 172, from SW's
          manuscript dated 28/11/1831.

Scraps for the Organ → 650, 652, 670 and 679

678   Variations [B♭]   1817
ms   BL Add 34089 (dated 1/12/1817), BL Add 69859 f 28ᵛ (VN, entitled
          'Variations on "God save the Queen"')

679   Vivace [E♭] ('Scraps for the Organ, no. 4')   [≤1808]
ms   RCM 4021 f 14, *RCM 1151 f 46ᵛ (J. W. Windsor, compiled in 1808, this
          work marked 'Allegretto cantabile' and designated as 'Scraps for the
          Organ')*
pr   In VN, *Short Melodies for the Organ* [1848–1858], p 237, described as
          'A continuous melody from an unpublished manuscript'.
ed   Robin Langley, *14 Short Pieces* (Oxford, 1981), p 9.
rmk   ♫

HARPSICHORD AND PIANOFORTE MUSIC

1. Works Printed before 1839

A. Sonatas and Sonatinas (in chronological order)

701   **Eight Sonatas** [B♭, D, F, C, A, E, G, E♭] [op. 1]   [1777?]
pr   *Eight Sonatas for the Harpsichord or Pianoforte.* (London, SW, Chesterfield St, [late 1777].[1]) RISM W920. *Facs* (of no. 7) *LPS* 51.
rmk   Dedicated to Daines Barrington. *See* Tryphena Bathurst→SW, 26/1/1778?, Philip Hayes→CW, 15/6/1778.

702   **Three Sonatas** [C, F, D], op. 3   [<5/1789][2]
pr   *Three Sonatas for the Piano Forte, Op. 3.* (London, SW, Chesterfield St.) RISM W922. Facs LPS 57.
rmk   Dedicated to Miss Mary Grignon.

703   **Twelve Sonatinas** [C, F, D, B♭, D, A, E♭, B♭, F, G,   [1798]
       G minor, E♭], op. 4
ms   BL Add 35007 f 91 (copy of no. 8, wmk 1834)
pr   *Twelve Sonatinas for the Piano Forte or Harpsichord, with the proper Fingering marked...Op. 4.* (London, SW; sold by Robert Birchall, 133 New Bond Street, [1799].[3]) RISM W923.
ed   Timothy Roberts (London, 1984)

---

[1] This publication date is substantiated in the note to Tryphena Bathurst→SW, 26/1/1778?.

[2] The printed title-page says work sold at Birchall and Andrews' Music Shop, 129 New Bond Street. Birchall and Andrews were in partnership from 1783 to May 1789 (*H&S*).

[3] SW→Latrobe, about 28/2/1799, states that this work is 'newly published'.

704   **Four Sonatas** [A, B♭, D, E♭] **and Two Duets** [F, D],   [*c*1801]
       op. 5
pr   *Four Sonatas and Two Duets, for the Piano Forte Op. 5.* (London, L.
       Lavenu, 29 New Bond Street, for the author, [1801].) BL copy wmk
       1801. Reviewed *MM* v 11 (1801) p 536.
rmk   Dedicated to 'the Honourable Miss Lambs'. Presumably *MW list* 52,
       described as 'Three Sonatas dedicated to the Hon. Misses Lamb'.

705   **Sonata** [D minor]   [*c*1808]
pr   *A Sonata for the Piano Forte, in which is introduced a Fugue from a
       Subject of Mr Salomon.* (London, R. Birchall.) Facs LPS 85. Reviewed
       MM, June 1808 p 341. In EW, *A Selection of Pianoforte Works* [c1880].
rmk   Dedicated to Charlotte Augusta Oom. *MW list* 51.

706   **The Siege of Badajoz**   [1812]
pr   *The Siege of Badajoz, a Characteristic Sonata for the Piano Forte.*
       (London, Preston, [1812].) Reviewed *GM* v 83 part 1 (January 1813)
       p 60.
rmk   *MW list* 53. Celebrates the British siege and eventual capture on
       6/4/1812 of the town of Badajoz, Spain.[4] *See* SW→VN, 6/5/1812.

707   **Sonatina** [ded. Miss Meaking]
pr   London, Goulding.[5] No copies located.
rmk   *MW list* 52. Possibly the Sonatina [C], work 754.

---

[4] The last movement, entitled 'Lord Wellington's March', honours SW's distant
relative Arthur Wesley [1769–1852, from 1798 Wellesley], commander of the
British forces in Portugal and Spain, who had been created Earl Wellington on
28/2/1812.

[5] The Goulding firm, variously styled, published music during the years 1786–
1834 *(H&S)*.

B. VARIATIONS

708   The Bay of Biscay   [1812?]

pr   *Nine Variations on the favorite Air of the Bay of Biscay.* (London, Clementi, Banger, Collard, Davis & Collard, [late 1812 or early 1813].) Reviewed *MM*, February 1813, p 69. Subsequently published by Monro & May.

rmk   Dedicated to Muzio Clementi. *See* SW→Muzio Clementi?, 6/1/1813.

709   The Favorite Duet in *La Cosa Rara*   [1789][6]

pr   *The Favorite Duett in the Opera of La Cosa Rara, varied & adapted for the Piano Forte.* (London, Birchall & Andrews, [1789].) RISM W927.

rmk   An arrangement of 'Pace, caro mio sposa' from *Una cosa rara* (Vienna, 1786) by Vicente Martín y Soler [1754–1806]. Presumably the composition listed in *Jacobs* p 56 as 'Du. in La Cora Rasu, in C. (Birchall)'. Reviewed *Analytical Review* v 2 (February 1789) p 237.

710   A Favorite Italian Air   [c1827]

ms   MA MAM P12C, BL Add 35007 f 107 (last variation only), *BL Add 35007 f 103 (EW)*

pr   *Variations for the Piano Forte on a Favorite Italian Air.* (London, Mori & Lavenu, plate no. 2236, [1827].)

rmk   *MW list* 75. Dedicated to the Rev. Robert Nares.

711   The Hornpipe and Variations from a favorite   [1820]
Organ Concerto

pr   *The Hornpipe and Variations* [the last movement] *from a Favorite Organ Concerto* [SW's Organ Concerto [D], work 414], *Performed with Great Applause at the Oratorios at the Theatre Royal, Covent Garden, Arranged with a new Introduction for the Piano Forte.* (London, Royal Harmonic Institution, plate no. 600, [1820], ESH 11/1/1821.)

rmk   *MW list* 45.

---

[6] Presumably composed after the first London performance of *Una cosa rara* on 10/1/1789.

712   **Jessy of Dunblaine**   [*c*1830–1834][7]
ms   RSCM, RCM 4025 f 88
pr   *Variations on Jessy of Dunblaine.* (London, J. A. Novello, *c*1837.)
        Advertised as 'in the press' on wrapper of 13/10/1837 *MW*. No copies
        located. *See* SW→Joseph Alfred Novello, undated, 7/1830–1834.

713   **Patty Kavanagh**
pr   *The Favourite Ballad of Patty Kavanagh.* (London, W. Hodsoll,
        [<1831].) Subsequently published by Zenas T. Purday.
rmk   *MW list* 64.

714   **A Polish Air**   [*c*1806]
pr   *A favorite popular Polish Air, with New Variations.* (London, Birchall,
        [*c*1806].) Reviewed *MM* v 21 (4/1806) p 256.
rmk   *MW list* 57. Dedicated to Georgiana Russell, Duchess of Bedford. *See*
        SW→Robert Birchall, undated, 1806–13/1/1810.

715   **Scots wha hae wi' Wallace bled**   [*c*1824]
pr   *Scots wha hae wi' Wallace Bled, A Scotch Air, with Variations for the
        Piano.* (London, Birchall & Co., plate no. 1612, [1824], ESH 9/7/1824.)
rmk   *MW list* 59.

716   **Sweet Enslaver**   [1816?]
pr   *Sweet Enslaver, a favorite Vocal Round of the late L. Atterbury, with
        Variations for the Piano Forte and an Accompaniment for a Flute or
        Violin (ad lib).* (London, C. Guichard, ESH 20/8/1816.)
rmk   On a round by Luffman Atterbury [*c*1740–1796].

C. RONDOS

717   **Bellissima Signora**   [<1819]
pr   *Bellissima Signora, A favorite Song Composed by M. P. King,
        Arranged as a Rondo.* (London, Phipps & Co., 25 Duke St, [1810–
        1818].)
rmk   *MW list* 66.

---

[7] SW's assignment of copyright in 'Jessy of Dunblane' to J. Alfred Novello
appeared in Sotheby catalogue 15/5/1996 lot 148, as part of a lot dated *c*1830–
1834 by the cataloguer.

718   **The Christmas Carol**   [*c*1815]

pr   *The Christmas Carol, Varied as a Rondo for the Piano-Forte.* (London, Clementi & Co., [1815].) *Facs LPS* 117. Reviewed *Repository of Arts*, 4/1815. Arr. for organ in VN, *Short Melodies for the Organ* [1848–1858] p 297. In EW, *A Selection of Pianoforte Works* [c1880].

rmk   *MW list* 58. On 'God rest you merry, gentlemen'. ♫

719   **The Deserter's Meditations**   [*c*1812]

pr   *The Deserters Meditations, A Favorite Irish Air arranged as a Rondo for the Piano Forte.* (London, Chappell & Co., [plate no. 82, 1812].) Facs LPS 111. Reviewed *MM*, 6/1812; *Repository of Arts*, 7/1812. Arr. for organ in VN, *Short Melodies for the Organ* [1848–1858] p 295.

rmk   Presumably *MW list* 65, 'Rondo on an Irish Air'. Dedicated to the Misses Harrison. *See* SW→VN, 2/7/1812.

720   **A Favorite Air by Weber**   [1824?]

pr   *A Favorite Air Composed by Carl Maria von Weber, & introduced in the Melo Drame of 'Der Freyschutz', arranged as a Rondo for the Piano Forte.* (London, Birchall & Co., plate no. 1651, [ESH 15/1/1825].)

rmk   On Weber's *Lied der Hirten* ('Wenn die Maien grün sich leidern'), op. 71 no. 5. Dedicated to Miss Burgh. *MW list* 53.

721   **A Favorite Rondo** [F]   [*c*1800]

pr   *A Favorite Rondo for the Piano Forte.* (London, L. Lavenu, 29 New Bond St, no. 61 in a series 'Le Melange'. BL copy has wmk 1800.) RISM W925.

722   **Fly not yet**   *Lost*

rmk   *MW list* 62. Described in *Jacobs* p 56 as on an Irish melody in F.

723   **I attempt from love's sickness to fly**   1830

ms   BL Add 69854 f 16 (dated 8/12/1830, includes instructions to engraver)

pr   *The favorite Air of I attempt from Love's sickness to fly: A Rondo.* (London, J. A. Novello.) Advertised on wrapper of *MW*, 13/10/1837.

rmk   On an air by Henry Purcell. Dedicated to WL. *MW list* 50.

724   Jacky Horner   [1815?]
pr   *Jacky Horner, a Favorite Air arranged as a Rondo for the Piano Forte,*
        with an Accompaniment for the Flute (ad lib). (London, Clementi &
        Co., ESH 20/7/1815.)
rmk   Dedicated to Graeff.

Kitty alone and I → 728

725   Lady Mary Douglas   [<1813]; *Lost*
pr   (London, W. Hodsoll, [<1813].) No copies located. Advertised in *A*
        Catalogue of Instrumental Music, Printed & Published by W. Hodsoll,
        at his Music Warehouse, 45, High Holborn, London, an undated
        catalogue printed in John Gildon, *The Siege of Badajos* (copy at RCM
        D553/5); as Badajoz was captured on 6/4/1812, the catalogue and hence
        this work presumably <1813.
rmk   *MW list* 67.

726   Moll Pately   [1815?]
pr   *Moll Pately, a Celebrated Dance...Arranged as a Rondo.* (London, C.
        Guichard at Bossange and Masson's [c1814–1815], for SW.) *Facs LPS*
        123. Reviewed *Repository of Arts*, v 1 (2nd series) no. 1 (1/1/1816)
        p 43.
rmk   *MW list* 56.

727   Off she goes   [<1813]
ms   *BL Add 35007 f 106ᵛ (EW, incomplete)*
pr   *Off She Goes, a Popular Air, Arranged as a Rondo.* (London, W.
        Hodsoll, [<1813].) Advertised in *A Catalogue of Instrumental Music,*
        Printed & Published by W. Hodsoll, at his Music Warehouse, 45, High
        Holborn, London, an undated catalogue printed in John Gildon, *The*
        Siege of Badajos (copy at RCM D553/5); as Badajoz was captured on
        6/4/1812, the catalogue and hence this work presumably <1813.
rmk   *MW list* 61.

728   An Old English Air   1830

ms   BL Add 69854 f 20 (dated 4/3/1830, includes instructions to engraver)

pr   *An Old English Air arranged as a Rondo* (dated 4/3/1830, the air
        identified as 'Kitty alone and I'). (London, J. Alfred Novello, 67 Frith
        Street, [1830–1834].) *Facs LPS* 142. [The title-page of the BL copy,
        facs LPS 141, reads: *A Rondo, for the Piano Forte, Composed &
        Inscribed to Jos*[h] *Street, Esq*[r] and notes that J. Alfred Novello also sells,
        apparently as a separate work, SW's *An English Air, arranged as a
        Rondo, for the Piano Forte.*[8]]

rmk   *MW list* 49, as 'Rondo on an old English Air, dedicated to Mr Street'.

729   Old Towler   [1794?]

pr   *Old Towler a Celebrated Air...Arranged as a Rondo, for the Piano
        Forte.* (London, Preston, 97 Strand, [1794?].)

rmk   Air by William Shield, first performed at Covent Garden on 24/1/1794.
        Dedicated to Miss Wyndham. *MW list* 60. *See* CW Jr→John Preston,
        undated, 2/1794–1797.

730   Orphan Mary [B♭]   *Lost*

pr   (London, Hodsoll) according to *Jacobs* p 56. No copies located.

rmk   *MW list* 63.

731   Polacca [G]   [*c*1830]

ms   BL Add 69854 f 24 'del Signor Pastorelli'[9] (with instructions to
        engraver)

pr   (London, J. A. Novello) as *Pastorelli's Polacca in G, Rondo*, according
        to *Jacobs* p 55. No copies located. In EW, *A Selection of Pianoforte
        Works* [*c*1880].

[8] No such separate work has been located. The apparent incompatibility of this
title-page with the music that follows it remains to be explained.

[9] SW apparently used 'Pastorelli' as a pseudonym.

732   **The Widow Waddle**   [*c*1808]
ms   BL Add 35006 f 35ᵛ
pr   *The Popular Air of the Widow Waddle, composed by Mr Reeve,*
      arranged as a Rondo, & inscribed to Mr Grimaldi. (London, Button &
      Whitaker, [*c*1808].) *Facs LPS* 105. Subsequently published *c*1827 by
      Paine and Hopkins.
rmk On the song (published on 12/10/1807) 'Mrs Waddle was a widow'
      from *The Cassowar* composed by William Reeve [1757–1815] and
      sung by Joseph Grimaldi, the dedicatee. *MW list* 55.

733   **Will Putty**   [*c*1809]
pr   *The favourite Air of Will: Putty, composed by Mr Reeve. Arranged as a*
      Rondo, and inscribed to the Composer. (London, printed without a
      publisher's name.) BL copy wmk 1809, with autograph inscription from
      SW to BJ dated '2 September'. RISM W936. *Facs LPS* 97.
rmk On William Reeve's song 'Will Putty was a glazier bold' from the
      pantomime *Thirty Thousand; or Harlequin's Lottery*, performed in
      April 1808. *MW list* 54.

D. MISCELLANEOUS COMPOSITIONS, INCLUDING DUETS

734   **The Cobourg Waltz**   [1816]
pr   *The Cobourg Waltz, for the Piano Forte.* (London, C. Guichard, ESH
      19/8/1816.)
rmk Marks the 2/5/1816 marriage of Princess Charlotte to Leopold of Saxe-
      Coburg-Saalfeld.

Duet in *La Cora Rasu* → 709

735   **An Exercise consisting of Prelude and Air**   [*c*1811]
pr   *An Exercise Consisting of Prelude and Air, with variations...for the*
      Piano Forte. In William Seaman Stevens, *A Treatise on Piano-forte*
      Expression...to which is added, An Exercise, Composed Expressly for
      this Work, by Mr Samuel Wesley. (London, M. Jones, 1811.) Reviewed
      GM vol. 84 part 1 (May 1814) p 483.
rmk *See* William Seaman Stevens→SW, undated, 1811.

736   **Fugue** [D] [ded. John Bernard Logier]   1825
ms   Private UK collection (dated 1825)
pr   *A Fugue for the Piano Forte.* (London and Dublin, I. Willis and Co., plate no. 'Royal Musical Repository 444', [1828].) *Facs LPS* 133.
rmk   *MW list* 51.

737   **Grand Coronation March** [D]   [1837]
pr   *Grand Coronation March, for the Piano Forte.* (London, Willis & Co., plate no. 'Royal Musical Repository 1674', [1837–1838].[10])
rmk   An arrangement of the march from the overture to 'Begin the noble song' (work 207).

Grand Duet → 604

738   **Introduction and Air** [ded. Mrs Stirling]   [*c*1827]; *Lost*
pr   London, I. Willis & Co., *c*1828. No copies located. Advertised on the title-pages of works 736 and 625, both published by Willis in 1828.
rmk   *MW list* 52. Dedicatee presumably the 'Mrs Stirling of Brighton' to whom SW dedicated work 121, dated 25/10/1827.

739   **Introduction and Waltz** [D]
ms   RCM 4028 f 72 (with instructions to engraver)
pr   *Introduction and Waltz.* (London, [George Alexander] Lee and Lee, [*c*1828–1834].) No copies located.[11]
rmk   *MW list* 68.

740   **An Italian Rondeau**   [1783?]; *Lost*
rmk   *See* Gasparo Pacchierotti→SW, 6/1783.

741   **Lunardi's March**   [1784?]; *Lost*
rmk   Probably relating to the first hydrogen balloon ascent in England by Vincenzo Lunardi on 15/9/1784.

---

[10] Victoria acceded to the throne on 20/6/1837. Her coronation, on 28/6/1838, followed SW's death.

[11] SW's correction of proofs for the Lees is mentioned in SW→SS, 11/10/1829.

742 **March** [D]   [1824?]
pr   No. 55 in *Collection of Duetts for Two Performers on One Piano Forte*
       (London, W. Hodsoll, [ESH 18/2/1825]).
ed   Basil Ramsey, *March for Piano Duet* (London, 1958)

743 **The Sky Rocket**   [1814]
prs *The Sky Rocket A New Jubilee Waltz for the Piano Forte.* (London, W.
       Hodsoll, [ESH 1/8/1814].) Reviewed *GM* v 84 part 2 (9/1814) p 260;
       Repository of Arts (2/1815).
rmk *MW list* 69. Dedicated to William Congreve, inventor of the Congreve
       rocket.

2. WORKS NOT PRINTED BEFORE 1839

A. LESSONS, SONATAS AND SONATINAS (IN CHRONOLOGICAL ORDER)

744 **Two Lessons** [D, G]   1774
ms   BL Add 34998 f 49 (dated 1774)

745 **Sonata** [G]   [1774–1775]
ms   BL Add 34998 (SW's 'pasticcio book, 1774–1775') f 15ᵛ (Allegro
       movement, incomplete)

746 **Sonata** [B♭]   [1774–1775]
ms   BL Add 34998 (SW's 'pasticcio book, 1774–1775') f 23 (one
       movement in B♭, the others in G; incomplete)

747 **Sonata** [B♭ and F]   [1774–1775]
ms   BL Add 34998 (SW's 'pasticcio book, 1774–1775') f 23 (one
       movement in B♭, the other in F)

748 **Sonata** [B♭]   [1774–1775]
ms   BL Add 34998 (SW's 'pasticcio book, 1774–1775') f 55ᵛ (in two
       movements)

749	**Sonata** [G]	[1774–1775]
ms	BL Add 34998 (SW's 'pasticcio book, 1774–1775') f 58^v	

750	**Sonata** [E♭]	1788
ms	RCM 1039 f 1^v (dated 8/11/1788)	

751	**Sonata** [B♭]	1793
ms	RCM 4018 f 1 (dated 28/1/1793)	

752	**Sonata** [A♭]	1794
ms	RCM 4018 f 7 (dated 5/10/1794)	

753	**Sonata** [C]	1813–1831
ms	BL Add 35008 f 8 (first movement dated 1813, dated 23/3/1831 at end)	
pr	EW, as 'Sonata in C (Posthumous)', in *A Selection of Pianoforte Works* [*c*1880].	

754	**Sonatina** [C]
ms	BL Add 35007 f 92
rmk	Possibly the same as work 707, described in *MW list* 52 as 'Sonatina inscribed to Miss Meaking'.

B. VARIATIONS

755	**The College Hornpipe**	[1837?]^{12}
ms	BL Add 35006 f 11^v	

756	**Le Diable en Quatre**	1801
ms	RCM 1039 f 11^v (dated 28/10/1801)	

757	**Fairest Isle** [B♭]
ms	BL Add 35008 f 20 (incomplete)
rmk	'An air [from *King Arthur* by Henry Purcell] with variations.'

---

[12] Date proposed from other works in ms.

758 **Happy were the Days** [1800–1807][13]
ms BL Add 14343 f 47, BL Add 71107 f 104[v]
rmk From a song in the 1798 opera *Ramah Droog* by Joseph Mazzinghi [1765–1844] and William Reeve.

C. RONDOS

759 **Drops of Brandy** 1837
ms BL Add 35006 f 40 (dated 20/7/1837)

760 **A Frog he would a-wooing go** [1837?][14]
ms BL Add 35006 f 14[v]

761 **The Lass of Richmond Hill** 1837
ms BL Add 35006 f 9 (noted by SW as given to EW for her 18th birthday on 6/5/1837), *BL Add 35007 f 98[v] (EW, incomplete)*
rmk 'A rondo.'

762 **Morgiana**[15]
ms BL Add 35008 f 18[v] (incomplete)

763 **Rondo [B♭]** [1774–1775]
ms BL Add 34998 (SW's 'pasticcio book, 1774–1775') f 14

764 **Rondo del Sig. R. S. Sporini** 1833
ms RCM 4025 f 86 (dated 25/10/1833)
rmk 'Sporini' was a pseudonym of SW.

---

[13] Dating range proposed from other works in BL Add 71107.

[14] Date proposed from other works in ms.

[15] In the story *The Arabian Nights* Morgiana is the faithful, clever female slave of Ali Baba.

D. MISCELLANEOUS WORKS WITH TITLE OR TEMPO INDICATION

765　　**Adagio** [E minor]　　　　　　　　　　　　　　　　[*c*1797?][16]
ms　　BL Add 35007 f 84

766　　**Air** [D]
ms　　BL Add 35006 f 6
rmk　　'Vivace moderato.' Based on the theme of the last movement of work
　　　　705.

767　　**Air** [D minor]　　　　　　　　　　　　　　　　　　1829
ms　　RCM 4028 f 65 (two copies, dated 10/7/1829), BL Add 35006 f 7ᵛ
　　　　(marked 'Con discrezione')

768　　**Air** [D minor]　　　　　　　　　　　　　　　　　[1837?][17]
ms　　BL Add 35006 f 14

769　　**Air** [E♭]
ms　　RCM 4021 f 39

770　　**Air in Tekeli** [G]　　　　　　　　　　　　　　　　　*Lost*
rmk　　Ms listed in *Jacobs* p 56. Presumably based upon an air from the 1806
　　　　melodrama *Tekeli; or, The siege of Montgatz*, the music of which was
　　　　composed by James Hook [1746–1827].

771　　**Allegro and Minuet** [D]
ms　　BL Add 35007 f 110ᵛ

772　　**Andante** [A]
ms　　BL Add 35008

773　　**Andante Grazioso** [A]
ms　　BL Add 35006 f 32, BL Add 35007 f 101 (incomplete)

---

[16] Date proposed from other adjacent works in ms.

[17] Date proposed from other works in ms.

774   Auld Robin Gray   1813
ms   Private UK collection (dated 31/7/1813, inscribed by SW to VN, and
         annotated by VN 'harmonised (and most beautifully) for me by my dear
         friend Sam Wesley'), *BL Add 65497 (VN, dated 3/1813, and noted by
         VN as 'harmonized by S. Wesley (for me)')*

775   Caprice   [1809?]
ms   Fitzwm 699 (noted by Crotch as presented to him by SW in 1809)

776   'Denmark'   [*c*1830]
ms   BL Add 35007 f 89
rmk   Based upon Martin Madan's hymn tune 'Before Jehovah's awful
         Throne' (DENMARK).

777   Diabases and Metatheses   1826
ms   BL Add 31239 f 22, 27^v, 30^v, 36^v (f 24 dated 4/8/1826)
rmk   17 'Diabases' and 2 'Metatheses': small keyboard pieces, some only
         four bars in length.

778   Divertimento [B♭]   1829
ms   MA MAM P12C (dated 1829)
rmk   In two movements: 'Lento con espressione' and 'Marcia'. Possibly *MW
         list* 54, 'Divertimento dedicated to Miss Walker'.

779   The Duke of Wellington's Return   1816
ms   BL Add 35083 f 63 (dated 4/7/1816)
ed   Jack Werner (London, 1966)

780   Fugue [G]   [*c*1836–1837][18]
ms   BL Add 35006 f 30^v

781   Gavotta [G minor]   [1818?][19]
ms   BL Add 35006 f 29, RCM 4022 f 29

---

[18] Dating range proposed from other works in ms.

[19] Date proposed because work is written in RCM 4022 on the same sheet as
work 796, which is dated 21/11/1818.

782 **March** [B♭]   [*c*1774–1778]²⁰
ms   BL Add 35006 f 6ᵛ, BL Add 35007 f 98 (annotated by EW 'composed when 8 years of age')

pr   In EW, *A Selection of Pianoforte Works* [*c*1880], no. 1, as 'A new march as perform'd upon the Parade and at St James's', with versions (i) for pf and (ii) for 2 hns, 2 obs or cls, and 2 bsns.

783 **March** [E♭]   [1837?]²¹
ms   BL Add 35006 f 7, BL Add 35007 f 97ᵛ

784 **Minuet** [F]   [1774–1775]
ms   BL Add 34998 (SW's 'pasticcio book, 1774–1775') f 61ᵛ

785 **Minuet** [G, ded. Miss Guisses]   [1774–1775]
ms   BL Add 34998 (SW's 'pasticcio book, 1774–1775') f 34ᵛ

786 **Minuet** [A minor]   1777
ms   BL Add 35007 f 67 (dated 16/9/1777, lacks beginning)

787 **Minuet** [B♭]   [1774–1775]
ms   BL Add 34998 (SW's 'pasticcio book, 1774–1775') f 79 (unfinished)

788 **Prelude** [C]   [*c*1834]
ms   BL Add 35007 f 95 (wmk 1834)

789 **Prelude** [D]   [*c*1834]
ms   BL Add 35007 f 95 (wmk 1834)

---

²⁰ In her *c*1880 edition, EW identifies this work with the march for oboes, bassoons and French horns, described in *Barrington* p 303, that SW was 'desired to compose' for 'one of the regiments of guards'. However, as Daines Barrington did not meet SW until 'the latter end of 1775, when he was nearly 10' (*ibid.* p 298), and was present with SW at the work's performance at the beginning of a 'military concert' (*ibid.* p 303), EW must have been mistaken either about this work's date of composition or its identity with the march described by Barrington. Another SW march for wind band, explicitly dated 24/6/1777, about the time of Barrington's reference, is extant (work 534).

²¹ Date proposed from other works in BL Add 35007.

790   Prelude [D]   [1836]
ms   *BL Add 35007 f 96 (EW, dated 1836)*

791   Prelude [G]   [c1834]
ms   BL Add 35007 f 95 (wmk 1834)

792   Prelude [A]   [c1834]
ms   BL Add 35007 f 95ᵛ (wmk 1834)

793   Presto [E♭]   [c1800–1807][22]
ms   BL Add 35006 f 8, BL Add 71107 f 97,) *BL Add 35007 f 96ᵛ (EW), BL*
        Add 65497 f 17 (VN), RCM 4038 f 57ᵛ (Marianne Merewether)

794   Quickstep [C]
ms   RCM 4025 f 94

795   Sarabande [G]   [c1801]
ms   BL Add 35007 f 86 (wmk 1801, incomplete)

796   Tempo de Walcia [D]   1818
ms   BL Add 31239 f 32ᵛ, RCM 4022 f 29ᵛ (dated 21/11/1818)

797   Tune [A]   1825
ms   BL Add 31239 f 15ᵛ (dated 10/6/1825)

798   Tune [A]   1828
ms   RCM 2141b f 45 (dated 1828)

799   Two War Songs: 'Amsterdam' and   1814
        'The Cry to Arms'
ms   BL Add 35008 f 17 (dated 28/3/1814)

---

[22] Dating range proposed from other works in BL Add 71107.

800 **Waltz** [D] [*c*1800–1807][23]
ms BL Add 71107 f 95, *BL Add 35007 f 96 (EW), BL Add 65497 f 16ᵛ (VN)*

801 **Waltz** [D]
ms RCM 4025 f 95

E. MISCELLANEOUS WORKS WITH NO TITLE OR TEMPO INDICATION

802 **Movement** [C] [*c*1800]
ms BL Add 35005 f 124ᵛ

803 **Movement** [C minor] 1829
ms RCM 2141b f 45ᵛ (dated 24/6/1829)

804 **Movement** [D] 1797
ms BL Add 35007 f 83 (dated 6/9/1797)

805 **Movement** [D] [1837?][24]
ms BL Add 35006 f 8ᵛ

806 **Movement** [E♭] [*c*1812]
ms BL Add 35007 f 87 (wmk 1812, incomplete)

807 **Movement** [E] 1826
ms BL Add 31239 f 23ᵛ (dated 3/8/1826)

808 **Movement** [F] 1822
ms BL Add 35007 f 88 (dated 18/11/1822)

809 **Movement** [F]
ms BL Add 35007 f 113

---

[23] Dating range proposed from other works in BL Add 71107.

[24] Date proposed from other works in ms.

810	**Movement** [G]	[1783]
ms	BL Add 35025 f 29ᵛ	

811	**Movement** [G]	[*c*1800]
ms	*RCM 4083 f 71 (Marianne Merewether)*	
rmk	On similar material to the Finale of the Sonata [D minor], work 705.	

812	**Movement** [G]	1813
ms	RCM 4025 f 91 (dated 23/10/1813)	

813	**Movement** [G]	[*c*1827][25]
ms	RCM 2141b f 12	

814	**Movement** [G]	1816
ms	RCM 2141b f 25 (dated 15/11/1816)	

815	**Movement** [G]	1834
ms	BL Add 35038 f 64 (dated 1834)	
rmk	'For Mr Glenn' [RG, who married SW's daughter Rosalind in 1834].	

816	**Movement** [G]	[1837?][26]
ms	BL Add 35006 f 39ᵛ (incomplete)	

817	**Movement** [A♭]	
ms	MA MAM P12C	

818	**Movement** [A]	
ms	Fitzwm Henderson bequest mus. v. 15	

819	**Movement** [B♭]	[*c*1800]
ms	BL Add 35005 f 124	

---

[25] Date proposed from other works in ms.

[26] Date proposed from other works in ms.

820	**Movement** [B♭]	$[c1836–1837]^{27}$
ms	BL Add 35006 f 47^v	

821	**Movement** [B♭]	[1774–1775]
ms	BL Add 34998 (SW's 'pasticcio book, 1774–1775') f 79^v	

3. PIANO DUETS

822	**Andante** [D]	1791
ms	BL Add 35007 f 124 (dated 13/6/1791)	
rmk	'A duet.'	

823	**Duet** [G]	1832
ms	BL Add 35007 f 115 (dated 19/1/1832)	

824	**'God Save the King' with Variations** [D]	[1834]
ms	*BL Add 35007 f 119 (copy by 'F. D.',^{28} dated 9/10/1834)*	

825	**Sonata** [G]	1791
ms	BL Add 35007 f 126 (last four pages only, dated 13/6/1791), *BL Add 14344 f 25 (VN)*	
rmk	Larghetto, Allegro spiritoso, Largo, Comodo, Presto. Perhaps *MW list 52*, described as 'Sonatas for the Pianoforte *à quatre mains*'.	

---

[27] Dating range proposed from other works in ms.

[28] Perhaps Frederick Davison [organ builder, c1815–1889].

4. THREE PIANOS

826   Trio for three pianofortes   1811
ms   Private UK collection (score, dated 20/4/1811),[29] *BL Add 14334
          (score), BL Add 35008 (score, SSW),* BL Add 35007 (parts, partly SW,
          partly SSW)
rmk   *MW list* 77, as 'Concerto for 3 pianos'. First performance by Stokes,
          VN and SW at Hanover Square Rooms, 27/4/1811. *See* SW→Stokes,
          6/6/1811; SW→VN, 1/7/1814, 19/7/1814; SW→RG, 22/7/1814.

5. UNTRACED WORK

827   The Young May Moon [C]
rmk   Work, described as an 'Irish melody', listed in William Winters, *An
          Account of the Remarkable Musical Talents of Several Members of the
          Wesley Family*, London, 1874, p 91. No copies located.

---

[29] This score was sold as lot 390 of the 21/1/1978 Sotheby sale to the
antiquarian book dealer Richard Macnutt.

DEDICATEES

Samuel Wesley dedicated several of his musical compositions to performers, pupils or friends, and a few works to larger groups of people.[1] These dedicatees, briefly identified where possible, are listed here in alphabetical order, followed by the title and number of each work dedicated to them. The following list does not include handwritten inscriptions that SW penned on some copies of his printed music.

Ad Libitum Society *See* Carter

Adams, Thomas [organist and composer, 1785–1858]
Preludes and Fugues [I and II] for organ, *606–607*

Anglesey, Marquess of *See* Paget

Attwood, Thomas [composer and organist, 1765–1838]
Voluntary [B♭] for organ, *622*

Barrington, Daines [lawyer and antiquary, 1727–1800]
Eight Sonatas [op. 1] for harpsichord or pianoforte, *701*

Bedford, Duchess of *See* Russell, Georgiana

Burgh, Miss [perhaps a daughter of the Rev. Allatson Burgh][2]
A Favorite Air by Weber, rondo for pianoforte, *720*

Carter, Thomas [singer and coal merchant, 1769–1800] and the Ad Libitum Society[3]
Near Thame's fam'd banks, song, *289*

---

[1] In addition to dedicating original compositions, SW 'presented' his 1826 edition of Handel's *Three Hymns* (arrangement II of work 913) 'to the Wesleyan Society at large'. SW generally used the synonym 'inscribed' rather than the word 'dedicated' on printed title-pages.

[2] *See* SW→VN, 13/9/1824, 28/9/1824.

[3] SW's dedication reads: 'Composed for the performance of Mr Carter and for the use of the Ad Libitum Society to whom it is respectfully inscribed'.

Clementi, Muzio [composer, piano manufacturer and music publisher, 1752–1832]
The Bay of Biscay, variations for pianoforte, *708*

Congreve, William [rocket inventor, 1772–1828]
The Sky Rocket, waltz for pianoforte, *743*

Drummer, William [friend of SW]
Voluntary [D] for organ, *623*

Gauntlett, Henry John [lawyer, organist and composer, 1805–1876]
Voluntary [G] for organ, *625*

Glenn, Robert [organist, 1776–1844]
Movement [G] for pianoforte

Graeff, John George [composer and flautist, 1762?–?]
Jacky Horner, rondo for pianoforte, *724*

Grignon, Mary
Three Sonatas [op. 3] for pianoforte, *702*

Grimaldi, Joseph [dancer, actor and singer, 1778–1837]
The Widow Waddle, rondo for pianoforte, *732*

Guisses, Miss[4]
Minuet [G] for harpsichord or pianoforte, *785*

Gwilt, Joseph [architect and musician, 1784–1863]
O sing unto mie roundelaie, madrigal, *233*

Harding, John [medical doctor of Kentish Town][5]
Three Voluntaries [1st and 2nd sets] for organ, *615–616*

Harrison, Misses
The Deserters Meditations, rondo for pianoforte, *719*

---

[4] This name may refer to two or more persons [not identified] named Miss Guisse.

[5] Harding appears in the calendar of correspondence several times, from John Harding→Sarah, 16/1/1822, to SW→Sarah, 8/1/1827.

Howell, Mark
What folly it is, song, *313*

Jackson, Thomas [Methodist minister and editor, 1783–1873]
All go unto one place, anthem, *77*

Lamb, the Honourable Misses [Emily Mary Lamb, 1787–1869, later Lady
    Cowper; and Harriet Anne Lamb, 1789–1803][6]
Four Sonatas and Two Duets [op. 5] for pianoforte, 704

Linley, William [author and composer, 1771–1835]
I attempt from love's sickness to fly, rondo for pianoforte, *723*
Voluntary [G minor] for organ, 624

Logier, John Bernard [music educator, 1777–1846]
Fugue [D] for pianoforte, 736

Marshall, Frederick [composer, 1790?–1857]
Grand Duett [I] [C] for pianoforte or organ, 604

Meaking, Miss
Sonatina for pianoforte, 707

Moore, Thomas [poet, 1779–1852]
When Bacchus, Jove's immortal boy, glee, *248*

Nares, Robert [editor, librarian and archdeacon, 1753–1829]
A Favorite Italian Air, variations for pianoforte, *710*

Oom, Charlotte Augusta [educator of ladies, 1783–1854][7]
Sonata [D minor] for pianoforte, 705

'Organists in general'
Twelve Short Pieces with a Full Voluntary Added for organ; later rededicated to
    'Performers on the Seraphine and Organists in general', *617*

---

[6] Identified from a comment in SW's *Reminiscences* in which he lists amongst
his pupils 'the Miss Lambs, daughters of Lord Viscount Melbourne', i.e., of
Peniston Lamb, 1st Viscount Melbourne, 1774/5–1828.

[7] In *Court and Private Life in the Time of Queen Charlotte: being the Journals
of Mrs Papendiek* (London, 1887, v 2 p 301), Augusta Delves Broughton
described her aunt Mrs Oom, who was Mrs Papendiek's eldest daughter, as 'a
musician of more than the usual calibre of an amateur'.

Paget, Henry William [1st Marquess of Anglesey, 1768–1854]
As on fam'd Waterloo the lab'ring swain, song, *264*

'Performers on the Seraphine' *See* 'organists in general'

Reeve, William [composer, 1757–1815]
Will Putty, rondo for pianoforte, *733*

Rudall, George [flute maker, 1781–1871]
Trio for pianoforte and two flutes, *514*

Russell, Georgiana, [1781–1853, 2nd wife of the 6th Duke of Bedford]
A Polish Air, variations for pianoforte, *714*

Russell, William [musician, 1755–1839][8]
Three movements for two violins and bass, *512*

Salomon, Johann Peter [violinist and concert promoter, 1745–1815]
Sonata [F] for violin and pianoforte, *508*

Stirling, Mrs [of Brighton][9]
Awake my glory, harp and lute, hymn, *121*
Introduction and Air for piano, *738*

Stotherd, Miss
O Delia, ev'ry charm is thine, glee, *229*

Street, Joseph Payne [?–<1852, secretary of the Madrigal Society]
An Old English Air, rondo for pianoforte, *728*

'The public'
Two Sonatas [op. 2] for violin and keyboard, *508*

Walker, Miss
possibly *Divertimento [B♭]* for piano, *778*

---

[8] This William Russell was the son of John Russell, SW's host at Guildford in 1776. *See* Sarah→SGW, 30/6/1776; CW→William Russell, 21/12/1778 and 24/2/1783.

[9] SW presumably met Mrs Stirling during his October 1827 trip to Brighton.

Wesley, Eliza
Organ Duets [D, G, F, A, G, B♭, A, G], *667*

Wyndham, Miss[10]
Old Towler, rondo for pianoforte, *729*

---

[10] As *Old Towler* was dedicated to Miss Wyndham about the year 1794, she presumably was not, but perhaps was related to, the Miss Wyndham whom SW began to instruct in 1806 (*see* SW→SGW, 12/1806).

DISCOGRAPHY

The following discography lists all known commercial recordings of Samuel Wesley's musical works, in the same numbered order as the list of these works. In addition, three barrels containing music by other composers that SW arranged for a barrel organ are extant: see the note to SW→Walter McGeough, 11/11/1822, in the calendar of correspondence.

SACRED VOCAL MUSIC: LATIN TEXT

16b   Ave Regina Cælorum [II]
Choir of Gonville and Caius College, Cambridge, Geoffrey Webber
    (ASV GAU 157, 1996)

22   De profundis clamavi ('Si inquitates observaveris')
Choir of Grace Cathedral, San Francisco, John Fenstermaker (Gothic G49098, 1998)
Gentlemen of Durham Cathedral, James Lancelot (Priory PRCD 625, 1998)

26   Dixit Dominus [II]
Choir of Gonville and Caius College, Cambridge, Geoffrey Webber
    (ASV GAU 157, 1996)

28a   Domine salvam fac reginam nostram Mariam
Choir of Gonville and Caius College, Cambridge, Geoffrey Webber
    Christopher Monks (organ) (ASV GAU 157, 1996)

33   Ecce panis angelorum
Choir of Gonville and Caius College, Cambridge, Geoffrey Webber
    (ASV GAU 157, 1996)

36   Exultate Deo
Choir of Ely Cathedral, Arthur Wills (Hyperion A 66012, 1980)

43   In exitu Israel
Choir of York Minster, Francis Jackson (LPB 793, 1978)
Choir of Christ Church Cathedral, Oxford, Christopher Grier (ALH 919, 1982)
Choir of St Paul's Cathedral, John Scott (Hyperion CDA 66618, 1993)
Choir of Gonville and Caius College, Cambridge, Geoffrey Webber
    (ASV GAU 157, 1996)

49   Magnificat Anima Mea [I]
Choir of Gonville and Caius College, Cambridge, Geoffrey Webber
   (ASV GAU 157, 1996)

54   Omnia Vanitas (Carmen Funebre)
Choir of Gonville and Caius College, Cambridge, Geoffrey Webber
   (ASV GAU 157, 1996)

55   Ostende nobis, Domine
Choir of Gonville and Caius College, Cambridge, Geoffrey Webber
   (ASV GAU 157, 1996)

Si inquitates observaveris → 22

68   Tu es sacerdos [I]
Choir of Ely Cathedral, Arthur Wills
   (Meridian E 77089, 1985, reissued as Meridian CDE 84276, 1995)

69   Tu es sacerdos [II]
Choir of Gonville and Caius College, Cambridge, Geoffrey Webber
   (ASV GAU 157, 1996)

SACRED VOCAL MUSIC: ENGLISH TEXT

71.2   Jubilate [F] (from Morning and Evening Service)
Choir of Gonville and Caius College, Cambridge, Geoffrey Webber
   (ASV GAU 157, 1996)

71.6   Nunc Dimittis [F] (from Morning and Evening Service)
Choir of Gonville and Caius College, Cambridge, Geoffrey Webber
   (ASV GAU 157, 1996)

80   Behold, how good and joyful [II]
Choir of Rochester Cathedral, Barry Ferguson (APR 302S, 1979)

101   O Lord God most Holy
Choir of Gonville and Caius College, Cambridge, Geoffrey Webber
   (ASV GAU 157, 1996)

139   Might I in Thy sight appear
Frances Cary, Andrew Arthur (ASV GAU 157, 1996)
Patrick McCarthy, Timothy Roberts (Hyperion CDA 67020, 1998)

Secular Vocal Music

233 **O sing unto mie roundelaie**
Invocation vocal ensemble (Hyperion CDA 66740, 1994)
Canzonetta vocal ensemble (SOMM SOM CD 204, 1995)

Orchestral Music

404 **Sinfonia Obligato**
London Mozart Players, Matthias Bamert (Chandos 9823, 2000)

406 **Symphony** [A]
European Community Chamber Orchestra, Jorg Faerber
 (Hyperion CDA 66156, 1985)
Milton Keynes Chamber Orchestra, Hilary Davan Wetton
 (Unicorn-Kanchana DKP 9098, 1991)
London Mozart Players, Matthias Bamert (Chandos 9823, 2000)

407 **Symphony** [D]
Bournemouth Sinfonietta, Kenneth Montgomery (EMI CSD 3767, 1976)
Milton Keynes Chamber Orchestra, Hilary Davan Wetton
 (Unicorn-Kanchana DKP 9098, 1991)
London Mozart Players, Matthias Bamert (Chandos 9823, 2000)

408 **Symphony** [E♭]
Milton Keynes Chamber Orchestra, Hilary Davan Wetton
 (Unicorn-Kanchana DKP 9098, 1991)
London Mozart Players, Matthias Bamert (Chandos 9823, 2000)

409 **Symphony** [B♭]
Milton Keynes Chamber Orchestra, Hilary Davan Wetton
 (Unicorn-Kanchana DKP 9098, 1991)
London Mozart Players, Matthias Bamert (Chandos 9823, 2000)

420 **Violin Concerto** [D]
Elizabeth Wallfisch, Parley of Instruments, Peter Holman
 (Hyperion CDA 66865, 1996)

Chamber Music

514 **Trio for pianoforte and two flutes** [F]
Anthony Robb, Janet Larsson, Richard Shaw (KLT 004, 1994)

524   **String Quartet** [E♭]
Salomon Quartet (Hyperion CDA 66780, 1995)
Bochmann Quartet (Redcliffe Recordings RR 013, 1997)

ORGAN MUSIC

602   **Fantasy** [F]
Christopher Dearnley (Move MD 3166, 1996)

604   **Grand Duet [I]** [C]
Hans Fagius and David Sanger (BIS 273, 1984)
Trevor Pinnock and Simon Preston (Archiv 415675, 1986)
Istvan Ella and Janos Sebestyen (Hungaroton 31464, 1993) (fugue only)
Stefan-Johannes Bleicher and Mario Hospach-Martini (Orfeo C341941A, 1994)
Elizabeth Anderson and Douglas Lawrence (Move MD 3180, 1996)
Timothy and Nancy LeRoi Nickel (Arsis Audio 104, 1997)

607   **Prelude and Fugue [II]** [G]
Margaret Phillips (AERL 30, 1981) (fugue only)

617   **Twelve Short Pieces with a Full Voluntary added**[1]
8, 9: G. D. Cunningham (HMV B 3483 [1926–1937], reissued: PHICD 136, 1999)
8, 9: E. Power Biggs (Columbia MM 954 [1950–1951])
8, 9: H. Wollenreider (HMV C 4192, 1951–1952)
8, 9: Nicholas Danby (ORYX EXP5, 1968)
5, 6, 8, 9, 11, 12, 13: Hans Musch (Musical Heritage Society MHS 4382, 1981)
1–13, Full Voluntary: Gerald Gifford (Libra Realsound Cassette LRWS 130, 1984)
8, 9: John Scott (Cirrus CICD 1007, 1987; Castle DDD 96)
8, 9: Hans-Dieter Karras (Prospect 03695/00490, 1990)
9: Jennifer Bate (Unicorn-Kanchana DKP 9099, 1990)
7, 12: Jennifer Bate (Unicorn-Kanchana DKP 9096, 1990)
6, 8: Jennifer Bate (Unicorn-Kanchana DKP 9101, 1991)
6, 8: Hans van Laar (VLS Records, VLC 0392, 1991)
1–13: Margaret Phillips (York Ambisonic CD 111, 1992/1995)
8, 9: Stephen Cleobury (Belart, 4500132, 1993)
8, 9: Ian Sadler (CBC Records, MVCD 1068, 1994)
1, 8, 9, 13: Joseph Payne (Naxos 550719, 1994)
2, 9: Barbara Owen (Raven 92, 1996)
6, 8, 9, 11, 12: Hans Fagius (Bis 140, 1996)
8, 9: Christopher Monks (ASV GAU 157, 1996)

---

[1] As noted in the list of SW's compositions this work comprises 13, not 12, short pieces, followed by a voluntary.

8, 9: Stephen Cleobury (OxRecs, OXCD 61, 1996)
5, 8, 9, 11: Christopher Herrick (Hyperion 67146, 2000)

620 Variations on 'Rule Britannia'
Gerald Gifford (Libra Realsound Cassette LRWS 130, 1984)

621 Voluntaries, Op. 6
1: Gerald Gifford (Libra Realsound Cassette LRWS 130, 1984)
1: Gerald Gifford (Libra Realsound Cassette LRWS 149, 1987)
1: Jennifer Bate (Unicorn-Kanchana DKP 9096, 1990)
3: Jennifer Bate (Unicorn-Kanchana DKP 9099, 1991)
3, 10: Hilary Norris (Priory PRCD 741, 2000)
6: Jennifer Bate (Unicorn-Kanchana DKP 9101, 1991)
6: Margaret Phillips (York Ambisonic CD 111, 1992/1995)
7: Jennifer Bate (Unicorn-Kanchana DKP CD 9106, 1991)
9: Gerald Gifford (Libra Realsound Cassette LRWS 130, 1984)
9: Andrew Millington (PR 147, 1984)
9: Catherine Ennis (Gamut MW 945, 1986)
9: Jennifer Bate (Unicorn-Kanchana DKP CD 9104, 1991)
9: Margaret Irwin-Brandon (Raven 92, 1996) (fugue only)
10: Jennifer Bate (Unicorn-Kanchana DKP 9105, 1991)

622 Voluntary [B♭, ded. Attwood]
Jennifer Bate (Unicorn-Kanchana DKP 9106, 1991)

623 Voluntary [D, ded. William Drummer]
Geoffrey Webber (ASV GAU 157, 1996)

647 Air [C minor]
Gerald Gifford (Libra Realsound Cassette LRWS 130, 1984)
Christopher Dearnley (Move MD 3166, 1996)

667 Duets ['for Eliza Wesley']
3, 6: Sylvie Poirier, Philip Crozier (Amberola, 1998)

669 Introduction to J. S. Bach, Fugue [E♭] ('St Anne')
Stephen and Nicholas Cleobury (VPS 1039, 1977)

679 Vivace [E♭] ('Scraps for the Organ, no. 4')
Jennifer Bate (Hyperion CDA 66180, 1986)

Piano Music

718   **The Christmas Carol** ('God rest you merry, gentlemen')
Ian Hobson (Arabesque Z6594, 1988)
Marian Ruhl Metson (on an organ) (Raven OAR 260, 1991)
Timothy Roberts (Hyperion CDA 66924, 1996)

WESLEY'S EDITIONS AND ARRANGEMENTS

1. Works Printed before 1839
(by composer of the work arranged, and then in chronological order of printing)[1]

901   [with CFH:] **J. S. Bach, Six Organ Sonatas**   [*c*1809–1811]
       [BWV 525–530]

pr   *No. [] A Trio, Composed originally for the Organ. By John Sebastian Bach, And now Adapted for Three Hands upon the Piano Forte.* (London, nos. 1–3, 'to be had only of' CFH, 25 Queen Square, and SW, Camden Town; nos. 4–6, 'to be had of' CFH, 25 Queen Square, Birchall, New Bond Street, and [James] Ball's Piano Forte Manufactory, Duke St, Grosvenor Square.)[2]

rmk   Each trio was published singly, with its number handwritten on the title-page. *See* SW→BJ, 17/10/1808, 3/3/1809, about 15/5/1809, 29/5/1809?, 24/11/1809; SW→CFH?, 1/10/1809?. This correspondence indicates that CFH lent to SW the ms used to prepare this edition,[3] that the first trio was published about May 1809[4] and the second trio was published about September 1809. As SW's Camden Town address appears on the third trio it presumably was printed before SW left that address in January 1810. K copy of trio 6 has wmk 1811.

---

[1] SW's arrangements in VN's *The Psalmist* are entered above, work 118.

[2] The CFH/SW edition was the first publication anywhere of the entire set of trios. AFCK had published the first trio ten years earlier on plates 58–67 of his *Essay on Practical Musical Composition* (London, 1799).

[3] CFH's ms of these trios has not been located. SW's ms copy of three movements from trios BWV 526, 529 and 530, now BL Add 14330 f 120–126, presumably was written before 25/8/1811, when SW presented this manuscript to Joseph Major.

[4] The first trio appears to have been published not later than 5/5/1809: in 1926, C. W. Pearce reported that he owned a copy inscribed 'Miss Scott, May 5, 1809' (C. W. Pearce→Editor, *The Musical Times, Musical Times,* 1/6/1926, p 544).

902   [with CFH:] **J. S. Bach, 48 Preludes and**   [*c*1808–1830]
        Fugues: The Well-tempered Clavier
        [BWV 846–893]

ms   BL Add 35023 f 27 (Part 1 Prelude and Fugue [C#], BWV 848, only,
        with SW's instructions to engraver, including changes to the plates)[5]

pr   *S. Wesley and C. F. Horn's New and Correct Edition of the Preludes
        and Fugues, of John Sebastian Bach.* This work, comprising four books
        (each containing 12 preludes and fugues), appears to have been issued
        in four states during SW's lifetime. The second and third issues differ in
        musical and other details from the first issue and from each other.
        ISSUE I: *Books 1–2:* (London, 'printed for the editors' [SW and CFH]
        by R[t] Birchall, 133 New Bond Street). Book 1 published 17/9/1810.[6]
        Book 2 published between 15/1/1811 and 22/5/1811.[7] *Books 3–4:*
        (London, 'printed for the editors' [SW and CFH] by R[t] Birchall, 133
        New Bond Street, and Chappell & Co., 124 New Bond Street). Book 3
        published between 27/9/1811 and 26/12/1811.[8] Book 4 was due for
        publication in July 1813.[9] Reviewed *GM* v 83 part 1 (1/1813) p 59.[10]

---

[5] SW and CFH appear to have owned or borrowed several mss of the '48'. Two
other mss of the '48' in SW's handwriting survive: BL Add 14330 f 1–119
(SW's transcription of the entire '48' from the edition published by Nägeli in
Zürich in 1801, presumably made in 1806 from Graeff's copy of this edition),
and RCM 4021 f 5[v]–10[v], f 30[v]–38[v], which contains copies of seven fugues. A
thorough study by Dr Yo Tomita of the manuscript and printed sources of the
'48' in England at this time, to appear in Michael Kassler (ed.), *Aspects of the
English Bach Awakening* (Aldershot, 2002, forthcoming), has established that
the Wesley/Horn edition was not prepared directly from BL Add 14330. We are
grateful to Dr Tomita for sharing his extensive knowledge of this subject with
us.

[6] *Morning Chronicle*, 3/9/1810 and 18/9/1810, quoted in 'Bach's music in
England', *Musical Times* v 37 no. 644 (1/10/1896), p 656.

[7] Although the *Morning Chronicle* announced on 24/11/1810 that Book 2 was
'in the hands of the engraver, and will shortly appear' (*Musical Times, loc. cit.*),
by 15/1/1811 the proofs supplied by 'Lomax the engraver' had not yet been
examined and corrected by VN (*see* SW→SS, 9/1/1811? and 15/1/1811). Book
2 was published by 22/5/1811 (*see* SW→VN, 22/5/1811).

[8] SW→VN, 27/9/1811, states that the proofs of Book 3 were ready for
correction. In the *Quarterly Musical Register* no. 1 (1/1/1812, advertised in *The
Times* on 26/12/1811), Books 1–3 are said (p 30) to be 'already printed'.

[9] SW→BJ, 10/5/1813, states that Book 4 should appear by 1/7/1813. However,
SW→VN, 23/6/1813, indicates that the proofs had not yet been received.

[10] The *GM* review ostensibly is of all four books, although the fourth book was
not yet published when the review appeared.

ISSUE II: *Books 1–4:* (London, 'printed and sold by R^t Birchall', 133 New Bond Street, [*c*1819].) BL copy (f.11.b) wmks 1817 and 1819; changes (from Issue I) of title-page plate presumably engraved before Robert Birchall's 19/12/1819 death, as his company became known after then as Birchall & Co. or as Birchall, Lonsdale and Mills.

ISSUE III: *Books 1–4:* (London, 'printed and sold by R^t Birchall', 140 New Bond Street, [1829?].) BL copy (Hirsch iv.1588) wmks 1829 and earlier.

ISSUE IV: *Books 1–4:* (London, C. Lonsdale (late Birchall & Co.), 26 Old Bond Street, [≥1834].)

rmk   *See* SW→Graeff, 21/5/1806?; SW→CB, 12/4/1808, 5/1808?; CB→SW, 5/1808?; SW→CB, 23/6/1808, 7/7/1808; SW→BJ?, 17/9/1808; SW→BJ, 17/10/1808, 19/10/1808; SW→Crotch, 25/11/1808; BJ→John Bacon, 12/12/1808; SW→BJ, 2/3/1809; SW→CB, 4/9/1809; SW→BJ, 25/9/1809; SW→CFH?, 1/10/1809?; SW→BJ, 24/11/1809; SW→SS, 9/1/1811?, 15/1/1811, 20/1/1811; SW→VN, 22/5/1811, 27/9/1811; SW→Bridgetower, 4/9/1812; SW→Charles Butler, 7/10/1812; SW→VN, 30/3/1813; SW→BJ, 10/5/1813; SW→VN, 23/6/1813, 28/1/1814?

903   **J. S. Bach, Six Little Preludes, nos. 1–3**   [1812–1813][11]
        [BWV 933–935]

pr   *No. [I] Easy Select Pieces, of Sebastian Bach, for the use & improvement of young students, on keyed instruments with the proper fingering marked throughout by Samuel Wesley.* (London, SW, Tottenham Ct, [1812–1813].) [Copy at RCM D553/2, on which the numeral 'I' is written by hand.]

rmk   SW's source was either a manuscript [not located] or the only prior publication of this work, JSB's *Six Preludes a l'Usage des Commençants pour le Clavecin* (Leipzig, C. F. Peters (Bureau de Musique), [1802]) which, besides SW's addition of fingering, differs from SW's edition in minor ways. It is not known whether SW's apparent intention to publish the three other preludes in the set, BWV 936–938, came to fruition.

---

[11] Date proposed on the basis of SW's residence at Tottenham Ct.

904   F.-H. Barthélemon, *Jefté in Masfa*, selections

pr   *Selections from the Oratorio of Jefté in Masfa composed at Florence in the year 1776 for the Grand Duke of Tuscany by the late F. H. Barthélemon.* (London, Clementi, Collard & Collard, [1827].)

rmk   Vocal score. The 'advertisement' on p 3 of this work, by Barthélemon's daughter Cecilia Maria Henslowe, thanks (amongst others who assisted her) Crotch, SW and Attwood for 'the several arrangements' that they made in this edition.[12] Reviewed *QMMR* v 9 no. 34 (1827) p 238.

905   John Wall Callcott, The New Mariners

pr   *The Volunteers Glee for 3 Voices. A Parody upon the Words of The New Mariners...Adapted to the Original Music of Dr Callcott by Samuel Wesley.* (London, J. Dale & Son, 19 Cornhill, [c1805-1809].)

906   G. F. Handel, He gave them Hailstones for Rain (*Israel in Egypt)* [HWV 54]

pr   *Handel's grand hailstone chorus arranged for two performers on the pianoforte by Saml Wesley.* (London, Preston, [1778–1787].)

rmk   Pf duet.

907   G. F. Handel, Cherub & Seraphim *(Jephtha)* [HWV 70]

pr   *Cherub & Seraphim, a Favorite Chorus from the Oratorio of Jephtha ...arranged for two performers on the Piano Forte by S. Wesley.* (London, L. Lavenu, 26 New Bond Street, [c1805-1807?]; subsequently published by C[harles] Mitchell.)

908   G. F. Handel, From the Censer curling rise *(Solomon)* [HWV 67]

pr   *From the Censer curling rise, A Grand Chorus from the Oratorio of Solomon...arranged for two performers on the Piano Forte by Samuel Wesley.* (London, W. Mitchell, 159 New Bond Street, [c1811].) K copy wmk 1811.

---

[12] In 1807 SW had 'corrected the copyist's blunders' in another Barthélemon oratorio, *The N.ativity. See* SW→Bridgetower, 15/6/1807.

909 **G. F. Handel, Hark! 'tis the Linnet** *(Joshua)* [1823–1824]
[HWV 64]

ms RCM 4026[13]

pr *Hark! 'tis the Linnet. Air, from the Oratorio of Joshua by G. F. Handel
newly arranged by Sam¹ Wesley.* (London, Royal Harmonic Institution,
plate no. 1551, [c1823–1824].)

rmk v, pf.

G. F. Handel, Cecilia, volgi un sguardo [c1824]
[HWV 89]→ 912

910 **G. F. Handel, Love sounds th'Alarm** [c1824]
***(Acis and Galatea)* [HWV 49]**

ms RCM 4026 (bears a 4-digit number which possibly is the plate no. of an
actual or intended Royal Harmonic Institution publication [not located])

pr *Love sounds th'Alarm.* (London, Cramer, Addison & Beale, plate no.
2357, [1838]; perhaps a reprint of a not located Royal Harmonic
Institution publication.)

911 **G. F. Handel, O, Lovely Peace** *(Judas Maccabaeus)* [c1824]
[HWV 63]

pr *O Lovely peace, a Song with recitative, arranged by S Wesley.* (London,
Royal Harmonic Institution, plate no. 1635, [1824].)

rmk v, pf.

912 **G. F. Handel, 13 Celebrated Italian Duets** [c1824]

ms RCM 4026 f 74–96 (five duets), BL Add 35005 f 119, 121, 123
(fragments only)

pr *[No.] A Collection of Duets, Trios, Quartetts, &c &c...by Handel,
Steffani, Clari, Jommelli, Marcello &c &c. arranged with an
Accompaniment for the Piano Forte.* (London, Royal Harmonic
Institution, various plate nos. from 1673 to 1740, [1824–1825].)

cont No. 1: arr. (v, pf) of 'Tre amplessi innocenti' from Handel's cantata

---

[13] RCM 4026 also contains arrangements (listed below as work 924) of other
oratorio songs by Handel on which four-digit numbers have been written. These
numbers possibly are plate numbers of actual or intended Royal Harmonic
Institution publications, of which no copies have been traced. In SW→CW Jr,
6/11/1824, SW wrote that he has had 'much employment' from the Royal
Harmonic Institution, arranging 'a multitude' of oratorios and songs.

'Cecilia, volgi un sguardo' [HWV 89]. Nos. 2–12: arr. (v, pf) of nos. 1–11 of Handel's *13 Celebrated Italian Duets* (London, 1777), as follows: 'Sono liete, fortunate' [HWV 194], 'Troppo cruda, troppo fiera' [HWV 198], 'Che vai pensando, folle pensier' [HWV 184], 'Amor gioje mi porge' [HWV 180], 'Va', speme infida' [HWV 199], 'A miravi io son intento' [HWV 178], 'Quando in calma ride il mare' [HWV 191], 'Tacete, ohime, tacete' [HWV 196], 'Conservate, raddoppiate' [HWV 185], 'Tanti strali al sen mi scocchi' [HWV 197], 'Langue, geme, sospira' [HWV 188].

rmk   *See* SSW→SW, 10/9/1824, SW→VN, 13/9/1824, SW→CW Jr, 6/11/1824. Although the last ltr states that SW has almost completed arranging 13 duets, only 11 printed duets have been located. RCM 4026 also contains SW's arrangement of the 12th of the *13 Celebrated Italian Duets* ('Caro autor di mia doglia' [HWV 182]). SW's arrangement of the 13th duet ('Se tu non lasci amore' [HWV 193]) is lost.

913   **G. F. Handel, Three Hymns** [HWV 284–286]   [1826–1827]
ms   RCM 4025 f 42 (of SW's arrangement II.)
pr   SW published two arrangements of these hymns:
         I. *The Fitzwilliam Music, never published. Three Hymns, the Words by the late Revd Charles Wesley, A.M....and set to Music by George Frederick Handel, faithfully transcribed from his Autography in the Library of the Fitzwilliam Museum, Cambridge, by Samuel Wesley, and now very respectfully presented to the Wesleyan Society at large.* v, kb. (London, SW, Euston St; to be had also at the Royal Harmonic Instution, [1826].)
         II. *Handel's Three Hymns from the Fitzwilliam Library, Arranged in Score for the Convenience of Choirs, by Samuel Wesley.* SATB, org. (London, SW, Euston St, to be had also at Messrs Kershaw, City Road, Stephens, City Road, and Kershaw, Paternoster Row, [1827].)
         The first and second hymns in II. were included as GILEAD and KEDRON respectively in VN, *The Psalmist* v 3 (1839), work 118.
cont The Invitation ('Sinners obey the Gospel Word'); Desiring to love ('O Love divine how sweet thou art'); On the Resurrection ('Rejoice the Lord is King!')
ed   Donald Burrows, as 'George Frideric Handel, *The Complete Hymns & Chorales*' (London and Sevenoaks, [1988]). Includes *facs* of I. and II.
rmk   Texts by CW. Handel's autograph ms (for S, bc), from which SW made arrangement I., is now Fitzwm 262. *See* SW→SS, 13/9/1826; Sarah→John Gaulter, 25/10/1826; SW→Tooth, 31/10/1826, 8/11/1826; SW→Jackson, 8/11/1826; SW→Sarah, 13/11/1826; Sarah memorandum, about 15/11/1826; SW→John Jackson, 29/11/1826; SW→Jackson, 19/12/1826; SW→Thomas Roberts, 6/1/1827; CW Jr→Langshaw Jr, 11/1/1827?; SW→Sarah, 22/1/1827?; SW→Jackson,. 12/2/1827; SW→Thomas Roberts, 8/3/1827; SW→Jackson, 17/5/1828;

SW→'Sir', 24/3/1829; SW→Stephen Francis Rimbault, 30/3/1829. This correspondence indicates that arrangement I. was published by 29/11/1826 and arrangement II. by 8/3/1827.

914 **attr. Matthew Locke, music for Shakespeare's** [*c*1816]
    Macbeth
pr *Shakspeare's Dramatic Songs...to which are prefixed a general Introduction of the Subject and Explanatory Remarks on Each Play, by Wm Linley Esqr Together with an appendix* [to volume 2] *containing a new Arrangement of the Music of Macbeth by Mr S. Wesley.* (London, Preston, [v 2 ESH 19/6/1816].) v 2 reviewed *MM* v 70 August, September and December 1816.[14]
rmk SSB, pf. WL states ('Introduction' to v 2, p 2) that, at his suggestion, SW 'in one instance only...varied a little from the harmony which has been received as Matthew Locke's'.[15]

915 **George Frederick Pinto, Four Canzonets, etc.** [1806–1808]
pr *Four Canzonets and a Sonata in which is introduced the admired Air of 'Logie o'Buchan' with an accompaniment for the Violin, likewise a Fantasia & Sonata for the Piano Forte.* (Edinburgh and London, to be had in London from Mrs Sanders[16], [1807–1808].). BL and RCM copies wmk 1807. Reviewed *MM*, 6/1808.
rmk SW's 'advertisement' which prefaces this work describes his role as making 'a correction of the whole' manuscript which had been left unfinished when Pinto died on 23/3/1806. Joseph Wölfl also assisted this publication by adding a few 'deficient measures' [i.e., missing bars] to one of Pinto's sonatas.

916 **William Russell, *Job*** [1825–1826]
pr *Job, A Sacred Oratorio, Composed by the late William Russell... Adapted from the Original Score, for the Organ or Piano Forte by Samuel Wesley.* (London, Royal Harmonic Institution, by Welsh & Hawes, [1826].) Reviewed *The Harmonicon* v 5 (5/1827) p 87.
rmk See SW→Mary Ann Russell, 16/4/1825; SW→VN, 10/5/1825; SW→ 'The Musical Public', 8/5/1826 [the preface to the publication].

---

[14] At least some of these reviews may be by SW himself.

[15] In this publication WL also acknowledges (p 5) that 'he has for many years reaped both profit and pleasure' from SW's 'general conversation, not only on musical, but other subjects'.

[16] George Frederick Pinto's mother, for whose benefit the work was published.

917   [with VN:] **Owen Jones Williams,**   [1816–1817]
       Brenhinol Ganiadau Sion

pr   *Brenhinol ganiadau Sion, neu Gynghanedd newydd Gymraeg yn*
       cynnwys... dau gant ac unarddeg a thriugain, o dônau Palmau [sic] *a*
       Hymnau a 4 o fawlganiadau atteb-leisiol ...yn ddau lyfr... Trefnwyd i'r
       Organ neu'r Pianoforte gan S. Wesley a V. Novello [*The Royal Songs*
       of Zion, or new Welsh Harmony, containing 271 psalm and hymn tunes
       and four polyphonic anthems, in two books. Arranged for organ or
       piano by S. Wesley and V. Novello], 2 vols. (London, W. Mitchell, for
       the author [1817].)

rmk   In the preface to his *Psalmodia Cambro Britannica* (London, 1826),
       Owen Jones Williams stated that he arrived in London from Wales in
       March 1816 and, 'while in London, during a period of eight months',
       wrote *The Royal Songs of Zion* for publication 'by the late W.
       Mitchell'. According to Williams's account, Mitchell had 400 copies
       printed and sent them to Wales for sale without remunerating Williams.

2. WORKS NOT PRINTED BEFORE 1839
(BY COMPOSER OF THE WORK ARRANGED)

918   **J. C. Bach, Andantino for [Gluck's opera]** ***Orfeo***   [1832?]
ms   BL Add 69854 f 14 (dated '23 June', with annotation by VN that SW
       arranged 'this tasteful and beautiful air on purpose' for him; ms dated
       1832 by VN)

rmk   Arrangement for organ of John Christian Bach's song 'Obliar l'amato
       sposo'.[17] Perhaps the 'beautiful song' that SW had recommended in
       SW→Mary Beardmore, 7/7/1808.

---

[17] This was one of seven songs composed by J. C. Bach as an addition to the
1770 London performance of Gluck's opera *Orfeo ed Euridice* and published by
Robert Bremner in *The favourite Songs in the Opera Orfeo* (London, 1770). *See*
Charles Sanford Terry, *John Christian Bach* (London, 2nd edition, 1967),
pp 117, 234–235.

919   **J. S. Bach,** *Quodlibet* **from** *Goldberg Variations*
       [BWV 988 var. 30]
ms   GEU Wesley Coll. item 81
rmk   Arrangement for string quartet.[18] VN notes on ms that he and SW often
       played this arrangement—a 'special favourite' of SW—as an organ
       duet, with SW taking the violin parts and VN the 'viola and bass parts',
       and that SW gave him this ms 'a few years before' he died.

920   **William Byrd, Antiphons from** *Gradualia*   [1825–1826]
ms   BL Add 35001 f 86–144 (some with instructions to engraver[19])
cont   'Notum fecit Dominus' (incomplete); 'Dies sanctificatus illuxit nobis';
       'Tui sunt cœli'; 'Viderunt omnes fines terræ'; 'Hodie Christus natus
       est'; 'O admirabile commercium'; 'O magnum mysterium'; 'Ecce
       advenit Dominator'; 'Reges Tharsis et insulæ'; 'Vidimus stellam ejus';
       'Ab ortu solis'; 'Surge, illuminare Jerusalem'; 'Alleluja! cognoverunt
       discipuli'; 'Ego sum panis vivus'; 'O quam suavis est, Domine'; 'Jesu
       nostra redemptio'; 'Quia illic interrogaverunt nos'; 'Quotiescumque
       manducabitis'
rmk   Ms is SW's transcription from Fitzwm ms 114, a score written *c*1740.
       SW's proposal to publish this transcription by subscription did not
       succeed.   *See*   SW→VN,   14/9/1825;   SW→RG,   4/4/1826;
       'Jubal'→Editor, *The Harmonicon*, 20/5/1826; SW→Sarah, 14/6/1826,
       8/7/1826?;   SW→SS,   13/9/1826;   SW→'Sir',   27/10/1826;
       SW→Jackson, 19/12/1826; SW→Street, 25/5/1830.

921   **Giovanni Clari, Nel suo bel prato ameno**
ms   RCM 4026 f 64 (marked '1835', possibly the plate no. of an intended or
       actual but not located Royal Harmonic Institution publication in 1825,
       perhaps in the same series as the publication of work 912)
rmk   2 treble voices, pf.

---

[18] SW's arrangement is limited to writing out each of the parts of JSB's
Quodlibet on a separate stave.

[19] SW→Street, 25/5/1830, states that nine plates [not located] have been
engraved.

922   **William Croft, Anthem[s]**

pr   Publication of the first number of an edition by SW and John Page of anthems by William Croft and Maurice Greene was noticed in *MM* v 27 (1/2/1809) p 66. The engraver was James Balls. No copies located.

rmk   See SW→BJ, about 15/5/1809. It is not known whether any further numbers of this edition were published.

923   **Giovanni Mane Giornovichi, Violin concerto** [E]   1782

ms   BL Add 35024 f 35 (score, entitled 'Concerto Jarnoviche' by SW, dated 9/4/1782), f 52 (parts)

rmk   Vln, obs, hns, str. According to John I. Schwarz Jr, SW provided 'new accompaniments' to the solo violin part that he copied substantially from an edition of Giornovichi's concerto printed by J. J. Hummel.[20] SW's arrangement first performed at the CW Jr/SW concert on 18/4/1782, and performed again at the CW Jr/SW concert on 6/3/1783.

Maurice Greene, Anthem[s] → 922

924   **G. F. Handel, Songs from oratorios**   [*c*1824–1825]

ms   RCM 4026 f 7 (all the following songs bear four-digit numbers consistent with Royal Harmonic Institution plate nos. *c*1824–1825 and presumably were arranged for publication, perhaps in the same series as the publication of work 912, although no copies of any prints of these songs have been located)

cont   'Again to Earth' (*Judas Maccabaeus* [HWV 63]); 'And ever against' (*L'Allegro ed il Penseroso* [HWV 55]); 'As when the dove' (*Acis and Galatea* [HWV 49]); 'Cease to beauty' (*Acis and Galatea*); 'Come and trip it' (*L'Allegro ed il Penseroso*); 'Come rather Goddess' (*L'Allegro ed il Penseroso*); 'Come thou Goddess' (*L'Allegro ed il Penseroso*); 'Consider, fond shepherd' (*Acis and Galatea*); 'Father of Heaven' (*Judas Maccabaeus*); 'Happy We' (*Acis and Galatea*); 'I'll to the well-trod stage' (*L'Allegro ed il Penseroso*); 'I rage, I melt' (*Acis and Galatea*); 'Haste thee nymph' (*L'Allegro ed il Penseroso*); 'Love in her eyes sits playing' (*Acis and Galatea*); 'Mirth admit me' (*L'Allegro ed il Penseroso*); 'Rejoice O Judah' (*Judas Maccabaeus*); 'Shepherd what are thou pursuing' (*Acis and Galatea*); 'Where shall I seek' (*Acis and Galatea*); 'Would you but gain the tender creature' (*Acis and Galatea*)

rmk   *See* SW→CW Jr, 6/11/1824, where SW says that he has arranged 'a multitude' of songs for the Royal Harmonic Institution.

---

[20] John Irvin Schwarz Jr, *The Orchestral Music of Samuel Wesley*, Ph.D. dissertation, University of Maryland, 1971, v 1 p 278.

925   **G. F. Handel, Zadok the Priest** [HWV 258]
ms   BL Add 35007 f 20
rmk   Piano duet. 'Coronation anthem.'

926   **W. A. Mozart, 'O God, when Thou appearest'**
      [K 336a(345)]
ms   BL Add 35007 f 27
rmk   Piano duet. 'O God, when Thou appearest' was Latrobe's arrangement,
      published in his *Selection of Sacred Music from the Works of some of*
      the most eminent Composers of Germany & Italy (London, v 2 p 17,
      1809), of the opening chorus from Mozart's *Thamos, König in Ägypten.*

927   **W. A. Mozart, Minuet** [F] [K 374e (377)]
ms   BL Add 35007 f 38
rmk   Piano duet. From the last movement of this Mozart sonata (vl, pf).

928   **Giovanni Pergolesi, 'Gloria in excelsis'** [I]   [*c*1824][21]
ms   RCM 4026 f 1
rmk   Piano duet. From Pergolesi's Mass [D].

929   **Giovanni Pergolesi, 'Gloria in excelsis'** [II]
ms   BL Add 35007 f 41, 45 (two copies)
rmk   Piano duet. On the same theme as, but longer than, work 928.

---

[21] Date proposed from other works in ms.

~ 5 ~

LITERARY WORKS

PRINTED WORKS

Only the first printings of Samuel Wesley's literary works are noted
here. Letters by SW printed in the publications *Bird*, *Liston*, *Logier*
and *Russell* or in newspapers and magazines published during SW's
lifetime are entered in the calendar of correspondence.

ORIGINAL WRITINGS

*Vindex to Verax. Or, Remarks upon 'A letter to the Rev. Thomas
Coke, Ll.D. and Mr. Henry Moore; and an Appeal and Remonstrance
to the People called Methodists'. Addressed to 'An Old Member of
the Society'.* London, printed for the author, by J. Moore..., 1792.[1]

'Advertisement' to Pinto, George Frederick, *Four Canzonets and a
Sonata in which is introduced the admired Air of "Logie O Buchan"
with an accompaniment for the Violin, likewise a Fantasia & Sonata
for the Piano Forte.* Edinburgh and London, *c*1806.[2]

'Advertisement' to Bach, John Sebastian, *No. I. A Trio, Composed
originally for the Organ...And now Adapted for Three Hands upon
the Piano Forte.* London, C. F. Horn and S. Wesley, 1809.

---

[1] This work was published anonymously, but a contemporary advertisement for
it, headed 'Just Published, Price Nine-Pence', identifies SW as the author. A
copy of this pamphlet with this advertisement is in the Methodist Archives. The
pamphlet is a response to the anonymous pamphlet *A Letter to the Rev. Thomas
Coke Ll.d. and Mr Henry Moore Occasioned by their Proposals for Publishing
the Life of the Rev. John Wesley A.M. in Opposition to that advertised (under
Sanction of the Executors) to be written by John Whitehead M.D. Also, a Letter
from the Rev. Dr Coke to the Author on the same Subject, Together with the
Whole Correspondence, and the Circular Letters written on the Occasion, and a
True and Impartial Statement of Facts Hitherto Suppressed, to which is added,
An Appeal and Remonstrance, to the People Called Methodists, by, an Old
Member of the Society.* London, printed for J. Luffman...[1792]. A copy of this
pamphlet is in the Methodist Archives. *See* Shepherd→SW, 24/4/1792;
Sarah→Penelope Maitland, about 1/5/1792.

[2] A copy of this work is in the British Library.

[with Charles Frederick Horn] Proposal to publish, by subscription, a new edition of the first twelve preludes and fugues of J. S. Bach's '48', with explanatory marks for young students. [1810][3]

[with Charles Frederick Horn] 'Introduction' to Bach, John Sebastian, *S. Wesley and C. F. Horn's New and Correct Edition of the Preludes and Fugues. Book 1st.* London, printed for the editors, by R[ober]t Birchall, 1810.

Explanation of All the Keys in Music. London, W. Hodsoll, *c*1814.[4] Subsequently published by Zenas T. Purday.[5]

Epistolary article quoting an extract from William Jackson's essay 'On Gentlemen-Artists', *European Magazine*, v 68 (September 1815) p 218–19.[6]

Two footnotes in C. J. Smyth, *Six Letters on Singing, from a Father to His Son.* Norwich, Stevenson, Matchett, and Stevenson, 1817.[7]

'Mr. Samuel Wesley's reply to the critique on his Church Service, in *The Harmonicon*', *Literary Chronicle and Weekly Review*, v 7 no. 317 (11 June 1825) p 377–380.

---

[3] This proposal, noticed in the 1 March 1810 *MM*, p 170, presumably was printed shortly before then. No copies of this proposal have been located.

[4] No copies of this work have been located. It was reviewed in the *GM*, v 84 part 2 (December 1814) p 573, under the title *Explanation of the Keys in Musick.*

[5] The title is listed in a catalogue of works 'published by Zenas T. Purday… late Hodsoll' inserted in the November 1830 number of *The Harmonicon.*

[6] This article, which has the form of a letter to the editor, was submitted by SW under the pseudonym 'Philomusicus'. The identification of 'Philomusicus' with SW is explained in the calendar of correspondence (*see* SW→Editor, *EM*, 1/9/1815).

[7] The two footnotes concern the vocal style of Sarah Harrop Bates [singer, *d*1811, wife of Joah Bates, *see* SW→William Seward, 16/6/1798], whom SW had heard sing 'numberless times' (p 13–14), and SW's preference of Latin to Italian as a language for singing (p 24–25). A third note by SW concering John Beard [singer, 1716?–1791] apparently was sent to Smyth, as it appears in a manuscript copy of his *Six Letters on Singing* (Bodl Ms Eng. Misc. e.464, f 38[v]), but was not included in the printed edition of Smyth's work.

Proposal to publish, by subscription, SW's transcriptions of antiphons by William Byrd in the Fitzwilliam collection, Cambridge. [1826][8]

'Preface', dated 10 July 1828, to SW's *Original Hymn Tunes, Adapted to Every Metre in the Collection by the Rev. John Wesley, A.M.*, [1828] p i–v.

'A sketch of the state of music in England, from the year 1778 up to the present time', *The Musical World*, London, v 1 no. 1 (18 March 1836) p 1–3.

REVIEWS

Review of John Wall Callcott, *A Musical Grammar, in Four Parts. British Critic*, v 29 (April 1807) p 398–407 and (June 1807) p 597–605.[9]

Review of George M. Slatter, *Maltese Hymn. The Cabinet*, n.s. v 1 no. 4 (April 1809) p 356.

Numerous reviews of music in the *European Magazine* from 1814 to the end of December 1816.[10]

---

[8] According to SW→Street, 25/5/1830, this proposal was printed in 1826, presumably before 'Jubal'→Editor, *The Harmonicon*, 20/5/1826, which appears to refer to it, but presumably after 1/3/1826, when SW was granted a grace by Cambridge University to publish music from the Fitzwilliam collection. No copies of this proposal have been located.

[9] This review appeared anonymously. A. F. C. Kollmann attributed it to SW in *The Quarterly Musical Register* no. 1 (January 1812) p 5. AFCK's attribution is supported by SW→CW Jr, 21/3/1807.

[10] SW's reviews for the *European Magazine* are discussed in Philip Olleson, 'Samuel Wesley and the *European Magazine*', *Notes* v 52 no. 4 (June 1996) p 1097–1111. SW→VN, 11/12/1816, indicates that the December 1816 reviews may have been written by SW in collaboration with VN. The music-review section of the *European Magazine* was discontinued after the December 1816 number (*see* SW→Stephen Jones, 13/1/1817).

REVISION

[John Wall] Callcott, *A Musical Grammar, in Four Parts.* Second Edition. London, Robert Birchall, 1809.[11]

ATTRIBUTED TRANSLATION

Rinck, Christian Heinrich, *C. H. Rinck's Celebrated Practical School, for the Organ...Translated from the Original, by the late Samuel Wesley.* London, R. Cocks & Co., *c*1838.[12]

---

[11] The second edition of Callcott's *Musical Grammar* was reported to be 'in press' in the 1 May 1809 *MM*; it was reviewed in the 1 September 1809 *MM*. According to the 'Advertisement' to this edition, p ix, SW 'carefully revised' and 'rendered correct' the 'erroneous passages' in the fourth part of this book, on rhythm, which he had criticised in his unsigned *British Critic* review of the first edition. At Callcott's request, SW's alterations were undone in the third edition of this book (*see* WH→SW, 8/1/1816).

[12] Although published within a year of SW's death—it is advertised in *MW* no. 127 (n.s. no. 33), 16/8/1838, p 267—the assertion that this work was translated by SW is doubtful. The attribution of the translation to SW is not confirmed by extant documentation from SW's lifetime, nor has evidence been found that he knew sufficient German to make such a translation.

MANUSCRIPT WORKS

An Explanation of the Gregorian Chant (BL Add 69853, f 1–15)

Lectures (BL Add 35014, BL Add 35015)

The following list of Samuel Wesley's lectures follows the ordering given on BL Add 35015 f 1 by Eliza Wesley, who bequeathed BL Add 35014–35015 to the British Museum. SW first lectured in March 1809, at the Royal Institution. He continued at various times to lecture there and at the Surry Institution, the London Institution and elsewhere, until he gave his final series of lectures in 1830 to the Philosophical and Literary Society of Bristol at the Bristol Institution. When known, the dates and places of SW's lectures are recorded in the chronology.[1]

　　SW's lectures were written and delivered over many years in various locations and contexts, and the surviving manuscripts contain numerous amendments, additions, cuts and alternative versions written on scraps of paper of different sizes and shapes. The text of each lecture preserved in these manuscripts presumably has the content that SW delivered last, and may bear little resemblance to lectures on the same subject that he wrote and delivered earlier.

　　The correspondence indicates that SW's lectures invariably included musical illustrations that he played at the piano or organ, sometimes assisted by singers or other instrumentalists.[2]

A　　Musical Prejudice. *[BL Add 35014 f 53]*

B　　The sublime, the beautiful & and the ornamental in Music—the church, the theatre, the concert room, the chamber. Gregorian Chaunt; Operatic Music; order in which vocal & instrumental concerts should be arranged. *[BL Add 35014 f 88]*

C　　Progress of music in general among us. *[BL Add 35014 f 99]*

---

[1] A few lectures have been annotated by SW with a date of composition or of first or later delivery. Other lectures have been dated by their position within a course for which a syllabus is extant. Some remaining lectures have been dated, more or less precisely, from internal evidence.

[2] SW appears to have been paid either £5/5/- or £6/6/- per lecture, about the same amount as he earned for playing the organ at a Covent Garden oratorio concert.

D   On the most eligible mode of advancing the cause of music theoretically and practically. *[BL Add 35014 f 155]*

E   On the distinction between good and faulty musical composition. *[BL Add 35014 f 128]*

F   The most eligible method of acquiring an easy command of keyed instruments. Transposition. Tuning, old and new method. Equal Temperament. *[BL Add 35014 f 2]*

G   On the advancement of musical knowledge and taste. Musical criticism. P.F Trio S Wesley. *[BL Add 35014 f 15]*

H   The rival merits of vocal and instrumental music—native and foreign musical artists. Difficulties of concert givers &c. *[BL Add 35014 f 39]*

I   What is the candid & judicious mode of comparing ancient music with modern church music? *[BL Add 35015 f 2]*

J   The difference to be made between *grave* and *solemn* music, & *heavy* music. *[BL Add 35015 f 20]*

K   In what respects may we be truly said to have improved in the knowledge & practice of music in the present period? Sensation playing & composition—musical instruments. *[BL Add 35015 f 32]*

L   Wind instruments—when desirable—when not so—in musical compositions. *[BL Add 35015 f 54]*

M   What appears to be the most rational, advisable & effective plan of ordering & conducting sacred musical performances in churches? *[BL Add 35015 f 68]*

N   The selection & mixture of pieces for public & private concerts—what is the best method to adopt? *[BL Add 35015 f 87]*

O   A candidly critical examination of the powers of vocal & instrumental music. Ought the former or the latter to be justly asserted more affecting & impressive? How should their comparative excellence by adjudged? *[BL Add 35015 f 100]*

P   Upon the acquisition of sound general knowledge of music. *[BL Add 35015 f 115]*

Q   A consideration of musical taste. *[BL Add 35015 f 144]*

R   The art & science of music. *[BL Add 35015 f 175]*

S   German hymn tunes. The general management of our own music both ecclesiastical & secular. Music in our cathedrals & churches. Opera. Music da camera. *[BL Add 35015 f 195]*

T   Requisites for the performance of grand sacred music. Improvement need in the soprano department of the choir. *[BL Add 35015 f 207]*

U   In the set of pieces for private or public concerts, which is the best mode to adopt? *[BL Add 35015 f 225]*

V   How to distinguish good music from bad. *[BL Add 35015 f 233]*

W   Church music. *[BL Add 35015 f 243]*

X   Art of music. *[BL Add 35015 f 249]*

Reminiscences (BL Add 27593, apparently written in early 1836)[3]

---

[3] The first part of SW's *Reminiscences* is dated 8/4/1836. BL Add 27593 also contains material presumably for SW's intended continuation of his article published in the 18/3/1836 *Musical World*, and possibly for other similar articles which never appeared (*see* SW→Street?, about 2/1836).

~ 6 ~

PORTRAITS

ICONOGRAPHY

Samuel Wesley was fortunate that, in his childhood, especially following the family's move to London in 1771, he was linked to his father's artistic and musical circle, which resulted in several early portraits of this child prodigy.[1] Moreover, this was at a time when portraiture of the English School was at its zenith, and child portraits were in particular favour.[2] SW therefore appears in these child portraits as a figure of charm and talent, intelligence and innocence.

Through his life SW retained such links,[3] resulting in the survival of a number of portraits and likenesses of an untypical quality which offer a particular insight into the nature of his life and achievement. His correspondence offers a few clues about these pictures.

SW wrote to Henry John Gauntlett in (presumably) 1836 that 'my picture has been lying at Mr. Huggins' in Leaden Hall Street for this last month: there were several gentleman he wished to shew it to, but Erasmus will bring it to you in his dining hour if he can find time'.[4] William John Huggins (1781–1845) was a marine painter and presumably also dealt generally in pictures. Unfortunately, this letter does not assist us to identify which portrait might be referred to here.

In an undated non-final will, SW's brother Charles Wesley Jr bequeathed an 'oval picture' of SW to SW's daughter Emma.[5] Although we cannot be sure which picture CW Jr meant, his description may refer to John Jackson's 1826 portrait of SW in a painted oval, now at the National Portrait Gallery, London.

It is necessary to insert a strong caveat, for the difficulties of tracing surviving images, and of piecing together the significance of

---

[1] The iconography section has been written by Peter S. Forsaith.

[2] See Pointon, Marcia, *Hanging the Head* (New Haven, 1993), especially Chapter 7, 'The State of a Child', p 177.

[3] For instance, in SW→SS, 26/1/1830, SW writes that he knew Sir Thomas Lawrence well.

[4] SW→Henry John Gauntlett, 30/9/1836?.

[5] CW Jr will, 11/1828–11/1830. CW Jr's final will (CW Jr will, 18/5/1831) does not mention this portrait.

isolated documentary references, leave ample room for uncertainty and speculation. It would be rash to claim that the following iconography represents a definitive account of images of Samuel Wesley, but it endeavours to be the best available with current evidence.

The following abbreviations are used to describe portraits:

attr.—attributed to
descr—description
engr—engraved
exhib—exhibited
exmpl—examples
HS—head and shoulders
HL—half-length
FL—full-length

inscr—inscribed
O/C—oils on canvas
prov—provenance
R—right (to viewer)
L—left (to viewer)
TQL—three-quarter length
u/d—undated
u/s—unsigned

A   attr. John RUSSELL, R.A. (1745–1806)   *c*1771

descr   O/C, u/s, u/d. HL standing to L, looking to front, and playing violin or viola left-handed. Collar-length dark hair, scarlet coat unbuttoned, scarlet waistcoat; frilled collar and cuffs to open-necked shirt. Pendant, and wide dark waist sash. Organ pipes in background.

Williamson, using Russell's diaries, notes that 'Master Samuel Wesley' sat to Russell in 1770/1771.[6] The left-handed playing in this portrait is problematic, and no easy solution suggests itself. It may be here and in **C** that SW is depicted wearing the 'suit of court scarlet'[7] bought for him by Garret Wesley, 1st Earl of Mornington.

Shortly after the Wesleys took up residence in London in 1771, John Russell painted portraits of members of the family.[8] Russell was then a rising young artist and, following a conversion experience in 1764,

---

[6] Williamson, G. C., *John Russell R.A.* (London, 1894), p 43.

[7] Telford, John, *The Life of the Rev. Charles Wesley* (London, 1900), p 265.

[8] Forsaith, Peter, 'Charles Wesley Junior: a portrait by John Russell', *Proceedings of the Wesley Historical Society* v 52 part 1 (February 1999) p 15–17.

was strongly linked to the Methodist movement.[9] Financially insecure until 1774, he painted many Evangelical clergy including John Wesley and George Whitefield.[10] SW and his sister Sarah spent a month at the home of Russell's father John Russell in Guildford in June–July 1776.[11]

exmpl   1. Charles Wesley Heritage Centre, Bristol (75×60 cm)

prov   Formerly in John Wesley's Chapel, The New Room, Bristol. Prior history unknown.

B   **attr. Nathaniel HONE (1734–1784)**   *c*1771–1774

descr   O/C, u/s, u/d. HL to R, face to front, collar length dark hair plain small collar, double-breasted coat, gilt buttons, 1 hand inserted in coat. Plain ground. The portrait has generally been known as 'Wesley as a boy'. Facial similarities to both **A** and **C** suggest strongly that the subject is SW.

Nathaniel Hone's 1766 portrait of John Wesley hangs in the National Portrait Gallery, London.

exmpl   1. Private collection, reputedly given in payment for a wine debt.

C   **John RUSSELL, R.A.**   **1776**

descr   O/C, FL facing L; collar length dark brown hair, scarlet coat and breeches, white waistcoat, frilled collar, black necktie, frilled cuffs; standing at desk composing music. By his feet a copy of *Ruth an Oratorio by Samuel Wesley Aged eight years*. Patterned carpet, ornate gilt and upholstered armchair, organ with drape in background.

This fine painting is visually linked with two other pictures. A companion portrait of Charles Wesley Jr (the two now hang side by side at the Royal Academy of Music) utilises a nearly identical chair,

---

[9] Rhodes, Iris C., *John Russell R.A.* (Guildford, 1986) provides a short biography.

[10] Forsaith, Peter, 'Portraits of John Fletcher of Madeley and their artists', *Proceedings of the Wesley Historical Society* v 47 part 2 (May 1990) p 190–191.

[11] *See* SW→SGW, 26/6/1776 and subsequent correspondence.

probably part of Russell's London studio furniture.[12] In a 'portrait of a cleric' of 1771 (possibly no. 269 in the 1771 Royal Academy exhibition), we observe the same desk: the sitter is unknown but may well be SW's godfather Martin Madan, whose preaching had led to Russell's Methodist conversion.[13]

exhib   Royal Academy 1777 (304).

exmpl   1. Royal Academy of Music, London (160×105 cm)
Presented with a contemporary companion portrait of Charles Wesley Jr.

prov   Owned by Matthias Erasmus Wesley and thence to the Royal Academy of Music.[14] According to Williamson, 'At one time this belonged to Mr Matthews of 21 Manchester Square, and then to Mr Martin Colnaghi, who sold it to the present owner' [MEW].[15]

engr   (mezzotint) William DICKINSON, 26 January 1778

D   (Thomas?) ROBINSON (*d*1810)   *c*1796

By 'Mr Robinson', according to SW's *Musical World* obituary, when SW was aged about 30.[16] Now lost. Possible reference in SW→James Asperne, 14/11/1812? to portrait painted '15 years ago'.

Thomas Robinson (who operated from 1770) was from Westmoreland. He was a pupil of George Romney from 1785 and was probably still in his studio when Romney painted John Wesley in 1789. Robinson was active in Ireland from about 1790.

---

[12] 'These portraits of Charles and Samuel Wesley...are perhaps [among Russell's] best works in oil.' Williamson, *op. cit.*, p 90.

[13] This picture was sold at Christie's, London, 26/4/1985 lot 94.

[14] Walker, Richard, *Regency Portraits* (London, National Portrait Gallery, 1985) v 1 p 543; see also Williamson, *op. cit., passim.*

[15] Williamson, *op. cit.*, p 150. The Royal Academy of Music possesses an invoice dated 6 January 1892 for MEW's purchase of this portrait, including its copyright, from Martin Colnaghi for £189.

[16] 'Professional memoranda of the late Mr Samuel Wesley's life (*continued...*)', *MW* v 7 no. 86 (3 November 1837) p 114.

E   William BEHNES (1795–1864)   *c*1807

Said to have been drawn when Behnes was '12 years old', and to
have been owned by Richard Clark (1780–1856, whom SW had
known as secretary of the Glee Club)[17] at the time of SW's death.[18]
Now lost.

F   John BACON (1777–1859)   **1809**

The first reference to SW sitting for Bacon is in SW→BJ,
17/11/1808?, where SW agrees to sit at Benjamin Jacobs's request.
SW arranged to meet Bacon with BJ on 21/12/1808 (SW→BJ,
8/12/1808; BJ→Bacon, 12/12/1808). The portrait presumably was
delivered to Jacobs in November 1809, as BJ→Bacon, 18/11/1809,
conveys BJ's thanks for Bacon's 'excellent' and 'correct' portrait of
SW and characterises it as 'a pretty fair specimen of painting
with…your pencil', suggesting that the work was a drawing. Now
lost.

John Bacon was a neighbour of John Russell in Newman Street and
their families were closely linked. Bacon pictured Russell's daughter
Jane (1776–1845) in 1791, and Russell painted Bacon and his family.

G   John James MASQUERIER (1778–1855)   **1813**

descr   TQL O/C: painted, according to Sée[19], for Sir Charles Forbes
[presumably Sir Charles Forbes, 1774–1849, from 1812 to 1818 M.P.
for Beverley, as a portrait of him by Masquerier was exhibited at the
Royal Academy in 1816]. Now lost.

Sée reports that 'musicians of the calibre of Samuel Wesley'
performed in Masquerier's home following Masquerier's marriage in
1812. SW→CLM, 27/3/1788 is addressed to CLM at 'Mrs
Masquerier's, Kensington', perhaps the mother or another relative of
the artist.

---

[17] *See* SW→Richard Clark, 4/12/1823?.

[18] 'Professional memoranda…', *loc. cit.*

[19] Sée, R.R.M., *Masquerier and His Circle* (London, 1922) pp 130, 239.

H   **John JACKSON, R.A. (1778–1831)**   **1826**

descr   O/C, u/s, u/d. HS facing L, receding hairline, medium length grey hair. High white cravat, dark collar. Outline of shoulders sketched in, plain ground.
Generally described as unfinished, this may not be the case. Compare Romney's self-portrait and Thomas Lawrence's portraits of George IV and William Wilberforce (all in the National Portrait Gallery, London) and some of Jackson's own work for *Wesleyan Methodist Magazine*, all of which seem unfinished, but which may be using this device deliberately.[20]

Although the canvas is undated, SW's *Musical World* obituary says that it was painted 'about 10 years ago',[21] and Kelly states 1826 explicitly.[22] SW and Jackson were in correspondence in 1826; of their letters, only SW→John Jackson, 29/11/1826, is known to be extant.[23]

exmpl   1. Wesley's Chapel, City Road, London (61×51 cm). This painting was cleaned and conserved in 1999 by John Burbridge of Granville and Burbridge, London.[24]
2. National Portrait Gallery, London; *NPG 2040* (57.8×47.6 cm, in painted oval).[25]

engr   Jackson 4.25×3.5 in. (= 11×9 cm) oval.

---

[20] Jackson's work, although not his portrait of SW, is discussed in Morgan, H. C., *Life and Times of John Jackson*, unpublished Ph.D. thesis, University of Leeds, 1956.

[21] 'Professional memoranda...', *loc. cit.*

[22] Kelly, Charles H., 'The Wesleyan Methodist Book-Room: pictures in the book steward's room', *Wesleyan Methodist Magazine* v 130 (1907) p 520.

[23] Jackson, a Methodist, desired to promote SW's publication that year of three hymns composed by Handel to words by CW, and SW sought Jackson's advice regarding this publication's engraved title-page. *See* SW→Tooth, 8/11/1826.

[24] This painting is reproduced as the frontispiece of this book.

[25] Walker, *op. cit.*, v 1 p 543.

I   **John James MASQUERIER**   **[1827]**

descr HS profile as old man with curly white hair. *inscr* 'sketched at Brighton by J.M.'.[26] *See* Walker, *op. cit.*, v 1 p 542–543.

exmpl 1. Sold through Christie's 9/4/1974. (19×14 cm)

J   **Frederick GILLING**   *c*1861

descr watercolour in an oval frame
exmpl 1. British Library Add 31764 f 2 'copied from the original miniature in the possession of Dr S. S. Wesley, Winchester'. Receipt 'for copying miniature' signed Fred Gilling, 28/2/1861, on the letterhead of John Wesley [son of SW and SS], 49 Paternoster Row. Possibly a copy of **F**.

K   **Anonymous (possibly John James MASQUERIER)**

descr Pencil drawing. HS facing. White hair, knotted white cravat, dark coat and waistcoat as an older man.

exmpl 1. British Library Add 31764 f 3.

L   **G. J. HUNT**   **1921**

descr FL facing L as a younger man wearing cutaway scarlet coat, holding book or musical score in L hand. R hand extended.

exmpl 1. Panel in S. J. King memorial window (1921), south side of nave, Bristol Cathedral. Made by Arthur Salisbury from Hunt's design. Source of image of SW unknown. This window also commemorates John Cabot, Edward Colston and William Worcester, all born in Bristol.

---

[26] SW is known to have been in Brighton only in October 1827. *See* SW→SS, 10/10/1827, 14/10/1827 and 16/10/1827. Masquerier lived in Brighton from 1823 (Sée, *op. cit.*).

M   *Death Mask:* **Frederick HEHL**   **1837**

descr   Recorded in BL Add 35027 f 2, an album compiled by Eliza Wesley, as taken by Hehl a few hours after SW's death.[27] Now lost.

---

[27] A Frederick Hehl, presumably the same man, worked for the Novello firm before becoming a music publisher in his own right *c*1844 (*H&S*, p 177). He probably was related to the Novello family, as VN's wife's maiden name was Mary Sabilla Hehl.

VERBAL PORTRAITS

We end by recounting some impressions of Samuel Wesley written by people who knew him. A consistent remark is that, throughout his life from the age of five, extempore organ performance was his greatest skill. Because SW lived before the development of sound-recording technology this leading aspect of his life has unfortunately not been preserved.

In an account of musical prodigies prepared for the Royal Society in February 1779, Charles Burney noted that:[1]

> ...the two sons of the reverend Mr Westley seem to have discovered, during early infancy, very uncommon faculties for the practice of music. Charles, the eldest, at two years and three quarters old, surprised his father by playing a tune on the harpsichord readily, and in just time: soon after he played several, whatever his mother sung, or whatever he heard in the street.
>
> Samuel, the youngest, though he was three years old before he aimed at a tune, yet by constantly hearing his brother practise, and being accustomed to good music and masterly execution, before he was six years old arrived at such knowledge in music, that his extemporary performance on keyed instruments, like Mozart's, was so masterly in point of invention, modulation, and accuracy of execution, as to surpass, in many particulars, the attainments of most professors at any period of their lives.

In September 1798 the *European Magazine* reported SW's organ playing as follows:[2]

> This great musician first played upon the organ with one hand at five years of age. He and the celebrated Mozart are two of the few early

---

[1] In Charles Burney, 'Account of an infant musician', *Philosophical Transactions of the Royal Society of London*, v 69 part 1 (1779) p 202–203.

[2] *EM* v 34 (September 1798) p 161. The writer probably was William Seward. The text appeared in the 'Drossiana' section of the *EM* to which Seward is known to have contributed and is preceded immediately by a reprint of a poem presumably by Seward concerning SW's visit to 'Mr S—' [Seward] at Richmond in the summer of 1798. See the note to SW→William Seward, 16/6/1798.

musicians, whose advancement in their art has born any proportion to their precocity of talent. Mr Wesley's power of improvisation on the organ is wonderful; his composition keeps pace with his execution; his melodies, though struck out on the instant, are sweet and varied, never common places; and his harmony is appropriate, and follows them with all the exactness and discrimination of the most elaborate and studious master; and his execution (however impossible it may be at times to follow his flying fingers with the eye) keeps its proper place, and is never sacrificed to the superior charms of expression.

In 1815 an anonymous writer said in the *New Monthly Magazine*:

The peculiar gift which Mr Wesley possesses of playing extempore, the depth of science, and the wonders of modulation which he displays in his masterly strains, rank him with the best organ players in England, we had almost said Europe. His regular pieces, though they exhibit superior talent, appear to us less happy efforts of his genius than those wild effusions which he puts forth in a convivial party, where, after throwing away on every topic that is started as much learning and wit as would set up an host of LL.D.'s, he places himself at the organ, where fugues double and treble, canons, imitations, subjects inverted, retrograde, and in all sorts of possible forms, seem to flow spontaneously from the magic of his touch.[3]

Describing a day spent with SW about eleven years later,[4] the musical amateur William Gardiner [1770–1853] wrote:

After service at St Paul's [Cathedral] Mr [Thomas] At[t]wood and Mr [George] Cooper, the organists, met Mr Samuel Wesley at the London Coffee–house for dinner. The conversation, at my instance, turned chiefly upon music; but to Wesley any other subject seemed more agreeable. I fell into his humour; and he told me many curious anecdotes of his uncle John, the celebrated founder of the Methodists. In the midst

---

[3] *New Monthly Magazine* v 3 no. 14 (1 March 1815) p 153. This passage is part of an anonymous review of SW's Voluntary for the organ, op. 6 no. 10.

[4] William Gardiner, *Music and Friends; or, Pleasant Recollections of a Dilettante.* London, 1838, v 2 p 652–654. Gardiner's meeting with SW appears to have taken place on a Whitsunday in a year when the St Paul's Cathedral organ had 'lately received an addition of pedal pipes of the largest size, descending an octave below the original notes'. This addition apparently was accomplished by James Chapman Bishop in 1826 (*Elvin* p 35, 162).

of our port and claret he called for a pen and ink, and wrote, from recollection, ...verses, composed by his uncle, upon the death of Whitfield,[5] which he said had never been published.

The divine [i.e., JW], he observed, was not the only celebrated man the family had produced. There was his cousin the soldier, Sir Arthur Wesley, or Wellesley, as they now had chosen to call themselves, for what reason he did not know, but it was within his recollection that they altered the spelling of the name.[6]

It was on the Sunday, after prayers at St Paul's, that we repaired to the tavern hard by. After dinner it was proposed that we should accompany Mr Cooper to the evening service at St Sepulchre's, where there is a fine organ. It was suggested that, if I were to ask Mr Wesley to play at the conclusion of the service, he probably would. ... As we walked together I said, 'Mr Wesley, these gentlemen wish me to ask you to touch the organ at the conclusion of the service; you may be a fine organist, that I know nothing about, but I am contented with you as a philosopher and man of letters, in whose company I have spent a pleasant day.' I saw, by a cunning leer at the corner of his eye, that I had pleased him by the remark, and the moment the service was over, with a smirk upon his countenance, he sat down, and began a noble fugue in the key of c♯ major. It was wonderful with what skill and dexterity he conducted it through the most eccentric harmonies. This extemporary playing was his forte, in which he had no rival. As a composer, if we may judge from his printed compositions, he had but little genius, scarcely deviating from the common routine of the old school. When he committed his ideas to writing he seemed to lose all freedom of thought, but, when released from the shackles of pen and paper, he was as wild and unfettered as he was stiff and precise before.

In 1829, Edward Hodges was astounded by SW's extempore organ performances. Hodges's journal entry for 1 October 1829,

---

[5] I.e., George Whitefield, pioneer Methodist leader, 1714–1770. The poem, which Gardiner prints, is not reproduced here.

[6] According to Christopher Hibbert, *Wellington: A Personal History* (London, 1997), Arthur Wesley (1769–1852, in 1814 created first Duke of Wellington), son of Garret Wesley (1735–1781, Mus. Doc., first Earl of Mornington), changed his surname to Wellesley in 1798, at the request of his elder brother Richard, second Earl of Mornington and then Governor–General of Bengal, who considered the name 'Wellesley' to be 'older and more aristocratic than Wesley with its associations of evangelical Methodism' (pp 4, 23). The distant relationship between CW's and Garret Wesley's families is described in *Stevenson* pp xi–xxiii and is charted in Stevenson's accompanying 'Pedigree of the Wesley Family'.

summarised in the calendar of correspondence, conveys his initial excitement vividly.[7]

SW's obituary in *The Musical World* describes his physical and musical characteristics in the following way:[8]

> Mr Wesley was, we should guess, rather below the middle size in stature; his features bearing a strong resemblance to those of his eminent uncle. His general frame was delicate, his hands and feet being small and the former very handsome. When composing, it was his custom to stand at a high desk…[and] so great was his power of abstraction, that he could go on writing while people around him were talking. … In composing he was remarkable for rapidity, at the same time his MS. remained clear, without blot. … So prompt, decided, and firm, was he in resolve, that having finished a composition he rarely found occasion for amendment. And having once begun, he never rested till he had come to a conclusion, but continued writing till four or five in the morning. …
>
> Of his talent in teaching he would say, 'I do not like teaching, because I have not studied music regularly as I ought to have done; and therefore I have no method as my brother has'. …
>
> Wesley has often declared that he never read a theoretical treatise on music. He had dipped into several, but had never gone through any one of them. …
>
> He took his position at the head of the [music] profession, perhaps more from his distinguished powers of extemporaneous performance than from a consideration of his character as a composer. … He set little consideration on many of his published compositions, observing, 'what can I do? they tell me to write something easy, and not to take more than six or seven [engraved] plates'. Still, no composition of Wesley's is without positive merit; and it is strange if before the performer gets through the first page, he does not meet with some bold chord or novelty of phrase.

A few years after SW's death, Mary Sabilla Novello, Vincent Novello's wife, portrayed SW's personality to the bass singer Henry Phillips in these words:[9]

---

[7] Later entries in Hodges's journal—especially that for 7/10/1829—are more subdued, reflecting his analyses of SW's subsequent performances.

[8] 'Professional Memoranda of the late Mr Samuel Wesley's Life', *MW* v 7 no. 84 (20 October 1837) p 81–93 and no. 86 (3 November 1837) p 113–118. As Henry John Gauntlett appears to have been much involved with this journal at this time it seems plausible to conjecture that he assisted in writing this obituary.

I have great pleasure in sending you two of Wesley's letters, which are particularly interesting as shewing the mind of the man in its opposite extremes of mad fun, & excessive depression, to which alternations Wesley was always subject. I knew him unfortunately, too well; pious Catholic, raving Atheist, mad, reasonable, drunk & sober—the dread of all wives & regular families, a warm friend, a bitter foe, a satirical talker, a flatterer at times of those he cynically traduced at others—a blasphemer at times, a puling Methodist at others—

Subsequently, Vincent Novello characterised SW as, 'with the exception of Henry Purcell, the greatest musical genius that England has produced'.[10]

On 17 February 1849 SW's friend William B. Kingston wrote to VN about 'poor, and most deeply lamented Wesley'.[11] 'I lov'd him as a brother for many years', Kingston reminisced:

for, in his happy moments, he was as truly amicable as he was highly gifted. During a long period, I believe myself to have had his entire confidence; & that, in our numerous conversations, he more fully revealed to me his *inner* Man, than to any other human Being; for, unless under the influence of unfavourable circumstances, or some, alas! fatal illusions, he was, at once, the most truthful & candid creature—even to his own disparagement—I ever knew. ...

Justice to the musical powers & genius of our poor friend was neither done, during his lifetime; nor has been since his death; & I am sorely afraid, never will be. He really seems to have been pursued by what, for want of a better word, is called *fatality*; or an inextricable web, & intervolved confusion of circumstances, which crushed him living, & still stand in the way of either himself, or his works being duly appreciated.— This is to *me* a very painful subject, & I must not dwell upon it.

---

[9] BL Add 31764 f 34. This letter is torn, with considerable text missing. From a reference to VN's daughters Emma and Clara being in Rome, it appears to have been written in late 1841 or early 1842.

[10] VN→Thomas Hawkins, 13/7/1843, BL Add 35027 f 36.

[11] BL Add 17731 f 37.

~ 7 ~

BIBLIOGRAPHY

WESLEY'S LIBRARY

No catalogue of Samuel Wesley's library is known to have been made, and information about the books and music that he owned accordingly is scanty. The calendar of correspondence identifies some publications that he had at particular times but, in view of his persistent financial insecurity, it would be unsafe to suppose that he kept his collection intact. The following remarks are limited to some printed works that SW is known to have possessed.

A ten-volume 1785 edition of Shakespeare's plays, with each title-page bearing the inscription 'Samuel Wesley, 1790' in SW's hand, was owned in the 1920s by Beatrice Little of Brighton, Victoria, Australia, who believed that SW had given these volumes to her grandfather. This set is now in the library of Queen's College, University of Melbourne. Each volume contains numerous annotations by SW which remark on Shakespeare's text and the interpretations of it by various commentators.[1]

A copy of the 1820 edition of Robert Southey's *Life of [John] Wesley*, inscribed 'S. Wesley 1829' and bearing SW's marginal annotations, was in private possession in 1960.[2]

SW's copy of Forkel's 1802 *Life* (in German) of J. S. Bach—the biography of which Charles Frederick Horn and SW had proposed in 1808 to publish an English translation[3]—is now in the Pendlebury Library, University of Cambridge. The book bears SW's inscription 'the gift of my very kind & respected friend, Mr William Drummer'. SW presumably received this gift after his unsuccessful efforts to publish a translation, as on 25/11/1808 he had written that he did not

---

[1] See Sugden, Edward H., 'Samuel Wesley's notes on Shakespeare', *London Quarterly Review*, v 139 (1923) p 157–172. Sugden's 51-page typescript of SW's annotations in this set is in the State Library of Victoria, Melbourne, Australia.

[2] See Taberer, Alfred A., 'Uncle and nephew: Samuel Wesley, junr.'s [i.e., SW's] comments on John', *Proceedings of the Wesley Historical Society*, v 32 part 6 (June 1960) p 140.

[3] See SW→BJ, 17/10/1808; *The Librarian* v 1 no. 5 (1/11/1808) p 238.

have the biography at hand, but could apply to CFH who had, or had access to, a copy.[4]

Some printed music formerly owned by SW is now in the library of the Royal College of Music. This includes JSB's *Clavier Sonaten mit obligater Violine*, BWV 1014–1019, published in Zürich c1801 by Nägeli, which SW purchased at Henry Escher's bookshop in London on 11/8/1809 for 18/-. Another volume in the RCM containins two books of JSB's *Choral Vorspiele* given to SW by Joseph Gwilt in 1809 and a Mass formerly attributed to JSB, BWV Anhang III 167, given to SW by Latrobe in the same year.[5]

The RCM also possesses a bound volume of printed music (shelf-mark D553) whose inside front cover bears SW's handwritten inscription: 'Samuel Wesley jun.[r] [i.e., SSW] the Gift of his Father. March 22. 1822'. Besides the only known copy of SW's arrangement of JSB's preludes, BWV 933–935, this volume contains copies of Introduction and Fugue for the organ by Timothy Essex, which is dedicated to SW, and the revised version of Muzio Clementi's Four Sonatas for the piano forte, op. 12, with Clementi's manuscript inscription 'Mr John Wesley from the Author with his best comp[ts]'. As this edition was published c1801–1802,[6] long after JW's death and when JWW was at most three years old, a plausible interpretation of Clementi's inscription is that he presented the work to SW but got his first name wrong.[7]

Other works dedicated to SW (of which he almost certainly would have received complimentary copies) include William Seaman Stevens's *Treatise on Piano-Forte Expression* (London, 1811) for which SW composed an 'exercise' consisting of a prelude and air, Joseph Major's *Specimens of Modulation from the Equivocal Chord*

---

[4] SW→Crotch, 25/11/1808.

[5] This book was originally bound during SW's lifetime. *See* SW→VN, 14/9/1814.

[6] Tyson, Alan, *Thematic Catalogue of the Works of Muzio Clementi* (Tutzing, Germany, 1967) p 49.

[7] We are grateful to Dr Peter Horton of the RCM library for showing us this volume and suggesting this interpretation.

to 26 Minor & Major Keys (London, *c*1818–1820), and a voluntary by James Hook.[8]

SW's library also would have contained works to which he subscribed. Printed subscription lists show that he subscribed for one copy of each of the following musical publications (arranged by year of first appearance), except in the case of Pinto's *Four Canzonets and a Sonata*, of which he ordered six copies. All works other than those by Pinto were published principally in London.

Barthélemon, Miss [Cecilia Maria]	*Three Sonatas for the Piano-Forte, or Harpsichord,* op. 1. *c*1776.[9]
Barthélemon, Mrs Maria	*Three Hymns & Three Anthems composed for The Asylum & Magdalen Chapels.* ESH 16/4/1795.[10]
Latrobe, C[hristian] I[gnatius]	*Dies Irae.* 1799.
Latrobe, C[hristian] I[gnatius]	*The Dawn of Glory. A Hymn...Set to Music.* 1803.[11]
Pinto, George Frederick	*Six Canzonets.* Birmingham, *c*1805.
Pinto, George Frederick	*Four Canzonets and a Sonata.* Edinburgh, *c*1806–1808.[12]
Webb, Rev. Richard	*A Collection of Madrigals for Three, Four Five & Six Voices.* 1808.
Novello, Vincent	*A Collection of Sacred Music, as Performed at the Royal Portuguese Chapel in London.* 1811.
Jacob, B[enjamin]	*National Psalmody.* 1817.

---

[8] See SW→VN, 23/6/1813. No copies of the original edition of Hook's voluntary have been located. However, a later publication by Wheatstone of a voluntary by Hook dedicated to SW is extant, and presumably is a reissue of the original edition with an altered title-page.

[9] SW's name appears on the subscription list as 'Mr S. Westley'.

[10] SW's name appears on the subscription list as 'Mr S. Westley'.

[11] SW subscribed from Highgate.

[12] SW subscribed from Camden Town.

Major, Joseph	*A Collection of Chamber Music for Churches & Chapels.* c1826.[13]
Russell, William	*Job, a Sacred Oratorio.* 1826.
Barthélemon, F.-H.	*Selections from the Oratorio of Jefté in Masfa.* 1827.
Bird, William	*Original Psalmody.* 1829.

---

[13] SW subscribed as Organist, Camden Town Chapel.

PUBLICATIONS ABOUT WESLEY

The following bibliography lists, by year of publication, articles and books that contain substantial information about Samuel Wesley. Articles in dictionaries and encyclopaedias are included only if they appeared during SW's lifetime.

Reviews of SW's musical compositions that were published while he was alive are noted in the list of his musical works. Subsequent reviews have not been entered in this source book.

PUBLICATIONS PRINTED DURING SAMUEL WESLEY'S LIFE

Burney, Charles, 'Account of an infant musician', *Philosophical Transactions of the Royal Society of London* v 69 part 1 (1779) p 183–206 [primarily about Crotch, but the abilities of CW Jr, SW, Mozart and other musical child prodigies are also discussed]

Barrington, Daines, *Miscellanies* (London, 1781), p 291–310,[1] reprinted as 'An account of the very extraordinary musical talents of Messrs Charles and Samuel Wesley', *Westminster Magazine* v 9 (1781) p 233–236, 289–295, and as 'Anecdotes of the early life of Samuel Wesley, Esq.', *Wesleyan-Methodist Magazine* v 13 (1834) p 596–599, 670–674

Barrington, Daines, 'Some account of little Crotch', in *Miscellanies* (London, 1781) p 311–325 [includes information provided to Barrington by SW 'who takes little Crotch much under his protection',[2] and describes some tests by SW of Crotch's musical abilities; it also discusses the capabilities of SW's relative Garret Wesley, 1st Earl of Mornington, as a musical prodigy]

---

[1] Barrington's essay on SW is in two parts. The first part (*Miscellanies* p 291–298) slightly abbreviates (e.g., by substituting initials for surnames) an account of SW prepared by CW, apparently at Barrington's request (*see* Daines Barrington→CW, 6/1776). The second part (*Miscellanies* p 298–310) contains Barrington's own observations of SW and includes a song that SW composed. CW's account of SW, without Barrington's alterations, is printed in Jackson, Thomas, *The Life of the Rev. Charles Wesley, M.A.*, (London, 1841), v 1 p 337–342. Manuscripts of CW's account are at MA DDCW/8/2, DDCW/8/24 and DDCW/10/2.

[2] See CW→JW, 23/4/1779.

S[eward, William], 'Lines addressed to Mr Samuel Wesley on his visiting Mr. S— at Richmond a second time, in the summer of 1798', *Whitehall Evening-Post*, 21–23/8/1798; reprinted *EM* v 34 (1798) p 161

[Bingley, William], 'Samuel Wesley', in *Musical Biography; or, Memoirs of the Lives and Writings of the most eminent Musical Composers and Writers...* (London, 1814) v 2 p 279–281 [substantially reprinted in *A Dictionary of Musicians from the Earliest Ages to the Present Time...* (London, 1824) v 2 p 535][3]

H[orncastle], W. F., 'Remarks on instrumental composers', *QMMR* v 5 (1823) p 292–9 [a letter to the editor about SW's 'extraordinary genius and wonderful powers']

[Hone, William], 'Mr Samuel Wesley', *The Every-Day Book*, v 1 (28 July 1825)

Gauntlett, Henry John, 'The ecclesiastical music of this country [from a lecture]', *MW* v 2 no. 17 (1836) p 49–52 [discusses SW's music]

OBITUARIES

'Death of Mr Samuel Wesley', *The Times*, 12/10/1837

'Mr Samuel Wesley' and 'Mr Wesley's last moments', *MW* v 7 no. 83 (13/10/1837) p 76

'Samuel Wesley', *Athenaeum*, 14/10/1837, p 771

'The late Mr Samuel Wesley', *The Times*, 18/10/1837 [account of SW's funeral and interment][4]

'Professional memoranda of the late Mr Samuel Wesley's life', *MW* v 7 no. 84 (20/10/1837) p 81–93 and no. 86 (3/11/1837) p 113–118

---

[3] A statement in the 1824 dictionary, printed for Sainsbury and Co., that 'S. Wesley died about the year 1815', led to SW→Editor, *The Times*, 11/10/1824 and subsequent correspondence.

[4] This report and the *Times* death notice were reprinted with slight revision in *GM* n.s. v 8, (1837), p 544–6.

'Christian Retrospect' [an obituary of SW dated 24/10/1837, probably by Thomas Jackson], *Wesleyan-Methodist Magazine* v 16 (1837) p 869–71

PUBLICATIONS PRINTED AFTER SAMUEL WESLEY'S LIFE

Jackson, Thomas, *The Life of the Rev. Charles Wesley, MA....* London, 1841, 2 vols. [includes, in v 1 p 329–455, CW's account of CW Jr and SW as child prodigies and other biographical information about SW]

Jackson, Thomas (ed.), *The Journal of the Rev. Charles Wesley, M.A.; to which are appended Selections from his Correspondence and Poetry.* London, 1849, 2 vols. [includes, in v 2 p 140–158, CW's account of CW Jr and SW as child prodigies]

'Memoir of Samuel Wesley, the musician', *WBRR* v 3 (1851) p 321–328, 361–370, 401–411, 441–453 [probably by G. J. Stevenson]

[Holmes, Edward], 'Our musical spring', *Fraser's Magazine* (May 1851) p 586–595 [discusses SW's role in the English Bach awakening; reprinted as 'The progress of Bach's music in England', *Musical Times* v 4 (1851) p 192–193]

Holmes, Edward, 'Cathedral music and composers', *Musical Times* v 4 (1851) p 207–208, 225, 233–234, 239–240

'Biographical sketches of eminent (deceased) freemasons I: Samuel Wesley, P.G. Org.', *The Freemason's Magazine and Masonic Mirror* v 5 (1858) p 151–161

Jackson, Thomas, *Recollections of my Own Life and Times* (London, 1874), p 231–232 [contains an account of SW's old age and death]

Winters, William, *An Account of the Remarkable Musical Talents of Several Members of the Wesley Family.* London, 1874 [reprints CW's account of SW, portions of SW's *Reminiscences*, and VN's list of some of SW's musical compositions]

Stevenson, George J., *Memorials of the Wesley Family.* London, 1876, p 490–538

Green, Everard, *Notes and Queries* 6th series v 4 (1881) p 147 [concerns a copy of SW's *Missa de spiritu sancto*]

Cummings, William H., *Notes and Queries* 6th series v 4 (1881) p 251–252 [responds to Everard Green's query and quotes Gianangelo Braschi→James Talbot, 4/5/1785]

A., L. A., 'Samuel Wesley, the composer', *Methodist Recorder*, 4/7/1884, p 476 [discusses letters from SW to Shepherd]

Higgs, J., 'Samuel Wesley: his life, times and influence on music', *Proceedings of the Musical Association* v 20 (1893–4) p 125–147

Hodges, Faustina Hasse, *Edward Hodges*. New York, 1896 [includes information about SW in Hodges's diaries and correspondence]

Kelly, Charles H., 'The children of Charles Wesley. II. Mr Samuel Wesley', *Methodist Recorder*, 16/2/1899, p 12–13

Edwards, F. G., 'Samuel Wesley 1766–1837', *Musical Times* v 43 (1902) p 523–528, 798–802

Edwards, F. G., 'Samuel Wesley a boy–poet', *Musical Times* v 48 (1907) p 91–94

'Letters of a Bachist: Samuel Wesley', *Musical Times* v 49 (1908) p 236–237 [discusses four letters from SW to Bridgetower]

Ford, Ernest, 'The Wesleys', *Monthly Musical Record* v 47 (1917) p 152–153

Squire, W. B., 'Some Novello correspondence', *Musical Quarterly* v 3 (1917) p 206–222 [includes several letters from SW to VN]

'Samuel Wesley and Byrd', *Musical Times* v 64 (1923) p 567 [concerns SW→Street, 25/5/1830]

Sugden, Edward H., 'Samuel Wesley's notes on Shakespeare', *London Quarterly Review*, v 139 (1923) p 157–172 [on SW's annotations in his own copy of Shakespeare's plays, now at VUQ]

Pearce, C. W., 'Samuel Wesley the Elder as organ composer', *Organ* v 6 (1926) p 36–41

Pearce, C. W., 'A notable eighteenth–century organ concerto', *Organ* v 7 (1927) p 38–41 [on SW's voluntary for organ, *Andante maestoso and Presto in D* (1788)]

W[allace], W[illiam], 'The Wesley family concerts, 1779–85', *RAM Club Magazine* no 84 (June 1929), p 7–11

Lightwood, James T., *Samuel Wesley, Musician: The Story of his Life*. London, 1937

Spink, Gerald W., 'Samuel Wesley, 1766–1837', *Musical Times* v 78 (1937) p 310–311

Dexter, Harry, 'Samuel Wesley and J. S. Bach', *Musical Opinion* v 74 (1951) p 427–428 [prints SW's letters to Graeff]

Taberer, Alfred A., 'Uncle and nephew: Samuel Wesley, junr.'s comments on John', *Proceedings of the Wesley Historical Society* v 32 (1960) p 140–141 [discusses SW's marginal notes in Southey's life of JW]

'Samuel Wesley, forgotten piano works', *Choir* v 54 (1964) p 162–163

Emery, Walter, 'Jack Pudding', *Musical Times* v 107 (1966) p 301–306 [on the Hawkes patent organ controversy]

Holman, Peter, 'The instrumental and orchestral music of Samuel Wesley', *Consort* v 23 (1966) p 175–179

Temperley, Nicholas, 'Samuel Wesley', *Musical Times* v 107 (1966) p 108–110

Wilshere, Jonathan, 'Samuel Wesley (1766–1837): A bi-centenary tribute', *Musical Opinion* v 89 (1966) p 297, 299

Routley, Erik, *The Musical Wesleys, 1703–1876*. London, 1968

Ambrose, Holmes, 'The Anglican anthems and Roman Catholic motets of Samuel Wesley (1766–1837)', Ph.D. dissertation, Boston University, 2 vols, 1969

Schwarz, John I. Jr, 'The orchestral music of Samuel Wesley', Ph.D. dissertation, University of Maryland, 3 vols, 1971

Matthews, Betty, 'Charles Wesley on organs: 2', *Musical Times* v 112 (1971) p 1111–1112 [on letters and papers in Dorset Record Office, including CW Jr's notebook entry for 25/6/1818 announcing SW's recovery from illness]

Baker, Frank, 'Samuel Wesley, Musician', *Methodist History* v 11 (1972) p 52–56 [prints and discusses SW→Pettet, 18/3/1824 and 6/4/1824, and SW→CW Jr, 1/6/1829]

Elvin, Laurence, 'The musical Wesleys', *Epworth Witness and Journal of the Lincolnshire Methodist History Society* v. 2 (1972) pp. 40–44

Marsh, John, 'Samuel Wesley's *Confitebor*', *Musical Times* v 113 (1972) p 609–610

Routh, Francis, *Early English Organ Music from the Middle Ages to 1837* (London, 1973) [discusses SW's keyboard music and lists manuscript and printed sources]

Schwarz, John I. Jr, 'Samuel and Samuel Sebastian Wesley, the English *Doppelmeister*', *Musical Quarterly* v 59 (1973) p 190–206

Matthews, Betty, 'Wesley's finances and Handel's hymns', *Musical Times* v 114 (1973) p 137–139

Marsh, John, 'The Latin church music of Samuel Wesley. PhD dissertation, University of York, 1975

Young, Percy M., 'Samuel Wesley and the sublime', *American Choral Review*, v 18 (1976) p 3–16

Brown, G. E., 'The organ music of Samuel Wesley'. MA dissertation, University of Durham, 1978

Fox, Peter, 'A biographical note on Samuel Wesley (1766–1837) the first Grand Organist', *Ars Quatuor Coronatum* v 92 (1979) p 64–81 [on SW and Freemasonry]

Ritchey, Lawrence I., 'The untimely death of Samuel Wesley; or, the perils of plagiarism', *ML* v 60 (1979) p 45–59 [on the controversy concerning the entry about SW in the 1824 Sainsbury and Co. dictionary of musicians]

Ogasapian, John, 'The organ music of the Wesleys', *Clavier* v 19 (March 1980), p 34–35

Norman, Philip, 'More Wesley organ duets?', *Musical Times* v 125 (1984) p 287–289 [on SW's eight duets for EW in BL Add 35007]

Routh, Francis, 'Samuel Wesley', *American Organist*, v 19 (November 1985) p 77–79

Carroll, William Pearson, *The Latin Choral Music of Samuel Wesley*. DMA dissertation, University of Cincinnati, 1988

Rogal, Samuel J., 'For the love of Bach: the Charles Burney–Samuel Wesley correspondence', *Bach* v 23 (1992) p 31–37

Langley, Robin, 'Samuel Wesley's contribution to the development of English organ literature', *BIOS Journal* v 17 (1993) p 102–116

Olleson, Philip, 'The Tamworth Festival of 1809', *Staffordshire Studies* v 5 (1993) p 81–106 [includes discussion of SW's contribution to the festival]

Olleson, Philip, 'Family History Sources for British Music Research', *A Handbook of Studies in 18th-Century English Music III*, ed. M. Burden and I. Cholij (Edinburgh, 1993), p 1–36 [includes discussion of SW's family]

Dirst, Matthew, 'Samuel Wesley and the *Well-Tempered Clavier*: A case study in Bach reception', *American Organist* v 29 (May 1995) p 64–68

Banks, Chris, 'From Purcell to Wardour Street: a brief account of music manuscripts from the library of Vincent Novello now in the British Library', *British Library Journal* v 21 (1995) p 240–258 [includes discussion of SW's manuscripts that VN had possessed]

Olleson, Philip, 'Samuel Wesley and the *European Magazine*', *Notes* v 52 (1996) p 1097–1111

Olleson, Philip, 'Organs, organ builders, and organs in the letters of Samuel Wesley: an index', *BIOS Reporter* v 20 (1996) p 10–18

Olleson, Philip, 'The organ-builder and the organist: Thomas Elliot and Samuel Wesley', *BIOS Journal* v 20 (1996) p 116–125

Olleson, Philip, 'The letters of Samuel Wesley: a work in progress report', *The Maynooth International Musicological Conference 1995 Selected Proceedings: Part Two*, ed. Devine, Patrick F. and White, Harry, Blackrock, Co. Dublin, 1996 (*Irish Musical Studies 5*), p 321–335

Jones, Peter Ward (trans. and ed.), *The Mendelssohns on Honeymoon: The 1837 Diary of Felix and Cécile Mendelssohn Bartholdy together with Letters to their Families*. Oxford, 1997 [includes Mendelssohn's account of his meeting with SW on 12/9/1837]

Olleson, Philip, 'The Music of Samuel Wesley on record: an introductory survey', *Proceedings of the Wesley Historical Society* v 51 (1997) p 31–36

Olleson, Philip, '"The Perfection of Harmony Itself": The William Hawkes patent organ and its temperament', *BIOS Journal* v 21 (1997) p 106–126

Olleson, Philip, 'Spirit voices', *Musical Times* v 138 (September 1997) p 4–10 [concerns SW's *Missa de spiritu sancto*]

Pelkey, Stanley C., 'Preludes in all the keys throughout the octave by Samuel Wesley: an introduction to a forgotten keyboard repertory', *Early Keyboard Journal* v 15 (1997) p 67–92

Olleson, Philip, 'The Wesleys at home: Charles Wesley and his children', *Methodist History* v 36 (1998) p 139–152

Olleson, Philip, 'Samuel Wesley remembered', *BIOS Reporter* v 22 (1998), p 19–22

Kassler, Michael, Letter to the editor, *Notes* v 55 (1998) p 222 [concerns SW→Stephen Jones, 13/1/1817, and responds to Philip Olleson's 1996 *Notes* article]

Olleson, Philip, 'Samuel Wesley and the *Missa de Spiritu Sancto*', *Recusant History* v 24 (1999) p 309–319 [an expanded and revised version of the 1997 *Musical Times* article]

Olleson, Philip, 'The obituary of Samuel Wesley', in Bennett Zon (ed.), *Nineteenth-Century British Music Studies*, v 1 (Aldershot, 1999), p 121–133

Olleson, Philip, 'Dr Burney, Samuel Wesley, and Bach's *Goldberg Variations*', in Jon Newsom and Alfred Mann (eds.), *Music History from Primary Sources: A Guide to the Moldenhauer Archives* (Washington DC, 2000), p 169–175

Olleson, Philip, 'Samuel Wesley and the music profession', *Music and British Culture, 1785–1914: Essays in Honour of Cyril Ehrlich* (Oxford, 2000), p 23–38

Pelkey, Stanley C., 'Handel and Samuel Wesley: A case study in Handel reception in the later Georgian Period', *Handel Institute Newsletter*, v 11 no. 2 (autumn 2000), p 2–5.

Olleson, Philip (ed.), *The Letters of Samuel Wesley: Professional and Social Correspondence, 1797–1837.* Oxford, 2001

Kassler, Michael (ed.), *Aspects of the English Bach Awakening.* Aldershot, 2002, forthcoming [includes information about SW's activities concerning J. S. Bach]

INDEX TO THE
CALENDAR OF CORRESPONDENCE

In addition to Samuel Wesley, the following persons are named in the calendar of correspondence on the pages indicated. An italicised page number indicates that the person wrote, or was the addressee of, a letter or document entered in the calendar on that page. The symbols '<' and '>' preceding a date stand for 'before' and 'after', respectively.

References in the calendar to SW's musical and literary works are indexed in the lists of these works. References to portraits of SW are given in the iconography section. Selected events in which SW participated are recorded in the chronology.